THE
FREE SPEECH
MOVEMENT

COMING OF AGE IN THE 1960s

Plus ça change, plus c'est la même chose

ON THE CAMPUS OF THE UNIVERSITY OF CALIFORNIA AT BERKELEY, OCTOBER 1, 1964.
JACK WEINBERG WAS ARRESTED FOR VIOLATING REGULATIONS PROHIBITING POLITICAL
ACTIVITY. STUDENTS SURROUNDED THE CAR IN WHICH HE WAS HELD AND PREVENTED
IT FROM MOVING. SPEAKERS USED THE POLICE CAR AS A PODIUM TO DEBATE FIRST
AMENDMENT ISSUES AND CIVIL DISOBEDIENCE. WEINBERG REMAINED IN THE CAR FOR
THIRTY-TWO HOURS. PHOTO BY HOWARD HARAWITZ.

THE
FREE SPEECH
MOVEMENT

COMING OF AGE IN THE 1960s

D A V I D   L A N C E   G O I N E S

TEN SPEED PRESS
BERKELEY, CALIFORNIA

Text and cover design by David Lance Goines
Typeset by Wilsted & Taylor

1☉

TEN SPEED PRESS
P.O. Box 7123
Berkeley, California 94707

Library of Congress Cataloging-in-Publication Data

Goines, David Lance, 1945—
    The free speech movement coming of age in the 1960s /
David Lance Goines.
        p.   cm.
    Includes bibliographical references and index.
    ISBN 0-89815-535-5
    1. University of California, Berkeley—Students—
History.   2. College students—California—Berkeley—
Political activity—History.   3. Student movements—
California—Berkeley—History.
I. Title.
LD760.G65   1993
378.794'67'09046—dc20   93-7929
                                                             CIP

Printed in the United States of America

1   2   3   4   5   97   96   95   94   93

For my sweet wife, Edie Sei Ichioka,
without whom,
no kidding,
this book would not have been possible

ON DECEMBER 3, 1964, EIGHT HUNDRED PARTICIPANTS IN THE FREE SPEECH MOVEMENT
WERE ARRESTED IN SPROUL HALL ON THE UNIVERSITY OF CALIFORNIA, BERKELEY
CAMPUS. THE ARRESTS TOOK SIX HUNDRED POLICE OFFICERS THIRTEEN HOURS.
PHOTOGRAPHER UNKNOWN.

CONTENTS

COME gather 'round people
Wherever you roam
And admit that the waters
Around you have grown
And accept it that soon
You'll be drenched to the bone.
If your time to you
Is worth savin'
Then you better start swimmin'
Or you'll sink like a stone
For the times they are
a-changin'.

Come writers and critics
Who prophesize with your pen
And keep your eyes wide
The chance won't come again
And don't speak too soon
For the wheel's still in spin
And there's no tellin' who
That it's namin'.
For the loser now
Will be later to win
For the times they are
a-changin'.

Come senators, congressmen
Please heed the call
Don't stand in the doorway
Don't block up the hall
For he that gets hurt
Will be he who has stalled
There's a battle outside
And it is ragin'.
It'll soon shake your windows
And rattle your walls
For the times they are
a-changin'.

Come mothers and fathers
Throughout the land
And don't criticize
What you can't understand
Your sons and your daughters
Are beyond your command
Your old road is
Rapidly agin'.
Please get out of the new one
If you can't lend your hand
For the times they are
a-changin'.

The line it is drawn
The curse it is cast
The slow one now
Will later be fast
As the present now
Will later be past
The order is
Rapidly fadin'.
And the first one now
Will later be last
For the times they are
a-changin'.

—Bob Dylan
"The Times They Are
A-Changin'"
New York City, October 24, 1963

9

A STUDENT ARRESTED IN SPROUL HALL ON DECEMBER 3, 1964, IS HUSTLED TO A
WAITING ALAMEDA COUNTY SHERIFF'S BUS. PHOTOGRAPHER UNKNOWN.

Here they come! Get ready!"

"Don't link arms; go limp and make them carry you. Do *not* resist in any way. All you have to tell them is your name, and be sure to ask for a lawyer and a phone call. Does everybody have a dime? Don't answer any other questions. When you telephone, call Arrest Central. Give your own name and the names of everybody with you, and say where you are. We want to keep track of everybody. Make sure you've taken anything sharp, like pens and pencils, out of your pockets. Take off your buttons, the sharp pins could stick you. Girls, make sure you've taken off any dangly earrings. No tied scarves, take off your necklaces or bracelets. If you see any instances of brutality, get the officer's badge number."

The cops start with the people nearest the elevator, and methodically work their way through the tightly packed crowd. I'm about two-thirds of the way down the hall, leading singing. It's amazing—I can remember every word to every song I've ever heard. Usually I have trouble, and bog down after a verse or two. Not this morning. Civil rights songs, FSM Christmas carols, Leadbelly songs, chain-gang chants, spirituals, folk songs—anything I can think of that has a call-and-response; it doesn't much matter, what's important is that we keep on clapping and singing. Everybody's excited, but it's a fragile sort of excitement. Some of the girls look like they're going to cry. That would never do.

Ain't gonna let nobody turn me 'round, turn me 'round, turn me 'round . . .

. . . we shall not, we shall not be moved, just like a tree standing by the water, we shall not be moved.

One of the cops points at me, two others nod their heads.

God gave Moses the rainbow sign, no more water but fire next time.

. . . and before I'll be a slave, I'll be buried in my grave, and I'll fight for my right to be free.

Lots of yelling up near the elevator. Girls' screams.

. . . deep in my heart, I do believe, we shall overcome some day.

They get closer and closer, and I guess they've gotten tired of my voice, because they skip over a bunch of kids to get at me. The girl next to me gives me a hard hug; she's shaking like a leaf, and hasn't got any color at all in her face, eyes as big as saucers. I look up at the giant policemen looming over me. My stomach turns over.

"You are the forty-third person to be arrested this morning. Will you walk or do we have to carry you?"

No answer.

Two officers pick me up with a "come-along" hold, and involuntarily I rise to my feet, cursing and trying not to show that it hurts; I don't want to frighten the others. It feels like they're trying to break my wrist. I clamp my mouth shut. I can hear the singing starting up again behind me. At the end of the corridor, they toss me underhand into the elevator.

The basement smells like sweat. An officer pats me down, but without much conviction. Pretty slim pickin's among these college kids. The guy behind me gets the once-over-lightly, too.

Another officer holds a piece of paper with a number on it in front of me. Flash. "Turn to the right." Flash. It's 5:06 AM.

"Empty your pockets." The policeman puts everything into a paper envelope. "You can keep your smokes."

"Name?"

"David Goines."

"Age?"

"Nineteen."

"Address?"

"2252 Bancroft, Berkeley."

"Race?"

"Human."

The policeman checks off "Caucasian," giving me a weary "nobody likes a wise-ass" look.

"Give me your right hand." As he fingerprints me. "Give me your left hand." He repeats the process. None too gentle about it, either. I wipe my fingers on my pants.

There's no room anywhere for us to be held and more students are piling in every minute, so we're escorted out to an Alameda County Sheriff's bus, barred windows painted over with grimy white. I light up. I swear to God, the first drag on that cigarette is better than sex. Sitting in the bus for half an hour while it fills, swapping stories about what we've seen and what's happened, singing more songs just to show them, and all the kids outside around the busses, that we're not slowing down for a minute.

If you're ever in Berkeley
Well, you better walk right,
You better not picket,
Or sit-in all night.
Or Alameda sheriffs will arrest you
And the boys will take you down,
And before you get free speech,
You're jailhouse bound.
Let the midnight special
Shine its light on me . . .

Then the Greyhound bus station smell of diesel exhaust as we take off on a long ride to we-don't-know-where. My wrist has stopped hurting. Dawn is just breaking as we file off the bus into the holding tank at Santa Rita.

Early December, and cold as a brass bra. I don't have a coat. I had one when we went into Sproul Hall at noon, but somewhere along the line I gave it to somebody. They run us through a police-paperwork gauntlet and herd us off in untidy groups to empty, dim barracks. Chilly, but we're issued thin scratchy blankets from a pile. Army-surplus bunk beds set up every which way, bare springs with a stingy striped mattress folded up on top. The whole operation looks like it was thrown together with no notice. Chattering excitedly among ourselves, waiting to see what happens now. No cops around anywhere. Nobody I'm with has ever been arrested before. After a while, most of us are asleep. Around noon we get a bologna sandwich.

Two in the morning and the lights come on without any warning; we stagger off through the unfamiliar compound, bright lights on lampposts and guard towers puncturing the darkness, guards at the head and tail of our straggling column. That sick feeling of not enough sleep and being abruptly awakened heart-pounding where am I what's happening. Wish I had a cup of hot coffee. Somebody's gotten our bail together, and we're being processed out. A faculty member greets me at the gate; parked on the side of the highway are hundreds of cars: faculty and Berkeley citizens waiting to take their students home.

ARRESTED STUDENTS FLASHED VICTORY SIGNS FROM THE WINDOWS OF AN ALAMEDA
COUNTY SHERIFF'S BUS AS IT PULLED AWAY FROM CAMPUS. PHOTOGRAPHER UNKNOWN.

The employers will love this generation. They are going to be easy to handle.

—Clark Kerr, Chancellor of the University of California at Berkeley, 1952–1958

A student who has been chased by the KKK in Mississippi is not easily intimidated by academic bureaucrats.

—Berkeley student Roger Sandall, 1965

I hold it, that a little rebellion now and then is a good thing, and as necessary in the political world as storms in the physical. It is a medicine necessary for the sound health of government.

—Thomas Jefferson, letter to James Madison, January 30, 1787

IN REACTION TO THE DECEMBER 3, 1964, SPROUL HALL ARRESTS, STUDENTS AND TEACHERS ON THE UC CAMPUS WENT ON STRIKE THROUGH THE NINTH OF DECEMBER. PHOTOGRAPH BY GARY MORETTI.

BRIGHT YOUTH PASSES SWIFTLY AS A THOUGHT

THIS BOOK IS ABOUT a four-month episode at the University of California at Berkeley, and what built up to it and what came after. It's made up of hundreds of details. Some of them come together and make sense; some of them don't. Sometimes it's from my own personal perspective, sometimes it's from the perspective of others. Sometimes I present the Big Picture, but mostly it's the small stuff. The grand sweep of history is all very well and good, but what I find compelling is the minutiae; personal recollections of insignificant parts of minor battles, scraps of contemporary conversations, laundry lists.

In June of 1984, Mark Kitchell interviewed me for his film *Berkeley in the Sixties*. Twenty years had passed since 1964; as much time as had passed between World War II and the Free Speech Movement. When I was nineteen that war was ancient history. The FSM is ancient history now, too, only I was in it.

Mark sent me a transcript of what I had said, and as I read it, that whole episode of my life came rushing back, murky and garbled, but with great intensity. I decided to copy the few pages of transcript, and flesh it out, to see just what I could dredge up out of the dim swamps of memory. The self-imposed task of auto-archaeology started getting out of hand; the more I wrote, the more I remembered. The initial mnemonic exploration was like the early excavations of Troy: great shovelfuls of priceless treasure unearthed at every turn, even the clumsiest effort returning wonders and marvels. After a bit of this, the going got harder. I was down to the whisk broom and dental tool stage in no time at all, attempting to assemble a whole event from shards, hints, half-remembered conversations, bright fragments of broken images; a reflection in a shattered funhouse mirror. It's hard to get things in the right order, to integrate bits of memory into a coherent framework.

It's all there, but deeply buried. I have become a placer miner of history; I pounce on little golden flakes of information. Though memory is tenacious, remembrance is a stew, matured over the years into a rich, amorphous sauce, ingredients blended and seemingly beyond individual distinction. Starting with soup, I work backwards, yielding at last a cutting board heaped with carrots, oxtails, onions, garlic, pepper. Some chunks remain identifiable, other ingredients seem lost forever, though they impart their elusive tastes.

The reconstruction of history is easier done with the help of others; everybody remembers different things about the same events. Strangely enough, most memories seem random, without regard for the apparent gravity of the circumstance they call to mind. I'm as likely to recall a specific garment, meal or glance as I am to forget whole weeks of what had to be desperately interesting living. Others' recollections shed light on dark corners, unswept by thought for years.

Whenever I've had a chance to compare my own recollections with those of someone else, I've often been surprised to find them at considerable variance, even in large matters. This doesn't bother me too much because there's nothing I can do about it; who's right and who's wrong is not an important question. Alternate realities are the fabric of history.*

This is the account of an historical event, but it wasn't history when we did it. It unfolded, day by day, and though we did our best to predict what might happen and prepare for it, we did not know how it was all going to come out. Looking back on things after they're all over, it seems almost inevitable that they should have resolved themselves the way they did. But that's not the way it was then—there was no inevitability, there were no best choices, there was no right answer. Tomorrow was as hidden then as tomorrow is hidden today. Tomorrow was filled with risk, danger and fear. We sized up our chances, made the best decisions we could, and leaped into the void.†

---

*Of course, as Tom Weller points out, "The one point at which these diverse, fragmentary and conflicting recollections are resolved comes when someone, such as yourself, writes it down in a book. At that point the story, be it purest malarkey, is fixed for all time" (personal correspondence, 1990).

†I thank Jeff Lustig for bringing this Nietzschean observation to my attention.

DUCK AND COVER

WHEN I WAS a trifle over two months old, the United States bomber *Enola Gay* dropped the first atomic device to be used in anger, obliterating 150,000 human beings in an instant. Three days later, the last bomb of the only nuclear war ever fought destroyed Nagasaki, snuffed out a few tens of thousands of human candles, and persuaded the Japanese war party that further resistance was futile.

The children of my generation were raised under the shadow of The Bomb. In school, we endured monthly air raid drills: crouch under your desk, put newspaper over your head, stay away from windows, don't look at the flash, wait for the all clear. We were shown demented Civil Defense films; animated characters instructed us in air raid procedure:

"This is Tommy Turtle. He knows how to duck and cover. Let's all do it: duck and cover, children, duck and cover."

It wasn't at all obvious to me what hiding under a desk and putting a piece of newspaper over my head would do to alleviate the hazards posed by a thermonuclear device demonstrated to be capable of annihilating an entire city. The suburban area of Sacramento where I went to elementary school was at the center of a triangle formed by Aerojet—where monster rocket engines were developed and tested for the military—Mather Air Force Base and McClellan Air Force Base. I lived smack dab in the middle of Northern California's prime military target, and I knew it.

When I was ten years old, my mother would awaken us to witness the nuclear test explosions in Nevada. As the first few morning birds quarreled musically over territory and foolish worms, my brothers and sisters and I stood about in the cool, silent black dawn still dressed in nighties and pajamas, feet chilly and wet with dew. Our hearts filled with awe and dread as the radio counted down: ten . . . nine . . . eight . . . seven . . . six . . . five . . . four . . . three . . . two . . . one . . . Noiselessly, the eastern sky flashed white as day. We trooped back to

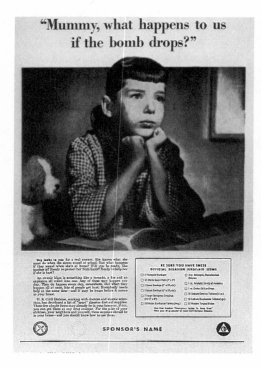

"Mummy, what happens to us if the bomb drops?"

bed and dreams of irresistible destructive might. Sputnik improved our science education, and our neighbors dug bomb shelters, stocked with all that was needful to live after nuclear holocaust had visited. My parents attended Civil Defense meetings, preparing for atomic war with Russia. The burning debate, turning neighbors into bitter enemies, revolved around who would you let in; presumably, you stocked enough for your own family, no more. The consensus was that others would be turned away, at gunpoint if necessary. Suburban split-levels and green grass yards would become a world of maddened dogs, tearing at each other for the scraps of survival. I often wondered, "Will today be the day? Will I be able to get home to my family in time? Will my father make it home from work to be with us? Will we die apart?" My thoughts never went beyond grabbing my little sisters and brothers out of their classrooms and dashing for home when the howling air raid sirens went off.*

---

*A U.S. Civil Defense advertisement of about 1955 demonstrates the skittish unreality of government information to the public, downpedaling the gravity of the matter with sugarcoated, useless advice:

"Mummy, what happens to us if the bomb drops?"

(picture of a soulful, worried little girl with a stuffed toy puppy, gazing up as though at an adult)

She looks to you for a real answer. She knows what she must do when the sirens sound at school. But what happens if they sound when she's at home? Will you be ready, like her teacher is? Ready to protect

her from harm? Ready to help her if she is hurt?

An atomic bomb is something like a tornado, a fire and an explosion all rolled into one. Any of these may happen any day. They do happen every day, somewhere. But when they happen all at once, lots of people get hurt. Everybody needs help at the same time—and it may be hours before it comes to your home.

U.S. Civil Defense, working with doctors and atomic scientists, has developed a tlist of "must" disaster first-aid supplies. These few simple items may already be in your home or, if not, you can get them at

At Cal, fallout shelter signs were posted all over University buildings. We thought they were a joke, and it was the fashion amongst surly youth to steal as many of them as possible, using them for macabre room decorations. Worked on them in black and yellow was the symbol for radiation, and inside a little circle was the maximum occupancy of the shelter. An arrow showed the direction to run in case of atomic attack. I had dozens of the things.*

All through my childhood, I'd been frightened beyond fear, and there hadn't been any reason for it. Adults had been silly, and dead-ass wrong about Russia, and the Communists, and Nuclear War, and every chance they got they made a big to-do about nothing, frightened of their own shadows. By the time I reached my teens, having been steeped in phony terror all my life, I wasn't afraid of anything anymore. I didn't take seriously what adults said, or place much credence in their ideas. In fact, if an adult said something, that as much as gave it the cachet of nonsense. In turn, they didn't like my music, they didn't like my haircut, they didn't like my clothes, they didn't like my morals, they didn't like my ideas, they didn't like my friends and most of them didn't like me.

Our parents, as well as the adults who would be key players in the FSM drama—Edmund G. "Pat" Brown, the Regents of the University of California, Clark Kerr, Chancellor Strong, Dean Towle, Arleigh Williams—had been born during or shortly after World War I; endured the deadly influenza epidemic that followed; suffered the debilitating silliness of Prohibition; were stripped of their livelihoods, possessions and security by the Great Depression; witnessed terrifying revolution in two immense, backward nations; and had seen the entire world dragged into

---

any drug counter. For the sake of your children, your neighbors and yourself, these supplies should be in your home—and you should know how to use them.

BE SURE YOU HAVE THESE OFFICIAL DISASTER FIRST-AID ITEMS

4 Triangular Bandages
12 Sterile Gauze Pads (3″×3″)
1 Gauze Bandage (2″×10 yds.)
1 Gauze Bandage (1″×10 yds.)
2 Large Emergency Dressings (7″×8″)
100 Water-Purification Tablets (4 mg.)
3 oz. Antiseptic, Benzalkonium Chloride
1 oz. Aromatic Spirits of Ammonia
1 oz. Castor Oil Eye Drops
50 Sodium Chloride Tablets (10 gr.)

50 Sodium Bicarbonate Tablets (5 gr.)
12 Wooden Tongue Blades

Get free booklet "Emergency Action to Save Lives" from your drug counter or local Civil Defense Director.

*Under the instigation of Wes Hester, Sr., who served on the Berkeley City Council from 1982 to 1986, in the early 1980s the council voted to amend the remaining signs: "There is no shelter from nuclear war. WARNING it is unlikely that any occupants of this building would survive a nuclear attack. Nuclear war has no cure. It can only be prevented." In 1990, the police department was the only building in Berkeley that still boasted the original 1950s shelter sign and the 1980s disclaimer.

NUCLEAR TEST SITE, FRENCHMAN'S FLAT, NEVADA, EARLY 1950S.
PHOTO © 1993 BY TED STRESHINSKY.

yet another stupid, pointless war resulting in nothing but a monumental loss of human life. Postwar depression, Korea and the cold war were the icing on the cake. Every time something good happened in their lives, something bad came right along behind it and gobbled it up. Our elders were desperate for order, calm, peace and quiet. They taught us to read from daffy books recounting the imaginary idyll of *Dick and Jane*, and passed laws against the comic books we relished, leaving only the tapioca eternal high school of Archie and Jughead, where nothing ever happened and nobody grew up. Veronica, despite her houri figure, remained a perpetual virgin. Archie and Veronica were Dick and Jane grown large, but never becoming adult. What *we* liked were EC horror comics, James Dean in *Rebel Without a Cause*, the irreverent *Mad* magazine, congressionally disapproved-of rock 'n' roll and Allen Ginsberg's *Howl*.

Like all children, we engaged our parents in a continual contest for independence. The difference between my generation and those which had gone before was twofold: First, there were more of us than there had ever been before, overwhelming our elders by sheer force of numbers. The population of the United States rose by 19 million between 1940 and 1950; between 1950 and 1960 by another 28 million; 4 million American children were born in 1947 alone. Between 1940 and 1950 California's population rose by 42 percent.

Second, we were the first generation in the history of the world that

WOMEN STRIKE FOR PEACE MARCH, JULY 15, 1962, MERCURY, NEVADA.
PHOTO BY HARVEY RICHARDS.

had never gone hungry. Our parents trembled at the memory of the
Great Depression, but it meant nothing to us. We didn't have much notion of not getting what we wanted, when we wanted it.

So what had been a matter of struggle and compromise for preceding
generations became for the first wave of baby boomers a matter of
fighting to win. We fought about hair, about clothes, about music,
about books, about sex, about education, about language, politics and
money. We fought about everything, and it got to be a habit.

The first fight that I remember was over a pretty basic First Amendment issue: comic books. In 1933, Max C. Gaines produced the first real
comic book, *Funnies on Parade.* By 1946, nine out of ten American children between the ages of eight and fifteen read comic books regularly,
consuming roughly forty million every month, increasing to fifty million a month by 1950.[1] In 1947, William M. Gaines inherited the firm
from his father and changed things around quite a bit with the 1950 publication of exciting, gory comic books. Entertaining Comics (EC)
printed war comics (*Frontline Combat, Two-Fisted Tales*), crime comics
(*Crime SuspenStories*), horror comics (*Witches' Cauldron, Tales from the
Crypt*), science fiction comics (*Weird Fantasy, Weird Science*) and humor
comics (*Mad,* in 1952), all of which were eagerly bought by kids, who
are genuinely delighted by things that their parents sincerely—and quite
mistakenly—believe will warp their little minds beyond repair.[2]

Will Eisner wrote for the comics, Ray Bradbury was liberally adapted and—posthumously—Edgar Allen Poe contributed memorable plots. The story lines were good, but the artwork was *great!* Wally Wood, Al Williamson, Frank Frazetta, Jack Davis, Graham Ingels, Reed Crandall, Bernie Krigstein, Johnny Craig, Joe Orlando, George Evans, John Severin, Bob Powell, Dick Ayers and Matt Baker—among others—churned out thousands of brilliant drawings every month, underscoring a rather bleak, Calvinist, horror-comic morality in which good was never rewarded but evil was always punished. Dr. Frederic Wertham, senior psychiatrist for the New York Department of Hospitals, presiding over a symposium titled "The Psychopathology of Comic Books," concluded that comic books glorified crime and violence, terming them "abnormally sexually aggressive."[3] When Dr. Wertham got up on his hind legs and condemned these popular publications in *Seduction of the Innocent,* linking juvenile delinquency to crime and horror comics, he particularly targeted the sex angle. "One of the stock mental aphrodisiacs in comic books is to draw girls' breasts in such a way that they are sexually exciting. Whenever possible they protrude and obtrude."[4] These fulminations of Wertham's diseased mind stimulated a U.S. Senate subcommittee on juvenile delinquency in the United States to hold public hearings on the deleterious effects of comic books on children and led to the creation of the Comics Code Authority in 1954, which effectively removed EC from the stands. "Gaines reached the last straw in late 1955, when the Comics Code refused to approve an anti-racism story in *Incredible Science Fiction* on the grounds that it was offensive because its hero, a Black man, was shown perspiring! Gaines denounced the Code, ran the story anyway with a bogus Code Approval Seal, and then shut down his New Directions comics at the end of 1955."[5] Gaines then converted his biggest selling comic book, Harvey Kurtzman's *Mad,* from a comic book format to a black-and-white magazine to circumvent the code. We lost the Battle of the Comic Books hands down, and it left a baffled, festering anger.

Even as the really neat comic books disappeared, in 1954 America heard the first rumblings of a new musical form. Adults hated it; kids loved it. My father thought rock 'n' roll was dreadful noise, and it reminded my mother of Kipling's "lesser breeds without the law," so, allying themselves against their children, they put Elvis the Pelvis, the Big Bopper, Buddy Holly, Chuck Berry, the Platters, the Everly Brothers, Screaming Jay Hawkins, Wolfman Jack, Little Richard, and that white trash Jerry Lee Lewis (who was in disgrace for bigamously marrying his—just barely—thirteen-year-old second cousin) on the shit list. In their fear and hatred of "jungle music," my parents linked hands with the solid citizens of the nation who, though unable to eliminate teenage racket from the airwaves, nonetheless pressured radio stations to ban particularly offensive songs. By 1958, plagued by inflated scandals and rocked by the untimely deaths of three of its greatest geniuses, rock 'n' roll was on the ropes. But the bell, in the form of my generation getting old enough to exercise considerable economic clout, rang just in time. Though the classic 1950s style of rock 'n' roll never really recovered, it turned in other directions and kept on growing with us as we wrested greater control over our own lives.

The fight was a hard one, and we were lucky to hold the grown-ups to a draw: in early 1958 I heard a song that burned its way into my mind on one single hearing. The powerful fuzz-tone guitar and drum instrumental was titled *Rumble*, and even though I, and other kids, loved it, it mysteriously disappeared from the air and I never heard it broadcast again. In 1990 I heard the song for the second time, and in the liner notes I found out what had happened:

> The "corrupting" influence of rock 'n' roll made some radio stations worry about offending parents, and a number of stations banned Link Wray's menacing guitar instrumental *Rumble*. Wray composed the song at a show in Fredericksburg, Virginia, after he was asked to play something for the popular dance, the stroll. Though Archie Bleyer hated it, he released the instrumental on his Cadence label because his daughter loved it (she named it after a scene in *West Side Story*). *Rumble*'s thick power chords and distorted guitar tone, which Wray created by punching holes in his amplifier's speaker, have led some to call it the first heavy-metal record.[6]

The important thing to remember is that this was an *instrumental*—not some inky savage lasciviously grunting the promise of primitive sexual delights into your daughter's shell-pink ear; not some greasy, sullen hillbilly thrusting his snake-hipped, denim-clad crotch into your children's virginal dreams; not peripherally intelligible dull-glowing words seducing youth into acts of mindless vandalism and lust: just a guitar and a drum.* Brothers and sisters, we really had 'em on the run. Our parents

---

*"As for three-chord party classics, the Kingsmen's version of *Louie, Louie* rode high on the charts in late 1963 and early 1964. Since then, the song has become a standard performed by artists as diverse as the Sandpipers, Julie London, Barry White and Blondie. The song's near-icon status was confirmed in the early 1980s when West Coast radio stations began holding *Louie, Louie* marathons, the longest being a program on KFJC, Los Altos Hills, California, which aired more than 300 different versions. The success of *Louie, Louie* derived in part from the sin-

were quite right, of course: this music was dynamite, and despite their efforts at censure it sold a million copies. Link Wray's challenging, insolent style influenced Bob Dylan, by whom our helpless parents were treated to taunting lyrics that far exceeded the vague terrors generated by holes poked in a speaker with a pencil.

The best-selling nonfiction book of 1959 was the treacle-voiced Pat Boone's pious fraud *'Twixt Twelve and Twenty*, which gave detailed, failsafe instructions on how to get kids to be good if you happened to live on Mars. The grown-ups of America were getting desperate.

If you think of the period between 1945 and 1970 as a battlefield, the fifties consisted of individual skirmishes of children against their parents, the sixties a more organized campaign of all of us against all of them, and the seventies a mopping-up operation. Because the University administration, like our parents, would not bend, it broke. In the end, we won because they were afraid, and we were not.

---

gle's crude recording quality. A rumor spread in late 1963 that buried within singer Jack Ely's garbled vocals were outrageous and obscene lyrics. Governor Matthew Walsh of Indiana banned airplay in his state, and the FBI and FCC held investigations at which Ely and the song's composer, Richard Berry, testified. After deliberating and playing the record at every speed, the FCC announced: 'We found the record to be unintelligible at any speed we played it' " (Joe Sasfy, liner notes to Time-Life's 1990 digitally remastered CD album *The Rock 'n' Roll Era, 1964*, 2RNR-10).

QUI TACET CONSENTIT

O<small>N</small> SEPTEMBER 30, 1964, eight University of California, Berkeley, students were suspended indefinitely by Chancellor E. W. Strong for violating rules regulating the form, place and manner of speech by students while on the University campus. After considerable uproar, culminating on December 3, 1964, in the largest mass arrest in California history, the University gave in and First Amendment rights were restored to the campus.

The First Amendment, "refreshed from time to time with the blood of patriots and of tyrants,"[1] guarantees us the right to speak; as citizens of this democracy we have an obligation both to speak and to act when fools and demagogues endanger our welfare and liberty.

We must be careful to recognize that the substance of much speech that today is taken for granted was, within living memory, and despite the black letter of the Bill of Rights, effectively illegal, for which the speaker, author, printer and publisher could be fined and imprisoned. That the battle for free speech is going on now and will continue forever has been illustrated not only by the Reagan and Bush administrations' apparent hostility towards the very idea of the Bill of Rights, as manifested in efforts to restrict, control and manipulate information that should without prejudice be available to the public, but in a recrudescence of arrests and convictions for images, words and actions displeasing to the reactionary sensibility, as well as a galloping erosion of the entire Bill of Rights under these administrations' Supreme Courts.[2]

This account of the Free Speech Movement can be introduced with the historical case of the colonial printer John Peter Zenger.[3] Under the British common law to which colonial America was subject, expression was protected only against prior restraint: government did not have a

---

Qui tacet consentit is often used as a motto for voter registration.
It means "Silence implies consent."

right to prevent citizens from publishing what they wished, but could punish them afterwards if what they said was seditious or offensive. The charge of seditious libel did not concern itself with the truth or falsehood of what had been said; if the sentiment endangered popular respect for the government, it was punishable. Indeed, "the law . . . did not regard truth as a defense. On the contrary, the theory of the law was, the greater the truth, the greater the scandal against the government."[4] Based upon the writings of "Cato" (the joint pseudonym of the Whig political journalists John Trenchard and Thomas Gordon, writing circa 1720), the defense of John Peter Zenger challenged this notion, and planted a triple precedent in the minds of colonial Americans: First, that the truth is a valid defense. Second, that citizens have a right and a duty to defend the state against corrupt officials and unjust laws. Third, that the jury has a right to judge the law as well as the facts of a case.

On Sunday, November 17, 1734, the German emigrant John Peter Zenger was arrested and imprisoned on a warrant from Governor Crosby and the Council of New York "for printing and publishing several seditious libels" in the *New York Weekly Journal*. The governor and council then ordered "burning by the common hangman, or whipper, near the pillory, [of] the libelous papers." Governor Crosby was a deeply unpopular official, and Zenger's case provided a focus for public anger. Zenger's attorney, Andrew Hamilton of Philadelphia, admitted that Zenger had printed and published the papers. Hamilton then introduced the argument that what had been said was true, giving it some strength by going on to point out that corrupt officials dishonored the Crown, and that it was a service to King and Country to expose them. The court did not admit the validity of his case (which indeed at the time had none), and instructed the jury to find Zenger guilty or innocent of having published the papers, leaving it to the court to determine the extent of the libel. The eloquent Hamilton told the jury that, despite these instructions, they had a right to pass judgment on the law itself. The jury retired for only a short time, and returned with a verdict of not guilty. Though this case had no immediate influence on common law, it captured the popular imagination and became a rallying point for Americans concerned with freedom of the press. "Today, with few exceptions, the states of the union—whether by constitutional provision, judicial decision or statutory enactment—substantially follow the Hamilton-Kent position, which derives from Andrew Hamilton's argument in the Zenger case."[5]

The precedent for citizen rights implied in this case was to be formally expressed on December 15, 1791, when ten amendments to the

Constitution were ratified by eleven of the thirteen original states; the most important amendment being the first:

> *Congress shall make no law respecting an establishment of religion, or prohibiting the free exercise thereof;* **or abridging the freedom of speech, or of the press;** *or the right of the people peaceably to assemble, and to petition the Government for a redress of grievance.*

What this meant was that Americans were, in principle, free to say or print anything, even to the point of being offensive or seditious. Of course, all this fine talk didn't amount to a hill of beans until the American Civil Liberties Union (ACLU), founded in 1920 by Roger Baldwin, became the champion of First Amendment rights. Until 1920, the First Amendment essentially did not exist, because nobody was around to stand up for it.* Elected and appointed officials, states, municipalities and courts routinely prohibited forms of speech that they found distasteful, including not only speech deemed offensive to the public morality, but the expression of unpopular political opinions as well; in this, they were commonly backed up by the primary defender of the Constitution, the United States Supreme Court, which—construing the First Amendment to apply to the Federal Authority only and not to the Several States—had yet to uphold a *single* free speech claim under the First Amendment.[6]

In 1919, in the matter of *Schenck* v *United States*, the renowned jurist Oliver Wendell Holmes, Jr., proclaimed for a unanimous court what has since become the watchword of all who would muzzle inconvenient expression:

> We admit that in many places and in ordinary times the defendants in saying all that was said in the circular would have been within their constitutional rights. But the character of every act depends upon the circumstances in which it was done. . . . The most stringent protection of free speech would not protect a man in falsely shouting fire in a theater

---

*"The persistent image of colonial America as a society that cherished freedom of expression is a sentimental hallucination that ignores history. The evidence provides little support for the notion that the colonies hospitably received advocates of obnoxious or detestable ideas on matters that counted. Nor is there reason to believe that rambunctious unorthodoxies suffered only from Puritan bigots and tyrannous royal judges. The American people and their representatives simply did not understand that freedom of thought and expression means equal freedom for the other fellow, particularly the fellow with hated ideas" (Leonard W. Levy, *Freedom of the Press from Zenger to Jefferson* [New York: Bobbs-Merrill, 1966], xxix).

and causing a panic. It does not even protect a man from an injunction against uttering words that may have all the effect of force. . . . The question in every case is whether the words used are used in such circumstances and are of such a nature as to create a clear and present danger that they will bring about the substantive evils that Congress has a right to prevent. It is a question of proximity and degree. When a nation is at war many things that might be said in time of peace are such a hindrance to its effort that their utterance will not be endured as long as men fight and no court could regard them as protected by any constitutional right.

The point concealed in this pre-ACLU decision is that—with a little imagination—*any* form of speech can be interpreted to be "a clear and present danger," and what actually emerged from this decision was a prohibition against shouting "Fire!" in a *burning* theater. In this celebrated suit, Charles T. Schenck and Elizabeth Baer, two New York Socialists, were on trial for opposing Selective Service law and for distributing pacifist literature decrying military conscription as "despotism arranged in the interest of Wall Street" to draftees and members of the armed forces. Like Zenger, they were accused of "seditious libel"; the difference was that instead of being brought before the hated representatives of a puppet government, Schenck and Baer were tried and convicted in an American court. If the same measure had been extended fifty years later to protesters of the Vietnam conflict, many Americans honestly opposed to what they felt to be an unjust, illegal war would by the same logic have been convicted of "conspiring to cause insubordination in the Armed Forces."

When Tennessee's new law prohibiting the teaching of evolution became effective in March of 1925, the ACLU at once sought a test of the statute's attack on free speech and secured John Thomas Scopes, a science teacher, as the defendant. William Jennings Bryan, three times the Democratic candidate for president and a rock-ribbed fundamentalist, volunteered to serve as chief counsel for the prosecution; Clarence Darrow, a member of the ACLU's National Committee and an agnostic, headed the volunteer defense team. Scopes was convicted and fined one hundred dollars. On appeal, the Tennessee Supreme Court upheld the statute but reversed the conviction, which made it impossible to appeal to the United States Supreme Court. The trial, however, played a major part in hastening the departure of religious indoctrination from the public schools.

By 1927 the U.S. Supreme Court had at least come to the point of active promotion of the ideals of free speech. Justice Louis Brandeis, in his concurrence in *Whitney* v *California*, made an eloquent defense of free speech in which he explained

> why a State is, ordinarily, denied the power to prohibit dissemination of social, economic and political doctrine that a vast majority of its citizens believes to be false and fraught with evil consequence.
>
> Those who won our independence believed that the final end of the State was to make men free to develop their faculties; and that in its government the deliberative force should prevail over the arbitrary. They valued liberty both as an end and as a means. They believed liberty to be the secret of happiness and courage to be the secret of liberty. They believed that freedom to think as you will and to speak as you think are means indispensable to the discovery and spread of political truth; that without free speech and assembly discussion would be futile; that with them, discussion affords ordinarily adequate protection against the dissemination of noxious doctrine; that the greatest menace to freedom is an inert people; that public discussion is a political duty; and that this should be a fundamental principle of the American government. But they knew that order cannot be secured merely through fear of punishment for its infraction; that it is hazardous to discourage thought, hope and imagination; that fear breeds repression; that repression breeds hate; that hate menaces stable government; that the path of safety lies in the opportunity to discuss freely supposed grievances and proposed remedies; and that the fitting remedy for evil counsels is good ones. Believing in the power of reason as applied through public discussion, they eschewed silence coerced by law—the argument of force in its worst form. Recognizing the occasional tyrannies of governing majorities, they amended the Constitution so that free speech and assembly should be guaranteed.

On an everyday level, however, free speech still struggled. In 1939, Mayor Frank "I Am the Law" Hague of Jersey City claimed the right to deny free speech to anyone he thought radical. Of his critics he said,

> We hear about constitutional rights and the free press. Every time I hear these words, I say to myself, "That man is a Red, that man is a Communist." You never hear a real American talk in that manner.

The ACLU, together with the Congress of Industrial Organizations (CIO), which was trying to organize in Jersey City, took Hague to the Supreme Court, which ruled that public places such as streets and parks belonged to the people, not the mayor, and that their use for free speech and assembly, though it could be regulated, could not be denied.[7]

This gradual expansion of First Amendment rights came to an abrupt halt on February 7, 1950, in Wheeling, West Virginia, when Wisconsin Democratic Senator Joseph R. McCarthy announced to the Republican Women's Club,

> While I cannot take the time to name all of the men in the State Department who have been named as members of the Communist party and members of a spy ring, I have here in my hand a list of 205 that were known to the Secretary of State as being members of the Communist party, and who nevertheless are still working and shaping the policy of the State Department.[8]

He offered no further proof and showed no one the list. During the stifling era of McCarthyism and the House Un-American Activities Committee [HUAC], Americans became afraid to speak their minds, and the First Amendment was eroded on the campuses of the University of California, as elsewhere, to the point of nonexistence. Dramatic change came in the 1960s, when citizens again awakened to their rights and duties.

TOWN AND GOWN

THE HISTORY OF THE CITY of Berkeley is inseparable from that of the University of California.[1] The site for the University was dedicated on April 16, 1860, and the University opened in 1873 with 191 students, 22 of them women. To ensure the isolation of the University from partisan influence, it was to be administered by a board of titular owners, called the Regents.* These powerful, wealthy citizens were given "full powers of organization and government, subject only to such Legislative control as may be necessary to ensure compliance with the terms of the endowments of the University and the security of its funds."[2]

In 1866 the fledgling city was named after George Berkeley, the English Bishop of Cloyne, whose bombastic *On the Prospect of Planting Arts and Learning in America*—

> Westward the course of empire takes its way,
> The first four acts already past,
> A fifth shall close the drama with the day:
> Time's noblest offspring is the last.

*There are twenty-four Regents; sixteen are appointed by the governor for terms of sixteen years each and eight others, including the governor himself, are public officials serving lesser terms as representatives of the public interest—the lieutenant-governor, superintendent of schools, Speaker of the Assembly, president of the State Agricultural Board, president of the Alumni Association, president of the University, and president of the Mechanics Institute, which was begun in San Francisco after the gold rush to teach skills to unemployed miners. In 1964 the members of the UC Board of Regents were Lt. Governor Glenn Anderson, Philip Brody Boyd, Governor Edmund G. Brown, John Canaday, Edward Carter, Dorothy Chandler, William Coblentz, Thomas Davis, Frederick Dutton, William Forbes, Cornelius Haggerty, Mrs. Randolph A. Hearst, Mrs. Edward Heller, Laurence Kennedy, Clark Kerr, Donald McLaughlin, Theodore Meyer, Samuel Mosher, Max Rafferty, William Roth, Edwin Pauley, Norton Simon, Jessie W. Tapp and Jesse Unruh.

THE REGENTS OF THE UNIVERSITY OF CALIFORNIA, 1964. UC PHOTO.

—inspired the citizens of what had formerly been known as Oceanview to bestow both his name and notions on their growing community.

The atmosphere of idealism and utopianism that surrounded the "Athens of the West" was reflected in the larger community. In such matters as progressive zoning regulations, a city-manager form of government to eliminate machine politics, vigorous public health measures and a forward-looking police force and fire department, the city was in the vanguard of civic consciousness from its earliest beginnings.

In matters of race relations, Berkeley was neither better nor worse than most other American cities. There were anti-Asian riots around the turn of the century, and as late as 1961 almost no Black employment in good mercantile or civic jobs.

When, however, the civil rights movement at last sparked the conscience of the community, Berkeley made dramatic, sweeping changes far in advance of others. In 1961 Berkeley elected Wilmont Sweeney, its first Black city councilman. Berkeley schools had never been overtly segregated, and the city was in the vanguard of bussing to rectify racial imbalance in public schools. University students and citizens picketed and boycotted downtown businesses that refused Black trade and did not employ Black people in good, conspicuous jobs, thereby forcing considerable change.

Berkeley's liberal, if not to say offbeat, leanings are rooted in the history of the city as well as that of the University. Radicals won office in the first city election of 1878. In 1911, quite counter to the surrounding area, the city voted in favor of women's suffrage and elected J. Stitt Wilson, a Canadian Socialist, as mayor. The city's large Bolshevik-leaning

Finnish population built the Finnish Hall in south Berkeley, which was later used as a base for the violent San Francisco general strike of 1934. Adherents to the Menshevik line, the "White" Finns, built a competing, though much less splendid, Finnish Brotherhood Hall up the road. In 1938 the "Red" Finns, with their history of socialism, had a large share in founding the Consumers Cooperative of Berkeley. In that same year, University students founded the cooperative living group Barrington Hall. Part of the larger student co-op movement, it was one of the few places that provided housing for minority students. The International House, established in 1930, was the other important residence for foreigners studying at UC, which in the late twenties had in attendance some 10 percent of all foreign students in the United States.

In the late 1950s and early 1960s the intellectual climate was one far more tolerant and welcoming of change than that of surrounding municipalities. Somewhat isolated geographically as well as culturally, the city is cut off by the San Francisco Bay from its glittering big sister, and from the monoculture suburbs to the east by a high hill range. Despite apparent blurring of civic boundaries to the north and south, Berkeley almost aggressively holds itself separate and maintains a clear civic identity, conspicuously contrasting itself to both the characterless bedroom communities of Albany and El Cerrito and the proletarian miasma of Oakland. Even the climate is distinctively its own; directly in line with the Golden Gate, Berkeley is cooler and foggier than the rest of the Bay Area.

STUDENT POLITICAL LEADER MIKE TIGAR SPEAKING AT A BANCROFT AND TELEGRAPH
RALLY ON THE BERLIN ISSUE, JULY 25, 1961. NOTE THE REGENTS' PLAQUE NEAR HIS
RIGHT KNEE INDICATING THE BOUNDARY OF THE CAMPUS.
PHOTO © 1993 BY TED STRESHINSKY.

FIAT LUX

D URING THE EARLY YEARS of Robert Gordon Sproul's UC presidency in the 1930s, left-wing student movements arose and proliferated in the United States and on the Berkeley campus. Their primary target was the escalating arms buildup, and the student peace movement, imitating the techniques of organized labor, made extensive, though ultimately ineffectual, use of rallies and brief strikes. In 1933, the Social Problems Club held rallies in front of Sather Gate to protest Japan's invasion of Manchuria. These rallies were dispersed by the police.

Real involvement in real social causes was in every sense contrary to the underlying philosophy of the University of California, whose charter echoes Cardinal Newman's belief that a university should be "the high protecting power of all knowledge and science, of fact and principle, of inquiry and discovery, of experiment and speculation; it maps out the territory of the intellect, and sees that . . . there is neither encroachment nor surrender on either side." Newman favored "liberal knowledge," and maintained that "useful knowledge" was a "deal of trash."* UC's glory has been in theoretical pursuits and Platonic "ivory tower" academics aggressively divorced from day-to-day practicality. The standing joke is that there have been doctorates granted by the College of Music to students who can't read music; the College of Architecture has the reputation for matriculating students who, despite a profound grasp of theory, can't build a doghouse; theoretical physics and abstruse mathematics, much furthered during President Sproul's

---

Fiat lux, "Let there be light," is the motto of the University of California, from the words of creation in the Vulgate.

*John Henry Newman, the English theologian most noted for his conversion from the Anglican church to Roman Catholicism, delivered a series of lectures on ed-

ucation in the 1850s, which were published as *The Idea of a University Defined* in 1873. The remarks here cited are quoted in Clark Kerr's *The Uses of the University* (Cambridge, Mass.: Harvard University Press, 1963), 2.

tenure, are UC Berkeley's bread and butter. Accordingly, Sproul did not believe that the University was the appropriate platform for social protest, and took steps to isolate the campus from radical influence.

Another aspect of Sproul's opposition to campus radicalism was the then generally current notion that a public university was a place to train those less fortunate children who were not of blue blood. Those born to the purple attended prep schools, Stanford University, and Ivy League colleges for the elite, who would after four jolly years of football and clambakes take their rightful places as the lords and masters of creation. Cal was for earnest climbers, honest sons of toil, and UC's constant uphill struggle for acceptance among the Eastern colleges could easily be tarnished by grimy bohemians. To allow students to blow their narrow chances through a lax administration's permissive tolerance of alien, dangerous thoughts could be seen as neglect of duty in the preparation of UC's students to take their places in society.

The first major change in University policy toward student political activity came in 1936, when the Berkeley Associated Students of the University of California (ASUC), previously opposed to antiwar rallies, sponsored a speech by the Socialist Norman Thomas on the Berkeley campus. Two weeks later Rule 11 appeared, requiring presidential approval for both off-campus speakers and the use of campus facilities by nonapproved groups. After this, flatbed trucks were pulled up to Sather Gate, then the entrance to the campus, to act as platforms for speakers.

In 1937, after Peace Strike planners at Berkeley suggested sending medical aid to Spain, Sproul announced Rule 17. It replaced Rule 11 and expanded the restrictions on campus political activity by forbidding fundraising for off-campus groups. Restrictions of on-campus political speech at last prevented any expression of political partisanship or advocacy of political action; the prohibition even extended to the speaking on campus of mainstream political campaigners. Thus in 1956 Democratic presidential candidate Adlai Stevenson could not enter the campus to speak to the students. The liberal candidate, widely popular in Berkeley, talked to thousands of students from atop an automobile parked at the corner of Bancroft and Telegraph.

Bob Gill: Stevenson was believed to have spoken from Stiles Hall, according to the people I knew. Stiles Hall, a building located a stone's throw from "new" Sather Gate, was itself an amazing place to us. Diagonally across the intersection from Harmon Gym, it was a lodestone of student radical and left-liberal activity through the sixties because its facilities were beyond the University's control. Stiles was where the

Wesleyan Foundation was based, the college-age movement of the Methodist church. Stiles Hall was the bastion from which we could sally forth into the community at any time because it was on the OTHER side of Bancroft and was definitely NOT on University sidewalks. I was told that Stevenson and anybody else rejected by University authorities would gravitate there as their first launching pad. By the time we got involved it was heavy into the American version of

BOB GILL, 1964. PHOTO BY CAROLE GILL.

the Campaign for Nuclear Disarmament [CND] and had been a mainstay of the burgeoning peace movement as well as the civil rights movement. For us it was great both for radical politics and for looking for girls. Before HUAC and FSM this was where we would find unconventional-minded bedmates, even if it was a nominally church-related locale. For a long time I didn't even know about the church aspect. I once went to a YPSL [Young People's Socialist League, the youth group of the American Socialist party] convention there and actually sang the Internationale at the closing, standing alongside hundreds of others with clenched fist held high. I almost cried. It was the only time I ever sang it like that.[1]

World War II put an end to campus political activity, and the return after the war of serious, older veterans, the escalation of the cold war, and the atmosphere of indifference and political repression combined through the late forties and most of the fifties to produce the "silent generation."* The last campus political protest of any significance until the loyalty oath controversy of 1950 was a peace strike on April 22, 1941.

---

*"If loquacity was one of the signs of the Great War—think of all those trench poets and memoirists—something close to silence was the byproduct of experience in the Second War. . . . Stephen Spender reports that early in September, 1939, a friend was traveling on a French train carrying British soldiers. They 'sat all the way,' he told Spender, 'in absolute silence, no one saying a word.' . . . they seemed

In 1946 the Regents passed a regulation that forbade a student to engage in "any off-campus activities in which he shall do anything intended [to], or which does, convey the impression that he represents the University or the student body" unless the student held written authorization to do so. Violation was grounds for dismissal.

Even as campus radicalism declined, the geography of the Berkeley campus changed. The University bought the land along Telegraph Avenue between Sather Gate and Bancroft Way and expanded the campus southward into the city. An administration building, Sproul Hall, was built on the east side of Telegraph, and in 1961 a new Student Union building, largely the new UC president Clark Kerr's project, opened on the west side. The area between was closed to traffic and became Sproul Plaza. Sather Gate, the former podium for off-campus political action, was now inside the campus and therefore off-limits, but the issue was more or less moot, since there weren't many student activists.

to feel that the less said, the better. . . . When the war was over, for most of the participants there was nothing to be said either. 'When I came back,' a Canadian soldier deposes, 'I didn't realize how silent I had been through those four years, and I became silent, or I continued silent. It was funny.' When the war was over, men of letters became silent too. As Karl Shapiro says, speaking of John Ciardi and the rest of the young writers who'd actually been in the fighting and had plenty to testify about, 'We all came out of the same army and joined the same generation of silence.' Kurt Vonnegut was of this group. When he returned from the war, he says, he wanted to tell everyone about the destruction of Dresden, which he had witnessed. He thought that it would be easy, 'since all I would have to do would be to report what I had seen.' But he found that it took him twenty-three years to overcome his urge to say nothing and to tell finally, in *Slaughterhouse Five*, what had happened in Dresden in 1943 and how it had affected his own life. . . . From this distance it's not hard to sense behind the Allied writing of the Second War what Susan Sontag will later designate, speaking of the plays of Pinter and Beckett, the films of Bergman, and the writings of Ponge and Robbe-Grillet, 'The Aesthetics of Silence.' 'As the prestige of language falls,' she says, 'that of silence rises.' . . . The war seemed so devoid of ideological content that little could be said about its positive purposes that made political or intellectual sense, especially after the Soviet Union joined the great crusade against what until then had been stigmatized as totalitarianism. After that embarrassment, less said the better indeed" (Paul Fussell, *Wartime* [New York: Oxford University Press, 1989], 129–143).

Eᴅɪᴛᴏʀɪᴀʟ ᴄᴀʀᴛᴏᴏɴ ɪᴍᴀɢᴇs of the cloak-and-dagger anarchist, the hairy Bolshevik and the shifty-eyed Commie union organizer were part of the standard repertory of American Types-That-We-Don't-Much-Care-For-In-A-Big-Way. Though we made *pro forma* condemnation of European Fascists, the American Bund and the Ku Klux Klan, it was generally agreed that these guys were fundamentally OK because they were themselves anti-Communist. (During a 1947 congressional session Congressman John Rankin of Mississippi called the Klan "a 100 percent American institution."[1]) One of the greatest culture heroes of this century, Charles A. Lindbergh, was openly pro-Fascist, and it didn't seem to bother anybody much.

In 1938, Congress established the House Un-American Activities Committee (ʜᴜᴀᴄ) to investigate "the cancers in our midst." Texas congressman Martin Dies, a fanatical anti-Communist, chaired the committee, which despite America's active preparation to engage in an all-out war with Fascism and to ally itself with "Uncle Joe" Stalin's Russia, interested itself in only one facet of "social cancer." The committee spent exactly one day hearing testimony about the American Nazi party, and on day two switched to Communism and stayed there, "opening its doors to anyone who cared to call anybody else a Red."[2]

Near the end of 1938, ʜᴜᴀᴄ's future chairman J. Parnell Thomas, a devout worshipper at the shrine of intolerance and swinish stupidity, instigated investigation of the American Federation of Labor (ᴀꜰʟ), the Congress of Industrial Organizations (ᴄɪᴏ) and the Federal Theater and Writers Project of the Work Projects Administration (ᴡᴘᴀ), which he called a "New Deal propaganda machine."[3] Even the idolized Shirley Temple was splashed with ʜᴜᴀᴄ's filth, for having inadvertently appeared in an interview in the pages of a French leftist newspaper.

These people were not merely anti-Communist. They were also anti-do-gooder, anti-urban, anti-intellectual, anti-second-generation-

American, anti-Catholic, anti-Jew, and very much anti-anyone holding "unsettling ideas about the condition of the negro [*sic*]." Without putting too fine a point on it, they were insane, and their insanity infected America. Congressman John Rankin may now sound like the very model of a Southern buffoon—the *Congressional Record* reports his idiot allegations that "Communism . . . hounded and persecuted a Savior during His earthly ministry, inspired His crucifixion, derided Him in His dying agony, and then gambled for His garments at the foot of the cross"—but his witch hunts intimidated the nation.[4] Before a congressional committee there were no rules of evidence, no cross-examination. The accused did not have the right to be confronted by his accuser. The anti-Communist films of the time may seem laughable now, but then they were the stuff of nightmares.

The most notable triumph of HUAC was the trial of Alger Hiss, then head of the Carnegie Endowment for International Peace and a former member of the State Department. Privately, I've always felt that he was successfully persecuted because of his name—"Hiss"—so like a snake's whisper: sibilant, sinister, easy to hate. Can you hear yourself saying, "I like *Hiss*. I think *Hiss* is a fine fellow. Let's give a cheer for *Hiss*." Probably not.

That aside, Whittaker Chambers, senior editor of *Time* magazine and a whimpering, self-proclaimed former member of what he called the "American Communist underground," fingered Hiss, who denied ever having been a Communist or even knowing Chambers from Adam's off ox. It wasn't easy to impugn the veracity of a man with such solid credentials, but California's enterprising junior congressman, Richard M. Nixon, figured out a way to trap him into committing perjury. Hiss was twice tried in a New York federal court. The first trial resulted in a hung jury, and a furious Nixon threatened to investigate both the twelve good men and true and the judge. Instead of being whipped like a dog and thrown out of office, Nixon got a more pliable second jury to convict Hiss and give him five years in prison, the maximum sentence for perjury.[5]

The American people were not stupid, and they learned this lesson fast: only a fool is going to get involved in some sort of political activity that half a lifetime later will set him up for prison and disgrace. America was panicked by a band of fanatics that presidents couldn't stop; Congress couldn't stop; even the military couldn't stop them. The late 1940s and early 1950s became a scramble to see who could climb onto the anti-Communist bandwagon fastest, bringing along at least one trophy set of ears before his own ears were cropped.

In 1953, Ethel and Julius Rosenberg were put to death for betraying atomic secrets to the Russians. With this bit of hard evidence of the menace in our midst, it looked like the beginnings of a real old-fashioned purge, but McCarthy's reign of terror broke down in 1954 when he overstepped his bounds and attacked the military. Television brought the Army trials into the living rooms of America, and a humiliated McCarthy was censured by the U.S. Senate.

Things are a lot harder to stop than they are to start, though, and the anti-Communist juggernaut kept on rolling for another half-generation. The original 1948 Mundt-Nixon bill, later the McCarran Act, was passed by Congress in 1950 over Truman's veto as the Internal Security Act. The McCarran Act demanded that the names and addresses of all members of Communist and Communist-front organizations, as well as the organizations themselves, be registered with the government; that provision be made for the construction of concentration camps to intern people dangerous to the security of the United States; and that trade unions, free speech movements, peace and ban-the-bomb organizations and Southern civil rights activists register with the government. (Many refused to do so and continued their activities more or less underground.) At this point, the First, Fifth and Sixth Amendments to the Constitution were dead by the hand of Congress itself.

THE YEAR OF THE OATH

A MAN IS GOING ABOUT HIS BUSINESS. A heavy hand falls on his shoulder. He is under arrest. Why? Perhaps he has criticized the political system that has taken over his country by force. And some stool pigeon has reported him. For this is happening in a police state, where no one is free to debate what is good for the country. One must accept, without protest, the ideas of the men in power. And we must never let the Reds turn our free America into that kind of fearful place.

With this bizarre quotation, from the 1955 trading card series *Fight the Red Menace*, published by the Children's Crusade Against Communism, I introduce the reader to the loyalty oath controversy.

On June 12, 1942, the Regents of the University of California adopted a resolution requiring that all employees sign the California loyalty oath:

> I do solemnly swear (or affirm) that I will support the Constitution of the United States and the Constitution of the State of California, and that I will faithfully discharge the duties of my office according to the best of my ability.[1]

Seven years later, on March 25, 1949, the Regents voted unanimously that all UC faculty and employees must sign a more strongly worded anti-Communist loyalty oath. Beginning June 24, 1949, each University employee was required to swear, in addition to the oath that all other California employees took as a condition of employment, that

> I do not believe in, and I am not a member of, nor do I support any party or organization that believes in, advocates, or teaches the overthrow of the United States Government, by force or any illegal or unconstitutional methods.[2]

I am not a member of the Communist Party, or under any oath, or a party to any agreement, or under any commitment that is in conflict with my obligations under this oath.[3]

The alternative was no pay. "Salary checks cannot be released until acceptance letters have been returned to this office properly signed before a Notary Public." So the Regents could change the rules in midstream whenever they wanted, and a tenured professor could be dismissed without so much as a by-your-leave if the Regents felt he was not jumping through some new hoop. As tenure rights were until 1958 a matter of custom rather than law, this created intense unease among the regular faculty, who felt "the oath to be discriminatory against the faculty in relation to other public servants, ineffectual in its purpose, and a violation of established principles of academic privilege."[4]

At an Academic Senate meeting on June 7, 1949, professor of psychology Edward Tolman objected vigorously to the amendment to the 1942 oath, but most UC professors and staff thought nothing of it and signed immediately.* Heavy pressure from within the faculty encouraged the lagging minority to conform, and by the end of August only 157 of the 9,450 UC employees had failed to do so. When the Group for Academic Freedom formed on the UC campus in July of 1950, that number had dwindled to 36. The Korean police action was going badly for the United States, and the general atmosphere was not friendly to a tiny band of principled nonsigners of what seemed to the public a perfectly reasonable anti-Communist oath—we *were* at war with them, after all. In August the Regents wearied of the power struggle and by a vote of 12–10 told the nonsigners that they had ten days to sign, resign or be fired. Three resigned, ten signed and of the remaining number, eighteen took the Regents to court. The case of *Tolman* v *Underhill* (Robert M. Underhill was the Regents' secretary and treasurer) went to court immediately and on April 6, 1951, a unanimous district court of appeals ruled in favor of the nonsigners. In May the California Supreme Court took the case along with several others then pending and, on October 17, 1952, ruled against the oath on the grounds that the original state of California oath took precedence and that UC employees could not be "subjected to any narrower test of loyalty than the constitutional oath prescribed."[5] The Regents met thirteen days later and voted unan-

---

*The Academic Senate is the whole body of regular faculty in the UC system. Throughout the text the Berkeley Academic Senate is called the Academic Senate, but it actually is a branch of the larger, statewide body.

imously to drop the matter. In November the nonsigners were offered their jobs back, but not their back pay. In March of 1956, by order of the court, the nonsigners were granted back pay for the period July 1, 1950, to December 31, 1952.

Professor Charles Muscatine: A vice president of the University, who was our lobbyist in Sacramento, dreamed up the loyalty oath as a way of pleasing some of the right-wing elements in the legislature. It wasn't even the president of the University who thought it up, or the Regents. It was totally uncalled for. Originally the Regents didn't even want it, but the president and the vice president talked them into it. Once the Regents got convinced they insisted on it.

I arrived in Berkeley in January of 1948, and at my first Academic Senate meeting an eminent professor of psychology, Edward Tolman, got up and said, "I've heard the disturbing news that the Regents have decided to impose a loyalty oath. That's wrong." He was the first one to rise up.

My view of the loyalty oath was based on the idea that the University was a place that was dedicated to freedom of thought, to the free pursuit of truth. A great many people objected to the loyalty oath, and there followed several years of controversy between the faculty and the Regents. My view, as I expressed it in my department, was, "I teach freshman English, and I teach my students to be honest about their opinions. I can't teach that if my own freedom is compromised. Signing would be in total contradiction to what I'm trying to do as a teacher; it would be a desecration of the gown. I have already signed an oath of allegiance to the United States of America; I'm a loyal citizen and a veteran. I can't sign this stuff. If you're committed to the free pursuit of truth, you can't say, 'I am not this and I am not that.' "

I wrote a letter to the president of the University which said, "I have signed an oath to support the Constitution of the United States of America, and I will not do anything to contravene that oath." I regarded signing that Regents' oath as a contravention of the First Amendment.

My position on the loyalty oath was the same as my position on art and literature and creativity: the whole essence of freedom of speech is freedom of imagination. That is, the imagination is the great creative agent, and if a person is not able to think thoughts that were never thought before, to feel feelings that were never felt before, to say things that were never said before, we're cut off from the greatest potential of humanity.

If you weren't living in the McCarthy era you wouldn't understand.

It was terrifying. People were being fired right and left. Let's say you're an associate professor with three kids and a mortgage. If you don't sign the oath you get fired. Then what? You're dead. The thing was incredibly painful for many people, including people like Ed Strong, who was really a liberal guy. Up until the last moment he didn't want to sign, and then finally had to. When Strong finally signed the loyalty oath, he sent it in to the Regents with a letter explaining his action and his deep anger over what he had been forced to do. Included with the letter was a rider, telling the Regents that if

CHARLES MUSCATINE.
UC PHOTO BY DENNIS GALLOWAY.

ever his letter were separated from the signed loyalty oath, they should consider it to be cause for his immediate resignation.

There weren't many who didn't sign, and those could be divided roughly into three groups: very, very eminent people, like Tolman, who was at the height of his profession, and Ernst Kantorowicz, the great medieval historian. Then some older folks with enormously secure personalities and powerful political convictions, like Jack Loewenberg and Margaret Hodgen. And then some cocky youngsters who figured, "Well, if I get fired, I'll get a job somewhere else." As for me, my wife wouldn't have let me sign, in any case.

There were three years of interminable faculty meetings. It was very important that the faculty speak with one voice in terms of what the Regents were doing. The Group for Academic Freedom, which was essentially the nonsigners, was responsible for organizing the faculty. Tolman was the chair, I was the secretary. We met once a week, and at first it was hundreds, and then dozens, and finally only a few. Early in the proceedings the leadership of the Academic Senate came to us and said—and it was very touching—"We have lost the right to speak, but you have not. So you

tell us what to do." So for about two and a half years we essentially managed the effort to get the faculty to say the right things to the Regents. At
last, some thirty of us were dismissed.

For the first year after I was dismissed I was totally unemployed, and
for the next two years I got a job at Wesleyan University, back East. After
we were fired, eighteen of us sued the Regents in the California courts.
Our lawyer, Stanley Weigel, now a federal judge, was one of the attorneys
for the State Banking Association; he was a true defender of civil rights,
and took the case at considerable professional risk. In three years, the California Supreme Court came down with a unanimous decision, saying
that the oath was unconstitutional, and directing the Regents to reinstate
us.

I didn't harbor a sense that the University was against me. To my mind,
the University is the faculty and the students. I've always thought of the
University as us, not them.[6]

The tension created by the loyalty oath confrontations provided a
subcurrent that ran all through the Free Speech Movement. The UC
faculty did not forget the insult, nor did it forgive the administration for
its actions, and in the eyes of many faculty members the treatment of
the protesting students was similar to that meted out to dissident faculty
in the 1950s.[7]

THE ADMINISTRATOR

THE UNIVERSITY IS BEING CALLED UPON to educate previously un-imagined numbers of students; to respond to the expanding claims of national service; to merge its activities with industry as never before. Characteristic of this transformation is the growth of the knowledge industry, which is coming to permeate government and business, and to draw into it more and more people raised to higher and higher levels of skill. The production, distribution and consumption of knowledge is said to account for 29 percent of gross national product, and knowledge production is growing at about twice the rate of the rest of the economy. What the railroads did for the second half of the last century, and the automobile for the first half of this century, may be done for the second half of this century by the knowledge industry; and that is, to serve as the focal point for national growth.
—Clark Kerr, President of the University of California, 1962

In 1952 President Sproul created the position of chancellor at Berkeley and named professor of industrial relations Clark Kerr to the post. Kerr was a Quaker, an active liberal Democrat, and had been among the leaders in opposition to the loyalty oath. After Sproul retired in 1958, Kerr, strongly backed by the faculty, became president.

Kerr began his tenure as president by ditching the old-fashioned notion that the pursuit of practical knowledge was a "deal of trash," and did his level best to make the university the servant of industry and government. A university, as Kerr saw it, was a "series of processes producing a series of results—a mechanism held together by administrative rules and powered by money."[1] And we're not just banging our gums here when we talk about mazoola. The 1965 budget for the University of California was 657 million bucks.[2] That's real money.

Kerr's idea of the university was in some sense the logical outgrowth of a peculiarly American view of education as the handmaiden of industry, a view rooted in the very foundations of American universities.

In the years following the Civil War, wealthy men returned part of their enormous plunder to the nation in the form of universities and colleges. Russell Conwell, famous for his "Acres of Diamonds" lecture, was a founder of Temple University. John D. Rockefeller was a donor to colleges all over the country and a founder of the University of Chicago. Near the end of his days, haunted by the terror of eternal damnation, that old pirate Andrew Carnegie spent fortunes on libraries, colleges and church pipe organs. Johns Hopkins was founded by a millionaire merchant, and the vainglorious robber barons Cornelius Vanderbilt, Ezra Cornell and Leland Stanford built universities in their own names. The institutions thus founded, as historian Howard Zinn points out,

> did not encourage dissent; they trained the middlemen in the American system—the teachers, doctors, lawyers, administrators, engineers, technicians, politicians—those who would be paid to keep the system going, to be loyal buffers against trouble.
>
> In the meantime, the spread of public school education enabled the learning of reading, writing, and arithmetic for a whole generation of workers, skilled and semiskilled, who would be the literate labor force of the new industrial age. It was important that these people learn obedience to authority. A journalist observer of the schools in the 1890s wrote: "The unkindly spirit of the teacher is strikingly apparent; the pupils, being completely subjugated to her will, are silent and motionless, the spiritual atmosphere of the classroom is damp and chilly."
>
> . . . . This continued into the twentieth century, when William Bagley's *Classroom Management* became a standard teaching text, reprinted thirty times. Bagley said: "One who studies educational theory aright can see in the mechanical routine of the classroom the educative forces that are slowly transforming the child from a little savage into a creature of law and order, fit for the life of civilized society."
>
> It was in the middle and late nineteenth century that high schools developed as aids to the industrial system, that history was widely required in the curriculum to foster patriotism. Loyalty oaths, teacher certification, and the requirement of citizenship were introduced to control both the educational and political quality of teachers. Also, in the latter part of the century, school officials—not teachers—were give control over textbooks. Laws passed by the states barred certain kinds of textbooks. Idaho and Montana, for instance, forbade textbooks propagating "political" doctrines, and the Dakota territory ruled that school libraries could not have "partisan" political pamphlets or books.[3]

Kerr's own view of history was, strangely enough in the light of what was waiting in the wings, one of the inevitability of events, and in his book *The Uses of the University* (1963), he made it clear that one must bow to the Wave of the Future. The choices are plain: participate willingly or participate unwillingly, but participate you will. The pre-destined future which Kerr so blandly presented was one that the students found particularly horrifying, the more so when it became obvious that Kerr *really meant it*.

In early October of 1964 the Independent Socialist Club published a pamphlet authored by Hal Draper. Titled *Behind the Battle of Berkeley: The Mind of Clark Kerr*, it presented the students with an unflattering portrait of their chief administrator, quoting selected passages from his writings that cast him in as poor a light as possible.

> Kerr, like many others, has perhaps forgotten that the very phrase [the wave of the future] comes from the 1940 book by Anne Lindbergh, *The Wave of the Future*, which presented the thesis that fascism or some type of totalitarianism was inevitably coming. She did not argue that this fascism be approved but only that it must be accepted. This was the identical approach also of Burnham's *Managerial Revolution*.
>
> The new type of "multiversity," Kerr writes later, "is an imperative rather than a reasoned choice." You cannot argue with an imperative. It is not Kerr's methodology to say, "This is what I think should be done." He represents himself simply as the interpreter of inexorable "reality."[4]

Kerr's 1962 speech about the factorylike university, producing knowledge the way other factories produce cars or soap, rubbed the students the wrong way, and in *The Uses of the University*, he warmed to his work, drawing the analogy even clearer:

> The university and segments of industry are becoming more and more alike. As the university becomes tied into the world of work, the professor—at least in the natural and some of the social sciences—takes on the characteristics of an entrepreneur. . . . The two worlds are merging, physically and psychologically.
>
> The campus and society are undergoing a somewhat reluctant and cautious merger, already well advanced. M.I.T. is at least as much related to industry and government as Iowa State ever was to agriculture.[5]

So did he alienate activist students the more. Underlying student and faculty antagonism to Kerr's academic assembly line was a bit of intellectual snobbery. Though we despised "ivory tower" academics, divorced from the real world and its real problems, we loved the idea of the pursuit of knowledge for its own sake, untrammeled by money-grubbing "what's it good for?" Babbittry. These seemingly contradictory notions coexisted in perfect harmony, and both collided with what were widely perceived as Kerr's nine-to-five, three-shifts-a-day trade-school ideas, dramatically manifested in the proposed "speed-up" change from semesters to the quarter system.

Kerr's vision of the university as the doxy of industry and government, distasteful as it was, paled beside his gleeful embrace of the concomitant domination of the university by the federal government, which was dumping huge piles of money into research and science and, in the process, transforming UC into one of the world's most important universities:

> The federal agencies will exercise increasingly specific controls and the universities dependent on this new standard of living will accept these controls. The universities themselves will have to exercise more stringent controls by centralizing authority, particularly through the audit process. In a few situations, self-restraint has not been enough restraint; as one result, greater external restraint will be imposed in most situations.[6]

Not only did Kerr foresee shining in the distance a glorious, bureaucratic, quasi-totalitarian future, he foresaw himself, mock-humble, at the helm:

> Instead of the not always so agreeable autocracy, there is now the usually benevolent bureaucracy, as in so much of the rest of the world. Instead of the Captain of Erudition or even David Reisman's "staff sergeant," there is the Captain of the Bureaucracy who is sometimes a galley slave on his own ship.[7]

And in his 1960 book *Industrialism and Industrial Man*, he presented the convergence of an authoritarian, bureaucratic, capitalist system and a softened-up Russian Communist system into an undifferentiated global industrialism.[8] In this society,

> The age of ideology fades; . . . industrial society must be administered; . . . The benevolent political bureaucracy and the benevolent economic oligarchy are matched with the tolerant mass; . . . Parliamentary life may appear increasingly decadent and political parties merely additional bureaucracies; . . . Not only all dictatorships but also all democracies are guided. . . . The elites become less differentiated . . . all wear grey flannel suits.[9]

Professional managers run the economy:

> Economic enterprise is always basically authoritarian under the guise of getting things done. . . . Authority must be concentrated . . . [Those in charge] will be bureaucratic managers, if private, and managerial bureaucrats, if public.

In this paradise there will be no war, no unrest, no strife: "Class warfare will be forgotten and in its place will be the bureaucratic contest . . . memos will flow instead of blood." The workers "will be subject to great conformity," and will accept this "as an immutable fact. The state, the manager, the occupational association are all disciplinary agents." The worker will have a certain degree of freedom:

PRESIDENT OF THE UNIVERSITY OF CALIFORNIA, CLARK KERR, 1964. UC BERKELEY PHOTO.

> Politically he can be given some influence. Society has achieved consensus, and it is perhaps less necessary for Big Brother to exercise political control. Nor in this Brave New World need genetic and chemical means be employed to avoid revolt. There will not be any revolt, anyway, except little bureaucratic revolts that can be handled piecemeal.

But what of the quality of life in Kerr's bureaucratic wet dream? Perhaps it will be found "in the leisure of individuals":

> Along with bureaucratic conservatism of economic and political life may well go a New Bohemianism in the other aspects of life. . . . The economic system may be highly ordered and the political system barren ideologically; but the social and recreational and cultural aspects of life diverse and changing. . . . The new slavery to technology may bring a new dedication to diversity and individuality.

53

Of course, there are snakes in Eden:

> The intellectuals (including the university students) are a particularly
> volatile element . . . capable of extreme reactions to objective situa-
> tions—more extreme than any group in society. They are by nature ir-
> responsible, in the sense that they have no continuing commitment to
> any single institution or philosophical outlook and they are not fully an-
> swerable for consequences. They are, as a result, never fully trusted by
> anybody, including themselves.
>
> Consequently, it is important who best attracts or captures the in-
> tellectuals and who uses them most effectively, for they may be a tool
> as well as a source of danger.

Protest, such as was rumbling all about him, and which had formed
the backbone of American unionization, was dismissed out of hand;
unions themselves were seen as a threat to the state, to be controlled or
destroyed:

> Today men know more about how to control protest, as well as how to
> suppress it in its more organized forms—the Soviet Union has indus-
> trialized and China is industrializing without organized strikes. A con-
> trolled labor movement has become more common.
>
> "Free trade unions" under some conditions become no more than
> Communist unions sabotaging efforts at economic development.
> Should they be that free? Completely free trade unions are sometimes
> not possible or desirable at certain stages in the industrialization
> drive. . . . The "free worker," in our sense, cannot exist in some social
> systems; in others he might exist, but to his detriment. . . . The "heavy
> hand of the state" over trade unions and enterprises may be the only
> substitute, at times, for the "invisible hand" of market competition
> which we have so long preferred. And some generals, in some situa-
> tions, may be by far the best leaders of an industrializing nation, all doc-
> trine of civilian control of the military to the contrary.

Was Kerr completely bonkers? Was this no more than the reflection
of a nasty adolescent power fantasy? Was Draper quoting everything out
of context? Did the students give a hoot in hell if he was? Nope. Were
any of the protesters going to sit down and read his books? Not a
chance. Students were much accustomed to synopses of course texts and
lectures, and Draper's pamphlet contained as much of Kerr's work as
we felt we needed to read. As far as we were concerned, Kerr had dug
his grave with his teeth.

Regardless of how he was quoted or to what end, there was no doubt that Kerr was profoundly arrogant and out of touch with the tenor of the times; his updating of 1930s Technocracy didn't even ring any new changes. The man was so caught up in his totalitarian idyll that he failed to notice what was actually going on right under his nose, and when he at last accepted the reality of social protest, tried to deal with it by following the blueprint that he himself had laid down. I'm pleased to report that it didn't work.

BANCROFT AND TELEGRAPH ENTRANCE TO THE UNIVERSITY OF CALIFORNIA, BERKELEY, CAMPUS, FALL 1964. PHOTOGRAPHER UNKNOWN.

His EDUCATIONAL THEORIES ASIDE, Clark Kerr was an amalgam of good liberal Democrat and dedicated bureaucrat. In 1959, Kerr granted an honorary degree to Professor Tolman, who had been dismissed for refusing to sign the loyalty oath, and in 1960 he induced the Regents to name a new building in Tolman's honor. Also in 1960, when Berkeley students were arrested for disrupting HUAC hearings, Kerr resisted demands to suspend or expel them, and he ignored similar outcries in the summer of 1964, when students were arrested for civil rights sit-ins at the Sheraton-Palace. The liberalization of faculty and student rights under Kerr's administration earned for him and the Regents the American Association of University Professors' (AAUP) Alexander Meiklejohn Award for conspicuous contributions to academic freedom, which was presented, ironically enough, in the spring of 1964.

The problem with Kerr's liberal principles, from the students' perspective, was that they tended to evaporate in the face of conflict: in any contest between the liberal's belief in civil liberties and the bureaucrat's desire for civil order, civil liberties were likely to draw the short straw—particularly if the disorder threatened Kerr's own turf. Challenges to the status quo might (or might not) be desirable, but should in any case proceed in an orderly manner—slowly, incrementally, through proper channels. Kerr's desire for order was yoked to a profound distaste for confrontation, and he viewed himself as "mostly a mediator," wryly acceptant of a certain inevitable unpopularity:

> The mediator, whether in government or industry or labor relations or domestic quarrels, is always subject to some abuse. He wins few clear-cut victories; he must aim more at avoiding the worst than seizing the best. He must find satisfaction in being *equally* distasteful to each of his constituencies; he must reconcile himself to the harsh reality that successes are shrouded in silence while failures are spotlighted in notoriety.

EDWARD W. STRONG. UC PHOTO.

It is sometimes said that the American multiversity president is a two-faced character. This is not so. If he were, he could not survive. He is a many-faced character, in the sense that he must face in many directions at once while contriving to turn his back on no important group.[1]

A master of the art of appearing to agree with everyone while siding with no one, Kerr became in moments of crisis particularly elusive, avoiding difficult situations and often dropping out of sight altogether.

Kerr's weakness was his personality. Like many political figures, he knew that confrontation was counterproductive; to avoid confrontation he preferred to leave the impression of agreement when he encountered opposition. A journalist, George N. Crocker, noted, "At one time or another—and often at the same time—every antagonist in a controversy thinks Kerr is on his side." The difficulty, of course, came when it was necessary to make a decision. Kerr used common bureaucratic techniques to minimize offending people. He avoided meeting those with whom he disagreed, he ordered bureaucratic underlings to make the decisions that would draw the most criticism, and he maintained a low profile—becoming, at times, almost invisible. One administrator said, "There is no Clark Kerr." In 1964 a Berkeley faculty member bitterly noted that while he and Kerr had worked on the same campus for sixteen years, he had never seen Kerr. The president's style was unusual. He often worked at home, where he managed massive flows of paper. Every afternoon eight secretaries packed a box of papers to be delivered to Kerr's home high above the campus in the hills of El Cerrito, and the next noon the papers were returned.[2]

On March 23, 1962, Edward W. Strong, a professor of philosophy, became the new chancellor. Making common cause with Kerr, in 1962 Strong was instrumental in persuading the Regents to abandon mandatory military training. Strong was "a traditionalist who turned brittle at the first sign of crisis, an almost total innocent concerning bureaucratic intrigue, and an idealist devoted to duty in a world run by accommodation and power. He lacked both the experience and the force of personality to be effective."[3] Strong's job, like Kerr's before him, was largely as a gofer and mouthpiece for the president's office, and Strong chafed under this much as had Kerr.

> *Charles Muscatine:* I suppose that President Kerr, an old Berkeley hand, did not want the Berkeley chancellor to rival him. But Ed Strong was particularly unfit to be chancellor at Berkeley to start with. He was an amiable vice-chancellor, a sweet man. He was a fine teacher, but did not have an imposing publication record; he filled that out with very distinguished service to the University, and rose through the ranks. When Kerr made a chancellor of Strong, who was not a powerful person to start with, it was obviously a signal that Kerr wanted Berkeley under his own thumb.[4]

Kerr's insensitivity to the feelings of his subordinates was part of a larger insensitivity to the outside world in general. His intellectual arrogance and personal isolation from the events of the day led him, in 1963, to the belief that the Left was dead and harmless, and he in consequence championed a campaign to repeal one of the last vestiges of McCarthyism: the Regents' ban of Communist speakers on any University of California campus. The Regents, however, were perfectly happy to let things stand as they were, and in order to complete the fight that he had inconsiderately begun, Kerr had to compromise.

> The old rule had banned communists but had allowed nonpolitical student groups to invite anyone else, except political candidates, to talk on campus. The new rule allowed communists to speak but required nonpolitical student groups to present balanced programs with opposing sides and a tenured faculty moderator whenever a speaker was "controversial." In practice, Kerr's new regulations left student groups at the mercy of the campus bureaucracy, which inconsistently and arbitrarily judged various speakers as controversial. For students, the greatest irritant was the requirement to find opposing speakers and faculty moderators. If such could not be found, then the program had to be canceled—or moved off campus.[5]

The students were not the only ones chafing under campus political restrictions; these rules applied to the faculty as well. UC professor John

Searle, in his essay "The Faculty Resolution," expressed their resentment:

> Although there have been some important liberalizations of late, the University of California has had a long tradition of political restrictions. The famous loyalty oath is its most spectacular efflorescence, but the more humdrum workaday civil liberties incident has set the campus atmosphere in recent years. An assistant professor is fired on political grounds over the protests of the Academic Senate Committees, a student gets a punitive F in ROTC for picketing while in uniform, a student group is refused permission to show a controversial film ("inconsistent with the educational objectives of the University"), a faculty group is reprimanded for asking an exam question not suitably respectful of the FBI, a speech by an assistant professor critical of the film *Operation Abolition* is canceled by the administration at the last minute, a Black Muslim leader is refused permission to speak on the campus.* And so on.[6]

Here we have, in terms of Berkeley's administrative bureaucracy, a recipe for disaster. The chief campus officer was a walking paradox. Kerr's confused liberalism, his slipperiness, his tendency to disappear at critical moments—leaving important decisions to weak underlings—his habit of stepping in at odd moments to countermand the actions of subordinates, would have a profound effect on how the UC administration mishandled the Free Speech Movement.

---

*The fired assistant professor was Eli Katz, of whom more in the chapter "Direct Action."

David Horowitz discusses the punitive ROTC event in his book *Student* (New York: Ballantine, 1962): Despite chief campus ROTC officer Colonel Malloy's threat that anyone picketing in uniform "will find it very difficult to pass the course," student Jim Creighton came in uniform to a December 15, 1960, picket of the ROTC at the drill field and, though an honor student with an A in ROTC, received an F for a final grade. Others who also picketed in uniform were not penalized (118–120). (ROTC stood both for Reserve Officers' Training Corps and Reserve Officers' Training Course. This minor confusion didn't bother anyone. The military training was compulsory for all male students until 1962.)

The banned film was Jean Genet's *Un Chant d'Amour*, of which more in the chapter "The Filthy Speech Movement."

The *Daily Californian* of March 8, 1960, reports on the troublesome question asked in the Subject A exam—an English test given to all entering freshmen to determine minimal English skills. The essay question was, "What are the dangers to a democracy of a national police organization, like the F.B.I., which operates secretly and is unresponsive to public criticism?" Hoover went crazy, and the composers of the question were sharply reprimanded by the UC administration.

Operation Abolition was an anti-Communist propaganda film distributed by HUAC. See the chapter "SLATE."

On May 4, 1961, Malcolm X was denied permission to speak on the UC campus on the grounds that he was the representative of a religious organization. He spoke at Stiles Hall instead.

IN LOCO PARENTIS

THE UNIVERSITY OF CALIFORNIA's postwar enrollment tripled the campus population from 7,748 in 1944 to 21,909 in 1946 and produced a housing crisis that led local residents to take in lodgers, build apartment units in basements and erect cottages in back yards. Between 1959 and 1964 the campus population jumped again by nearly 7,000 students; the first wave of baby boomers was beginning to hit college. In 1964 alone the freshman class enrollment increased by a whopping 37 percent, and the overcrowding and consequent neglect made undergraduates feel alienated and resentful. "California's five-year-old Master Plan for Higher Education guarantees college, tuition-free, to every high-school graduate in the state who wants it. Only the elite—the top eighth of the class—can apply to the nine campuses of the university. Others in the top third can attend one of 18 state colleges. For the rest, there are 73 two-year junior colleges. Nobody is left out, unless he wants to be."[1]

Students coming to UC Berkeley were the cream of the crop of California scholars, accustomed for thirteen years of kindergarten, elementary and secondary education to the fond attentions of their doting teachers. At Berkeley, so far from being big frogs in small ponds, they found that nobody gave a tinker's damn about them; required lecture classes were attended by as many as eight hundred students, broken up into study squads of fifteen or twenty under the often indifferent and only peripherally competent tutelage of grossly exploited graduate-student teaching assistants. Professors, obsessed with their own professional reputations and the gun held to their heads by "publish or perish" policies, had neither time for nor interest in their less important charges. The shocking transition from a warm, concerned, friendly and helpful school environment to the impersonal, disinterested, 1,232-acre knowledge factory caused me to flunk out almost immediately; I was readmitted in the fall of 1964 on academic probation with no brighter prospect of succeeding in my inappropriately chosen major of classics than before. I was bitterly disappointed with the kind of education I was getting, and was actively looking for remedies.

Renée Melody: When I was a small child, I lived in San Francisco. I had a view across the Bay of the city of Berkeley, and there was something over there that magnetized me. I would ask my dad, "What is that? What's over there?"

"Oh, that's just Berkeley!"

So I grew up always looking over there and thinking that my future was actually over there, and wanting to grow up so I could go over there and find it, because it was waiting for me. When I was in high school and at Foothill Junior College in Palo Alto, I could not *wait* to get out. My boyfriend said that I would really love Berkeley, that it was the place for me and that I really had to go there. When I finished Foothill, I was accepted at Stanford *and* at UC as a junior transfer student. If I'd gone to Stanford, I would have had free tuition, because my mother and all my ancestors had gone there; my sister was going there; my father, my grandmother, my great-aunt had been there. And I turned them down—a big slap in the face for my family—because I had to go to Berkeley!

It wasn't long before I found that what was happening outside the classroom was a lot more interesting than what was happening inside. At Foothill I'd had really exciting professors—it was a new school and they'd had their pick of interesting instructors. When I got to Berkeley, there were these old, dead professors who were giving the same lecture word-for-word from the Fybate notes; every joke that they'd been telling for twenty years, and I was really, really disappointed.* And I was pissed off, because this is what I'd been looking forward to and I expected it to be an improvement on Foothill—a *major* improvement— and the classes were duds. The best class I took—physical anthropology in Wheeler Auditorium—had a thousand people in it. The only class I got an A in. The others were really lame; the TAs were doing all the instructing, and it was just really boring.[2]

To add insult to injury, academic indifference was countered by an all too active administrative interest in the private aspects of students' lives. The doctrine of *in loco parentis* ("in the place of a parent"), by which students could be academically disciplined for "conduct unbe-

---

*Fybate notes were course notes provided by a commercial service that took notes in eighty-four major undergraduate lecture classes, then mimeographed them up and sold them in the bookstores around campus. At least half of the students enrolled in the huge lecture courses did not attend lectures, buying Fybate notes instead.

coming a student," deeply angered the undergraduate population. Parietal rules rigidly prescribed sexual mores, and girls were "locked out" of dorms and residence halls if they missed curfew, facing consequent expulsion for immoral behavior; students were liable for punishment by the University for civil crimes; and the student body chafed under the watchful eyes of student spies and congressional investigating committees. The administration kept

RENÉE MELODY, CIRCA 1964.
PHOTOGRAPHER UNKNOWN.

personal dossiers on its wards, and student extracurricular activities were organized under the chilling pall of University supervision. In consequence much student political activity was reminiscent of outlaw cells meeting in secret under a repressive regime.

Nobody was much interested in student complaints until the Free Speech Movement lit a fire under both faculty and administration, who in 1965 took a perverse delight in pointing out to each other that the horse was indeed gone, and that the door was indeed open, and yes, it was all somebody's fault:

> By any reasonable standard, the multiversity has not taken its students seriously. At Berkeley, the educational environment of the undergraduate is bleak. He is confronted throughout his entire first two years with indifferent advising, endless bureaucratic routines, gigantic lecture courses, and a deadening succession of textbook assignments, and bluebook examinations testing his grasp of bits and pieces of knowledge. . . . It is possible to take a B.A. at Berkeley and never talk with a professor. To many of the students, the whole system seems a perversion of an educational community into a factory designed for the mass processing of men into machines.[3]

A diagnosis of the malaise afflicting the American university would have to say a good deal about the increase in the size and power of administrative bureaucracies which regard the university as essentially "their" institution to be spared the troubles of restlessness and innovation. Something would have to be said about that prime vulgarity known as "publish or perish," a travesty of scholarship and common sense. And something more would have to be said, as I am glad the Berkeley students did, about the pressures faced by state universities from boards of regents heavily weighted toward conservative and business ideologies and almost always without faculty or student representation.[4]

Although disappointing, it is no surprise that the breakdown of communication across generations and between fragments of our society should also be present in the universities. "The administration," hero of a generation ago when salvation seemed to lie in organization, is an obvious target; but the growth of administrative power, in any institution, is not a simple phenomenon. The students' complaint about being manipulated by a group of conspirators to serve the economic needs of business, or whatever, is naïve. On the other hand, their sense of alienation is painfully real and justifiable. The proxy-parent—the administration rather than the faculty seems everywhere to play this role—is more powerful and more impersonal than any mother and father, and less inclined than many parents to treat the students with the dignity and respect accorded adults. The reasonable-sounding suggestion that the students had avenues of appeal open to them is simply not true in practice. In this context, it should be clear, I think, that until the students are really given responsibility, they should not be charged with being irresponsible.[5]

SLATE

STUDENT DISSATISFACTION with the way things were going at UC Berkeley was nothing new, and the administration did everything in its power to stifle organized protest except, of course, address the problems that the protesters were protesting about. In the late 1950s students unhappy with the University had begun to get organized, running candidates for the ASUC student government who interested themselves in matters of genuine social concern.

By 1964 the student organization SLATE occupied a key position in all campus political activity. Cheerfully beavering away at the underpinnings of Clark Kerr's multiversity, SLATE had begun in the spring of 1957 as TASC (Toward an Active Student Community), an umbrella group formed to run candidates on a single slate aimed at eliminating racial and religious discrimination in living groups. That October TASC expanded under graduate student Fritjof Thygesson and undergraduate Mike Miller to include ban-the-bomb and campus free speech issues. Interested in getting on-campus status, TASC reorganized on the UC campus in 1958 as SLATE. The pseudo-acronym was adopted because the organization decided to run a "slate" of candidates in the spring 1959 ASUC elections. When TASC became involved in student politics in 1957, the number of students voting doubled. Its successor SLATE got a large percentage of the undergrad and the majority of the grad votes, putting into office two graduate representatives, five representatives-at-large and an ASUC president over a two-and-a-half-year period. An all-around pain in the neck to the administration, SLATE tripped lightly from student affairs to ROTC protests, demonstrations against the death penalty, "No on 14" organizing, and confrontations with HUAC.*

*Proposition 14, the controversial "fair housing" measure coming up on California's November 1964 ballot, aimed to re- peal the Rumford Act, a law passed by the state legislature in 1963 to ban racial discrimination in housing. The initiative pro-

Graduate students, dragged unwillingly into the ASUC when it was made compulsory, made the best of a bad job by heavy participation in SLATE politics.* In a ploy to get SLATE supporters out of the ASUC, in January and February of 1959 the administration held an "informal poll" of graduate students to see if they would like to "dissociate" themselves and be exempted from the student body fee. The alternatives presented were no representation at all or a new, grads only, student association. A majority of the grads expressing an opinion opted out of the ASUC. Additionally, the administration counted abstentions as "yes" votes. Most graduate students felt that the student government had nothing to offer them, and that the paying of fees for things that catered only to the gay and carefree undergraduate taste was a burden; they viewed student government with indifference and did not see getting out of the "sandbox" of student politics as any great loss.

Although the poll had not been presented as a vote, on April 27, 1959, the ASUC Executive Committee approved the dissociation of the grads from the ASUC, and on September 22, 1959, at the beginning of the fall semester, the two graduate representatives were made nonvoting members of the Student Executive Committee. So the administration's ploy had succeeded, and grad students were cut out of student government. Later in the semester, the grads actually voted to secede from the ASUC and form their own association. A new graduate organization— the Graduate Student Association—was created, but never amounted to much, and by 1964 the GSA had withered away. "When graduate students concerned with the suppression of political freedom on campus tried to contact GSA officers, they were informed that no officers presently existed and that the last president was in Germany, along with all the organization's records. The field was therefore clearly open for a new graduate student organization."[1]

An important consequence of this permanent solution to a temporary problem was the destruction of any mechanism through which the administration could communicate with the graduate students. Teaching assistants (TAs) were all graduate students, and in late 1964, when the administration desperately needed a channel to them, it was forced

posed that residential and commercial property owners should have the right to sell, lease or rent their property at their absolute discretion, and that no state or local ordinance should prevent them from doing so. Sponsored by the California Real Estate Association, it was opposed by Governor Pat Brown. It won by a margin of two to one. In Berkeley it was defeated by the same margin.

*The ASUC was a voluntary student association until 1955, when, in order to finance the Student Union building, Kerr's baby, membership was made mandatory for both undergrads and graduates.

to acknowledge and deal with the hostile Graduate Coordinating Council (GCC) that had been formed by Free Speech Movement activists.

On May 15, 1959, SLATE's David Armor narrowly beat out Dan Lubbock, a fraternity-backed independent candidate, for student body president, 2,133–2,100, despite the fact that the fraternities and sororities had gotten out close to a 100 percent vote by requiring members to show a ballot stub in order to get their evening meal. Both the administration and the Greeks, who had long controlled the student government, were alarmed.

The administration had good reason to fear SLATE's victory. New ASUC president David Armor, not letting any grass grow under his feet, honored his campaign pledges to work for a co-op bookstore, a "Fair Bear" minimum wage of $1.35 per hour for student employees of local businesses, married student housing, and an end to housing discrimination. He had also promised to reopen the long-standing controversy over voluntary ROTC.* On September 22, 1959, a letter in the student newspaper, the *Daily Californian*, signed by freshman in philosophy Richard Casey, notified the campus that he had withdrawn from UC and forfeited his Regents' Scholarship rather than enroll in ROTC. The matter was brought to a head on October 19, 1959, shortly after the beginning of the fall semester, when freshman Frederick Lawrence Moore, Jr., the son of an Air Force officer, began a hunger strike on the steps of Sproul Hall to protest compulsory ROTC training. On October 21, after consultation with his parents, he ended his fast and withdrew from the University. That same day SLATE held a rally at Sather Gate to criticize the Regents for not taking action on ROTC, it having been three years since the undergraduate men had voted in favor of making military training voluntary and two since their position had been formally presented to the Regents. (ROTC remained compulsory until 1962. In May 1962, President Kerr presented a proposal to the Regents that it be made voluntary, and the proposal was accepted at the Regents' meeting of June 29.)

> *Paul Richards:* In 1961 I went with my father and stepmother to the Soviet Union where my father, Harvey Richards, made a film with my stepmother's help called *Women in Russia*. This was arranged through the Soviet Women's Committee. Madame Nina Papova, the head of the Soviet Women's Committee, had greeted us and provided us with inter-

---

*In the 1930s, the U.S. Supreme Court had interpreted the Federal Land Grant Act, which required that any college using lands donated through the act must have an officers' training course, to mean that the training had to be offered but did not have to be compulsory.

preters and helped to arrange an itinerary; we saw schools, factories and whatnot. Then we came back and I came to Cal and went into ROTC. I almost didn't go to school because I sat there having to either sign this loyalty oath and sign up for Reserve Officers' Training Corps, or not go to Cal. When they forced me to take it, that really pissed me off. You had to take two ROTC courses a year for two years. You had to march and you had to wear a uniform, and you learned how to break down an M-1. I made my decision and went to Cal and took ROTC. I'm sitting there in the back of the classroom and they're showing a movie, and the movie is "Who is the Enemy?" and there flashes up on the screen Madame Papova. She was the enemy. I'm sitting there at my desk and I hit the guy next to me and said, "Hey! I *know* that woman!" and he says, "What?!" and I say . . . wait a minute . . . "Nothin'."

You were supposed to wear your uniform going to and coming from class, and go home and change, but I would take off my hat and coat and walk home. Sometimes upperclassmen officers would say, "Hey, you! Come on over here and put on your uniform!" And I usually said, "Fuck you and drop dead, asshole!" and I walked off. "We'll get you!" they'd say, and I'd just walk away, "Ahh, fuck off." I'd ripped up my uniform in a motor scooter accident and I went in and said, "Hey, it's broken," and the guy threw me another one across the room, but I was happy because I'd cost them money. Every way I could I tried to make trouble for them. I'd walk behind these military brass around campus and shout and yell and make an embarrassing scene for them, "Bloody hands! You've got bloody hands! If we don't get out of Vietnam you've got bloody hands!" and they'd turn around and say, real hurt, "I don't have bloody hands!" I didn't want to flunk, but I got D's. I participated in the picket lines against ROTC, which was abolished shortly after I'd walked on the picket line; from this I gained the false impression that we were going to kick butt.[2]

In his 1963 Godkin Lectures, Kerr lightly dismissed the growing atmosphere of political activism at the University of California at Berkeley:

One of the most distressing tasks of a university president is to pretend that the protest and outrage of each new generation of undergraduates is really fresh and meaningful. In fact, it's one of the most predictable controversies we know; the participants go through a ritual of hackneyed complaints, almost as ancient as academe, while believing that what is said is radical and new.[3]

His actions in 1959, however, demonstrated a deeper concern. On October 22—a day after Frederick Moore ended his fast and left the Uni-

PAUL RICHARDS IN FRONT OF THE W. E. B. DU BOIS CLUB HEADQUARTERS, SAN FRANCISCO. A FEW WEEKS LATER, THE SHOPFRONT WAS DESTROYED BY A BOMB. PHOTO BY HARVEY RICHARDS.

versity—President Kerr issued rules governing political activity by students, aimed directly at SLATE and stressing that the ASUC was only to discuss and vote on campus issues, and that the chief campus officer (himself) was to decide what was a campus issue and what was not:

1) The preamble of the student government on each campus shall be changed to make it clear that the student governments are directly responsible to the appropriate chancellor's office.
2) Student governments are forbidden to speak on off-campus issues.
3) Amendments to student government constitutions are subject to the prior approval of campus officials.
4) To be recognized, student organizations must have an active adviser who is a faculty member or a senior staff member; such groups must declare their purposes to be compatible with the educational objectives of the University; they must not be affiliated with any partisan political

or religious group; and they must not have as one of their purposes the advocacy of positions on off-campus issues.

Protest against the Kerr Directives was prompt and widespread. The UC Berkeley *Daily Californian,* the UC Riverside *Highlander* and the UC Santa Barbara *Gaucho* complained that the directives infringed on the tradition of student government; the student government at UCLA, where distribution of literature of any kind was already prohibited, condemned the directives by resolution; and students at Riverside picketed the chancellor's office. SLATE hammered away for three years at what it called "The Big Myth" of liberalized campus rules under Kerr.*

In April of 1960 assistant professor of biology Dr. Leo Koch, a Cal alumnus teaching at the University of Illinois, was dismissed for "breach of academic responsibility" because he had written a letter to the student newspaper, the *Daily Illini,* advocating "free love" and suggesting that students who found themselves sexually frustrated stop their pitiful public necking, visit the nearest drugstore and buy some prophylactics. When the Cal student government heard about the firing, it asked University officials if espousing Koch's cause would be a violation of the Kerr Directives. Though told that it would be, on May 3, 1960, the SLATE-influenced Executive Committee of the ASUC nonetheless passed a resolution condemning the University of Illinois administration and supporting Koch's right to express his ideas. Shortly afterwards, Vice-Chancellor Alex Sherriffs told the ASUC Executive Committee that if it did not get in line, student government would "change drastically," i.e., be abolished, and members would be subject to expulsion.

The academic year of 1959–1960 saw the UC Berkeley chapter of the Congress for Racial Equality (CORE) picket the local Kress and Woolworth stores for the entire year over the issue of discriminatory hiring practices. Likewise student chapters of the National Association for the Advancement of Colored People (NAACP) investigated allegations of discrimination in off-campus housing. Led by SLATE co-founder Mike Miller, a committee on capital punishment formed and protested the San Quentin execution of "the red-light bandit," Caryl Chessman. Joining in the Caryl Chessman protests was Edmund G. "Jerry" Brown, future governor of California. (Though he later expressed hostility towards the FSM, after the Sproul Hall arrests Jerry asked his father, Governor Edmund G. "Pat" Brown, to listen to what the students had to say.)

---

*SLATE published a pamphlet titled *The Big Myth?* in November 1961, presenting its argument to the student community concerning the Kerr Directives. Authors were Carl Blumstein (bacteriology), Jerry Miller (chemistry), Mike Miller (social science) and James Walker (psychology).

ANTI–HUAC DEMONSTRATORS DRAGGED DOWN WET STAIRS IN SAN FRANCISCO'S
CITY HALL. PHOTO SAN FRANCISCO CHRONICLE, MAY 14, 1960.

This series of incidents aroused the unwelcome attentions of the vindictive, despotic madman J. Edgar Hoover, and a consequent low-grade running gunbattle between the University-based radicals and the FBI led to a violent confrontation with HUAC, which in May of 1960 served eighteen-year-old sophomore Douglas Wachter a subpoena on the grounds of the UC campus.* Subsequent protests on Friday, May 13, 1960, at San Francisco City Hall led to fire-hosing of the crowds and the

---

*FBI director J. Edgar Hoover (1895–1972) served under eight presidents—from Calvin Coolidge to Richard Nixon. His immense power stemmed, in large part, from his long tenure and his consequent extensive collection of dirt on absolutely everybody. American political and financial figures feared him and made an effort to stay on his best side, or at least not arouse his anger.

Hoover—a racist and fanatical anti-Communist—was greatly frustrated by the FBI's inability to ride roughshod over sixties civil rights demonstrators. When FSM and civil rights attorney Mal Burnstein demanded that FBI interviews of six civil rights demonstrators be conducted in the presence of their attorneys (this was against FBI policy), the agents in charge were sharply reprimanded by Hoover in an internal memo of March 12, 1965: *"Tell Sac to get some backbone. I don't care what these people think. The complainants are to be interviewed in our office and we are not going to be run by Defense counsel. I am astounded at Sac. [signed] H."* (Handwritten memo quoted from FBI files on David Lance Goines.)

I direct the interested reader to Curt Gentry's *J. Edgar Hoover: The Man and the Secrets* (New York: W. W. Norton, 1991).

PAGE B SAN FRANCISCO CHRONICLE, Saturday, May 14, 1960

Clubs, Fire

Water Sweeps Students; Screams Break Up Song

Continued from Page 1

their way backwards against the smash of the water, but they couldn't keep their footing on the slick marble and tumbled back, to get up again and make another try.

The voices of the singers echoed in the big rotunda of the City Hall like a choir in a cathedral.

"We shall not be moved, we shall not be moved," they sang in a chant.

IDENTIFICATION

Behind the line of policemen I saw one of the Un-American subcommittee staff pointing out people in the crowd. "That one's a Commie," he said, "that one's a witness."

Mostly what I saw were students, youngsters, and they were being very stubborn.

Then someone ordered the hose turned off, and the police line broke and came swarming down the stairs at the mob.

In a matter of seconds the enormous stairway was alive with struggling groups in wild confusion.

A big, red-bearded man was the first grabbed by the police. As he came down the stairs, he slipped and they dragged him like a sack of grain out through the lobby and into the sunlight of Polk street.

LIMP

I did not see any of the kids actually fighting with police. Their resistance was more passive. They would simply go limp and be manhandled out of the building. At this point it got very rough.

One plump girl was shoved from the top of the stairs and tumbled and slipped down two flights to land like a bundle of clothing at the ... The crowd of ... and civil servants ... and Jeanne and Deirdre into a roar of laughter the I. S. H. girl started to cry.

Another young man carried bodily by four policemen, kicked out as he went through the big revolving doors at the Polk street entrance. The glass shattered and tinkled on the marble floor.

CLUBBING

"They're using clubs," the crowd screamed. "They're hitting them!"

I saw one slightly built lad

Police pulled sprawling pickets down slick stairs

SAN FRANCISCO CHRONICLE, MAY 14, 1960.

arrest of sixty-four people, of whom thirty-one were UC Berkeley students.

Bob Gill: The HUAC demonstrations on May 12, 13 and 14 were the official opening day of the sixties. Never since the thirties had so many and such a diverse group of radical activists come together in one cause. Radical experiences were replicated around the Bay Area (with the notable exception of Stanford and the interesting addition of Reed College in Oregon) from this point on, and gave an evolutionary push for what came after.

Formally, this led to the Mount Madonna Park gathering of student activists—liberal religious and civil rights groups and ban-the-bomb types —who met over a weekend in July 1960 to form the Bay Area Student Committee Against HUAC (BASCAHUAC). That was the first time I'd ever seen ditto machines and typewriters in a park. Position papers were written, mimeoed and passed around, workshops were formed and "plenary" sessions were planned, but all these traditional academic forms paled beside the endless groupings and intellectual gropings of American kids who got together and asked each other just why things were the way they were and how they could do something about it.

The activists' purpose was to help in court cases or with University discipline procedures, but what they mainly ended up doing was to organize the many popular showings of the congressional propaganda film *Operation Abolition*, a heavy-handed pseudodocumentary meant to show the students as mere playthings of the shadowy Communist party.* The movie itself was a howler, complete with low music and talking-head shots of committee members who would later serve time for criminal corruption. BAS-

SAN FRANCISCO CHRONICLE, MAY 14, 1960.

CAHUAC organizers would list its countless errors of fact and film editing, and students coming of age at the time got a good glimpse of the American Establishment's basic deceitfulness and lack of principles that they would protest against for the rest of the decade and after.† The Mount Madonna gathering's germinal influence may never be fully understood, but it came to stand for the coalescing of general student

*"The center of this attack [on students who had protested HUAC hearings in San Francisco], which included a report by J. Edgar Hoover, was a film entitled 'Operation Abolition' made from newsreels that the Committee had subpoenaed from television stations KPIX-TV and KRON-TV. These films were edited by the Committee and then printed by Washington Video Productions" (David Horowitz, *Student* [New York: Ballantine, 1962], 82).

The film *Operation Abolition* actually served as a beacon to advertise radical activity. By 1964, tens of thousands of high school students had seen the film, and the more socially conscious high school and college students, such as Frank Bardacke and Lee Felsenstein, were in consequence drawn to Berkeley like bees to honey.

†David Horowitz presents an alternate origin of BASCAHUAC. "A meeting was

called at Barrington Hall on the evening of May 13, 1960, of participants in the HUAC demonstration. Arrested students met with attorney Jack Berman. On June first, Judge Axelrod dismissed charges against 62 of the 63 arrested. Shortly afterward the defense committee for Robert Meisenbach was formed. Meisenbach was accused of felony assault, of which he was found not guilty in May of 1961. The first Bay Area showing of *Operation Abolition* was on August 7, 1960, at the American First Baptist Church in San Francisco. Former defendants Burton White and Irving Hall put together a rebuttal, 'In Search of Truth,' and on September 11 the film and its rebuttal were shown. At that meeting, BASCAHUAC was formed, Burton White chairman and Irving Hall secretary-treasurer" (*Student*, 88–89).

One demonstrator caught full force of water when police turned on fire hose

SAN FRANCISCO CHRONICLE, MAY 14, 1960.

discontent over the way in which the American University was trying to form them into commodity products for the Establishment to consume. It meant that for the first time in a long time, students not only rejected the University as their alternate "parents" but demanded the status as adults their real parents had never been allowed to achieve.

This coalition supplied a core of veterans, training and experience that passed through to the FSM, the antiwar movement and the student civil rights movement.[4]

At the beginning of the academic year 1961–1962, SLATE representatives to the ASUC Ken Cloke and Roger Hollander wrote a *Daily Cal* article challenging the Kerr Directives in which they argued:

1) A true open forum is hindered by the requirement that one week's notice must be given for a rally or meeting, since it makes the spontaneous public discussion of issues impossible on campus, especially under emergency situations.

2) Relegating social and political actions to off-campus status is detrimental to the educational process. The University must prepare students for participation in society, and that includes teaching them to put ideas into action, as well as to consider ideas objectively.

3) The California constitution cannot be invoked in defense of the prohibition of social and political action on campus. The constitution (Article IX, Section 9) is meant to protect the University from outside forces which might try to influence its policies for political or sectarian reasons. It is not meant to restrict the actions of on-campus groups, such as SLATE.

4) Something must be behind the decisions, without precedent, to eliminate previously existing student rights. What forces are behind those decisions?[5]

Kerr responded, also in the *Daily Cal*, that things were better than they'd ever been, and if Hollander and Cloke didn't think so, they were welcome to return to the old Rule 17. If the ASUC wanted it, Kerr would toss his new directives into the garbage and immediately reinstitute the 1937 Sproul rules. The ASUC (SLATE representatives opposed) then slavered all over Kerr and told him how keen‾ they were on the much superior Kerr Directives.

ABOLISH HUAC MARCH AND DEMONSTRATION, 1961. PHOTO BY BOB GILL.

Cloke and Hollander answered Kerr in another *Daily Cal* letter that the question was not whether the new regulations were better than the old ones, or that the old ones were bad, but whether the administration had the right to set arbitrary rules governing the political and social behavior of students and campus organizations. "In a democratic society, the source of authority for such regulations is rightfully derived from the society's constituents, which in the case of a student community are the students and not the university administration."[6]

By March the requirement of prior notice was reduced to seventy-two hours, and the Student Civil Liberties Union (SCLU) was campaigning for a further reduction to twenty-four, as well as for other changes: that student groups be required only to notify the administration of intended meetings, without the necessity for approval; that any group—recognized or not—composed of only UC people could use campus facilities for meetings; and that the administration deal with the problem of appointing a faculty adviser.[7]

In March 1961, SLATE invited the secretary of the Citizens' Committee to Preserve American Freedom, Frank Wilkinson, to speak on campus. Wilkinson had been convicted for contempt of Congress and was just about to go to jail; the contempt citation had been incurred in Atlanta, Georgia, when Wilkinson had aided the Emergency Civil Liberties Committee and the Southern Conference Educational Fund in their efforts to reduce the damage done to the civil rights cause by HUAC investigations.

A local passel of anti-Communist ministers violently protested his invitation, provoking a storm of controversy. In response, Governor Brown said,

> This country has become great because we let everybody speak their piece . . . if they violate the law, if they urge revolution by force or violence, then we can put them in jail. But to ban them before we know what they are going to say, I think that is a very serious mistake.

At the March 20, 1961, Charter Day ceremonies, Clark Kerr similarly defended the controversial invitation:

> The University is not engaged in making ideas safe for students. It is engaged in making students safe for ideas. Thus it permits the freest expression of views before students, trusting to their good sense in passing judgment on these views. Only in this way can it best serve American democracy.[8]

Two days later Frank Wilkinson was heard on campus by some thirty-five hundred students and faculty.

SLATE organized noisy campus protests of the April 17 Bay of Pigs disaster and, under SLATE influence, the ASUC passed resolutions supporting Southern civil rights activists and opposing the NDEA (National Defense Education Act) loyalty oaths. The May 1, 1961, SLATE candidate for ASUC president was Mike Tigar, an announcer for Berkeley's left-liberal listener-sponsored radio station KPFA. Tigar was a popular fellow, who had added to his notoriety by narrating the spoof version of *Operation Abolition*. He came in a respectable second (Brian Van Camp 3,593; Mike Tigar 2,864), and two other SLATE candidates won office. Doing its best to irritate Vice-Chancellor Sherriffs, SLATE invited Dr. Leo Koch to speak on campus, which he did, to a large and appreciative audience on May 11, 1961. SLATE by now had been elevated to a place on the permanent all-time shit list of the UC administration, which was looking for any plausible excuse to get the organization out of its hair.

When TASC had reorganized as SLATE in May of 1958, it had applied for on-campus recognition as a "campus political party." This was denied. It had then reapplied as a "student organization concerned with the ASUC" and was accepted as such in September 1958. On March 30, 1961, Dean of Students William F. Shepard warned SLATE chairman Michael Myerson that a leaflet identifying SLATE as a "campus political party" was in violation of the terms of its recognition. Myerson apologized, explaining that a member of SLATE had prepared the leaflet without his knowledge. Shortly there-after a telegram was sent by SLATE to the Ohio State *Lantern*. The telegram was signed "Michael Myerson, chairman of SLATE, a campus political party." Myerson again explained that he had not authorized the manner of signing the telegram, but to no avail. This flimsy technicality formed the ostensible basis for kicking SLATE off campus, and on June 10, 1961, its recognition as a legal campus organization was revoked. This provoked a response from SLATE that the administration would have done well to ponder:

MIKE TIGAR, 1961.
PHOTO © 1993 BY TED STRESHINSKY.

> SLATE has objected to the administration's arbitrary actions, but it has never led a sustained and deter-mined campaign to challenge the legitimacy of this complete power and to institute students' rights. The administration has shuddered at the implications of the party idea, but we have never carried that implication of student autonomy to its logical conclusion. Perhaps the most recent and most blatantly un-justifiable action against SLATE should serve as the signal for a student rebellion for student rights.

No campus political party can hide from the battle with the administration. The question will always be: what status in the hierarchy of priorities should this battle occupy? Should it be central from the beginning and the basis on which you appeal for support from students? Should the party take the initiative in defying the administrative authority demanding fair and uniform procedures and rights? Or should the issue remain peripheral until the administration commits such an obvious injustice that the party can issue the plea of the martyred to the oppressed students to rise up and demand their rights?

"WHO APPROVED THE WAR IN VIETNAM?" 1962
CHARTER DAY PROTESTS. PHOTO BY BOB GILL.

And what sanction can such a group find to make its power felt? Would a student strike be effective? Would it flop for lack of support? Would judicious use of the press and the ever-present threat of bad press for the administration be a powerful enough instrument? Could the courts be used?[9]

SLATE was not, in fact, slowed down a bit by being thrown off campus. Under University regulations, the organization could still sponsor campus candidates and schedule speakers and other campus events. If anything, SLATE took its activities a step further.

President John F. Kennedy was to speak at the March 23, 1962, Charter Day ceremonies. The administration considered this a star in its crown, but the campus radicals saw it as an occasion to showcase dissatisfaction over atomic testing, U.S. relations with Cuba, civil rights, the bracero program, discrimination in housing, enforced military training and the activities of the House Un-American Activities Committee. Frank Bardacke was chairman of the Ad Hoc Committee for March 23, incorporating just about every left-liberal political organization in town, especially SLATE. This full-scale general protest deeply embarrassed the campus administration and drew heavy fire from Hugh Burns (D-Fresno), a powerful anti-Communist California senator.

Realizing that student control of the ASUC was not only ineffective but almost impossible, SLATE began a serious campaign to develop a strong student following by providing a service that would actively involve students and give them something they both needed and wanted. Beginning in the academic year 1963–1964, SLATE handed out forms for course and teacher evaluations, which it then gathered and published over the summer as a supplement to the University's *General Catalog*.

The *SLATE Supplement to the General Catalog* was among the first student-initiated evaluations of teachers and courses in the United States, and as such was not welcomed with cries of joy by the administration. Everyone knew that the University took an exceedingly dim view of both the *Supple-ment* and its parent organi-zation. Adopting a general tone of realistic cynicism, it took more than a few sly digs at the administration in passing. Distributed on September 10, 1964, with the *SLATE Supplement* Vol-ume I, Number IV, was a thirteen-page "Letter to Undergraduates" signed by former student Brad Cleaveland, the campus rabble-rouser manqué, call-ing for "open, fierce, and thoroughgoing rebellion."

"JFK STINKS," 1962 CHARTER DAY PROTESTS.
PHOTO BY BOB GILL.

I'd had only a little contact with Cleaveland, but it was enough to dis-cover that his monomaniacal educational theories escaped me completely.

> The "Big U" does not deserve a response of loyalty and allegiance from you. There is only one proper response to Berkeley from undergradu-ates: that you <u>organize and split this campus wide open!</u>
> FROM THIS POINT ON, DO NOT MISUNDERSTAND ME. MY INTENTION IS TO CONVINCE YOU THAT YOU DO NOTHING LESS THAN BEGIN AN OPEN, FIERCE, AND THOROUGHGOING REBELLION ON THIS CAMPUS.
> I would like to briefly explain to you now why such a course of ac-tion is necessary, and how, if such a revolt were conducted with unre-lenting toughness and courage, it could spread to other campuses across the country and cause a fundamental change in your own futures.
> Go to the top. Make your demands to the Regents. If they refuse to give you an audience: start a program of agitation, petitioning, rallies, etc., in which the final resort will be CIVIL DISOBEDIENCE. In the long run, there is the possibility that you will find it necessary to per-form civil disobedience at a couple of major University public ceremonies.
> And if you get this far you will also have witnessed a nation-wide publicity which will have exposed Berkeley for the undergraduate sham that it is. Not to say that the public in general will feel that way, what with the press "red-baiting" you, but that students all over the country

TOM WELLER. PHOTO BY ANNA BELLE O'BRIEN.

will read between the lines. By this time you may also be able to call for a mass student strike . . . something which seems unthinkable at present. If a miracle occurs, or two, you might even get to say that you were the seeds of an educational revolution unlike anything which has ever occurred.

Tom Weller: The idea of a student guide to classes seems obvious today. Indeed, within a few years the SLATE *Supplement* was taken over by the ASUC as an official function, and most schools around the country now have something similar. But at the time you'd have thought we were trampling the flag. Concern primarily came from the faculty. Curmudgeonly Joseph Fontenrose of the classics department was particularly critical, forbidding anyone in his classes to contribute questionnaires and otherwise raising Cain.

There were some good arguments on that side of the question. Faculty were jealous of the traditional sanctity of the classroom and of peer-based hiring and tenuring, and feared a possible entering wedge for more administrative control. And not unreasonably: the recent loyalty oath struggles were fresh in their minds.

Indeed, in recent years that fear has partly come true, particularly at schools like the California State colleges where the lofty independence of the faculty had never been that well established. Occasionally student evaluations have been used by administrations as yet another club against the faculty, or as weapons in internal political fights. On the other hand, this seems to arise in situations where the students have lost control of the thing.

I got involved with the *Supplement* through my friend Jon Petrie and contributed two of my skills—editing and stapling—to one or both of the first couple of issues. That's how I met Phil Roos, the prime mover of the project, and Jerry (now Joaquin) Miller.

Phil had a concept of writing and editing as not merely a collaborative but a communal activity. He and I and others, perhaps Jerry, would get together and edit the summaries written by the supervising grad student of each department into a consistent style. I was surprised that rather than parceling out the work, Phil led us through the text line by line, word by word, each of us making suggestions aloud until by consensus the *mot juste* had been achieved. But it seemed to work.

Usually when the work was nearly done, a fresh-faced Jann Wenner would finally blow in, clad in baggies and with surfboard under his arm, and inquire brightly, "Are we finished yet, fellows?"

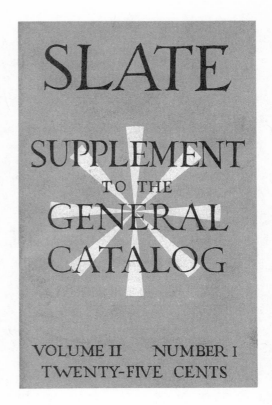

SLATE

SUPPLEMENT

TO THE

GENERAL

CATALOG

VOLUME II   NUMBER I
TWENTY-FIVE CENTS

Brad Cleaveland was full of ideas about educational reform and could convey a great sense of enthusiasm to a group of people face to face, I'd heard. But he couldn't write worth a darn. He had written this long rant and Phil gave it to me to edit.

It was a mess, all CAPITALS!!! and exclamation points!!! and underlines!!!, and resembled the style of strange religious pamphlets or Dr. Bronner's Peppermint Castile Soap bottles. I worked on it for a while but then, being a feckless youth, started to dawdle. Phil finally got impatient and took it away to give to someone else. I think it went through several more hands before it was finally published. So for all I know, I may have written that stirring phrase calling for "open, fierce, and thoroughgoing rebellion" that the administration apparently found so terrifying. I couldn't tell you.

I haven't seen the document in the intervening years, but it's my recollection that, despite the ruckus it caused, it was mostly concerned with boring old educational reform and was not a call to the barricades in any but a highly metaphorical sense.[10]

Bob Gill: The SLATE *Supplement* represented one of the basic tenets of University reform, namely to plan your own learning experience. The thing about school in general was that you had to struggle through it in order to get out and do the things you wanted to do in the first place. Why bother with this kind of schooling at all? British students told us that this kind of grade-unit-semester bullshit didn't exist over there, but there didn't seem to be much to do about it over here. The *Supplement* was the first chance to say or do anything about the force-fed pablum approach to education since the introduction of Fybate notes. It transcended Fybates because instead of merely regurgitating class content it added an actual value judgment on the class itself, the teachers in particular and the consequences of taking the damn thing in the first place. Here was another split with the campus faculty liberal: we were actually *judging* them, crossing the boundary that kept the inmates from running the asylum. The *Supplement* sowed the seed of the short-lived Free University, self-guided course planning, pass-fail grades and other feeble but noteworthy attempts at educational innovation. [11]

For all the headaches it gave the administration, SLATE was oriented toward moderate policies, working with or within the Establishment for gradual change, and friendly to such political organs as labor unions, the Democratic party and the student government of the ASUC. The chairman of SLATE for the academic year 1963–1964 was Art Goldberg, assisted by his sister Jackie Goldberg and his friend Sandor Fuchs. As 1964–1965 chairman, Sandor headed SLATE throughout the life of the FSM. Jackie Goldberg and her brother Art, Sandor Fuchs and Brian Turner believed that "boring from within," gradually taking the system over, would attain the desired end, and they inclined throughout the FSM toward negotiation, enlisting faculty cooperation, and a "go slow" attitude. In this they differed markedly from students in the campus civil rights organizations, who tended to be activist and confrontational, eschewing established political avenues, parties and individuals. Art's personality also grated on many members of other campus and off-campus organizations, and by September of 1964 a genuine rift, based on fundamental political differences, political goals, personality conflicts and activist tactics, had developed between SLATE adherents and the student civil rights groups.

CIVIL RIGHTS

By THE EARLY 1960s, student peace protests had given way to civil rights activism aimed at the plight of American Negroes and, incidentally, the civil liberties of the students themselves.* The old National Organization for the Advancement of Colored People was a go-slow, conservative organization, unable to respond to the demands of activism made by the young people who were the center of the new civil rights movement. Student activists gravitated toward the more militant Con-

*Throughout this century, the terminology for Americans of Black African ancestry has constantly evolved. When I was a little boy, I was sharply reprimanded for referring to a man as a "Black." This disparaging term was not used in polite conversation, as it was reminiscent of former slavery and degradation. The polite term was "colored," as it both implied that the person had at least a soupçon of white blood and did not automatically exclude other nonwhite people (hence the "National Association for the Advancement of Colored People," founded in 1909 with a predominantly white membership). "Negro" was also polite. A further bone of contention was whether the word was capitalized or not in print; almost as an overt insult, many publications had no policy to capitalize the word "Negro," and its appearance in all lowercase was a subtle insult that persisted in American journalism well into the 1960s. Following the ideology of Elijah Mohammed, Malcolm X consistently said, "the so-called Negro," and in his May 4, 1961, speech at Stiles Hall said that he was as offended by "Negro" as by "nigger." In the mid-1960s, when the Black Power movement began to gather steam, the politically correct term became "Black," and later "Afro-American" (which never really caught on). In the 1990s, "African American" or "American of African Ancestry" and, in reference to nonwhite races and peoples, "persons (or people) of color" became the politically correct usages, though there is an interesting revival of both "Negro" and "colored" among African American people themselves. All this aside, the term used during the early civil rights and free speech movements and well into the mid-sixties was "Negro," and in the interests of historical accuracy as well as a desire to avoid an ex post facto kaleidoscope of shifting political tides, I shall leave contemporary usage intact where appropriate. As the term "Black" is now used in direct reference to Americans of Black African ancestry, it seems to me appropriate to capitalize it. I have occasionally seen "white" capitalized when used in reference to Americans of European ancestry, but it seems a bit too much to follow this model, even though it would actually be more consistent.

gress of Racial Equality (CORE) and Student Non-violent Coordinating Committee (SNCC). CORE was a national left-of-center civil rights organization, founded in Chicago in 1942 by James Farmer. It was integrated, activist, confrontational and espoused the philosophy of nonviolence. At Berkeley, Campus Friends of CORE had a strong Independent Socialist Club influence. SNCC (pronounced "snick") was a more radical, youth-oriented organization dedicated to registering voters and organizing in the South. Impatient with Martin Luther King's nonviolence and reformism, and with the adult-dominated CORE, Black college students founded SNCC in 1960, and in 1964 it was headed by the militant Stokely Carmichael. Though CORE openly welcomed whites into its ranks, SNCC displayed an ambivalent attitude, and in 1966 expelled whites from the organization. Despite its name, SNCC's commitment to the philosophy of nonviolence was not at all deep. In the early 1960s these distinctions were not so clear, and in the Bay Area, many members of SNCC were also members of CORE, and participated in the same demonstrations. Though we routinely referred to ourselves as members of "CORE" or "SNCC," outside of the South the local chapters were actually called "Campus Friends of SNCC" or "Berkeley Friends of CORE."

> *Bob Gill:* The student movement revolved on the three areas of civil rights, civil liberties and University reform. Civil rights was the delicate but determined fight against racism both locally and in the South. Civil liberties was the holding action against right-wing and liberal repression (both government and otherwise) that attacked our efforts, mostly through simpleminded Red-baiting. University reform of course meant taking care of administrative pressure where we lived. Ban-the-bomb-type resistance should be included, but at the beginning of the Movement it was being pushed aside as a sort of childhood disease we were outgrowing.[1]

The 1963–1964 academic year was ushered in by escalating student participation in the civil rights movement, given impetus by the June 12, 1963, assassination of Medgar Evers, the NAACP's Mississippi field secretary, in Jackson, Mississippi. In November 1963, extensive picketing of the San Francisco branch of Mel's Drive-in was designed to force the hiring of minorities. Court orders limited the number of picketers and the nature of the action, and because these were constantly violated, police arrested 111 protesters. On November 8, Mel's in

Berkeley was also picketed.* On November 21, Berkeley CORE announced that it planned to picket Sather Gate and downtown Berkeley firms during Christmas.

In February 1964, Campus CORE brought into play the new tactic of the "shop-in" at the Lucky supermarket at Telegraph and Haste. CORE members filled shopping carts with groceries, had them checked out and then declared that they would not pay for the groceries until the store ended its discriminatory practices. The demonstrators dressed nicely—because after all they were totally screwing up the store and didn't want to give anybody a reason to call them bums or beatniks—but the CORE or SNCC pin on the lapel was a giveaway.

Shopping cart filled to overflowing with small, expensive items (it was fun playing like you actually were on a shopping spree even though you couldn't take anything away for real). The checker looks up, sees an attractively dressed young woman. Sees the CORE pin. Laboriously rings everything up.

"Peas, nine cents. Harry, how much is this paté stuff? Dollar ninety-nine each. OK, Miss. That'll be nineteen dollars, please."

"I'm *so* sorry, but I seem to have forgotten my purse until you hire some Negroes in public positions."

The guy behind her is wearing a sports coat, tie and CORE pin. Shit.

After ten days of this highly disruptive action, CORE and Lucky's signed a hiring agreement affecting all Lucky stores in the Bay Area. Not long afterward, that particular Lucky store was permanently closed.

On the day that the Lucky agreement was announced, a picket line was established outside the Sheraton-Palace Hotel in San Francisco. On Friday night, March 6, a thousand demonstrators, mostly UC students, appeared at the Sheraton-Palace; by Sunday, the number of pickets had increased to two thousand. After hundreds of demonstrators had been arrested for blocking the hotel lobby, the Hotel Owners Association signed an agreement promising to hire more members of minority groups.

On March 16, picketing began at a Cadillac agency in San Francisco;

*"On November 8, Mel's in Berkeley was picketed, 180 taking part under the leadership of a high school group. Campus CORE refused to endorse the picket, arguing that it was politically motivated since one of Mel's co-owners was a candidate in San Francisco's mayoralty race. (He lost.) Campus CORE was also unhappy because no provision had been made to monitor the picket line in order to prevent violence. After three days more of picketing, Berkeley CORE claimed victory" (Max Heirich and Sam Kaplan, "Yesterday's Discord," *California Monthly* 75, no. 5 [February 1965]: 30).

this time, one hundred were arrested. Over the course of the spring and summer, more than one thousand participated in the Auto Row demonstrations that continued throughout the summer.

Paul Richards: I was chairman of the Berkeley Du Bois Club when I went to jail for Sheraton-Palace, Cadillac and Mel's, and was one of the chief instigators in those protests. My level of alienation was complete. It was in the context of HUAC protests and compulsory ROTC that I sought out the student protesters, SLATE and Mike Tigar and Ken Cloke.* That's when I met people in the Communist Party, who were active in the Du Bois Club. The Du Bois Club was a semi-secret recruiting device, with only a few open meetings.† I met Bob Kaufman, who'd been with the Freedom Riders in the South and gotten a fractured skull. He was the philosopher of the Movement, a quiet, wonderful guy. He really inspired me. Those were the kinds of guys I wanted to be associated with.

People experienced racism in their lives, and out of this came a struggle to the death over an issue that was in your soul. I was raised by a Black man, and my heart burned against racism. I believe that type of commitment is what really characterized the civil rights movement; the SNCC students and Freedom Riders and others who simply threw the gauntlet down and said, "We're not going to take this anymore." Out of this comes a response that everything is based on. We were responding in a very childlike fashion. It was pure, it was absolute, it was intransigent. This moment—from 1960 when HUAC started to break up, until 1965 when the Vietnam War drowned us in blood—this was a moment of immense power for the people, of immense change. It was the breakup of segregation, which was vastly important to the shape of the American Establishment. But it wasn't the end of racism. My mistake in the sixties was to think it was the end of racism, because I didn't live in the segregated world, and I really didn't understand that. We saw the outward forms change, and thought somehow that was connected to the substance.

*Both Jeff Lustig and Wayne Collins, Jr., recount that Ken Cloke was being groomed as the successor to Mike Tigar as SLATE's ASUC presidential candidate. Just before he was to have declared his candidacy, Ken was apprehended for shoplifting a book from the ASUC bookstore. Usually nobody paid much mind to this sort of infraction, and it certainly would not have done much harm to his standing among the students. However, the matter was referred to Alex Sherriffs, who told Cloke that unless he dropped out of the race, he would be prosecuted to the full extent of the law and expelled. Cloke dropped out of the running for ASUC president, quit Cal and went to UCLA.

†Named after the American educator, sociologist and co-founder of the NAACP, the W. E. B. Du Bois Club was founded in the early 1960s as a youth organization closely tied to the Communist party.

I was greatly inspired by what was going on in the South. I wanted to jump on that bandwagon, but I didn't want to go South: I wanted to hit it here. In the South, they were fighting against legal segregation. In the North, we were fighting racism—discrimination in hiring, discrimination in schools. I went to a couple of CORE and SNCC meetings, and saw that they were support groups for civil rights activism in the South, and I was not moved by that. They were "Friends of the Student Nonviolent Coordinating Committee," and "Campus Friends of the Congress of Racial Equality," and I wanted to do it right here, right now.

The Du Bois Club had decided to concentrate on discrimination in hiring, and I'm sure the Party had decided on that focus before the Du Bois Club had. So, the Old Left was there, in the background. Things were discussed with old-line Communists like Rosco Procter and Mickey Lima, and we formed the core of political youth who were active in the early civil rights movement in the Bay Area.

Mel's Restaurant was first. Mel's didn't hire any Blacks. Maurice Dobbs was the owner of Mel's in San Francisco and Berkeley, and he was the Republican mayoral candidate in San Francisco against Shelley, the Democrat. When we started to picket Mel's, the Democrats came up to us and said, "Oh, don't picket Mel's, because then Dobbs will win." We went ahead and picketed Mel's anyway, and it hurt Dobbs a lot and Shelley won handily, but he turned out to be a wishy-washy guy. There were a lot of people in the Communist party who were really in the Democratic party, and worked through the Democrats and really believed in it. They did not oppose our demonstrations but were silent about it. For the students, for us on the ground who weren't part of the Establishment political life, it seemed like a sellout, that they wanted to co-opt us. Our attitude was that we had some objectives that were just—*just* was the word—and our attitude was, "We're right, you're wrong, fuck you." We would not budge one single inch, and that's what made us different from them.

We didn't really succeed in Mel's, because Mel's closed down, at least temporarily. But Mel's was the launching pad for Sheraton-Palace and Auto Row. That's when the Ad Hoc Committee to End Discrimination was formed, and it involved SLATE, SNCC and CORE and people in the community civil rights groups.

We picked Sheraton-Palace because it was, as my father said, "the citadel of Establishment culture." We won at Sheraton-Palace, and went on to Auto Row. I don't know why. It was an anticlimax. There weren't that many jobs involved.

Hundreds had been arrested, and we made a deal that we'd get tried in groups of ten before all different judges. Some were acquitted, and some were convicted. My ex-wife, Susan Alland, was arrested three

TRACY SIMMS AT THE SAN FRANCISCO CADILLAC DEMONSTRATIONS.
PHOTO © 1993 TED STRESHINSKY.

times in all three demonstrations, right alongside me, but she got off and I got convicted and went to jail.

A lot of people got busted in Mel's but didn't have to do time on it, because the next demonstrations clogged the courts so much that they just cut everybody loose. But I got two months for Cadillac and three months for Sheraton-Palace with one month suspended.

The co-chairmen of the Ad Hoc Committee to End Discrimination were Mike Myerson and Tracy Sims. When it came time to serve our sentences, Mike left the state and never came back. Tracy took a big fall; after serving time in jail I never saw her again. Jail took it out of her. The fact that Myerson wasn't there to help her when the shit came down didn't help. It's bad in jail. I remember guys in jail crying, "Oh, I'll never do this again, I gotta get out!" The loudest, most vocal protesters just bawling, wishing that they were out of there. People cracked up. In jail I saw the consequences of what we did more clearly. I'd had no clue when I was arrested.

Maybe two or three others got the kind of sentences I did. In August of 1966 I served my time in the San Francisco county jail, and I was alone in there most of the time. I came into the jail after everybody else had been in for almost a month, and all of these guys were making a protest because the San Francisco county jail was segregated. It's a six-story jail, with two wings with a rotunda in the middle. The first story housed the "dormitory" floor. The Black dorm is on one side, and the white dorm is on the other side. The Blacks were downstairs in the laundry and the kitchen, and the whites had everything else. So the demonstrators immediately formed a grievance committee to end discrimination in the jail. This committee, through the Hallinan brothers, was putting a lot of political heat on the jail about segregation. Willie Brown showed up, and put on a lot of pressure merely to keep the demonstrators safe, because it was a vicious situation in there.

At first, I worked in the jail administration office where I shared a desk with fellow inmate Conn Hallinan, and there I was privy to all the information about how the sheriff's people were handling the demonstrators and the grievance committee. I became the liaison with that committee right away. This grievance committee found non-demonstrators in the jail who wanted to affiliate themselves with its goals. The people who were in that committee were of mixed motives, to say the least. The political people were interested in keeping the guards off their ass, in keeping a high profile, and making a further dent in the Establishment scene. I don't know what the regular prisoners wanted; in jail you learn fast that people are not what they seem.

The grievance committee was all a part of continuing the struggle. The grievance committee had a meeting with Sheriff Carbury—

drunken red-nosed creep that he was—where I called him a liar and walked out. Immediately thereafter I got thrown in solitary—locked into my cell—in the isolation wing on the sixth floor, where I served the rest of my time. The television faced away from my cell over my head blaring from nine in the morning until nine at night. While I was in lockup, all the other demonstrators got out. Meanwhile—this is in 1966—riots are going on all over the United States; when the Fillmore–Hunter's Point riots occurred, some inmates in the Black dormitory burned mattresses in sympathy. The jail locked down, and they brought in sixty cops, armed to the teeth. They walked right into the Black dorm and arrested the remainder of the grievance committee for rioting, even though they hadn't done the mattress burning. They lost their good time; I lost my good time. One Black car thief was severely beaten during the police action. After that, there was not a meeting, there was not a peep out of anybody in that jail. That was the end of the grievance committee and that was the end of the effort to end segregation in the San Francisco county jail. At that moment I realized what "talk is cheap" meant. We'd done the talking and the non-demonstrator prisoners paid the price.[2]

Tom Miller: Most people that are in the ISC [Independent Socialist Club] are in CORE. To tell you the truth, the CORE people aren't very friendly to the SLATE people at all, and they didn't want what was going to happen to fall into the hands of SLATE. We figured there'd be a big blowup. The SLATE people politically disagree with the CORE people.

The type of thing the SLATE people did in the Ad Hoc Committee to End Discrimination in San Francisco is an example. Tracy Sims was the leader there and got screwed by the ad hoc committee. She was a great leader. The ad hoc committee said they'd fight the arrests all the way to the Supreme Court, but when it came down to attacking the people who were putting us in jail, the local Democrats, who they claimed they'd gotten elected, they wouldn't do anything. They just let everybody get slaughtered in the trials, and in effect killed the San Francisco civil rights movement for a long time. It was very explosive at Cadillac; at least three thousand people were demonstrating, and at least a thousand were ready to get arrested. SLATE was a part of the ad hoc committee, and they constantly attacked Campus CORE, which offered other alternatives to the way it was being run. SLATE wanted to be the main civil rights group on campus, and so did CORE. So there was conflict over domain. Ego conflict. The ideology of the various groups was different, and there were a few personalities that conflicted, such as Art Goldberg's.

CORE is civil rights activists. None of the CORE people work with the Democratic party. We demonstrated when Johnson showed up, and that shook a lot of people up. When the FSM formed there was a split right away between the SLATE people and the CORE people, SDS [Students for a Democratic Society] falling in the middle most of the time; sometimes they'd side with one, sometimes with the other.

At the first meetings of the FSM we tried to get as many CORE sympathizers as possible on the Executive Committee. We got Jack Weinberg, plus three CORE people plus two ISC people, plus a couple of suspended people; David Goines, who although he had been cited at a SLATE table was sort of close; he'd started going towards us. I was elected the ISC representative to the Executive Committee. Barbara Garson was in CORE.

I was elected to the Steering Committee, Savio was elected, Art Goldberg was elected, David Friedman was elected—he quit in a week because he was in CORE and Jack was in CORE and I was in CORE. We had three CORE people. Sid Stapleton was on, Bettina Aptheker was on, and right away we had problems with Goldberg. He would never sit down in a Steering Committee meeting and discuss anything. He would always jump up when others were speaking; he would never listen when others would talk. It was very frustrating with Goldberg. Jackie, after all, didn't show up at most of the meetings. Bettina was good. I left the Steering Committee in November; the meetings were too long; I just couldn't keep it up and go to school. I had to graduate, it was my fifth year.[3]

The CORE and SNCC activists, such as Jack Weinberg, Mario Savio and Suzanne Goldberg, believed that change was best accomplished by confrontation and direct action. They eschewed cooperation with those whom they perceived as their "class enemy." In the instance of student rights, the administration represented the ruling class, the faculty the middle class and the students the working class. The activists in the power structure of the FSM outnumbered the moderates, and took control of the Movement almost immediately, ousting their ideological enemies and relentlessly pursuing this bitter internal conflict throughout the FSM's existence.

Most of the students involved in the Free Speech Movement fell into neither camp, though their sympathies may have lain with one fundamentally different attitude or the other. Though I was aligned with the activist element, I was a nascent anarchist.

The anarchist philosophy was inarticulate in the FSM, but formed the essential activist core for everything that followed: the Filthy Speech Movement, anti–Vietnam War activism, the drug culture, hippies, Yippies, the Weathermen, People's Park and so on.

CORE PICKET, SAN FRANCISCO, DECEMBER 1, 1963. PHOTO BY HARVEY RICHARDS.

Students for a Democratic Society (SDS) was aligned with neither CORE nor SLATE, and though the FSM tactician Steve Weissman was a member, SDS ideology was of no great importance to the FSM's philosophy. At that point, SDS could have gone one way or the other: just another Young Democrats or, as it happened, the apotheosis of sixties anarchism. The Weather Underground—which is what the SDS turned into—could stand for the organized aspect of late 1960s anarchism, whereas the whole hippie movement could be seen as the unorganized aspect. After the FSM, we were without ideology or formal leadership, seeking only the destruction of the repressive, murderous established order. Our plans for replacing it with something better were extraordinarily vague.

FREEDOM SUMMER

MARIO SAVIO: I got involved in the Student Non-violent Coordinating Committee when I was living in this horrible boarding house. It was rather like a dorm I'd lived in at my first year at Manhattan College—water bombs flying around, constant noise. There's a place for all that, but this was *constant!* You have all these people, very crowded, yet you really feel alone. You don't feel you can communicate with anybody. The roommate I had was a Goldwater conservative. As long as we didn't discuss politics, I could communicate with him. As a matter of fact, as long as we didn't discuss anything *important* I could communicate with him. I didn't really know much of anybody on campus. The kind of people I wanted to know were the kind of people who were involved with Campus SNCC. I didn't want to find people I could go to parties with. I had a very romantic view of what college *could* be, even if it wasn't.

Civil rights activity was one of the things that was part of the community that I wanted to be a part of. A frame of reference that constituted the community. Here were people more or less like myself, who seemed by the things that they said to have a well-developed sense of justice and injustice. By contrast, the very things that seemed to be defended by the merchants seemed wholly other.

The appeal of the subculture, in part, I'm sure, was rebellion. In part, the lively interest in politics, where that means a real concern for and engagement with public issues, as opposed to what politics means in our society: the brokerage that results in this little bill being passed here that wasn't passed there. I was dimly aware then, and really believe now, that the lack of politics in the first sense in society creates a real thirst, a real hunger, which this particular community was able to begin filling. There was a very strong vicarious identification with the national civil rights movement, which for several years was the most interesting thing that one *ever* read about in the newspapers, that one *ever* heard about on television. Seemingly the most unsullied thing, certainly.

I think, in part, the attraction of all these things was a desire to be an actor in one's own life. In a way, I think the civil rights movement represents that to people who are otherwise quite passive in their own lives. Causing things to occur, rather than having things happen to them. It's really easy to see how white, middle-class youths could identify with the civil rights movement. Very different from watching television or being a spectator at sports. It seemed to be a real wedding of thought and action. I found that here in Berkeley, in this subculture we've been discussing, it comes close to being my ideal of what college should be like.

Brian Turner lived next door, though I didn't meet him for the better part of a semester. It turns out, he'd been involved in some kind of civil rights activity in high school, and attended SNCC meetings with me.

I first found out about the Sheraton-Palace demonstrations from a leaflet passed out at Bancroft and Telegraph. People were talking about it, and the arrests, so we knew about that. I hadn't decided whether I was going to go, and had more or less forgotten about it. I was at a "welcome to spring" party with my girlfriend and the three fellows with whom she shared an apartment. Altogether there were about seven or eight people there. The subject of the Sheraton-Palace thing came up, and we all said, "Why not? Let's go!" So we all went over to Stiles Hall, where you knew there would be cars—one of the standard facts was that you knew there would be cars there to go. And we piled into a Volkswagen bus and went across the bay. I'm sure that there were many, many people at that demonstration who had planned just as carefully as I had.

I really didn't know what would happen. I was one of those in favor of going to the upper floors and waking people up. It seemed to me that the people in the hotel ought to be disturbed. We stayed on the bottom floor, because the upper parts were closed off by the police. But we made a lot of noise on the lower floor. A peculiar thing happens. You're in a hotel lobby, and you have no particular experience before of clapping, stamping and marching around in hotel lobbies. But then, you're in this hotel lobby with hundreds of other people, and the purpose of being there is one that you accept. In this case, half-trying to communicate to large numbers of people that something is seriously wrong here, but also to make it clear to the management that unless they do something about this condition, that they're not going to be able to run this hotel. While, at the same time, not going around breaking things. By your presence, by your numbers, by the noise you're making, making it very clear that the hotel runs only if it runs in a more just fashion.

Once you're in the hotel, something else takes over. There's this *community* within the hotel. There's all these people engaged in common in this worthwhile endeavor. You're close enough to people where you can

MARIO SAVIO, 1964. PHOTO BY HOWARD HARAWITZ.

see the people that are doing it with you. It's not the kind of common activity that you're engaged in within a nation, where you don't have any idea who the people are who are engaging in this supposedly common activity. Maybe in some nations at some times this feeling can be engendered for brief periods of time, though that usually is quite dangerous.

Tracy Sims urged that people block the doors, and if the police arrested us we would get arrested. The idea was to get the protest into the courts, and to make it further difficult for people to use the hotel. This

SHERATON-PALACE DEMONSTRATIONS, SAN FRANCISCO, 1964.

was the kind of mark of ultimate commitment to this internal community here. So if someone asks, "Was it justified?" you ask, "In what
context, to what end?" What actually makes you decide? You sit there
looking at your finger, and there comes a point at which you realize that
you have lifted your finger. I was arrested there. There were 160 people
arrested, and I was one of them. In the case of each individual there are
a lot of factors that relate directly neither to the external community nor
to this community of protest, but to something even more personal:
well, there I was, I was at this demonstration with the girlfriend that I'd
just come with. There's another reason for being arrested. When I look
back on it, there was no single reason as *the* reason for being arrested.

If the thing is to be analyzed in political terms, the thing to analyze
is, why people come to the demonstration. Once you're at the demonstration, once you're in this thing which has a character of its own,
there are several roles within it that you can play. If you've already accepted yourself as an actor in this context, then it's a matter of your own
personal dispositions of various kinds, derived from factors that aren't
strictly political, which will determine which ones of the possible roles
in this you play.

After the Sheraton-Palace demonstrations, I was in jail with Jon King

PHOTO BY HOWARD HARAWITZ.

and Jack Weinberg, and Jon told me about the Mississippi Summer Project, and I thought about it and decided to go. I was in two different places. Half the summer I was in Holmes County, doing voter registration and Freedom Democratic party organizing, which meant, really, just convincing people to join. Door to door; sometimes sitting down for an hour with a person or a family and then being told, "Sorry, we decided no." We saw quite a few people that way. Within the difficulties of that situation, I found that I could get along comparatively easily. We lived in a Freedom House.

I went to McComb for the other half of the summer. In transit, while in Jackson, I and a friend got into a little trouble with a couple of rednecks who got out of this car, right in Jackson, with two police billy clubs and they came after us. I ran. I got one or two blows on my back, but my friend went the wrong way, and they started beating up on him. I started back toward them, and they ran away back to their car. I got the fellow's license plate, and through that we were able to track him down. They came to trial, and I testified against them, as did the friend who was beaten up and a local person, who got away without being hit at all. The local person was a young Negro fellow. That's how they identified us: we were walking down the street together. It was one of the few convictions that SNCC ever got, but it was a non-record court, so it may well have been reversed on the second shot. They start all over again: the guy gets another trial, essentially.

In McComb I was teaching American Negro history at a freedom school. I was learning it at the same time I was teaching it. Some mathematics, Spanish, English, something like civics—what your constitutional rights are—that's about all.

I came back different, though I didn't realize how different until the FSM started. I'd been changing over a period of a number of years, what with time in Mexico, and civil rights activities around here. I was at Cadillac, Mel's Drive-in and Lucky. By the time I came back, a long process had come to fruition.*

With Jack Weinberg, I was one of a group of people who were active in Friends of SNCC and Berkeley or Campus CORE who had set up a tutorial program in West Berkeley for elementary and high school students. It was remedial work in different subjects: arithmetic, algebra, geometry, reading, writing. It met in three sessions once a week. It wasn't very successful. We tried to keep it down to small groups. Four, maybe five at the most to each instructor. Sometimes one person to an instructor. But it was a finger-in-the-dike operation and we seemed to be running just to stay where we were. It had the effect of convincing me personally that other, more political means of attacking the problem were what was called for, rather than setting up tutorials for junior high school students. When someone was responsive, you had the feeling you weren't preparing them for anything at all. When they'd leave the

---

*W. J. Rorabaugh's description of Mario's background summarizes some of the elements brought to fruition in 1964: "Savio, the son of devout Italian Catholics, had been educated at the Christian Brothers Manhattan College until he had transferred to Queens College. In the summer of 1963 he had worked for a Catholic relief organization in rural Mexico, and that fall, after his parents had moved to Los Angeles, the former altar boy had entered Berkeley as a junior. During the summer of 1964, he taught a freedom school for black children in McComb, Mississippi; conditions there, he told the press, had made him 'very angry.' By the fall of 1964, this philosophy major had had an unusually broad experience that stimulated his passionate dedication to the causes he held dear. Savio's father, a machinist, was proud of his son's Catholicism and devotion to social justice. When the son entered Berkeley, he appeared to be searching for new roots; he began to call himself Mario instead of the more prosaic Bob of his childhood.

"In 1964 the 6'1", 195-lb. Savio was proud and cocky, angry and defiant. He scowled beneath his longish, sandy-red hair. He was not cool. His power came from his ability to articulate a tone that expressed the frustrations and anxieties of his generation. While others were as angry as Savio, they found it impossible to articulate their anger. Savio had the gift, perhaps the result of his Catholic education, to discourse rationally." (*Berkeley at War: The 1960s* [New York: Oxford University Press, 1989], 21–22.)

session and go back to school, whatever curiosity had been excited would just as quickly be quashed. We tried to make some contact with the schools, but they weren't particularly cooperative.

After a while the Women Mobilized for Berkeley wouldn't renew our arrangement. The involvement of CORE in the Shattuck Avenue Project had something to do with this. This was when we were picketing merchants on Shattuck.

The defendants' meeting for the people arrested in Sheraton-Palace was my introduction to that mysterious thing, sectarian politics. There wasn't enough room to have it indoors, so we had it outside in the parking lot adjoining the office of one of the attorneys, who addressed us from the balcony window. Arlan Tussing raised the question that there weren't any defendants' committees. Now, Arlan Tussing is associated with the Socialist party and the Young People's Socialist League. There were people in the back, who I later found out were Du Bois Club members and they were shouting Tussing down and attacking what he was saying: "If you don't like the present defense, if you don't like what the lawyers are doing for you, why don't you get your own lawyers?" This wasn't completely reasonable. There were two people at this meeting who I knew had no particular axe to grind, who were also making suggestions, such as we not put in any pleas. Those two people were Jack Weinberg and me. I think that we were identified with Tussing and his group, and it was thought that we were being divisive, which was how the Social Democrats acted in general. I didn't know what a Social Democrat was! That night, I went with Jack to the Du Bois Club meeting. At the meeting, there was this person who said that he hadn't been at the meeting, but that he had it on the best authority that a group of Social Democrats had tried to break the meeting up. Now, I know that wasn't true, because at least two of the people who were trying to "break up the meeting" were me and Jack. I discussed that later with Jack Kurzweil, who was prominent in the Du Bois Club.[1]

Jack Weinberg: I think "radical politics" or even "politics" was secondary to what the Movement was all about. All of us were dissatisfied with the world and wanted change. Racism presented itself to us as the obvious flaw in American society—Jim Crow in the South, systematic, de facto racial discrimination in the North. The movement to fight it offered purpose and meaning that was otherwise hard to find. Events presented an opportunity for us to believe our efforts and commitment could make a difference—could be a part of a movement that was changing the world. What a heady feeling.

In those days, being "radical" meant to me being a person who was willing to act on his or her beliefs whatever the consequences. It meant being willing to go to jail, willing to risk death. It was as much a matter of attitude and style as it was "politics." Organized political radicalism played a significant role in this milieu, but did not define the Movement.

I and others talked about expecting an "explosion" of activism when students came back in the fall. People high up obviously had the same concern—a fear that the momentum of the Bay Area civil rights movement that had seen mass demonstrations with hundreds of arrests in the spring and summer might reach new heights when the students came back to school after that eventful summer. It was a fear that student involvement might catalyze events and have a real impact on race relations in the Bay Area.

Pressure was put on the University to head off growing student involvement in the civil rights movement. The University acted to keep the students from engaging in "forays" into the larger community and in large part succeeded. The expected "explosion" occurred. But it was limited to the campus, and student impact on the Bay Area civil rights movement never returned to previous levels. However, a year later the anti–Vietnam War movement became the beneficiary of the student rights fought for and won by the FSM.

The events of the summer had an enormous effect. It opens a window into what put me—and many others—in a mood to behave the way we did in fall of 1964.

Martyrdom was the theme of the summer. It was as if a righteous war had been declared and we were all ready to march off. Before 1964, the Student Non-violent Coordinating Committee had been putting out the message that the murder of Black civil rights workers was a common event in Mississippi, but that the rest of the nation didn't care. The main purpose of Freedom Summer was to create a presence in Mississippi so that the nation could no longer ignore what was going on there. True to expectations, white civil rights workers—college kids— were murdered along with the Black.* Mississippi racial injustice had finally been uncloaked—or so we thought. But in early fall of 1964 the national Democratic party, with full support of its liberal, Hubert Humphrey wing, rejected the Mississippi Freedom Democrats in favor of "greater political interests." This event was a watershed in American

---

*On June 22, 1964, three civil rights workers, Michael Schwerner, Andrew Goodman and James Cheney, were arrested by Deputy Sheriff Cecil Price in Neshoba County, Mississippi, held in jail until after dark and then turned over by Price to the Ku Klux Klan. Six weeks later, on August 4, the FBI found their bodies buried in an earth-fill dam near Philadelphia, Mississippi. On October 20, twenty-one white men were arrested and later convicted by an all-white federal jury of conspiracy in the slayings.

JACK WEINBERG, PICKETING THE BERKELEY BANK OF AMERICA, SUMMER 1964. THE
BLACK ARM BAND IS FOR CIVIL RIGHTS WORKERS SCHWERNER, CHENEY AND GOODWIN,
MURDERED IN MISSISSIPPI. PHOTO BY HARVEY RICHARDS.

Andrew Goodman   James Chaney   Michael Schwerner

political life. The experience caused me personally—and large numbers of others—to lose my last vestiges of faith in the American system.

Before the Free Speech Movement, several different activist and/or radical student organizations existed, each with its own agenda. Civil rights activism had been growing for about a year in its national context and was the one issue that could bring various groups together in common action. Before the FSM, this occurred only in the context of some larger civil rights struggle with roots in the off-campus Bay Area civil rights movement (like for example the Sheraton-Palace demonstrations). But we had nothing like a machine—there was no financial base, no paid staff, no printing press.

The closest thing to a "machine" for causing trouble might have been the Berkeley Campus CORE chapter. We had maybe twenty-five activists. Other campus civil rights groups had less. Though the people involved in civil rights had just come through a very radicalizing experience, they had no thought of looking for a fight on campus. Our orientation was activities in the community. The campus was a base for drawing support. At first, all we wanted from the University authorities was to be left alone.[2]

BONE OF CONTENTION

The war began, like many wars, over a boundary dispute.
—John Searle, 1965

WHILE MARIO SAVIO and Jack Weinberg (among others) were participating in civil rights activity in the South, UC students back in the Bay
Area continued their own activism throughout the summer of 1964.
Besides the Auto Row demonstrations, University activists organized
anti-Goldwater pickets at the Republican National Convention in San
Francisco, and there was an ongoing campaign against former state senator William F. Knowland, California manager of Goldwater for President and owner and editor-in-chief of the *Oakland Tribune*. The
ultraconservative Knowland was the arch bugbear and easy target for
the campus left, and as much as he editorialized against the campus radicals and particularly the civil rights movement, so much the more did
he come in for their unwelcome attentions.

> *Bob Gill:* It was such a joy to tweak Knowland's nose. The bastard had
> been notorious in the fifties both as a repressive employer (I had suffered
> at the tender age of twelve as a paper boy for the *Tribune* and for me it
> was personal!) and as a U.S. senator from California so well known as
> a flunky for the hated China lobby of California/Taiwan millionaires
> that he was called the "Senator from Formosa."[1]

Things had come to such a pass that the *Tribune* building in Oakland
was being regularly picketed, and SLATE chairman Art Goldberg was
calling for a series of civil rights demonstrations to bring Knowland to
his knees:

> We have got to get solid community support, and it's not going to be a
> one-weekend thing. So what I'm asking now, is for people in this room
> who are dedicated to bringing some kind of change in the power struc-
> ture in the East Bay. If Knowland falls, and I think that Mr. Knowland
> realizes this, it'll be much easier in the East Bay to negotiate for hiring
> policies, if the biggest and the most anti-Negro hiring policy man is

BANCROFT AND TELEGRAPH, FALL 1964. PHOTO BY HOWARD HARAWITZ.

beaten. So, I'm asking the students in this room to make a dedicated effort to for sure come this week to the picket line. We've gotta have a bigger picket line every week. There might be some form of direct action, I'm not sure.[2]

The powers that be were not pleased, especially since the pickets were organized from card tables set up at Telegraph and Bancroft. Since Sather Gate was now a hundred yards inside the campus, activists observing rules banning political activity had from the early sixties distributed literature, solicited donations and gathered sign-ups for protests from card tables set up on the wide brick sidewalk between the concrete pillars at the entrance to the campus and the street. The 26-by-90-foot strip of sidewalk that concerned the administration was a portion of the whole sidewalk, whose total depth is something like 34 feet, of which the 8 feet closest to the street belong to the city of Berkeley. Nothing differentiates the 26-foot and the 8-foot strips except a small bronze plaque embedded in the bricks that says:

UNIVERSITY OF CALIFORNIA
—

PROPERTY OF THE REGENTS OF
THE UNIVERSITY OF CALIFORNIA.
PERMISSION TO ENTER OR PASS
OVER IS REVOCABLE AT ANY TIME.

As far back as September of 1959, Kerr had foreseen trouble with the strip because there was no logical basis for exempting it from the no-politics rule that applied everywhere else on campus, and he got the Regents to agree that it ought to be turned over to the city for use as a public plaza. However, the University's treasurer never got around to carrying out instructions to deed over the strip.* For more than two years, the University administration had sent students to City Hall to get permits for the area, and though the permits did not specify the exact location, students operated under the assumption that University property began at the pillars 26 feet north of Bancroft Avenue, and that what went on outside them was city business. The administration understood that this

*The reason may have been that the University did not actually own the strip of land in question. W. J. Rorabaugh notes that "in a twist of irony, years later it was discovered that the city of Berkeley actually had retained the area when the city had deeded Sproul Plaza to the University; the area subsequently was—and is—covered with city-licensed food vendors" (19).

DEAN OF MEN ARLEIGH WILLIAMS.
PHOTOGRAPHER UNKNOWN.

area was only partly city property, but viewed it as a safety valve, and turned a blind eye.

Dean Arleigh Williams: In essence, it was utilized as though it were sort of a no-man's-land and a safety valve where students could use the facilities. They got their permission from the city, yes. Actually, the permission from the city was permission to be able to use that portion of the property that was from the curbing that delineates the walkway from the road, and up to the bronze plaques that were embedded in the brick. But the city of Berkeley could not have authorized the use of University property.

We never issued permits; the property was just used as a means to permit students to scratch an itch on any issue or candidate. I think this came about as a result of the structure of this area. When Sather Gate was the original entrance, this was the area for open discussion and when these [new] buildings [Sproul Hall and the Student Union] came into play, that was taken away. The boundaries of the campus changed, so there was an effort to provide a space for them out here. I think originally, they thought they might be able to use this patch right out near where there are benches, and that didn't work out very well. It was not in a center of traffic, and students felt that they had to be in a center of traffic. Prior to that time, you may recall, an open discussion area was established in the lower plaza. This must have come about a year preceding September 14 [1964]. This was assumed to be able to be the safety valve, or the University's action to permit a

"NO ON 14" AND ANTI-GOLDWATER MARCH, SAN FRANCISCO, 1964.
PHOTO © 1993 BY TED STRESHINSKY.

so-called Hyde Park, where students could go at any time they wished and advocate whatever they wished to advocate.* No restrictions were to be placed on that. That, I'm sure, failed because it was out of the way.[3]

Alex C. Sherriffs, vice-chancellor for student affairs and a psychology professor popular among fraternity and sorority students, demonstrated open dismay at the activists' presence.† Sherriffs' office was in

---

*The official Hyde Park area on the UC campus was established on March 15, 1962. "Hyde Park" is the name of a park in central London, of which a part, called "Speaker's Corner," has been from the late nineteenth century traditionally the scene of impassioned soapbox oratory. The term came to refer to any area in which orators were allowed to expound on any of a wide range of subjects with no interference from the authorities. The Student Union Plaza, also called Lower Sproul Plaza, was the huge, utterly deserted area to the west and below the Student Union, between the Student Union and Zellerbach Hall. You could let off an atom bomb there and nobody would notice.

†The SLATE Supplement (Volume II, Num-

ber 1) did not think highly of Mr. Sherriffs or of his course: "PSYCH 33 is the departmental course for non-majors; a general, superficial, fun course in personality; simple, no papers, no muss, no fuss. . . . Mr. Sherriffs is rated entertaining, fun, not terribly challenging, and not at all profound. He freely wholesales his personal opinions on events of the day, both on and off campus. Exams are based primarily on readings. If you like this course, do not major in psych."

Tom Weller took the course, and remembers it as a "Mickey" (short for "Mickey Mouse," i.e., a course that was easy and of little value). He also remembers Sherriffs as pandering to the coarsest tastes of his mostly freddy and sally (fra-

CIVIL RIGHTS DEMONSTRATORS AT THE REPUBLICAN NATIONAL CONVENTION, COW PALACE, SAN FRANCISCO. PHOTO © 1993 BY TED STRESHINSKY.

Sproul Hall, and though he certainly was displeased by the left-wing political activity, he was more dismayed by its high visibility. He was also much annoyed by the incessant jungle beat of bongo drums that wafted from the intersection up to his office. The first thing encountered at the main entrance to the campus was a rat's nest of tables, post-

ternity and sorority) students, who roared with delight at his fulminations against every kind of group not in the mainstream of American culture. The impression among my acquaintances was that he was incompetent, obnoxious and more than a little mad.

Germaine LaBerge, in her interview of Arleigh Williams, asked the dean about Sherriffs' popularity as a professor: "Somebody made the comment—I can't remember where I got this—that when Alex Sherriffs was a professor, he was very popular and the students loved him and there was this wonderful rapport between him and the students. Something in him seems to have changed when he came from the faculty to the administration . . ." Williams responded, "What I'm saying now is going to be critical. Alex being very articulate, being very capable with

words, knowing just exactly what he wants, also was a person with great needs to be extremely popular and being a wonderful guy in the eyes of the students. I don't know that there is anything wrong with that except that the emphasis should be on the teaching and the emphasis should be on how well a person is doing, but not making every effort just to please and to be a guy that is worshiped and well liked and so on. Each one of us needs to be loved, I have to admit that, so you do what you can." (Arleigh Williams, *Dean of Students Arleigh Williams, The Free Speech Movement and the Six Years' War, 1964–1970*, interviews conducted by Germaine LaBerge, 1988 and 1989, Bancroft Library Regional Oral History Office, University of California, Berkeley, 1990, 115.)

ers, leafleters, colporteurs, orators and picket signs—a sight not likely to give a favorable impression of the University to visitors and passersby.

Oakland Tribune reporter Carl Irving, reacting to the UC students' organizing of pro–William Scranton, anti–Barry Goldwater demonstrations at the Republican National Convention at San Francisco's Cow Palace, asked the University's public affairs officer, Richard Hafner, Jr., why the rules that applied to the rest of the campus were not applied to UC property at the Bancroft-Telegraph border.* Hafner took the question to the office of Chancellor Strong, who was in Ha-

ALEX SHERRIFFS

DAILY CAL PHOTO.

waii. In his absence, Vice-Chancellor Alex Sherriffs got the ball, and presented the question at an administrative meeting on July 22, 1964, in which he implied that an order to ban the tables had come directly from Kerr. (The meeting, originally called to discuss problems with bicycles on campus, became known as the "bicycle meeting.") When directly

---

Arleigh Williams: . . . I didn't realize it was out of bounds, and that was one of the reasons we ran into difficulty. We had an enterprising reporter and a very nice guy ask the question.
Germaine LaBerge: Was this somebody from the *Oakland Tribune*?
Williams: Carl Irving.
LaBerge: Do you want to comment more on that? What I have is that he asked Dick Hafner, who was the Public Information officer, to clarify the University's policy about students organizing on University property. Is that what you're referring to?
Williams: What happened is that Carl Ir-

ving looked at that spot and he recognized that it was not University property; he wanted to know, "Why are you permitting things to take place on campus and not out there?" That question was asked and Dick, as I recall, brought it up and said, "Here we have it. We've got to do something about it." This relates to the time that Katherine was on vacation and I was here and we had the meeting [on July 22] with Dick Hafner, Frank Woodward, the chief of police, Forrest Tregea, and others. . . . (Williams, *Dean of Students*, 119.)

asked by a concerned dean of men Arleigh Williams under what authority he proposed an outright ban, he pointed a finger into the air and replied, "God." By this, Williams understood Sherriffs to mean Kerr. This was not, of course, at all true, and when Kerr asked Williams later how he had managed to make such a mess of things, Williams was astonished; Kerr denied that he had ordered anybody to do anything. Edward Strong, of course, was a big law-and-order man, and may have instructed Sherriffs to lower the boom. But, if he did so, he acted without Kerr's knowledge or consent. In any event, Williams went along with it, much against his better judgment, and on July 29 it was decided that the tables should be banned.

As the beginning of the fall semester approached, Clark Kerr was in Tokyo on his way home from a seven-week economic mission to iron curtain countries, and Sherriffs instructed a reluctant dean of students Katherine A. Towle (pronounced "toll") to come down like a cartload of bricks on the increasingly obstreperous student activists. Towle, a former colonel in the Marine Corps, was not happy about the ban (she felt that "the tables were harmless and useful as an escape valve"[4]), but it fell to her lot to send out the letter officially notifying student groups that tables would no longer be allowed in the Bancroft-Telegraph area.* *Iacta alia est.*†

Arleigh Williams: . . . There was a meeting in the office in the summer [July 22, 1964]. Dick Hafner, Frank Woodward, the chief of police, I'm not sure who else, were at the meeting in Katherine [Towle]'s office to see what we can do about bicycles upon campus. . . . We noted that the area outside the posts at Bancroft and Telegraph was being mis-used according to University policy and that we could not turn our heads. . . . [from memo, July 22, 1964] There was some concern about the strip. I refused to let the committee vote upon that because Katherine was away. I know darn well that she was not going to do something that egregious before the students returned; that was accepted.
Germaine LaBerge: And it had to be, for what reason?
Williams: We asked that question for that very reason and the answer was, "Because God said so."
LaBerge: Who gave you the answer?
Williams: Alex Sherriffs. I assumed, Kath-erine assumed, that we were talking about Clark Kerr. Clark Kerr was not around. I don't know the answer to why that was so but that was the answer.
LaBerge: So the letter went out over your objections?
Williams: The letter went out over our objection. I hate to do this. But I think for your information—and I told the same thing to Clark Kerr.
LaBerge: It's been documented in other people's oral histories also.
Williams: Is that so?
LaBerge: Yes, and you want to tell the truthful story. Were there other people who objected, too?
Williams: Not really, not that I recall. I think Katherine and I were the only ones. Verne Stadtman chronicled that in his book [*The University of California 1868–1968* (New York: McGraw-Hill, 1970)]. I don't know whether he speaks about the two of us or not but I think he does.
LaBerge: I have read that, but I haven't

read it recently so I'll look it up. So that letter really . . .

Williams: That letter took the freedom away.

LaBerge: And began the sequence of events that followed. How did you feel having to deal with what happened, after you had objected to the letter in the first place?

Williams: I guess I couldn't understand it. I think I was still . . . I'm certain Katherine felt that there was still room for negotiations. In fact, negotiations did continue for a while. I guess we're down to the twenty-ninth or so of September that the whole thing broke loose. Now, that was a difficult period of time, a particularly serious one because I think, too, as a result of that, Alex also published something in the paper and blamed Katherine for this. That didn't set well with a lot of us because that was something that was not needed, not intellectually honest, not right.

I came here and got to meet Alex Sherriffs in '57. I met with him frequently. He had a part to play in my going on over to the dean's office. It bothered me very, very much. I never knew a man who had more potential to be successful with students than he. But unfortunately I lost my respect for him and for what he did. This was one of those things when Katherine Towle was written up in the *New York Times*, that it was her responsibility . . . [Katherine Towle had an interview with Wallace Turner in the *New York Times*, March 14, 1965. He was the only reporter to interview her personally during the FSM.]

LaBerge: You mean, the article said that it was her responsibility for sending the letter?

Williams: Yes. Alex was covering his tracks.

LaBerge: Were both you and Katherine responsible to him, as one of your superiors, in your job?

Williams: I was responsible to Bill [Shepard].

LaBerge: But in that meeting . . .

Williams: He was acting as if . . . He had a step higher administratively; there's no question about that. This is one of the reasons that we couldn't understand why "God" was responsible. We couldn't get in touch with him: he was labeled. But it hurt the worst from my standpoint—what bothered me the worst—was his response in statement to the newspaper; that was not right. Katherine finally got a correction made, I think, but that stopped the relationship with a guy I admired very much. I found out I was in the wrong ball game. I say this because I think it's a fact, and you say it's documented; it needs to be documented and emphasized. . . .

LaBerge: What was the reaction of Chancellor Strong and/or President Kerr after this letter went out? It sounds like they didn't know it was going to happen.

Williams: I wasn't in the position to know what the response of the Chancellor and President were. I knew of the response of Alex. I went to his [Alex's] office; Alex at that time was walking around his desk checking for bugs. He thought somebody had posted stuff at his office so they could get all of the information they wanted from him. He was worried about the communists taking over. He gave me hell; he said that Ed Strong was upset because I hadn't been moving fast enough on the job. . . .

Then we went to the [Richard E.] Ericksons' house after the first football game. Clark Kerr showed up and we went out onto a little outdoor porch. Clark told me at that time, "You guys really bungled that one." I almost fell through the floor, because I thought that he was the one who was God . . . (Williams, *Dean of Students*, 91–93, 95; appendix, 235)

†"The die is cast," i.e., there's no going back now. Proverb quoted by Julius Caesar as he crossed the Rubicon.

OAKLAND TRIBUNE PICKET AND DEMONSTRATION, SUMMER 1964. PHOTO BY MARSHALL WINDMILLER FROM "THE LIBERAL DEMOCRAT," JANUARY 1965 (PAGE 7).

QUESTION AUTHORITY

W<small>E TOLD THEM</small> they had to go back on the streets where they'd been traditionally for this kind of activity; and they then took the position that "we want to undertake these activities on campus property itself," and we said that this is not possible.
—Clark Kerr, October 1964

On September 16, 1964, the bombshell, in the form of the letter from Dean Towle, exploded. Presidents, chairmen and faculty advisers of every on-campus student organization were told that, as of September 21,

provisions of the policy of The Regents concerning "Use of University Facilities" will be strictly enforced in all areas designated as property of The Regents . . . including the 26-foot strip of brick walkway at the campus entrance on Bancroft Way and Telegraph Avenue. . . .

Specifically, Section III of the [Regents'] policy . . . prohibits the use of University facilities "for the purpose of soliciting party memberships or supporting or opposing particular candidates or propositions in local, state or national elections," except that Chief Campus Officers "shall establish rules under which candidates for public office (or their designated representatives) may be afforded like opportunity to speak upon the campuses at meetings where the audience is limited to the campus community."

. . . Section IV of the policy states further that University facilities "may not be used for the purpose of raising money to aid projects not directly connected with some authorized activity of the University. . . ."

Now that the so-called "speaker ban" is gone, and the open forum is a reality, student organizations have ample opportunity to present to campus audiences on a "special event" basis an unlimited number of speakers on a variety of subjects, provided the few basic rules concerning notification and sponsorship are observed. . . .

KATHERINE A. TOWLE
Dean of Students

DAILY CAL PHOTO.

It should be noted also that this area on Bancroft Way . . . has now been added to the list of designated areas for the distribution of handbills, circulars or pamphlets by University students and staff in accordance with Berkeley campus policy. Posters, easels and card tables will not be permitted in this area because of interference with the flow of [pedestrian] traffic. University facilities may not, of course, be used to support or advocate off-campus political or social action.[1]

According to Towle, the new ruling had become necessary because of "the growing use and misuse of the area," which had "made it imperative that the University enforce throughout the campus the policy long ago set down by the Regents."[2] This "use and misuse" undoubtedly included the continuing pickets of the *Oakland Tribune* launched from Bancroft and Telegraph (on September 15 the Ad Hoc Committee to End Discrimination had announced plans to picket the *Tribune* for the third Friday in a row*); Knowland contemptuously referred to the University of California at Berkeley as the "little red schoolhouse," and his fulminations

---

*In "The Naked Emperor," Paul Krassner reported that a student attending the chancellor's reception for holders of the Regents' Scholarship at University House had "overheard someone question Chancellor Strong about the reason for the University's new policy. [Strong] replied that the *Oakland Tribune* had called him and asked if he was aware that picketing activity (protesting alleged racial discrimination in the *Tribune*'s hiring practices) was being organized on University property. Strong said he didn't know it *was* University property, but that he would investigate" (in Michael V. Miller and Susan Gilmore, eds., *Revolution at Berkeley: The Crisis in American Education* [New York: Dell, 1965], 245–246; reprinted from *Cavalier*, April 1965).

no doubt influenced the University's administration to try to keep the lid on the students, particularly as this was a time when the University's budget was being reviewed by the very people to whom the Left was giving so much shit.

WILLIAM F. KNOWLAND
PHOTO BY DOUGLAS WACHTER.

Charles Muscatine: A lot of the tension was just budget anxiety. From the point of view of the faculty, I say that the University is a sacred place. From the point of view of the administration—vis-à-vis the state legislature and the atmosphere of McCarthyism—the University is a *clean* place. By "clean" I mean politically nonthreatening. In a sense, the faculty and the administration are working at cross purposes.[3]

The administration was also unhappy about the anti-Goldwater picketing during the Republican National Convention; in February of 1965, Kerr remarked in an interview with A. H. Raskin in the *New York Times Magazine* that "whatever pressure preceded the order involved the loading of the galleries at the Republican convention with Berkeley students whooping it up for Scranton against Goldwater."*

*A report by Chancellor Strong to the Berkeley division of the Academic Senate in October of 1964 emphasized the administration's displeasure with the anti-Goldwater pickets: "The situation was brought to a head by the multiplied activity incidental to the primary elections. Representatives of the Chancellor's office, the Dean of Students' office, the campus police, the Public Affairs office, and the ASUC had the problem on the agenda of meetings of July 22, July 29, and September 4. They agreed that the situation would worsen during the political campaign, and steps should be taken at the beginning of the semester to assure the use of the Telegraph-Bancroft area in accordance with University rules."

On September 16 representatives of the student groups affected by the ruling held a meeting in front of the Bancroft-Telegraph gate. It was conducted by Bob Wolfson of the Congress of Racial Equality. ABC newsmen interviewed participants, and Mario Savio, Tom Miller, Michael Rossman and Larry Marks addressed a small crowd.

Mario Savio: Then one day, the sixteenth of September, I was at a Campus CORE meeting at Stiles Hall, and Ed Rosenfeld was reading this fantastic, unbelievable letter that Campus CORE had received from Dean Towle. People were pretty exercised over it. I hadn't been taking part in the meeting, but I volunteered to go with a group—Bob Wolfson and Ed Rosenfeld—to the administration. There were others from other groups. There was no formal organization.

Betty Garmon had left SNCC at this point, and Ed Wilson and I were going to be co-chairmen. When Betty left, there was no organization. She'd been too essential to it. While she was there, it was magnificent. I went representing SNCC to that meeting. Jackie Goldberg had been informally selected as spokeswoman, but we didn't maintain too much order. I played an increasingly assertive role in the meeting, but was by no means a spokesman or leader. By September 30, I was playing a very, very active role.

It seemed pretty simple: this totally absurd ruling had come down. Maybe it was a mistake. In any case, maybe there was a way that we could in some way modify the ruling. That's what we wanted to know. We offered tongue-in-cheek to have an independent organization do a traffic survey, because the only reason they'd given was that we were interfering with pedestrian traffic. Of course they said no, and later they just said, "It's the rules, and they've got to be obeyed." Everything was very vague. We couldn't find who was responsible for it. Dean Towle seemed awkward. She wasn't really suited to passing down other people's absurd regulations and then having to make up excuses for them. By Monday they granted the mechanical points—where you could set up tables and so on, which dashed their argument that we were interfering with traffic—but didn't grant any of the substantive points—that you could do politics from these tables.

I'd been engaged during the summer and previous spring in political activity. I found out about the Sheraton-Palace demonstration when somebody gave me a leaflet in just this area. I'd been down to Mississippi; I'd seen people treated pretty shabbily, and here was one of the main outlets in the free part of the country for information and recruiting people to go down there. It seemed fantastic that the University would presume to cut this off, because of what an important role it was serving. It seemed the most important thing going on in the country at that time. I reacted in terms of my memory of Negro Farmer "X," whose home had been shot into.[4]

On September 17, nineteen student political organizations formed a nonsectarian United Front to protest the new rules.* Representatives met with Dean Towle and expressed surprise that the presumed city-owned strip of land had overnight magically become University property. The organizations depended completely on this small strip of land for all their high-profile activities,

ART GOLDBERG. PHOTO BY RON ENFIELD.

and taking it away from them would spell their collective doom. None of the organizations were interested in any sort of confrontation, and most of the students concerned thought there had been some sort of mistake that could be ironed out with a little sweet reason. They asked for the right to advocate any political viewpoint and to distribute political literature, and for permission to put up posters so that passersby would know what they were doing. Since the problem seemed to center on traffic flow, they volunteered to conduct a traffic survey, and to police themselves for future violations. Dean Towle held to the hard line, and maintained that the Regents' policy was clearly set down for all campus areas, including the disputed Telegraph-Bancroft trouble spot, and that

*The conservative campus publication *Man and State* summarized: "The new regulations were immediately opposed by all campus political organizations. . . . The initial conversations with the administration left no doubt but that the regulations were a result of outside pressure and were intended to stop any political activity on campus. . . . The negotiations failed" (quoted in Hal Draper, *Berkeley: The New Student Revolt* [New York: Grove Press, 1965], 32).

the University administration was under an obligation to enforce that policy. She also said that the administration had repeatedly asked for co-operation in the matter of too many tables and posters, and hadn't gotten any. "Some of the students," she noted, "have been both impudent and impertinent."[5] She was probably talking about Mario, who was perhaps the first among the fledgling activists to realize that being conciliatory and polite was a big fat waste of time.

Casting about for some gracious, easy way out of what was promising to become a much bigger deal than anyone had anticipated, Dean Towle said that it might be possible for the University to substitute the Hyde Park area in the plaza behind the Student Union building for the Bancroft-Telegraph area. The students were by this time much less conciliatory than they would have been a year earlier, and rejected the compromise out of hand. Everybody knew perfectly well that the Student Union Plaza was well off the beaten track, and that as far as genuine effectiveness went, tables might as well be set up on the dark side of the moon. The students insisted on their right, and "duty to society," to remain at the South Gate entrance posts. The irony of the situation was not lost on the older SLATE members, who remembered that in 1960 SLATE had asked the administration to declare a portion of that same plaza a Hyde Park area. This request had been ignored.

Art Goldberg called the new policy "another in a long series of acts to curtail either right or left wing political action on campus," and charged that

> as the students become more and more aware of America's social problems, and come to take an active part in their solution, the University moves proportionally the other way to prevent all exposure of political action being taken. The most important thing is to make this campus a market place for ideas. But, the University is trying to prevent the exposure of any new creative political solutions to the problems that every American realizes are facing this society in the mid-Sixties.[6]

On September 18, the United Front asked Dean Towle to allow student groups to set up tables, distribute literature and accept donations at the entrance to the campus, subject to conditions that answered any reasonable criticism about traffic flow: the tables would be manned at all times; the student groups would provide their own tables and chairs; there would be no more than one table in front of each pillar and one on either side of the entrance; posters would be attached to the tables only, and not to the entrance posts; and students would police themselves, publishing and distributing the rules to the student organizations. The United Front did not, however, budge an inch on the main issues: solicitation of donations and distribution of "literature advocating action on current issues" would continue, subject to "the understanding that the student organizations do not represent the University—thus these organizations will not use the name of the University and will dissociate themselves from the University as an institution."[7] The United Front did not actually believe that the traffic problem was any-

MONA HUTCHIN.
PHOTO BY HOWARD HARAWITZ.

thing more than an excuse; both sides knew that much more was at stake, and antagonisms were beginning to clarify and harden.

In an evening meeting on September 20, the United Front agreed to picket, conduct a vigil, hold rallies and—though the conservative organizations declined to go this far—adopt the civil rights technique of civil disobedience if the University made no concessions after a meeting with Dean Towle that was scheduled for ten-thirty the next morning.

Mona Hutchin: At one of the first United Front meetings Jack Weinberg was arguing against all the activities that people were proposing, picketing and things like that, and he was saying, "No, no, we shouldn't worry about this, we shouldn't worry about picketing and getting out a lot of leaflets. It's an artificial issue, we have to get back to the business of what the civil rights movement and CORE are trying to do. We have to concentrate all our efforts on our real goals, and not get hung up on this side issue." There were some people who agreed with that, and there was a general debate. Most people said that they just wanted to get the Bancroft-Telegraph area back, and didn't want to make a bigger fuss. They wanted to get back to doing what they were supposed to be doing, but others said, "No, no, no! The question is not whether we get the Bancroft-Telegraph area back, it's a question of morality!" But most people weren't interested in that. People hadn't had time at this point to think about the fact that there could be broader issues involved.*

On September 21—the first day of classes—Dean Towle met with representatives of the United Front and accepted the traffic proposals without demur. She said that the organizations would be allowed to distribute informative literature from their tables, which made everyone happy as larks until they asked what the information could say, which turned out to be nothing. Dean Towle drew a careful distinction between informative and advocative literature. Students were forbidden to advocate specific action, recruit for specific causes, or solicit funds and donations "to aid projects not directly connected with some authorized activity of the University. . . . It is not permissible, in materials distributed on University property, to urge a specific vote, call for direct social or political action, or to seek to recruit individuals for such action."[8] To back up her argument, Towle (perhaps unknowingly) misquoted a clause in the state constitution prohibiting partisan political activity on the UC campus.[†]

---

*Vice president of the University Society of Individuals (USI) and the very image of propriety, Mona Hutchin was later to gain fame as the first woman to demand to ride standing on the running board of a San Francisco cable car. Customarily, when a cable car was full, men were expected to rise and offer a seat to any woman, and themselves stand on the running board; women were not allowed, under any circumstances, to ride standing on the running board. Able-bodied men were also expected to help the gripman turn the cable car around at its terminus. I recollect an incident in the early sixties when a man refused to give up his seat to a woman and was kicked off the car, to the warm applause of all the passengers. (All this may seem strange, but if you look at contemporary photos, you will notice that men wore coat and tie to baseball games, too.) As reported in the *San Francisco Chronicle*, Mona boarded a cable car on April 27, 1965, wearing a button proclaiming "I Am a Right-Wing Extremist," and insisted that she had an equal right to stand, as men were permitted to, on the running

board. In this she was resisted by the gripman, and after she still refused to move, and six cars were backed up at the Market Street turntable, she was forcibly removed by three policemen, taken to the Hall of Justice, lectured and released. The gripman acted with the blessings of Tom McGrath, the president of the Amalgamated Transit Union. All to no avail, however: the "men only" tradition had been shattered and succeeding women who tried it were left entirely in peace.

(All quotations of Mona Hutchin are transcribed and edited from an interview taped by Marston Schultz on October 19, 1965.)

†In her interview of Arleigh Williams, Germaine LaBerge observes that in 1964 Alex Sherriffs asked the counsel for the Regents, Thomas Cunningham, for an opinion on the legality of the University's rules regarding the use of University facilities. In his response, LaBerge notes, "Thomas Cunningham reminds Alex Sherriffs that he [Cunningham] previously gave him a memorandum in 1961 on the same subject and noted, with respect to

As a sop, Dean Towle told the students that a second Hyde Park free speech area had been created "on an experimental basis" on the entrance steps in front of Sproul Hall, where

JACKIE GOLDBERG. PHOTO BY RON ENFIELD.

individuals are free to speak at will . . . provided they are registered students or staff of the University of California and observe the policies pertaining to use of University facilities. Since the University reserves such areas of the campus for student and staff use, those who speak should be prepared to identify themselves as students or staff of the University. It is suggested that speakers use as their podium the raised part of the wall on either side of the main stairway or the lower steps flanking the main stairway. Because of possible disturbance to persons working in Sproul Hall offices, voice amplifiers will not be permitted. There must be no interference with traffic or the conduct of University business.[9]

Jackie Goldberg, the Delta Phi Epsilon pledge mother and longtime Women for Peace activist, acted as a spokeswoman for the protesting groups. Jackie had been selected by the United Front as a spokeswoman not only because she was articulate, but because her appearance con-

political material, 'that there is no federal constitutional prohibition of such activities, and the state constitution and University regulations require only that the University, as such, may not become involved in political activities.' Then he goes on to state, 'There would appear to be no legal reason why partisan political literature, not only specifically supporting or opposing a candidate or a proposition but also urging the victory or defeat through appropriate votes for a proposition or candidate and suggesting action and recruiting individuals therefore may not be permitted.' And then later, 'In other words, the limitations suggested with respect to the type of non-commercial literature which may be distributed in the Bancroft-Telegraph area is not consistent with the existing Berkeley campus regulation and that regulation would have to be amended accordingly.' . . . Katherine Towle [didn't know] . . . that the counsel had already spoken about the legality of this in 1961 and somehow that memo was lost; had she known about it she would have acted differently . . ." (Williams, *Dean of Students*, 122–123).

founded accusations that we were all a bunch of social eccentrics, the boys scruffily bearded, the girls uniformly accoutred in black eye-makeup, long straight hair and dark stockings. Sorority girls were not allowed to go on campus casually got up, so Jackie always dressed nicely and looked respectable, her sorority pin conspicuous. She had already acquired a following from her activities as a campus activist, having earlier in the year organized a Women for Peace "pack-in" in a fallout shelter, tricking the authorities into thinking that it was official. The pack-in demonstrated that if the allotted number of people were in the room for any length of time, they would all die from lack of air, food and water.[10]

Speaking for the United Front, Jackie insisted:

> The University has not gone far enough in allowing us to promote the kind of society we're interested in.
>
> We're allowed to say why we think something is good or bad, but we're not allowed to distribute information as to what to do about it. Inaction is the rule, rather than the exception, in our society and on this campus. And, education is and should be more than academics.
>
> We don't want to be armchair intellectuals. For a hundred years, people have talked and talked and done nothing. We want to help the students decide where they fit into the political spectrum and what they can do about their beliefs. We want to build a better society.[11]

Dean Towle stood fast, giving a nonexplanation that the restriction on advocacy was not directed specifically at students; even nonstudents invited to speak on campus were informed that on-campus advocacy of direct political or social action was prohibited. Dr. Saxton Pope, a special assistant to Vice-Chancellor Alex Sherriffs also present at the meeting, explained that the University was trying to discourage "advocacy of action without thought."[12]

On that same day, the twenty-first of September, the United Front set up tables at Bancroft and Telegraph, and held its first rally on Sproul Hall steps. About a hundred students remained to hold an all-night vigil. Some of the students marched to University House, where the chancellor lived, to protest the regulations.

Jackie Goldberg: I started getting involved the day the letters came out. I got one of those letters, I guess it was dated the fourteenth, but I don't think we got them until about the sixteenth. It was the week before school was to begin. On the twenty-first was the first day of school; it was reg [registration] week. I called my brother, who was the outgoing chairman of

SLATE, and he said he'd gotten one, and then he called someone from the Du Bois Club. We were both calling people to find out who got them.

We arranged a casual meeting at his apartment, and about sixteen people came, from various groups. It was rather a dismal session, because at that point it looked like we were all through. Sandor [Fuchs] was there, Art, me, Sid Stapleton, Brian Turner, Cahill, Jo Freeman, Pam Horner, Dan Rosenthal, Dick Roman, Mona Hutchin. CORE was there, SLATE was there. I think YPSL was there.

Then I made an appointment with Dean Towle, and with the chancellor for all of us. That's when I found out from his secretary that he didn't have anything at all available in the way of appointments until after the first week in October. But we figured we were going to see the dean, so maybe she could get us an appointment.

The day of the [first] meeting with Towle was in reg week. About an hour before the meeting, we met in a room in Wheeler that no one was using, and I was sort of, very informally, made the spokesman, since I had set up the appointments and since the right-wing groups trusted me more than they did any of the others. Bettina [Aptheker] was around, but she wasn't representing any group, so she wasn't with us at that point. Mario and Weinberg weren't with us.

We decided that our tactic with the dean was first, to find out what's up, then to find out what can be done about it, and then explain to her in as strong a way as possible what this decision meant to our groups. Not in a threatening way, but in an informative way explain to her that we *weren't* going to just let it go if nothing could be done through channels. Of course, with the composition of the group we had, we didn't know exactly what we *could* do. That's the first time those groups had ever worked together, and that includes some of the left-wing groups, let alone the left and the right.

So we went to the dean, and she was fairly receptive. She explained to us that she had been given this ruling. We asked her, "How did it come about?" And she said, "It was found out over the summer that this was property of the Regents, and that as such it was subject to the same rules as the rest of the campus, which were 'no political activity.'"

Actually, it was Article IX, Section 9 of the [state] constitution, which is, "The University of California shall be kept free of all political and sectarian influence." I might add, parenthetically, that upon looking up that section, one finds the finish of that statement to be, "free of sectarian and political influence *in the selection of its Regents and other officers.*" And has nothing to do with student activity at all. But that, nonetheless, is the article of the constitution that these things were outlawed under. The only ruling under which they could forbid that area was a Kerr Directive. It was not in the constitution at all.

The most important reason for the tables being taken away from Bancroft and Telegraph was traffic. It was not political yet; she mentioned that, but the most important reason was traffic. At that point, we offered to have the planning studies department run a traffic study, and police the tables ourselves, and the whole bit. To cooperate fully, and that didn't seem to do much good.

I started the speaking and ended it, and in the middle everyone spoke. It was quite obvious that Dean Towle was disturbed about it. I told her halfway through the meeting that I wasn't able to see the chancellor, and this, facially, seemed to disturb her. Because that was one of the first things she told us, that we'd have to see the chancellor. There was very little she could do about it. But she did say before we left that meeting that if we would draw up for her the types of proposals and things necessary for us to continue existence, she'd see what she could do.

So, we left, and we made an appointment with her for 10:00 AM, Monday the twenty-first, the first day of school.

Sandor and I left the meeting to draw up the proposals, and we had planned a weekend meeting for the whole group. We drew up proposals that said, basically, that we needed the tables, that we needed to be able to collect money, and pass out literature. We would limit it to six tables, and we would limit it to one person sitting behind a card table and we would use only our own tables and chairs, instead of borrowing them from the Student Union.

Once the tables could not be put up legally, more groups, in terms of defying the regulations to find out what would happen, put up tables. And students who were not in groups seemed to think it was more important to find out what was going on. So they were more around the tables. I think that they created more interest in political activity, I don't think it made the tables necessarily any more important than they had been. It was an increased interest in politics in general that made the tables seem more important.

We submitted our proposals to her, and in the ten o'clock meeting on Monday she abandoned totally the idea of the traffic problem. We came in, and she said, "Before we begin, we've found out that under the kinds of rules and regulations that you've submitted yourselves, last Thursday, the traffic problems will be alleviated. So you can have your tables back." Which was very nice. And that was the end of it, until somebody asked, "Well, what can we do at these tables?" And we got the bad shock again. Only informational literature could be given from the tables. In other words, we still couldn't collect any money, we couldn't advocate anything. We couldn't collect membership lists, or even mailing lists. No selling of anything. We could give away bumper stickers—as long as they didn't advocate anything. We found this rather unsatisfactory.

After about an hour and a half of meeting, we informed her that at noon we were going to set up tables as we had before, and do exactly as we'd always done before. This was the twenty-first, the first day of school. We said that it wasn't with any intention of being defiant or rebellious, yet, but the whole point was that, if we didn't do something now, it would mean, for sure, political death to all of our groups. This way we had a chance.

Before the meeting with Towle we had met and decided what to do. We made up hypothetical cases; if we got blank, blank, blank, then we would do blank, blank, blank in response.

The weekend meeting we decided something like this: that we would draw lots for whose tables would go up; that the right-wing groups that felt they could not participate would not in any way, either publicly or privately, undermine the action. This seemed satisfactory to everyone.

We did set up the tables, and I expected arrests or some action. A lot of kids didn't. A lot of kids figured that they were just going to let it go, because they knew we were going to stick with it, and it didn't really bother them anyway, and they had done what they had to do for whomever they had to do it. And, sure enough, nothing happened. Had the tables up all day Monday; lots of cameras and photographers, lots of television coverage; and deans came down, I don't think they took any names. SLATE was there, the Young Democrats were there, CORE was there, I think the moderate Republicans were there, I think Women for Peace drew one, but I can't remember. Either Du Bois Club or YPSL or YSA [Young Socialist Alliance], one of those three drew one. It's hard to remember. There were only two groups that didn't put in their names to draw.

Monday night we had a meeting about an all-night vigil on the steps of Sproul on Wednesday. I think that's where Mario and Dusty Miller came the first time. We decided on it because we felt it was a tactic that everybody in the United Front could participate in fully. There was nothing illegal about a vigil, and it was a protest. Everybody agreed to participate in it. The tables we decided would continue to go up at Bancroft and Telegraph.

We had fairly good participation at the vigil considering that the groups expected almost no help from the rest of the campus. We sang songs and discussed among ourselves what would happen and what the future would bring, and tried to encourage people to get their groups involved with the United Front. I think we had about 800 at the beginning and it dropped down at its lowest point to probably about 200 to 250.

Maybe half of the group went over to Dwinelle because they thought that the chancellor was having a meeting; that was around midnight.[13]

Tom Miller: There were just two meetings with Dean Towle. She stressed, "We're not going to negotiate, I'm telling you," although she said it nicely. At times she was apologetic; she'd be the typical administrator type in that "You're students, I've listened, be nice children," except it was more subtle than that. There were indications that she didn't support what she was doing; we were putting forth valid arguments, and valid alternatives to the rule she was putting up; we'd offered to make a study of blocking traffic and a lot of times she was forced into a corner from which she reasonably couldn't argue. That's when I sprung the question, "This is all because of civil rights this summer and last year, isn't it?" and she said, "Yeah," and then she shut up.[14]

Students and faculty who came to campus early on September 22 were startled by the spectacle of Sproul Hall steps festooned with sleeping students. That day the ASUC Senate got into the act, and by a vote of 11–5 petitioned the Regents "to allow free political and social action to be effected by students at the Bancroft entrance to the University of California, up to the posts accepted as the traditional entrance"; to allow funds to be solicited there for off-campus activity; and to extend the right of advocacy and fundraising to the eight other campus locations where only non–advocative literature was permitted.[15] In a real effort to defuse what was looking more every day like a gathering storm, the ASUC Senate also got the bright idea of buying the land from the Regents and establishing it as a free speech area outside the official cognizance, thereby saving everybody's face. Not quite up to speed, they took the allegations of traffic problems seriously, and suggested that an ASUC board of control be put in charge of the area to prevent congestion and aggressive leafleters. Nobody paid any attention to them.

Chancellor Strong responded to the outburst of political activity, the vigil and the rally, with a statement on September 23 insisting that the University's "Open Forum" policy allowed a "full spectrum of political and social views" to be heard in the Hyde Park areas, and reiterating the contention that "University facilities are not to be used for the mounting of social and political issues directed at the surrounding community." The University's position, he maintained, had been clearly laid out in President Kerr's Charter Day address on the Davis campus, May 5, 1964:

The activities of students acting as private citizens off-campus on non-University matters are outside the sphere of the University. . . . Just as the University cannot and should not follow the student into his family life or his church life or his activities as a student off the campus, so also the students, individually and collectively, should not and cannot take the name of the University with them as they move into religious or political or other non-University facilities in connection with such affairs. . . . The University will not allow students or others connected with it to use it to further their non-University political or social or religious causes, nor will it allow those outside the University to use it for non-University purposes.[16]

On September 25, Kerr made the fatuous point—one that haunted him for the rest of his tenure—that learning could and indeed should be divorced from action:

The Dean of Students has met many requests of the students. The line the University draws will be an acceptable one. . . .

I don't think you have to have action to have intellectual opportunity. Their actions—collecting money and picketing—aren't high intellectual activity. . . . These actions are not necessary for the intellectual development of the students. If that were so, why teach history? We can't live in ancient Greece. . . .

The University is an educational institution that has been given to the Regents as a trust to administer for educational reasons, and not to be used for direct political action. It wouldn't be proper. It is not right to use the University as a basis from which people organize and undertake direct action in the surrounding community.[17]

During the first week of classes, the chancellor traditionally held an open meeting to welcome new students and faculty. The chancellor's University Meeting in 1964 was to be held in the Student Union Plaza (also known as Lower Sproul Plaza), the large open area bounded by Zellerbach Hall to the west, the dining commons to the north and the Student Union to the east. On the twenty-eighth, the same day as the University Meeting, the United Front planned to set up tables at Sather Gate and hold an unsanctioned rally from the old 1930s site of free speech, the oak tree in front of Wheeler Hall.* The protesters then

---

*The original Wheeler Oak from which student radicals harangued crowds in the 1920s and early 1930s was cut down in 1934, and the speakers moved to the steps of Wheeler Auditorium. With the completion of Dwinelle Hall in 1954, students began speaking from Dwinelle Plaza. The Wheeler Oak under which the United Front rallied on September 28, 1964, and that stands there today, in 1993, is another tree planted in the same spot as its noble predecessor.

MARIO SAVIO SPEAKING UNDER WHEELER OAK, SEPTEMBER 28, 1964.
PHOTO BY RON ENFIELD.

planned to march to the University Meeting while it was in progress and picket. The conservative organizations planned only to participate in the march, since the rally and tables were illegal and they disagreed with the idea of a picket.

Jackie Goldberg: Things were fairly quiet the rest of the week [of September 21]. We were still having meetings, we were still setting up tables. The following Monday, the twenty-eighth, was when we were going to picket the chancellor's University Meeting. We decided that there was going to be a rally over by the old Wheeler Oak, and then a picket line that would circle the area of the meeting. At first, we thought it was going to be in Dwinelle Plaza, which is one of the biggest reasons that we were at Wheeler Oak. Then the meeting was in the Lower Student Union Plaza, and we decided to leave the rally at the tree anyway, and walk over. I *know* that Mario was there. I know Dusty Miller had come into the picture. I think Jack Weinberg had entered the scene. I know that Brian Turner was around, I'm pretty sure David Goines was around,* of course the Stapletons were there, I think Dick Roman, Pam

*I remember seeing the vigil on the steps, but I do not believe I participated in it. I remember the picketing at the University Meeting, in which I may have partici- pated. I did participate in some picketing at Bancroft and Telegraph. I do not re- member attending or participating in any meetings before October 3, 1964.

PICKETS AT THE CHANCELLOR'S UNIVERSITY MEETING. PHOTO BY RON ENFIELD.

Horner, Cahill, Rosenthal, Sandor, Art, myself, Stephanie Coontz and Patti Iiyama were coming now, Jo Freeman. Always Jo Freeman.

The loudest speakers were Art, Mario, Dusty, Sandor and myself. We usually pretty well yelled it out. The old shouting test: who can shout the others down? There wasn't so much disagreement as sort of playing by new rules for the first time. It was very difficult to predict what the response of the University would be, what the response of the rest of the campus would be. We knew only one thing: at that point we could not afford to break apart our coalition. I must admit that most of our tactics were planned much more around keeping the coalition together than actually defeating the administration's position. We knew we had no hope of ever getting to a point where we *could* defeat the administration's position if we broke down our coalition too early. Then they could claim it was just a bunch of tired old left-wing radicals trying to stir up some trouble, and the campus would believe 'em. And we knew that would be the end. So we had to really court the middle of the road and the right wing.

Of course, a picket is a picket, and there's nothing dangerous about a picket. I'm sure there were more militant things than that proposed, but what we ended up with was a picket.

Meanwhile, I was still trying to make an appointment to see the chancellor, and we still were unable to. This is the twenty-eighth of September, now.

Art, and Sandor and Mario did most of the speaking at the rally. I was still sort of the provisional spokesman, although that was beginning to change slightly with all these powerful new characters coming onto the scene. Usually before we went out there, we planned who was going to speak, but usually that was whoever wanted to speak. The group wasn't really aware of Mario at this time. He was just another representative for SNCC as far as we were concerned.

We had a phenomenal turnout. In terms of anything we had ever hoped for, it was out of the question. This is the first point that any of us ever realized what we might have tied ourselves onto. It was a very odd feeling. There were all kinds of people picketing; the lines were three or four or five abreast, tightly packed, and circling the whole area. Faces that none of us knew, whereas up to that point it was only the people we knew and could coerce into doing things with us. But this was a different type of thing. I remember being elated, saying, "My God, we may have a chance." Because most of us in the left wing had looked at the United Front as a way of going out in style. It was the biggest shot in the arm.[18]

Just as picketing began, Chancellor Strong announced a "reinterpretation of Regents' policy," allowing campaign literature advocating "yes" and "no" votes on propositions and candidates, campaign buttons and bumper stickers to be distributed at Bancroft and Telegraph as well as the eight Hyde Park areas on the campus proper. This accomplished two unwanted ends: first, since poor Dean Towle had just told the United Front that the Regents' police unequivocally prohibited distribution of literature advocating either a "yes" or "no" vote, the credibility of the administration was thrown into serious doubt and, more important, the students learned the absolutely correct lesson that pressuring the administration worked just fine. Later that day we discovered that the about-face had resulted from UC administrators realizing that, in contradiction to what Dean Towle had said, the University was itself actively throwing its weight behind the November ballot's Proposition 2, a bond issue to fund UC and state college construction.

When told of Strong's announcement, Art Goldberg crowed: "And you're asking me if picketing is effective?" Another protest spokesman said, "The Bancroft-Telegraph issue has alerted us to the free speech issue all over campus. We won't stop now until we've made the entire campus a bastion of free speech."[19]

ASUC president Charles Powell, however, was unhappy about the disruption of the chancellor's address and University Meeting, and complained, "Placards like 'Sproul Hall Will Fall' and constant heckling and disruption among the audience . . . are . . . unnecessary at this stage of the issue, and a reflection of student sentiment of which I can no longer be proud."[20]

Jackie Goldberg: When that picket line was planned, we had no idea at all that the chancellor was going to make any statement. In fact, I don't even believe that any of us heard him make it. I think we found out about it later that night. He hadn't really conceded anything: all he'd given was the right for us to advocate ballot issues. One of the reporters called us later that afternoon: "Got a tip for you about why the University changed their policy on ballot issues." The next day, on September 29, paid for by the University of California stamps, on University of California stationery, a University of California endorsement for the ballot issue Proposition 2 was going out. He felt that this announcement was made so that this wouldn't seem in contradiction to *us* not being able to advocate ballot issues. The University was handing out Proposition 2 propaganda everywhere: football games, and everywhere.

So this was the point, when we felt that we had some numbers—when the University had made two concessions: first, the tables coming back and now ballot issues, but we knew they weren't going to concede the things we needed—that we decided on a picket all day, move the tables from Bancroft and Telegraph to Sather Gate on the thirtieth, and at the same time, we had an appointment with Dean Towle. We would picket Sproul Hall. We were talking in terms of a sit-in, but we didn't plan one for that day. At this point, we had a lot of trouble with Dan Rosenthal.* Bancroft and Telegraph he could understand, but why did we have to go to Sather Gate? Now [Paul] Cahill didn't agree with him. Cahill was with us on everything we did, all the way. He was president of USI [University Society of Individuals] and he had a lot of trouble with his group, because they thought he was completely wrong. They thought he was playing into the hands of the Communists, being duped, but he was fighting to keep his group alive. If we didn't win, his group was going to fold, too. But Rosenthal didn't look at it that way. He abstained, but he didn't vote no, and he did agree, at least up to this point, not to cut our throats publicly.[21]

The administration was becoming impatient with the continued violation of rules, and Dean Arleigh Williams issued a warning that students persisting in "illegal politics" might be expelled. This was a serious

---

*Dan Rosenthal was a contentious member of the conservative organizations Young Americans for Freedom and Cal Students for Goldwater.

SDS TABLE AT SATHER GATE, SEPTEMBER 28, 1964. PHOTO BY RON ENFIELD.

threat, and one that was not taken lightly, though its most significant effect was to make the general campus population aware that something very much out of the ordinary was going on.

On September 28 and 29, the United Front drew straws and set up tables at the disputed area of Telegraph and Bancroft, and made a strategic advance into the campus proper, drawing lots and setting up tables at the old boundary just outside Sather Gate. Some of the organizations had gotten permits, but in the cases of SNCC, CORE and SLATE permits were out of the question. Permits were issued only to "qualified organizations," which SLATE certainly was not, and the whole point of the civil rights organizations was to do all the things that were prohibited, so they would not promise to conform to the regulations merely to get a permit. Dean Williams said, "Every effort will be made to remove those tables."[22] At this point, things got serious. Dean Williams and campus police visited each Sather Gate table, warned that what they were doing was against University regulations and asked for identification. The students manning these tables now had a reasonable assurance that if they continued to violate the rules, their academic careers were on the line.

> *Mario Savio:* They'd told us that there were about eight areas on campus in which we could do the kind of things we wanted to do at Bancroft and Telegraph, *minus* politics. They included Sather Gate. So it was perfectly logical and perfectly consistent to set up tables at Sather Gate; since we didn't recognize their right to prevent us from doing things at Bancroft and Telegraph, likewise it was perfectly consistent to do those things at Sather Gate. So they couldn't get us for having tables at Sather Gate, they could only get us for doing certain things at those tables. That's the rationale.
>
> The *emotional* force of it was our moving one hundred yards inward, putting those damn tables right where they could see them. On the first of October, we moved them to a place that *wasn't* one of the eight. So while there was a perfectly good rationale for setting them up at Sather Gate, it provided a momentum that enabled us to move them to the foot of Sproul Hall. You get one foot in the door, and then the thing is moving.[23]

Mario and Art, both of whom had spoken and organized pickets from Wheeler Oak, were told to make appointments with Dean Williams. This was understood to be the first step in serious disciplinary proceedings against them, and was interpreted by the United Front as an act of war. Right after he cited Mario and Art, Dean Williams sent the following memo to Chancellor Strong:

> October 1, 1964
> MEMORANDUM TO: Chancellor E. W. Strong
> RE: Individual Student Violations of the University
>   Policy on the Use of Facilities
>
> *Mario Robert Savio*
>   On Monday, September 28, Mr. Savio addressed a pre-announced (*Daily Californian*, September 28, 1964) and unauthorized student rally

at the oak tree in line with Sather Gate and within the broad areas of Dwinelle Plaza. His apparent purpose was to urge students to join in picketing the University Meeting (11:00–12:00 AM) which was in progress in the Student Union Plaza.

I talked with him during the rally and at a time when he was not speaking to the group. He was informed by me that this rally and his conduct were in violation of the University Policy on the Use of Facilities. In addition, I told him that I had no alternative but to initiate disciplinary procedures against him and that if a student organization was involved that the disciplinary authority of the University would be invoked against the organization. I stated that individual students were free to picket as long as they did not interfere with or disrupt a University exercise. I urged him to listen to your statement of clarification relative to the privileges of student organizations, and I informed him that you were going to make this statement at the University Meeting then in progress. He replied that he was aware that he was in violation of University rules and that he as well as others had violated the University policy during the week. Further, he emphasized that he couldn't stop the plan to picket the University Meeting. Again, I informed him that he was in violation of the Use of Facilities policy and that I would have to initiate disciplinary action against him.

In my conversation with Mr. Savio on Tuesday afternoon, September 29, 1964, he acknowledged his conduct as reported above. He explained his actions in terms of his conviction that University policy violates the guarantees of free speech and equal protection under the law contained in the spirit of the first and fourteenth amendments of the Constitution of the United States. He stated his belief that any person, student or non-student, inherently possesses the right to speak on any subject (other than advocating the violent overthrow of the Government) at any time and at any place upon the campus, and that both groups or individuals (student or non-student) have the right to set up tables in designated areas to collect money, to solicit membership, to advocate any position or course of action, and to distribute literature. This reasoning prompted him to be a leader of the unauthorized rally and to take an active part in exhorting the listeners at the meeting to join a picket line and march upon the University Meeting. Further, purposefully and admittedly in violation of University policy, he set up a table at Sather Gate in the afternoon of September 29, 1964, on behalf of S.N.C.C. for the purpose of demonstrating his belief in the rights of students and non-students.

Mr. Savio identified the "principle of double effect" as further justification for his actions. This principle appears to state that when one is seeking an end which is morally sound (quite apart from its legality or illegality), the selection of the means employed must be governed by the judgment that the probable good effects outweigh the probable bad effects which are inherent to the method under consideration. In his judgment, his actions had satisfied this philosophical requirement.

Arthur Lee Goldberg

On Monday, September 28, Mr. Goldberg addressed a pre-announced (*Daily Californian*, September 28, 1964) and unauthorized student rally at the oak tree in line with Sather Gate and within the broad areas of Dwinelle Plaza. His apparent purpose was to urge students to join in picketing the University Meeting (11:00–12:00 AM) which was in progress in the Student Center Plaza.

I talked with him during the rally and at a time when he was not speaking to the group. He was informed by me that this rally and his conduct were in violation of the University Policy on the Use of Facilities. In addition, I told him that I had no alternative but to initiate disciplinary procedures against him and that if a student organization was involved that the disciplinary authority of the University would be invoked against the organization. I stated that individual students were free to picket as long as they did not interfere with or disrupt a University exercise. I urged him to listen to your statement of clarification relative to the privileges of student organizations, and I informed him that you were going to make this statement at the University Meeting then in progress. He replied that he was aware that he was in violation of University regulations but that he could not stop the plan to picket the University Meeting. I informed him that I would initiate disciplinary action against him. He asked if the pickets could go into the area where the program was being held. I responded that they could not because this would be considered as interfering with a University exercise. After this exchange I repeated that I would initiate disciplinary action against him.

In my conversation with Mr. Goldberg on Wednesday, September 30, 1964, he would not verify that he had acknowledged to me on the preceding Monday his awareness of the fact that he was in violation of the University's policy on the Use of Facilities. At this time he opined that a controversy existed about the interpretation of the rule, and that the accurate interpretation would have to be defined by the courts. He did, however, admit the fact that I told him that he was in violation of the Use of University Facilities policy, and he did acknowledge that I expressed the University's interpretation of the policy. He emphasized that I had not read a law to him, and that I gave him a verbal statement only. He argued that my statement to him was hearsay and that it required him to accept the word of an authority figure of the University.

He did admit that I explained the policy on pickets, and that I stated that pickets could not interfere with University exercises. He affirmed that he asked if the pickets could go into the audience attending the University Meeting and that I said they could not because such action would be construed as a violation of the picket policy. I did tell him that pickets could stand on the outer perimeter of the audience.

He classified himself as one of the leaders who organized and planned the announced and unauthorized rally, and he verified that he played a very active role as a leader in the meeting and the picketing. He spoke at the rally and he was observed by Deans Van Houten and Murphy and Lt. Chandler of U.C.P.D. as one of the apparent directing forces of the pickets. Further, Dean Van Houten and Lt. Chandler watched him as he directed the picket line into areas he was told they could not go, and it appeared to Dean Van Houten that he was involved in turning the picket line down the aisles. Goldberg claimed he could not control the pickets, that their actions were spontaneous, but at no time did he attempt to control them other than getting them to positions he seemed to desire.

As the leader of Slate, he verified to me in my interview of him that he played an active role in setting up tables upon campus. These tables were in evidence during the last three days. They were not authorized by the Dean of Students' Office. Slate Supplements were being sold at the tables, and they were soliciting membership lists. He believes that it is questionable whether he is in violation of the Use of Facilities policy and he charges that this issue cannot be settled until the courts decide whether or not the specific policy violates the first amendment of the Constitution of the United States.[24]

REBEL WITH A CAUSE AT LAST

> "What are you revolting against?"
> "Whaddaya got?"
> —Marlon Brando in *The Wild One*, 1954

Late in the summer of 1964, together with some of my friends and roommates, I participated in picket lines at the *Oakland Tribune* and at the entrance to the campus, but what it was all about was a little murky to me. I was becoming aware of radical politics as an entrée to friendships and excitement, and Lord knows I was itching for trouble and looking for some excuse to make it hot for anyone in a position of authority. But I cannot honestly say that at the time I understood, or was more than superficially interested in, the politics themselves. I hailed from ancestors who, beyond a vague allegiance to either the Republican or the Democratic party at election time, had no political opinions of any kind. They did their work, exercised their franchise and served their country honorably if called upon to do so, but otherwise lived lives completely outside any political arena, and until then, so had I. My roommate Carl Foytick characterized those of us engaged in such gratuitous troublemaking as "not having the convictions of our courage."

Another of my roommates, Jon Petrie, was the business manager for the SLATE *Supplement*, and he introduced me to the editor, Phil Roos.* I designed the cover and improved upon most of the ads with my unpolished calligraphy and insignificant graphic skills. Aside from mimeographed illustrations for dances and the high school student newspaper, this was the first work I'd ever done that actually got printed.

Near the end of September, I became aware that considerable ferment and turmoil was going on; I'd read the *Daily Cal*'s commentaries

*The SLATE *Supplement to the General Catalog* cost twenty-five cents and came out five times a year. The one I worked on, Volume II, Number 1, was edited by Phil Roos. The editorial staff included Doug Brown, Sue Currier, Joe Freeman, Steve Plagemann, Ron Rohman, Joan Roos, Pete Sessions, Marston Schultz, Al Solomonow and the not-yet-publisher of *Rolling Stone* magazine, Jann Wenner. Production staff included Carl Blumstein, Marston Schultz, Terry Stauduhar and David Goines. Advertising sales were done by Jon King (later the founder of Velo-Sport Bicycles) and Art Goldberg. Cover design was by David Goines. Jerry Miller was the managing editor, and the business manager was Jon Petrie.

SANDOR FUCHS. SLATE CAMPAIGN FLYER, 1965.

and had seen people walking around in circles holding signs and chanting, and had even participated briefly in a picket line. On September 30, I was told that the University no longer allowed the distribution of the *SLATE Supplement* or any literature of a political nature, the urging of people to join any political organization or the solicitation of funds for them. From what I understood, a student had been called before the dean the previous day for doing just that.* In effect, students were to check their lifetime subscriptions to the Bill of Rights at the door to the campus, retrieving them upon departure.

*"At approximately 10:40 AM on September 29, 1964, Frank Miller, Business and Finance Officer of the Berkeley Campus, and I approached a student sitting at a table on the south side of the east pillar of Sather Gate. I introduced myself to the student and asked him if he had a permit for the table at which Slate Supplements were being sold. He stated that he did not have such a permit. I asked him if it was his table, and he responded that it was not his table, but that it was a Slate table. I explained to him that he was in violation of the University Policy on the Use of Facilities and that he had to remove the table from the area. He was informed that if he did not respond to my order that I would be forced to initiate action against him as an individual and that if an organization was involved that I would have to initiate action against the organization. I asked

him for his registration card. He presented the card to me and the card identified him as Sandor Fuchs. I repeated the information stated above and I asked him if he understood that I had stated this to him. He acknowledged that my statement had been made to him, that he was in disagreement with the rule, and that he refused to move the table, and its materials. I reemphasized that he was in violation of the University Policy on the Use of Facilities, and that I would initiate disciplinary action against him.

"Mr. Fuchs made an appointment at my request to see me at 4:00 PM on Tuesday, September 29, 1964. He did not keep the appointment." (Arleigh Williams, memorandum to Chancellor E. W. Strong, October 1, 1964, in Williams, *Dean of Students*, 232.)

So my artwork and design were all for nothing. Damn! This was just a little too familiar, and all the years of being told that I couldn't do things that I felt were perfectly reasonable erupted in me at that very moment. Furthermore, this abrogation of civil liberties smacked too strongly of the arbitrary parental authority that I had just escaped, the old "no particularly good reason, you just can't do it" guff. Authority and I had never gotten on all that well, I didn't like this place all that much anyway, and I was generally in a piss-poor mood: *I wasn't going to put up with it anymore!* There

STUDENTS AROUND SNCC TABLE, SEPTEMBER 39, 1964. PHOTO BY HOWARD HARAWITZ.

was, in addition, an undertone of that fiendish delight a child takes in doing something he's not supposed to do when he has some justification for doing it.

That very morning over coffee, Tom Weller, Peter Paskin, Peter's roommate Charlie Cockie and I had all agreed that we'd just plain had it up to here with the whole system. That week and the previous week, the *Daily Cal* had been filled with agitated letters about student rights, and the undertone of outrage and excitement permeated the whole campus, sort of sloshing around and looking for a place to burst out.

The exhilaration mounting in my blood was like drunkenness, like a drug. I was suddenly a young man filled with joy, the ecstasy of destruction; running into battle, invincible, I feared nothing. I dashed across Bancroft Way to Jon Petrie's apartment where the booklets were stored, got a big box of SLATE *Supplements*, and a card table, and a money can, and hotfoot brought them back to campus and set up a table right under Sather Gate. I sat there for about an hour, after which time Peter Paskin was going to spell me, but he had to go to class.

As I sat there, I got madder and madder. I realized in my dim way that this was a first-class example of me being right and them being

THE AUTHOR, 1963.
PHOTOGRAPH BY W. C. GOINES.

wrong, and that was all there was to it. Although I don't remember what I said, I was outraged eloquence to an extremely indiscriminate audience; people didn't particularly care what I was saying as long as I was on the right side and saying it loudly and passionately; I managed to whip up quite a crowd. Through it waded two deans, George S. Murphy and Peter Van Houten. One of them said, "Are you aware that you are violating University rules and regulations?" And I said, "Are you aware that you are violating my constitutional rights?" And he said, "Are you going to take your table down?" And I said, "No." And then I said to the dean, "Would you care to engage in debate? If you beat me in debate, I'll stop and go away." And the dean said, "No, not today." And I said, "What's the matter, don't you know what you're talking about? Don't you believe in what you stand for?" I flew into a fury and jumped up on top of my chair and began to harangue the crowd around me, screaming at the top of my lungs. I understand it was a good speech. But I'd never delivered a speech before in my life, so I really can't say.

They took my name and told me, "Show up at Dean Arleigh Williams' office at three o'clock," and left with little dignity.*

As I thundered and fulminated, a slender, pretty, dark-haired girl sidled up and fixed her liquid gaze on me in the classic "come hither" expression. I was experiencing the first fruits of being a hero.

---

*"On Wednesday, September 30, at approximately 2:00 PM, Deans Murphy and Van Houten returned to the Sather Gate area and approached the table identified as representing Slate. . . . Upon request . . . the student produced his registration card showing him to be David L. Goines. He was directed to report to the Office by 3:00 PM" (Arleigh Williams, memorandum to Chancellor E. W. Strong, October 1, 1964, in Williams, *Dean of Students*, 233).

Renée Melody: My classes were such a disappointment, and I was kind of looking around for something more exciting there in Berkeley. I was very idealistic, and I felt that things were wrong. I happened to be in Sproul Plaza and some guy was sitting at one of the tables, saying, "Free speech," and he kinda goes like this (*beckons with her finger*). You were trying to get people over to your table, and I sort of laughed at you at first, and you said, "No, come on!" And I said, "Oh, well. What the hell, I'll go see what this guy wants; what he's got going," and you started telling me about SLATE. And I said, "Why should I be interested in your cause?" We got into this really witty, sarcastic give and take, and more people gathered around to listen, and then the deans came.

It was more than a sexual thing: it was a rebellion thing; it was coming out of being oppressed by my mother; it was being in a new exciting place where I'd wanted to be all my life, and finding it every bit as exciting as any of my vague fantasies from when I was seven years old, looking across the bay at this golden, glowing place. I finally caught up with my future. That year when I was nineteen was the most alive, exciting part of my life.[1]

It seemed that I was not the only one actively violating the rules. Although I had no idea of who they were, or even where, others had also been summoned to a rendezvous with destiny, or at least with Dean Williams.

Jackie Goldberg: On the thirtieth, there was a name-taking. Brian [Turner], and Beth Stapleton. They were at Sather Gate. SLATE was at Sather Gate, YSA was at Sather Gate, SNCC was at Sather Gate. Sandor was manning a table. Women for Peace lost the draw; we were still at Bancroft and Telegraph at this time. They just took people at Sather Gate, not at Bancroft. There was a crowd around, and we decided to keep the tables manned all day. The United Front had a meeting with Dean Towle at four o'clock. We decided to gather as many petitions as we could.[2]

Tom Miller: I was up on a chair saying, "There's the dean taking his name. Tell us why, Dean!" Then he came up to me and he says, "Gimme your reg card," and I says, "You're not getting *my* reg card 'til you explain the rules here." And he said, "Gimme your reg card," and I said, "Nope! You get up here and explain the rules and I'll give you my reg card." So he just left, he didn't take my reg card.[3]

Overwhelmed by the crowds and the tone of open rebellion, the deans began to withdraw. They had actually cited only five students—Brian Turner, Elizabeth Gardner Stapleton, Mark Bravo, Donald Hatch and me—and, despite eager students almost demanding to be cited, they refused to take more names. Soon pieces of paper torn out of notebooks began circulating, saying, "We the undersigned have jointly manned tables at Sather Gate, realizing that we were in violation of University edicts to the contrary. We realize that we may be subject to expulsion," or words to that effect.[4] There was no particular uniformity among the certificates of complicity; all they had in common was the general idea that the signers would have been perfectly delighted to have been cited. Hundreds of signatures were gathered by midafternoon.

Mario Savio: On the twenty-ninth, Brian Turner was manning the SNCC table near Sather Gate, and was approached by the deans and folded up his table and left. On the thirtieth, he set it up again, and the deans told him to come to the office at three. Brian got up, and Donald Hatch sat down. Same thing. Donald Hatch got up, and Mark Bravo sat down. Same thing again. Before Brian sat down and had his name taken he came to me and said, "Yesterday I got up and took the table away, and I really think I ought to sit down again. What do you think? What would you do?" I said, "I would sit down." He also asked if he would be supported, and I said, "If I had anything to do with it."* Then other people started to sit down, and the deans started to walk away. I and other people called them back and said, "There are plenty of other people who want to violate your regulations. Will you please stay here and take down their names?" But they wouldn't. Then we started the petition of complicity, and all the people who had signed it went into Sproul Hall at three.[5]

We figured that it would be a really swell idea if we all went to the dean's office together. Despite the mob scene that resulted in Sproul Hall, Mario managed to get a communication through to Dean Williams. The first demand was to drop all the charges. The second was to treat everyone the same—cited students and those who only said they'd

---

*Brian Turner, who'd only been a member of SNCC for a week, made quite a good statement to the *San Francisco Chronicle* on October 3, 1964: "I backed down on Tuesday because I didn't want to go alone. I folded up the table and went home. But I thought about it overnight and I went back. When they came up to see me again, my own principles prevented me from leaving. I had decided that the freedom of 27,000 people to speak freely is worth the sacrifice of my own academic career at Cal."

BRIAN TURNER AT A SNCC TABLE BESIDE SATHER GATE, SEPTEMBER 30, 1964.
PHOTO BY RON ENFIELD.

broken the rules—and that he see us all. Dean Williams was not in a position to agree to either demand and replied, "I cannot make any guarantee to concede to any request. We are dealing only with observed violations, not unobserved violations. And, we will continue to do this."[6] Williams then let it be known that the United Front representatives need not show up for the scheduled four o'clock meeting in which they and Dean Towle were to discuss University policy concerning the new regulations. At four o'clock, Dean Williams again asked the five cited students, plus three leaders of earlier demonstrations—Mario Savio, Art Goldberg and Sandor Fuchs—to come unaccompanied into his office to face disciplinary procedures. None of us did so.

Jackie Goldberg: We went up to 201, we had everybody sit down leaving aisles and space along the hall, gathered all the petitions, and asked to see Dean Williams. Dean Williams came out into the hall, and said he wanted to see the six that were cited, leaving out Mario and Art. He went in, and came out in about twenty minutes and read the list again, this time adding Mario and Art, making it eight he wanted to see, right then and there. At that point, he also announced that the meeting with Dean Towle had been canceled. It was at this point that we decided to stay. We had no hopes of seeing anybody at that point. We weren't going to leave the eight people there, so we all stayed. At that point we started sending people out for food, and Mario started making a number

SEPTEMBER 30, 1964, SPROUL HALL SIT-IN. PHOTO BY RON ENFIELD.

of speeches outside Sproul Hall urging people to come in. CBS television and reporters from the newspapers interviewed me, and I was issuing information about what was happening.[7]

Arleigh Williams: When we were making every effort to prevent this from escalating into something which would be much more difficult, I requested eight people to see me at three o'clock in the afternoon. Instead of receiving eight people, I received three hundred and eight people. That was the beginning of the first sit-in. That was the time that Mario Savio acted as spokesman for the group, and stated that there were problems with the First Amendment and the Fourteenth Amendment, and he was advising no one to see me unless I was willing to see each person who had come up to the office on the second floor. I requested to see the eight, because I was dealing with them separately. I told them I couldn't see the group as a whole, and stated that I *would* not talk with the group as a whole, that I had to see these and also inform them that we had planned a meeting that afternoon in 221 Sproul Hall with representatives of the political action groups and advisers of the political action groups. I wanted to be able to hold this meeting, but I didn't feel that I could hold it in this kind of an environment, and requested them to leave the second floor. Well, they didn't feel they could leave the second floor, and remained there. I came back here, and again went out at four o'clock and requested the individuals to see me, and then added the names of a few others who I was going to see at four o'clock and asked them to come in at the same time. At that time they said, "No," they rejected that and said, "We will not unless you see each person." I'm not sure if again the emphasis was placed on the First and Fourteenth Amendments, but I'm sure that this was the essence of their driving thought at that time. Then they stayed in the hallway and remained in the building until around two o'clock, three o'clock in the morning, I don't recall that any stayed overnight.

There wasn't any hostility in this group. In fact, quite the opposite.[8]

In his memo to Chancellor Strong, Dean Williams expanded his report on Mario to include the cited students and Sproul Hall sit-in:

October 1, 1964
MEMORANDUM TO: Chancellor E. W. Strong
RE: Individual Student Violations of the University
    Policy on the Use of Facilities

Mario Robert Savio
    On Wednesday afternoon, September 30, 1964, Mr. Savio brought three hundred or more students to see me in my office. I met him and them at the entrance door of the Dean of Students' Office. He identified himself as the spokesman for the group and described their purposes, i.e., that they knew of several students who had been directed to make an appointment with me for violating the University Policy on Use of Facilities and that each person with him acknowledged violation of the same policy and was desirous of making a similar appointment. My first response was to request five students who had been observed violating University regulations (Elizabeth Gardner, Mark Bravo, David Goines, Donald Hatch, and Brian Turner) to go into the Dean of Students' Office and talk with Dean Murphy and Dean Van Houten about their conduct. This request was not accepted by Mr. Savio, [by] the specific students noted or by the group in general. Savio again spoke for them. He indicated that I misunderstood apparently his statement of position. He repeated it and suggested clearly that I would have to talk with each member of the group if I wanted to talk with any of them.
    I repeated the direction to the five students named, and then informed the group that it would be impossible to talk to all of them at that time. I requested each to leave his name with me if he wished to do so, and I stated that I would determine if and when appointments would be made for them. I informed the group that I was concerned only with observed violations. I reminded them that upon the request of students,

arrangements were made to meet with the leaders of each organization actively involved in the protest, that the advisors of each organization had been urged by us to attend this meeting, and that the meeting was scheduled for 4:00 PM this date. I declared that we wished to hold this meeting, but that we could not conduct it unless it could be held in an environment conducive to good exchange of statements. I concluded my remarks with the request for them to leave the building.

Mr. Savio responded

1) that equal protection under the laws was at stake;

2) that the group was prepared to leave only if I would guarantee that the same disciplinary action would follow for each member of the group; and,

3) without such assurances he would urge everyone to remain right where they were.

I spoke again and told them that I would not make such guarantees, that I was committed to support University policies and that I had every intention of doing so. To the best of my recollection I believe that I told them again about the scheduled meeting of student leaders and their advisors and of my hope that this meeting could be held. I asked them again to leave the building because they were interfering with the ability of neighboring offices to continue their University work.

At the termination of my remarks Mr. Savio organized the sit-down.

At approximately 4:05 PM I approached the group again and requested Elizabeth Gardner, Mark Bravo, David Goines, Donald Hatch, Brian Turner, Sandor Fuchs, Art Goldberg, and Mario Savio to see me as each was involved in a personal disciplinary problem. Further, I announced that the scheduled meeting of the presidents and advisors of the groups was canceled. I should note that none of the students listed above responded to my request to see them.[9]

Larry Marks: All of the people that were milling around in Sproul Hall went and sat down in front of Strong's office. There was a little bit of singing, and a little bit of ogling at Strong's secretary, who was a pretty luscious thing. Very interesting, she looked like a very, how shall I say it, beatnik type.[10]

Mario Savio: It wouldn't have been impossible for Dean Williams to see all the people on the list. Start at the bottom with five at a time, or maybe get a big room and talk to us all at once. Some arrangement so that he wouldn't just talk to those five who had been cited. Because if he talked to those five *first*, then it was over. There were good reasons for not letting him talk to those five.[11]

SEPTEMBER 30, 1964, SPROUL HALL SIT-IN. PHOTO CALIFORNIA MONTHLY (FEBRUARY 1965, PAGE 13).

At a few minutes past four o'clock, Mario announced that we would stay in Sproul Hall into the night. Things had happened with astonishing speed; that morning the campus had been relatively peaceful with perhaps a subcurrent of unrest, but by the afternoon it was Katy, bar the door.

SHERATON-PALACE AND AUTO ROW SIT-INS PROVIDED A MODEL FOR THE SIT-IN AT UC BERKELEY. CADILLAC SIT-IN. PHOTO BY HOWARD HARAWITZ.

THE FIRST SIT-IN

> We want equal action. And that's no action, because they can't take action against all these people who are here. They're scared. We're staying.
> —Mario Savio, Sproul Hall, September 30, 1964

Without any actual premeditation, the student invasion of Sproul Hall had turned into a sit-in: we all sat around because we couldn't really leave, having caught a tiger by the tail. The building was then closed, and they said, "You have to get out," and we said we wouldn't, and so they left, instead. Money was collected, food was purchased, and a few coeds assembled sandwiches and distributed chow to the troops. I worked as a monitor.

At about eleven-thirty that night, Dean of the Graduate Division of the University Sanford Elberg stood before the assembled students in Sproul Hall and mechanically read a leaden statement issued by Chancellor Edward W. Strong:

> Students and student organizations today enjoy the fullest privileges in the history of the University, including discussion and advocacy on a broad spectrum of political and social issues. Some students demand on-campus solicitation of funds and planning and recruitment for off-campus social and political action. The University cannot allow its facilities to be so used without endangering its future as an independent educational institution. The issue now has been carried far beyond the bounds of discussion by a small minority of students. These students should recognize the fullness of the privileges extended to them by the University, and ask themselves whether they wish to take further actions damaging to the University.
>
> The University cannot and will not allow students to engage in deliberate violation of law and order on campus. The SLATE Supplement report this fall urged "open, fierce, and thoroughgoing rebellion on the campus . . . in which the final resort will be Civil Disobedience." Individual students must ask themselves whether they wish to be part of such action.
>
> When violations occur, the University must then take disciplinary action. Such action is being taken. Eight students were informed indi-

SIX OF THE EIGHT SUSPENDED STUDENTS, LEFT TO RIGHT: BETH STAPLETON, SANDOR FUCHS, BRIAN TURNER, DAVID GOINES, DONALD HATCH AND ART GOLDBERG. NOT PICTURED, MARIO SAVIO AND MARK BRAVO. PHOTO SAN FRANCISCO EXAMINER, FRIDAY, OCTOBER 2, 1964.

vidually by a representative of the Office of the Dean of Students that they were in violation of University regulations and were asked to desist. Each of the eight students refused to do so. I regret that these eight students by their willful misconduct in deliberately violating rules of the University have made it necessary for me to suspend them indefinitely from the University. (*A roar of protest, followed by shushings and "We're here for free speech, let him speak!"*) I stand ready as always to meet with the officers of any student organization to discuss the policies of the University.[1]

Thus it was announced that the five students who had manned tables and the three protest leaders had been, we called it, "expended." We weren't quite expelled, for if we repented of our ways we could come back, but we were indefinitely suspended until we did. This punishment was unusual in that it did not exist in the code of conduct but had been created specially for the occasion—a fact that we immediately argued emphasized the illegality of the administration's reaction.

As soon as I heard the news, I realized with a thrill that I was having the best time I'd ever had in my entire life. I was up to my ears in excitement and getting to know new people. Out of nowhere, a pretty girl had paid attention to me. I had absolutely no interest in doing anything but keeping right on doing what I was doing. All my life, I'd had a terrible headache and because I'd always had it, I didn't even know that I had it. The terrible headache was *school*. In an instant I understood that I *hated* school, and that I'd *always* hated school, and that now, suddenly, miraculously, my headache was gone. I wouldn't have gone back for pie. At last I had a focus for the rage that had been building in me. This general rage egged me on throughout the entirety of the FSM, and kept me going for a considerable amount of time afterward in the Congress of Racial Equality. I was overwhelmingly angry at the whole works, and as I became more aware of what I was angry at I became even angrier. This anger gradually became less the outraged sputtering anger of the first couple of days, and more a calculated fury.

Immediately after Elberg's announcement, Mario came forward and, in ringing tones, addressed the excited group of his formerly fellow students, who greeted his words with profound, rapt silence:

Well. This started out as a completely spontaneous response of students at this University against arbitrary action taken by the dean's office here against certain students who thought they had the right to free expression at this University. Well, free expression, for the University, means that you can talk about lots of things, but as we just heard in the statement from Chancellor Strong, those things you can't do are the taking of action on various ideas that you discuss. Now, I'd like to connect that, right here, very, very clearly, with statements that have been made by President Kerr in his book on the multiversity. President Kerr has referred to the University as a factory; a knowledge factory—that's his words—engaged in the knowledge industry. And just like any factory, in any industry—again his words—you have a certain product. The product is you. Well, not really you. And not really me. The products are those people who wouldn't join in our protest. They go in one side, as kind of rough-cut adolescents, and they come out the other side pretty smooth. When they enter the University, they're dependent upon their parents. That kind of dependency is the sort of thing that characterizes childhood and adolescence. When they're in school, before they enter the University, part of that dependency is shifted to the various schools that they're in. Then they come to the University. And now, instead of suckling at their mother's or at the breast of their schools, they suckle at the breast of Holy Mother University. So here they are. Now, they're dependent upon the University. They're product. And they're prepared to leave the University, to go out and become members of other organizations—various businesses, usually—and I hope I'm not offending anyone in this, but I'm speaking *my* mind— which they are then dependent upon in the same way. And never, at any point, is provision made for their taking their places as free men! Never at any point is provision made—you know, someplace in society, some things you can do which in some ways can be expressive of your individuality. You just can't do that unless you have no intention of making it in this society. You can be poor and have dignity, but if you have

MARIO SAVIO SPEAKING IN SPROUL HALL,
SEPTEMBER 30, 1964.
PHOTOGRAPHER UNKNOWN.

any intention of making it in any way, you're out of it, you're just completely out of it! You've gotta be a part; part of a machine. Now, every now and then, the machine doesn't work. One of the parts breaks down. And in the case of a normal, regular machine, you throw that part out; throw it out, and you replace it. Well, this machine, this factory here, this multiversity, its parts are human beings. And, sometimes, when *they* go out of commission, they don't simply break down, but they really gum up the whole works! (*Scattered laughter.*) That's what we're all doing here. We've kind of gone out of commission. We won't operate according to the way the parts of this machine should operate, and the machine started to go out of commission. But the remedy is the same! In the case of a regular machine, in the case of *this* machine, you throw the parts out! And that's what they decided to do. That's what the statement says. They're an indefinite suspension—I presume that's close to the words he used—of those students who went out of commission; those students who weren't good enough parts, who didn't function well enough. For one brief moment, there were lots of people, lots of students, whose imaginations were fired. Maybe we would not have to likewise be parts. Maybe somehow we could take our place as free men also! So those students said, "We're with you! We stand right with you! Not behind you. We're next to you! We're brothers!" They signed that sheet! That sheet said, "We want you to treat us *all the same way*." Now, you know it was an unreasonable demand. It was unreasonable in this regard: it's not a demand the University could have met without completely dropping any kind of disciplinary action against anyone. And they knew it! And . . . we knew it.

Well, they've decided, instead, to disregard your protest, and to assume that you had never come in here, nothing like that had happened, that instead what it is—the eight students, they refused to speak with the proper authorities, and they've been axed.

We can do various things. I suppose that's really what we want to talk about. We can do various things. We can—and this is what I would hope the group here would want to do—we can make as the issue of our continued protest three things: First, whatever action has been taken against these particular individuals singled out by the administration, this action be dropped, completely! (*Thunderous applause and cheers.*)

Are there any abstentions? (*Laughter.*)

The second thing is that we here, all of us, the committee of the whole, we demand those particular demands I read to you from that yellow sheet earlier today concerning freedom of expression on this campus. We are putting our weight behind those demands. (*Applause.*)

In particular, our protest is demanding a meeting with Chancellor Strong—none of these little guys, we're done with that. (*Laughter and applause.*) We're demanding a meeting with Chancellor Strong to discuss those demands!

Third, we demand that, at least until that meeting has taken place, if there are any groups on campus who exercise what they believe to be their rights of free expression, there will be no disciplinary action taken against them, at any time! (*Cheers and applause.*)

I presume that, from the basis of the response, in the name of all the people assembled here, and hopefully in the name of the University of California, we can make these demands public, and make them to the administration; to the chancellor. Is this something we can do? (*"Yes! Yes!" Great applause.*)[2]

Had I been in the shoes of the administration, I would have trembled at this oratory, and carefully examined my motives and what I hoped to gain and what I stood to lose. This is not the speech of fractious, willful children deprived of a glittering toy. This is the speech of the Americans who dressed up in war paint and threw taxed tea into Boston harbor. This language promises fire and blood.

Dean Sanford Elberg left in anger and disgust, and was replaced by the obviously rattled Assistant Dean Barnes, who spoke to the demonstrators sympathetically but without yielding any ground:

My interpretation of these rules is simply this: that anybody on this campus can advocate; they do not have to be restricted to purely informational material, but may advocate positions. Positions on any issue. This advocacy as I understand it is restricted to some nine places on campus. Hyde Park areas. One of which is the old Hyde Park area down by the Student Union; [one is] out by Bancroft and Telegraph. I think three tables can be placed in front of this area; [and there is] unlimited right to speak out here on the steps of this hall, right underneath here on

Sproul Hall [steps], and I think also Sather Gate and some other areas I'm not really familiar with.* Advocacy. What cannot be done is to solicit funds for any cause off-campus. What cannot be done is to recruit members for off-campus organizations. What cannot be done is to mount political action, off-campus, here. There is nothing, as I understand it, and I may be proven wrong, that prevents any speaker here, any group speaker, any distribution of literature by any group, which calls for a meeting off-campus for the purpose of discussing political action. But that political action must not emanate from the campus. It seems to me that it has to begin off-campus. Stiles Hall, or elsewhere. This, it does not seem to me, is a restriction of free speech! It may be a restriction of political action, and I can't argue that. It obviously is. But it is not a restriction of free speech. The distinction is essentially a legal one. A legalistic one, if you wish. Sure. But, advocacy here; action begins there. But by this distinction, quibble though it may be, legalistic though it may be, the University places itself in a posture where it can honestly say, to those who would pressure it, that this University is not a forum for political action. And you, who would attempt—I don't mean you—I mean the outside pressures, the outside forces, who would like to turn it into your own particular political bailiwick, have to stay out! We stay out of your action, you stay out of ours.

("*Boo! Who's 'we'? Boo!*") The University, of which you're a member, of which I'm a part, of which all of us [are a part].

The request has been that I direct my attention to the question of the suspension of students. All right. Here. What I cannot do is deliver myself—because I am not informed well enough—is deliver myself on the suspension of Mario and these other seven students, tonight. I can't do this.

Second of all, what I fear, and this again I do not know, but what I fear is, that if there is continued disobedience of the rules and regulations concerning this policy, that further suspensions may, in fact, result. (*Applause.*)

This is what I *do not* want to see. I don't know how other people feel about it in this community. But what worries me ("*Quiet! Let him finish!*"), what worries me precisely is this: that much of the best willpower and manpower in this University is up here tonight. I have no doubt about that. I think that you can, within this existing framework of policy announced on Monday, work effectively for the political ends you want. I have no doubt about this. I think that if you disobey these

---

*Hyde Park areas were actually eight in number: Wheeler Oak, Bancroft and Telegraph, Sproul Hall steps, Student Union steps, North Gate, Student Union Plaza, Mining Circle and the steps of Harmon Gymnasium.

rules then you are in jeopardy as individuals, and the organizations that you are working with are in jeopardy as organizations. (*Angry responses. "Let him talk!"*) Go ahead.

From the crowd: I want to ask you one question, just concerning the students. If this University is so rotten and so corrupt at its base, that a simple demonstration by students asking for free speech will cause this University to *collapse* from outside pressure, I ask you if you can stand there and solicit my support for it! (*Whistles, cheers and prolonged applause.*)

Dean Barnes: I deny, first of all, that this University is that corrupt, at base or anywhere else. (*Heckling from the crowd.*) Second of all (*"Shh!"*), secondly of all, it is not a demonstration that is involved. It is the continued, and I fear willful, breaking and violations of regulations (*laughter, babble, "Shh!"*) which the University went into.

From the crowd: Question! You have stated that the University must withstand the outside pressures. I maintain that the University is walking hand in hand with the outside pressures! (*Enthusiastic applause. "Yes! Yes!"*) In its participation in the cold war manufacturing of weapons. (*Confused crowd response. "Let him speak!"*) In the Giannini Institute over here that has made a decision that the bracero program is OK for the growers, isn't that using the University, and the University's name, for the outside community that it's supposed to be withstanding?*

Dean Barnes: No. Because I deny, first of all, that involved in this is a Giannini Foundation position on braceros. I don't know whether it is

---

*The bracero program was one which allowed California growers to import Mexican field laborers, grossly exploit them, and deport them when they had no further use for them. UC's position on the bracero program was an extremely sore point. The conviction that UC was working under the thumb of agribusiness was supported by suspicious suppression of reports and stifling of criticism. In the fall of 1963, the Division of Agricultural Sciences published a report that concluded that some form of cheap foreign labor had to be maintained after the bracero program ended on December 31. It was revealed by Thomas L. Pitts, president of the AFL-CIO, that seventeen pages had been removed from the report. These pages would have shown that no bracero program was needed. It was believed that both Governor Pat Brown and Jesse Tapp, chairman of the board of directors of the Bank of America, head of the State Board of Agriculture and a UC Regent, had seen the report in its unaltered state and had ordered the passages removed. In addition, a study, "Harvest of Loneliness," prepared by Henry Anderson, a researcher employed by UC to study health conditions of braceros, was believed to have been confiscated and destroyed by a University committee. In 1958 the American Friends Service Committee had asked Anderson to write a statement on the bracero program, which fell into the hands of the Farm Bureau Federation, which pressured UC to terminate his project. In 1960, Anderson published a hundred draft copies of his report, which were ordered recalled and destroyed. (This information is abstracted from an undated Independent Socialist Club leaflet that was probably printed in the spring or summer of 1964.)

or not. I can't answer that. (*Confused crowd response.*) The Giannini Foundation, I know nothing about the Giannini Foundation itself. (*"We want Mario! We've only heard one speaker! Let him talk!"*) I know nothing about the Giannini Foundation. I just don't know. I know that most of the people in this University probably oppose the bracero program. I certainly do very potently. I think, by the way, that a great many of the statistical studies [that] have proven that the bracero program does not need to be continued in this state emanated from this very University; from the faculty of this University. So, there are balances here, too. Now, with respect to the cold war; it is a perfectly respectable position for many people to believe that the cold war is in fact a reality, and that this University, and any American university, must partake, must at least be cognizant of the existence of the cold war, and must, to some extent, as it sees fit, and as individuals see fit, contribute to the winning of that cold war. (*Disapproving sounds.*) You may not agree! I am not worried about what you think, as you're probably not worried about what I think on this matter. But this is at least a responsible position.

Voice from the crowd: This University is giving you guys the axe for something that you've been doing for years. And now, they all of a sudden call up this law which they've never enforced, without telling you why they're enforcing it now. They prefer to hide in the maze of their machine. I want to ask Professor Barnes, if he is trying to explain their position, why are they enforcing it now?! Is it because they're responding to outside pressure? I'd like him to answer that, because if he can't, that's a pretty terrible admission. They won't even tell you *why* they're giving you the axe!

Mario Savio: I would definitely like to hear from him on that very question, and before he makes his remarks, I want to say something which Dean Towle said, so that he can't tell us something different first! She said the following to the second meeting of the representatives of the political organizations: She said, after she had decided, "No, traffic violation wasn't the thing," and, "No, tables in wrong places, it wasn't any of that," someone asked her, was it the fact that we've been asking people to come down to picketing, did this trigger this action, this new enforcement?" and she said, "Yes, that definitely had something to do with it." With that preface, we'll let Professor Barnes speak.

Dean Barnes: I can add nothing to what you've just heard. First of all, I don't know what is behind it, and secondly of all, if that is what Dean Towle in fact said, fair enough, I can certainly not go above any higher authority than that. I don't know.

One more point that was raised. Yes, the basic issue is the question of the continual functioning of off-campus political and social groups on campus. I think that is the basic issue here. I do believe that these

rules and regulations, and I know that the speaker before Mario disagreed, I think we can work under these rules and these regulations. I
don't think they're as crippling as people feel they are. Fine, fair enough,
it's a disputable point. The point is, advocacy of any position, as I understand it, is now definitely *OK!* It has been since Monday. Advocacy
of *any* position—here's what isn't allowed—not saying, "Now, let's go
picket this place or let's go picket that place." No.

From the crowd: Isn't that a position?

Dean Barnes: That's a position. That is advocacy, sure, of one sort.
But what we are talking about are advocacies of a particular political or
social position. That is advocacy. This is a call to action. That call to
action is not allowed.

The other point is, you can do more than pass out bumper stickers.
You can urge people to vote, or not to vote. For Goldwater or anybody
else. [Tape ends.][3]

Following the lead of others, I gave an enthusiastic, largely incomprehensible speech from the second-floor balcony of Sproul Hall. It generated a good deal more heat than light, but the hour was late,
everybody was hyped up and nobody seemed to mind. What was said
from the balcony was scarcely intelligible to the crowd below anyhow.
I was taken off by Tom Miller, who told me my speeches were alienating people. I was in effect saying, "If you're not in here, you're screwing *me,* and you're screwing *yourself,* and you're screwing everybody."
I referred to the University as a cloister instead of an educational institution. I don't know if they were good speeches. I imagine they weren't.
But they were passionate. A group of six people came in and said,
"You've convinced me," and another group of six said, "I'm never
gonna go in because of *you,*" so I imagine I *was* alienating people. I was
very angry. I was almost in tears.

I got my picture taken and made a statement to the press. It was probably pretty dumb, and I'm glad that it didn't get printed. I met the other
people who had been thrown out; I didn't know any of them. They all
seemed to know each other, though. I found out later that they were all
political people and knew each other from way back. They were bewildered that *I'd* gotten thrown out, because they didn't know *me.*

There was a meeting on the first floor in the north end of the building
in a little cubicle where all the eight suspended students and several others talked. It became very hot and stuffy. We were arguing about
whether we should leave or not leave. The arguments for staying were:
if we leave, it will seem that we're chickening out; we fought for this,
and kept it for so long, we really shouldn't leave now; we've got this far

STUDENTS IN SPROUL HALL, SEPTEMBER 30, 1964. SEATED FACING THE CAMERA, SANDOR FUCHS. PHOTO FROM THE FEBRUARY 1965 CALIFORNIA MONTHLY, PAGE 39.

and we really shouldn't split. The arguments against—which I thought were much stronger—were that, staying is kind of absurd, we can't gain anything, we're not disrupting anybody's anything. If we want to do something, come back in tomorrow morning about seven o'clock. If we want to disrupt things, we should disrupt things then. But, we're not doing *anything* now, it's purely symbolic, we're wearing everybody out, everybody's tired, we want to go home and go to bed. That argument won out. The Sproul Hall sit-in ended around three in the morning, except for a few diehards, who refused to leave. Before it broke up, a free speech rally was announced for noon the next day on Sproul Hall steps.

Jack Weinberg: During the sit-in there was a debate over strategy. Some wanted to stay as long as necessary until the University withdrew the suspensions. But others told of a sit-in that spring at the University of Chicago. The students sat in the administration building for two weeks without encountering punitive action. At the end, they were isolated and discouraged and quit.

We weren't ready for such a long sit-in and so decided to take our protest back to the plaza. It was decided to set up as many tables as possible the next day at noon, this time on Sproul Hall steps. We also decided that when the deans tried to cite anyone, the person would refuse to identify themselves. This was an effort to keep on escalating the confrontation while keeping the locus on the plaza where the largest number of people would be directly affected.

That night, after leaving Sproul Hall, the Campus CORE activists met. We sent a telegram to the CORE national office saying to expect a major confrontation the next day, and requesting a telegram of support back from James Farmer, the CORE director. We also arranged to set up a seven-foot-long table on campus the next day, surrounded by a dozen activists.[4]

Jackie Goldberg: Not too many speeches were being made inside Sproul Hall. Mostly people were sitting quietly studying, the secretaries went on about their business, the life of Sproul Hall was not interrupted. Around eleven the United Front had a meeting to decide what to do: here we had a sit-in that we hadn't planned! The discussion was, should we keep this going, should we call it off, and we didn't conclude much, because we got word that someone from the administration was going to make an announcement. About midnight, we came back up the stairs just in time to hear that the eight were suspended indefinitely. At which point, most of the eight made speeches standing on a chair in the hallway.

At that point, we resumed the meeting that had been broken up, and by two-thirty we decided to break it up and everyone went home by three. Some people didn't want to leave—Arnie Eagle was one. We explained that it would be better to leave now, and make plans for a period of time beginning tomorrow morning, and just run them right through until we got what we wanted. I don't know when Arnie and his friends left.*

The United Front adjourned to Art's apartment to decide on the next day's activities. Now, about this point, a vote was taken that Mario and Art should be the spokesmen and I faded. The press didn't know this for a couple of days. We decided to set up every table possible in a long line in front of Sproul Hall. We had all kinds of people committed to taking someone's place as soon as someone's name was taken. We were going to get as many people on the list of those to be suspended as possible. We decided to picket, we decided to collect money; the money would all go into a common fund. Every table had as much advocative literature as they could, everybody was collecting names for membership lists. We were going to break every rule and force them into a showdown.[5]

I went off with my friend Peter and his girlfriend, and slept at their house. I woke up the next morning about eight o'clock and took off for school again, with the fantastically elated feeling that I'd been thrown out and I didn't have to give a good goddamn about anything. I hadn't much liked the idea of going to school that semester anyway, but I hadn't been able to think of anything better to do.

---

*The *Oakland Tribune* of October 2, 1964, reported: "As the students filed out of Sproul Hall last night, one young man, who refused to identify himself, loudly protested that he would not leave. 'That's OK, kid,' said one officer as he locked the door. 'Be my guest.'"

IN THE LATE 1950S AND EARLY 1960S, PEACE ACTIVISM PROVIDED A FOCUS FOR SOCIAL
PROTEST. JEFFERSON POLAND AMONG "BAN-THE-BOMB" MARCHERS, 1962.
PHOTO BY BOB GILL.

JACK WEINBERG AND THE POLICE CAR

THE NEXT DAY, October 1, the whole campus was hot to trot. That was the day of Jack Weinberg and the police car; the most dramatic, wonderful thing I'd ever seen in my entire life. I cannot begin to describe how much fun it was. It was like being in Valhalla, in a war where nobody got killed. I was rid of the burden of going to school, and simultaneously an incredible, exciting, wonderful new world was opening up.

Around ten o'clock that morning, Gretchen Kittredge and Tom Miller of the Campus Congress of Racial Equality drove Jack Weinberg, balancing an old door on the car roof, to Telegraph and Bancroft. Jack carried the door onto campus and set it on trestles in the middle of a row of smaller tables at the foot of Sproul steps, facing Ludwig's Fountain.*

I helped set up tables and was quite elated at the whole works; especially so at the sight of CORE's huge table. All involved had purposefully set out to violate the University's regulations against distributing information and collecting donations for non-University causes on the campus.

---

*Ludwig's Fountain is the large, centrally located circular fountain in Sproul Plaza. It is so called after a large German shorthair mutt named Ludwig von Schwarenberg that was each day taken to campus by its graduate-student master and left at the fountain, in which it cavorted joyfully in all weather. After a while, Ludwig came to campus on his own at eight and left promptly at five-thirty. The dog was taken up as a campus mascot and, honoring student requests to do so, the Regents officially named the fountain in Ludwig's honor in 1963. In September 1965, Ludwig moved with his masters, Mr. and Mrs. John W. Littleford, from Berkeley to Alameda, where the president of the Alameda First National Bank offered him the use of the bank's fountain. "Forrest Tregea, executive director of the Associated Students of the University of California, thanked [bank president] Spillman for the offer, but suggested that the bank fountain be made free of 'beatniks, radicals, subversives, communists and troublemakers.' These people, said Tregea, have had Ludwig 'very troubled' during his six-year tenure at Cal" (*San Francisco Chronicle*, 14 August 1965).

OCTOBER 1, 1964, 11:50 AM. JACK WEINBERG IS
TOLD BY DEANS MURPHY AND VAN HOUTEN
THAT HE IS UNDER ARREST.
PHOTOGRAPHER UNKNOWN.

Mario Savio: Not showing reg cards was a way of upping the ante. They could either arrest you, or do nothing. It also did not allow them to distinguish between students and nonstudents. It took the initiative out of their hands, and was another way of refusing to follow their rules.[1]

Tom Miller: After the sit-in, CORE held a meeting at Gretchen Kittredge's place. About twenty-five people showed up, and we went through our whole strategy. I had this big table at my place—it was a huge door that had legs on it, and was the table Jack was arrested from. I still had the lists of names of people who said that they had also violated the rules; and we decided to put those lists on the tables. If they came up and asked us for identification, we'd say, "We won't give you any. Our name is on that list and if you want our name you take the whole list; everybody on there is responsible." So we got to bed around four o'clock that night, and up again at seven, getting that door to campus. I think I carried it in my car. All kinds of people trying to hold it on. We didn't think that they'd come and drag us off; we thought they'd suspend us like the other students. When they came up to the table, Jack told them his name was on the list, and they arrested him. We had scheduled a rally for noon, which was very convenient, because people were pouring in to the plaza just as Jack was being arrested.[2]

Jack represented Campus CORE. He was not a UC student at that time, having graduated "with great distinction" in mathematics the year before. But instead of being an alumnus, or graduate, or former student, or former teaching assistant in mathematics, Jack was miraculously transmogrified into a "nonstudent," and was called that from there on out by newspapers, magazines and campus officials. Considering the difficulties they'd had the day before, I imagine that the authorities—in the person of the luckless Dean Towle, who had drawn the short straw and was carrying the can for the administration—figured they would have a better case if they moved against what they could call an outside agitator than against another one of the students. Jack was also being very loud in his debate on the subject, and as he saw the deans approaching, became louder yet, switching gears from debate to diatribe.

OCTOBER 1, 1964, 11:59 AM. A POLICE CAR PULLS UP TO THE CORE TABLE. PHOTOGRAPHER UNKNOWN.

Jack Weinberg: I was the one nonstudent ringleader. They couldn't have suspended me when they got Mario, Art and Sandor, so they chose to go after me that day. When I refused to identify myself they called the cops.[3]

The authorities, again in the persons of Deans Murphy and Van Houten, accompanied by University police lieutenant Merrill F. Chandler, told Jack that if he was not a student he was trespassing, and if he was a student, he was violating University regulations. Jack would not identify himself, saying that his name was on the list on the table. He was warned that he would be arrested.

"Oh, please Br'er Fox, don' throw me in de briar patch!"

An excited crowd was milling about, mostly craning their necks and goggling at all the excitement, but seemingly willing to go along with whatever irritated the administration and made the most fuss. Chandler told Jack that he was under arrest, and asked him if he would come peacefully. If not, he would be taken by force. Echoing Wednesday's statements of complicity, the cry went up, "Take all of us!" Lieutenant Chandler went off to get help. The dean stood by, and Jack took this golden opportunity to deliver a rousing speech to the intensely excited and rapidly growing crowd:

I want to tell you about this knowledge factory, while we're all sitting here now. It seems that certain of the products are not coming out to

JACK WEINBERG IS SEIZED BY UNIVERSITY OF CALIFORNIA POLICE
Students staged a sit-down in front of police car to block his removal

OCTOBER 1, 1964, NOON SHARP. JACK
WEINBERG IS ARRESTED. OAKLAND TRIBUNE
PHOTO BY RUSS REED, OCTOBER 1, 1964.

standard specifications. And I feel the University is trying to purge these products so that they can once again produce for the industry exactly what they specify. This is a knowledge factory—if you read Clark Kerr's book, these are his words. This is mass production; no deviations from the norm are tolerated. Occasionally a few students get together and they decide they are human beings, that they are not willing to be products, and they protest; and the university feels obliged to purge these nonstandard products. We want to see social change in the world in which we live. We want to see this social change, because we are human beings who have ideas. We think, we talk, we discuss, and when we're through thinking and talking and discussing, well then, we feel that these things are vacuous unless we then act on the principle that we think, talk and discuss about. This is as much a part of a university education as anything else. (*Here Jack sees the cops coming for him through the crowd and raises his voice.*) We feel that we, as human beings first and students second, must take our stand on every vital issue which faces this nation, and in particular the vital issues of discrimination, of segregation, of poverty, of unemployment; the vital issue of people who aren't getting the decent breaks that they as individuals deserve . . . (*The cops grab him and he goes limp.*)[4]

The campus fuzz came up to Jack, warned him that he was under arrest for trespassing, and told him to come with them, please. Instead of

STUDENTS JAM UC PLAZA TO TRAP POLICE CAR CONTAINING A CORE LEADER
Note the orators using the car's hood and top as a podium to address the crowd

MARIO CLIMBS ONTO THE POLICE CAR TO ADDRESS THE CROWD. PHOTO SAN
FRANCISCO EXAMINER, OCTOBER 2, 1964.

standing up and walking off with them, he just went limp. At the stroke
of noon, Jack Weinberg was then carried off in the classic, approved civil
rights method. It created quite a sensation; those in the crowd not previously involved with civil rights actions had never seen anyone just flop
down like that: when the cops said, "Come with us, please," you came
with them, if you were half-smart. Each policeman took an arm or a
leg, and began carrying Jack through the students. He had a bored look
on his face, and I was delighted at this expression of James Dean cool-
as-a-cucumber indifference and patted him on the stomach as he went
past.

Someone—my memory is that it was my buddy Peter Paskin,
though just about everyone remembers somebody different starting the
ball rolling—yelled, "Sit down!" and I repeated it, and everybody in the
vicinity sat down, boom! just like that, so the cops had to walk over
seated people. It couldn't have taken more than ten seconds for everybody to sit down, and there must have been two or three hundred people

JACKIE GOLDBERG ADDRESSES THE CROWD FROM
THE ROOF OF THE POLICE CAR.
PHOTO BY RON ENFIELD.

around. *Then* I noticed that a car had been brought on. I don't know when the car was brought on, but I know it was when my back was turned. Instead of toting Jack into police headquarters in Sproul Hall, University police had brought a car into the center of Sproul Plaza, intending to spare their backs and remove him by automobile. Five of them carried him about twenty feet, popped him into the back seat of the car, and made as though to drive off, though they were clearly unable to do so.

I turned around, saw the car, ran over to the car, and sat down behind it. The engine was still running, and exhaust fumes were coming into my face. There were people sitting down everyplace, and they happened to be sitting down right around the car. I'm sure it was an accident that they sat down around the car. Everybody repeated the cry, "Sit down!" and so everybody sat down and the car happened to be there. There were hundreds of people in front of it, and hundreds of people behind it, and people lined themselves up behind the car in rows, about twelve people to a row, stretching back about ten rows, and more coming every minute. For a short while, students around the car chanted, "Release him! Release him!"[5] I was sitting next to a girl whom I've never seen since, and we had a conversation about "wasn't it all grand." I still didn't quite know what was happening, but it was really great. "These bastards they're gonna throw me outta school I'll show *them!*"

The police kept the motor running quite a while, in hopes perhaps that we would all evaporate or something equally improbable. After ten minutes or so, it was turned off. The engine started up again for a short time, and then went off again. Somebody crammed an apple into the exhaust pipe, and someone else poured a generous glass of lemonade into the gas tank. I positioned myself and three friends around the car by the tires, with pocket knives, and I told them that if the engine started up again, to stab the tires. Which was kind of dumb, because they could have simply slit the valves. But I'm sure they figured that out for themselves. As I recollect, I let the air out of my tire by pushing my thumbnail against the valve. That way I wouldn't have to watch it. That car was not going anywhere if we could help it.*

JACKIE GOLDBERG ON TOP OF THE POLICE CAR, ABOUT 12:30 PM, OCTOBER 1, 1964. PHOTOGRAPHER UNKNOWN.

A couple of hundred students are sitting around the car, Jack is in the

*Bob Starobin, in a July 23, 1965, interview taped by Marston Schultz, recounted a precedent for the police car incident: "The year before, in October '63, at the time of the Madame Nhu demonstration, they arrested a foreign guy and had him in the cop car and Lennie Glaser was trying to get people to free him from the cop car; which they did. They released him, which is sort of an interesting precedent for what happened to Jack."

Another precedent occurred in the Caryl Chessman protest in 1960, as reported by Michael Rossman in the *Daily Cal*. "A long moment of silence hung like a clock-stroke above us all, guards and marchers and spectators alike. Then, as a large, expensive press car started down the road to our stunned circle, the cry went up: 'Sit down! Sit down!' Once started, it was echoed again and again: 'Keep your hands in your pockets! Put down the signs, keep your hands in your pockets, sit down!'

"Immediately marchers and spectators sprang to the center of the road and sat down. The car tried to edge past on the side, but a dozen seated figures appeared before it. Thirty of us sat there, acting in unison, without leadership, as if by instinct. Then the guards came charging from behind the barricade, shouting and cursing. They picked us up one by one and tried to carry us off the road; but as soon as a sitter was released he walked back onto the road and sat down again. Frustrated by twenty hours without incident, the guards grew angrier and angrier, and finally discovered a way out: they began to kick several of the seated demonstrators, kick them in the legs, groin and kidneys. One man lost consciousness; we gathered around the guards, who jostled him and another limp figure to a squadcar down the road. The press car pulled hastily past, somehow neglecting to take pictures, as we ran after the guards. A marcher lay down before the squadcar, blocking its passage; the guards jerked him up and threw him in the back seat. The squadcar pulled away with a squeal of rubber amid cries of reassurance from the imprisoned demonstrators." (Quoted in Horowitz, 38–39.)

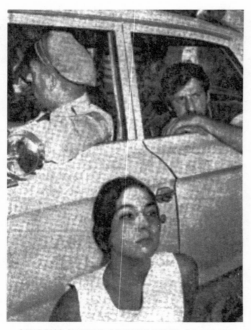

STUDENT SITTING AGAINST DOOR OF POLICE
CAR. SF EXAMINER PHOTO, OCTOBER 2, 1964.

car, the car now has at least one flat tire, a solid object up the exhaust and sugar-water in the gas. Then Mario Savio takes off his shoes—he was wearing white socks—jumps up on the car and begins addressing the crowd. One of the policemen pleaded, "Be careful of the antenna! Be careful of the antenna!" And Mario said, "Alright, I will," and began to speak:

We were going to hold a rally. We didn't know how to get the people. But, we've got them now, thanks to the University. . . .

Strong must say no to the suspensions. He must agree to meet with the political organizations. And, there must be no disciplinary action against anyone before the meeting! And, I'm publicly serving notice that we're going to continue direct action until they accede.[6]

Jackie Goldberg: At noon Jack Weinberg was arrested. It was the most completely spontaneous thing I'd ever seen; kids jumping in front of the car, and I did the same thing. At that point I went with two other people down to University Hall and tried to see Kerr. We got the runaround, and so I came right back.

I went up to the police car, and asked if we could use the car to speak from. And the policeman said, "Sure, if you take your shoes off." Mario went up first, before I asked, and there was one guy trying to grab him; he kept moving around and speaking as the guy was trying to grab him. It would have been just as easy to ask. He stood on the hood at first, and they told him to get off, and later he got up on the roof real quick. But by the time he got up there, I'd already asked permission. Some guy told him to take his shoes off, and the other guy stopped chasing him.[7]

Mario Savio: Why did I climb up onto the police car to speak? It seemed like the thing to do. With all these people sitting around, the physical

JACK WEINBERG IN THE POLICE CAR SHORTLY AFTER HIS ARREST. NOTE THAT THE ANTENNA IS NOT YET BROKEN OFF. PHOTO BY AL SILBOWITZ.

A vast throng of 3,000 students milled in front of Sproul Hall at the University of California at

OAKLAND TRIBUNE PHOTO BY LONNIE WILSON OR RUSS REED, OCTOBER 2, 1964.

.C. Campus

Oakland Tribune

Fri., Oct. 2, 1964

Tribune photos by Lonnie Wilson and Russ Reed

height of demonstration. They engulfed police car in which Jack Weinberg was being held

layout of things presented certain possibilities: one of the possibilities was that sooner or later somebody would stand up on the police car and start talking, where you could be seen by as many people as possible, whose focus, after all, was the police car. It was just a question of who, in that situation, was so disposed as to be the first one to do it. And that was me. It's not that hard to understand.[8]

I had neither met nor heard of Mario Savio until the previous night. He was a man of fiery eloquence when aroused, otherwise he had a terrible stutter.*

There was an uninterrupted succession of speakers and gradually the roof and sides got dented in more and more. Somebody pasted a "No on 14" sticker on the car, and the car squatted lower and lower as the suspension gradually gave up the ghost. By early evening, people stopped taking off their shoes, and the antenna finally got busted off. If you look at the frontispiece, you'll see that we put newspaper under the microphone stand to protect the automobile's paint, though I imagine that the wear from shoes scuffling around took off quite a bit of the finish, anyway.

Those desiring to speak signed up on an orderly list, and awaited their turns, three minutes each (more or less). The orators argued every side of the question. A student speaker, Dusty Miller, took up the highly relevant issue of civil disobedience in a bantering tone:

> We get back to civil disobedience. Civil disobedience doesn't mean throw a brick through the window; it doesn't mean punch a cop. (*Laughter.*[†]) It doesn't mean tip over this police car, and don't do it! Don't do it! (*Voice from the crowd: "Not while Jack's in it!"*) Not while I'm on it! (*Laughter.*) Civil disobedience comes when there's no higher authority who has anything to do with the whole scene—not the legislature, nobody else. The governor is an *ex officio* of the Board of Regents; and the Board of Regents, and Clark Kerr, and Chancellor Strong, those are the

---

*In an interview taped by Marston Schultz in July 1965, Patti Iiyama recalls, "Before Mario went down to Mississippi I remember we were horrified that he was elected chairman of SNCC on campus. He was such an ineffective speaker that we said that SNCC is just going to fall apart completely. But in the FSM he could explain something *well* and understandably. I've always thought that he was never really that eloquent unless he was angry; if he was really furious about something; and *then* he got very eloquent. But then, I noticed even when he wasn't really that mad his speech deteriorates. He's got to be really furious. After the FSM he went back to being a bad speaker."

†I vaguely remember that one of the cops looked up at him inquiringly, and that the crowd were laughing because of this interchange.

STUDENTS SURROUNDING THE POLICE CAR LISTENED INTENTLY TO THE DEBATE
CONDUCTED FROM ITS ROOF. PHOTOGRAPHER UNKNOWN.

people you're talking to, and *there is no legal way to get at 'em!* The only
way is to stand here, to sit here, to block the whole scene. (*Applause.*)

The best acts of civil disobedience are the mildest *effective* forms of
civil disobedience. Not the wildest, the mildest! But not the mildest; the
mildest *effective!* (*Applause.*) I say you've got one hell of an effective
thing, I'm proud of you all. (*Applause.*) . . . I've got a pair of shoes over
there . . .[9]

Professors gave lectures on Law and Order (Seymour Martin Lipset
compared the demonstrators to the Ku Klux Klan, sparking a lively debate between himself and the crowd), and Charles Powell, ASUC president, somewhat recanted his anti-demonstrator position of a few days
before, saying, "I can see now that your cause is just."[10] At Powell's suggestion, he and Mario went into Sproul Hall to meet with Dean Williams. Williams shuffled them off on Strong, and Strong told them to
get lost.

Mario Savio: We saw the chancellor with three points: release Weinberg,
drop the charges against the students, and set up negotiations concerning the Bancroft-Telegraph area. That meeting was completely fruitless.
He said, "No. We can't do that. We're not going to discuss things while
you have this demonstration going on. No negotiations while you have
a gun to our head."

We were considering proposing a moratorium on demonstrations and a moratorium on use of the Bancroft-Telegraph area for one week. If after a week we didn't have the right *de jure*, we would reassert it *de facto*.[11]

A textbook on Marxism was among the crowd

Savio and Powell returned from their meeting with Chancellor Strong about a quarter of two in the afternoon. Powell got back up on the car and suggested to the crowd that the ASUC Senate should be given authority to negotiate on the behalf of the protesters. The crowd turned him down flat, and he left. From this point onward, Powell was relatively hostile to the methods, though not the goals, of the Free Speech Movement. Throughout the life of the Movement, he tried repeatedly to gather the reins of power into the hands of the elected student government, but in this, as well as in attempting to be a mediator between the students and administration, he was entirely unsuccessful.

Even I favored the multitude with some garbled but sincere harangue. Next morning's paper ran a photograph of me bellowing from the roof of the stranded car. In the foreground, looking suspiciously like it was planted there, is a textbook labeled "Marxism" lying right next to a coed who is sitting down listening to the speech.* The San Francisco papers and the *Oakland Tribune* ran head-and-shoulders photos of the suspended students. Thus were my parents rudely made aware that their eldest son had abandoned his academic career for one more suited to his immediate temperament.

By about four o'clock that afternoon I had become clear enough on the issues from listening to the speeches to discourse on what I was doing, and why. I had all the issues down, absolutely pat, to about a one-and-a-half-hour spiel. I'd talk *continuously*, uninterruptedly, and rattle off every fact and figure I could think of. I got about ten more people convinced. Two of these people were in the December Sproul Hall sit-in; one of the people I talked to when I was haranguing from my chair was also at the sit-in. It took about an hour to convince him. But mostly it was just sitting around the car. People were singing, and I was wandering around, but always, always by the car. Sitting down sometimes, sometimes up.

---

*The photograph ran in the *Oakland Tribune* on Friday, October 2, 1964, with the caption "A textbook on Marxism was among the crowd." It features me holding forth from the top of the police car, with the "Marxism" textbook in the extreme foreground. Something about this photo always bothered me, though it wasn't until I'd been a printer for twenty-five years that it struck me what was so very odd about it. The published photograph is a composite of two or perhaps three photos.

The left side of the photo, below the car, is cut out of another photo, taken at about the same time of day—though the shadows of the two halves do not fully agree—and is superimposed on the photo that shows the speaker, the crowd around the car and the seated woman in the foreground with her back to the camera. The dark cut-line separating these two original pictures runs around the couple sitting at the upper left, touches the near seated woman's left shoulder and runs down her left side, cutting her arm off above the elbow, and continues around the shadow at her butt—where a bit of clumsy cutting creates a thin white line which separates the outline of her dress from the shadow—and along the edge of the pile of papers at her lower left.

The actual title of the book is *Essentials of Marxism*, a Bantam paperback required for the freshman course, Social Studies 1A (Colin Miller, "The Press and the Student Revolt," in Miller and Gilmore, 318). The shadows on the book do not correspond to the shadows immediately around it, and a shadow on the lower right piece of notebook paper is drawn in. The oddest thing about the papers and the book is that the perspective is quite different from the rest of the picture, as though they were propped up or, as is more likely, they were photographed with a different camera lens at a different angle.

This image printed in a major metropolitan newspaper is a fake. The purpose of the fake was to make us look bad in a way that the general public could easily understand. Though it was indeed a common practice to enhance or embellish photos—the October 1, 1964, *Tribune* photo of Jack being arrested is enhanced to make the policemen stand out—real newspapers, newspapers that report rather than manufacture news out of whole cloth, are not supposed to wander quite this far into the territory of shameless distortion of actual fact.

ART GOLDBERG AND BRAD CLEAVELAND ON TOP OF THE POLICE CAR, OCTOBER I,
1964. PHOTO BY HOWARD HARAWITZ.

THE SIMPLE JOYS OF NONFATAL COMBAT

Forty-five minutes after Charlie Powell and Mario returned from Chancellor Strong's rebuff, Mario escalated the confrontation: "I recommend that 500 of you stay here around this auto and others join me in taking our request back to the deans."[1]

A few hundred students left the car and went into the building, where they sat outside the dean of students' office. In an hour or two, there were five hundred students blockading the deans, and more than a thousand outside around the car.

> *Jackie Goldberg:* There were enough people to protect the car, so I took in a group to see the deans, and it was there that I walked up and there were three cops, in back of two or three secretaries, and I said, "Excuse me, I want to go in to make an appointment with one of the deans." And the policeman informed me, at that point, that if I tried to enter the room or even leaned into one of the secretaries, he would arrest me on a felony assault charge. At which point I got extremely infuriated, and said, "If you're not letting us in, we're not letting you out." And we completely jammed up the area, so no one could get in or get out. There were three votes: one was sit and clear the aisles; one was just sit down, and if they have to walk over you they have to walk over you, but you'd let people go by; and the third was pack in tight. We voted to pack in tight. There were all kinds of arguments, and the faculty finks came in and told us not to pack in tight. I remember Sue Currier, who was six or seven months pregnant, planting herself in front of the doorway. While I was there, a couple of students who were in decided to go out, but nobody came in.[2]

Even though it would have been the simplest thing in the world for Dean Towle and the various secretaries to walk out over or through the demonstrators, they played up to the drama of the moment and crawled out windows and over rooftops to seek safety from the mob. As a bizarre

Professor Nathan Glazer and Dr. William Petersen urge students to truce

PROFESSOR NATHAN GLAZER AND DR. WILLIAM
PETERSEN URGE STUDENTS TO TRUCE. OAKLAND
TRIBUNE PHOTO, OCTOBER 2, 1964.

consequence, Jackie was charged for a time with felony kidnapping.

Around five-thirty Mario told the crowd that members of the faculty had contacted him and offered to negotiate with the administration on our behalf. He thought that we were entering an important stage in our efforts, with the faculty and the students allying themselves against the administration. A vote was taken, and it was understood that the faculty would tell the crowd as soon as they made a start at talks with the administration. If they were successful, the students would be told of it; and if we agreed with the results—though earlier we had rejected the faculty's right to negotiate on our behalf—the demonstrators would leave the building. Meanwhile, Sproul Hall was supposed to be left open in case the talks broke down.

> *Mario Savio:* We had a difficult situation: we'd caught a police car, and we didn't know what to do with it. At one point, I suggested that we reenter Sproul Hall and leave a group around the car. It seemed a bit more abrasive. We surely couldn't keep this up indefinitely, and the more trouble we could cause with the resources that we had, the better.
>
> At some point along then, while I was upstairs, [Professor John] Leggett came up and said, "A group of faculty members is trying to make contact with the administration," [and that] when that contact is made, as a sign of our good faith, we should leave Sproul Hall. So the conditions that were set up over the several yards between Leggett and me were: Sproul Hall closes at seven. This faculty group sends us word when they have contact with the administration. Soon as we receive word, we'll leave Sproul Hall. We will return to Sproul Hall under the following conditions: if the faculty has not made progress in this meeting by a quarter to seven—so we have time to get back in—or, at such point before a quarter to seven that they tell us that the meeting has failed, or that they tell us that the meeting has been successful, in which case we won't go back in.[3]

The faculty committee made contact with Vice-Chancellor Alex Sherriffs and began negotiations. The sit-in should now have been called off, but two things went wrong: nobody called Professor Leggett, who was supposed to tell the student leaders around the car that contact had been made, and Nathan Glazer, the faculty member who had been appointed by the committee to bring the message to the students in front of Sproul Hall, dawdled along and stopped for coffee instead of coming right away to the plaza where the students and the police were waiting. So, though the police and the administration thought that the students were supposed to leave, we didn't.

Tom Miller: On October 1 we met with Lipset, Scalapino, Petersen, and Glazer, who were the faculty negotiators. Stampp was there, but he wasn't so bad. I was sitting next to Scalapino and Lipset all of a sudden blew up. He tears off his glasses and says, "You people aren't interested in free speech! You're just hoodlums! Hoodlums!" and his face is getting all red and his eyes are bulging out, and the other faculty people are getting very embarrassed, and I said, "Mr. Lipset. Will you please control yourself." All of a sudden Scalapino noticed that the other faculty were laughing, and he said, "Does this mean that this meeting's through!?" and gets up and walks out. At this meeting we agreed that we would pull out of Sproul Hall as a sign of good faith, that we weren't trying to be antagonistic or anything, if that would help in getting the negotiations going with Kerr, who refused to negotiate. We gave 'em a time that they would have to negotiate with us, and that they wouldn't close the doors, so we could go back in if Kerr refused to set up a meeting. And we didn't hear that a meeting had been set up; somebody was supposed to tell us that the meeting had been set up, and then these professors claimed that we were breaking good faith because we didn't pull the people out. But, we hadn't been notified that a meeting had been set up.[4]

About five forty-five that evening, I was on the upper part of the plaza—the wide place between the flights of steps leading up to Sproul Hall—talking to friends. Everyone I knew showed up at the demonstration at some point or another: my summer roommates Tom Weller and Carl Foytick; skinny motorcycle racer Peter Paskin and his big, healthy girlfriend; the whole SLATE crowd, at least all the ones that I had met; my high school Latin teacher Ernie Karsten and his friend Van Burdick; another Castlemont teacher and friend Gita Kornfeldt and her husband Mel. Ernie and Gita said that they'd seen me on television. The crowd was being entertained by some pretty good civil rights singing and guitar playing, and students were filing out of Sproul Hall.

As I was talking to them, pretty much alone on the plaza, I noticed that a large group of policemen was starting to close the doors in Sproul

SINGER ON TOP OF THE POLICE CAR. PHOTOGRAPHER UNKNOWN.

Hall. During all that day we'd held the hall I had never been in there; I'd stayed by the car, not straying more than a hundred yards from it. We'd made an agreement—I'd gathered by osmosis—that the doors wouldn't be shut before seven.

We saw this closing of the doors as an example of the blackest perfidy, to break their side of a bargain, especially as Sproul Hall was ordinarily open until seven anyway. Echoed by a woman's voice in the crowd, I began to yell, "They're closing the doors!" and ran up to the middle door and slammed myself up against it and at that precise instant Mario reached the other door and slammed *him*self up against it. That's when I formally met Mario. And then Ronn Pickard came up, and then Mike Rossman. Then more and more people began to come. We threw ourselves up against the door in two rows, facing each other, and people behind us and beside us, and a couple of people inside, but not very many. People in the crowd yelled, "Stay with the car!" which most of them did. The crowd booed the police. Then the police came up, and Mario was arguing with the police and asking on what grounds they were trying to close the doors, and the police said they were given orders, and he said, "By whom?"

"By the Captain."

"Who gave the Captain orders?"

"I dunno, I just follow orders."

"Well, at least this is one order you're not gonna obey!"

"Oh, yeah?"

STUDENTS BLOCK THE DOORS OF SPROUL HALL.
LOOK PHOTO BY PAUL FUSCO.

Policeman is sent sprawling during scuffle

OFFICER MOWER IS KNOCKED DOWN, OAKLAND
TRIBUNE PHOTO, OCTOBER 2, 1964.

"Yeah!"

"Your mother!"

"You're another!"

And, "So are you!" This is just how it went. We were getting angrier and angrier. As the crowd sang "God Bless America," we called out badge numbers. One larger-than-ordinary policeman started walking through the dense group, avoiding toes and legs until his second trip, when he became careless. We said, "Hey, you're stepping on us. Take off your shoes, at least, if you're going to walk on us."

Officer Philip E. Mower (badge number 24), with a high and mighty look, glanced down at the crowd from his cloudy height and kept on walking. So we pushed him down and took off his shoes. Well, he was much alarmed, suddenly being in the middle of about thirty people who were holding him down and messing with his feet. This also got the other cops all excited. They realized that although nothing particularly bad was happening, even not-so-bad things were not supposed to happen this way. During the scuffle (although it was vigorously denied by everyone both then and later) Mario got carried away and bit Mower on the leg—I saw it with my own eyes—at which the downed man let out a powerful yell, galvanizing the other cops. There were twenty-five of them exactly; I counted them up afterwards. The cops started diving in, and we had a mêlée of sorts. It was short of an actual fist fight; more of a shoving match, and that's about as far as it went: not much kicking or

—Examiner Photo by Bob Bryant.

BERKELEY OFFICER PHIL MOWER, TRYING TO LOCK SPROUL HALL'S FRONT DOORS, LOST HIS BOOTS TO DEMONSTRATORS
Some 80 students stormed up the steps and shoved police aside. "Take his shoes," some of the students shouted

AND HIS SHOES REMOVED. OAKLAND TRIBUNE PHOTO, OCTOBER 2, 1964.

gouging or hair–pulling, and no nightsticks. I got one young cop by both wrists, and was spitting and cursing into his face. He couldn't have been more astonished. He got away, and a couple of bigger ones pitched me into the foyer. The police finally got command of the door area; students were rushing up the steps at them, and the cops were grabbing and toss-ing them through the doors behind them. A moment's reflection would have shown them that this was a really bad idea, but they didn't have a moment. People would get tossed in, skid on the polished floor, twirl around, bounce off the wall and run back the way they'd come. An enormous crowd surged up from around the police car. I think the police car could have gotten away right then if it had wanted to, and of course it would have been easy enough for Jack to hop out and scamper off, though probably the cops in the car were mesmerized by the battle at the door and didn't even think of it. Soon the cops at the door were caught between two fires, namely all the people they'd tossed into the building as well as the people who were trying to get up the stairs and through the door. At that point, they abandoned ship, and retreated to the stairway that led to the second floor. The dumbfounded police then held the high ground, which nobody wanted, and the students held the lobby and the entrance. The barefoot officer's shoes and hat were tossed to him, and he put them on, looking sheepish. We were shaking our fists at them shouting, "This is what you'll get again if you try it!" Mak-

183

ing insulting remarks. Then we occupied the building with half the people inside and half the people outside.

Mario Savio: A decision was made by the group. It's kind of like the police car—who was running the police car demonstration? Nobody! It was running itself! People were meeting who were part of the original United Front, would try to think up possible things that could be done, suggestions and so on, but the decisions were much more collective than that and much more informal than such a thing as taking votes.

When police tried to close the doors of Sproul Hall, a couple of us saw this was happening. I ran up there and called to people to help block the doors. I had no legitimate authority over these people; I couldn't *cause* them to block the doors, but I happened to be there, saying something which at a particular time and under those circumstances was something that a lot of people were prepared to hear and act on. Protecting the rights which existed in the context of our community.[5]

Bob Starobin: They had agreed that we could keep the doors open until seven, then around five a whole bunch of Berkeley and campus cops massed inside just by the door. And a whole bunch of us got in the doorway, some lying down, some standing up. The doors open outward, and the cops couldn't figure out any way of closing the doors because there was a mass of human bodies piled up, which they couldn't move. This one big, tall cop—Mower—jumped on top of all the bodies, and reached up with his arms outstretched to grab both of the doors, thinking he could pull them shut. Once he got on top of everybody, he had no footing, so he was completely off balance. So the kids who were sitting down reached up and pulled him down, and then they passed him out the door and down the steps.

While Mower was standing on the kids, the cops inside were trying to pull kids out of the doorway. [Michael] Rossman was there, with his shirt off—baring his breast—Ron Pickard was there—he got his eye cut a little bit. I was standing right next to Lenny Glaser, and he was yelling, "Get the cops! Kill the cops! At 'em! Charge! Get the cops!"* He was

---

*Jeff Lustig recalls Lenny Glaser as "the first soapbox speaker. He was the guy who legitimized the Hyde Park tradition at Cal. In October of 1963 Madame Nhu spoke at Harmon Gym, and afterwards Lenny Glaser stood on one of the balustrades outside and started speaking to the students streaming past. 'That was just a course that you took. You took a course in politics, and you failed. It was not just a course in political science. When you fail a course in *real* politics, you pay, and you're going to pay in the jungles of Vietnam, in the pampas of Argentina, in the deserts of Africa.' He changed quite a bit after he got out of jail, went kind of crazy. But before that, he was a terrific orator" (conversation with the author, 11 June 1992).

"Virtually every day Glaser stood at the corner of the campus and argued politics

hitting Mower—pulling at him, hitting his arm and chest—but there was a right-wing guy on the outside who was also engaged in a little fight with Lenny, so Lenny was having a tough time. I kept saying to Lenny, "We're doing all right without killing the cops; it's impossible for them to get us out of this door." But he wanted to turn this into a big thing against the cops.[6]

Right about then, the tardy faculty representative showed up and gave us the lowdown on the meeting between faculty and administration. History is full of heroic battles that occur after peace has been negotiated but before word arrives.

After all the hoorahing was over, Professor John Leggett explained to the protesters around the car what had happened:

from different, sometimes contradictory viewpoints. In 1962 he broke new ground by lecturing on the virtues of marijuana. Although the *Daily Californian* covered his talk, it attracted little interest. Late the following year, however, Glaser wandered along Telegraph Avenue, 'very high,' and after police found a small quantity of marijuana on his person, he was arrested. In February 1964, during one of the Lucky's shop-ins, Glaser was arrested for throwing food; CORE, the civil rights organization, told police that Glaser was not part of their protest, and the charges were dropped. A month later, at Glaser's trial on the 1963 marijuana charge, the defendant challenged the government's portrayal of marijuana as a dangerous substance. Although he displayed considerable erudition and unveiled the prosecutor's ignorance, Glaser was found guilty. He received probation. In a letter to the *Daily Californian*, Jerry Rubin angrily attacked the trial. Glaser continued to hang around Telegraph Avenue and urge the use of drugs. In October of 1964, during the Free Speech Movement, he apparently started the sit-down around the police car. His role drew notice, and shortly afterward Glaser was stopped, searched, and after marijuana was found on his person, arrested; his parole was revoked" (Rorabaugh, 129–130).

The cops were out to get Lenny, and from all indications he was set up for a fall.

Sometime after the events of October 1964, Lenny was holding forth at Bancroft and Telegraph when a suspiciously (in retrospect) straight-looking guy said, "Hey Lenny! Have a beer!" and handed him a can of beer. Lenny took it, and a cop showed up and busted him for public drinking. He had thereby violated the conditions of his three-year probation, and the judge locked him up for one to ten years. It was plain as the nose on your face that he was busted for advocating on October 1 and 2 that Jack Weinberg be freed from the car by force.

Lenny Glaser was, throughout the FSM, a loose cannon and all around pain in the ass, and when he was arrested most people were glad to see him go. He'd "denounced the Du Bois Club for supporting Johnson, he embarrassed the YSA by his commitment to 'non-political' issues such as reform of the narcotics laws, he differed with PL [Progressive Labor] on the question of Stalin, he attacked the FSM for dilettantism and lack of nerve" (Michael Klein, "Political Prisoners, 2. The Case of Lenny Glaser," *Spider* 1, no. 4 [3 May 1965]: 22–23). After his arrest, his problems came up in an Executive Committee meeting, where both Mario and I made impassioned speeches about solidarity and not letting him fry all alone. The body was persuaded not to abandon him, but I do not recollect that anything further was done on his behalf.

It was agreed that the faculty would try to initiate contact for the purposes of mediation with the administration. It was also agreed that if such contact was made, that those inside Sproul Hall would leave. It was also understood that I would communicate the coming about of such contact if it were to occur. What happened was a breakdown in communication. A number of faculty members did contact important people in the administration; discussions did go on. However, I was not notified. I sat in my office from five-thirty to six-thirty waiting for the phone call, and nothing happened. I came down here about fifteen minutes ago, only to find out that contact *had* been made, that several faculty members, including Nat Glazer, [William] Petersen and Matson, had been talking about the problems with Vice-Chancellor Sherriffs. I also understand that it was very difficult to get the administration to compromise, or to back down on some of their positions. Your group had agreed originally, that in the event the administration refuses to compromise, or to begin to seriously open negotiations, under those circumstances the group should remain inside Sproul Hall. It was understood that if negotiations were to begin, that the group would leave. Unfortunately, those who were engaged in the negotiations did not contact me, so that I could contact the leaders of your organization. Consequently, the people stayed inside Sproul Hall rather than coming out. As it turns out, perhaps they were wise to stay inside the building. (*Thunderous applause, cheers, whistles. Shouts of "Bravo! Bravo!"*)[7]

Jackie Goldberg: We had a United Front meeting on the steps of the Student Union, where we discussed a pre-concession of leaving Sproul Hall; everybody returning to the police car.

Being a Greek, I had gotten word that the fraternity boys were coming that night. So we knew in advance they were coming. It was a planned event. The Phee Gees and probably SAE had called a lot of the houses, who were all having their drunken brawls, and said, "Look, let's take the police car back." They got pretty stewed beforehand. It was my opinion that it would be good to leave Sproul Hall before they came, and make it look like a pre-concession, and everybody agreed. I was sent in just before that, to get everybody down to the first-floor level, and to try and encourage everybody to leave. There were two or three people around the doorway, making sure it stayed open. That's how I got in. I didn't see any policemen near the doorway.

Again, there were a million votes, but I explained that this would be a good tactical thing to do, and that since there was no one in the building, we weren't really doing any good staying there, while we might be doing some good out there by the police car. After we voted to pull out, we all went back around the police car again.[8]

People spoke from the car, there was a debate, there was a vote, and we decided that we would occupy the building until nine o'clock, to show that we could do it if we wanted to, and then we would get out, because we didn't want to divide our forces, and have half inside and half outside. Divided forces would give the police an opportunity to rush the car, and we were assuming that they would probably want to do something like that. At nine o'clock we abandoned the building, and they locked it up, and we all went back around the car.

Tom Miller: After the sit-in had been abandoned, and the students had returned to surround the car, an interesting thing was happening. Petersen and Glazer and a few other professors were going around and gathering groups of students around them and trying to point out how we had been dishonest in not pulling out the people, and generally denouncing the leadership and saying, "Go home, go home." We were running past them saying, "This guy's a liar, we just came back from a meeting and he's deliberately telling a lie here; he knows we haven't heard anything about the meeting set up." So he shut up for a while and walked off to the side. I think he was deliberately lying.[9]

Glazer, Lipset, and a few other young professors who took an active interest in the controversy never wearied of efforts to set up negotiations between the students and the administration, even going so far as to work directly against the student leadership, and to oppose the clearly expressed will of the participating student protesters. Generally their efforts, no matter what they were or how motivated, were not appreciated by the students, who felt that they were not really on our side so much as they were yearning for a quick fix for a serious problem. We felt that, with the exception of a few professors not numbering more than the fingers of one hand, the faculty was on the side of the faculty. Though many of them agreed wholeheartedly with the goals and aspirations of the students, almost none of them condoned the means or recognized that without those means there would be no ends.

Charles Muscatine: I had no problem with the idea of First Amendment rights; I had a problem with the *locus*. As I saw it, the center of the conflict was a revolution in the notion of what the university was. I and a lot of other people had been nurtured in the old medieval idea of the university as a special place which is purposely insulated from the rest of the world so that contemplation can go on. The idea was that society needed to provide a place that was free of political passions, controversy and prejudice, for what was then thought of as the free pursuit of truth.

It was still possible in those days to think, "You're a student; you're only temporarily here. You're not even here all year. You live in Bakersfield, you live in Sacramento; go exercise your civil rights in Sacramento or Bakersfield.* This is a different kind of place. We don't have ordinary civic activity by students in this place, because this place is a different place, a sacred place." That idea was under major attack.

The faculty animal is almost bred to be nonpolitical. We think, we talk, we vote, but we do not *act*. It's not our thing. When the Free Speech Movement first broke out, my reaction, nurtured on this medieval tradition, was, "OK. But why don't they go exercise free speech in the city? That's where citizens exercise free speech. The campus is a special place. The police never come here, we don't have politics. You have all of Berkeley before you. Why here, for Christ's sake? Why did you pick this little spot?" That certainly was a part of the reason that people like me and a lot of the other liberal professors didn't get it at first.

What the students achieved was a redefinition of the campus as the *polis*, or civic home, of the students. If it isn't your civic home, go demonstrate someplace else; but if it is, OK. It took those months of turmoil for a lot of us to recognize that this was the students' civic place. They forced that idea upon us, and it turned out to be right.[10]

---

*Before 1972 the residency requirements for voting in California were one year in the state, ninety days in the county and fifty-four days in the precinct. The voting age was twenty-one, and the majority of undergraduates were younger. National and many local elections were held in November, when students were away at school, and Berkeley elections were held in June, when most students were back home. College students were effectively disenfranchised.

THE CATBIRD SEAT

At ten o'clock that evening, the leaders met and decided that the demonstrators would attempt to remain on the steps and in the plaza through Saturday, October 3. Things were looking good for the demonstrators: Family Day was October 3, and we were sure that the potential for embarrassment would force the administration to give in before then. Nobody could quite imagine students towing their bewildered, alarmed parents through a few thousand demonstrators around a demolished cop car. There would be no easy explanation of this to the Pater. This would do big nothing for the University's image, and we knew it, and they knew it, and we knew that they knew it, and we knew that they knew that we knew it. We figured that we had the whip hand, and that we could force them to make some major concessions before Saturday morning.

If the demonstration continued through Friday, we intended to set up more tables at Sather Gate, hold a noon rally from the cop car, and afterwards reinfest Sproul Hall. The experienced civil rights activists drew a parallel with the Sheraton-Palace demonstrations, in which the Hotel Owners Association simply could not afford the bad press that the demonstrations were giving them. They couldn't afford to lose patronage over a few measly jobs for a few carefully selected Negroes; they didn't want policemen and kids scuffling around on their expensive carpets and making everybody look bad; they didn't want arrests and noise and disruption, so they settled when we had convinced them that we meant it, and that we would make their lives a misery until they did what we wanted. There was nothing wrong with this reasoning except that the University of California at Berkeley did not approach the controversy from the same perspective as the San Francisco Hotel Owners Association.

At the beginning of World War I, nobody imagined that the war

FAMILY DAY, OCTOBER 3, 1964. PHOTO BY DAVID LINN.

could continue for more than a few weeks. Each side reckoned without understanding the immense resources of its enemy, and the incredible damage that the contestants could sustain before utter collapse. At the beginning of the Free Speech Movement, nobody thought that things could possibly go on for long. But they did.

NEAR RIOT

By early evening of october 1, the crowd had swelled into the thousands, at least half of whom were unaligned or hostile spectators. The Indian summer weather continued, a balmy evening becoming a shirtsleeves night. Many demonstrators had gone home and returned with sleeping bags, intending to stay the night.

Around midnight there was a lot of trouble with the fraternity boys. A crowd of them had marched down Bancroft Avenue, chanting and shouting. Their march was fragmented by the masses of people at the campus entrance, but they re-formed at the top of Sproul Hall steps. Maybe fifty or a hundred of them were lined up, chanting and catcalling, and throwing eggs and lighted cigarettes. It seemed clear to us that they were working up their courage to rush the students surrounding the car, and drive them away so that the police could take Jack away to the pokey. We were having none of it, and the taunting and name-calling was just short of coming to blows. Just at that point, around midnight, the Student Union lights were turned off, and the plaza was plunged into total blackness. Peter Paskin and I and a few others argued with the openly hostile building superintendent, Forrest Tregea, to turn them back on again, and finally convinced him to do it. Earlier in the afternoon, psychology undergrad Ron Anastasi had noticed that the crowd around the car was so large that people on the fringes were having difficulty hearing the speakers, so he had gone out on his own hook and rented two loudspeakers, a microphone, an amplifier and a battery. When the battery gave out, we'd run an extension cord into the Student Union. We got that turned on again, too.

Amazing as it may seem, Jack was let out to stretch his legs and his tonsils, because he thought that he could calm the crowd a bit, and the cops, willing to try anything, let him out to do it. He addressed us from the top, rather than the inside, of the car. His brief speech was, in essence, "Be cool, and if I should fall, carry on." Very noble and inspiring.

MARIO SAVIO ADDRESSING THE CROWD AROUND THE POLICE CAR,
APPROXIMATELY 2 AM, OCTOBER 2, 1964. PHOTO BY DAVID LINN.

A little bit after midnight, a fire engine came roaring up, and, re-
membering the 1960 HUAC hearings in San Francisco, I was positive that
they were going to hose us all away from the car. The fraternity boys
chanted, "Hose 'em, hose 'em." Many others also believed that the fire
engine was there to do just that, although if that had been their intention
it seemed rather strange for them to come up there with red lights flashing and siren going like the Fourth of July. However, the fire engine
was going after something in Dwinelle Hall, and took care of it and
went away.*

Mario announced that the fire engine had responded to a false alarm,
and asked that all members of the demonstration remain calm, remain
seated and be silent. He then addressed the crowd, and the fraternity
boys, and explained why we were there and what we were doing. Cat-
calls continued throughout. ("Buy the car from the University and then

*We found out the next morning that the
fire in Dwinelle Hall had been started by
sunlight shining through a glass paper-
weight, and was put out by a student who

yelled to a coed to call the fire department.
By the time they got there, the fire was out
and the heroic student was gone.

stand on it!" "Go home!" "Get off the car!" "Go sit on a flagpole!" "If you don't like Cal, go somewhere else!" "Where's your reg card?!" A woman's voice from among the demonstrators: "He lost it defending *your* rights!" Cheers and applause from among the demonstrators.)

Mario's didactic speech was less intended to explain what we were doing than to keep the two groups from clashing. He repeatedly attempted to calm the frat boys, and continually urged the crowd to silence and calm. As he talked through the loudspeaker, the crowd around the fringes quieted down.

No question about it, there was going to be Big Fat Hairy-Ass Trouble. We were all thoroughly aware that there were Berkeley and campus cops standing out of sight at the edges of the crowd.

Mario then quixotically attempted to explain the knotty question of civil disobedience. No small feat in the teeth of catcalling, jeering, chanting, bellowing, drunken fraternity boys.

I would like to explain—please, would the people here at least keep quiet—I would like to explain the principle, as I said before, and see if you're willing to accept it, on the basis of which we took the action. Are you willing to listen? (*"Get off the car!"*) Alright, I'll try! (*"Get off the car and we'll listen!"*) Have you ever heard of a man named Thoreau? (*Mario's voice almost drowned in jeers.*) The man's name was Henry David Thoreau. Part of his life was during the time the United States engaged in a war with Mexico. At that time, there was no slavery in Mexico, and there was in the United States. This man believed that he could not in conscience support a war to extend slavery into Mexico. And, so do you know what he did? He disobeyed the law! He refused to pay any taxes! He disobeyed the law! He believed that there were certain matters of conscience which exceeded any legal matters in importance. We likewise in this instance, we believe that there are matters of conscience which greatly exceed the question of disobedience to law. Do you recognize that there at least could be circumstances . . . (*"We want Thoreau! We want Thoreau!"*) . . . I wish I could give him to you! That's a start! You'll be on our side in a little while if you keep chanting that! What I'm asking you is this, if you would just keep quiet and think for a moment on the principle. Do you agree that there are times when questions of conscience exceed in importance questions of law? That's the question.

(*An object flies past him.*) You missed me, fortunately. Alright, we're going to sing for a while. Maybe that will calm us. (*Mario leads the demonstrators in singing "We Shall Overcome" while the fraternity boys chant, "We want the police," and counter by singing the Mickey Mouse song.*)[1]

JERRY GOLDSTEIN

DAILY CAL PHOTO.

About two o'clock in the morning, what with taunting back and forth and things being tossed, fights breaking out, the tension was so thick you could cut it with a knife. Dean Louis Rice tried to calm the fraternity boys, but got the raspberry for his pains.

Jerry Goldstein, ASUC vice president and a fraternity member, tried to talk to his fellows without success, and asked that the police clear a path between the two groups.

I hate to think that a few of you, just a few, might even get injured a little as well. Whether you realize mob rule and mob violence or not, the potential is sitting right here now with your heckling and all. Negotiations can't proceed when you guys are kicking everybody here and forcing them closer. (*"We're gonna get the car if you don't move it!"*) You're going to get the car? And, maybe happen to *kill* a few people on the way, huh?! (*Cheers from the frats.*) Are you kiddin' me?![2]

The frats booed and hurled epithets at him, too. Alex Sherriffs later characterized them as the "only true Cal supporters."

Right at the moment when things had quite nearly gotten out of hand, Father James Fisher of Newman Hall got up on the car and began pleading for peace, calming the crowd. In his prayerful manner, he took the fuse right out of it:

This is Father Fisher from Newman Hall. I'm not a student; I once was. I don't know whether I'm the only impartial member of this crowd. I think I know some of the issues that are involved. The right of free speech, great as it is, and the right of authority, greatly as it must be respected, should not be brought into conflict if a human life is going to be endangered. John Kennedy once asked, "Do not ask what your country can do for you, but what you can do for your country."

And what you can do for your countrymen is to respect their differences without bloodshed, and hatred begets bloodshed. The kind of catcalling that's gonna go on here will get worse as the night goes on, unless somebody calms down. He who hates his brother is a murderer. And those who begin in hatred and resort to abuse are going to produce murder. It's easy in a crowd to get carried away. It's a lot harder to face yourself in the mirror in the morning.

MARIO AND A FRATERNITY BOY ADDRESSING THE CROWD, APPROXIMATELY 2 AM, OCTOBER 2, 1964. PHOTO BY DAVID LINN.

I'm not sure of all the issues involved, but I am convinced that in a free society rational men can discuss and solve their differences without bloodshed. You presumably have come to this University because you are rational men seeking to perfect your rationality. Tonight is your chance to prove it. I have nothing more to say. (*Decorous, enthusiastic applause.*)[3]

Father Fisher climbed down from the car, and no one else stood up to speak. Every single one of the demonstrators fell silent. No noise at all. There was only one remark made among the demonstrators during the next thirty minutes, and the speaker was quickly shushed. The only sounds were shushings from a couple of thousand people. Soon it became painfully obvious who was standing up and who was sitting down, and who was being noisy and who was being quiet. The standing crowd began to drift away, leaving only the demonstrators. One of the fraternity boys observed that they didn't want to hurt anyone, and went on to say that the students had remained peaceful when a representative of the Nazi party spoke on campus, but had shown their opinion of him by walking out in the middle of his speech. They had made their opinion of the demonstrators clear, he said, now they should walk out on them, too. And the forty or fifty students with him walked away.

The other freddies began to go, too—"C'mon fellahs, let's go!" and

MIKE SMITH. PHOTO BY RON ENFIELD.

"Gee, this is a drag, let's beat it!"—breaking off in little bunches of twos and threes and twelves, and by two-fifteen or two-thirty, they all were gone.

Mario Savio: Basically, the demonstrators had greater internal resources than those who were heckling us. Finally, one of the people who was acting as a spokesman for them said, "Give up the car. But if you won't give it up, we want one too." A fantastically poignant thing. It's a heartbreaking thing, when you come to think of it. We were the only people on campus who had this beautiful thing, that sense of community and importance, and these people felt out of it. And the only way they could express it was by striking out in some way. Whereas that's not what they really wanted to do. But they would had to have overcome much too much in terms of their internal barriers of all sorts to take part in what we were doing.[4]

Brian Shannon: Interesting regarding the pacifism of the students. Because, had there been a general attack of the freddies, they would have fought back. There would have been a real fight, and the idea of lying down or pacifism would never have entered their minds. It's different so far as the police are concerned. So in a way, so far as theory is concerned it doesn't make any difference. Maybe it's that they're the law, or that they have big clubs, and it isn't smart tactics to take them on. But it's interesting the division they made. It was Larry Schum, a member of the YSA [Young Socialist Alliance], that thought of going and getting the priest who quieted the whole thing down.[5]

Mike Smith: The Thursday night when the fraternity guys threw eggs, it was just their reaction to something they didn't understand. Most of them don't realize the significance of what the Free Speech Movement was to the people involved. To them it was just another chance to party and throw eggs and play around. Most of them weren't even acting out of conservative conviction. They were just harassing the dirty beatniks. The Phee Gees and SAEs were well represented and when I took the petition around I didn't even go to houses like that, because all they would do was throw food at you and insult you.

I was in school, and I was working at San Quentin as a guard, and they were trying to get rid of me. I really didn't know anything about the protest about changing the rules at Cal besides what I'd read in the *Daily Cal*. The day that I'd concluded work at San Quentin I was driving across the bridge and I saw twenty or thirty highway patrol headed toward campus, and I went down, and people were sitting around the car, and I sat around the car and then it broke up. The next thing was that there was somebody sponsoring a petition against the FSM, and so I sponsored a petition in the fraternities and sororities supporting the goals of the Free Speech Movement, because I thought that this would break up the conservative backing of the administration. We got about 850 signatures from thirty-seven fraternities and sororities, and on October 8, presented it to Chancellor Strong and Dean of Men Arleigh Williams, and there was a write-up in the *Daily Cal*.[6]

Bettina Aptheker, Stephanie Coontz and I set up a monitors' patrol to watch for freddies and for police. We were anticipating a rush in the early hours of the morning from the police, to try and get the car away when most of the people were gone. I noticed that there was a police car sitting out there all night, cruising back and forth, sitting by the corner and cruising back and forth again.

JACK GOES TO THE CAN

IT'S REALLY NOT SO UNCOMFORTABLE. Why, I think I easily would be able to hold out for a week. I was a little worried about the roof at first, but after I watched it for hours and it didn't get any worse, I've sort of eased off thinking about it. But I don't sit under the side that's caved in the worst. You really don't get to think too much about yourself in something like this. It's not necessarily that the cause engulfs your whole personality. No, it's not that. It's more like there are so many things going on you just don't have time to think of personal comforts.
—Jack Weinberg, Friday, October 2, 1964

I made the acquaintance of the man in the car and shook hands: "Hi." "Hi, how are ya." He didn't pay much attention to me and I didn't pay much attention to him. He was a somewhat incidental guy to the whole thing. Just the guy in the car.* Out of fear that the police would hustle Jack away in the small hours, many of us stayed around the car all the time. Bringing up a subject that every single one of us had thought about, Mario humorously made the point that if we were to succeed, we'd better stick around:

> This car's here. It's been here for a long time. I'm gonna request that they bring Jack a chamberpot. You know these things, right? (*Laughter and applause.*) This car, I hope, if you stay sittin' here, is gonna stay here *all night*, and as long tomorrow morning as necessary! All night, this car's gonna be here, is that right?! (*Cheers, applause, "Yeah! Yeah!"*)[1]

*In her interview with Marston Schultz, Patti Iiyama expressed the initial reaction of the politicos to Jack: "I remember at the very beginning, several of us who'd been very political before, when we found out it was Jack in the car we got all panicked 'Eeeee! Ye Gods! No! Anybody but him!' (*Laughs.*) Because we had this concept of him as being this fellow who just went around making trouble without any sense of strategy, without any sense of tactics, who was just one of these alienated types of people that just didn't contribute much to a movement."

Earlier, the call of nature had been answered by a pee into a bottle, but around three in the morning, old number two reared its ugly head, and Jack simply had to go into the Student Union. We struck a bargain with the cops that two of them would escort him and two of us would escort him as well. Just as we feared that Jack would be taken away from us, so did the cops dread a rush of students to free him. We agreed that we would do no such thing, and they agreed that they would do no such thing, but as insurance, Jack's trip to the can was a fairly public event.* On the whole, the police and the crowd got along well. Just business on both sides, nothing personal. It was probably as exciting for them as it was for us.

Jack says it didn't happen:

After the first few hours, I figured it might be a long haul and decided not to eat. I do remember being told I could go into Sproul Hall for a shit with a promise I could come back to the car. But it seemed to me it was a trick, and so I refused.[2]

---

*Tom Weller recollects this event as having happened much the way I recount it. Patti Iiyama remembers that as Jack was being taken away from the car, the people sitting around it became greatly concerned, thinking that he was being taken away to jail. The protesters who had ne- gotiated the bargain with the police reassured them that Jack was only going to the bathroom and would be right back. The main difference between Patti's memory and mine is that she places the event in the late afternoon.

Mario savio: [The police car capture] was a beautiful coup. It wasn't clever, because we hadn't planned it. First of all, there was an ironic aspect. This was the symbol of how the other side was cleverly going to take away Jack Weinberg, and this had turned out, by some stroke of good fortune to us, to be their major weakness. It began with the physical layout. Everybody there was needed. It wasn't like an all-night vigil, where it didn't make any difference if you came or went. It was *essential* that a few hundred people, at least, stay. They had a job to do, and they had a job they had to do night and day; namely, keep this car. There was the beauty of that, of everyone pulling together in this common work that they had to do, which they could all see immediately the value of. One of the things required for a sense of community is that people feel that they're needed, for something the importance of which touches the deepest part of you. It wasn't a political thing; it wasn't an organization which parceled out work, and directed you to do X, Y and Z. Each person, in terms of the personal ability which *he* had, and the particular thing which *he* saw needed to be done, was there to do it. They felt a personal responsibility to the well-being of all. This is something which must be described as beautiful.[1]

Early on the morning of October 2, my grade school buddy Janis Zimdars and I sat on the bricks around Ludwig's Fountain, talking about what we were doing and marveling at our surroundings. She introduced me to her new roommate, Pam Mellin. As it turned out, Pam became fairly important in the FSM, since she worked in the dean's office and could get us copies of everything that passed through there that was of any importance. We got some embarrassing inside dope and put the administration on the spot a few times. Why they failed to figure out where the leak was, I can't imagine. It could have been her looks. She was a slender, severely attractive blonde who wore those awful black "harlequin" eyeglasses that make anyone look like an angry cat; just the sort who really does fit your idea of a conservative secretary if she wants to.

Most of the people bedded down; I didn't go to sleep. I was too keyed up. I didn't sleep worth discussion during that whole five-day period. As a consequence, I sort of cracked up afterwards for a couple of days.

I met a girl and we wandered around on patrol, and talked to people and each other and bummed cigarettes. The feeling of comradeship was growing much, much stronger. I felt

JEFF LUSTIG, 1964. PHOTO BY PAUL FUSCO.

like we all shared the same breath and blood. About five in the morning somebody went out and bought three or four cartons of cigarettes, and I went around passing them out. Handing out cigarettes to somebody who needs cigarettes, handing out Marlboros and Pall Malls, handing them out by whether you liked filters or nonfilters. The group had dwindled to about four hundred. Maybe even fewer than four hundred. But they were behind the car, and in front, and a few on each side. Some were on the grass. The administration guys let off an alarm clock, way up in Sproul Hall, but the tinny rattle didn't wake anyone. A little after five o'clock the lawn sprinklers went off, and got a lot of people wet. The people in the administration building looked out their windows and thought it was pretty funny, so I assumed at the time that they'd turned the water on, but in reality, the sprinklers were automatic. A little bureaucratic serendipity. I ran up and got the people off one lawn, and then got people off the other lawn onto the pavement. A couple inside a tent, which was bobbing around remarkably for that hour of the morning, told me to go away, not to bother them, and I guess it was a waterproof tent, because the sprinklers didn't slow them down a bit.

Jeff Lustig: I slept, or tried to sleep, with my girlfriend Margie on the bricks around the car. Not far from us was a couple trying their damnedest to sleep on the bricks comfortably and affectionately at the same time, and not having much luck. In a whisper that seemed to amplify their conversation rather than hide it, the girl was saying things like, "OK. Let's try it with me on top and you underneath . . . No, that's not working, try putting your leg over this way . . . my arm's getting squashed . . ." Finally, she whispered, "Let's just pretend like we're married and sleep back-to-back," and everybody around them within a twenty-five person radius burst into laughter.[2]

There had been no police trouble at all. The police were pleasant, sort of tired. Somewhere between twelve and three I knew they changed shifts, because I saw some new cops. About six, we picked the lock of the maintenance shed below the ASUC building and hauled out the big vacuum cleaner and some brooms and rakes and cleaned the whole area up. By about seven o'clock the plaza and lawns were tidy, a thin mist had given way to bright morning sun and everybody was awake except for maybe one or two who just did not want to get up.

I was outraged by the careless, biased sensationalism of the reporting in the morning papers, and learned not to trust anyone who looked like a newspaperman. I roundly cursed every newsman I saw, and they were very hurt. I didn't understand at the time that they were not responsible for this. I didn't understand that the newsman takes pictures and reports and the editorial desk does what it wants. The papers completely distorted the events. They said "riots," and they said, "beatniks and Communists," and I knew that none of this was true. Since the reporting of the news that I knew about was baloney, I concluded that reporting of the news that I didn't know about was also baloney. Others shared the mistrust created by the coverage of events in which we had all participated, creating a ready market for the host of alternative newspapers and magazines that sprang up as the sixties wore on.

In particular, there was no love lost between the demonstrators and the *Oakland Tribune*, which was, needless to say, our particular enemy, losing no opportunity to distort events, belittle our accomplishments, pooh-pooh our goals, bemire our reputations and emphasize whatever damning evidence could be ferreted out. I tried to stay out of the way of newsmen, but I got in the newspapers often enough. No way around it.

Tom Weller: The great Lucius Beebe, one of the most colorful journalists of all time, was still writing a column for the *San Francisco Chronicle* at that time. I recall reading it with delight the morning of the second as I sat by the police car. Beebe easily showed his mettle as king of curmudgeons by demanding that the demonstrators be hung *and then shot with crossbows.*[3]

An industrial-sized coffee maker had materialized. We plugged it into the extension cord winding out of the Student Union and served free coffee and donuts to the demonstrators, and to the newsmen, and to the cops. Anybody else wanted it they had to pay a dime, but that didn't go over very well so everybody got free coffee. More and more the day picked up, and more and more people came by; fewer and fewer people on their way to classes actually went to class. They stopped and stayed around the car. They figured, "Well, hell's bells. We can cut a class today. Something like this doesn't happen all the time."

The maintenance man came out and looked very wounded that the whole place had been cleaned up. Perhaps, in the annals of maintenance men, he was looking forward to a red-letter day. So he got out his big vacuum cleaner and went over the whole area again. Because after all, you know, you got a job to do, and you gotta do your job whether it's been done or not. The whole area was immaculately clean. But he cleaned it up all again, anyway. This improved my mood.

JACK WEINBERG AFTER SOME 24 HOURS IN THE POLICE CAR. PHOTO BY DON KECHLEY.

THE CAPTURED COP CAR: DAY TWO

Responding to the sit-ins, California Governor Edmund G. Brown issued a statement supporting the administration, calling for "law and order," and maintaining that "this is not a matter of freedom of speech" but "purely and simply an attempt . . . to use the campuses of the University unlawfully. . . . This will not be tolerated."[1] Chancellor Strong issued the usual rehash, embellishing his flat denial that freedom of speech was at issue with a bit of academic weasel-wording and casting the University in the role of the great defender of a "public trust: namely, that the University will never allow itself to be dominated nor used by the parties, sects, or selfish interests. . . . The consequence of defaulting on this public trust would be the erosion of the independence of the University."[2]

Charles Powell, still conceiving that his duty as ASUC president extended to that of mediator and problem solver, advanced a timid, inaccurate statement calculated to appeal to the moderate element of the crowd, and serving as well to convince the more radical that he was no more than the puppet of the administration:

> The facts are these:
> The prohibition on the solicitation of funds and memberships on campus for partisan issues is not a ruling of the Chancellor or of President Clark Kerr.
> It is, in fact, a State law.
> Therefore, the only rational and proper action at this point is to seek changes in the law. Those opportunities are not here on the campus—but in the houses of the State Legislature.
> In a conference with President Kerr, I have been told that mob violence and mass demonstrations directed at the Administration will, in no way, do anything to alleviate the problem.

1964 ASUC PRESIDENT CHARLES POWELL.
PHOTO BY STEVE MARCUS.

In fact, we are indeed losing support among the Regents for concessions which have already been made.

I am certain, and President Kerr has confirmed this fear, that if demonstrations such as today's continue, we will lose the Open Forum policy.

This is a tradition for which all students and President Kerr have fought long and hard, and one which we need not lose.

I appeal to my fellow students.

I ask that you not oppose the Administration—the Administration can do nothing to meet the demands being made.

But this I do ask, write your State legislators, then give your full-hearted support to the ASUC Senate which will ask the property at Bancroft and Telegraph be deeded to the City of Berkeley for municipal administration.

Above all, I ask you to discontinue demonstrations which are endangering lives, property, and the Open Forum policy which the entire University community enjoys.[3]

Even the conservative organizations showed more gumption than the ASUC; though they did not officially participate in the sit-ins in Sproul Hall or around the car, some members did picket on Sproul Hall steps, and the groups came out with a collective statement supporting the goals of the protesters.* "The conservative campus groups fully

*The statement of support was reportedly made by Mona Hutchin, vice president of the University Society of Individuals, but in her interview with Marston Schultz she denied having made it: "The *Daily Cal* reported that I issued the conservative or-

agree with the purpose of the sit-ins," it read in part; "the United Front still stands."[4]

Except for the small hours of the morning, when most of the demonstrators were sacked out, speeches went on all the time from the top of the car, which got more and more beat up. By nine in the morning of October 2, the microphone and loudspeakers were blatting away again, and turn after turn, a lively debate went on from the groaning podium. Although we had voted to have another sit-in, Sproul Hall was locked and guarded by campus police all day. Many people directly involved or just sympathetic wore black arm bands. Blue buttons with a white FREE SPEECH F. S. M. appeared by the end of the next week; selling for a quarter, they helped finance the cause.*

A can for contributions passed around continuously, and the money collected went for sound equipment, pink lemonade and soft drinks for the crowd. The lunchtime rush of students and curious onlookers swelled the crowd to four or five thousand. The Bear's Lair cafeteria went into overdrive and ran out of everything.

I took a bag of small change and hitchhiked to the Telegraph Avenue Co-op at Telegraph and Ashby for as many bottles of soda pop as the money would get. The man who picked me up took me directly there, accompanied me into the store, paid for the two cases of Coca-Cola and drove me back to the campus. The excitement of events had communicated itself to the whole community, and the general air was one of an exuberance I had never felt before. On Sproul Plaza I handed out Cokes and dropped the money back into the general fund.

It was hot, and luckily the prowl car was white. Stuck in the back of a police car for two days, Jack had a bit more than he had bargained for, but the constant presence of the car with its arrested occupant galvanized the campus in a way that nothing else would have. Questioned about his comfort, Jack, with his drooping proletarian mustache and look (as

ganizations' statement, but I didn't. It was Warren Coates for the Young Republicans and Paul Cahill for USI and Danny Rosenthal for Cal Students for Goldwater expressing solidarity for the United Front even though they didn't particularly agree with the sit-in. I didn't sit in around the car; I was against it—it didn't appeal to me. After the conservative organizations left the United Front I went back to studying. I was inactive until just before the [November] march on the Regents."

*Tom Weller recalls that political buttons "proliferated to such an extent that by the late 1960s the average activist's bebuttoned breast came to resemble that of a Russian general" (personal correspondence, August 1990).

Calvin Trillin later characterized it) of Sacco and Vanzetti rolled into one, said:

> I have spent many a day in jail for civil rights work in the South and imprisonment is just something that sometimes must be put up with. Actually, I think this car is better than that jail. It certainly isn't any worse.[5]

The media had a field day, and from October 1 to early January, the Free Speech Movement was never off the front page.

A CHAT WITH DAD

ON THE AFTERNOON OF THE SECOND DAY, when there had been plenty of time for everything to get into all the papers, I felt that I should let my parents know how I was doing, and why I was doing it. They were learning of my career at second hand, and I felt that a bit from the horse's mouth would be only right. I also wanted them to understand that I was no Communist cat's paw, as they surely feared. I wanted everything that I did to be understood as deriving clearly from principle, and well considered, and not by any stretch of the imagination did I wish them, or anyone, to think that I was a leaf blown along by winds from Moscow, or anyplace else for that matter. I was doing the blowing. After a lengthy conversation, I demanded of my father,

"Are you for me or against me?"

"Well, son, I guess we're for you. We love you, son, be careful."

My poor parents.

Warren Goines: I was scheduled to go to South America with a team of Bechtel engineers, and that required a first-order security clearance. Those guys who do the investigations are masters of guilt by association, and my first thought was for myself and my job. But when my co-worker Irving Joseph heard of what the students at Cal were doing, he said to me, "You should be proud of your son. He's standing up for what he believes in."

This brought me to my senses; I also remembered that I'd done the same damn thing myself, only I had a wife and six kids on the line. In 1957, we were living in Fair Oaks, California. The State Water Rights Board that I was working for had a loyalty oath floating around. It was circulated among all the employees; four pages about conduct expected of us, and a lot of it related to issues that were none of their business— particularly participation in so-called subversive organizations. At the end of this four pages, given to every employee of the State Water Rights Board, was a little statement at the bottom that said, "I have read

WARREN CHARLES GOINES.
PHOTOGRAPHER UNKNOWN.

this material, I understand this material, and I will comply therewith." And you were to sign it. Most of this was commonsense morality, you know, "You don't steal, you don't lie, blah, blah, blah." But a lot of it was none of their business. It is completely unconstitutional to tell people that you will influence their political opinions—that's none of their business. So I looked at this thing, and y'know I felt, "This is a real dilemma." I finally decided the best way out of it was this: I crossed out everything except "I have read this," and signed it. And the shit hit the fan.

I was the only one in the whole office who had said, "I won't sign this thing." Even the lawyers had signed it. I was a member of the professional staff. I was a registered engineer at this time—I wasn't just a clerk.

They held a hearing, at which this issue was raised, and I said, "I take the position that what you've asked of me is totally outside of your sphere and is a violation of my constitutional rights as an American citizen, and I refuse to sign it."

I went to a lawyer, and told him what I'd done, and asked him if I had a leg to stand on.

He says, "Yes. You can bury them, but you'd better be prepared for a real fight, and you'll probably get fired."

Sure enough, my boss, Larry Spencer, came in one day and said, "Warren, they're gonna fire you."

I said, "Go right ahead. I need the job, but I don't need it that bad." And I told him I wouldn't sign it.

As a result of my objections, a full hearing was held at which it was decided that all the signed statements were to be withdrawn. Subsequently they were all destroyed.

About three months later, I got promoted.

There's one thing I learned: never lie. Never. Every organization needs someone that tells them the bitter truth. If they don't have that, they will not survive. That's the route I took as a professional. I was not a person who made it a point to get along with any asshole, but my boss knew that what I told him was to the best of my knowledge and ability *absolutely* true. I told him when he was in trouble, and many times he was. That's why I was respected.

I got the security clearance anyway, but didn't end up going to South America.[1]

STUDENTS AROUND POLICE CAR ABOUT 6 PM, FRIDAY, OCTOBER 2. CENTER STANDING FIGURE IS PATTI IIYAMA. SEATED JUST BELOW, LOOKING AT THE CAMERA, IS STEPHANIE COONTZ. PHOTO BY PAUL FUSCO.

BETTER A LIVE DOG THAN A DEAD LION

ABOUT FIVE O'CLOCK ON OCTOBER 2, a number of people who had been doing a good deal of the speaking disappeared, and other speakers took over who weren't quite so good. The better orators were recognized as spokesmen, and that, combined with a desire on the part of the news media to have identifiable leaders, pushed Mario Savio and others into the position of negotiating with President Kerr and Chancellor Strong for some resolution to the impasse that had developed.

Tom Miller: The night of October 2 at about five o'clock we called all the political groups to the Student Union on the steps, and we selected a negotiating committee, which was myself, Bob Wolfson, Mario, Eric Levine, Jo Freeman—Jackie wasn't on the original one; Sandor [Fuchs] got in by accident, too—the negotiating team was six or seven people. It was dominated by the civil rights groups.[1]

Mario Savio: The negotiating team was chosen to be representative. But that's not how you choose negotiators: you choose negotiators because they can negotiate. It was an ill-balanced team, and it was too large. We were learning to be political, but it was still much more a rebellion than a revolution.[2]

Jackie Goldberg: Mario and Jo Freeman and Sandor Fuchs and Eric Levine, Paul Cahill and Tom Miller from CORE, were the people who were chosen to be negotiators. Somebody else didn't show up, so they said to me, "You're it." I wasn't on the negotiating committee before the minute we went up there. That's when Dan Rosenthal appeared and said that if he didn't go, he was going to do everything he could to undermine what happened, because it wouldn't be fair for all of us lefties to go without him. And we made the foolish mistake of putting him on.

Before we left, they had delegated me to be the spokesman—this was still the United Front. By the time we got to the elevator, all of a sudden

Mario was the spokesman. I don't know how it came about; didn't bother me. When we got there, about four-thirty or five, some kids from the religious community joined us, and of course Charlie Powell at the request of Kerr; Strong was there, too.[3]

Mario Savio: We tried to talk about issues. I questioned Kerr on just what the University's position was on the advocacy question. I said, "It's direct political and social action that you want to restrict. Well, I want to see just what that means. Let's say that we had a poster which said, 'Hubert Humphrey to speak, Oakland Municipal Auditorium, Thursday, 7:00 PM.' Could we have such a sign displayed on campus?" And he said, "Yes." Then I asked, "What if we had a sign that said, '*Oakland Tribune* to be picketed, 7:00 PM Thursday.' Could we have that sign?" And he said, "No." So I said, "Well, they're both instances of *legal* action, and I think *you* in any case would agree that they're *both* instances of political action, even if I wouldn't; how do you distinguish between them?" He didn't answer that question.

The original form of the agreement was "Student demonstrators will agree to abide by legal forms in their protests against the University regulations." And that wasn't acceptable. I told Kerr, "If that stays, I won't sign it." Others wouldn't sign it either. I'm sure that Tom Miller wouldn't sign it. Whereas Jackie, she wanted to take it just as it came out of his hand! She was ready to go. I don't think it was because of any bad inclination on her part, it was just a question of style. She more easily accepted a kind of paternalism, it seemed to me. The thing I remember about her was having to oppose her. Tom Miller and I were the most belligerent at the meeting. Also good were Jo Freeman and Bob Wolfson. While Bob seemed to be able to stick to these principles quite well, he was more levelheaded and equable than I, and that seemed to be useful. I had already developed a knack for being quite impolite.

So it was suggested that it say, "The demonstrators will cease their present demonstration." He said no. Finally we hit upon "Demonstrators will desist from their illegal protest of University regulations." We weren't completely happy with it, but he understood why we insisted on that form. He tried not to comment. We didn't want to be prevented from future protests. Our point was that we can't bind our consciences indefinitely into the future; circumstances may make it appropriate to use who-knows-what kind of means. We explained the sense that we put on it, but the important thing was what the demonstrators understood by it. It was explained in front of the demonstrators what we had agreed to, and what we meant by it.

Another change was "The case of the eight suspended students will be submitted within one *week* to the Academic Senate." So that they wouldn't wait indefinitely. That didn't happen. At one point Kerr said, "You really have to hurry. I've asked the police not to break up the demonstration, but I can't control them."[4]

Jackie Goldberg: We sat outside Kerr's office waiting. We saw his secretary, and she told us to wait. We waited about fifteen minutes. We got in the conference room, and Kerr was standing up. We had brought in with us some proposals, and Kerr had some proposals.

First thing we did when we sat down was we made him give us his word that while we were there no police action would take place. Because we could not have all the leaders of the demonstration in his office when there were arrests going on. And he gave us his solemn word that it was he who had called the police; it was from him that the orders to move or not to move would come; and that he would not issue any orders regardless of what happened until we were safely back with the demonstration. Later, he told us that the police were on their own and that they could act without his orders.

It started out with Kerr saying, "I'd like to read these proposals and then I'll hear yours." Kerr made the point that his were drawn up by faculty members: Lipset, Glazer and Petersen, so we were not terribly set up to hear something good. Glazer's my adviser, and he's the only one I was surprised about. Lipset we knew and no one trusted; Petersen no one trusted. Glazer I kept defending until I couldn't defend him anymore. He'd always been fair, and always been a nice guy, and always seemed to be inclined to be with students on this point. He'd helped me out when I was in the Sheraton-Palace; he'd helped me out when I had a couple of midterms; he seemed to want to give breaks to kids who were involved in these activities. So I assumed, incorrectly, and sadly, that he was with us. I'd like to believe that he was just a fool and naive—that his heart was in the right place—but I'm not so sure now. I've seen some of the stuff he's written and I'm not sure.

Kerr made an introductory speech that went something like this: "I'm a good guy, you gotta trust me, I've been the students' friend, you can look at my record, any good things that have happened to students have happened since I've been here, you must realize that I'm in a difficult position, we gotta trust each other, and this is no different."

Kerr read his proposals, and we told him that we'd like him to hear ours, and he did. We were explaining that all those people out there were not United Front people; a lot of them were nonpolitical students and we had a responsibility for why they were sitting there; there were things that we could sign and that we couldn't sign. When we left the demonstration, only about a third of the police that eventually came were there.

My position was that we should get as much as we could and sign no matter what we had to do. That we'd have to work it out; that I didn't trust that he'd live up to any agreement that we had signed; we wouldn't have to worry about getting out of it later. He wanted it signed. He also had a stenographer taking a report of what was said. That was a mistake, because though we thought it was a verbatim report, she was rather selective in what she remembered of the conversation. You know the trouble we got in later on when they quoted from the record. When he appointed from Friday to Monday ten of the twelve people on the CCPA [Campus Committee on Political Activity], he was telling us, "We never agreed on any number."

Most of the talking was done by Mario and myself, until one point when Dan [Rosenthal] sold us out so bad. The whole conversation started around the area of Charlie Powell's suggestion that the students buy from the University the area at Bancroft and Telegraph. If we couldn't buy it, maybe the city would lease it from the University, and on Berkeley property we could do what we wanted to do. None of us really liked the idea, but we talked about it for a while. Kerr said that the University would do all in its ability to lease this land to the city of Berkeley. We thought that this was not desirable, but more desirable than the way it was. We all sort of let it go; none of us really thought it would come about.

The first point was Jack Weinberg: we wanted him to be released, never booked. Kerr proposed that he would be booked, but that the University would not press charges. In our caucus, we decided that would be good enough.

Then we started talking about the suspended students. We wanted them reinstated immediately. Now, this is where Kerr tricked us. He said that he would have them turned over to the Faculty Committee on Student Conduct. We didn't know that there was no Faculty Committee on Student Conduct. The only committee on student conduct was the *Chancellor's* Committee on Student Conduct, and that's not the one we wanted; we were trying to avoid that. When he said, "faculty," not "chancellor's," we assumed that they were not one and the same. Again, we fought over that. In the caucus, most of the kids wanted to accept it, and I wanted to accept it. I believed, and I still believe, that if we didn't come up with some agreement, no matter how bad, that when those policemen moved in on those kids on open pavement, after the demonstrators had been awake for thirty-two hours, and the cops had driven their motorcycles through, which they were wedged in a position to do, and they'd come in with the clubs, and they were mostly Oakland cops, I believed that someone was going to get killed. I really did. I still *do!*

The arguments for refusing were that we could get something better, he was only bluffing. Either immediate reinstatement, or that the faculty's decision would be final and not advisory to the chancellor. The final agreement was an advisory hearing without reinstatement.

The biggest debate was over that point and over the first point in Kerr's statement which was that all forms of illegal protest shall cease. We fought over this first proposal, because we thought it meant we were going to have no more protests, and that we were binding all groups for all time. The only thing that we could really bind was the United Front, and we weren't even sure that we had the authority to do that. The way the statement sounded was that there shall be no more illegal protests about anything forever and ever and ever amen. That's the way it read. I proposed an alternative word in there, which was "desist." It was accepted, because in my understanding of the word "desist" it means to end, singularly, and I interpreted it to mean that we would desist from our illegal protest. The one that was going on now. I don't think he interpreted it that way, because he accepted it too readily.

After our first caucus, Dan Rosenthal said, "I have a statement to make." At which time our hearts dropped into our stomachs. He made a statement to Kerr about how his group by not having participated in an illegal protest had been seriously hurt because we'd had an unfair advantage all this time by setting up illegal tables and his group hadn't been able to, and he demanded that the students *not* be reinstated, that they be suspended, that disciplinary action be taken against all groups that had participated in the illegal protest, and that Jack Weinberg, who had in fact broken a law, be arrested and prosecuted. Kerr, of course, took it all in. Then Paul Cahill pulled a real guts-ball move. He says, "I don't know who Dan's speaking for, but he's not speaking for me, or my group, or for the conservatives that I'm representing." So Kerr had a lot of the wind blown out of his sails, because he couldn't make any kind of a statement that the conservatives opposed everything that was going on because Cahill had just blown it out completely. I wish you could possibly understand: we're fighting to get the most out of Kerr and then this bombshell is dropped on the floor with the cops out there waiting to move in. It was just the most hideous thing. I haven't said a word to Rosenthal since then. It was just one of those unforgivable things; even if he believed that, he had no right to come in as a part of *our* negotiating team and make that statement. He could have come in and said he was a student, but not on our negotiating team.

About an hour after we'd been in there, Kerr's secretary started coming in saying that the police were getting ready to move, and that she could not convince them that they should hold off any longer, and that we had better hurry. She said this to Kerr, but she said it loudly enough for us to hear. She sounded scared. Of course, I believed that it was the case. I still do. I don't believe they were bluffing at all. I don't trust those Oakland cops as far as I could throw any one of them. She came in five or six times.*

Also, Kerr was called out of the room once, for a long-distance call which we believed was from Sacramento.

Glazer and Petersen came into our caucus to urge us to make a deal. They looked tired and draggled out, like they'd put all of their soul and guts into that goddamned agreement. We caucused in the conference room—Kerr and Strong left, and we sent Charlie Powell out, too. Strong didn't say very much, and when he did, Kerr seemed perturbed with him.

In the caucuses, the biggest fight was over whether Kerr was bluffing us with the police. At first, I was the only one who said, "I don't want to take the chance." I kept saying over and over again, "If this were a revolution, a real revolution, you expect some of the troops to die." But this was no revolution, and I didn't care what anybody says, it's not a revolution, and I'm not going to live with, to go home with it on my mind, that someone *died* out there, was maimed, or seriously injured. I'd seen too many cops in action to know that on open pavement, without press there to take pictures and a mass arrest scene with people thirty-two-hours tired, that *anything* could happen.

I felt that Mario was being reckless at this time. Mario was a little rash during the negotiations. I thought that part of what he was doing was directed more at me than at Kerr; he didn't like me or didn't trust me or both. I was scared about Mario and Tom [Miller] reinforcing each other and making it impossible for either of them to sign anything. I was frightened that we might not get back in time.

Kerr responded the most favorably to myself. I had a long talk with Mario afterward, after he made some rather harsh remarks about my actions. And I tried to explain to him that he had damn well better get used to the idea that there are all kinds of styles of negotiating, and one of them is not being rude. That I'm not claiming that my style is the most effective. I've never found that being rude or insulting is a good negotiating style. This talk was not too long after he tried to keep me off the Steering Committee, during the formation committee of the

---

*According to Hal Draper in *Berkeley: The New Student Revolt*, early Friday morning Kerr and Strong had gotten together with the police and in a three-hour session hammered out the plan for action. Representatives of Governor Brown joined the session, and an agreement was reached among them for a six o'clock deadline, at which time Chancellor Strong would read the riot act to the demonstrators, warning them to disperse or else. They did not at this point contemplate negotiation, but as the crowd swelled, they were more or less forced to consider it.

FSM. In fact, he apologized for it all. He said, "Yes, I've got to understand it's a difference in style." But, I was purged later, so . . .

Tom was not insulting. He was firm, and cocky.

Kerr looked pretty relaxed, like an old labor negotiator.

I don't know where they were getting their information, but both Mario and Tom Miller *knew* that they were bluffing. They also gave the impression that even if the cops did attack, that it wouldn't be so bad. Eric Levine felt the same way that I did. Sandor finally said the same thing exactly; Cahill agreed with me. But Tom Miller and Mario felt that I was losing my cool, and that I shouldn't be in negotiations if I wasn't willing to risk all on a bluff. We had a number of rather violent arguments.

We got that there would be no action against organizations that had participated. We said that we'd have the right to recommend and have a say about who was to be on the committee; we agreed that leaders from among the students would be included. We understood that the recommendations would come from each of the three groups.

Eventually, we signed, and there was the mad dash back to the demonstration. More cops than I'd ever seen. This was the first time Mario was completely assertive: he said, *"I'm going to make the statement."* And, not being in the mood to argue, nobody did. Art was still up on top of the police car explaining what to do when the police came. He was looking excited and nervous. I said to him, "We've signed an agreement; Mario's going to announce it. He should be here any minute."[5]

Tom Miller: On October 2 about three o'clock we were notified by Charles Sellers that Kerr had changed his mind; that he would negotiate. So we showed up there, and we found out that Jo Freeman—I think that this is very sneaky, now that I think back on it—Jo Freeman had contacted one of her Democratic party people, and he showed up and said that he had arranged the meeting, like he was doing us a favor. But not to tell anybody. "Keep this silent."

So an interesting thing happened, Jackie Goldberg and Dave Jessup were there, Cahill was there, and this right-wing guy, Rosenthal, and he demanded to go also. So the negotiating team said, "OK, come along," because we didn't want to wreck the United Front. That was a big mistake we made, because when we got to the office, there was no discipline on the negotiating team. First Kerr went into this long speech about how he was such a great defender of rights and everything like that. Sue Johnson, the editor of the *Daily Cal*, was sitting there crying, and Edward Strong spoke about Clark Kerr, how he defended liberty and everything else. Like he was there to build up Kerr's image.

One of the ministers was there, and we asked that they be kept there, because they had taken our position. Kerr had asked them to leave. Dave Jessup wasn't inside. He had stayed outside to keep us informed of what was happening with the car.

Kerr threatened us, saying that "You have five minutes before the police are going to arrest." So I said, "Let us talk to ourselves for a minute, we can't be threatened by this. This is ridiculous. We're not going to *talk* to you if you're going to give us five minutes." So he says, "No, what I really mean is that I have complete control of them, they won't do anything until we get back to the demonstration." So we asked him explicitly, "You mean they will not act until we get back there? Not 'til after we have either rejected or signed this, but 'til we get back?" And he said, "OK."

There was no discipline in the meeting. He used Jackie Goldberg very effectively. He kept on calling her by her first name, she kept on agreeing with him, she was a tool for him—not a voluntary tool, but a tool. A negotiator will pick out the weakest person and start calling him by his first name, and be very familiar, shoving out the other people. Then work through him to get his position accepted. He was a very smart negotiator, no doubt about that. It's interesting, he called Jo Freeman by her first name, too. Those were the ones he could manipulate. They weren't experienced negotiators.

We were constantly being interrupted by his secretary coming in and telling him that the police were going to attack, and he was constantly going in and out of the room; when we asked about changes, Kerr wouldn't make 'em then; he would go into this other office. We thought he was phoning Governor Brown about it, because he was talking to somebody else about it on the phone. The faculty group, including [Professor Lewis] Feuer and Glazer, while we were deliberating, came in and insisted that we go for it. All through this whole thing, they had been playing this role. "This is the best you'll get, it's a miracle that we've gotten to negotiate at all." This type of routine. The faculty came in twice. The crowd had dropped to about three hundred before we started negotiating. All these things add up.

I kept demanding that we take five minutes alone to discuss this. Then we talked about discipline in those five minutes, and agreed upon some type of discipline. Except some people didn't. The problem was that we didn't have a leader. I suggested that Mario talk, mainly because I didn't want Jackie to talk. Sandor wouldn't want me to speak, so I said Mario or Bob Wolfson should speak. Bob Wolfson is a very good negotiator.

I knew those cops, and knew what they were capable of, and figured that if they charged the crowd that somebody would get killed. But Kerr *also* knew this. Kerr doesn't want a University of Mississippi any more than anybody else does.* In fact, his whole image would have been ruined. That was a strong point on our side, when you have legitimate demands. People who took a strong position were actually myself and Mario. It seemed to me that everybody was caving in there except Mario and me.

When Kerr came back in again, it completely fell apart. He started in on Jackie again. We suggested the word "desist" instead of the word that implied that we won't demonstrate again, and we had a hassle about this. First we said, "We'll end our demonstration now." But Kerr *knew* what that meant, and we found this compromise, which satisfied us in a sense because it meant we will desist *now*. Kerr felt he could use it to effectively mean, "they won't do it again." So it was a face-saving device for both of us. Also, I requested in the end the sixth point about buying the land. All these things add up. So we signed that. We all signed it; Dave Jessup ran in and signed it, too.† It was implicit in the agreement that nobody will get in any trouble and the suspensions will be dropped immediately. It wasn't written, but it was understood. We believed that the Student Conduct Committee was to be a formality to save face. We were told that the suspensions were to be dropped within a week, and that there wouldn't be any recriminations.

Before we went in, the crowd had dropped to about three hundred people, and this had affected the negotiations. Just as we signed it, I got a note from Jessup, which was late, saying that there were three thousand people out there. Now if I'd had that before, we could have pushed much harder.

Gretchen Kittredge: I kept trying to phone in to you, and Jessup wouldn't answer the phone.

Tom Miller: He was outside, and supposed to be answering the phone, and he didn't. We asked him to do that.

Gretchen Kittredge: See, I called down there. There was a woman there who answered the phone, and I said, "I'm supposed to ask for Dave Jessup," and she said, "Oh, I'm sorry, just a minute," and didn't find him.

Tom Miller: I thought the agreement was OK when I thought there were only three hundred people there. I thought we couldn't do any better than this, though I was very mad at the negotiating team. The demands we stated up on the car were freedom of speech, change the rules, im-

---

*On September 30, 1962, Governor of Mississippi Ross Barnett defied a federal order to admit a Black man, James Meredith, to the University of Mississippi, and blocked his path with state troopers. President Kennedy sent federal troops to force compliance. A massive riot ensued

in which at least three people were killed and fifty injured.

†The agreement was signed by Clark Kerr, Jo Freeman, Paul Cahill, Sandor Fuchs, Robert Wolfson, David Jessup, Jackie Goldberg, Eric Levine, Mario Savio and Thomas Miller.

STUDENT HANDING OUT BLACK ARM BANDS,
OCTOBER 3, 1964.
PHOTOGRAPHER UNKNOWN.

mediately dropping the suspensions. Very high demands. I don't know what we would have gotten with a skilled team and knowledge that we had a big crowd.

I was feeling very bad, and some YSA people, Sid Stapleton and his wife, Beth, were out there the next morning passing out these black arm bands. And that made me feel really good, and I started passing out bands.[6]

The administration was getting a good deal of heat from Sacramento, and was being pushed hard to get the whole thing over with one way or another. If Kerr couldn't do it through sweet reason, Sacramento was going to do it by brute force.

Near dusk, the rumor went around that a stupefying horde of cops was closing in on the campus. There must have been more than five thousand students in Sproul Plaza, five hundred or so of them sitting around the car, and above their debating and the loudspeaker's arguments, we heard what sounded like every motorcycle in Christendom massing at Bancroft and Telegraph. It sounded like tanks. The motorcycles started up all at once. I was standing next to two people and we all three simultaneously thought that it was tanks. For some reason it seemed to run through the whole crowd. Everyone I talked to later was convinced it was a tank, or two tanks, or several tanks. For real, that they'd brought up *tanks!* There'd been a rumor that the Army and Navy would participate, and there *were* Army and Navy paddy wagons, because I noticed them later running around. They'd blocked off Bancroft and Telegraph for several blocks down each way, and they were just chuck full of cops.

The state of California had declared war on the students of the University, and it was going to be real unpleasant. Governor Brown never did understand, then or later, what the hell was happening. He would have machine-gunned us all with tears of liberal grief pouring down his jowls, unable to imagine another way of solving the problem except to get a bigger hammer.*

I was tired beyond exhaustion, and I was keyed up, and I didn't understand what was going on. Somebody here was making a plea for us to stay, somebody there was making a plea for us to go, and right about this time we began forming concentric rings about the car and locking arms and getting set for a big rush from what we had heard were fantastic num-

STUDENT HANDING OUT BLACK ARM BANDS, OCTOBER 3, 1964. PHOTOGRAPHER UNKNOWN.

bers of police. "Fantastic numbers" were anywhere from hundreds to thousands of police. I was fully equipped to believe this, because though

---

*According to Bob Gill, "Governor Edmund G. 'Pat' Brown had a shitty reputation early on in the decade. Besides the shifty liberal stands he had taken so far—bracero program, water plan, execution of Caryl Chessman—by the fall of 1960 he had signed the evil new vagrancy law. It meant that any time we might be hitchhiking down to L. A., we would stand the chance of taking the weekend off in some little town's jailhouse if we didn't have at least five dollars in our pocket. When JFK first campaigned in the Bay Area, he stopped by San Jose, where a tiny band of us state college radical youths greeted him with his first giant anti–nuclear weapons banner. Leaving the area, he and Brown shared the same back seat of an open-air limo, side by side, sitting up on the back seat with their feet on the cushions, per-

haps the very same that Jackie would climb over trying to retrieve the president's brain fragments. No crowd restrictions then, the entire mob was right there in the street swelling around and I realized that I could actually get within two inches of JFK's ear and yell one precisely chosen *bon mot* as he cruised by in the deafening roar. To my horror, I saw that it was Brown on my side of the street and it would be his ear presented to me and I had no time or room to rush to the other side before the limo came by. When His Honor's balding head pulled up, there was only one grand public policy issue I could think of in that split second. 'What about the goddamn vagrancy law, Brown!' I screamed. He kept right on smiling and waving like a horn-rimmed Buddha" (written communication, November 1990).

THE FREE SPEECH MOVEMENT

I hadn't seen any of them, I'd heard that there were *seas* of Oakland cops swarming all over the campus.* I was fully prepared to fight to the death this time. I was right next to the car, and the feeling of both the demonstrators and the policemen in the car was that we were in for a lot of trouble.

For no reason that I can put my finger on, I had the distinct impression that those particular cops were going to be fighting on our side, if it came to that. I'd had the same feeling the night before, when the freddies were trying to start a riot. The cops had been divided up on sides, to some extent: the Berkeley and campus cops were on the side of the demonstrators, the Alameda and Oakland cops were on the side of the freddies. If it came to a fight, it seemed to me reasonable that the Alameda County sheriffs would be fighting the Berkeley police. I had great faith in the Berkeley and campus police, who were quite decent throughout. They had no real choice but to enforce the law as they were ordered to, but they weren't nasty and truculent about it.†

---

*According to contemporary KPFA tapes, there were 637 Oakland, Alameda and highway patrol officers in addition to the Berkeley and campus police. The *Examiner* reported 965 police present.

†Some time later, in 1990, I heard a corroborative anecdote related by Ray Bolerjack, senior systems analyst for the city of Berkeley, who worked with the Berkeley police department in the late 1960s. Though he was not present at the event itself, the particulars were related to him by Berkeley police sergeant Bob Peters, who was. In response to one of the anti–Vietnam War demonstrations, hundreds of Alameda County sheriffs, Oakland police and law enforcement officers from surrounding communities were called in. Among this number were eight Berkeley police officers and one lieutenant, who had responded as part of the "mutual aid" agreement among the Bay Area's various police agencies. The lieutenant happened to overhear instructions to the Alameda sheriffs that they should maximize efforts to break heads and cause injuries to the demonstrators, "teaching them a lesson so that they will never come back." The Berkeley lieutenant then deployed his eight officers between the Alameda sheriffs and the demonstrators, turned them to face the sheriffs, and told the officer commanding the sheriffs that he understood that the police had been instructed to inflict as much injury on the students as possible, and that, as this was contrary to his understanding of proper police procedure, the sheriffs would have to confront the Berkeley police first, who could be depended upon to give as good as they got. He acknowledged that the Berkeley cops would no doubt get the shit kicked out of them, being outnumbered as they were better than twenty to one, but the commanding officer would have to admit that it would sure look bad on TV, what with cops battling cops and all. The commanding officer of the sheriffs saw the reason in this and the subsequent arrests took place in an orderly fashion, with little gratuitous injury to the demonstrators. As a consequence, relations between the Berkeley police and the Alameda County Sheriff's Department were strained for some years. A *Time* magazine article about the Berkeley police department's actions of October 1965, "Finest of the Finest," alludes to an incident for which protesters "applauded the police." The reference is probably to the interference of police with Hell's Angels who were attacking a crowd of anti–Vietnam War demonstrators (*Time*, 18 February 1966).

I was about the fifth circle out, standing with arms locked to two people next to me. We kicked the girls out because we figured that they couldn't form anything strong enough to hold. I had two real bulls beside me; *really* enormous guys, and they'd taken off their shirts. We were taking off our glasses, and we were taking pens out of our pockets and political buttons off and undoing belt buckles so they couldn't drag us by our belts, and really setting up for a knockdown, drag-out, blood-and-guts fight. Which we were fully prepared to undertake; a fight to the death. And I'm sure there would have been somebody killed if the Oakland cops had been let loose on us, because we weren't giving any more or budging anywhere from that car. Then the Berkeley cops rushed the group; there was a photograph on the front page of the *Chronicle* of the cops rushing and several of us yelling, "Lock arms!" We were pushed back and down on the demonstrators behind us. Somehow they'd caught us by surprise and managed to break through. It occurred to me, for a few moments, that they were going to rush the car and try to take it, and then it became clear that they weren't trying to rush the car at all, they were just trying to get around it; they just posted a guard around the car, and that was all, and they didn't do anything more. I'd expected when they started at us that they were going to try to break the ranks and promote confusion, but they didn't. I think they were worried about their buddies in the car. Those guys were not in an ideal position if things started to get rough.

Sam Slatkin: People were linking arms and legs, and preparing for an attack of this army. I was sitting towards the Bancroft side of the car, just about due south of the car, towards the outside of the circle, which is where the four policemen tried to break through from. I was about two circles in from the outside. We hadn't the slightest idea of what they were doing. All of a sudden I noticed that the monitors who were standing up kind of toppled over, inward, and over them started crawling the policemen. UC cops, as I remember. They were being very careful; they looked where they put their feet to be sure that they were stepping on the ground and not on anybody. We packed in and tried to make it difficult for them to get in because we didn't understand what was going on, and then they just picked their way rather slowly through an awful lot of commotion into the center of the crowd. To the car. Nobody was injured, and that was about it. They just went to the car and stood there. Two on either side, near the doors.[7]

As the likelihood of police action increased, we were instructed from the car top on "how to be arrested" by experienced civil rights workers from SNCC and the Congress of Racial Equality. We were told to remove

STUDENTS SINGING AROUND POLICE CAR,
ABOUT 6 PM, OCTOBER 2, 1964.
PHOTO BY PAUL FUSCO.

sharp objects from our pockets, take off pins and earrings, pack close together, go limp and not link arms. When arrested, give only your name and address, ask to see your lawyer, do not make any statements. Everyone under eighteen, noncitizens, people with small children, and those on parole or probation were advised to leave. Many of us felt that we were going to be charged by the motorcycle police, and that some of us were going to be killed.* But by now it was their pride and honor against *our* pride and honor, and though theirs would probably win out, we weren't going to go down without a fight. From atop the car Art Goldberg warned of the real danger we were facing and urged us on into the fray:

> There's a *big* risk. There's no doubt about it. Anybody who tries to tell you that there's no risk in sitting here is *lying* to you. There is a risk! But you have a choice to make. You have a choice to *act!*[8]

During negotiations with Kerr, Jackie was terrified that people around the car were going to be killed in a police charge; while others argued the virtues of martyrdom, she was for any solution at all that

---

*Arleigh Williams told Germaine La-Berge, "I was not privy to any of the discussions at the President's office relative to the [police] car. I couldn't describe those things. I have to admit though—and I did tell Clark Kerr this recently when we met for purposes of oral history—that I think, had he not called off the troops as he did, that there would have been multiple killings on that plaza. I have to admit that at the beginning I did not feel that way. I thought that this is fine, we'll get them out of there, so on and so forth. But in retrospect the more I looked at it, learned from it, the more I was convinced that there would have been just a massacre" (Williams, *Dean of Students,* 96).

MOTORCYCLE POLICE AT BANCROFT AND TELEGRAPH, OCTOBER 2, 1964.
PHOTO BY DOUGLAS WACHTER.

would prevent violence. One of the negotiators—probably Tom Miller—expressed the sentiment of the more militant protesters when he said that "in a revolution people get hurt." The students asked Kerr to leave the room, and a violent emotional clash ensued in which Jackie's feelings ran head-on into Mario's. There were more students around the car than at any other time, almost none of whom were affiliated in any way with any of the United Front organizations, and it was uncomfortably clear that the leaders didn't really represent these protesters adequately. Only a few days before, the United Front had legitimately spoken for a small, well-defined student federation. In the space of three days, things had gotten explosively out of hand, and the student leaders and spokesmen were catapulted into a position where they suddenly were required to speak for masses of students whose intentions they did not well understand.

Part of the group felt keenly that they had no business negotiating with Kerr at all, and that their real place was out there with the students who were, as far as anyone knew, putting their lives on the line for the right to speak freely on campus. The caucus felt that they could not reach an agreement unless Kerr clarified the administration's position. When Kerr reentered the room, a member of one of the more conservative groups stood up and declared that neither he nor his organization any longer supported the United Front or its goals, and left. This somewhat weakened the student position, which was even more compromised as the revving of police motorcycles rattled the windows. Kerr's secretary, in a ludicrously obvious ploy, came in twice and in a stage whisper said to her boss, "I don't think the police will wait any longer," and "The police say that they don't need your permission to break up the student protesters."

The issue more or less resolved into the conflict between taking a bad deal or letting things run their course and seeing what happened. The moderates favored a bad deal that spared bloodshed, feeling that this was not a time to force violence on the protesters. The more militant wanted to see what happened, come what may. Mario underestimated the concern that the negotiators felt for the physical welfare of the students packed in around the car, and when the matter came to a vote, Jackie's more moderate position carried.

Because of this, as well as because of her now suspect credentials as a sorority sister, Mario developed a deep mistrust of Jackie, and accused her of ingratiating herself with Kerr. When the FSM was founded that weekend, replacing the United Front, Jackie was effectively edged out, and though initially included as a member of the elite Steering Committee, had such grave differences with both Mario and Jack that she resigned. This outraged her brother Art, who was all for pulling SLATE out of the FSM in sympathy. However, Jackie refused to introduce a split in the ranks and quietly accepted the peripheral role of sorority and living-group organizer that she had chosen; thereafter, she did not speak at rallies and was accorded no prominent public role in the FSM. This was, however, so well managed by all parties that there was no outside suspicion of a break in the ranks, and Jackie was believed throughout the life of the Movement by the students, the administration and the press to be a central character.

MARSTON SCHULTZ. PHOTO FROM A SLATE CAMPAIGN FLYER, 1965.

We around the car, unaware of the moral struggles and caucusing going on among our representatives, were at last informed, through the car-top news agency, that the administration and student leaders were meeting, and that until the meeting was over, there would be no police action. Out there in the gathering dark was such a frightening rumble of motorcycles, and such a huge mass of cops, that despite our numbers, the singing, cheering, chanting crowd was genuinely afraid.

Marston Schultz: I had it figured out how they were gonna do it: they had two columns of cycles, and the way I figured it they was gonna pull in, and go straight into the demonstrators. And then the cops would come in right between them. And they would just pull the demonstrators out, the cycles blocking off everybody from getting in. I couldn't imagine why those cycles were there for any other purposes. We were convinced, then, that they were going to take the motorcycles and just *run* the motorcycles into the crowd. That's what we thought they were going to do. And then when the crowd was all broken up, in the con-

MOTORCYCLE POLICE AT BANCROFT AND TELEGRAPH, ABOUT 6:30 PM,
OCTOBER 2, 1964. PHOTO BY ROBERT R. KRONES.

fusion the cops would charge. I thought it was an awfully big fuss over
one police car.[9]

Just as the first stars were coming out, Mario appeared to address us
in measured, stately tones that were probably due as much to his extreme exhaustion as to the gravity of the situation. The newsmen shined
lights right in Mario's eyes, and he became angry at them and, with the
assistance of others, pushed them away. This moment is when he became the official leader of the Free Speech Movement.

I would like to request that we have silence. I want everyone here to
understand very carefully, very, very completely, the seriousness of the
circumstances in which we find ourselves here and now. You all see how
many are assembled. The demonstrators know the nature of certain of
the people who are assembled here who are *not* demonstrators, and likewise, I'm sure we're all aware of the presence of large numbers of police. Until this time we have tried our very best to submit all statements
to a vote of those present. However, let us consider what a vote means.
A vote should be the result of an intellectual decision. Such a decision,
if we have respect for our dignity as free men, cannot, I believe, be made
under the circumstances of a meeting of this sort, with the police present, as they are, with our knowing full well the kinds of things they, or
hecklers, may do. However, as a preface to these remarks, and because

I have a very deep respect for popular process, I would like to call a meeting for Monday, twelve o'clock, to be addressed from the steps of Sproul Hall. At this meeting, all those with a vital interest in these proceedings will have an opportunity, one with another, to discuss the nature of the documents which I'm going to read here. This will give adequate time for the free men involved to consider carefully the very serious issues involved in this matter.

Mario seemed almost in tears as he read the terms that he and other representatives of the students and Clark Kerr himself had signed:

I would like to read the statement through once, then I would like to call special attention to a change which was made in the wording of one of its provisions, in order to protect all of us who have engaged in this demonstration. I want to make it very clear that as representative of University Friends of SNCC, I could not have in good conscience subscribed to the statement before that change. And I think you will clearly understand why. I should now— (*Crowd noise, catcalling, chanting from fraternity boys and sorority girls on the fringes.*)

Please maintain silence! I appeal to you, please maintain silence! Retain your dignity and self-respect in this matter, please! I think you're aware of some of the pressures we're under, so please! I implore you! Maintain your composure, please.

I should now like to read the document. The first provision: the student demonstrators shall desist from all forms of their illegal protest against University regulations. (*"No! No!"*) Please, please.

Number two: a committee representing students—including leaders of the demonstration—faculty and administration will immediately be set up to conduct discussions and hearings into all aspects of political behavior on campus and its control, and to make recommendations to the administration.

Three: the arrested man will be booked, but released on his own recognizance, and the University, which is the complainant, will not press charges. (*Great cheering and applause.*)

This is four: the duration of the suspension of the suspended students will be submitted within one week to the Student Conduct Committee of the Academic Senate. Not to the administration! (*Cheering and applause.*)

Five— (*Chanting from the fraternity and sorority members on the fringes.*) Please, please be silent! Please! Please be silent! Five: activity may be continued by student organizations in accordance with existing University regulations. That is, in other words, none of the groups originally involved have had their privileges suspended. (*Scattered applause.*)

Sixth and last, and then I should like to explain the first, as I said. The president of the University has already declared his willingness to support deeding certain University property at the end of Telegraph Avenue to the city of Berkeley or to the ASUC Senate. Now, do you understand what that means? You will be able to do there—if this goes through— (*From the crowd: "How about here?"*) One minute. A committee will be set up immediately to discuss what we may do here. You will be able to do there—if this goes through—what has been done there for years. (*Cheering and applause.*)

Now, I have only two more points. The first, I should like to briefly explain article one. The original wording of that article was as follows: "The student demonstrators promise to abide by legal processes in their protest of University regulations." This, I felt, would have been an impossible bind upon the consciences of those who, perhaps at some time in the future—and this was my opinion as representative of just my organization, but there were others who joined me in this—this we felt would have had the effect of binding for an indefinite period of time the freedom of the protesters to engage in actions which they may feel at some time, though technically illegal, are the only ones they can take. We could not have accepted that provision. (*Applause.*) Instead, we accepted the wording that I read the first time, with the understanding that this would not indefinitely bind anyone, and it was, "The student demonstrators shall desist from all forms of their illegal protest against University regulations." I would like that those who have taken part in this protest will agree, by acclamation, to accepting this document, and as soon as they have done so, to rise, quietly, and with dignity, to walk home. May I please have that decision? (*"YES!" Cheering and applause.*) Will you please then rise at this point, and will you please follow me away from this area quietly and with dignity, please! (*Babble of voices as the students disperse.*)[10]

The crowd broke up into furiously arguing knots, and the first great moments of the coming avalanche were over. We took the crippled victory that this seemed to offer, and as the crowd dispersed, displeased at the outcome, I could see hundreds of California highway patrolmen muffler to muffler at Bancroft and Telegraph.* The freed police car was started, and limped off the campus trailing an environmentalist's nightmare of dense blue smoke. We later on took up a collection to pay for

---

*The *Oakland Tribune* of October 13, 1964, reported that Alameda County billed UC $34,613 for providing 102 sher- iff's deputies, the city of Oakland billed $4,580 and Berkeley billed $2,171.

the damage to the police car, though there is some confusion as to whether the money actually made it to the city of Berkeley or not.*

> *Patti Iiyama:* Our first reaction was "My God! He had no right to make that agreement without coming back and taking a vote of everybody sitting around the car," because here we were willing to get our heads bashed in, and Mario and several other people had signed this agreement. You could see this terrible stress they were under, but they should've come back, and I know I was very mad and several people around me, they all were muttering, nobody wanted to leave, and you could *see* it on people's faces that nobody wanted to leave, and they said, "Why should we go," and then they started muttering to themselves a little bit, and then they left, but they were very unhappy. You could see it on everybody's faces. I saw unhappy faces. Everybody was very disappointed at the outcome.[11]

> *Jack Weinberg:* I remember being disappointed with the agreement that was reached ending the police car incident. However, it turned out pretty good. It set up a framework for negotiations on the outstanding issues and, in labor/management terms, made it possible for the FSM to force the administration to recognize it as a bargaining agency. This was a critical ingredient in the FSM's winning the overwhelming support of the student body.[12]

> *Brian Shannon:* I thought that the agreement recognized the right of students to independently negotiate, and that was the key thing. They should have known they weren't going to get anything out of the agreement, and used that as the basis for a political campaign. They should have *immediately* issued their newsletter, should have sent organizing teams into the co-ops, into the fraternities at the very beginning, gotten a few simple ideas into their heads. But above all, make it clear what their real demands were: most of the students didn't understand what they were fighting for.[13]

Clark Kerr, interviewed in Sproul Plaza as the students were dispersing, seemed to think it was all over:

---

*Estimates of damage to the police car vary wildly, from a high of around six hundred dollars to a low of only two or three hundred. "In an effort to atone for damage to the police car during the Thursday and Friday demonstrations, the stu-dents began a collection of funds to help pay the $334.30 in damages to the police car" ("Chronology of Events: Three Months of Crisis," *California Monthly* 75, no. 5 [February 1965]: 45).

The students have agreed to abandon their illegal protests against University regulations; they've agreed also that the student who is in the car can be booked by the police, in the proper course of events. We have always been willing to have discussions about our policies. We would as a matter of course always review the length of a suspension. When you suspend people indefinitely, it's quite obvious that you have to set some term, and we would set that before the Committee on Student Conduct. So we feel that law and order has been preserved on the Berkeley campus without the use of violence. I think it's a great triumph for decency and good will and reason in what was an extraordinarily difficult situation.

I met with the students at about five o'clock this afternoon. There were about ten from the different groups involved, also Charlie Powell, the president of the Associated Students, Sue Johnson, who is the editor of the *Daily Cal,* and then there were two representatives from the Interfaith Council: one student and one of the ministers of one of the student religious organizations.

Chancellor Strong was in on most of the discussion. [The] agreement carries, however, the name of these students and myself. He fully agrees with that, quite obviously. We're very happy to have law and order restored, and that the processes of law enforcement can go ahead and the student will be booked in the normal course of events. We don't want to be vindictive. The student in the car became kind of a prisoner of everybody. It was fully understood with the students that what the district attorney may do, we of course cannot commit, but we ourselves will not press the charges.

I've been through some tough ones. You know, my field is industrial relations. I've been arbitrator and mediator in some of the biggest disputes on the Pacific Coast, and in the United States. I used to be the impartial chairman on the West Coast waterfront under the so-called old look. They now have a new look where things are going better. In those days, you were in the midst of the International Longshoremen's Union, the ILWU, and the Waterfront Employers Association. I can assure you, you were an awful long ways away from anybody else.

It's hard to say if this is the toughest; there have been many of them in the life of a University president. This I certainly would rank as one of the more difficult ones that I've had to go through.[14]

Immediately after the demonstration had broken up, KPFA also interviewed Mario as he was on his way from the plaza. In the background is the chatter of thousands of dispersing people, and announcements over a bullhorn for people who wanted to clean up ("Put all garbage bags and stuff like that in a central area so it can all be picked up later on"), telling all others to clear the area around the car. A few remarks from police, "Break it up, come on."

Mario, would you say that you backed down or that the University backed down, which?

I would say that no one has as yet backed down, especially when we consider provision one. We're willing to wait. I think this is an expression of good faith on the part of the demonstrators. We're willing and anxious to conduct discussions not with guns at anybody's head. I think that we understand what *could* have happened tonight, and neither we nor the president wanted those to be the conditions under which discussions go on.

Is this cooling-off period until Monday a part of the concession?

No. This is simply a meeting which the leaders of the demonstration have called for the following reason. I've been in many situations in which action being taken is decided by a small elite without even adequate information being given to the people involved. It's been my feeling in this matter that everything should be done completely in the open, and I feel that all the people involved should have a right, in open forum, to discuss these matters. However, I think it's clear for those who are aware of the power circumstances involved in this particular situation, that this agreement could not possibly have been submitted to a vote.

So is it actually accepted, or what is the situation?

The agreement was accepted by representatives of the off-campus political organizations, provisionally, in the name of the demonstrators. It is clear that we cannot bind the consciences of those who have not, themselves, agreed to do so. (*Man's voice: "On Monday a vote will be taken." Woman's voice: "Can we go home and get some sleep, please?"*)

On Monday a vote will *not* be taken on this agreement. Some other things may be decided by the group on Monday. We must leave now. It's absolutely essential.

One other question, Mario. Can you continue to collect funds on this campus, in this area or not?

In accordance with this agreement, we cannot.[15]

Jack went to the station, was booked and released. The University explained that it was "powerless to have the charges dropped," broadly hinting to the DA that if Jack were to be prosecuted it would not be an entirely unwelcome event, though as far as I know no charges were ever pressed. The FSM went into high gear the next day.

I was so tired, and so fuzzy in the head, that if Mario had said, "Stand on your head and click your heels together," I would have done it. I just got up and walked away, with several of my friends and a couple of the people there. We walked down the street. By then I was out of my head; I ran into a group of people on the corner and made a big, rousing speech, and got dragged off again by my friends. Then I went home, and drank a whole bunch of beer. Renée, the dark-eyed beauty who had latched onto me in front of Sather Gate, and of whom I had lost track after the initial hoopla, found out where I lived, somehow, and showed up, shy but determined.

That was the last time I was in my old apartment, with my old buddies, before I completely abandoned my former life. From there on out, for food and shelter, it was catch as catch can.

Early in the morning I walked Renée back to Stebbins Hall, and on my way home I ran into a freddy—this is about five o'clock in the morning—and had a discussion with *him* that lasted until about nine o'clock in the morning. He was friendly to the whole idea of what we were doing, though quite confused by it. By that time I had such a stock of facts and figures under my belt that I could stun an ox by their weight alone. I pretty much convinced him that what we had done was kosher. Then I went to a friend's house, because it was closer—my apartment was way to hell and gone, down by Ashby and Grove. I stayed there, tried to sleep, got up after maybe an hour and went to Art Goldberg's ground-floor apartment on Dwight and College, where I'd been told there was to be a morning meeting. There we had the first meeting of the FSM.

THE FREE SPEECH MOVEMENT

THIS FREE SPEECH FIGHT points up a fascinating aspect of contemporary campus life. Students are permitted to talk all they want so long as their speech has no consequences.

One conception of the university, suggested by a classical Christian formulation, is that it be in the world but not of the world. The conception of Clark Kerr by contrast is that the university is part and parcel of this particular stage in the history of American society; it stands to serve the need of American industry; it is a factory that turns out a certain product needed by industry or government. Because speech does often have consequences which might alter this perversion of higher education, the university must put itself in a position of censorship. It can permit two kinds of speech: speech which encourages continuation of the status quo, and speech which advocates changes in it so radical as to be irrelevant in the foreseeable future. Someone may advocate radical change in all aspects of American society, and this I'm sure he can do with impunity. But if someone advocates sit-ins to bring about changes in discriminatory hiring practices, this cannot be permitted because it goes against the status quo of which the university is a part. And that is how the fight began here.

—Mario Savio at the first FSM rally, October 5, 1964

On Saturday, October 3, the campus was filled with dismayed parents and nervous students, walking around and trying to act like everything was going to be OK and the place hadn't just yesterday been a complete mob scene with cops and rioting students and squashed cop cars and everything. Edward W. Carter, chairman of the University's Board of Regents, treated the whole thing as though it were all over—a big-time panty raid that had gotten out of hand—and, heaving an almost audible sigh of relief, issued the following statement to the press:

> Law and order have been re-established on the Berkeley campus of the University of California. That this was accomplished without violence

is a tribute to President Clark Kerr and his administrative staff. All applicable University rules remain unchanged; the non-student arrested has been booked by the police; the eight suspended students are still on suspension, and the regular procedures for review of student conduct and grievances are functioning.

A faculty committee will review individual cases in an orderly manner, and in due course will make recommendations for their disposition by the properly constituted administrative authorities.

It is regrettable that a small number of students, together with certain off-campus agitators, should have precipitated so unfortunate an incident.[1]

Someone among the politicos had figured out who I was and where I lived, and had told me where a meeting of the other suspended students was going to be. They were more than a little curious about me, and some feared that I was an *agent provocateur*. I was not entirely welcome; I had come out of left field, as it were, with no connections and no coherent politics. Although I was plainly a real ball of fire, I didn't fit in. Everyone else who had been suspended was a member of some political club, and they all seemed to know each other, and appeared to me to have planned out to the last jot and tittle who was going to do what and when. I, on the other hand, was the unplanned child. The Congress of Racial Equality people, who had taken pains to stack the deck in their favor, were particularly dismayed because I had been cited at a SLATE table, and they figured that I was part of the SLATE camp. When it became clear that I was not, in actuality, part of any camp or organization at all, the CORE people became much more amiable. Soon Jack Weinberg took me under his wing, and any fears that I was not the Genuine Article went West.

To quote the philosopher Ludwig Wittgenstein, "We cannot think what we cannot say."[2] Before you can do anything, you've got to have a name, and that was our first order of business. We tried on several—Students for Free Speech, United Free Speech Movement, University Rights Movement, Students for Civil Liberties—but none seemed really to fit.

Mario Savio: I had the feeling that "FSM" was suggested by Jack. There were a lot of possibilities. But we wanted the initials to be something like "FLN" which was easy to say.* Not something like "URM," which

*The "FLN" was the Algerian Front Libération National, much in the press at the time.

sounded kind of "earthy." "University Rights Movement" was OK, but not "URM." It's a great name, but there's a certain kind of humor floating around in "URM" that isn't appropriate to the Free Speech Movement.[3]

Bob Starobin: The name "FSM" was proposed by Jack Weinberg. Another name was "Students for Civil Liberties." I favored Jack's suggestion because it was something that could be written on the walls, like in Paris or Algiers. The name was adopted by a margin of one vote. The mood of this first meeting, at Art Goldberg's place, was naive and with no conception of the struggle we were entering. Nobody had any idea that this was going to last for very long.[4]

During this meeting, the Executive Committee concept was created, and when the committee was at last assembled on the eighth, it consisted of the suspended students and representatives of all the involved campus political organizations; at times, it had more than fifty people active in it. Becoming more important later on, the graduate students also elected representatives to the Executive Committee, many of whom went on to organize the Graduate Coordinating Council (GCC) which, in turn, organized the campuswide strike after students were arrested in Sproul Hall in December.* Recognizing that not all or even most of the students participating in the FSM were affiliated with established political organizations, a group of Independents met at Saint Mark's, and elected seven delegates to the Executive Committee. The meeting was so crowded that people were actually hanging from, and sitting on, the rafters.

Brian Shannon: At the Independents' meeting, a lot of spirit was shown, and new people were elected out of that meeting. Katie Coleman was

---

*Delegates elected were Robert Kauffman, Robert Starobin, Robert Richheimer, Myra Jehlin and Charles Vars. Alternates elected were Brian Mulloney and Suzanne Goldberg. Stephan Weissman served as GCC chairman. Subsequently, a graduate representative was put on the FSM Steering Committee (Suzanne Goldberg), and in November, when GCC representation in the FSM was expanded, Stephan Weissman and Michael Abramovitch were elected delegates and George Batzli and Bob Wyman alternates. Weissman also served on the FSM Steering Committee. Actually, there were more than this number of graduates on the FSM Executive and Steering Committees, since the political and social action groups and the religious groups often sent graduate representatives to the FSM. Other graduates, such as Michael Rossman and Benson Brown, were co-opted to the Steering Committee (Robert Starobin, "Graduate Students and the Free Speech Movement," *Graduate Student Journal*, Spring 1965, 25).

elected as a representative, as were David Kolodny, Betty Linsky and Ron Anastasi, none of whom had previously been involved in campus politics. Dusty Miller and Julie Blake were new too. From then on, it should have been their responsibility to call meetings of the Independents and explain what was going on. They did this once or twice, but never really took that as their responsibility. They acted like they represented six or seven hundred people, but really they represented nobody but themselves. After they were elected, who were they? Just individuals.[5]

Giving the large and slow-moving Executive Committee direction, and empowered to make rapid decisions, was the Steering Committee. The Steering Committee was elected by the Executive Committee. The people who were initially selected for the Steering Committee were those who had been in on the negotiations and had proved themselves capable of leadership. Though there was an effort to include a broader sampling of campus activists, these people didn't work out. Jack Weinberg, Art Goldberg and his sister Jackie, Mario Savio, and a few real heavies from among the established campus politicos provided the effective core. Bettina Aptheker, Michael Rossman, Sidney Stapleton (a member of the Young Socialist Alliance and suspended student Beth Stapleton's husband), Dusty Miller, Suzanne Goldberg (a graduate student in philosophy), Benson Brown, Steve Weissman, Ron Anastasi, Martin Roysher and Mona Hutchin were all members at one time or another.* The Steering Committee waxed and waned throughout the FSM, generally having around a dozen active members, of whom only a few really ran the show: Jack, Mario, Bettina and later Steve Weissman. The Steering Committee was to be responsible for negotiations in the administration–faculty–student Campus Committee on Political Activity (CCPA) and to select the negotiators.

Most of the wrangling resulted from the preexisting conflict between SLATE and CORE. Realizing that CORE was getting control, members of the Young People's Socialist League seemed to want much more than one club, one vote; they wanted representation on a membership basis, which would have given SLATE total control. This was such an obvious

---

*The conservative campus organizations, such as the University Society of Individuals, the Young Republicans and Cal Students for Goldwater, left the United Front after October 2, though they rejoined the FSM after the faction fight that preceded the resumption of confrontational tactics on November 9. This was when Mona Hutchin, who had been active in the United Front, became a member of the Steering Committee. Though she spoke only rarely and frequently slept or did homework, outside of meetings she was quite active and vocal.

ploy that it failed, leaving the more militant faction in control. With the objections that the moderate element was insufficiently represented, Jackie Goldberg and Dick Roman were initially included, but soon either were edged out or resigned. Except for Bettina Aptheker, who was generally perceived as a reasonable if not actually moderate influence on the Steering Committee, this lack of moderate representation created considerable friction, and later nearly led to a split in the FSM.

Mario Savio: There was a power play between the SLATE people and the new people. There had been a demonstration over this Negro student who was not allowed to be an escort in the beauty contest, and Art seemed to be prominent in that.* I felt a bit of awe. When I came back from Mississippi, and saw how he conducted himself, I came to feel that he was often very well intentioned, but wasn't equal to the situation.

By the end of the first sit-in, already there had occurred a shift away from the SLATE leadership; Art and Sandor and Jackie. The two people who most began to dominate were me and Jack [Weinberg].

Jack has a consummate talent for determining what the tactical possibilities in any given situation are, enumerating and analyzing them, and deciding what to do next and why. Sometimes he overdoes it.

I was good at public presentation. I had the ability to put visceral reactions into words. The ability to say the way a large number of people were feeling, but no one had yet said they were feeling. Maybe the best example of this was on September 30. We all marched into Sproul Hall, and there we were, just a glob of people there in Sproul Hall. And there was Dean Williams at the other end of the hall. Just Dean Williams and this glob of people. So I just started talking for all these people across the hall. It was an emotionally tight scene, and there was no formal legitimacy for my talking, but it was and continued to be clear that what other people were feeling, I was expressing. This kind of ability I had went hand in hand with a great distaste for detail and organizational matters.

Bettina [Aptheker] played an extremely important role, and—press reports notwithstanding—bearing as far as I can determine no relation

*In fall of 1963 "a storm broke over a racial incident involving University participation in an annual football festival sponsored by Berkeley's Junior Chamber of Commerce. Lynn Sims, a Negro student who was vice president of the junior class at U.C., had been chosen to escort one of the girls competing in the queen contest that was part of the festival. The JayCees, however, requested Sims not to escort her. The University launched an investigation, the JayCees apologized, but the University withdrew from the festival. With that, the JayCees withdrew from the festival themselves, and it was scheduled elsewhere for the '64 football season" (Heirich and Kaplan, 30).

to her ideological connections.* A very spirited, effective, pragmatic and *balanced* approach to politics. Both Jack and I tend to be unbalanced. Better than anyone else, she combined these two poles. Better than anyone I know she is able to keep a large number of involvements going at once, and well organized.[6]

Jackie Goldberg: The friction between Mario and my brother grew up a little later. All of us were doing pretty well together until October 2. On Saturday afternoon at Art's place, we'd come together to form an organization to include nonpolitical people.

Dusty Miller was urging a nonpolitical involvement. He had become more important since his talking on top of the car. We got around to the idea of taking two votes from each group for the Executive Committee, and some sort of organization for the nonpolitical people, and that the Executive Committee would nominate the Steering Committee. I wasn't there during this part. I wasn't there when Mario made his first attack. I had been nominated, and he said after I'd been nominated that I had been trying to ingratiate myself with Dr. Kerr during the negotiations and that I couldn't be trusted. At which time my brother probably chose him off to fight—but everybody calmed down and I arrived, and Sandor withdrew from the running to support me. He said that it was mostly to keep Art, because Art probably would have been elected. I may not have [been], but if I hadn't been after what Mario said, then Art probably would have withdrawn. So I was elected, with Art, Mario, Jack, Bettina, Brian Turner and Sid Stapleton.

Spider no. 1, page 15, says what a Steering Committee meeting was like.† "I walked in the room. It was obvious from the stench that they'd been at it for hours. The discussion was an important one; sweat was streaming from every pore. I exchanged nods with everyone and instantly began sweating to show my solidarity. The fight was raging; it seemed we had come to the end of our rope. There'd always been an answer before, why not now. Whiner stood up and began to explain the historical necessity of action, and of course everyone immediately knew he was correct. He was our brilliant tactician he oughta know alright. Then I spoke out; I pointed out that there was an answer to the question that could be found by careful analysis. Happily I sat down and the gang nodded approval of what I had said. Savior stood up. The room fell

---

*Bettina was the daughter of Herbert Aptheker, CPUSA theoretician, and herself a member of the Communist party.

†*Spider* was a campus literary magazine first published in March 1965 by Jackie

and seven others. In this interview with Marston Schultz on July 27, 1965, she is reading from her own satirical article in the first number of the magazine.

silent. Sweat poured more freely now in anticipation. Savior said, 'Democracy is good, you know, but it must be carefully guided to ensure the correct democracy.' I sat thinking, 'How does he always know the right thing to say, it's remarkable.' And then some people have got it and others don't and he does. The discussion continued until we ran out of cigarettes; then instinctively we knew where to go, what we needed. We knew it because a sign had come. A sign so obvious that no one could miss it. A sign that not even the ignorant and uninformed masses could miss. A sign that had to appeal to everybody's sense of humanity. A creeping, crawling, screaming sign, it was the sign of sleep. We were all but dead on our feet, and because of all this the solution must come now it always had done so before. Whiner stood up, the flow of his sweat ceased, he groaned moaned and laughed, and then he said, 'We need walkie-talkies.' "

And that's the way a Steering Committee meeting was. We spent hours and hours and hours and hours and hours telling each other all of the things that could go right or wrong with any single plan that we had. A plan for every complete contingency until we were so exhausted that we couldn't go on anymore and then we made decisions like (*snaps fingers*) that. Just before everybody passed out. Or left.

The decisions were most often based on what could have been decided in the first hour we were there. But unfortunately we were all much too long-winded; let's put it this way: it is *impossible* to decide all of the things that could possibly happen, and to make an alternative plan for each one of them. You just can't plan like that. But we tried to. Of course there were arguments: long arguments. Vehement arguments. Disagreements. Very often, blocs started to set up. Mario and Jack very often with others coming in and going out. My brother didn't attend most of the Steering Committee meetings at first. Brian and Dusty and I very often were on one side, and Mario and Jack and Sid were on the other.

Sherry Stevens was the FSM secretary. Suzanne [Goldberg] first appeared as a secretary at the Steering Committee meetings and then sometimes Suzanne would just come with Jack. Suzanne was elected because she was a graduate, and because the graduates needed [a representative]. The rumor was that she got there because of Jack, but it turns out that none of the graduates had any time except her and so she got there by default.[7]

Brian Shannon: I began chairing the meeting—did a pretty good job of chairing it, despite my political bias—and then we had the idea of the Independents' meeting, and I chaired that.

There was a vote, and we chose the Steering Committee. A number

MICHAEL ROSSMAN.
PHOTO BY WALTER TSCHINKEL.

of names were suggested and there was a vote of the whole body. It turned out that the most radical people were most of the people on the Steering Committee, with the exception maybe of Jackie Goldberg. Steve Roman was elected and then resigned—probably because there weren't more people like himself on the committee. Roman didn't play any positive role at the time.

On the Sunday [October 4] Steering Committee meeting tempers got very bad—Mario stalked out at one point, and Jack made a very undiplomatic speech and denounced Jackie Goldberg, with a very strong attack on the Democratic party, on the CDC [California Democratic Council]—which hadn't done anything in this big fight—on Governor Brown, President Johnson. Saying he didn't want her on the Steering Committee. Before the elections he'd stated that he didn't want her elected, and she was elected anyhow, and afterwards he attacked her. Jackie played a big role at the beginning, and thought she was running it—matter of fact that's the impression that I had—and had all the leadership ability, but was very quickly nowhere. Many people on the hill thought she was a leader, and the press thought she was a leader, and the fact that the administration cited her as one of the four probably indicates that they thought she was still a leader, too, though it's possible that they cited her merely to be consistent, because they were citing for events that happened before the FSM was even formed. The administration always wanted to keep the appearance of legality.

Once they had the Steering Committee, they should have selected a negotiating committee, and they could have put a couple of these liberals on the negotiating committee with themselves. After all, that's what these people wanted to be on anyway—they didn't care about the Steering Committee, they wanted to be on the negotiating committee, which gave them more prestige in the eyes of the campus. Jo Freeman was one of those people, for instance. What the Steering Committee did was turn *itself* into the negotiating committee, which meant that the hard organizational work of building the FSM was not done.[8]

Jack Weinberg: Art and Jackie had been the people who had talked with deans, and Jackie was on more friendly terms with Dean Towle. Mario was

SID STAPLETON. PHOTO BY STEVE MARCUS.

very bitter, for some reason, about the manner in which Jackie was functioning in the negotiations with Clark Kerr. When Jackie's name came up for nomination to the Steering Committee, he spoke against the way she was negotiating, and in a rather insulting way. After which Art got up, absolutely furiously defending his sister, and things got very messy. Sandor Fuchs of the SLATE people was nominated instead of Art, but declined the nomination. Jackie was nominated and she and Art were both elected, but by then there was a lot of bitterness. Mario's attack was based on real political considerations—he felt she was very conciliatory and weak as a negotiator—but he lacked tact. This problem re-emerged later in a much more bitter way.[9]

The "participatory democracy" demanded of the evening meetings of both the Executive and Steering Committees meant that they went on for hours and hours; the meetings were not closed, and were often crowded with vociferous observers. People slept, did their homework, went out for dinner and came back again, but it was generally agreed that no decision could be arrived at except by consensus, so it was necessary that everyone understand and agree with everything before the group committed itself to words or deeds. The first meeting of what became the FSM, for example, lasted one full week.

Mona Hutchin: I went to a lot of meetings, and they were all pretty much alike. The Steering Committee meetings left me with a feeling of in-

SUZANNE GOLDBERG.
PHOTO BY MICHAEL ROSSMAN.

credible annoyance: the fact that the meetings were interminable (the meeting on the Sunday after the Regents march went on for twenty-one hours with a break for dinner). You could tell from the very beginning that there was something that had to be discussed, and I knew what everybody was going to say about it and sure enough they'd go through the same script and they'd have the same fights night after night after night, hour after hour after hour, and it would usually be resolved in approximately the same fashion.   Psychodrama and soul searching, and Michael Rossman and his long, long lectures on morality. Bettina very practical and down to earth. The militant faction and their "Let's take the most militant course of action no matter what it is and no matter what it's going to do." And Steve Weissman sort of wavering back and forth, trying to look like a revolutionary intellectual. Jack sitting and twisting his hair,* and announcing that we couldn't rely on anybody and that we'd get sold out if we tried to make any kind of overtures toward the faculty and only militant action would get us anywhere because that's all that had got us anywhere in the past and that's all that would get us anywhere in the future and we were going to build a great new student movement and how can we get some civil rights people to speak at our rallies. Mario was about the same only on a higher plane. Jack was less an intellectual and more of a person who knows what he wants and goes out and gets it in the most militant way possible, while Mario was interspersing his militancy with vague ideals and intellectual refer-

---

*FSM participant Janis Zimdars describes Jack as "twisting his hair as the intensity of conversation increased until, by the end of a meeting, he looked like a Topsy doll" (personal correspondence, 7 May 1991).

ences. Suzanne was always of the "Let's do the most militant thing possible because everybody else will sell us out if we don't and furthermore the revolution is coming and we're going to be the vanguard." Art Goldberg was so well-meaning. It wasn't a question of expediency with him, or attachment to some sort of vague ideals. He always was talking about the people involved, he was always worried about them: "What about the kids who are going to do this, we don't want them to get hurt, or get disil-

JACK WEINBERG AND RON ANASTASI.
PHOTOGRAPHER UNKNOWN.

lusioned. We don't want to do anything that would be bad for them." In that sense you might say that he was naive, especially compared with all of those schemers and plotters around him. Mostly it was a question of Art Goldberg versus the Steering Committee. He wasn't as militant as the rest of them. He's so bungling—always wandering into the middle of things or not showing up. Art was always bringing things to a very personal level, and the rest of them depersonalized everything. They looked at it as goals and militancy and what we want and things to do, and I think that they got a little bit annoyed with his always saying, "Well, maybe we shouldn't do this, maybe it isn't the best thing to do."

The feeling in general was "Oh boy! We're building a great student movement and soon students will rise all over the world realizing that they have nothing to lose but their administrations." There was a feeling of unreality about it. All of these people sitting in a little room cut off from the world for twelve hours at a time discussing things to the point where they really lost all of their meaning. Off in the clouds somewhere; instead of Plato building the ideal society, all of these people were building the ideal revolution without paying any attention to what was going on and what kind of support they could get. I felt like they were sitting in a glass tank and I was watching them. I never got a feeling of belonging. I could talk if I wanted to, and they would listen, but they

STEVE WEISSMAN. PHOTOGRAPHER UNKNOWN.

wouldn't hear what I had to say. So I didn't talk. I kept on going because I wanted to see what was happening. Probably this was as close to a search for abstract knowledge as I've ever done. I wanted to understand. How often does one get a chance to really witness something like this?

I felt that what we were doing was important, and it meant a lot to me, and it bothered me that they were looking at it from such a detached, unrealistic point of view. I got the feeling that something tremendous was just *happening*, and though we were leading it to a certain extent, the resentment at the administration had been there before the beginning of the year. All this tremendous resentment was coming out into the open. People who had felt stifled for a long time and who were tired of standing in long lines and being handed green, pink and orange forms for everything [they] wanted to do and having to go through all this crap every time [they] wanted to get something done were coming out. There wasn't any turning back.[10]

Andy Wells: Jack Weinberg was the ultimate weapon in tactics. Mario was a tactician and the Movement philosopher; he was able to pick out with incredible accuracy the various holes in certain documents. Suzanne spoke well when she was with a small group of people, but when she got in the Steering Committee she was sort of eclipsed by Jack. She didn't speak much at all, and when she did speak it was usually a reiteration of what Jack said. Bettina was a very forceful speaker, very clear thinker. She never presented a particularly hard line; she was always one for taking various proposals and clearing up difficulties with each one. She had a mind for organizing; she knew where we were in a particular meeting. She would be able to say, "Here's where we've gotten so far." Anastasi was the workhorse. He just got things done. Rossman spent a lot of time talking about the moral force that we all had: "This has been

going on for eight years . . . I'm just sick of this (sigh)." Rossman
would sigh his way through most meetings. But he added a certain fla-
vor of rightness to the cause. Weissman was a parliamentarian. Weissman was SDS and a radical from the beginning; he was willing to shove
and push every chance he got. He knew how to handle a meeting, he
was always able to cut off debate at an appropriate moment. He knew
what he wanted and was generally able to chair a meeting so that he got
it. Mona Hutchin never said a word. I never could figure her out, I never
could quite believe it: she never said anything at all. She almost always
chose a corner in the Steering Committee meeting room and quietly
went to sleep. She was very tired most of the time.[11]

Jack struck me as the only sensible person in the whole group. I more
or less fell under his political aegis, and in all matters voted just as he did
and assiduously followed his lead. Since I had no political savvy, and
meetings bored me to tears, I turned my enthusiasm to a variety of
things that seemed real and useful, and that I could actually do. I understood that I was defending the First Amendment, and that I was having
a wonderful time, but not much more.

On Monday, October 5, I had a telephone conversation with my
boss at the Institute of Governmental Studies library, where I was a
page. She tried every way she could short of actual fraud to keep me on
the payroll, but I would have none of it. I was free and intended to stay
that way, and anyhow I didn't think that I would have time to do anything but fight the administration.

PETER PASKIN, ART GOLDBERG, BETTINA APTHEKER AND DEWARD HASTINGS IN FRONT
OF SPROUL HALL, DECEMBER 1964. PHOTO BY DAVID LINN.

HELLO, CENTRAL

DURING FRIDAY'S DEMONSTRATION, Tom Weller had volunteered his telephone number and apartment as a clearinghouse, so those who had participated in the demonstration could get hold of each other, not reflecting that his new roommate, Steve Memering, might want to have a say in the matter. When Steve got home, it was to a house filled with excited, jabbering demonstrators; the phone was ringing off the hook, and his house was, in short, no longer his home. Not unreasonably, Steve pitched a fit. The number was supposed to be secret, or at least not common knowledge, but on Saturday we discovered that someone had posted it on the main display screen in Wheeler Auditorium for two hours. *Then* we found, to our horror, that the number was on a unit account, not an unlimited account, which meant that every outgoing call was costing about ten cents. So we abandoned both the number and Tom's apartment.

Between the afternoon and evening meetings on Sunday, October 4, Sandor Fuchs and I were together at Art Goldberg's apartment, where we hatched the idea of forming a central communications bureau. Deward Hastings agreed to let us use his apartment up in the hills above campus, and before the dust had settled around Tom's destroyed telephone number, I hiked up to Deward's place and set up shop. I had conceived an elegant system: Our big problem was that nobody knew where anybody else was, and communications were impossible. So I put the twenty or so main people on a staggered list, and told them that they were supposed to call me every half hour and tell me where they were. The idea was that somebody would be calling me every five minutes, and I would always know where everybody was. This did not work. But I finally got through to them the importance of everybody knowing where everybody else was, and gradually, after about two days' service, the place really was running like a Swiss watch, and I knew where almost everybody was almost all of the time. Whenever anybody would

THE AUTHOR AT CENTRAL, EARLY OCTOBER,
1964. PHOTOGRAPHER UNKNOWN.

call, I'd ask, "Where's everybody?" and they'd tell me where everybody had last been seen or heard of. So pretty soon somebody would call and ask the whereabouts of Mario and I'd say, "Two minutes ago he was walking down Telegraph toward Pepi's." And they'd call up again, "Found him, and Jack is on his way to Bettina's." I was gradually getting to know all these people. By the end of the FSM I knew two or three thousand people, either on sight, by name or as a nodding acquaintance.

More people pitched in, and we soon developed a small staff. Tom Weller helped, Peter Paskin and his girlfriend helped, Renée Melody, Larry Marks and Deward Hastings did a little and then Marilyn Noble came onto the scene. Marilyn Noble ran around doing quite a bit of the shit work that I didn't want to do. She answered the phones and cooked food and bought groceries and did laundry. I was there at Central for about two weeks, and when it was running well enough without me, I left and started doing other things. I became commissar in charge of You-Name-It-I-Can-Get-It-For-You.

Then Deward's neighbors started making a fuss about all the twenty-four-hour traffic disturbing their quiet hillside homes and he kicked us all out, which was OK because the place was too small and too far away from the action. Rosemary Feitis offered her house on Panoramic, but it was even farther away and Rosemary and Marilyn Noble were engaged in a bare-knuckle bout anyway, so we declined her offer and moved Central down from the hill, to Mario's apartment at 2536 College, and set it up again. We kept Deward's telephone number and had it switched to Mario's place. Though 848-2930 remained under Deward's name, everybody, including the telephone company, knew that it was the FSM's.

This more public location also made it convenient for all the crackpots who sent us hate mail, as well as for the poor soul who left a note on the garbage can asking that the trash not be picked up so that the fire department would have an excuse to close us down.*

I got a lot more workers, a lot more regular staff and more telephones. In two weeks the whole works was running smoothly, and again I gave up direct control. We ate there, many of the leaflets were written there, some of the work, planning sessions and meetings went on there. The Central staff ate supper at Kathleen Whitney's for a while, until Marilyn Noble took over the housekeeping tasks, when Central became a boarding house for many of the people who were doing so much of the work that they weren't living at home anymore. Jack Weinberg lived there, Mario lived there—of course it was his house—I lived there, quite a few other people lived there. After a month Central boiled down to a steady crew who both lived and worked there day and night, and did an admirable job, considering the general level of anarchy. The core Central staff became Marilyn Noble, Sam Bader, Sam Slatkin, Donald Dean, Kitty Piper, Wendy Dannette, Shirley Dietrich, Bob Mundy and John Sutake.

Marilyn Noble had been there by the police car on October 2, and she stayed to clean up afterward. Her master's thesis in sociology was on student movements in the United States, and she'd come to Berkeley to complete her studies. She latched onto Mario at the earliest moment, deciding that he needed a mother. She defined herself as the house-mother for Central, and saw herself as specifically defending Mario from the madding crowd—giving him some space. Mario was somewhat bemused at this. She annoyed the sand out of me—I was contemptuous and exceedingly rude to her (though in mitigation I must say that, without discrimination, I was rude to almost everyone), but she ignored my bad manners. Much of her own behavior was overlooked because she was both genuinely useful and actually pumping money into Central. She bought food and to some extent took on the responsibility of making and serving it to the people that worked there. She was always at Central, and fancied herself as being in charge of it, though in fact was most of the time under foot.

Though many things went on there, Central's primary responsibilities were internal communications: to know where people were, and

---

*"Please don't take *any* garbage. The fire department *needs* an excuse to close down this communist sponsored, pinko-oriented, slack jawed, rabble-rousing, unpatriotic, dribble-spouting, root-gnawing, malodorous, *mafia* of overprivileged, underbrained, bleeding-hearted megalomaniacs" (anonymous note quoted in Rorabaugh, 26).

call them together for meetings, and to convey messages from one party to another.

Sam Slatkin: Central was one of the most amazing things I've ever seen. It was the workhorse and backbone of the whole thing. Central was what did most of the jobs that had to be done. We had myself and John Sutake and Don Dean and for a while Bob Mundy working there twenty-four hours a day. Periodically we had others working there full-time, as well as streams of helpers for an hour or two here and there—between classes or whatever they were doing. What we did was recruit people for various jobs that had to be done. Seems to me what took up most of the time was making phone calls. We had lists of everybody who had cars, and everybody who had telephones and was willing to do phoning, and everybody that had something that we'd be likely to need, like the ability to type, and when we needed something we would just call down these lists until we got somebody who would do it. We worked out a force of people that generally did, and we worked them to death, too. Central was terribly hectic because there were so many things going on: aside from all this telephoning, we had to make sure that the leaflet was getting printed up properly, and make sure that we had leafleters to hand it out, and we had to get the sound equipment down to campus for the noon rallies, and then there was the handling for a while of press relations—before Press Central was set up. All the incoming telephone calls came here, from the press and everybody. We kept files, as good as we could—all the leaflets, newspaper clippings—we had a pretty complete morgue as I remember. We had a kitchen staff of sorts that fed us and kept us alive. We had Marilyn Noble—when she was there—who coordinated the whole thing and at the same time managed to make it pretty damn hectic. The kitchen was also used for ironing and mending clothes and late-night meetings. Mario and Suzanne sat down late one night and wrote a leaflet in the kitchen.

One of the most important things we did was get people together for meetings. There was often contact with faculty going on there. People tried to handle everything from this office.

We had two phones—at the end we got three. The third was supposedly a "hot line" between Central and Nexus, and supposedly *nobody* was supposed to know the number so it could be kept free for that purpose.* It worked for a while, but there were all sorts of problems with

---

*Located in the out-of-the-way West Berkeley house of Ed Rosenfeld, Nexus was a late and largely unsuccessful attempt to create a "super Central" to coordinate the activities of the many subsidiary Centrals that had evolved. See the chapter "Happy New Year."

Nexus. We had a couple of typewriters, and no real filing equipment except for wooden crates. There always seemed to be a shortage of something or other.

In the building next door was John Sutake's room, which people slept in and which we used for storage. There was an attic up there—we feared at one point that somebody might ransack Central so we took all the records up there.

The height was just after the arrests [at the Sproul Hall sit-in, December 3]. Activity depended on whether there was a crisis—an obvious crisis that students could see, not just some big meeting. This was when Central operated the best. This was when people came in offering their help. It fluctuated pretty much with the mood of the student body as a whole.

The arrests and the strike [in December] created a hell of a lot of interest. I came in about three or four on Friday morning after getting out of jail, and there were people pouring in—even at this hour of the night—wanting to help. The place was cluttered with people and we had great difficulty getting anything done.

There was one mass phoning on the weekend of the strike. We tried to contact the whole student body—I heard estimates that we contacted twenty to twenty-one thousand. We took our lists of people who had volunteered to do phoning in the past, and we called them up and asked, "Would you be willing to call a couple of pages out of the student directory for us?" We used just about all the manpower we had on that. We had to get people in to call the phoners to get the phoners to get the phoners. We just got a couple of copies of the student directory and ripped them up and passed them out. There was an instructions-to-phoners sheet, with a very specific wording that was to be followed. Something like, "How sympathetic are you to the sit-ins? What is your reaction to the arrests? What is your reaction to the strike? Would you cross a picket line?" There were a few basic questions like that. It was a poll to test public opinion; of course the wording was very carefully worked out to present the FSM in a favorable light. But there were no out-and-out requests for support. There may have been some question about, "Would you help us, have you ever participated and would you consider participating in the future?" But this was really to get a sampling of what people were thinking.

We had to arrange to get the [arrested] people out of Santa Rita [jail], and we were calling people to bring cars. A few cars had followed the first busses to find out where they were going, and there were rumors that the police had given them trouble. Before I got back to Central there was a lot of work done to get the bail bond together. We tried to compile lists of defendants from lists of arrestees in newspapers and information from people who had been arrested.

Command Central was over on Durant. It was set up after people were in jail. Ron Anastasi and Barry Jablon and Kate Coleman and Karen Spencer were there. This was a much quieter scene. This was where the brain work was going on and the working out of the plans and coordination of the other places. What was going on there was mostly telephone communication with the other Centrals.[1]

As the needs of Central expanded, it budded and more Centrals came into existence: Print Central, Work Central, Communications Central, Strike Central, Press Central, Legal Central; they all just grew. It was always awkward. The only one that ran well, aside from Central Central (as it was called at one point), was Legal Central, which kept track of all the defendants after the arrests of December 3. David Stein was in charge of it for two and a half years, and it's the only one that ran as well as it could have, with almost no hang-ups or personality difficulties.

Beyond telephonic communications, my immediate role was factotum and gofer. I attended all the Steering Committee meetings, which were pretty boring and happened three or four times a day. I'd make my reports, and we'd hash out this and that and decide what was going to happen that day and the next, and the leaflet would get written and off I'd go. Soon I had expanded my efforts to where I had a finger in just about every pie. Print Central was my baby. At the beginning, Jack Weinberg was printing the leaflets, then he trained me how to do it, and I took over. Usually I worked alone, but I would occasionally draft people to help me. There wasn't really any person I could totally trust to be in charge, because it called for being awakened at every conceivable hour of the day or night and working solid until the job was done. I ran off the longer-run leaflets on a fast, fancy Gestetner mimeograph machine located in Ruth and Hal Draper's basement; we paid them a small rental for the use of their machine. Often I also lettered the headline. To prevent confusion of one leaflet with the next, we used a different color of paper every day. Merely printing the leaflet was not enough; as soon as the leaflets were done, I would call for my ride and one or another of the small crew of faithful, self-appointed taxi drivers would drag himself out of bed and give me a lift from Oakland back to the campus. At seven-thirty every weekday morning, a half-dozen dedicated leafleters would be awaiting the daily ration of FSM propaganda, and would share out the five thousand leaflets among themselves, dashing to the four corners of the campus to hand them out to the hordes of eight o'clocks. Peter Israel—slight, ginger-bearded, chipper—was there every day. Patti Iiyama and her inseparable companion Stephanie Coontz set up shop at Sather Gate each weekday morning, one on either side passing out leaflets as fast as they could. Getting the FSM line out was not a problem: people snatched them from the hands of the pamphleteers. The art of distributing them was to keep enough in reserve so that there would be some available for the next wave of students at nine. They were always all gone by ten. If something big was in the offing, I

PRESS CENTRAL. PHOTOGRAPHER UNKNOWN.

would print ten thousand. Leaflets *never* ended up in the trash or on the ground. This was exciting war news, to be read and passed along until ragged and illegible.

Dunbar Aitkins, publisher of the student science journal *Particle*, had revived an old Multilith 2066 offset press that had been bought in the early 1960s to print the student journal *Root and Branch*.* On this he and Deward Hastings managed occasionally to get out the FSM *Newsletter*, each issue of which gave a four-page analysis of the FSM position on an important topic.

Shorter-run leaflets and other mimeographed communications were run off at all hours at Press Central, located in Tom Irwin's basement on Milvia. Since it was part of a house, to avoid disturbing the residents we ordinarily entered and left through the basement windows.

Tom Irwin ran the press liaison with the help of a couple of other people, but mostly single-handedly, throughout the entirety of the FSM. It was a relatively miserable task because no one knew or cared what he was doing, and he was always being neglected. People wouldn't tell him what was going on, and he would have to rely more or less on leaflets and bits and pieces of information. He was always screaming for more

---

Root and Branch, a Radical Quarterly, was founded by Phil Roos, Robert Scheer, Maurice Zeitlin and David Horowitz, *inter alia*. The first issue came out in the winter of 1962. Editorial board: Richard Currier, Gerald Dworkin, Victor Garlin, Cyril Wolfe Gonick, David Horowitz, Irving L. Markovitz, Ruth Markovitz, Manuel Nestle, Serena Turan Scheer, Robert Scheer, Robert Starobin, Brian Van Arkadie, Maurice Zeitlin. Production manager, Carl Blumstein.

information. His job was all responsibility and very little thanks or praise. He was never in the public eye, he missed almost everything by being in his basement all the time. But without him we would have had an even more violently distorted view coming from the press. The press did report our releases, and whenever we were going to do something we'd prime the press for it via Tom.

Tom Weller: One night I wandered into Press Central to see if they needed any help. The two guys there must have been on a long shift without food, sleep, or whatever; they looked at me like I was an angel from heaven.

"Yeah—phone this press release into the city desk at all the papers," one guy said. Then he stuck a piece of paper into my hand and they both instantly vanished before I could ask any questions.

I rummaged around the office awhile and found the phone numbers.

"City desk," barked the guy who answered the phone. Just from his voice, I could see this tough old guy with a cigar clenched in his teeth and a battered fedora jammed onto his head, pounding an old upright typewriter and slugging whiskey from the bottle. I would have bet you a million dollars that's what he looked like.

"Uh, I've got a press release from the FSM that I'm supposed to call in . . ." I ventured.

"How many words?" he growled, cutting me off.

I stared blankly at the piece of paper. No one had ever asked me for an impromptu word count before. "Gee, uh, I don't know. Uh . . . maybe two or three hun—"

"Doesn't anybody there know how to write a goddamn press release?" he interrupted. "OK, give it to me."

I read it to him and heard keys banging on his end. "Do you want to read that back?" I asked. I think it was the wrong thing to ask a city desk reporter.

"No," he barked, and slammed down the phone.

After I'd done it a few more times, I felt like I'd learned a trade.[2]

Lee Felsenstein: I came to Berkeley from Philadelphia. I had read in a book called *True Bohemia* about the beatniks in San Francisco, and I'd heard some tape recordings of "songs of social significance"; the thrilling thing was that at the end of these subversive songs, on came an ID from KPFA. These songs had actually been *broadcast* on the air! Then I saw a presentation of *Operation Abolition. I* wanted to be *there.* I applied to Cal, and was accepted. I took a train out here and picketed Madame Nhu in 1963, and got into the work-study program after my freshman

year.* I went to work for
NASA at Edwards Air
Force Base, where they
finally got around to processing my security clearance. They kept asking
me, "Do you know any
Communists?" and I said,
"No." They finally told
me, "Well, your *parents*
are Communists!" I
swear the personnel offi-
cer, Richard Stratman,
was drunk at this point—
he probably had to be. A
crushing blow, because I

LEE FELSENSTEIN.
PHOTO BY HOWARD HARAWITZ.

actually had absorbed the anti-Communist indoctrination that kids got.
I went out in the hall and called my dad and asked him, "Are you or
aren't you?" And he said, "I don't want to talk about it right now."

There I was looking out the window at the Mojave Desert, into
which I was about to be cast. I took the train back to Berkeley, and arrived on the sixteenth of October.

I had been sent into exile with the understanding that if I kept my
nose clean for a couple of years I would have no trouble getting back
in. I read the FSM pamphlets and leaflets and realized, "Yeah. These guys
are right." Within ten days I decided that I was going to go with the
FSM. I knew that the people that had exiled me were always watching;
they would know what I did. I wasn't going to be able to do anything
secret. Some people took less time to make the decision—how many
people's lives were changed the same way? God! Impossible to estimate!
It almost makes me wish you could create these events to order. But you
can't.

I sniffed around, and after the existential work of deciding to get into
this uproar found out where I could go to be of help. I had no student

---

*Madame Nhu (Ngo Dinh Nhu), the
black-clad "Dragon Lady," was the sister-
in-law of Ngo Dinh Diem, the South
Vietnamese premier. She was the wife of
Nguyen Cao Ky, "the Flying Cowboy,"
head of the South Vietnamese Air Force
and later prime minister. After her
brother-in-law's death in 1963, Madame
Nhu spoke all over the United States,
trying to drum up support for her falter-
ing government. Her appearances were
the occasion of loud protest from those
who were aware of American involvement in Vietnam, though at this time
most Americans did not know that Vietnam existed, let alone that we were busy
getting into a war there.

duties—lucky me—I was still on the cooperative work-study program in engineering, and only had to work eight hours a day; no homework. I was then defining myself as an audio man—I had this big, good tape recorder—so I figured, let's turn my massive technological skills to use. So I inquired, and somebody said, "Go down to Press Central." There was an A. B. Dick Model 91 mimeo in the basement of 2413 Milvia—Press Central. I decided I could use the recorder to make audio press releases—that came to nothing. We did make one tape—I really didn't know anything about editing tape at all, so you had this five-minute spiel, a quote from Mario, that I wound up dropping in the slot of a couple of TV stations. So that all came to naught, but at least it introduced me to the place. I had learned in sixth grade to run a mimeo machine. I was involved in taking care of the old Barringer sound equipment—the stuff that was stashed at 2538 Durant. Barringer Sound was run by this old Red: we were renting the equipment first by the day, and then by the week and then by the month. We always kept it in that basement hiding place. Security was tight.

The Freedom Singers came to town, to sing on Sproul steps. It was a group, but we only had one microphone. So I exercised my technical prerogatives by going to a surplus store and getting a little gray crinkle metal box, and I took the microphone cord and cut it, and put it through the box, and wired up a fitting for another microphone. So we were able to run a little tiny hand-held crystal microphone along with the other microphone. I wrote on the box, around the microphone connector, "Manufactured through the Good Offices of the FSM Engineering Department."

This box was on the microphone and the sound equipment that went into Sproul Hall during the [December] sit-in, and was seized by the cops. During the trial, there was a point at which we all were sitting there in the Veterans' Building; the prosecutor and [FSM attorney Mal] Burnstein were sparring, and when he referred to us as seven-hundred-odd individuals, Burnstein objected to being called "odd."

The prosecutor was attempting to prove that this was a "military-style operation." They had a policeman on the stand, and asked, "What did you find there?"

"I found this amplifier system."

"Could you describe what you found on the amplifier system?"

"Well, there was this cable; there was a box with sort of a fitting."

"Could you describe to us what was written on the box?"

I was out in the audience, and *sotto voce* said, "Oh, my God!" to heighten the drama.

He said, "It was something to the effect, 'Manufactured through the Good Offices of the FSM Engineering Department.' "

A tremendous roar of laughter went up, including from the bench. One of the lawyers was on his feet, saying, "The FSM is not on trial here; who's on trial here are seven-hundred-odd individuals." Then Judge Crittenden, still laughing, said, "Mr. Burnstein will object to that," and the whole place just dissolved.

They'd also gotten all exercised about the walkie-talkies we'd had all over the place. The idea that there was a continuous cabal of engineering sorts hanging around was an exaggeration. There was a set of about ten people—I can't think of all their names, but there was me, Deward Hastings, Dunbar Aitkins (sort of), Tom Irwin, Bob Dietrich and Roger Muldavin. Brian Mulloney every now and then was involved in plugging together some wires. The major tasks that we had to contend with were printing and mimeography, and tending the amplifier.

We had defined ourselves, me and this little crowd of techies, as people whose identity was their ability to work with technology. So there was nothing less at stake here than one's self-definition. I had expected or hoped that somebody would tell me what I should do. Sort of like the engineer's prayer, "Use me."* I was hanging around Central, waiting for someone to tell me what to do with all my skills. Then came an incident which directed the rest of my life: Art Goldberg and his usual retinue came into the office all excited, shouting that the campus had been surrounded by cops. Led by the hysteric Marilyn Noble, suddenly everyone turned to me and said, "Quick! Make us a police radio!" Now, I knew what they meant—back in 1939 the police band was just above the broadcast AM band, and you would be able, just by twisting some screws in the radio, to de-tune it so you could get police broadcasts. But those days were long in the past. Now it was up in the 30 to 50 megahertz region, and FM—how do you explain that to these guys? "You don't understand, it takes more time than that, it's more complicated." To which the answer was, all in unison, "Never mind about that, make us a police radio!" At which point, I mentally started a project to make a police radio, which would wind up in a three-tube amplifier at FSM Nexus, which was supposed to be the secret headquarters, but it didn't work out. But I realized in this crystalline moment, that I would never get anywhere by waiting for my intellectual betters to tell me what it was that I should do, because it was me and people like me who put things on the shelf that they would then reach for, and that meant that I was out ahead of them, and I wasn't going to get any advice, because they simply didn't understand the environment in which I was working.

---

*The character Spiegel, in the 1959 Ingmar Bergman film *The Magician*, has the line, "I have prayed just one prayer in my life: 'Use me.'" Bergman's films were de rigueur for all intellectually rebellious university students.

So at the age of nineteen I stopped waiting for orders. The only orders that would make sense to me would be ones that I would give myself—I had to do the work in terms of developing and working with technology *beforehand*, and have things on the shelf, so that when they came running to me saying, "Quick, give us this or that," I would say, "Well, you can't have that, but here's what I've got."

I had a particular view of myself as a member of the "black gang." That's a nautical term for the engine room crew. The despised bunch who, as the name implies, didn't even have features—covered with coal dust and grease. But they made the damn thing run. To me, that was where I belonged; casting myself almost into the role of an object.[3]

We were obsessed by the fear that somehow the police would come and take away our sound equipment. As a result, we had a small flying squad, usually headed by Bob Mundy, and a trifle before noon we'd jump in a car, go down to where the rented microphone, batteries, amplifier and loudspeakers were hidden away in the parking garage of an apartment building near Sproul Hall, load it all in, come up to campus and rush it in, pursued by phantasms. A large group of monitors stood near the sound equipment during each rally, serving double-duty to keep the speaker area clear. Otherwise, the speakers were smushed by the crowd. After the rally, we'd rush it all out and put it back in its secret basement garage. We did this every time.

During the December sit-in we lost five hundred dollars' worth of equipment, some of which we recovered, and some of which we did not recover. We had to pay that all off.

Tom Weller: One day I ended up on the loudspeaker detail. Having wired up the battered old junk, we discovered that the car battery that powered it was stone dead. The news crews from the TV stations were setting up their cameras for the scheduled rally. We asked one of them (I can't remember which station) if they had an extra battery. In those days, the big, clunky 16mm film cameras the TV crews used were run off car batteries, believe it or not.

They said, "Sure," and lent us a battery. By this point the news folks and the FSM people had spent so much time together they were old friends. Besides, if we couldn't get the loudspeaker running, they'd have nothing to film.[4]

I was also in charge of the rally monitors, a group of 100 to 150 students who saw to it that doorways were not blocked, that a fire exit lane was at all times kept open and that any litter was picked up following a sit-in or rally. We couldn't clean up Sproul Hall after the December 2 sit-in, because we were all in jail, and were reproached in the press for leaving a mess, which we felt as a keen injustice, especially since most of it was the numbered sheets of paper that the cops had held up in front of us as we were mugged, which they then threw on the floor.

The fire lanes were an index of our innocence: down the center of each huge crowd of people, stretching from the doors of Sproul Hall to the top of the Student Union steps, was a clear lane about five feet wide and straight as a die. At the biggest rally, where we had something like twelve or fifteen thousand people,

FIRE LANE AT A RALLY.
PHOTO BY LOREN WEAVER.

we still had a beautiful straight aisle running right down the middle. The Berkeley fire marshal had requested it, and we complied faithfully, just in case Sproul Hall caught fire, and the people inside had to get out fast. What a sweet bunch of children we were. We got nasty later.

The monitors were more or less FSM policemen, running around and making sure that people were sitting down so that everybody could see; they also were useful in case of any kind of disturbance. They were well trained and followed orders to perfection. The chain of command was short; it went from me to the monitors, or from the Steering Committee to me and then to the monitors, though it was rare that we even had to tell people what to do, because they understood their duties so thoroughly and the general level of public cooperation was so high.

After a rally was over, late in the afternoon, I made the campus rounds and collected the contribution cans, hopping on a borrowed motorcycle or scooter and toting the hoard of small change and crumpled bills to Gretchen Kittredge's apartment across from the Telegraph Avenue Co-op. Dumping the money out on her kitchen table, we would tot it up in marathon counting bees and enter the day's receipts in the FSM's books. During the trial, Adrienne Thon did some of the books.

MONITOR'S ARM BAND, STENCILED BLACK ON SPRAY-PAINTED FLUORESCENT ORANGE.

There was a period when Lee Goldblatt, daughter of Lou Goldblatt of the longshoremen's union, did similar work, while Legal Central was still at 2431 Dwight at Anya Allister's house—the old YPSL bungalow just below Telegraph.

Each night, after the evening Executive Committee meeting adjourned and the general tone of the next day's sentiment was agreed upon, the elite politicos would hammer out the wording for the new leaflet between midnight and four in the morning. I would sleep until awakened by whoever had typed the stencil (usually Pam Mellin), call for a ride, and get to the basement mimeograph by 4:00 AM. The slightly giddy, mildly nauseated sensation due to extreme lack of sleep was a normal part of my life.

The absolute dependability and unfailing fidelity of the people who had appointed themselves to each task was something that I came to rely on as I did the sun's rising in the east and setting in the west. For everything that needed to be done, small or great, there was a person or group of people who materialized at the exact right moment, saw the job out to the end, and then went back to whatever they had been doing before, only to come back the next day and do it all again: at eleven-thirty the monitors were ready and waiting; at a quarter to twelve I went to Telegraph and Bancroft, and there as sure as Death and Taxes was a small coterie of fellows who went with me to get the sound equipment; the leaflet was always typed up on time; the door to the basement housing the mimeograph machine was always unlocked; my rides were always ready when I needed to go to Oakland and came promptly to take me back to campus, where the leafleters were always hot to get at it before their classes began. Whatever was needed was provided; each person who felt the justice of the Free Speech Movement's goals gave time, money and energy in "good measure, pressed down, and shaken together, and running over."[5]

FREEDOM'S JUST ANOTHER WORD FOR
NOTHING LEFT TO LOSE

As I SAT THERE ON THE FLOOR at the first FSM meeting, listening to incomprehensible arguments about parliamentary procedure and marveling at the political hipness of it all, this really beautiful girl next to me edged her hand over to mine to where they were just touching. I could scarcely believe my good fortune. Was it an accident? Or did she mean it? I responded by edging my hand closer to hers. Soon, while feigning interest in the proceedings, we were passionately holding hands. We left the meeting together to get some refreshments for the group, and on the way back from the store were making out with our hands all over each other, and necking in the doorway of the Christian Science Church. To my delighted astonishment, we ended up in bed that very evening. This was my second introduction to the wonderful world of bold-eyed girls who wanted to do it as much as I wanted to do it. Striking and tall with a show-girl figure, Nina had transparent blue eyes and straight, black, amazingly heavy wirelike hair hanging down to the small of her back. It must have put an unusual strain on her neck. I've never seen anything like it before or since. She had been involved in the civil rights demonstrations at Sheraton-Palace and Auto Row, and was selected by the media as something of a spokeswoman for the students during the days around the squad car.

Coming from L.A., she claimed a considerable sexual background. She did teach me a good deal about technique, mainly through example but also by praising those efforts that pleased her. My impression was that she had a wide but shallow experience, mostly with boys who, like myself, knew damned little besides the rude basics.

Before the Free Speech Movement began, my sexual experience had been limited to one glorious holiday with my high school girlfriend, whose father hated my guts and had late in the summer of 1964 at last succeeded in destroying our love affair. Following hard on the heels of meeting Renée, this new relationship with Nina contained nothing at all of love and everything of lust. What I wanted was sex, and I resolved to

BRIAN TURNER'S MERCEDES. NOTE "FSM"
BUMPER STICKER. PHOTOGRAPHER UNKNOWN.

cut as wide a swath through the ranks of Berkeley's maidenhood as I possibly could. I was at last completely at liberty to do as I pleased, accountable to no one. I had no job, no place to live, no sweetheart, and I had been expelled from school. Perfect.

I spent the next three months in a blur. Though my home base was Central, I stayed some of the time at Rosemary Feitis' house at 498 Panoramic. Rosemary was a wonderful woman; she seemed to me to be amazingly sophisticated and worldly-wise. She was a high-tone New Yorker with a faint New England accent, but not a trace of that classic New York nasal thud so grating on the Western ear. She had Taste. She had Style. She had Class. She seemed to me to be a great deal older than the rest of us—almost *thirty*.

This was when turning thirty was a major disaster. People would have black birthday cakes with black candles and black icing, sing "Happy Birthday" to the dirgelike tune of the "Volga Boatmen" and even go so far as to do away with themselves. Some of this misery can be laid at the feet of Jack Weinberg, whose "Don't trust anyone over thirty" became the watchword of our generation; at least until we turned thirty ourselves.

During the FSM Rosemary cooked for me and washed my clothes, and in later years did indeed become to some degree a surrogate mother or, more realistically, a big sister. Aside from the meals she cooked me, I think I lived off nothing but peanut butter sandwiches and apples, which were always abundant at Central. The occasional plate of turkey dressing at Robbie's when the Steering Committee felt flush padded out the protein.

Rosemary was fond of me the way older women so frequently were: they thought that I was cute, and found my anarchistic behavior amusing. Something in my appearance or personality brought their maternal urges howling to the fore, and they indulged me outrageously, and saw to it that I didn't actually starve or freeze to death, and that my nakedness was decently covered.

I drove her Peugeot like a maniac, filling her neighbors with rage and apprehension. Not only was I a reckless driver, but I had never bothered to get a license. This caught up with me later.

I also made free with Marilyn Noble's black 1962 VW. The fan belt on the car broke once and I seized the engine up; didn't seem to do it any harm. I borrowed it one Saturday evening without telling anyone and went with Renée to San Gregorio Beach, where we spent a cold, uncomfortable but romantic night strolling under the full moon and making love in the back seat. No small accomplishment to do it in a VW without crippling yourself.

I also drove Brian Turner's big black Mercedes from time to time, but it made me nervous. It was noisy, steered like a truck, and stuck out like a pig amongst chickens. I preferred the anonymity of a small foreign car, or a junky American behemoth.

THE FREE SPEECH CONTROVERSY DEBATED ON DORMITORY WINDOWS.
PHOTO BY BILL MENKEN.

WE ARE THE CHILDREN OUR PARENTS WARNED US AGAINST

ONE OF THE MAIN things that motivates youthful activity is sex.* The FSM, following soon after the introduction of the Pill to middle-class American girls, was the beginning of what was for me and many of my comrades in arms a continuous process of vigorous sexual activity.† Not precisely every second of every minute, twenty-four hours a day, because we had a revolution on our hands, but in any off moment people were shucking their old morals along with their clothes, though we behaved with an innocence that seems unbelievable now. The image in my mind's eye is of a big pile of puppies in a basket; clambering all over each other in a fuzzy, polymorphous heap, wide-eyed and eager.

We were little concerned with the possibility of venereal disease. There was not much of it in our social stratum, and what there was could be cured easily and quickly, being mostly nonspecific urethritis, yeast infections and such no-account trash. Syphilis and gonorrhea were quite nearly unheard of in our circle, and neither I nor anyone I knew came up with anything like them, though they began to be a problem by the late 1960s.‡ The real heavyweights, herpes and AIDS, had not been invented yet.

---

*Before the FSM began Clark Kerr remarked, only half in jest, that the ideal university provided "sex for the students, sports for the alumni and parking for the faculty" (Rorabaugh, 12).

†Commissioned by birth control pioneers Margaret Sanger and Katherine Dexter McCormick, an effective birth control pill was developed by 1955. Approved for general prescription in 1960, by 1965 it was used by one American woman in five.

‡Between 1955 and 1958 the incidence of reported syphilis cases reached a low of 4 per 100,000, rising by 1960 to 12 per 100,000 because of a cutback in federal funding for disease control.

Around 1978, when a significant number of women began reporting severe fertility problems, it was belatedly discovered that what had consistently been diagnosed as "nonspecific urethritis or vaginitis" was actually chlamydia, a kissing cousin of the nasty parasite that causes trachoma. If treated in a timely manner with tetracycline, it was easily cured; the problem was that often it exhibited no symptoms.

The Pill was the favored means of contraception, to the near exclusion of other forms of birth control. In the late 1950s and early 1960s contraceptives were not all that easy to come by;* in the Hyde Park areas on campus, where students were free to say whatever they wished, frequent demands were made for "the right to smoke marijuana, to be able to buy contraceptives at the University Bookstore or for other far-out objectives."[1]

I slept with what seemed to me to be a phenomenal number of girls, but—with notable exceptions—recollect them only indistinctly. In this, as in many particulars, I am able to call to mind little beyond the sensation of wild good cheer that pervaded my mostly sleepless existence for that three months.

I have a vague but (only now) humorous recollection of awakening early one morning in a girl's apartment with the sinking feeling that I couldn't for the life of me remember her name, and stealthily going through her purse, looking for her driver's license and hoping that she wouldn't awaken and think I was pilfering.

One night up at Deward's house on the hill, I went to sleep with a girlfriend and woke up in the morning with Mario Savio. The girlfriend had gotten up to do her shift on the phones. Seeing the apparently empty bed, or perhaps too sleepy to inquire or reluctant to awaken the occupant, Mario crept in and sacked out. When I awakened, he and I were entwined in a loving embrace. I looked at him, and he looked at me, and, entirely unembarrassed, I remarked to his startled, unshaven face, "Well, politics makes strange bedfellows!" and was as pleased with the *bon mot* as I have been with anything I've ever said in my life. He hit me, and we went back to sleep. Mario was looking terrible, absolutely ghastly. He was getting thinner and thinner, and he hadn't shaved in days; he was looking wretched. I don't imagine that I was any champion pig either, but I was already so skinny that I doubt I could have lost any more weight, and I hadn't started shaving yet.

---

*Indeed, contraceptives were illegal in many places. Prophylactics were sold "for the prevention of disease only" in most locations, and birth control devices of any kind were available in many states of the union by prescription only, and then for the health of the woman rather than for contraception per se. By this logic, birth control was not often prescribed for single women. Indeed, not until June 7, 1965, in *Griswold*, did the U.S. Supreme Court establish the fundamental right to contraception. Speaking for the court, William O. Douglas said, "The right to privacy is not found in the letter of the Constitution, but in its penumbra."

WHY WE HAD THE BULGE ON THEM

OCTOBER AND NOVEMBER were our allies. The fall weather was hot and dry, and although there was a bit of wet weather around Thanksgiving, the rainy season did not begin in earnest until late December, by which time the show was over. I imagine that if the weather had been unpleasantly wet, or foggy and cold, the FSM would have fizzled out. But it was the administration's bad luck that it was lovely days and nights, right down the line.

Aside from good weather and lots of happy sex, it should not be overlooked that we were winning, hands down, on every count. We had no thought but that what we were doing was absolutely correct. No flicker of doubt troubled the clear pools of our ideology. Our strength was as the strength of ten because our hearts were pure. Not only were we right in our hearts, not only were we having a rip-snorting good time, not only were we fucking our brains out, but we were winning. We were at all points far more than one step ahead of the administration. Everything they did was necessarily in reaction to everything we did; we calling the shots and they scrambling to clean up the mess. Everything they would try to put their fingers on would squish out and disappear; as if they were trying to corral a puddle of mercury, they couldn't actually get their hands on what was happening, and they absolutely did not understand the issues.

Our University president was turning out not to be the mighty Wizard of Oz, but only Professor Marvel: a small, smug, bald, bespectacled nerd living in cloud-cuckoo land, still thinking he was lording it over us when we were actually standing behind him, watching him pulling levers, releasing clouds of hot air and projecting his no-longer-awesome face on a screen. When the poor son of a bitch actually ran into the real world, history blindsided him and his theories left him woefully unprepared. He was a boardroom warrior; when it came to scuffling around in the dirt with the students, he was a wimp. A clever, dangerous wimp, but a wimp nonetheless.

Perhaps his greatest tactical errors were twofold: Most important, the muffled, muddled responses of various bureaucrats threw the entire administration into confusion; they were repeatedly forced to withdraw from positions either because they were obviously untenable or because the president moved in and contradicted positions taken by the chancellor. Kerr's silence and inaccessibility forced deans to make decisions based on policies that they often neither understood nor agreed with, and when these decisions only served to muddy the waters Kerr stepped in and humiliated them by dealing with the students himself. In no time the students dismissed everything said by lower officials as unreliable and subject to change at the whim of the president, and as the president continued to ignore advice and contradict the actions of the chancellor's office, the entire orderly structure of the University's disciplinary administration collapsed.

Secondly, neither Pat Brown nor Clark Kerr quite realized until fairly late in the game that this was a serious proposition. From the outset, they treated us like children, and even when we seemed made of tougher stuff than what they were prepared for, they were doomed by their official, quasi-parental viewpoint to make the cardinal error of any confrontation: underestimating their enemy. Kerr never, at any time, realized that this was not just an exalted panty raid. He never took the students seriously, at all points underestimating their strength, numbers and dedication. Unlike a labor union, we were not out to cut a deal. The techniques that worked so well in management theory did not work at all when one of the parties, in this case the students, did not accept the possibility of defeat, was not going to compromise and was never going to give up.

While the FSM had to win support from the students and the faculty, the administration had to woo just about everybody, and whatever they did to make one party happy made all the others mad as hornets. Kerr needed the voters of the state of California, who were footing the bill; the legislature, which was giving him the money; the alumni, who were coughing up huge chunks of dough (or not) if they were happy with the University (or at least the football team); the governor; the press; the cops; the American Civil Liberties Union; the faculty; and last but not least, the students themselves. We didn't have to do any of that stuff, and could single-mindedly go straight for what we wanted without having to worry about who it might piss off into the indefinite future.

Furthermore, for a loose coalition of college students, we were extraordinarily well organized. Within hours of the breakup of the sit-in around the car, a clearinghouse for information and communication was set up; the first of many similar nodes of the FSM's nervous system, it ran wide open twenty-four hours a day. We, most of the time, knew what the administration had done, was doing, was proposing to do or wanted to do, and could in consequence prepare for it. They had few but the most blatant clues to our plans, did not know who was doing what, did not know who was for or against them, and when they did know that we were going to do something, their behemoth bureaucracy prevented them from doing anything about it. They had weight and reach on us, but we were fast on our feet.

Last, the FSM had an "advantage in personnel over the administration":

As everyone has said, the Movement had leaders and followers who were trained in the techniques of protest, while the administration lacked experience in dealing with sit-ins and other kinds of civil disobedience; but what has been much less commonly remarked is that the FSM simply had more talent than the administration. And why not? At an eminent university, especially one with a vast graduate program, the number of intelligent students had better exceed the number of intelligent bureaucrats.[1]

GOVERNOR OF CALIFORNIA EDMUND G. "PAT" BROWN.
STATE OF CALIFORNIA PHOTOGRAPH.

REACTIONS

BY OCTOBER 4, we had begun hearing from the general community. We had attracted the attention of some real heavy hitters in the area of First Amendment issues, and gained much heart from their good offices. At the instigation of Berkeley attorney and SLATE co-founder Peter Franck, the executive director of the Northern California chapter of the American Civil Liberties Union, Ernest Besig, intervened on the behalf of the eight Berkeley students who had been suspended indefinitely by Chancellor Strong. As it turned out, the charges against the students were not spelled out until almost two weeks after the suspensions and then they failed to specify the rules that had been violated. To have the ACLU beating the drum for us must have had the liberals among the Regents and administration seriously doubting the rectitude of what they were about. The ACLU was right on top of things, and had become interested in the student free speech cause even before the FSM had officially formed. Peter Franck and Ernest Besig had both pointed out that the state constitution said nothing at all about student political and sectarian activity on campus, and on the eighth of October the ACLU officially involved itself with the student cause by representing the suspended students before the committee that reviewed their punishment.

> The ACLU does not share the opinion of the University Administration that the constitutional ban on political and sectarian activity is aimed at students.

> The ACLU's position is that the regulations which the students were alleged to have broken violate their political rights as guaranteed by the first amendment . . . the ACLU will challenge the suspensions as a violation of due process of law.[1]

Important support came from the Executive Committee of the Association of California State College Professors: "Participation in social action, whether it is political or non-political ought not only to be permitted, but actively encouraged, so long as it does not interfere with the regular instructional program."[2] The Inter-Faith Staff Workers and Student Leaders put in a good word for us, too: "We affirm the right of members of the campus community to solicit funds, distribute literature and recruit members for involvement in common action."[3]

A group of graduate students, primarily from the departments of history and economics, circulated two petitions addressed to the administration. The first, signed by some seven hundred teaching assistants and graduates, read:

> We . . . believe: Freedom of speech and expression are both inalienable constitutional rights of students as citizens and a necessary part of the educational process. True freedom of speech requires that students and student organizations be free to promote the causes they support by any peaceful action on or off the campus. Free speech can only thrive in an atmosphere of mutual trust. This atmosphere cannot be sustained when student leaders are suspended for political actions, when force is threatened by one party to negotiations, and when irresponsible statements are made to the press. The Free Speech Movement is composed of responsible students whose goal is to secure for us all the right to freedom of speech and expression on the Berkeley campus. We support this goal and the leaders of the Free Speech Movement, who are working to achieve it.[4]

The second petition was circulated by grads among the faculty. It endorsed the position of the American Association of University Professors—a group which had supported the students' rights to organize political activity—that students should enjoy the same freedom of speech, press and assembly that citizens generally possess, and urged that the faculty should support these freedoms.

Cal Students for Goldwater supported the Regents and wondered why they were so lax in enforcing rules applying to campus political activity. The *Daily Cal* came down firmly on the side of the administration.*

---

*On October 21, 1961, the *Daily Cal's* forthright editorials on HUAC and an editorial supporting the candidacy of SLATE chairman Mike Tigar had prompted a resolution by the Executive Committee of the ASUC to suspend the paper's by-laws. The editorial staff was also given a punitive one-week suspension. The by-laws were changed to give the Executive Committee "final authority with respect to the supervision and direction of [the *Daily Cal's*] affairs, policies, and conduct." In response, the entire editorial board and staff—excepting the business staff—re-

Despite offered assistance, the FSM did not pursue remedies through the courts.

Brian Shannon: There was no test case on the suspensions because we were afraid we'd lose in the lower courts. Going to the courts tends to stop all demonstrations—people think, "You don't have to act, the courts will settle it." During the early period it would have dulled the FSM. Second, even though we were sure we were right on constitutional grounds, it could have been two or three years before it got to the Supreme Court. Finally, you could have a writ of certiorari denied, without any real final resolution.* We didn't know what we were—who were we and what legal rights did we have? You can be legally right, and never even get to court unless you're a genuine party in conflict. We thought that if anybody should bring that case, it should be the student body government. They passed a resolution and said they were going to but never did it. They were the person who actually had a legitimate case as a party in conflict, despite their being set up by the chancellor and all that. Given all those various things, it was not considered worthwhile. It's quicker to get into the courts when you try to do what you want to do, and become a legitimate party to the case—you have a real legal interest because you've been arrested for doing what you want to do. There's therefore no question about whether you can get into court or not, because they've *brought* you into court. This is the way that most of these cases in the United States are fought. It's true that it's more difficult to get yourself declared a party in conflict when you're just in violation of University rules. You speak on a street corner and get arrested, it's clear. But here, there's a problem of who owns the University. The legal fiction is that it's owned by the Regents, and that's a problem. Are the rights of a student separate from the rights of a person who just comes on the campus? It's a complicated legal maneuver. In any case, the main thing is, why should *we* bring the case? If the Uni-

signed, as did the editors of all other ASUC publications. They then got together to form the *Independent Californian*, which, without the *Daily Cal*'s business staff, could not attract sufficient advertising. Though the *Daily Cal* was free, the *Independent* had to sell for a dime, and this, combined with a lack of advertising revenue, forced the *Independent* to shut down after only a month. The students willing to scab for the ASUC house-organ were less than the highest caliber, and well into 1965

the *DC* was politically backward (Horowitz, 109–110).

*A writ of certiorari is a writ issued by a superior court to call up the records of an inferior court or a body acting in a quasi-judicial capacity—in this case Brian is probably referring to the University of California itself—in order that the party may have more sure and speedy justice or that errors and irregularities may be corrected (*Webster's Third International Dictionary*).

versity thought that they had a right not to allow us to put tables up on the campus, or to speak where we wanted to when we wanted to, why shouldn't *they* bring the case to determine it? After all, they were the ones who were changing the rules, not us.[5]

Governor Brown pledged to maintain Law and Order on University campuses, and asked Kerr to prepare a report on the demonstration as soon as ever he could: "I would like a detailed account of its causes, what actions were taken and why, what issues were involved, and what recommendations you have for preventing similar situations in the future." Kerr said that the administration had jumped on the opportunity like a duck on a June bug, and that a report was already in the works.

> Law and order were restored to the Berkeley campus without the use of force—a result the Governor desired as much as I.
> . . . . All applicable University rules remain unchanged; the nonstudent trespasser has been booked by the police. The eight suspended students are still under suspension and the regular procedures for review of student conduct and grievances are functioning. . . .
> Students with left-wing and right-wing political orientation are more active than ever before. Off-campus elements excite this orientation. As a consequence, the historical position of the University against being made a base for political direct action is placed under unusual attack.
> At the same time, the world and national situations have most unfortunately placed more emphasis in the minds of a few students on direct action, even outside the limits of the law, than on compliance with law and order and democratic process.
> Nevertheless, the University is fully responsible for the maintenance of law and order and the guarantee that it remain an educational institution.[6]

What Kerr didn't know was that the entire arsenal of UC Berkeley civil rights machinery had just swiveled around and leveled itself square at his head. A newly formed FSM was scrambling to line up outside support wherever it could and was bee-busy organizing itself and an excited, highly receptive campus. Student anomie had been all dressed up with nowhere to go for ten years or more, and all of a sudden, it was Saturday night and we had a date.

RED-BAITING

Reds on campus trumpeted the banner headline of the *San Francisco Examiner* on October 3, 1964. In the *Oakland Tribune*, a handful of students who had visited Cuba in the summer of 1964 were puffed up into "Cuba trained" instigators. The *San Francisco News Call Bulletin* quoted Kerr as saying that "the University was contending with a hard core of Castro–Mao Tse-tung line communists" during the demonstrations; "49 percent of the hard-core group are followers of the Castro . . . line." Mario responded angrily that the specter of Communism was the "great bogeyman raised . . . whenever a group is working for social change. No one wants to admit that large numbers of people are sick and fed up with the way things are."[1] Red-baiting continued as a stock administration ploy throughout and even beyond the FSM, and in Davis on October 15, Kerr again maintained that some of the demonstrators "had Communist sympathies." The FSM, which was at that time attempting to negotiate with the authorities in good faith, responded,

> The FSM has every hope that the negotiations which we are entering into with the administration can be productive.
> However, we hope that President Kerr's attack upon us is not an indication of an unhealthy attitude with which the administration is entering these negotiations.
> It is regrettable that the President has resorted to such attacks and that the Board of Regents has permitted President Kerr's attack.[2]

So far from being "49 percent followers" of anybody's line, we had exactly one, count 'em, one, for-real genuine honest-to-God Communist and she was the most reasonable person on the whole Steering Committee. Bettina Aptheker had remarked during the FSM's first meeting, "I've got a last name that's dynamite." At the time, I had no idea what she meant, though I was told not long after that her dad, Herbert

BETTINA APTHEKER. PHOTO BY STEVE MARCUS.

Aptheker, was a big-deal Communist theoretician and historian. Though Bettina admitted privately that she really was a no-fooling, card-carrying member of the American Communist party, she publicly shied away from discussion of her politics. Mario proposed her to speak at the first FSM rally on the Monday after the police car precisely because, as he said, "We should throw the only *real* Communist we have in Kerr's face."[3] However, her ties to the Party were not to be flaunted in quite that public a manner. At that time and until June of 1966 it was against the law to be a member of the Communist Party of the United States of America (CPUSA), and the penalties for belonging were stiff. Most of her parents' friends had been in jail during the 1950s—some for as long as eight years—and Henry Winston had only been released in late 1963 on a pardon from John Kennedy.

I made like I thought it was just terrific that she was a Communist, but secretly it disturbed me considerably that she was under Party discipline. It worried me that if the Party told her to do something, she would do it. Members of the CPUSA had, it seemed to me, given up thinking, and let the party line do it for them.

I had given up thinking, too, for the duration of the FSM, but wasn't aware of it. Basically, I put myself completely in the hands of Jack Weinberg, and let him do all my thinking for me. After the trials of being a student, and wrestling with the imponderables of love, I was glad to be on autopilot for a while. I relished the sensation of being a willing, unquestioning tool in the hands of a trusted comrade.

In retrospect, I realize that my harsh judgment did Bettina an injustice. She may, indeed, have done a fairly courageous thing by admitting her membership; this was probably her first real break from Party discipline, foreshadowing even more dramatic independence. No Communist *ever* admitted being a member of the Party. When confronted they would stand foursquare on the position that their political belief

was none of the questioner's goddamned business; their right to espouse
any political sentiment or belong to any organization was fully protected
by the Constitution, and they weren't even going to recognize the validity of that line of questioning. I guess that Bettina got tired of all that,
and made a real political stance all on her own. But I didn't understand,
and nobody wised me up.

Having spent the sleepless weekend of October 3 and 4 forging a coherent organization out of the jigsaw pieces of campus political clubs, on Monday, October 5, the FSM held its first official rally on Sproul Hall steps. Concerned faculty members had warned us that Chancellor Strong intended to arrest Mario if he spoke, and suggested that we have someone read Mario's speech for him, or that he be introduced by a professor. We weren't about to let Strong scare us off, so the notion of physics professor Owen Chamberlain reading Mario's speech was firmly rejected. The idea of a faculty member introducing him, however, seemed a good one, and Professor Glazer did just that.

The rally was technically illegal under University regulations regarding nonstudent speakers. It was permitted, however, under a "special waiver" signed by Dean of Students Katherine A. Towle, which we took to be an acknowledgment by the administration that as long as they couldn't stop us, they would maintain at least the illusion that we weren't acting in open defiance. In reality, we had not sought a permit; many of the speakers were either suspended or nonstudents, and as University regulations on the time, place and manner of public addresses clearly stated that nonstudents had to wait seventy-two hours after officially requesting permission from the dean's office to speak on campus, the administration was putting the most face-saving interpretation on Mario's Friday announcement that a rally would be held on Sproul Hall steps the following Monday.

About a thousand students showed up to hear Mario state, "Although the whole war is far from over, we have won the biggest battle."[1] In the war over the basic issue of free speech on campus, our first victory in battle was twofold: first, the administration now admitted that there was an issue to discuss, and second, the administration had recognized an ad hoc student group—the signers of the agreement with Kerr—as a legitimate negotiating body which, together with representatives of

MARIO SPEAKS FROM SPROUL HALL STEPS, OCTOBER 5, 1964.
PHOTOGRAPHER UNKNOWN.

the administration and faculty, was to form a committee to work things out in a manner satisfactory to all parties. Art took a surprisingly strong stance on the basic issue of free speech, foreshadowing his later involvement with the issue of obscenity:

> We ask only the right to say what we feel when we feel like it. We'll continue to fight for this freedom, and we won't quit until we've won.[2]

Professors John Leggett of sociology and Charles Sellers of history, as well as most of the suspended students, also spoke. We took this opportunity to display the statements of support that had come in over the weekend, including one signed by forty-three political science and economics teaching assistants.

When I stood up to talk, the muse was no longer with me. My speech was confused and ineffective, and my words fell flat and dull. After this time at the mike, both the other speakers and I realized that I understood the issues only poorly, that I expressed them from the narrow viewpoint of an individual, and I wasn't any good at public speaking anyhow. Speaking for yourself alone was confusing and divisive. The best and most convincing speakers were those who never consulted the personal pronoun, who spoke for everyone, who had the right kind of rhetoric ready to their hand, and who were already part of the political scene. The more lofty expositions of the experienced handmaidens of social change made better sense, so I gave over the job to others better skilled.

That day Chancellor Strong announced the appointments to the faculty-student-administration Study Committee on Campus Political Activity (CCPA) and the FSM was deeply shocked.* We were greatly displeased at the ominous words "Study Committee," which sounded as if a lot of serious backpedaling had been done over the last forty-eight hours. We did not think that we were here to study the problem of free speech on campus; we thought that we were here to get free speech on campus as fast as possible. This "study" stuff sounded mighty bad to

---

*Chaired by Dean Arleigh Williams, the CCPA was also known as the Williams Committee. Appointees included faculty members Robley Williams (virology), Theodore Vermeulen (chemical engineering), Joseph Garbarino (business administration), and Henry Rosovsky (economics); administration representatives Katherine Towle (dean of students), Milton Chernin (dean of the School of Social Welfare), William Fretter (dean of the College of Letters and Science), and Alan Searcy (recently appointed vice-chancellor for academic affairs); and, to represent the students, ASUC president Charles Powell and Marsha Bratten (both winners of the 1964 Robert Gordon and Ida W. Sproul awards). This left, on a committee of twelve, two student slots to be filled by FSM representatives ("Chronology," 45).

us. We were even more displeased at the makeup of the committee: four hostile administration representatives, four hostile faculty representatives, and two student slots filled by administration stooge Charlie Powell and somebody named Marsha Bratten whom nobody had ever heard of, but whom we could safely assume was not going to be of much help. As Mario had announced at the rally, we thought that the students who had negotiated with Kerr were to be the students on the committee, or that the FSM was to be able to appoint its own representatives. The FSM pointed out that ten of the chancellor's appointees were openly hostile to the students' position, and that there was damned little chance of getting anything done fairly if the administration insisted on stacking the deck before starting to deal. At that night's FSM meeting it was decided that the administration had little, if any, intention of playing fair and that its real goal was to talk us to death. A majority felt that we should try to work within established channels or change the channels to make them go where we wanted them to go. A minority felt that we could get nowhere by cooperating with the administration. Everyone, however, accepted that it was absolutely critical to avoid the impression that we were hotheads who would not even sit down at the table and talk before flying off the handle again. But in order to have any chance at all of doing things through the CCPA, we had to either get rid of the whiz kids and replace them with FSM negotiators or get more FSM people on, and in order to do *that*, we had to convince the administration that we wanted a new deck, a new shuffle and a new deal.

On October 7 the CCPA held its first meeting. Ten FSM spokesmen walked in, presented a statement condemning the committee as illegally constituted, and walked out. On Tuesday, October 13, the CCPA held its first public meeting at 7:30 PM in Harmon Gymnasium. Some three hundred students showed up, most of whom were there to tell the committee that it was illegally constituted and should either disband or reconstitute itself with the faculty appointing its own members and the protesting students theirs. A leaflet included with the first edition of the FSM *Newsletter* had urged this position, and after hearing fifty students parrot the same advice, the tedious parade spiced by one student who did not agree, the committee announced that the public meeting was at an end.*

Student negotiators had extracted a promise from Kerr that the cases

*The FSM *Newsletter* was edited by Barbara Garson and Stephen Gillers, and its staff included Deward Hastings, Truman Price, Mickey Rowntree, Marston Schultz and Linda Sussman.

of the suspended students would be turned over to the Student Conduct Committee of the Academic Senate within a week. When Strong was given the job of doing so, he was publicly humiliated by the discovery that there *was* no "Student Conduct Committee of the Academic Senate." The Academic Senate had once controlled student discipline, but had given up much of that power in 1921, and had lost it completely by 1938. They didn't want to be bothered, and the task of student discipline for nonacademic infractions fell to the dean's office.[3] It was also impossible for the Academic Senate to comply with a one-week deadline. There was a "Faculty Committee on Student Conduct" that existed as an ordinary part of the machinery of student discipline, but it wasn't what had been agreed upon, and its members were administration appointees guaranteed to be on the wrong side of the fence, as far as the students were concerned. When we kicked up a fuss about the nonexistent committee that had been palmed off on us, Strong made the reasonable response that he had referred the suspensions to the only possible committee that could have been meant. We were not convinced.

> *Charles Muscatine:* The expelled students would not necessarily be brought before a faculty committee. There's a division of jurisdiction; the faculty had jurisdiction over academic matters, but the administration had jurisdiction over student conduct and sports—there's a dean of students and there's a dean of faculty. The faculty traditionally consider student high jinks as the dean of students' department. The Academic Senate has virtually no regulations concerning student conduct, unless it would be plagiarism or cheating on exams or something like that.[4]

Kerr responded to accusations of "bad faith" on the part of the administration in a manner that the students found only to be another example of the same thing:

> A question has been raised about the appointment of the joint advisory committee. The minutes of the meeting show the following:
> "Kerr: This committee would have to be appointed by the administration."
> It was noted that it was the only agency with authorization to appoint faculty, students and administrators.
> A question has also been raised about the "Student Conduct Committee of the Academic Senate." This is a misnomer. It was used in a draft prepared by an informal group of faculty members. I did not catch the misstatement at the time; nor did anyone else. The only such committee that exists is the "Faculty Committee on Student Conduct"

which is composed of faculty members. The minutes show the following:

"Kerr: We need to understand that the Committee does not make final determinations. You would have to be aware that you would be dependent also on whatever confidence you have in the decency and fairness of the Administration and respect for it."

The campus administration went ahead promptly to show its good faith in appointing the joint committee and submitting the suspension cases to the Faculty Committee on Student Conduct. The campus administration reserved two of four student places for representatives of the demonstrators as they clearly represent only a minority of students.[5]

So not only did the Student Conduct Committee of the Academic Senate not even exist, but if it had existed it would only have been advisory to the administration, requiring us to "be dependent . . . on whatever confidence" we might have "in the decency and fairness of the Administration and respect for it." Since we didn't have any confidence in the administration except that it was going to try to screw us any way it could, this just made things worse. Between the high-handed packing of the CCPA with those guaranteed to be unfavorable to the demonstrators' position and the probable kangaroo court of the Faculty Committee on Student Conduct, we started off very much on the wrong foot. Art called it "almost a breach of good faith on the part of the administration. . . . It is dangerous to start out so arbitrarily. The University has put us in an impossible position before we start."[6]

On October 8 the Academic Senate was asked to appoint an Ad Hoc Academic Senate Committee on Student Suspensions to hear the cases of the suspended students. Ira Michael Heyman, professor of law, was appointed chairman, and the committee was in consequence known as the Heyman Committee.* Also on the eighth, during a speech before the San Diego Chamber of Commerce, Clark Kerr again emphasized that a "minority" of students were involved in the incident around the car, and made a large point that those involved were acting under the influence of outside agitators:

The situation [at Berkeley] is new in that students are more activist than before and that diverse groups . . . are attacking the historic policies of

*Other members of the Heyman Committee were Robert A. Gordon, professor of economics; Mason Haire, professor of psychology and research psychologist in the Institute of Industrial Relations; Richard E. Powell, professor of chemistry and chairman of the chemistry department; and Lloyd Ulman, professor of economics and industrial relations and director of the Institute of Industrial Relations.

the University. Students are encouraged, as never before, by elements external to the University. [It was] one episode—a single campus, a small minority of students, a short period of time.[7]

I dare say those actively involved in the FSM were indeed a small minority of the campus population; actively involved folks always are. This small minority, however, was at the long end of the lever, and we knew it; we remained unimpressed by Kerr's whistling in the dark, and kept right on with our work.

With the American Civil Liberties Union and others on our side we felt that we had a wider base of support than just a few liberals in the immediate community. This was reinforced when, on the twelfth, Chancellor Strong was given a petition signed by eighty-eight faculty members favoring reinstatement of the suspended students. The petition was ignored.

FSM representatives tried repeatedly to meet with Kerr to negotiate "interpretation and implementation" of the October 2 pact, asking, among other things, that the composition of the CCPA be modified to give a more acceptable student representation. Kerr was "unavailable," and his office referred them to vice president of administration Earl Bolton, who told them that they'd have to meet with Chancellor Strong. On October 11 and 12, FSM representatives went to Strong, who sent them back to Bolton. On the thirteenth, Bolton finally met with the FSM, but said that he couldn't do anything.

The Regents were scheduled to meet at Davis, and the FSM sent telegrams to Governor Brown and chairman of the Regents Edward Carter, requesting that FSM representatives be allowed an hour before the Regents to present their case. On the fifteenth, the day of the meeting, the Regents responded in the negative:

> The Regents have concluded that in view of the study being conducted by the appropriate committee, no useful purpose would be served by considering whether your group should be heard by the Regents at this time.[8]

At this point, the FSM concluded that the administration not only had absolutely no interest whatever in playing fair, it had no intention of playing at all. Though we did not feel that we could continue wearing holes in the carpets of administrative waiting rooms, we also felt that there was no real chance of getting student support for renewed activism unless we could convince everyone that the committees were nothing but a charade. We were stuck up to the axles in administrative mud.

On the evening of the fourteenth, professor of industrial relations Arthur Ross attended an FSM Steering Committee meeting at Sid Stapleton's apartment and—assuring the students that he was empowered within limits to make deals—worked out a provisional agreement concerning the composition of the CCPA. He was to take the role of chief negotiator, and the number of student negotiators was to be expanded by the addition of four FSM appointees. Though Powell and Bratten would remain, anything they might say or do would be neutralized by the FSM majority. Two more faculty would be added, and the faculty would select them, rather than the administration. Decisions would no longer be by simple majority—which meant that the faculty and administration could team up and get anything they wanted—but had to be by consensus. The committee would remain advisory, but Ross strongly implied that the administration would rubber-stamp anything it recommended. Ross seemed to be a real hope—he was reasonable and intelligent, and gave us to believe that while the official channels were not working out because of obstructionists in the administration, by negotiating unofficially we could devise a deal that everyone could live with. After the incredible runaround that we'd gotten from Kerr, Strong and the Regents, things were starting to look up.

On October 15 the revised committee was announced to a meeting of the Academic Senate. Kerr and Strong were at the Board of Regents meeting in Davis, and gave the revised committee their blessing in absentia.

Jack Weinberg: Ross gave this whole line about the honor of mediators, they're nonpartisan. We bargained back and forth, he won a few points, we won a few points. I was fairly impressed with him until he started backsliding on what he had promised.

The Study Committee was expanded from twelve to eighteen members, with the new members appointed in a manner more agreeable to the students. The FSM's appointees to the Committee on Campus Political Activity were Mario Savio, Bettina Aptheker, Sidney Stapleton and Suzanne Goldberg. In the Heyman Committee hearings, the students were represented by Ernest Besig and Wayne Collins, Sr., and the University's case was argued by University lawyers. Administrators, such as Arleigh Williams and Dean Towle, found themselves in a position of being witnesses for the committee, and were cross-examined at length by the lawyers for the students.[9]

Jackie Goldberg: Dean Towle and I had become close when, the previous semester, she had been instructed to see that racially discriminatory clauses in sorority charters were removed, and that they all signed non-discrimination pledges. The alternative being that she would have to take away their legal status, and this she did not want to do. The Greeks had been given five years to abolish their systematic exclusion of minorities, and hadn't done much of anything yet. She'd encountered considerable resistance, until I came up with the idea of asking sorority representatives from the deep South to come and speak on the subject, and their outrageous racism so horrified the Berkeley sorority members that on the first vote they resolved to drop all references to race as the basis for membership.* Though the discriminatory practices did not stop, at least they weren't down in black and white anymore.[10]

I had seen Dean Towle several times, on my own mostly, about that [October 2] agreement, and I explained to her in full honest detail how we were completely disillusioned with the administration and were sure we'd been tricked in the lowest possible way, and that I didn't know who she could convey this to, but whoever she could she'd better let 'em know that if they wanted to solve this thing without any more demonstrations they sure were going about it the wrong way. She didn't say she agreed with me, but she didn't say she disagreed with me either. Then I told her that she could not expect anyone from the newly constituted FSM to appear at that first [October 7] committee meeting. That meeting was called without the FSM delegates being [officially] notified.

I only did two more things as a Steering Committee member. One was I went as a member of the negotiating committee to the [October 11] meeting with Strong. It was a pretty ridiculous meeting all right. This meeting came about through an attempt to see Kerr and then Vice President Bolton. I'd first been told to see Kerr, but he couldn't see us for some reason. Then I tried to set up a meeting with Bolton, but Bolton said we'd have to see Strong first, and that's why we went on the eleventh to see Strong. Kerr had sent in some faculty; Ross was there—that fink Ross. Mario blew his cool in the middle of it, and made some pretty wild, insulting statements. I wanted to applaud. I agreed with everything he said, but it almost destroyed the whole meeting. The faculty started to walk out. They said, "We don't have to sit around and listen to this," but Art convinced them to stay. Of course, the whole gist of the meeting was "go talk to Dr. Kerr about it." So we tried to set it up with Kerr and it didn't work out. I kept getting told he wasn't

---

*The nondiscrimination pledge was due on September 1, 1964. In December 1964, the University chapter of Pi Beta Phi sorority filed suit to prevent expulsion by the national; the sorority had been put on probation preliminary to expulsion for signing the nondiscrimination clause. Pi Beta Phi was the first sorority to face the problem of going against its national charter, which specifically included racial and religious discrimination (*Daily Cal*, 5 March 1965).

there, or he wasn't going to be there. Nobody ever said that he *wouldn't* meet with us. They'd say things like "I'll give you Vice President Bolton's number, perhaps he can help you." So I called Vice President Bolton. At first he seemed extremely cooperative, because he called me back right away, which none of those administrators ever do when you leave a number, and he called Kerr right away and Kerr gave him absolute one hundred percent authority to speak in the name of the University, as if he were president of the University, to sign and negotiate as if he were president of the University—wow, God! this is going to be simpler than I thought it was going to be. And then we started talking about who could come to the meeting. Then Bolton informed me that only signers of the original agreement could come. But I explained to him that some of them were not with us at all anymore—we didn't want Dan Rosenthal back with us. I didn't say that, but . . . Some of them are not on the Steering Committee anymore, and we're now an organization. And he says, "Well, I'm so sorry, but only the people . . ." So there we were. We got over that hump sort of by him agreeing that other people could observe, and that we could caucus. Then we got to the topics of discussion, and there was really only one: the October 2 pact. We couldn't talk to him about the suspended students, we couldn't talk to him about the issue itself! Here it was, after October 11—this began September 14—and except for Dean Towle, who had no power, we had not talked to one administrator who would talk about the issue itself. Bolton just kept finding all sorts of reasons why we couldn't talk about things that we thought were important. He kept saying, "I can see you, and everyone else that was there that night, on the issue of what happened that night, and that's it." He was very amiable throughout the whole thing, but he didn't give in. We never managed to talk about the basic issue of setting up tables on campus.

Another strange thing happened, and that was the Arthur Ross intervention. I remember trusting him. We were completely taken in the first time—never again, but the first time. He phoned on Wednesday the fourteenth in the middle of an evening Steering Committee meeting at Sid Stapleton's house, and said that he wanted to come over and talk to us before we did anything rash. We said we'd call him back, and discussed it, and sang folk songs and had dinner and figured we had nothing to lose and called him back. He came over that evening—we were still singing and he sat down and joined in—and said that no one knew he was here; he had talked to Kerr, who was a personal friend of his, and he was doing this on his own, but he wanted to mediate between us and Kerr. He gave a very straight hard-line type of statement, "I'm not here because I think you're right." And he seemed very honest. The reason we trusted him was because he didn't say, "I'm with you all the way." We weren't trusting any faculty that said that, anymore. He said he was a mediator, that he'd been in labor relations, that "if you give some, I can get Kerr to give some. Tell me what you can give, and we'll tell you what they can give." He didn't say "we," he always said "they." The next day I met him at his office, and he told us that they would set up a faculty committee, and that the CCPA would be reconstituted, and the faculty would select their own members. The biggest concession we made was that the faculty decision on the suspended students wouldn't be final, that it would be subject to the chancellor.

Most of us felt pretty happy about the whole thing. At that moment, it looked like the kids were going to get reinstated, and it looked like we were going to get negotiations with the faculty and the administration, and we even had something about a veto put in—if any group votes against a proposal that it vetoes it. That gave us more power than we'd had before, because we couldn't trust a two-to-one decision.[11]

The campus science club Particle Berkeley was the only nonpolitical organization that had participated in the United Front. On the twentieth, it was warned by the dean of students that its membership in the Free Speech Movement jeopardized its on-campus status. Jack Weinberg responded:

We hope that this is not an indication of future punishment to be given on-campus groups involved in the FSM. "On- and off-campus" means "what we like and what we don't like" to the administration. This is a bad omen, especially at the start of negotiations on the free speech issue.[12]

Also on the twentieth, Chancellor Strong issued a statement echoing Kerr's frequent harping on the Communists in the FSM, and reiterated that the campus had an Open Forum policy which, nonetheless, did not allow the "planning and implementing of political action." He maintained that the students were led by "hard core demonstrators" who had been involved in Freedom Summer in Mississippi—"professional demonstrators, but I won't smear all the other good kids by calling it Communist-led." Clearly, he was letting his mouth get away from him a bit. Art hotly retorted,

If "hard core demonstrations" means that we are still going to fight for our principles and the Free Speech Movement, then Chancellor Strong is right. . . .

[There are two types of] political action. It's sort of like the double

U.C. Admits 'Politics' Variance

The eight U.C. students seem in a happy mood as they appear for the hearing. L. to r., front: Brian Turner, Sandor   Fuchs, Art Goldberg and Elizabeth Stapleton Gardner. Rear: David Goines, Mark Bravo, Dan Hatch, Mario Savio.
—News Call Bulletin Photo.

THE EIGHT SUSPENDED STUDENTS. LEFT TO RIGHT, FRONT: BRIAN TURNER, SANDOR FUCHS, ART GOLDBERG AND ELIZABETH STAPLETON. REAR: DAVID GOINES, MARK BRAVO, DONALD HATCH AND MARIO SAVIO. SAN FRANCISCO NEWS CALL BULLETIN PHOTO, OCTOBER 28, 1964.

standard. We are the girls, with lock-out, and the administration is the boys, with no limitations. When they want to talk about their Democrat and Republican politics, it's "University policy." But, if we say anything about social action, or something that might make people think, it becomes "too political." If the University has a true Open Forum, why can't we advocate social action? It seems we have a closed Open Forum.[13]

On October 25, the Ad Hoc Academic Senate Committee on Student Suspensions suggested to the administration that, during the course of the hearings, the eight suspended students be reinstated. This was denied on October 26. The students' attorney, Ernest Besig, then said that if the Heyman Committee did not satisfactorily resolve both the issues of First Amendment rights on campus and the suspensions, the ACLU would take the University to court.

The FSM felt that this would be a good time to escalate its demands beyond the basics. Not only did we want to be able to advocate action, to recruit members and to solicit funds, we wanted to get rid of restrictions that made it difficult to do those things. The things that had to go were: the seventy-two-hour rule, which made it difficult to respond to

---

STATEMENT

BUSINESS OFFICE: CASHIER

THE REGENTS OF THE UNIVERSITY OF CALIFORNIA

Berkeley, California

In Account with: Date. DEC 1 4 1964

> Campus Core
> c/o David Friedman
> 3044 Telegraph, Apt. B.
> Berkeley, California

NOTE: University accounts are on a cash basis and settlement must be made promptly.
Please return this statement with your remittance or give bill numbers shown herein. Any irregularity should be taken up immediately with the Business Office—Cashier, Room 107, Window C, Sproul Hall. Make checks in favor of THE REGENTS OF THE UNIVERSITY OF CALIFORNIA.

Date	Bill Number	Description	Amount
6/18/64	78657	Police charge for the Tracy Sims & Bill Bradley speech held in 2000 Life Science Bldg. on Wednesday, June 17, 1964	$21.80
		This charge is long past due, please remit by return mail. Thank you.	

---

changing political events; the necessity of having a tenured faculty moderator at meetings; and the insult of not only having University-mandated police present at arbitrarily selected meetings but having to pay for them as well.*

On October 28, we turned the heat up a bit more when Sid Stapleton presented the Committee on Campus Political Activity with a simple solution to the seemingly complex problem. He suggested that the First Amendment to the U.S. Constitution be the only policy regarding political expression on campus, as it was everywhere else in America.

---

*A Campus CORE leaflet dated December 14, 1964, reproduced a bill from the UC Business Office for police services of June 18, 1964: "Police charge for the Tracy Sims & Bill Bradley speech held in 2000 Life Science Bldg. on Wednesday, June 17, 1964. $21.80. This charge is long past due, please remit by return mail. Thank you." CORE refused to pay the bill, which it termed "protection money."

Mario backed this up with a threat that if the CCPA did not adopt this motion, the FSM would "have to consider more direct action." Dean Towle said that it would be OK to recommend action, but that it was not OK to advocate action.

> A speaker may say, for instance, that there is going to be a picket line at such-and-such a place, and it is a worthy cause and he hopes people will go. But, he cannot say, "I'll meet you there and we'll picket."[14]

While the students' argument had the simple elegance of an appeal to the Bill of Rights, Dean Towle was put in the uncomfortable position of proposing that speakers, to dodge the intent of University regulations, engage in sophistic word games. This did not sit well with either the students or faculty. The FSM's response in its daily leaflet was "We repeat: when the morass of mediation becomes too thick to see through, action must let in the light."[15]

On November 4, the FSM put up an informational picket on Sproul Hall steps to focus attention on the free speech issue, and to call attention to the afternoon meeting of the Heyman Committee, which had completed its hearings on the suspensions the day before. The committee's recommendations and the administration response to them would dictate what the FSM would do. If it looked like negotiations were getting results, then the FSM would stick with them; if, on the other hand, negotiations were apparently no more than a stall tactic, then the FSM would resume direct action. Though we agreed that action would be risky and divisive, the activist contingent felt that we had no choice but to force the administration's hand if they weren't sincere.

Earl Cheit, professor of business administration, introduced a proposal to the Committee on Campus Political Activity which became the center of debate on both the fourth and fifth of November:

> That in the Hyde Park areas, the University modify its present regulations by dropping the distinction between "advocating" and "mounting" political and social action. Although we could find no case in which this distinction has been in issue, the position of the students and the recent resolutions of the Academic Senate and the Regents all support a University policy which (subject only to restrictions necessary for normal conduct of University functions and business) permits free expression within the limits of the law. Subject only to these same restrictions, off-campus speakers invited by recognized student groups to speak in the Hyde Park area should be permitted to do so upon completing a

simple registration procedure which records the inviting organization, the speaker's name, and the topic of the talk.

The administration felt that it needed protection from charges that the campus was a launching pad for illegal activity. The students argued that the critical phrase, "within the limits of the law," gave the University the power of prior restraint. Sanford Kadish, professor of law, then proposed a modification of the Cheit proposal which would get around the problem of prior restraint by emphasizing that the University was not protecting those who advocated illegal action, but merely abiding by the Constitution.

> The advocacy of ideas and acts which is constitutionally protected off the campus should be protected on the campus. By the same token, of course, speech which is in violation of law and constitutionally unprotected should receive no greater protection on the campus than off the campus.

Students and faculty agreed on the Kadish proposal, but the administration wanted something that made it clear that UC was not a revolution mill and did not condone the mounting of unlawful action from its campuses. All parties felt that we were almost in agreement, saving the thrashing out of some kind of wording that would make everyone happy. The committee took a recess while Professor Kadish, dean of educational relations Frank Kidner and FSM attorney Malcolm Burnstein went out in the hall and tried to hash something out that everybody could agree on. They returned with this amendment:

> If, as a direct result of advocacy on the campus, acts occur in violation of U.S. or California laws, the University should be entitled to take appropriate disciplinary action against the speakers and their sponsoring organizations, to the extent that the person or organization can fairly be found to be responsible for the unlawful acts.

No good. The students rejected this amendment claiming that it would, in effect, give the University the power of prior restraint, as it left interpretation of unlawful acts up to the University.[16]

On November 7, the University position hardened up. Dean Kidner felt that the University should be able to discipline students who had committed illegal acts, whether or not those acts were committed on the campus, if those acts had been advocated or organized from the campus.

If acts unlawful under California or Federal law directly result from advocacy, organization or planning on the campus, the students and organizations involved may be subject to such disciplinary action as is appropriate and conditioned upon [a] fair hearing as to the appropriateness of the action taken.[17]

Kidner and Mario got into a shouting match, during which Kidner went overboard and said that even if an act was not declared unlawful, the administration could still take disciplinary action. Sid Stapleton brought up the problem of outside pressure on the University, and maintained that it would not be possible for the University to conduct a fair hearing if it had not only to administer discipline but also to decide arbitrarily whether discipline was called for in the first place. Vice-Chancellor Alan Searcy turned to Sid and emphasized that the University administration was made of men of good will. Mario said that he didn't think so, and that he didn't want to depend on their good will when matters of free speech were involved. This offended the administration members. Everybody thought that everybody else was being unreasonable. Dean Kidner's amendment failed—administration "aye," faculty "abstain," students "nay."

The student representatives then countered with this amendment:

In the areas of First Amendment rights and civil liberties, the University may impose no disciplinary action against members of the University community and organizations. In this area, members of the University community and organizations are subject only to the civil authorities.[18]

The student proposal was also defeated, with the administration and faculty voting against. All of a sudden things had fallen apart. It became apparent to the students that nothing was ever going to happen with the CCPA. It wasn't so much a stalling technique as the normal way the administration and faculty did things. We, on the other hand, had work to do and this dicking around in an endless, pointless committee was not getting us anywhere at all.

Jack Weinberg: We had developed a new perspective on the CCPA, which was that from now on we would use the CCPA merely to work out a platform. Our delegates were instructed to deadlock on this issue or that. We would gear our direct action on factors other than our performance in the CCPA. Up 'til that time we had not tried to do that. We had found the issue that we thought was most important, and we were trying to get the CCPA to go one way or the other on it, or to deadlock on that issue. So that we would either deadlock or win on what we considered was the main point. Since we knew that they weren't going to give us the main point, we instructed the delegates, rather than deal with other matters, to disregard everything else until we had won that point. That was the point of advocacy.[19]

The Committee on Campus Political Activity continued to debate, but nobody was willing to budge an inch, and nobody was getting anyplace. Mario's favored tactic was to blow up at members of the committee.

Bob Starobin: In the CCPA meeting Mario really lost his cool and got in a fight with Meyerson—Meyerson was only on the committee for one day—he replaced Letters and Science dean Fretter, because Fretter was too weak. He got in a fight with the dean of the Social Welfare Department, too. He was always losing his cool—constant fireworks.[20]

Now that the CCPA had come to a complete deadlock, Mario felt it was time to push Strong a little harder.

Mario Savio: We asked the chancellor, "Would you dissolve the CCPA and reconstitute it in a way that has been arrived at in negotiation with the FSM, and will you send the cases of the suspended students to the Academic Senate, or reinstate them at once?"

On the point of the Academic Senate, the chancellor said he could do nothing without Kerr. On the point of dissolving the committee, he said, "It's an advisory committee; advisory to the chancellor, and therefore I'd have to ask Kerr's advice as to whether I can dissolve it." Fruitless but instructive.[21]

From the third of October until the early November stalemate of the CCPA the FSM had distributed daily bulletins on the progress of all aspects of negotiations and committees. Almost every day there had been, somewhere on or near campus, huge public meetings of interested students. Meetings, proselytizing, leafleting, organizing, fundraising, informational rallies, debating and negotiations had gone on night and day, but the FSM had honored the letter of the pact of October 2 and as a gesture of goodwill had not engaged in any direct action, on or off campus. Campus political organizations had scrupulously set up their tables outside the official campus boundary. Now, however, it became clear that it was time to light a fire under the administration, which we felt was perfectly delighted at the prospect of talking the FSM, and all it stood for, to death. Time was on their side, and we had to seize what opportunity we had by the forelock because, as we knew full well, Fortune is bald behind. Our excuse came in the form of intercepted letters from Kerr and University general counsel Thomas Cunningham.

In the original FSM meeting, cards had been handed out so that people could sign up if they wanted to work, and in answer to "What special talents do you have?" Sherry Waldren had put down on her card, "I work in Kerr's office." Kitty Piper and I were responsible for going through the cards, and pounced on it like a cat on a mouse. However, we felt that we had to be scrupulously moral about using her, because she could lose her job and get blacklisted if she gave us something and we screwed up and it could be traced to her.

Sherry photocopied two letters dated the thirteenth of October dealing with University regulations and, we felt, tipping the hand of the administration's real intentions. One letter, from Clark Kerr to the Regents, included an addition to University Regulations on the Use of University Facilities. "University facilities may not be used for the purpose of recruiting participants for unlawful off-campus action."[22] The second letter, bearing the typewritten name of Thomas Cunningham, was addressed to the Regents and proposed legislation to be presented to the state legislature making it a misdemeanor to advocate illegal activity from the University campus.

Neither letter had been signed. Kerr said that he had not written the letter bearing his name, that he disagreed with it and had never signed it. "I made no proposals for any changes in the rules at the October [Regents'] meeting, neither those in the letter nor any others." We did not believe him. Cunningham said, "I prepared it. The president discussed it with the chief campus officers, and decided he would not recommend it."[23] We did not believe him, either. Kerr's little tricks and dodges had come home to roost—if he'd been generally trustworthy these letters would have meant little or nothing. An unsigned letter could come from anyplace. But we'd been led down the garden path one too many times, and now we didn't believe a word Kerr said.

If these letters were authentic, the whole CCPA was a fraud, because the issue had already been decided by executive fiat. We'd known about the letters since October 26, but hadn't figured out what to do with them except make deeply veiled allusions to underhanded dealings on the part of the administration. We had decided not to release the letters unless we could protect our source, which we had not done. Our plan was to make copies and mail them anonymously to some liberal professor, who would then bring the letters to our attention.

BRIAN MULLONEY

GCC CAMPAIGN FLYER

Things had gone badly in negotiations on November 5, and without consulting Ex Com, Mario and Bettina unilaterally released the letters. Kitty Piper and I were angry at this, and went over to Sherry's house about one in the morning and warned her and her husband that the letters had been released, and that she should watch out. We felt that the release of the letters was inconsiderate and dangerous, and we didn't want her to walk into work the next morning and have the sky fall on her head. As it happened, nobody in the administration ever figured out how the letters had been leaked until somehow or another the matter came up in the trial, where Pam Mellin, who was known by the staff in her office to be sympathetic to the FSM, was blamed for it.

Andy Wells: The Cunningham letter changed my thinking a great deal.* Before that time I felt that the administration had just fucked up; that they didn't know what was going on and had no conception of how this thing affected students, or how far students were willing to go to regain their rights. Then I heard about the letter—it was read in an Executive Committee meeting at Westminster House—and I just about shat. We saw that there was proof that despite all the negotiations Clark Kerr was going ahead with the Regents anyway. It changed my view—if they were going to pull that crap, then I had no compunction about doing anything that was needed. If they were going to fight dirty, then we would fight just as dirty. The Cunningham letter made everybody considerably more radical. That's what the process of the FSM was, the rad-

---

*Since both letters had been drafted by Cunningham, they were often referred to collectively as "the letter," without too much regard for exactly which letter was being talked about.

icalization of the whole body. After that we understood more why Mario had yelled and screamed at the administration.

It was decided to make the letter public; Clark Kerr denied it and that was the end of it. We decided to keep on with the negotiations anyway. The general opinion was that we were stupid to get into these things, but now that we were in it, how were we going to get out of it without looking like we were acting in bad faith. We concluded that no rational argument was going to change anybody's mind.[24]

Brian Mulloney: The meeting at Newman Hall where the Cunningham letter came in, where people kept holding things up because they had this or that particularly hot piece of information, was total chaos. The Cunningham letter had been muttered about before, that such a thing was under way and that we were being double-crossed. I'm still annoyed at myself and other people there for not asking if the damn letter was signed, because that was stupid. An unsigned letter has no meaning. What was voted on was tactics for negotiations, what to do with the CCPA. Whether to pull out, whether to stay in, whether to unmask them all as a fraud. Mario was arguing that we had *real* evidence that they were going to double-cross us, and when people asked what it was he said that "we can't reveal it because that will jeopardize our source of information." That's why nobody asked if it was signed. From that came the fiasco later in the year of releasing the letter, and Kerr being able to deny it because it was unsigned. I remember David Kolodny— almost alone—arguing that we couldn't reasonably be asked to vote for a drastic action for reasons which they couldn't even tell us, let alone tell the general public. So, it was stupid to pull out of the CCPA.[25]

On Saturday, November 7, Professor Cheit proposed that the committee report substantial agreement, and that a joint student-faculty statement be issued on the nature of their disagreements. Mario strongly disagreed that they were almost in accord; he said that the main point of disagreement was also the only point that mattered. At this time, it became evident that the faculty representatives did not understand the issues of advocacy and prior restraint, and were concerned solely with University regulations on what the FSM negotiators considered window-dressing. Cheit would not back down, the FSM would not back down, and the student negotiators left the meeting with a firm resolve to resume direct action.

A further perception led the FSM toward direct action: the University administration, so far from making concessions toward a solution in which each side gave a little and got a little, seemed by subtle stages to be making further inroads on First Amendment rights, adding to its

PETER FRANCK. PHOTOGRAPHER UNKNOWN.

original demand for control of on-campus activity a growing insistence on its jurisdiction over the legality of off-campus activities as well. This accusation came as something of a surprise to the administration itself, which may not have realized the trend of its own position.

Mario Savio: Our position was the pure, aesthetic position that there shall be no regulation of the content of speech. At Friday's rally I said, "On Monday I can see tables set up here on Sproul Plaza."[26]

The precious resource of student interest—the lifeblood of the FSM—was dripping away into an endless, tedious, pointless bureaucratic morass. The Steering Committee realized this and decided that the only solution was to create new confrontations, new excitement, new martyrs. The moderate participants in the FSM, who believed that renewed confrontation would provoke violence and bloodshed, strove with all their might to keep the contending parties at the negotiating table. These factions came into serious conflict over the weekend of November 7 and 8, and the FSM was almost destroyed.

INTERNAL COMBUSTION

Over the weekend of the seventh and eighth of November, so many things happened so fast that nobody knew what was going on. Even now, trying to sort out the events is a formidable task. In order to make it somewhat clearer, I will preface the account with a brief synopsis:

On Wednesday, November 4, about two hundred students picketed on the steps of Sproul Hall. On Thursday, November 5, the FSM made public the letters from Clark Kerr and University counsel Thomas Cunningham which implied an absence of good faith on the part of the University. At the Friday rally, Mario unilaterally announced that the FSM intended to resume direct action on Monday. On Saturday, November 7, the CCPA reached a deadlock on the matters of advocacy and prior restraint. It was generally agreed within the Steering Committee that the time had come to bail out of the CCPA and go on to direct action. This conclusion, so crashingly obvious to the negotiators, was not shared by more than a marginal half of the Executive Committee.

In part, this was because the matter of advocacy itself, crystal clear to the Steering Committee negotiators, was as clear as mud to everybody else, including the FSM membership. At this point, about half the FSM Executive Committee felt that we'd gotten all that we could get and that the issues of advocacy and prior restraint were radical excuses to resume direct action. Though the FSM leadership had more or less abandoned the CCPA as a viable organ of change, many of the students did not agree, and wanted to pursue this moderate path further. In an Executive Committee meeting on Saturday night Art Goldberg argued for continuation of the CCPA and Mario, Bettina, Sid and Jack argued for abandonment. Art's position was bolstered by the support of Mike Tigar, a Boalt Hall law student who had been one of the most important activists in building SLATE's campus following.

In general, there was a high degree of dissatisfaction with the manner in which the leadership was handling negotiations. The active members of the Steering Committee, which had dwindled in size to those directly involved in the negotiating, had become isolated from the membership. When they became aware of the extreme unhappiness of the Executive Committee, they agreed, fearing a split, that a reorganization would be in order. The new Steering Committee was elected on Saturday night, at the same meeting that debated the Kadish proposal, the Cheit proposal, getting out of the CCPA and the resumption of direct action. The inactive members—Art and Jackie in particular—were not reelected, and some new members were added. Though these new members were elected to appease allegations of isolation and unbridled radicalism, they either did not participate or were politically neutral, and had little effect on the further course of the Steering Committee, which continued to be dominated by the radical Congress of Racial Equality faction. To appease SLATE, Art was reinstated a week later, but did not participate in meetings any more than he had before.

Despite a vote endorsing the resumption of direct action, many Executive Committee members wanted to discuss the issue further. They demanded another meeting on Sunday night, but did not get it. The disgruntled Executive Committee members then caucused for a meeting on Monday morning before the tables were set up. This was opposed by the Steering Committee, which had publicly committed itself to action and did not want to back down.

To complicate matters, a faction headed by Young Democrat leader Jo Freeman had during the previous week entered into separate negotiations to cut a deal with Clark Kerr, essentially promising that if the FSM wouldn't go along with it, she and her faction would pull out of the Movement. Jo had been involved in the United Front and the October 2 negotiations with Kerr, but had been cut out of the action since and had developed a bad case of the bent nose. Hearing of the faction fight over setting up tables, she managed to involve several members of the Executive Committee in her plans, one of whom was Brian Turner, and incorporated the Monday morning meeting into her agenda. Brian was reluctant to get involved in any deals with Kerr and did not quite understand or agree with what she was doing.

Nevertheless, agreeing that things needed to be discussed, and believing that the necessary twelve signatures required to call an Executive Committee meeting had been gathered, at midnight on Sunday Brian Turner instructed Central to call the meeting for Monday morning. The Steering Committee heard of the attempted Freeman coup, and confusing it with the other demands for a Monday meeting, instructed me to stop all efforts to call an Executive Committee meeting. To what degree Brian Turner, Art Goldberg and Sandor Fuchs were cooperating with Jo Freeman and her goals is not clear. They certainly were trying to get an Executive Committee meeting to discuss the resumption of direct action, and their insistence on having the meeting before direct action was resumed coincided with Freeman's hopes that Kerr would call on Monday morning and confirm their pact.

The Steering Committee realized that a meeting had to be called, and that four urgent matters had to be dealt with. First, the resumption of direct action, which would mean the death of the CCPA. Second, the alienation of the membership from the leadership and the isolation of the leadership from the membership. Third, the threat of a public split in the leadership, and last, the threat of a separate peace in the name of the FSM.

The moderates packed the Monday meeting with every organization that had any claim to a vote. The first vote, in which only active members of the Executive Committee participated, was to decide if the half-dozen inactive organizations could vote. It was decided that they could. The second vote was for or against the resumption of direct action, and direct action passed. This scotched Freeman's coup attempt. Kerr did not call by ten o'clock and Jo and the others discovered that Kerr had not dealt fairly with them, intending only to disrupt the FSM. With this preface, I now enter into the particulars.

On Saturday night, November 7, SLATE spokesman Art Goldberg and the law student and former SLATE leader Mike Tigar supported the continuation of the CCPA and voiced opposition to the resumption of direct action. Mario spoke in favor of setting up tables again and Tigar opposed this, on the grounds that we could only hope to win through the CCPA, and that direct action would destroy our chances; he argued that by sticking with the moderate path, "You may not get more but you won't get less." Mario replied, "Ah, that's what we thought." The debate split along SLATE and CORE lines, and the more militant position prevailed, though by a narrow margin. Many members of the Executive Committee felt that direct action had been ramrodded by the Steering Committee, and wanted to explore the matter further. It was generally felt that Jack, Mario and Bettina had become inflexible and could not lead the FSM to victory if they persisted in their uncompromising demands.

Brian Mulloney: It was because of that meeting that Kolodny and Anastasi and I were dissatisfied with the Steering Committee. We wanted the whole thing to be gone over by a much larger Executive Committee, because this meeting was underrepresented and had been called at short notice. Then we found that we couldn't call a meeting because there was no mechanism for doing so. The Steering Committee said, "What's your beef? If you lose a vote you can't go around demanding a new meeting." Which was reasonable, at least from their point of view.

Then the next day we called a larger meeting of about ten people whom we thought might be sympathetic to this viewpoint: it included Jo Freeman, Dusty Miller, Andy Wells and Bob Kauffman. Jo Freeman eventually left in a huff, because we told her we weren't going to sell out, but she tried to co-opt us anyway afterwards. It was agreed that we'd go and talk to the Steering Committee before doing anything foolish or drastic. From this came the reorganization of the Steering Committee and changes in procedures that I think worked to the good.[1]

Tom Miller: It was obvious that the professors had backed down from supporting free speech and had come to the administration's position, and we were just going around in circles. The professors could deal in these abstract circles all the time, and it was like a spider's web—you go around and around and around and it's got this sticky stuff on it and you go slower and slower and pretty soon you just fall in exhaustion.

The general discussion was that we've got to get out of this quagmire. Jack and Mario were the most vocal proponents of setting up the tables again. There were some people who were opposed because they thought it would wreck the negotiations. The Saturday night Ex Com meeting with Mike Tigar considered the Kadish proposal. Before the tables were set up, there was still a chance to save the CCPA, though in effect the Kadish proposal was like setting up your own loyalty oath and then getting screwed by it; it would be self-incriminating to agree to it, because eventually you'd violate it, and then you'd have two things to face. The people arguing for it were Brian Turner and SLATE. Tigar came in—he's an effective speaker—and spoke for the Kadish proposal. After debate, Tigar changed his position and agreed that we couldn't accept it. We won the vote, but Art and Brian didn't change their positions. Then Art and some other people tried to arrange something with Kerr—tried to arrange some compromise.[2]

Andy Wells: A lot of us thought that as long as we were in negotiations we should not set up the tables. If we were going to play the game with the committee, we should play it the whole way. Otherwise we should get out of the negotiations. But there was a decision to set them up, and it was pretty much already decided before we had even had the meeting.

Mario had announced on Friday that we were going to set up tables, and when Monday came there were the tables and it pissed us off.

The group dissatisfied with the way the Steering Committee was running the FSM invited Bettina to come over and talk to us. There was oftentimes a lot of friction between the Independent delegates and members of the Steering Committee. We felt they were moving too fast without consulting the student body and there wasn't enough communication between the Executive Committee and the Steering Committee. We felt that though we agreed with a lot of the proposals, the Steering Committee was very skilled in parliamentary maneuverings and it seemed that an awful lot of railroading was going on. We felt we were being led around by the nose—we'd even developed our own plot theory. It seemed like a lot of secrecy was going on. A lot of people felt that the Steering Committee was really looking for action, and that they always moved fast enough and in the right direction so that they were always going to get action no matter what the issue was. Our position was that we could afford a little time to discuss things, whereas the Steering Committee moved right ahead to the next thing. There was a feeling of being useless on the Executive Committee, because things were pretty well run by nine guys on the Steering Committee.

The Steering Committee would come in with proposals already made up, and they had the skill and the force of rhetoric to get them passed, and it was pretty difficult for anybody to disagree with them or get their arguments across. A lot of us were pretty upset about the way Mario was conducting himself in the meetings with the administration—yelling and screaming. You can be damned tough without having to do that sort of stuff.

Jack Weinberg and Mario and particularly Steve Weissman (though he wasn't on the Steering Committee at the time) defeated some proposals that we thought were pretty sound.[3]

Jack Weinberg: The issue was whether or not the University had the right to discipline students when their activities on-campus could be connected to violations of law off-campus. The FSM argued that if laws were broken off-campus, the authorities could use police, courts and jails to deal with it, but there was no justification for the University to get involved. The University argued that it needed the power to discipline students who wished to use the campus as a base from which to launch "illegal attacks" on the community. By then, it had become clear that the FSM could win just about everything else it was fighting for if it agreed not to push this one issue. It had also become clear that the University administration was prepared to fight to the death on this point. Tigar led an effort to convince the FSM to yield. Art Goldberg supported him. Mario, a few other leaders and I made a private pact that if Tigar's position passed, we would resign from the Steering Committee rather than be party to a sellout. To us, it was a matter of high principle.

The meeting with Tigar and the Executive Committee was over the Cheit proposals. There was the last CCPA meeting at which we refused to go along with what the administration was trying to do, which Turner had supported and which the administration and faculty voted for. We had a Saturday meeting, in which it was decided that we were going to set up tables on Monday. There was a vote on it, of the Executive Committee meeting at Westminster [House].

The Steering Committee during this interim period had pretty much fallen apart. Myself and Mario and Sid Stapleton and Bettina and Suzanne—these four negotiators, plus myself—were functioning as the Steering Committee. But it had really stopped meeting. People weren't attending, and we needed a Steering Committee that could meet all the time.

It was at this Executive Committee meeting that we suddenly realized that we were getting into direct action again, and we needed a group with tactical responsibility. So we began by trying to elect a new group to run the tactical part of the campaign—a new Steering Committee. The entire discussion was over tactics of trying to set up tables—the decision had already been made by the time of that Saturday meeting.[4]

Larry Marks: The Executive Committee meetings were frankly rather boring; if there was any debate on a subject they were factionalized along well-defined lines. The lagging groups in the Executive Committee were the Young Republicans—the rare occasions when they were taking part, of course, most of the time they weren't even a part of it—the Young Democrats were moderate; SLATE was moderate; the right-wing socialist groups were moderate. The left-wing socialist groups and the civil rights groups were the activists.

There was no question in anyone's mind that the Steering Committee had to be reconstituted. The call to reconstitute the Steering Committee was frankly overwhelming. Mario was conferring with groups of professors and making decisions, and that made people very mad. Sometimes the Steering Committee did overstep its bounds. Art was voted off the Steering Committee—they decided to elect a nine-man committee.

Art showed up later on and nominated himself and wasn't elected. A couple of days after that Art and Sandor and I went up to the Steering Committee meeting and had the big thing; and then it was at the Executive Committee meeting the next day that they agreed to see about provisionally adding one more member. And then about a week later they finally provisionally added Art to the Steering Committee again, even though Art was considered incompatible with the Steering Committee. Art was the major cause for reconstitution of the Steering Committee in the first place, because people were really unhappy with Art's performance. Dusty [Miller] was deadwood, and so they weren't interested in having him around. Another piece of deadwood who was reelected to the Steering Committee, and I don't know why he ran, was Sid Stapleton. He later resigned, because he frankly wasn't participating.

The tone of the speeches was direct action, and that was what was really going on. Art was talking "let's be politic," and he was pretty soundly defeated. Jack made a speech and everybody copied it; after that Mike Parker got up and made a speech that said, "I'm not going to vote for anybody, because you're all trying to show who can be the most radical," and he got laughed down.

Goines was an unofficial part of the Steering Committee through the whole thing. Not a voting part; he was a liaison; he implemented whatever they'd decided on.[5]

Jackie Goldberg: The people who weren't reelected to the Steering Committee were Dusty, myself, Brian Turner and my brother.* They put Art back on even though he hadn't been reelected, because if Art hadn't been on it, SLATE would have pulled out. I wasn't happy with the new Steering Committee, but at least it still had Bettina on it. Bettina I trust. I can't say a *thing* except that I trust. She's just got more good common sense politically than just about any person I've ever met in my entire life. What she and Mario agree on I'd be almost sure to agree on also, and to trust. Even if I wasn't sure I agreed I'd trust their decision. Given the kind of information we had, which was always sort of half guess, half reality, I would say that they'd come up with as good an analysis as any other two people.[6]

Brian Mulloney: The Steering Committee was making far more of the decisions than had originally been intended, and people were very unhappy. Ron Anastasi and David Kolodny and I went to the Steering Committee and explained our position. After about twelve or fourteen hours of meeting they saw our point. The main thing that healed the difficulty with the Steering Committee was the YDS [Young Democrats, Jo Freeman's organization] trying to sell us out. Jack Weinberg, who was

*Brian viewed this as part of the purging of the moderates; his biggest complaint was that the Executive Committee had been pressured into allowing a major decision to be made by the Steering Committee with no further consultation.

at that time the most politically savvy guy, was smart enough to see that there was real political trouble here. Essentially they did the intelligent thing, which is to take someone who is concerned into your confidence. So they agreed that Ron would be recommended to the Steering Committee, and he was voted on, as was Marty Roysher.[7]

Bob Starobin: Rossman was taken into the Steering Committee because he was editor of the Rossman Report.* He also was able to articulate a certain position which was in vogue at that time, which I would call a position of the alienated, romantic revolutionary student, mixed in with a lot of nihilism. That was really going over well up until the [November 20] Regents' meeting. After the disillusionment that followed the Regents' meeting, he gave an hour-long speech to the Steering Committee on the Saturday or Sunday afterwards at the Wesleyan Foundation. He had this ability to catch people up in his rhetoric, but that was beginning to break down. People said that Rossman had entranced the Steering Committee, that he had turned them all on to his way of thinking, especially in the week before the Regents' meeting. But I would say this trance was broken after that.

He'd been to a few Steering Committee meetings before. When Goldberg was put back on, it was also suggested that the Steering Committee be expanded to twelve. So they had to have three more, and the three turned out to be Art, Mona [Hutchin] and Rossman. By this time Rossman had put out the Rossman Report, and had insisted that they step up their PR, and everybody said, "Yeah! Yeah!" So he got on the Steering Committee, there was this sort of feeling that everybody at one point was looking to Rossman for the answers. Everybody was jazzed. That weekend [November 14 and 15] they were meeting at Ron Anastasi's place, and that was the time that they were under surveillance, there were police agents watching the house and taking down license numbers. There was one period there where there was a real cloak-and-dagger scene going on, and the people on the Steering Committee were having a real ball with that. This was the same time that Rossman was holding forth.[8]

---

*The Rossman Report, more formally called *Administrative Pressures and Student Political Activity at the University of California: A Preliminary Report*, was a massively documented work compiled by a group of graduate and undergraduate students and edited by mathematics graduate Michael Rossman, reporting on the administration's restriction of student political activity and expression. It was presented to the Williams Committee (CCPA) by the FSM, and a synopsis of its findings was distributed to the campus as a whole. Lynne Hollander was responsible for editorial coordination, Marston Schultz and Tom Irwin for production (Starobin, "Graduate Students and FSM," 19).

Brian Shannon: Ron Anastasi was noteworthy, though I had differences of opinion with him later on. From the very beginning Anastasi started doing some hard work. Anastasi was in charge of the microphones, as I recall. Continuously during the FSM he did some concrete organizational work. He seemed to know where all the committees were; he kept his fingers on the pulse more than any other person on the Steering Committee. The problem there was that politically he was not that good, and so he was a person that did take an active interest in sub-organizations, but it should have been somebody stronger. But maybe because he wasn't that strong, he was good for them to use.

Sid Stapleton played a very strong role in the FSM until his studies and the necessity of getting a job interfered. For the first two-thirds of the FSM he was very active. He's not a strong speaker, especially before large numbers of people. Very thoughtful speaker—in a meeting inside you'd sit there and listen to him, but not out on the steps—he'd never cut a big role there. For instance, Sid was the person that convinced Savio to go for the [December] strike.

Even in the beginning Art Goldberg treated things too lightly. He's got a good political mind, but he's cynical toward what he reads and what he thinks about. Another thing is that some of his cynicism at those meetings was because they just took too long, and he would willingly have them shorter even if he lost his point. He had a lot more political experience than most other people and got bored because other people were ignorant.

I understand Jackie Goldberg joined a sorority mainly because she thought it was important to get sorority people to support you in the long run. Why do you educate that group? It has to do with the fetishism that those are the important people in the society. It's also acceptance of the status quo—you don't transform sororities from the inside—it's an acceptance of their long-range viability as an institution. It's a fetishism that people have toward those who are in a position of authority.[9]

The Steering Committee was reorganized on Saturday night and, without further consulting the Executive Committee, on Sunday, November 8, the new FSM Steering Committee issued this statement:

> Ever since Oct. 2 the organizations composing the Free Speech Movement have voluntarily refrained from exercising their constitutional liberties on the Berkeley campus of the University of California. The FSM imposed this moratorium in the hope that agreement with the administration regarding any regulations could soon be reached. Although we continue to be a party to the Campus Committee on Political

Activity, we feel that we must lift our self-imposed moratorium on political activity because the committee is already deadlocked over the issue of political advocacy and appears headed for a long series of radical disagreements. . . . We must exercise our rights so that the University is not permitted to deny us those rights for any long period and so that our political organizations can function to their maximum capacity. Many students and organizations have been hampered in their efforts in the past election and in civil rights activity because of the moratorium.

Saturday the CCPA became deadlocked over the issue of the student's [*sic*] right to advocate off-campus political activity. . . . [The administration proposed an amendment] directly aimed at student participation in the civil rights movement and . . . totally unacceptable to the students. The administration would give themselves the right (1) to decide on the legality and the "appropriateness" of the students' off-campus political activity, (2) to decide the legality of the students' on-campus advocacy of off-campus action, and (3) to discipline the students in the area of their civil liberties.

. . . . The Free Speech Movement proposed [an] amendment which is the position of the American Association of University Professors and the American Civil Liberties Union.

. . . the administration vetoed our position and insisted on the ability of the University to discipline students in the area of their civil liberties. The FSM believes that the University is not a competent body to decide questions concerning civil liberties, especially since it is subject to strong political pressures. Because students' rights have great political impact as well as legal significance, the courts should be the only body to decide upon them.

The AAUP has declared that "students should enjoy the same freedom of religion, speech, press and assembly, and the right to petition the authorities that citizens generally possess." The Free Speech Movement intends to exercise those freedoms on Monday.[10]

Despite the Saturday night reorganization of the Steering Committee, and despite the vote that had agreed on renewed action, a substantial minority of the Executive Committee was still extremely unhappy with the way things were going. Brian Turner had become embroiled with Jo Freeman; Art Goldberg and Sandor Fuchs had gotten into some sort of tar-baby mess that never became clear to anyone; a group that had formed earlier in the week to demand a Steering Committee reorganization had gotten itself mixed up with the Young Democrats and their plot to make a deal with Kerr; the SLATE faction was desperately unhappy that Art had more or less been purged. In short, the deep dissatisfaction with the high-handedness, isolation and escalating radicalism of the Steering Committee had reached a climax. A minority faction formed to demand a new Executive Committee meeting. At first they wanted a meeting called for that very night. The Steering Committee refused, on the parliamentary point that a meeting could only be called if the Steering Committee were informed twelve hours in advance. This angered the dissidents further. They then demanded a meeting for the following morning, to precede the setting up of tables. This the Steering Committee also refused, saying that the death of the CCPA and renewed action had been agreed upon in the Saturday meeting, and an endless rehash was inappropriate after action had publicly been promised. The dissatisfied faction then argued their own parliamentary point, claiming that they had a right to call a meeting if twelve or more Executive Committee members so petitioned. This the Steering Committee reluctantly granted, and a frantic effort to get twelve signatures ensued.

Andy Wells: We wanted to reorganize the Steering Committee, which we felt was lopsided. Ron Anastasi, Brian Mulloney and I were the most concerned. There was a meeting at Ron's place; Mulloney was there, David Kolodny, Betty Linsky, Julie Blake, I don't remember if Dusty Miller was there or not. The Young Democrats were there; Jo Freeman was there. As a matter of fact, we had a big argument about whether Jo Freeman should get into this thing or not. Everybody thought Jo Freeman was sort of a fink; we couldn't tell what she was going to do next. She showed up anyway, and was *very* interested in the whole thing— her eyes glistened when she heard about it. Our intentions were never to split up the Free Speech Movement; what we wanted was to see the Steering Committee reorganized. We were counting votes, to see how the Executive Committee was going to line up. We calculated it up on paper, and then we started calling people. I think we got somewhere around eleven or twelve votes for sure, and calculated another five or six that might be going with us. We needed eighteen. We were really steamed up about this, and were working every way we could to get the Steering Committee to come around to listen to us. Then Ron Anastasi got elected to the Steering Committee, so we kissed him off.

We had the meeting, and the Steering Committee found out about it. They found out about it because I blew it. Ron happened to be there at a Steering Committee meeting when they found out about it. The Steering Committee seemed genuinely concerned with the feelings of the Executive Committee, and worried about the chances of a split. We talked the whole thing over, and straightened things out. Things weren't half as bad after that.

A new Steering Committee was elected over the weekend. Mike Tigar came to the meetings—he was in favor of the Cheit number two proposal—it was very confusing, everybody had proposals. The Steering Committee meetings were held at Sid Stapleton's after that, and then at Marty Roysher's.[11]

Meanwhile, back at the ranch, Jo Freeman and her faction had secretly negotiated a separate peace with Clark Kerr and the administration. Kerr urged the group to break with the FSM; when the five students refused to do so without concessions, Kerr offered a settlement that involved the reinstatement of the suspended students, the dropping of any plans to institute further penalties against students and organizations, and the reinstitution of campus political rights. In return, the moderates would get the FSM to abandon the ideas of advocacy and prior restraint. If the moderates could get the FSM to accept this settlement, well and good; if not, the moderates would publicly pull out. The moderates would force a meeting before activism resumed and try to stop it. Kerr would call before ten o'clock Monday morning to consolidate the deal. It is here that the plot thickens to the point of melodrama.

Ron Anastasi: Jo Freeman suggested to Mona [Hutchin] that she infiltrate the Steering Committee, and Mona said, "She practically suggested that I should sleep with Jack Weinberg in order to seduce him over to the conservative cause!" Apparently Jo had suggested to Mona that she work on Betty Linsky, Brian Mulloney, David Kolodny and Ron Anastasi. That they represented potential converts.

Jo wanted Mona to contact Dick Roman of the YDS and YPSL [Young People's Socialist League], to get Mike Eisen from UCLC [University Civil Liberties Committee], Paul Cahill from the YRS [Young Republicans], YPSL, SLATE, UCLC, the Conservatives for an Open Campus, SDS with Bob Jervice (someone from SDS was supposed to have been at the secret meeting with Kerr), CCR [California Campus Republicans], Brian Turner from the Student Non-violent Coordinating Committee, and Don Hackett and Greg Moore from Conservatives at Large; this was apparently the faction that she was developing.[12]

Patti Iiyama: [On Sunday night] Brian Turner went to Stephanie [Coontz]'s place and said, "I want to talk with you about this, but it's gotta be top secret." He told her that he and a small group of people were negotiating on their own with the administration. He wanted to see if she was in on it, and she lied and said she'd go along. Then he left Stephanie's and said he would call back again at twelve. She was completely panicked and didn't want to be on her own, so she called me up and said, "I've got to talk with you." She wanted to have me along with her as another witness. So around midnight Brian called her up and told her where to go and Lewis Lester and the both of us went over. They were really hamstrung by the fact that it had to be awfully secret. Mike Abramovitch was there, and Jo Freeman, and Brian Turner. They had a plan that Brian Turner didn't agree with: in the middle of the rally they were going to suddenly get up and say, "We don't agree with this at all and we don't approve of setting

STEPHANIE COONTZ.
PHOTOGRAPHER UNKNOWN.

up the tables," and they were going to walk away and try to carry the rest of the crowd with them. They got into this huge argument over whether or not that was the right tactic because Brian Turner didn't agree with it.

Mario called and he wanted to speak to Brian. Evidently what had happened was Brian had also called up Mike Tigar and told him about it, and asked him if he would come in with them and also get up and say something about how he disagreed with what was going on. Mike Tigar of course had called up the Steering Committee and let them know what was happening. Stephanie talked with Mario after Brian had, and told him what was going on. We asked who else was in on it; we kept asking, "Where's Art and Sandor?" And they said, "Well, they've been negotiating." They said that they were going to get an answer from Kerr by ten o'clock the next morning, and so they wanted to have a meeting before then at eight o'clock in the morning to get support, so they could give Kerr an answer.

We left at about one o'clock. It wasn't really a meeting! It was just a bunch of people standing around talking, trying to figure out what they were going to say to the press later on. Whether they were going to say, "Yes, we are part of the FSM," or even to say, "Well, we're a part of FSM but no longer a part." Brian Turner was very confused; Jo Freeman was really running it.

So we left on the pretext that I had to go home and Stephanie was going to drive me. We left Lewis there to report on what was going on while we were gone. Then we went over to the Steering Committee meeting at Ron Anastasi's. We walked in and just as we walked in, Art and Sandor walked in. This was about one, one-thirty, so we stepped out of the room in a hurry. We thought that Art had seen us, but we weren't sure, so we closed the door, and we were listening to what he was saying. We got *furious*, because he was lying through his teeth, he said he had *nothing* to do with the thing, all he wanted to do was make sure that a meeting would be called because of democracy; that every side should be heard and that the issue had not been fully discussed in the other Ex Com meetings; it had been rushed through. And he was going on and on like this, and at the other meeting everybody was waiting for Art and Sandor to come back, because "Art and Sandor are leaders, they're the ones who know everything about what's going on and we're not really that sure." So we talked with Bettina and she said, "Well, come on in and confront them." We came on in and Art and Sandor evidently didn't realize at first what role Stephanie and I had played. When she started contradicting them, they left in a big huff. They kept saying they were innocent, that they hadn't promoted this at all; that Brian Turner had come up to them and said that he was negotiating on his own and would they help and arrange a meeting. Art never admitted that he was lying. He just said, "Well, we'll see at the meeting tomorrow, what happens." And I *think* he had agreed to abide by the decision at the meeting. But everybody on Steering Committee felt that he was [lying]. After they left we stayed and discussed what we should do. We knew they were going to try and pack the meeting the next morning.

We never really fully discussed it afterwards. Everybody tried to forget about the split, and tried to heal it up, although it's very hard because there were very bitter feelings on *my* part, anyway. That they would even *think* of trying to negotiate on their own![13]

Though the Steering Committee had no direct information about this attempted coup, vague rumors were circulating, which the Steering Committee conflated with the efforts to call an Executive Committee meeting early Monday morning. The Steering Committee didn't know how far the attempted coup had proceeded, or if it was connected with the oddly persistent demands for an Executive Committee meeting *before* the tables were set up. Already on the brink of paranoia, it reacted violently, assuming that *this* was the group trying to pull off the break, and condoned drastic action. Mario and Jack instructed me to confiscate the FSM files and in general try to scotch those bent on calling the meeting.

About eleven-thirty Sunday night, I got a call at Central from Jack Weinberg that there'd been some political shenanigans on the part of a dissident minority. The Steering Committee didn't know what was happening, and they considered it important to prevent a coup. He told me to get all important files and all important materials and information and get out of the house with them as fast as possible and take them over to Anastasi's. I did just that and got in Marilyn's car and split.

I then returned to Central and sat on the phones. I said that I would be the only person answering or receiving calls, and if anyone tried to do anything I'd pull the phones out of the wall. This really shook the staff up, as they had no idea that anything was amiss. Then they discovered that I'd taken all their files and went through the roof. Art and Sandor Fuchs came in, convinced that setting up tables again would touch off a bloody riot and that the whole student movement would be crushed. They asked to use the phone, and I let them. They called their own group and got the ball rolling again for the morning meeting.

The dissidents claimed to have the required number of names to call a meeting, but when asked to produce them, could not. An hour later, they came up with a list of twelve names, though upon checking it was discovered that four of the names were illegitimate. One person had never heard of the meeting, one denied that he had ever sympathized with the dissidents, one was not even on the Executive Committee, and one was me. I then remembered that Art had asked me, "Do you object to a meeting?" I'd replied, "No, I don't object to a meeting, but it has to be done right." He took that out of context and put me on the list, which was pretty dumb, because everybody knew I was a part of the CORE crowd. After we'd gotten into a big argument about whether I'd agreed to be on his list or not, I left and went back to the Steering Committee meeting at Anastasi's. The Steering Committee perceived that, whatever the hell was going on, it was serious, and that it would be far better to have a meeting and find out all about it. Thus, a meeting was officially called for the next morning at eight.

Marilyn Noble: That day [Sunday, November 8] at about five-thirty, Sam Bader and Brian Turner went over to dinner at Kathleen Whitney's, and Brian had gone through the box with addresses and telephone numbers, and had said to me, "Marilyn, I will call you later on for some more names. I'm working on something." By this time the Steering

Committee meetings had become very secretive, going on at Ron An-astasi's. Nina Spitzer had been kicked out of a meeting, and she was our own press representative! It was really getting very paranoid at this point. I believe that Brian had called me once during the evening, get-ting more names, and told me to call an Ex Com meeting for the next morning. I think this was around nine o'clock. Then a phone call came through for David Goines, and Goines talked on the phone a while, and then for a little bit he was rambling through the files—I mean, the files were just sitting there—and then he asked for the car. He said he had to deliver something, and he'd be back. So he went. And then he came back. And I reached for something, afterwards, and I couldn't lay my hand on the file. I said to Sutake, "Where is that file?" And then David said, "They're at Steering Committee." He'd pulled the list of members and the card files, and maybe three or four of the Ex Com committee lists. I was just furious, and said, "These are our files! We need these files!" We had some substitute lists, and I started calling names, and all of a sudden the operator's voice came on and said, "Is this 848-2930? You have an emergency call," and Mario's voice came on, just scream-ing, saying, "You will not call that meeting!" And I said, "What? It's been called by Ex Com!" And Mario was just screaming, that they hadn't given [twelve] hours' notice. By this time I was getting hysterical. Ex Com's coming at us one way, Steering Committee the other, and we're paralyzed. I said, "I'm going to do what I think is right," and Mario said, "No, you're going to do what I think is right!" and I said, "No, I'm going to make whatever information we've got left available to whoever is in this organization!" And I just hung up. I was in total hysterics, and I called Keith Chamberlain and said, "Will you come down here, I'm scared for my life. I'm scared for my physical safety." And I got hold of Father Fisher, the same way. They came flying through the door in about ten minutes. It must have been one-thirty, and by this time David had wandered off somewhere. He knew he was pretty unpopular at that point.

The next afternoon, after the meeting, Bettina called and wanted me to get ahold of somebody, and I said, "I can't. You have my files," and she said, "Oh. Do you want us to bring them or will you come and get them?" Kitty [Piper] and I went over to Ron Anastasi's and 'Tina [Bet-tina] and Suzanne gave them back to me and said that they were very sorry over all this mix-up. They were trying to be nice. The boys were nowhere around. As far as I know we got everything back. From that point on, David Goines was never trusted in the office again. We felt that he was Jack Weinberg's hatchet man. The next day we made copies of everything and hid it at Don Dean's house, and we gave a bunch of stuff to Kitty to take home.[14]

Larry Marks: I was at Central at the time the files were taken out. Paranoia was running rampant; Marilyn was on the ceiling—she was always out of her mind, she was a nervous wreck, falling apart—Father Fisher and Keith Chamberlain from Westminster came over and they talked her to bed finally, and they sat there worrying for a while; Art was there; Art and Sandor and I were talking with Father Fisher. I'd come in about eleven; it was at ten o'clock that the news had come that Brian Turner had finked out. So things were in an uproar there and all of a sudden Goines popped in around midnight—he appeared on the scene for a moment, and then was gone. He had Marilyn's car—she was still running around not seeing anything, she didn't get to bed until around one. We shoved some tranquilizers down her. She was inflicting hysteria on everyone; she was a moderate, she was on Goldberg's side, but she had this thing about taking care of Mario. This was sometime before she started sewing people's initials in their underwear. That was the point at which Goines quit—she was doing the laundry for everyone, and so that she could identify everybody's underwear she started embroidering their initials in their underwear and their undershirts, and Goines took a look at this and said, "I've *had* it!" and he moved out, and that was the last Central ever saw of him.

I looked out the window at Goines, and I saw something under his arm, and then we started looking for the work files, and we noticed that the work files and practically everything else from Central had been taken. This as far as I could ascertain was at the direction, for the most part, of Weinberg. I don't know if Weinberg had gotten much sleep at that time, but I can tell you that Weinberg's actions were very sick at that time. When I went to the [Steering Committee] meeting, his face was very tense, and his voice was tense and it was raised, and it seemed like someone was trying to murder him or something. Jack had ordered it, because the phone rang and I answered it and it was Weinberg, and he asked for Goines, and I handed the phone to Goines and the next thing I knew was that Goines was going out the door with the files. So as far as I know it was directly at the order of Weinberg.

We were trying to get ahold of Turner, and he finally called in and Art talked to him. He wanted to see that a meeting was called, and that he and the Young Democrat faction had figured out that there had to be this meeting. Turner didn't even get it as bad as Art did. The Steering Committee thought that Art led the thing, but he didn't.

The three of us went to the Steering Committee meeting to try and convince them that we were not with Brian Turner. Because this even made the three of us a little unhappy. We went up to plead with the Steering Committee to have an Executive Committee meeting the next day. We were not convinced that direct action was a good idea, and we did not think that the Steering Committee had the support of the Executive Committee. Frankly, it was a very close vote at the Executive Committee meeting and it had appeared that way at the time.

The Steering Committee meeting was a group of very paranoid individuals; and I think that the sickest of them was Jack. It's no secret that the moderates had no great love for Jack, nor he for us. We were in conflict.

I knew Jack when he was a very straight math student and happily married, before he had ever taken part in any civil rights activities, and the next time I saw him he was the chairman of Campus CORE. Something had come over him. All of a sudden he became very direct-action-oriented and very impatient. One of the problems of the FSM was the lack of communication between the administration and the students. Certainly the administration was of no help in this respect, but the students weren't a great deal of help either. Jack was a prime example of this; Jack would rather fight than talk. I saw the necessity for a fight when it finally came; but one of the bases on which the FSM operated was that the FSM would exhaust all the alternatives before then. Art was very politically oriented, and frankly he thinks that Jack was a very impolitic person. Jack in his private life is a hell of a nice guy, but in his political life we don't get along.

I took Art home, and he spent the next couple of hours on the phone calling the moderates. He was sincerely working under the notion at this time that direct action would be impolitic.[15]

Jack Weinberg: The so-called purge occurred after the CCPA meeting. [On Sunday] Turner and his group were having a separate meeting somewhere else. We [the Steering Committee] were at Anastasi's house, it was pouring cats and dogs—really coming down. We get the report that Turner had requested a meeting of the Executive Committee for Monday at eleven o'clock in the morning. Turner had told Mario, and Mario had replied by saying that eleven was impossible—we had another meeting then and had planned an Executive Committee meeting for twelve. But Turner insisted.* We had a ruling that a petition of twelve

---

*The tape throughout most of this interview with Jack is extremely difficult to understand: the microphone is in the middle of the room, Jack has a bad cold and is mumbling half the time while eating crackers or potato chips, a dog is barking and traffic sounds obscure vital passages. From what I can gather from this and other sources, Brian Turner wanted to

have the Executive Committee meeting at eleven in the morning because Jo Freeman had promised to telephone at ten o'clock giving the results of her negotiations with Kerr. If she had managed to strike a deal, then Turner's group would have a concrete alternate platform to present at the Executive Committee meeting. The meeting actually occurred at eight in the morning

names could call an Executive Committee meeting. It never had been resolved that by getting twelve names you could pick the time and place, it was just that it had to be reasonable. Turner was of the opinion that by calling an eleven o'clock meeting he could preempt our activity. But he never gave us the petition. So we had a report that the bureaucracy was phoning people for this meeting; we called up Central for David Goines, who was there, and said, "What's happening there, what's going on?" We told him to take the files and bring them to Anastasi's house. It was our opinion that the files were the property of the FSM, and that the Executive Committee had the ultimate power over this property. We felt that calling this meeting with the FSM files was clearly an effort at sabotage.

Patti Iiyama and Stephanie Coontz had been at the Turner meeting and brought a report. As the word came out of what was going on, Anastasi's house just got fuller and fuller and fuller. People we'd never seen before, like Barry Jablon for instance; Dave Rynon came by, and Myra Jehlin, and Bob Kauffman came by, Dunbar Aitkins came by—Dunbar didn't understand what was happening, he was very confused by all this confusion. Later on Art came by, and Art clearly was politically siding with Turner; he apparently hadn't been meeting with him, though at the meeting we thought that Art was totally together with Turner. Art argued that we just had to have this meeting no matter what at eleven o'clock the next day. Even if we never did receive an official petition. We kept on trying to get this list. What finally happened is that Turner gave us names over the phone. We checked out the names and a lot of the people on the list had never even heard about this thing. David Goines was one of the people who they gave as one of the twelve; apparently Turner had come up to him and said, "What do you think of the idea of a meeting . . . think it's a good idea to have a meeting?" and he said, "Sure." So Goldberg was saying, "Even if the petition wasn't signed, I think we should still have a meeting." A whole bunch of people were throwing questions at him, and he was saying that he didn't really understand what was going on but that we should have a meeting. After Goldberg left, the girls who had been at Turner's house said, "He's lying. He knows all about what's going on, he was in a phone conversation with Turner."

After he left a lot of people said, "We've got to have a meeting early

and the moderate position was voted down. In consequence, Jo had nothing to report to Kerr, who in any event did not call her at ten o'clock as had been agreed. When the moderates met with Kerr again, he denied that he had made any deals of any kind. Kerr had not intended to abide by any agreements and had only intended to introduce a split in the FSM.

in the morning just to get this thing over with," and word got out and people called their friends, and there was a meeting next morning with a long debate.[16]

Mario Savio: They had told Marilyn Noble to call an Executive Committee meeting, and we had told her nothing doing without a petition signed by twelve names, and she had gone ahead anyway, and then we went over and got the books. They were countermanding our orders. Stephanie came over with the information about the sellout, and I got angry with Brian Turner and yelled at him on the telephone. I felt really bad about that afterward.

They were going through the list and guessing at people whom they thought might agree with them. When we contacted people on this list of names, we found that some of them had either not been asked at all or were in complete disagreement with their position. We consented to the meeting even though we thought that their list of names was bogus, but we put a time limit on it.[17]

Mona Hutchin: There was a meeting called by Brian Turner and a minority faction to try to stop setting up the tables. This meeting was attended by the conservative organizations because the moderate faction was frantically getting out votes and tried to get all the conservative groups and representatives to come and vote with them. It was at eight in the morning at Barry Jablon's house and everybody was falling asleep. It was a yucky meeting, challenges to credentials and endless debate going back and forth. Danny Rosenthal and I were all set to vote against the moderates just on general principles, but we didn't because we were afraid we'd be disowned if anybody ever found out. Jo Freeman had called out our groups and we felt that it would be a good act on our part to vote against her. Probably if we'd known then what we found out later we would have. After this the conservative organizations decided to keep on sending people to meetings, and I was one of the representatives that went.[18]

Bob Starobin: The final CCPA meeting was the Saturday before the tables went up. There was a pretty deep division among the graduates on whether to set up tables, though not within the graduates on the Executive Committee, who were unanimously in favor of it. Jo Freeman was working along with [Dick] Roman and Jim Burnette, and she approached Mulloney to try and bring him into her group. He wasn't interested in what they were trying to do, which was to split the FSM, but he went along with them to a certain extent to find out what they were doing.

There was a division within the Executive Committee on the question of setting up tables, though a clear majority favored the return to activism. Jo Freeman was having all kinds of negotiations with Lipset and Kerr at that time, and there was a meeting at Barry Jablon's apartment on Ridge, early in the morning [of November 9], just before the tables went up at eleven or twelve. I was at the meeting, and they were waiting for a telephone call from somebody, which was supposed to come at ten o'clock, and this concerned whether Kerr was going to accept what Freeman and Roman were proposing, but the telephone call never came. So their whole tactic fell through and we went on putting up the tables. Brian told me that Jo Freeman was in contact with Governor Brown, and that she contacted him because of her position within the Young Democrats, and told him of the situation and the problem with militancy, and claimed there was Communist infiltration and domination. Governor Brown wrote back to Jo Freeman and Jim Burnette, in late October or early November, and thanked her for the information and said that he too was worried about Communist infiltration and would meet with her. Then Jo tried to get graduate support for her deal, and she contacted Brian Mulloney. Brian went to a meeting, but he never participated in what was going on. There's no question that she was in contact with the governor.[19]

Brian Mulloney: Jo Freeman was in the Young Democrats. She showed me a letter that she had from the governor; it was a blatant attempt, at that point, to sell out. The letter thanked her for her letter to him explaining the YD position and encouraged her attempts to bring a reasonable resolution, and if anything could be done where the YDs and she could collect some student support; if they would come part way then he would go the rest. Her coalition was pretty small: Jo Freeman, Dave Jessup, Dick Roman, Ann Kilby, Sue Schwartz. The YPSL people and that whole collection of people of that general ilk.

Early in October the YDs and YPSLs had pulled out, had denounced the FSM at various points, had done no work, and had been sneaking around behind the scenes and had just generally been obnoxious about the whole thing. They'd *clearly* withdrawn. And then they showed up in all their various and sundry manifestations, you know, the Democratic Socialists, the Young Democrats, YPSL, all claiming their seats and wanting to vote. They were all there that morning, making a threat of publicly denouncing that the FSM was antidemocratic and Communistic. They were given the vote eventually, probably as a result of those threats. But they were voted down anyway, and their whole business failed.[20]

Mario Savio: The Democrats and Social Democrats only come to meetings to vote against the ongoing momentum of the Movement, and then they go back into their holes. When would Jim Burnette come to a meeting? To vote against what we were doing. These people were the ones who we found out had conspired with Lipset and Kerr. Their letter said, in effect, "We couldn't possibly sell the Movement out—unless we got something for it."[21]

Bettina Aptheker: My recollections of that unfortunate episode involving the sellout deal was that Seymour Martin Lipset and Nathan Glazer were the real culprits and had the power because they were on the faculty and had Kerr's ear. They initiated the contact with the students.* Also, far more important in that episode was the role of Jo Freeman, who was in the political science department and very close to Lipset.[22]

At the meeting Monday morning the Steering Committee walked in en masse, late, and with a haughty air. There was no screwing around. It was a matter of getting right down to business, because the meeting had a time limit on it. The meeting convened at about eight o'clock with the parties divided geographically in the room. Brian Turner looked guilty and confused. It became clear that Jo Freeman was the inspiring influence, and was actually running the whole show. The other groups were obviously following her lead. Jo made a couple of speeches attempting to defend her position, but she would have done better to save her breath to cool her porridge.

The room was filled with paper organizations and nonfunctioning, defunct organizations—organizations we'd never heard of—and the split was pretty even. The rules of the Executive Committee had never really made clear who should be a member and who should not be a member. Basically, any legitimate student organization had the right to send two representatives. Since the rules weren't clear, they had us in a cleft stick. We were afraid to censure a portion of the Executive Committee right then and there, because they had too much power. Both we and they recognized that it wasn't legitimate power, but they still had

---

*Andy Wells, in his taped interview with Marston Schultz on October 17, 1965, recollects two young faculty members sneaking late at night into Ron Anastasi's apartment and meeting with Mario, presenting a half-baked plan for reconciliation which Mario rejected out of hand. Andy's memory was that the faculty members were tremendously excited by their plan, and that they insisted on the proviso of "advocacy of *legal* action," which was by that point in negotiations the central issue. He recounts that they were much disappointed that their program was not well received by the FSM representative. It is likely that they then attempted to approach the FSM by another route. Although Andy could not remember who the two faculty members were, Glazer and Lipset fill the bill.

enough power to gum up the works. There was a considerable amount of debate, and all of it was being pressed by time. We wanted to get the tables set up and wanted to prepare for the rally.

There were two significant votes. The first was 18–17: whether the six inactive groups *could* vote.* That's why the vote was smaller on the first vote than on the second vote. Dan Rosenthal made a nasty scene, and a big display of himself, and made threats about smearing the FSM publicly, and almost got into a fistfight with somebody. The argument was that his organizations didn't belong anymore, that they'd quit. The rule set out at the formation of the FSM was one club, one vote, and it was agreed that any legitimate campus organization could be a member of the FSM Executive Committee. Nobody had ever said anything about remaining active or losing your membership, so we finally agreed that these groups, by virtue of having once been active and having originally been members of the United Front and having originally sent representatives to the Executive Committee, had a right, no matter how manipulative and counterrevolutionary, to vote. The second vote, on the main issue of whether we were going to set up tables or not, was 21–20 in favor of setting them up.

Afterward, we found out from Brian Turner what had gone on between the dissenting faction and the administration of the University. In return for dropping disciplinary charges against the suspended students and granting immunity from discipline to students who had participated in campus political activism since the Free Speech Movement began, the FSM minority faction would publicly accept the CCPA and stop hanging things up on the ill-understood issues of advocacy and prior restraint. The split would force the radicals out, and the matter would be resolved. After the moderate faction agreed to this, another meeting was set for later. On the ninth of November, the moderate position did not prevail and the tables were set up. Kerr did not call Jo Freeman, which didn't matter because Jo Freeman had nothing good to tell Kerr. If the moderates had prevailed, Jo Freeman would then have had the ammunition to negotiate with Kerr. They did not, and the bitterest pill to be swallowed by the breakaway group was Kerr's later repudiation of his implied cooperation; when they met with him the next day, he

---

*Although it is not now and was not even then entirely clear just what these six organizations were, I can give the reader a rough idea of which ones they must have been among: CCR (California College Republicans), UCLC (University Civil Liberties Committee), YD (Young Democrats), YR (Young Republicans), YPSL (Young People's Socialist League), YAF (Young Americans for Freedom), COC (Conservatives for an Open Campus), and CAL (Conservatives at Large).

acted as though he had never agreed to anything. They then realized that Kerr had intended only to divide and conquer, and that they, in a sincere effort to seek a resolution to the conflict, had only fallen into a trap. Everyone profited by this demonstration of administrative duplicity; and Kerr was, forevermore, viewed as manipulative, unprincipled and completely untrustworthy.

Facing the concerted wrath of the whole body, the breakaway group was unable to continue, and as the students knew nothing of their treaty with the University, the majority faction was able to repudiate the arrangements as not representative of the FSM's true desires.

After the meeting at Barry Jablon's and the close vote, Brian Turner got up and said, "We've taken the vote, and this is what has been decided upon. We all have a duty to go ahead with it now, and continue as a united FSM." Everybody applauded. Despite Turner's heavy involvement in the moderates' coup attempt, nobody seemed particularly inclined to hold it against him, and he was welcomed back into the fold with no hard feelings to speak of. The upshot was that the Steering Committee made a serious effort to behave in a more open, democratic manner, taking care to avoid the appearance of railroading. On November 14, the Executive Committee elected three more members to the Steering Committee: Mona Hutchin, Mike Rossman and—mainly to appease SLATE—Art Goldberg, but Goldberg's stock was flat, and he scarcely attended further meetings.

John Searle, who argues that the faculty had a dominant role in the resolution of the conflict, presents a more benign version of the event:

> after the failure of the official negotiations several informal groups were formed attempting to produce a solution. One of these, composed mostly of members of the department of history, produced a compromise agreement. It involved only such University restrictions on free speech as were constitutionally allowable, and it provided for due process and the possibility of University cooperation in test cases before the courts. The FSM leaders informally agreed to this and there were many informal talks about it with the administration. In the end the administration did not accept it. This incident deserves to be better known, for it demonstrates that the FSM leaders were willing to compromise, at least in mid-November.[23]

DIRECT ACTION

O<small>N</small> NOVEMBER 9 Chancellor Strong issued a statement in the *Daily Cal*:

> If the FSM returns to direct action tactics, this will constitute a clear breach of the agreement of October 2. Students and organizations participating will be held responsible for their actions.

At noon, speakers addressed a rally from the top of an old dresser, set up in the exact spot where the police car had foundered on October 2. Mario thundered:

> By its continuing acts of political oppression, the University Administration has abrogated the Pact. . . . Accordingly, the students have lifted the self-imposed moratorium on the exercise of the constitutionally-guaranteed political rights. . . . No institution, except the courts, has any competence to decide what constitutes the abuse of political freedom. The students shall not cease in the responsible exercise of their rights.[1]

Card tables were set up by the FSM and eight other off-campus organizations with sign-up sheets and cups for donations. Seventy-five people had their names taken by underling administrators, called "the little deans." As Deans Rice and Murphy took names, a microphone was held so that their interrogation was broadcast for all to hear. The student emcee also took the opportunity to introduce Berkeley mayor Wallace Johnson, FBI agents, representatives of the district attorney's office and the lumpish Berkeley "Red Squad"*—the branch of the Berkeley police

---

*Every police department in the United States had a Red Squad or something like it. To supplement the FBI, some states had an official or semiofficial undercover department dedicated to nosing out Communists. In the 1950s and early 1960s,

NOVEMBER 9, 1964 LEAFLETER. PHOTO © 1993 BY TED STRESHINSKY.

department whose calling in life was to keep track of all the Commies and Bolsheviks, most of whom were conveniently located on campus.

It was raining, and the rally was not particularly well attended. This did not improve the FSM's leverage, though the statements that the rallies would continue, and that they would include tables at which students

Robert Mates' family was routinely shadowed by the Michigan Red Squad. Through the Freedom of Information Act the Mateses discovered that after they'd sold their car in 1961, the Red Squad followed it around for years to places where its new owner took it, none of which had anything to do with Communist activities. Wayne Collins, Jr., told me that in 1965 undercover policeman Jim Majors of the Berkeley police department infiltrated the Vietnam Day Committee and participated in making a documentary about the VDC. Police agents were often the most vocal in favoring *agent provocateur* activity and "let's you and him fight" sort of stuff. The police had a vested interest in the amount of trouble caused by left-wing groups, and because they were immune to prosecution, made sure that plenty of trouble was available. It came to be common knowledge that those who most espoused violence and who strove to "out-Herod Herod" in their every word and deed, egging others on to greater outrages and risks, were themselves often cops. Precisely who was who, of course, was never quite clear. Bob Gill told me that it was discovered after a 1969 demonstration against the draft and Vietnam War in Fort Collins, Colorado, that there were more police agents, police informers, FBI informers and agents, CIA agents and stoolies, military intelligence officers and paid spies, snitches and double agents of various other descriptions than genuine demonstrators. When we figured out who was who we generally left the agent undisturbed, figuring that the devil we knew was better than the devil we didn't. To my knowledge the FSM was not, properly speaking, infiltrated by police agents, though we were fully aware that the police attended our many open public meetings.

would break the rules against on-campus political activity, may have given a greater impression of strength and solidarity than was evident from the sparse turnout. Another problem for the administration peeked its head out: this being a threat that if police attempted to arrest the student protesters, the graduate students would refuse all cooperation thenceforth, implying the ability and willingness to call a strike of teaching assistants and faculty.

DETAIL OF LEAFLET.

As a result of the rally and of statements by both the FSM and administration that the other side was acting in violation of their previous agreement, the Committee on Campus Political Activity was de facto no more. That evening, Kerr and Strong formally brought the CCPA to an end:

> FSM has abrogated the agreement of October 2, and by reason of this abrogation, the Committee on Campus Political Activity is dissolved. . . .
>
> We shall now seek advice on rules governing political action on campus from students through the ASUC and from the faculty through the Academic Senate. . . .
>
> . . . students participating in violation of rules will be subject to penalties through established procedures.[2]

On November 10, the seventy-five violators were issued official warnings by Chancellor Strong, and on the sixteenth were mailed notices requiring them to report to the dean of students' office for interviews. Nobody showed up, though in place of students we sent the deans 835 letters concerning our constitutional rights.[3]

Mike Smith: I was one of the students cited, and was elected chairman of the Cited Students Association, which was kind of a joke because the organization never did anything. I was actually a representative without a

MARIO SPEAKING AT THE NOVEMBER 9 RALLY. PHOTO BY HOWARD HARAWITZ.

constituency. But I was elected to the Executive Committee, and was given a vote. Stephanie Coontz was elected too. The day after we were cited, there was a meeting with the American Civil Liberties Union, and they advised us to go in to the deans like we were requested, but if they took any action against us the American Civil Liberties Union would represent us. They called up the dean's office and asked if rather than have seventy individuals come in they could just meet with our attorneys and they turned it down, so we all went in.* In order to provoke the administration further we continued to set up a Cited Students table, which I manned pretty much by myself.[4]

The cited students met at Westminster House, where Malcolm Burnstein told them:

*Now, either the cited students went into the dean's office, or they didn't. Seventy-five students pouring into the dean's office all at once would more or less have qualified as a sit-in, and some note would have been taken; nobody mentions anything of the sort and I don't remember anything like it. I believe that Mike is mistaken in his recollection, and nobody showed.

The regulations attempt to deprive you of a kind of speech, not a place to do it in. It is the opinion of all of us who have read the regulations that the University cannot legally do this.[5]

THE OLD DRESSER USED AS A PODIUM AT THE NOVEMBER 9, 1964 RALLY. PHOTO BY HOWARD HARAWITZ.

November 10 was also "graduate day." A hundred or so graduate students and TAs sat at tables, and many more signed a statement that they supported the actions of their colleagues. Letters were sent to the graduate students ten days later, in which the graduate students were asked to affirm that they had signed the statement that they had sat at the tables, or the matter would be dropped. The graduates responded that they had signed the statement and that unless they heard from the deans again, they would assume that the administration's rules were in violation of the Constitution. Nothing was heard from the deans again on this matter, and the tables continued to be manned throughout November without incident.[6]

Bob Starobin: Tables were set up and the Strike Committee started organizing. Between then and the Regents' meeting [on November 20] there was a lot of exchange of letters between the students and the deans. I was responsible for writing up, with Walter Stein, another grad, the reply that we sent, which everyone signed and we put in a big mailbox. I have the receipt that Goines kept from Arleigh Williams. There were two versions: one for the people who were actually cited, and one for the people who supported it. Also we were building for the November 20 Regents' meeting. The problem there was that we had to a certain extent lost contact with the people who were sympathetic, and there was a tremendous need to go out to the people again and explain to them why we had to go to the Regents. Arthur Goldberg was very instrumental in organizing that, going around to living groups and talking wherever he could on campus.[7]

Addressing the ASUC Senate on the evening of the eleventh, Mario demanded equal rights for the students, both on and off the campus. Bringing out the naked sword, and brandishing it before the administration (represented in this case by Dean Frank Kidner), he said, "If the

FSM ATTORNEY MALCOLM BURNSTEIN.
PHOTOGRAPHER UNKNOWN.

FSM must resort to mass demonstrations, they will not be halted unless we receive substantial concessions from the administration." Kidner listened to Mario's remarks "with some interest and some sympathy," and reported that "the administration will continue to consider revisions in its policy."[8]

On November 12, Kerr released the report of the disbanded CCPA. The report recommended substantial liberalization of University rules regarding on-campus political activity, including on-campus mounting of legal off-campus action. It also recommended, however, that if on-campus advocacy resulted in illegal action, the students and organizations responsible be subject to University discipline.

On the thirteenth, the Heyman Committee issued its report and recommendations on the student suspensions:

> The procedures followed [in suspending these students] were unusual. Normally, penalties of any consequence are imposed only after hearings before the Faculty Student Conduct Committee. Such hearings were not followed here with the result that the students were suspended without a hearing . . . in hindsight, it would have been more fitting to announce that the students were to be proceeded against before the Faculty Committee rather than levying summary punishments of such severity. We were left with the impression that some or all of these eight students were gratuitously singled out for heavy penalties summarily imposed in the hope that by making examples of these students, the University could end the sit-in and perhaps forestall further mass demonstrations.
>
> Moreover, we believe that these students viewed their actions in operating tables as necessary to precipitate a test of the validity of the regulations in some arena outside the University . . . [the chancellor] had made it clear that the President and the Regents had rejected in final form the request of the ASUC Senate for changes in the rules to permit solicitation of funds and membership and organization of political and social

action campaigns on campus. The door was thus seemingly closed to any negotiations on these central issues.

The procedure by which the University acted to punish these wrongdoings is subject to serious criticism. The relevant factors are: first, the vagueness of many of the relevant regulations; second, the precipitate action taken in suspending the students some time between dinner time and the issuance of the press release at 11:45 PM; third, the disregard of the usual channel of hearings for student offenses—notably hearings by the Faculty Committee on Student Conduct; fourth, the deliberate singling out of these students (almost as hostages) for punishment despite evidence that in almost every case others were or could have been easily identified as performing similar acts; and fifth, the choice of an extraordinary and novel penalty—"indefinite suspension"—which is nowhere made explicit in the regulations, and the failure to reinstate the students temporarily pending actions taken on the recommendation of this committee.[9]

The Heyman Committee advised reinstatement of six of the eight students as of the day of their suspensions. It recommended six-week suspensions for Mario and Art, the suspensions to begin September 30 and to end November 16. It further recommended that the penalty of indefinite suspension be expunged from the students' records and that the penalty be recorded as that of "censure" for a period of no more than six weeks. The heavier punishment for Mario was because he had led the Sproul Hall sit-in of September 30, and for Art because he'd led the picket which interfered with the University meeting on September 28.

The administration was not amused. Strong was particularly annoyed that the committee had addressed its report directly to the Academic Senate instead of to himself. This was, as Strong should have perceived, no accident. The faculty, displeased at being slighted by the administration and angered by the threat of force on campus, was flexing its muscles.

In a statement issued by Chancellor Strong, the administration stressed that it was not going to let bygones be bygones and did a little saber-rattling of its own:

As the report stresses, the committee, with the assent of the parties, "has been concerned only with events occurring through September 30, 1964, and has not been asked to, nor has, considered any event after that date." Much has happened since September 30. Some of the students mentioned in the report have . . . engaged in serious misconduct since that date and with regard to those actions, regular disciplinary procedures will prevail, including the immediate filing of charges by appropriate officials and hearings before the faculty committee on student conduct. In a recent conversation with Professor Heyman on November 9, he agreed recent violations of rules should be referred to the faculty committee on student conduct.[10]

Strange as it may seem, the FSM took no particular offense at this threat and simply went on about its ordinary business of raising Cain. On November 16 and 17, tables again appeared on Sproul Hall steps. No attempt was made by the administration to remove them. The FSM *Newsletter* announced that "the illegitimate tables will remain until they have become legal, through repeal of restrictive rulings." It went on to denounce the diffident faculty in stinging terms:

> They allow their colleagues to be victimized one at a time. They are loath to use their power to fight for their own freedoms or anyone else's. . . . They may think like men; but they act like rabbits.[11]

As well as a spur to action in the present instance, this was a blunt reminder of the hated loyalty oath and the scarcely forgotten cause célèbre of Eli Katz, who in the academic year 1963–64 had held a temporary position as acting assistant professor of German. The German department and the Senate Committee on Privilege and Tenure had recommended that he be promoted to assistant professor, and the matter was referred to the chancellor for a routine rubber stamp (though everyone knew that Kerr would have a say in the matter). Although Katz had signed the legislatively mandated loyalty oath, rumors had surfaced concerning his involvement in Communist politics in earlier years, and Katz refused to discuss the allegations with Strong. Strong therefore blocked the appointment, and Kerr concurred. Both the German department and the Academic Senate were angered, and by a vote of 267–79, the Academic Senate condemned the administration "for its disregard of and contempt" for the senate in the handling of the Eli Katz case. Katz had left the University under a cloud. The FSM's jab at the faculty's tepid support shrewdly exploited a residual ill-will between the faculty and administration that was already more than apparent.

On November 17, the somewhat conservative Boalt Hall law students came out in favor of the goals of the FSM:

> . . . a free society can tolerate no less than an unrestricted opportunity for the exchange of views on the political and social questions of the day

. . . we believe that the University's restrictions raise serious constitutional questions.

We believe that the spirit and perhaps the letter of our Constitution command that these restrictions be withdrawn. Where the choice is between expediency and freedom of speech, a nation of free men can have no choice.[12]

The same evening, the ASUC Senate proposed a solution for the free speech issue to be delivered to Kerr by ASUC president Charles Powell and first vice president Jerry Goldstein.

The University shall maintain that 1) all legal activity is allowed on campus, and 2) illegal activity off the campus is, as always, the private business of the student as a private citizen.

In addition, the ASUC recommended an extraordinarily cumbersome process for dealing with students suspected by the chancellor to have "used University facilities to incite, plan or organize illegal off-campus action or used criminal speech on campus."[13]

On November 19, the state board of directors of the California Democratic Council (CDC) asked the University administration and Regents to protect "the constitutional liberty" of the students, stating that "advocacy of ideas and acts which are constitutionally protected off-campus should be protected on-campus. . . ."[14]

The administration seemed to be unable to respond effectively to student violations of campus regulations; the FSM was harvesting a bumper crop of endorsements; student support was on the rise; and it seemed like a good time to take our case right to the top.

ON NOVEMBER 20, 1964, THOUSANDS OF STUDENTS MARCHED TO THE UC REGENTS'
MEETING AT UNIVERSITY HALL TO PRESENT THEIR POSITION ON THE FREE SPEECH
CONTROVERSY. PHOTO BY DON KECHLEY.

CHILDREN'S CRUSADE

On NOVEMBER 20, following a noon rally conducted from Sproul Hall steps, three thousand students marched across campus to sit on the lawn across from University Hall where the Regents were meeting. A petition to be presented to the Board of Regents read:

> We the undersigned resolve that:
> Only the courts of law should have the power to judge whether the content of speech on campus is an abuse of constitutional rights of free speech. Only courts of law should have the power to impose punishment if these rights are abused.
> Therefore, we ask the administration to recognize that it not usurp these powers.[1]

As advertised in the morning's leaflet, Joan Baez sang on Sproul Hall steps for the crowd and walked with us as we marched to University Hall on Oxford Street. The march was preceded by a banner declaring "Free Speech," carried by members of the Executive and Steering Committees. To give the lie to news accounts that we were "beatniks," everyone participating in the march was asked to dress nicely. The boys mostly wore coats and ties, and the girls dressed as though they were going to church. In light of later events, photographs of that march are almost surreal.

Andy Wells: Ron Anastasi had a big thing about Joan Baez. I had to keep Joan Baez secretly concealed until the time to lead the students. He had the big idea of having Joan Baez come up before the whole student body and play these stupid songs and lead the procession to the Regents. It seemed to me that it didn't have a damn thing to do with Joan Baez; if Joan Baez wanted to come along and support the demonstration, then that was all right with me. But the idea of having Joan Baez kept in seclusion until the moment of the great rally, at which time she was going to lead the troops, really pissed me off. Like Joan of Arc.* Ron had a big complex about it, and we had a big argument about it after the Regents' meeting. The argument was about this elitist tone that the Steering Committee was taking up again: "Sorry Andy, and the rest of you guys, we can't tell you anything now . . ." It was necessary to have a militant cadre to lead the thing, but sometimes it was grating.[2]

JOAN BAEZ SINGING TO UC STUDENTS BEFORE THE MARCH TO THE REGENTS' MEETING. PHOTOGRAPH BY AL SILBOWITZ.

A delegation of five FSM representatives requested a hearing before the Regents. The five negotiators chosen to go into the Regents' meeting were Mario, Steve Weissman, Mona Hutchin, Mike Rossman and Ron Anastasi. Mona was picked as the

---

*Joan Baez had also been in town for a concert on October 2, the night that the sit-down around the police car came to an end. Brian Shannon recounted, "Joan Baez was scheduled to sing that Friday night. Some friends of hers wanted to convince her not to sing, because of what was going on down below. But they didn't think they could speak as well on the phone and present the issues as clearly, so they introduced me to her on the phone and I spoke to her and told her what was involved, and she said, well, she had a commitment, and she really didn't think she could [break it], she'd think about it and could I call her back later. I called her back later, and again she said definitely that she couldn't [break it], she'd think about it and could I call her back later. I called her back later, and again she said definitely that she couldn't [not sing], that she would make some kind of statement. I

could not persuade her not to go. But I was working on persuading her first to come down to where we were sitting around the car and hoping that she would be affected by that so that she would not sing. Or, at least to come down and maybe do a separate concert afterwards. But then the next time I was able to call her right back and tell her that the issue had been settled, and so she went on. She gave me two free tickets to the performance.

"The next night I understand that after her performance she wanted to see Mario, so Mario went over and talked to her. He came back a half hour later and said, 'I don't know what she wanted to talk to me about—out of her mind or something. Bombed, taking a trip.' People had gotten the impression that she was high during that second performance anyhow." (Schultz interview.)

conservative representative, Mike because of the Rossman Report, which we understood that at least some of the Regents had read, and Ron because he was known as a moderate. Although the delegation was admitted to the Regents' meeting room, they were not allowed to speak.

With the demonstrators standing across the street, the Regents considered the recommendations submitted by Kerr and Strong:

1) That the sole and total penalty for the six students be suspension from September 30 to date.

2) That the other two students be suspended for the period from September 30, 1964, to date and that they be placed on probation for the current semester for their actions up to and including September 30, 1964.

3) That adjustments in academic programs be permitted for the eight students on approval by the appropriate Academic Dean.

4) New disciplinary proceedings before the Faculty Committee on Student Conduct will be instituted immediately against certain students and organizations for violations subsequent to September 30, 1964.

5) That rules and regulations be made more clear and specific and thus, incidentally and regrettably, more detailed and legalistic; and that explicit penalties, where possible, be set forth for specific violations.

6) That the Berkeley campus be given sufficient staff in the Dean of Students Office and the Police Department so that as nearly as possible all students involved in violations be identified with the fullest possible proof since the incompleteness of identification of participants and collection of full proof have been held against the University; also that the General Counsel's office be given sufficient staff so it may participate, as necessary, in the legal aspects of student discipline cases, particularly since a more legalistic approach is being taken toward student discipline.

7) That the right and ability of the University to require students and others on campus to identify themselves be assured by whatever steps are necessary.[3]

The Regents hearkened to Kerr's recommendations, and passed them all. Though minor concessions were made to student political speech, the gist was that they had it in for all the students who had broken rules after the thirtieth of September, that they had a particular hard-on for Mario and Art, and that they would not relinquish the University's right to sit in judgment on students who, on-campus, broke the law, contributed to breaking the law, or advocated breaking the law:

FSM STEERING COMMITTEE MEMBERS LEAD THE REGENTS' MARCH.
PHOTO BY RON ENFIELD.

1) The Regents restate the long-standing University policy as set forth in Regulation 25 on student conduct and discipline that "all students and student organizations . . . obey the laws of the State and community . . ."

2) The Regents adopt the policy effective immediately that certain campus facilities, carefully selected and properly regulated, may be used by students and staff for planning, implementing or raising funds or recruiting participants for lawful off-campus action, not for unlawful off-campus action.[4]

Mona Hutchin: I was a delegate to the November 20 Regents' meeting. We walked in, and they were having a really animated discussion on the budget. Then they came to the free speech thing. They took the first one and they read it, and they asked, "Is there any discussion?" and there was no discussion. "Are we ready to vote?" Yes, everybody was ready to vote. "All in favor," and there's this chorus of "ayes"; "All opposed," and there's this dead silence. So then they come to the second measure, and Rafferty says he wants to split it, and is everybody in favor of this and there's this chorus of "ayes," and "Anybody opposed," and silence. And they take the next measure, "Is there any discussion?" No discussion. "All in favor of this," and there's this chorus of "ayes." "All opposed," and there's this silence. And they come to the last measure, and the same thing happens except that two people say they want to go down in the record as opposed, and Rafferty also says that he wants to go down in the record as being opposed to it. Then it was announced that there were requests from groups that wanted to present their views on the FSM, but the chairman didn't think that it would be expedient at this time to have them present their cases and they would invite all the groups to submit written reports for the consideration of the Regents and "Is there anybody who wants to oppose the policy of not having people come up and address the Regents?" and there's this silence. OK, on to the next issue. And that's about how long it took, and in this weird room, too—deep in the middle of University Hall and no windows. Rows of seats in tiers like in a lecture hall. Down in the center behind a barrier is this table with the Regents all sitting around it, having their discussion, oblivious to the people watching them. It was an incredible feeling, sitting there and watching these people with all the power they have deciding your fate and not being able to do anything. Just sit there and watch them. I was stunned and didn't realize what they'd passed; I didn't understand what it meant.[5]

WAITING FOR THE REGENTS' DECISION. PHOTO BY ELSA GARCIA.

LOOK BEFORE YOU TAKE THE GREAT LEAP FORWARD

Iɴ ʀᴇsᴘoɴsᴇ ᴛo ᴛʜᴇ ʀᴇɢᴇɴᴛs' dilly-dallying around and the generally unsatisfying response to the march, there was a muddled sit-in on November 23. Jack addressed the administration, and told the crowd that the proposed sit-in was

> a plea, sort of an existential cry: Listen to my voice; you haven't heard me before; you ignore me. I came out in five thousand and you didn't recognize me. You didn't even mention me. I sent in petitions; you didn't read them. I put forward platforms; you didn't study them. You cannot ignore me any longer, and I'm going to put myself in a position where I cannot be ignored, because you're going to have to look at me. You're going to have to look at me as you go about your business, and you're going to have to take me into account.[1]

After a lengthy debate on Sproul steps, involving Vice-Chancellor Alan Searcy (who used his own microphone and comparatively wimpy loudspeaker), Mario, Jo Freeman, Art and just about anybody else who wanted to put his oar in, a few dozen students went into the building and were followed by more, until three or four hundred were inside. There the debate continued about whether we were willing to risk the welfare of the Movement in a possible arrest for trespassing, or whether we should leave at five o'clock. After bitter disagreement, the Steering Committee voted 6–5 to leave. The split, combined with the feeling that nothing was happening, left us with a feeling of deep discouragement. I had gone in with the first wave and, ignoring the debate, fell sound asleep with my head on Patti Iiyama's lap, which is how we met.

Brian Mulloney: We [the Graduate Coordinating Council] were against the abortive sit-in. It was just rage and frustration. We were sitting in because we were pissed off because we weren't winning. Arguments for sitting in were that we were losing our drive, that we needed to do something to galvanize the people, some bold step forward to draw new support. Our arguments against it were, bold steps forward have to occur in some context, and just smashing the band makes no sense at all, people will think you're stupid. You'll get no support; you'll just drive away the support that's already fairly peripheral. The original motion passed was that the Steering Committee was empowered to call a sit-in if things had not materially changed between that Saturday night [November 21] and Monday [November 23]. We argued that it was stupid to have the authority and not to have one, and that if they *did* have one, they were being criminal. So, we went to bed Sunday knowing that on Monday there'd be one in all its full-blown glory.

At the abortive sit-in, Jo Freeman engaged in long, bitter denunciations; personal attacks on Savio and Jack Weinberg; red-baiting; pretty shocking stuff. A denunciation of the FSM; essentially saying in public the sort of things she'd been saying to us in an attempt to buy us off.[2]

Tom Miller: The usual vultures were there at the abortive sit-in—Lipset and Feuer and Glazer; I remember Jo Freeman getting up and denouncing it. She got up after the rally and really came out and denounced everybody. She said very heatedly that just a small group was making decisions, "they don't really represent the majority of you students on campus." She was denouncing it as a conspiratorial Leninistic small group that was trying to wreck things. It fit in with the role she had taken.

I urged that they shut the microphones off after her speech. People were walking in, and they left the microphones on for anybody that wanted to speak. So some people walked in, but many hung around outside to hear what this or that person had to say—this doesn't work well at all. Inside people were up on the card catalogue speaking.

Art Goldberg was threatening to urge people not to go in unless he got to speak; he was using this as a club over the people who were running the rally; they were trying to get up a consensus to sit in. He was partially wrecking the rally—in fact he did wreck it. He forced Mario and others to compromise their position of urging people to sit in by saying, "*I* am going to sit in, but it's a personal decision," and so on. This wrecks a political movement. He was being an emotional kid. The rally was destroyed because people were talking about individual decisions, going in as a testimony to what you think is right instead of as an effective means of forcing the administration to accept our demands.

There was a definite split at the earlier Executive Committee meeting on sit in or not to sit in, and there was a general agreement that you would have people speaking for and giving a minority report also; which was a disaster to agree to do anyway. When you're at that step you don't start going through the pros and cons of doing it because then you might as well not have it. Parker and the ISC [Independent Socialist Club] people—Dave Friedman and Joel Geier—argued for the sit-in. I didn't see how it would gain that much. The rationale that came out was that the sit-in would be a moral witness—which I disagreed with completely. The tactical consideration was that it would somehow force their hand, but it seemed so ridiculous because it was so far away from our demands: to attach the sit-in to our demands would be very difficult. That's why I couldn't see it accomplishing what we wanted—it didn't strike a chord with the student body.

Bettina was arguing that we should save what face we could and leave at five. Mario seemed destroyed at the time, things were so bad. He finally just acquiesced and sided with Bettina.

After the abortive sit-in, I was really mad at what had occurred. It was a complete defeat for the FSM and I thought we were going to fold—blackmailing had really screwed things. Once you've decided on the sit-in you've got to go the full force and try to get as many people as possible, or you lose the point of a sit-in. What do we do now, we've wrecked it. How the hell are we going to get out of this mess. We even talked about putting the FSM to sleep.[3]

Jack Weinberg: There was enough of a split on the issue that you really couldn't say, "Everybody who isn't a fink come sit in." The meeting in the stairwell, everybody knew how they were going to vote before the meeting; discussion wasn't necessary.

I was very upset by the decision to leave at five. But I told people that even the people who were in the minority council would go along with the majority decision. I thought the Movement was all over. I personally was going to drop out at that point, so was Mario. The reason why I mentioned the vote, it was my feeling that the whole sitting-in and then leaving was so clearly a disjointed activity—the result of bungling.[4]

Bob Starobin: Over the weekend before November 23, Benson Brown [a GCC member elected to the Steering Committee during the November 8 reorganization] was opposed to the sit-in, and apparently the personal and tactical conflicts got so heated within the Steering Committee—they split fairly evenly—that by the time of the sit-in on Monday, he could no longer sit with them, and resigned [from the Steering Committee]. Even though he was opposed, he went in with everybody else. A lot of people who were opposed went in anyway, because they didn't want to split the Movement.

I was also opposed to the sit-in, and once the people got inside the building most of them realized that they couldn't stay in there past five o'clock. They had made a mistake and didn't have enough people in there to carry the thing off. So the Steering Committee started meeting again under the southeast stairs. I insisted on taking Benson's place, and a close vote accepted that, and I had Benson's vote. Now, the vote on whether to leave at five o'clock was 5–5, and my vote made it 6–5. So, you might say that in terms of that one vote, had I not taken Benson's place, it would have been an even split, and they wouldn't have been able to come back out and recommend that they leave at five, though I think that they would eventually have done that anyway.

In favor of staying were Mario, Jack, Suzanne, Rossman and Anastasi. The people who were for leaving were myself, Bettina, Roysher, Weissman, Mona and Art (even though Art wasn't at the meeting, they knew what his position would be—there was always a lot of that going on). Everyone knew the Steering Committee was split—they'd already said that outside. The meeting under the stairs was short—only a few minutes. It was a very quick decision.

Arguments opposed to continuing the sit-in were: there wasn't enough support; Jo Freeman was holding forth outside, confusing everybody; we hadn't educated the campus on what the new situation was.

The arguments for staying were simple: as long as we're in here let's stay; this is the only thing we have left to do.[5]

Steve Weissman: From the administration's side we were this monolith; we all worked together and were just like machines. But within the Movement, there was always serious debate about everything.

There was so much disagreement about the wisdom of sitting in that we decided to allow both sides to be presented at the abortive sit-in, and let the crowd make a decision. It usually pays off to let the opposition speak: you're controlling the microphone, you're talking after them. If there is that much disagreement among the leadership, then you shouldn't engage in direct action. Mario was a majority of one when he said that he was going to sit in anyway.

Art spoke against it. There was a sit-in, and I was organizing outside. I walked into the sit-in and talked for leaving. I thought that leaving at five was a real victory, and Jack thought that it was all over.

There was a lot of bitterness, and Bettina was very important that weekend in keeping things together.[6]

Larry Marks: The destruction of the late November sit-in was something for which Art was personally responsible. The only way that the Steering Committee could reach agreement was with a compromise with Art, and Art wouldn't agree. The other reason was that there was no legitimate reason for a sit-in at that time. To this day I don't know why relatively intelligent individuals would have called that sit-in. After the abortive sit-in there was a feeling that it was all over. The issues at stake seemed too small to worry about. Nobody gave a damn.[7]

DEUS EX MACHINA

O<small>N THE TWENTY-FOURTH</small> of November, the administration announced new rules for political activity on campus:

Authorized student organizations will be permitted in designated areas (these designated areas to include the Bancroft-Telegraph area, North entrance, and areas in the Student Center to be delineated by the ASUC Senate), to accept donations and membership signups, and to distribute political and social action material from tables provided by the organizations. On an experimental basis, the administration of this activity is delegated by the Dean of Students to the ASUC President.

The following conditions shall apply:

A. Permits for tables must be obtained from the ASUC.

B. Tables for the student organizations shall be manned at all times.

C. The organizations shall provide their own tables and chairs.

D. At Bancroft and Telegraph there shall be no more than one table in front of each pillar and four at the east side, and three at the west side of the entrance way. No tables shall be placed in front of the entrance posts. No posters shall be attached to posts or pillars or set up on easels.

E. In using the tables for purposes of political action, organizations must not use the name of the University and must dissociate themselves from the University as an institution by means of a printed disclaimer.

F. Donations may be solicited at the tables.

Participation in the activities described above shall be limited to members of the University—students, staff, and faculty.[1]

The same day, an important motion was narrowly defeated (274–261) in the Academic Senate, which would have allowed the University to limit speech and political and social action only to the extent "necessary

---

Deus ex machina is a god lowered onstage by means of machinery. From the practice in classical performance of bringing in a god to solve superhuman difficulties or clumsy play writing.

to prevent undue interference with other University affairs."[2] Had this motion passed, the administration would have been faced with an eventual two against one in any reincarnation of the CCPA, and might have considered negotiation on the substantive issues of prior restraint and advocacy.

John Searle: The regents' meeting of November 20 produced major liberalizations in the campus political rules. Indeed, assuming they meant what

JOHN SEARLE. PHOTO BY WALTER TSCHINKLE.

they seemed to mean, and ignoring the status of the then existing rules there was only one major area of disagreement left. The regents said that the students could have freedom of speech in designated areas of the campus, except that they could not advocate any illegal acts. Now that might sound reasonable enough (though of course it is unconstitutional, since the first amendment makes the act of advocacy legal even in many cases where the act advocated is illegal) but for the fact that, as is generally recognized, only one sort of student group is at present likely to advocate any illegal acts: the civil rights movement. CORE, SNCC, etc., are the only student groups to which the rule would seem to apply, so the students, quite naturally, took the regents' policy as equivalent to an attempt to destroy the campus civil rights movement. Still, organizations like the FSM exist only by polarizing the issues and after November 20 the issues were not nearly as polarized as they had been. I, for one, was convinced that the FSM was dead and that the war was over, with the students winning a partial and ambiguous, but still substantial, victory. A proposed Sproul Hall sit-in on November 23, against which several of us on the faculty had argued with the students, was a failure, as only about 300 students sat in. The size of rallies was declining, and there was a distinct feeling of impending peace all around. A more or less pro-student motion failed narrowly in the Academic Senate on November 24—partly because after much amending its wording was so confused that nobody knew quite what it meant anymore.[3]

There it was; we were screwed. By the end of the Thanksgiving break it was clear that though we had won most of the battles we had lost the war; the new rules were almost word-for-word what had been requested by the United Front on September 18, and though they would at that time have been exactly what we wanted, we were now more politically savvy and realized that these concessions had a hole in them you could drive a truck through: the University was hanging onto its *in loco parentis* privileges like grim death and, though it did not say so anywhere in the proposed rules, clearly intended to retain absolute control over who could say what, and where they could say it, and furthermore preserved to itself the ability to disband fractious organizations, kick out politically volatile students, and somewhere down the line get at the students who had inconvenienced and embarrassed it so badly these past several months. The FSM itself was completely ignored, and the patsy ASUC, which had throughout the affair been trying to spread its legs for the administration, was to be put in charge of student political speech. It is well understood in circles of higher education that student government exists at the pleasure of the administration, and this had been demonstrated not long before with the extirpation of the graduate students from the ASUC when they seemed a group that favored the upstart SLATE. To have the ASUC in charge of the First Amendment was to have a hen guarding the hen coop.

Pro and con factions formed within the faculty, leading to a broad split that resulted in the formation of a group called "the Two Hundred," which put together a platform in favor of the goals of the Free Speech Movement.

Bob Starobin: An early November faculty meeting in 155 Dwinelle was attended by about 450 faculty. This is the meeting where they came out for the misnamed "maximum political freedom." They more or less excluded students, but it wasn't the tight security that they had later on. You can see the embryo of the Two Hundred in this meeting. It came out of the history department, and mainly was being pushed by Professors Laurence Levine and Charles Sellers. Levine was really the only guy that had the guts to get up and make the kind of resolution that he made. The problem at that meeting was that the [free speech] question was not on the agenda; you have to give three weeks' notice in the Academic Senate in order to get something on the agenda—the way it's set up you have to circulate the stuff to every faculty member—a very cumbersome process. You can, however, put a sense motion on the agenda immediately.* They got the thing on the floor, but they bollixed it. They

---

*A "sense motion" is a nonbinding expression of the general sentiment of a body. The parliamentary purpose is to find out how a group feels about something, generally to the end that some other body is given the information so that it, in turn, can act appropriately.

were under a lot of pressure and it was very tense; Levine really didn't know what he was doing and Sellers was trying to be a little tricky.

The guys who were in favor of the students were Mo Hirsch in math, Levine in history and Sellers in history. Whereas the other side even at that meeting were Ross—quite prominent—Cheit, Heyman sort of in the middle, and Henry May in history. These guys later became involved in the departmental chairmen's nonsense around Scalapino.* May red-baited quite a bit, Ross said that "progress has been made and it's not the time for harsh and dogmatic judgments." He felt that Strong's regulations represented progress. Neilands in biochemistry seconded the Levine proposal. Hirsch said at that time that free speech was a right and not a privilege, and that the faculty had the power in this matter—quite a radical position.

They got the thing on the floor finally and they debated it. Levine got very nervous and he kept misreading the motion. This confused people; he misread it about five different times—for example he said that "it is the sense of the Academic Senate," whereas they wanted to say, "it is the sense of the Berkeley division of the Academic Senate." He confused people and started alienating people, so the vote for the Ross thing was 232–205. So even right there the senate was pretty well split.

The vice-chancellor, Alan Searcy, gave a report where he said that as a result of Strong's regulations the students now have maximum political freedom. There was some snickering and laughter at this. Heyman then delivered his report from the Heyman Committee, and he said that he believed that the substance of the Heyman Committee's recommendations had been met. Of course, we know that the penalties were made greater. Then Levine got up and read a statement, and moved the last paragraph of the statement. Nielands of biochemistry seconded it, Sellers then got up and defended the motion. The chair ruled the motion out of order, Sellers then appealed the ruling of the chair, the motion was then ruled in order Henry May then got up—he was against the motion and said that the preamble was wrong, the faculty's relation to the Regents was misstated—in other words the faculty didn't have this power—he said that demonstrations need regulation and that he was against any kind of demonstrations, he red-baited the students, he said the administration and not the faculty should have power over political questions, and he got loud applause. Then Ross got up with a substitute sense motion. He said that the faculty had not been ignored by the administration, that the new regulations were based on the faculty's position in the CCPA, he said that progress has been made and it's not the

---

*On Professor Scalapino and the Council of Departmental Chairmen, see the chapter "Necktie Party."

time for harsh and dogmatic judgments, and he resolved that they re-affirm their support for "maximum political freedom" and that Strong's regulations represented progress.

Then Cheit got up and said let's not act foolishly, like the students and the administration. The faculty recommendations have been accepted by the students and the administration, the students love the faculty delegation and the Williams Committee, and the students agree to accept the Cheit proposals. None of this of course was true. Hirsch got up and said that free speech was a right and not a privilege and then they voted 232–205 in favor of the Ross substitute motion, which was to re-affirm their October position.

The Two Hundred really formed in a matter of two weeks after that.[4]

Shortly after the administration issued the new rules, public radio station KQED gave airtime on its "Profile" series to Professor Arthur Ross, Vice-Chancellor Alan Searcy and Bettina Aptheker, allowing each to give a brief explanation of the position they represented. Ross explained the faculty position:

The viewpoint of the faculty throughout this controversy can be stated in two points: First, there should be the maximum freedom for student political activity. That not only includes speech in the pure sense, but also organization, advocacy, and political action. Our second point, to which we've adhered throughout the controversy, is that there is no room for force or violence at the University of California, and that the differences should be settled by debate or discussion. I think the faculty feel that the recent action by Chancellor Strong, in promulgating new regulations today, does represent considerable progress. However, we are not out of the woods by any means. There are still important issues which remain to be decided. But it is true, nevertheless, that upon the recommendation of the faculty, the right to solicit funds has been restored, the right to solicit membership, the right to sell literature, the right to advocate social and political action, and on the recommendation of the senate committee, the eight students who had been suspended have been reinstated. Although some of the other recommendations of the committee were not accepted. It's my feeling that some progress has been made, but that we have to continue the debate.

Vice-Chancellor Alan Searcy spoke for the administration, claiming,

Free speech is not the issue at the University of California at the present time. The University is quite aware of the issue of free speech, not only as a general right of citizens, but as a particularly important right for students and faculty of the University. The expression of ideas is essential to the educational process. I must insist that the present regulations of the University allow free speech, they allow the students free expression of opinion, they allow them to hear freely expressed opinions of all spectra of political and social opinion.

Bettina spoke for the FSM:

> Our position is quite simple. It is the position of the Free Speech Movement that the administration does not have the right to arbitrarily decide whether a student has advocated something which is lawful; that only courts of law have the right to determine whether such advocacy is lawful. We will continue to press on this question.[5]

These were nice points, though, and hard ones to get people to understand. The administration's concessions and proposals made enough sense to the student body in general, and to the faculty, *Daily Cal* and ASUC representatives in particular, that the FSM's continued arguments seemed like graceless nit-picking, evil-tempered dissatisfaction with a workable solution, and gratuitous prolonging of an affair that most people were getting sick and tired of hearing about.

> *Tom Miller:* The problem was that you had the administration agreeing upon everything except the main point—as far as the political people saw it. You had the problem of communicating that to the campus, and getting the campus to fight over that one point, which was in a sense abstract, because it wouldn't occur until the administration actually wanted to use it. So some people wanted to put the FSM to sleep until the administration acted. The general impression was that the FSM's decision-making body was disintegrating. People had taken all types of weird stands—there was no direct conflict and it was hard to fight—and we didn't want it to turn into a Frankenstein's monster. We agreed once and for all that there would be no minority report, and then we went on vacation.[6]

This was a major episode in the political maturation of the FSM's activists. What would have been perfectly acceptable only two months before was no longer acceptable: in the meantime, we had learned that the whole free speech question was not actually at issue, or was at best peripheral to the real, the central matter; what was actually at stake had at last emerged. What we were *really* fighting about was that the University wanted to *control our lives*, and we wanted to control our own lives. We were struggling to become adults, to throw off the benign parental authority and become full, responsible citizens. The FSM was the coming-of-age of our generation; we were confronting the old men who would not stand aside for the young. Success or failure was vital; it had to be win or lose, yes or no; there could be no middle ground, no shades of gray. Either we were to be free now, or our term of indenture, of childhood, was to be indefinitely prolonged. The Free Speech Movement was not about the First Amendment: it was about power—they had it and we wanted it.

Thus, essentially defeated (though neither the students nor the administration thought so), the FSM leadership stood helpless until the administration, unable to resist a stupid Parthian shot, pulled our chestnuts out of the fire. A part of the resolution adopted by the Regents on November 20 bore its fruit on the twenty-eighth when the administration instituted the "new disciplinary proceedings" it had promised "against certain students and organizations for violations subsequent to September 30, 1964."

On November 28, Mario Savio, Jackie Goldberg, Brian Turner and Art Goldberg received letters from the chancellor's office initiating new disciplinary action; they were going to be raked over the coals for their post–September 30 violations. It was likely that they were to be expelled, and that campus organizations that had also received letters were to have their on-campus status revoked. The Regents and outraged alumni wanted somebody's hide, and they didn't care whose, and they didn't care what it cost, though they had good reason to believe that it wouldn't cost much, since the splits in FSM leadership and the abortive sit-in were not signs of a healthy organization. It graveled the administration's ass that they had to reinstate all the bad boys, and almost give us a victory into the bargain. Art was charged with leading and encouraging people to sit in around the car and threatening Sergeant Robert Ludden with bodily violence. Mario was charged with trapping the car, packing-in Sproul Hall and biting Officer Mower on the left thigh.

The selection of recipients was rather odd; Art, Jackie and Mario were recognized leaders, but why Brian alone and not the whole list of suspended students? Who the hell knew what was going on in the administration's hive mind. However, one pleasant consequence of these disciplinary letters was to provide a bridge for reconciliation between Jackie and Mario. Mario evidently figured that if Jackie had been singled out, she must be OK after all, and she was welcomed back.

In fact, the administration had once again done the devil's work for him, and once again Chancellor Strong had been stuck with the dirty work, though Alex Sherriffs likely was the instigator, if not the actual framer of the letters themselves.*

That administrative blunder was all we needed. It was almost impossible to explain to people that the concessions made by the administration were baloney, that they really avoided the whole First Amendment question, that the administration wanted to exercise prior restraint on all speech and furthermore that if they could paternally grant us what we perceived as inalienable rights, so could they take them away again. But it was easy to explain that they had singled out four people at apparent random to suffer for what we all had done. Though we had no idea how many students would understand the simpler issue, to our intense gratification the flagging student interest revived in an unexpectedly big way.

Larry Marks: The FSM was at a low at that point; if Strong hadn't made his proclamations, no one would have doubted for a moment that the FSM was dead. The administration had so many opportunities to kill the FSM: I can think of several separate and distinct opportunities they had to kill the FSM. The first one was to take a minor disciplinary action against the eight, because none of this would ever have happened if there were a reprimand; second, if the administration had even stuck by its original line that it was causing a traffic problem, but no. If the administration had showed the slightest good faith in negotiating, but they didn't. If Strong hadn't sent out the notice that the four were going to be disciplined, there wouldn't have been nearly the support.[7]

Brian Mulloney: As soon as those letters came, we were in the driver's seat. You couldn't ask for more; we were off and running. At that point,

---

*In her interview of Arleigh Williams, Germaine LaBerge asked Williams who he thought was responsible for the letters: "Just from hearing these people discuss the chain of command and who was making decisions and the Regents' policy, the fact that Chancellor Strong sent these letters— would that have been his decision or would it have been somebody else's decision and he had to put his name to it?" Williams responded, "He had made that decision sometime before. Whether Alex was the one who wrote the letter or whether it was the chancellor, I do not know. Again, Alex, as I can remember

. . . My effort to be able to prevent it from happening was, 'Let's call it quits; we've got enough blood right now.' His answer was, 'Over my dead body.' This time, it wasn't 'Jesus Christ' or 'God.'

"I don't know just exactly who was in charge, what the chain of command was. Alex was the vice-chancellor of student affairs; Katherine was the dean of students. I think it was he who must have prepared the letters, convinced Ed Strong that this would be done. He was very, very intense about having this action taken. . . ." (Williams, *Dean of Students*, 114–115.)

we could talk about a strike instead of just piddley-ass sit-ins. It was decided to have both a strike and a sit-in, and that the two would reinforce each other.[8]

Realizing that it was now or never, the FSM girded up its loins for a final assault, and began planning for a massive sit-in on Wednesday, December 2, bringing the matter of First Amendment rights before the whole world and forcing the administration's hand. The meeting deciding on the sit-in was crowded to the doors, and after we initially voted to keep the doors open to whosoever wished to attend, went on nearly all night. There must have been administration spies in the crowd, but judging from the administration response, either the information they gleaned was ignored or it was not communicated to the proper authorities.

On December 1, after Strong had formally rejected FSM demands that charges against the four be dropped, the FSM issued an ultimatum, and the Graduate Coordinating Council announced that teaching assistants would strike on Friday, December 4, "if conditions warrant." The administration ignored the ultimatum.

Ron Anastasi: My conversation with Dean Bolton the day before the sit-in went something like this: He suggested that we talk to Chancellor Strong. Then he said that he had an informal request to make of me; he said, "I know the Steering Committee is getting current and separate legal counsel. What I want to know is, are you taking advantage of it?" He went on to say that "the situation that you are planning tomorrow is a premeditated action. Are you aware of the great difference legally between this sort of action and the October 2 sit-down around the car?" He was obviously talking about the possibility of conspiracy charges being brought. He also said that he could assure me that there would be no discussion at all after the action starts. He said that the urgent need here is that a single gesture of goodwill be forthcoming from the FSM. He accused us of leapfrogging the Berkeley administration. He said that no formal communication is possible. He repeated this several times, and I got the distinct impression that he was under direct orders not to enter into formal communications with us. He did say later on that it would be possible to set up a three-way phone conversation, but that he couldn't meet with us in his office. I think that he meant by three-way, three FSM representatives and him.

He asked me why we made the existence of the letters to the four students public, and said that they would never have been made public if we hadn't made them public. I then asked him what procedures would be necessary for us to open some kind of communication with the administration. He said, and I think he was reading from a memorandum, "One, you must follow the procedures outlined in the letters, which is that you must go through several committees." Two, if after we have talked with the authorities on the Berkeley campus, we still think it is desirable to talk to the statewide administration, we can under the following conditions only: One, the FSM, or any organization in it, cannot be in recent violation of University regulations. It must be a sufficient period to demonstrate that we are willing to act sincerely and in good faith.

I told him that it was very difficult for us to do that, because the past actions of the University never led us to believe that by doing so we would get any results. Our experience was that the only way to get results was by pressing.

The second condition of meeting was that he would read to us at the beginning of the meeting a set of ground rules. The first ground rule would be a statement of his authority. The second would be a statement from the FSM as to what we wanted to discuss. There would be a stenographer present, and we would get a copy. And he must be able to fit the meeting into his schedule. There must be no back recriminations, and he said as an aside that he felt that the sit-in on Monday was the saddest thing that had ever happened. He then repeated, "Please be sure that you are using your excellent legal counsel in connection with the planning of events. This is an extremely serious matter. When crowded meetings take place," and I think that he was referring to the Executive Committee on Sunday which voted to sit in, "who voted, and who voted in what way, is known." He was apparently telling me that they knew who had voted which way, and if conspiracy charges were brought, they would know who to bring them against.

He went on to say, "Wednesday is not a student matter, like a rally." I said, "Is there any way that we can meet with you to stop this situation from occurring on Wednesday?" And he said, "There is no way of meeting with me unless you go through these preconditions." I said, "Is there any way we can prevent it? Because I don't think that's going to be possible, although I'll present that to the Steering Committee." I said I wasn't very optimistic. And he said, "Give my girl a call in the next couple of days if you can meet them." And that was the end of the conversation.

Although I'm sure that the administration would have given anything to prevent what was coming, they distrusted us so much that they set up impossible conditions before they would meet with us.[9]

A LITTLE PREPARATORY SABOTAGE

Here was the official plan: if it was not raining, and Sproul Hall was open, we would have the rally in the plaza and go into Sproul Hall. If it was raining, and Sproul Hall was open, we would go directly into Sproul Hall. If it was not raining, and Sproul Hall was closed, we would have the rally in the plaza and go into the Student Union. If it was raining, and Sproul Hall was closed, we would go directly into the Student Union. If the police didn't arrest, but just dragged people outside, the plan was to pack in around the doors.

To forestall the chance of Sproul Hall's being locked before we could get in, Pam Mellin and I got a bunch of toothpicks, and went around to every entrance plus main inside doors, behaving like a madly passionate pair of lovers. We'd stroll arm in arm, feeling each other up and looking goo-goo eyes, and when we'd get to a door, I'd throw my arms around her, and she'd throw her arms around me, and we'd kiss passionately, and I'd feel her up and grab her ass, and she'd feel me up and grab my ass. Of course any decent person averts their eyes. Meanwhile, I was cramming the lock full of toothpicks. As we were not sure that the sit-in was actually going to be in Sproul Hall, but might be in the Student Union building, we got its doors, too.

When we finished, we found that fellow FSMer Barbara Garson had come up with the same idea, quite independently, and had been busy all morning sabotaging locks on her own. I'd *thought* that some of those locks already had something in them.

Benson Brown and I had discussed the idea of using epoxy glue and match sticks, and we had it all mixed ready to squirt into the locks. But we decided against it because it might look less like kid-stuff, and somebody might get all worked up and make a federal case out of it.

I had forty-eight hours to get ready for the sit-in. I gathered equipment, organized monitors and gave monitors briefing meetings, and set things up for nonviolent resistance. Getting arm bands ready, getting food ready, figuring out who was going to do what. Setting up the supply lines for a sit-in of indeterminate length. Command Central was set up at Bob MacClaren's bizarre apartment at Bancroft and Telegraph, right across from Sproul Hall.

The leaflet handed out on the morning of December 2 exhorted students to "Come to the noon rally (Joan Baez will be there): bring books, food and sleeping bags."

MARIO SAVIO. PHOTO BY RON ENFIELD.

THE BIG SIT-IN

WE HAVE AN AUTOCRACY which runs this university. It's managed. We were asked the following: if President Kerr actually tried to get something more liberal out of the Regents in his telephone conversation, why didn't he make some public statement to that effect? And the answer we received—from a well-meaning liberal—was the following: he said, "Would you ever imagine the manager of a firm making a statement publicly in opposition to his board of directors?" That's the answer! I ask you to consider: if this is a firm, and if the Board of Regents are the board of directors, and if President Kerr in fact is the manager, then I'll tell you something: the faculty are a bunch of employees, and we're the raw material! But we're a bunch of raw material[s] that don't mean to have any process upon us, don't mean to be made into any product, don't mean to end up being bought by some clients of the University; be they the government, be they industry, be they organized labor, be they anyone! We're human beings!

There is a time when the operation of the machine becomes so odious, makes you so sick at heart, that you can't take part; you can't even tacitly take part, and you've got to put your bodies upon the gears and upon the wheels, upon the levers, upon all the apparatus and you've got to make it stop. And you've got to indicate to the people who run it, to the people who own it, that unless you're free, the machine will be prevented from working at all!

Now, no more talking. We're going to march in singing "We Shall Overcome." Slowly; there are a lot of us. Up here to the left—I didn't mean the pun.[1]

Mario, the machinist's son, at his most eloquent.* On December 2, following a huge noon rally in Sproul Plaza, about fifteen hundred people

---

*Recollect that Mario had cited Thoreau to the fraternity boys around the car, and compare this December 2 speech with Thoreau's words in *Civil Disobedience*: "If the injustice is part of the necessary friction of the machine of government, let it

STENTS FILING INTO SPROUL HALL, DECEMBER 2, 1964. PHOTOGRAPHER UNKNOWN.

packed all four floors of Sproul Hall. A young student was at the door of Sproul Hall right after Mario had finished his speech, standing in a truculent posture with balled fists, as though to defend the doors against all these Communists. As the waves of students approached and passed him, he looked astonished, put down his hands and walked away.

Charlie Powell urged the crowd to disperse, but was booed by the demonstrators. Mario said that he was "not only a strikebreaker, but a fink."[2] Throughout the afternoon, students ambled in and out at will, and the initially tightly packed mass declined to a more comfortable number.

Sue Stein: I was wandering around in Sproul Hall in the afternoon, and on one of my jaunts, a delegation of nice little girls came up to me and said, "We need Enovid [birth control] pills, or else we can't stay the night." So I said I would go and get some from my house. I went home, and got my pills, and gave them out to people.[3]

Just before seven in the evening, University police told us that the building would be closed, and that anyone who wanted to leave could

go, let it go: perchance it will wear smooth,—certainly the machine will wear out. If the injustice has a spring, or a pulley, or a rope, or a crank, exclusively for itself, then perhaps you may consider whether the remedy will not be worse than the evil; but if it is of such a nature that it requires you to be the agent of injustice to another, then I say, break the law. Let your life be a counter friction to stop the machine" (*Walden and Other Writings of Henry David Thoreau*, ed. Brooks Atkinson [New York: Modern Library, 1950], 644).

SPROUL HALL, DECEMBER 2, 1964. PHOTOGRAPHER UNKNOWN.

do so, but no one could enter. At this point, the cops discovered that they couldn't lock the doors, and as pairs of policemen guarded each entrance, locksmiths were brought in to do what they could.

Ropes dangled from the second-floor balcony, and food and a few demonstrators were hauled into the building. A line was passed across the plaza between the Student Union and Sproul Hall, and baskets of food and messages went along it from the Student Union to the eight or nine hundred remaining demonstrators.

Tom Weller: It's my distinct recollection that there was a contingency plan to construct a full-scale bridge between the Student Union and Sproul Hall at the second-story level, should the sit-in continue long enough. Looking at the site today, it seems impossible just from an engineering standpoint, apart from being totally loony; but at the time it seemed perfectly reasonable.

Did we not, after all, have an Engineering Central, staffed by people like Lee Felsenstein, who was later to be pivotal to the development of the personal computer? Did we not take over the University mainframe to keep track of our legal affairs during the trial? Could all of this have really happened?[4]

363

STUDENTS SITTING ON DRUMS OF CIVIL DEFENSE EMERGENCY FOOD AND WATER IN THE
BASEMENT OF SPROUL HALL. PHOTO BY BOB GILL.

Steve Weissman claimed that in Peace Corps training he'd learned to
make rope bridges, and that we should send out for the equipment to
make a bridge between Sproul Hall and the Student Union building.
Steve's plan for building a rope bridge had been discussed in the Steering
Committee meeting and we voted against it. (I was a voting member

JEFF LUSTIG AND LEE GLICKMAN PLAYING CHESS IN SPROUL HALL.
LIFE PHOTO BY PAUL FUSCO.

of the Steering Committee during the sit-in.) We had people who were ready, willing and able to do it, but we felt that it would be just too risky, and if someone were hurt or killed on it, it would be really disastrous for us.

The floors were divided up for various activities: first floor was for sleeping, second floor was wide open for anything anybody wanted to do, third floor was study hall and fourth floor was study and sleeping area. Every floor had monitors on it in proportion to the number of people, and members of the Steering Committee made themselves highly visible, talking with people and entering into impromptu discussions.

After movies (two comedies: a Laurel and Hardy film and *Operation*

FREEDOM SCHOOL SAMPLE CLASS SCHEDULE	
COURSE DESCRIPTION	INSTRUCTOR
1) MUSIC & NON-VIOLENCE	JOAN BAEZ + IRA SANDPERL
2) THE NATURE OF GOD AND THE LOGARITHMIC SPIRAL	MICHAEL ROSSMAN
3) WILD SPANISH CLASSES [AND MORE]	BOB MACLAREN

FIRST MEETING TONIGHT
7:00 PM   SPROUL
ON   HALL

MARIO READS LT. CHANDLER THE RIOT ACT. SPROUL HALL, DECEMBER 2, 1964.
PHOTO BY BOB GILL.

Abolition), Chanukah services, dancing and speeches, people settled down for the night, either to sleep or to study. Jeff Lustig and Lee Glickman played a giant game of chess on the linoleum-tile squares, using coke bottles for pawns and playing cards for the other pieces. Informal classes were held in corners and under stairwells. Hand-drawn posters advertised "Free University of California" courses.*

At about four in the afternoon, I had seen Lieutenant Chandler going up to a bathroom door on the third floor at the far end. He had keys in his hand and it looked to me like he was going to start locking bathroom doors. I got between him and the door, and told him that if he locked the door we'd piss in the hall; we'd sector off a part of the building as a latrine and God damn it we'd piss in it. He got very shaken up and took

---

*The poster is from a photograph by Bob Gill taken inside Sproul Hall during the sit-in. The Free University of California began spontaneously in Sproul Hall during the sit-in and bore no offspring. The FUC had unfortunate initials and the name was not continued with the Free University of Berkeley—founded in emulation of Alan Krebs' Free University of New York by Jeff Lustig, Bob Mates and Stew Albert in spring 1965. The first location of the Free University of Berkeley (from spring of 1965 to November of 1965) was at 2819 Telegraph; the second was at Walden School (from November 1965 through June of 1966); and its final location was at 1703 Grove. I taught a calligraphy course under the auspices of FUB for five or six years.

off. He was the easiest guy
to intimidate that I knew of;
you'd just yell at him and
he'd fall apart. We were
afraid that someone else
would try to lock the doors
to the bathrooms, so I told
several monitors to take the
doors off their hinges or
jam the locks. When we
heard that the police were
coming, we put some of
the doors back on their
hinges.

FOOD PREPARATION IN SPROUL HALL, DECEMBER
2, 1964. PHOTO BY RICHARD MULLER.

Most of my time was
spent running up and
down, carrying messages
and making sure that every-
thing was OK everyplace. I was up the roofs some of the time looking
around and finding ways in and out of the building. I discovered a weird
way in and out: you climb out a window in the women's john on the
second floor, then up a flight of stairs, and then you're on the fourth
floor on a little verandah that overlooks two offices. It seemed to have
been built for faculty teas. You climb off that onto the roof. The Steering
Committee held meetings in a small women's john and on the roof.
Anything for quiet and privacy.

As the evening wore on, the possibility of arrest seemed to lessen;
and at midnight we heard from Mrs. Kerr that there would be no arrests.
Joan Baez, who had sung our generation's anthem, "The Times They
Are A-Changin'," during the rally and walked into the building leading
us in "We Shall Overcome," left—though not before companionably
sharing peanut butter sandwiches with the students.*

During the sit-in a campus policeman peered into President Emeritus
Gordon Sproul's office, and seeing papers strewn about reported that the
demonstrators had broken in. This was not true, and the report was later
shown to be in error, as Sproul was a notoriously untidy man (his secretary later confessed, "We kept a messy office"), but it led the assistant

---

*Just why Joan Baez left before arrests be-
gan is not clear. Since at midnight we did
not think we were going to be arrested,
the most reasonable explanation is that she
was tired and wanted to sleep in a real bed.

But Janis Zimdars (now Dolphin) recollects that someone told her that Joan Baez
had left because she was on probation
from another demonstration and couldn't
afford another arrest at the moment.

JOAN BAEZ SINGING TO STUDENTS IN SPROUL
HALL. PHOTO BY ROBERT R. KRONES.

county prosecutor—Edwin Meese III—who was sitting in the campus police headquarters in Sproul Hall basement, to call the governor and tell him, "They're busting up the place. We have to go in." Brown then issued orders to arrest us, and Strong, who had been closeted in University Hall with Kerr all

evening, was elected to give us the news. This was not what Kerr had wanted. Kerr had decided to ignore the sit-in for as long as he could, figuring that the initial excitement would die down, the majority of the students would lose interest and become disenchanted with the demonstration, and the numbers that he would have to deal with would dwindle to a few hard-core activists. In this, as in other matters, he was frustrated by agendas beyond his control.*

Though strictly speaking we had not broken into Sproul's office, we had indeed broken in elsewhere:

> *Kate Coleman:* During the Sproul Hall sit-in we actually did break into some of the offices. There we found stuff on the University's contracts with A. P. Giannini's Bank of America, agribusiness and federal weapons research. All along, the administration had been going on about "off-campus" influence on the FSM, but it paled beside the "off-campus" influence on UC that we discovered there. We felt totally vindicated. This was a big step in my own radicalization; after others had gotten into the offices and were rifling through files, I came in and looked too. The room I was in was on the east side of the building and was full of filing cabinets. It was a big thing for me to be prowling around where I didn't belong, finding out things that had been hidden. I think that's what got me into investigative journalism: if you do only what you're allowed to do, and ask questions only where you're supposed to ask them, you never find out the truth.[5]

---

*W. J. Rorabaugh, in his book *Berkeley at War*, supports the theory hinted at by Arleigh Williams that Alex Sherriffs had something to do with the order for the arrests: "Two men played crucial roles in the police action. One was Alex Sherriffs, who had been appalled at Kerr's oscilla-tions all fall and now grimly sought to win his battle against the activists. The other was Edwin Meese III, the prosecutor who had made the crucial call to Brown and who, as liaison between the police and the prosecutor's office, supervised the arrests" (32).

At twelve-thirty everything was quiet, and I went down to the first floor and conked out on a sleeping bag. At about a quarter of two a newsman's lights woke me up, and shortly afterward I heard that police were on their way. Suzanne Goldberg and I were appointed fourth-floor monitor captains. We held two practice "pack-ins" like the one that we'd had around the dean's offices on October 1, got fire extinguishers ready to douse tear-gas bombs, and stacked everything that might hurt if you got dragged over it in a glassed-off section near the main door.

CHANCELLOR STRONG TELLS THE STUDENTS TO LEAVE SPROUL HALL OR FACE DISCIPLINARY ACTION. PHOTOGRAPHER UNKNOWN.

At 3:00 AM, Chancellor Strong announced that we were to leave or face disciplinary action:

> May I have your attention? I am Dr. Edward Strong, chancellor of the Berkeley campus. I have an announcement.
>
> This assemblage has developed to such a point that the purpose and work of the University have been materially impaired. (*Loud cheers and applause.*) It is clear that there have been acts of disobedience and illegality which cannot be tolerated in a responsible educational center and would not be tolerated anywhere in our society.
>
> The University has shown great restraint and patience in exercising its legitimate authority in order to allow every opportunity for expressing differing points of view. The University always stands ready to engage in the established and accepted procedures for resolving differences of opinion.
>
> I request that each of you cease your participation in this unlawful assembly.
>
> I urge you, both individually and collectively, to leave this area. I request that you immediately disperse. Failure to disperse will result in disciplinary action by the University.
>
> Please go.[6]

OUTSIDE SPROUL HALL, DECEMBER 3, 1964, 4 AM. PHOTO BY HOWARD HARAWITZ.

The elevators had been turned off around seven o'clock, and we'd taken all the standing ashtrays and green metal wastebaskets and put them in front of the elevator doors to act as a warning of sorts in case some sort of surprise got past the sentries. When Strong came out of the elevator on the fourth floor, he didn't see them, and kicked them over with a big operatic crash. It startled him, and made him even angrier, and instead of saying "Please go," he spat, "Now go! *Git!*" as though we were animals. We were shocked by the venom in his voice. I was standing behind him and beside Lieutenant Chandler, and when Strong finished his announcement, I moved to the back of the corridor and Suzanne to the front.

Lieutenant Chandler succeeded Strong, announced that we were in violation of the law and gave us five minutes to clear out. Nobody went.

Forty-five minutes later, Governor Brown announced that he had directed the California Highway Patrol and the Alameda County Sheriff's Department to arrest the demonstrators. As though awaiting his signal, the elevator doors opened, policemen came out and the arrests began.

This was the same Governor Brown who in a 1961 speech at the University of Santa Clara had applauded students for their political activism:

> Far from discouraging your students' social and public interests, I propose that you positively exploit them.
> Here is an honorable source of college spirit; here is a worthy unifying and organizing principle for your whole campus life.
> I say: thank God for the spectacle of students picketing—even when

UNIVERSITY OF CALIFORNIA POLICE IN SPROUL HALL. PHOTO BY AL SILBOWITZ.

they are picketing me at Sacramento and I think they are wrong—for students protesting and freedom-riding, for students listening to society's dissidents, for students going out into the fields with our migratory workers, and for marching off to jail with our segregated Negroes.

At last we're getting somewhere. The colleges have become boot

371

STUDENTS SLEEPING OR STUDYING IN
SPROUL HALL DURING THE SIT-IN.
PHOTOGRAPHER UNKNOWN.

camps for citizenship—and citizen-leaders are marching out of them. For a while, it will be hard on us administrators. Some students are going to be wrong and some people will deny them the right to make mistakes. Administrators will have to wade through the angry letters and colleges will lose some donations. We Governors will have to face indignant caravans and elected officials bent on dictating to state college faculties.

But let us stand up for our students and be proud of them.

If America is still on the way up, it will welcome this new impatient, critical crop of young gadflies. It will be fearful only of the complacent and passive.

On December 3, 1964, however, the "critical crop of young gadflies" was endangering his chances of reelection and Brown sang quite a different tune:

I have tonight called upon law enforcement officials in Alameda County to arrest and take into custody all students and others who may be in violation of the law at Sproul Hall. I have directed the California Highway Patrol to lend all necessary assistance. These orders are to be carried out peacefully and quietly as a demonstration that the rule of law must be honored in California.

I assume full responsibility for this in every shape, form, and manner. I felt it was the right thing to do. The overriding matter became one between the people of the State of California versus the demonstrators.[7]

Bob Starobin: Command Central was set up by Marty Roysher in an apartment behind Wells Fargo Bank; they had two phones and a walkie-talkie and were in communication with Sproul Hall, which was right over the roof.

I was at Command Central until one-thirty, and then went home. Everyone thought that there weren't going to be any arrests until the next day. At Command Central, we were sending out kids on motor

JACK WEINBERG INSTRUCTING STUDENTS IN NONVIOLENT CIVIL RIGHTS TECHNIQUES.
SPROUL HALL, DECEMBER 3, 1964, APPROXIMATELY 4 AM. PHOTO BY AL SILBOWITZ.

KPFA REPORTER BURTON WHITE.
PHOTO BY BOB GILL.

scooters to all the police stations to see if there was any activity, and there was nothing. Every half hour, a guy would come back with a report. All of a sudden, around a quarter of two, they started up. We knew that the police were coming almost an hour before they arrived at Sproul. Then I got a call about four-thirty—they were arresting people.[8]

Sam Slatkin: Some plainclothes high-up official pointed at Jack Weinberg, and two or three Oakland or Alameda sheriffs went after him. Jack tried to get out of their reach—he was standing in between the balcony windows and one of the tables and looking the other way—and he didn't get very far before they got him. They tried to pull a similar thing with Weissman, but we opened up a passageway for him and closed it after him and he got out the window.

There were two charges, one was to get Jack and one was to get the microphone. When they did get the microphone it was replaced—one that somebody happened to have, it wasn't very good but it did the job—and they didn't get that one again.[9]

Ron Anastasi: Jack was arrested early Thursday morning in the sudden police raid on the microphone. After we got the microphone back in working order, we decided to pack in around it to prevent another successful raid. Everyone was very upset by that first raid. Jo Freeman was screaming, "Link arms! Link arms!" and I had to pull rank on her, saying, "It is a Steering Committee decision not to link arms." Then several of the Steering Committee members decided that Steve Weissman should stay on campus and direct the strike. Steve really protested, but finally we all agreed that he should go out and direct the strike, and we set up a rope from the window, and if the police came Steve was to go down the rope. We had realized that we had too much leadership inside and not enough outside. When Steve left, he was about two feet ahead of the cops. They were hopping over people behind him.

Immediately after the building was closed, at seven, we'd started having communication problems. Walkie-talkies had been rented for $5 the first day and $2.50 the second day. My girlfriend Sally picked them up in San Francisco. Andy Wells had one inside, and some random person had one on the outside, and we weren't getting the information we needed. So we decided that a Steering Committee member should go outside, and sent Marty Roysher. He really didn't want to. No one wanted to leave. We argued about who should go out, and Marty was the worst arguer, so he had to go.

MARTY ROYSHER. PHOTO BY LOREN WEAVER.

We got a report that the police were going to use tear gas, and Mike Smith, who'd had experience with tear gas, said that it was heavy and sinks. Because of that, we decided to move people to the upper floors. Tear gas used in confined spaces could be toxic or cause panic. He suggested that the only thing to do would be to use wet handkerchiefs over our noses and mouths. It wouldn't be much, but it would be better than nothing. So members of the Steering Committee went to the different floors with pitchers of water. I was going up and down the aisles pouring water on handkerchiefs and scarves that people were holding up, some of the girls were sitting there holding up embroidered handkerchiefs and kerchiefs, and these kids were just shaking, and I was shaking, we were all so scared. And yet, they were staying there and doing it. That was the most profound moment. I really felt an incredible oneness with everyone; we are not going to give in.

We'd decided that people would grab the tear-gas cylinders and throw them out the windows. People from CORE—people who had been arrested before—were supposed to be on each floor, to keep things under control if the police showed up.

During the second attack on the microphone, I was standing on top

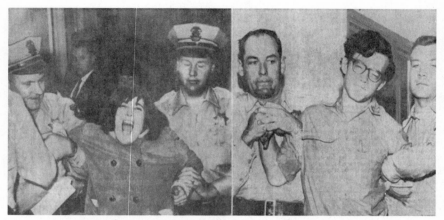

AN UNIDENTIFIED COED AND THE AUTHOR ARE ARRESTED IN SPROUL HALL,
DECEMBER 3, 1964, 5 AM. OAKLAND TRIBUNE PHOTO.

of the card file. A policeman was hitting people, and when the panic
and noise level were at a peak, all of a sudden an American flag came
shooting through the air and hit the guy, and he picked it up, and it
looked like he didn't believe it somehow. Myself and Hilbert [Coleman]
grabbed the end of the staff and started a tug-of-war between ourselves
and the police officer, and we finally got it back and handed it back to
the guy who had thrown it. It seemed very symbolic.

Thursday morning at about eight o'clock, I got a call from Command Central that twenty cars were on their way to park in around the
police cars and that a phone chain had formed to get more cars. And I
said, "What!? Tell them to stop that right now!" The action had already
been initiated, and the cars were on their way. Can you imagine what
would have happened then? People would have sat down around their
cars . . . There would have been a full-scale war. Jesus.[10]

The arrests began on our floor, and Suzanne and I led singing and
did our best to keep up morale. As the cops ground along, methodically
busting everyone in their path, Suzanne and I amused the crowd with
old vaudeville routines:

"What are pennies made out of?"

"Dirty copper!"

"What does your old man do for a living?"

"Nothin'! He's a cop!"

"Is he honest?"

"No, he's like all the others!"

(Big laughs. Who knows what the cops are thinking of these
chestnuts.)

THE PROCESS OF ARREST IN SPROUL HALL. PHOTO BY RON ENFIELD.

"Brass buttons,
"Blue coat,
"Couldn't catch a nanny goat!"

As we ran out of stock repartee, we got inventive. The comedy duo was broken up when the police arrested my sidekick. Leave 'em laughing. I was on my own, and kept up a running commentary on the clumsiness of the police as they arrested students. I made particular fun of Sergeant Glenn, who didn't pay too much attention. When the police got within a few rows of me, I sat down—I'd been on my feet to make my voice carry better, and to keep a high profile for the crowd. Glenn and three others held a tête-à-tête and skipped over the people in front to get at me. Though it was 5:06 AM, I was only the forty-third person to be arrested; the police had a long day ahead of them.

I went limp and was carried by two cops, one of whom bent my left arm sharply behind me, while the other put a "come-along" hold on my right wrist; the net result was that I was completely off the ground for most of the trip. Although it hurt a lot, as indeed it was meant to, I managed to keep relatively silent and made the front page of the morning *Oakland Tribune* with my mouth shut. A full-face photo was captioned

THE PROCESS OF ARREST IN SPROUL HALL. PHOTO BY RON ENFIELD.

"Tight-Lipped Demonstrator." My brothers and sisters were simultaneously horrified and thrilled, proud of their big brother's notoriety and ashamed of his being hauled off to jail on the front page of the newspaper. My parents were aggressively defensive, and publicly proclaimed that they were proud of me for standing up for my principles. My mother has a scrapbook of every newspaper or magazine account and photo of me.

Tossed into the elevator, where I landed on a fellow demonstrator, I broke my vow of silence and called Sergeant Glenn a son of a bitch. Accompanied by a policeman, the five or six of us rode down to the basement for preliminary booking. One of the guys made like the cop was an elevator boy, asking, "Mezzanine, please." We thought that was rich. We were fingerprinted and photographed, and when we were questioned amused ourselves by deviling the booking officers. When they asked "race," I replied "human," instead of Caucasian or Negro or whatever they obviously wanted. Everyone who heard me followed suit, to the ill-concealed annoyance of the already bone-tired cops. Just as dawn broke we were ushered into a waiting Alameda County Sheriff's bus for a ride to Santa Rita county jail.

The police had decided to let gravity do some of the work and began arresting demonstrators from the fourth floor down. The relatively small population of the fourth floor was entirely in custody before the third

STUDENT CARRIED TO THE BOOKING STATION IN THE BASEMENT OF SPROUL HALL.
PHOTO BY RON ENFIELD.

floor got any attention at all. They'd only arrested some of the students on the third floor before they switched to the second floor, where demonstrators had moved from both the first and third floors to form a massive people-jam. Police spent most of the day clearing the second floor. Men were taken directly to the small campus police station in the basement, fingerprinted and searched. Women were taken first to the dean of students' office, searched by a police matron, and then taken to the basement for fingerprinting. Though any demonstrator was free to go at any time before arrest, I do not believe that many left; indeed, quite a few climbed into the building during the day in order to participate.* In all, the arrests of some eight hundred students, University employees and former students took almost as many policemen thirteen hours.† As the jails filled up,

---

*In *Berkeley: The New Student Revolt*, Hal Draper says that about two hundred left between Strong's announcement and the point of actual arrest. I was arrested early, so I can't say for sure, but nobody mentioned anything then or later about people leaving the building, and if one-fifth of our number had done so, you'd think the

newspapers would have crowed about it. What's more likely is that from the fifteen hundred or so that went in at noon, the number dwindled to the sub-thousand that was in the building around midnight.
†Estimates are from a low of 367 to a high of 635 policemen.

JACKIE GOLDBERG ARRESTED IN SPROUL HALL. PHOTO BY RON ENFIELD.

amazed rummies and short-timers found themselves awakened and un-ceremoniously cut loose. Berkeley, Oakland and Santa Rita jails over-flowed, and a loosely guarded group ended up in the National Guard Armory in San Leandro. This, the largest mass arrest in California history, got headlines all over the world, even, to our delight, in Uganda.

> *Mona Hutchin:* During the sit-in, some poor girl found out that arrests were going to be made, and she said that she didn't want to leave, she felt committed to stay and she'd decided she was. She was really worried and was almost in tears because she had a midterm tomorrow and she didn't know what she was going to do. Everybody was very comforting and talked about all the midterms *they* had tomorrow and they were sure the professors would understand and she would get it taken care of. And she just sort of got this stricken look on her face because she was taking the course from Alex Sherriffs. So we generally agreed that it was pretty hopeless for her.[11]

> *Andy Wells:* The most startling thing about the sit-in was the amount of individual initiative. Out of the blue people would come up with tables and food, and some guy got those films [Laurel and Hardy and *Operation*

Abolition], and some people were organizing classes. It was a process of people doing what they thought was a good idea.

My only function was to find out what was going on outside so that the people on the inside could find out what was going on. So I spent the night on the roof with a walkie-talkie. I was not supposed to get arrested until the end. I was one of the last ten people to get out of the building. They came out and cleaned out the fourth floor, and at that time I was on the roof. Then they started cleaning out the first floor, and I figured that they were going to come right up the floors.* So I went to the third floor. I had an escape hatch: I had a rope. If the police came up on the roof, I would climb down the rope and come in another window in the bathroom downstairs and come in on another floor.

When the police were making arrests, they would determine who was the leader on each floor, and hold them up in front of the crowd and rough 'em up a little bit. They grabbed me by the hair and balls and sort of shook me in front of everybody until I winced, then they threw me down the stairs. God, I was annoyed at that. I'd told them I would walk, too.

I was with a group of people who had been thrown into the bull pen. About five guys would pick us up and sail us across the room into this bull pen. One guy got sailed the wrong way, and he smashed his head on the wall. And he was unconscious, so we asked them if we could have a doctor. You never heard such laughter in your life, from the police. He came to, though.

In jail, we wondered where the lawyers were. We heard there was a lawyer in the jail, so we asked if we could see him. The guard said, "Fill out this form," so we filled out the form—David Kolodny and I wrote a nice little message on the note, sending it to Burnstein—and handed it to the cop and he crumpled it up and threw it back into the cell and said, "Later, Mac."[12]

Jackie Goldberg: I was the fourth female Goldberg to arrive in Santa Rita, and two of them had been isolated already because they didn't know which of them was Art's sister. I got isolated, too.

Right after I was arrested I was interrogated by the Berkeley Red Squad for about fifteen minutes:

"When did you enter the building?"

"I wanna see my lawyer."

"Who did you enter the building with?"

---

*Actually the first floor was empty by then. Because we were afraid of tear gas, everyone had gotten out of the basement and first-floor areas before the police had begun the arrests.

STEVE WEISSMAN ESCAPES FROM SPROUL HALL.
PHOTO BY HELEN NESTOR.

"I wanna see my lawyer."

"Were you in on the planning of this sit-in?"

"I wanna see my lawyer."

"Will you answer any other questions I ask you with the same response?"

"I wanna see my lawyer."

There were about eight of us that left Sproul Hall basement at the same time, and I was the only one that was dragged completely on my back all the way. The others were carried at least part of the way.[13]

Steve Weissman: My voice had gone out, so I went to sleep, waiting to be arrested. About seven in the morning, someone awakened me and told me that Jack had just been arrested, and that no one was at the microphone. So I went up to take the microphone, which we called "Radio Free UC," telling people that if they still felt they had to go to class, they should go around and watch the police. It was part of our strategy that we were going to make the arrests take as long as possible, so that as many people as possible could see it.

When I came to the microphone, I thought it would be a good idea if I got arrested outside. I didn't go until the police came at me; I asked the people around me if maybe I should go down the rope. It was like the Red Sea parting for me and closing up again on the cops. I vaulted over the balustrade and I grabbed the rope, and I didn't know what to do; I'd never climbed a rope in my life. So I chiminied down, between the pillar and the wall.

When I got down the rope, I ran like hell to Dwinelle, and the police didn't come after me. So I came back and we pulled up the microphone, and I spoke from the steps. I was one of the few people on the outside who had any authority. If someone would come up to me and ask if something was a good decision, I would say, "If you're sure you can

ALAMEDA COUNTY SHERIFF'S BUS FULL OF FSM ARRESTEES. PHOTO BY RON ENFIELD.

defend it tomorrow morning, go ahead and do it." I was too giddy to make decisions, but it gave people a certain amount of confidence that there was someone from the Steering Committee there.

About nine o'clock [in the morning of December 3], I went and got a Dexedrine, and had some coffee, and went back to set up the rally.

When the cops came to get the microphone, [Jim] Petras immediately signaled everyone to split. Someone took off with the battery and we passed everything else through the crowd, over people's heads.[14]

Bob Starobin: I was right on the steps of Sproul Hall during the arrests: they had a PA system set up inside, by the windows on the little balconies. Barbara Garson was up there holding forth, so the police—this was around eight or nine in the morning—made a dash for the amplifier, and the kids were sitting around it on the second floor. The police broke a lot of windows trying to get the microphone, which was out on the window sill. The police just came charging through, there was a lot of screaming and yelling—they got part of it. Then there was another set which they set up afterwards, and that lasted a while longer. Later they passed it down so the cops couldn't get the second microphone. They were holding a rally outside, and they had the amplifier and the batteries and microphone sitting at the top of the steps, plus two big speakers. All of a sudden, cops in a column came either out of the door or along the lawn by the tree, charging right for the amplifier. Well, the people saw them coming, and they passed all of the equipment over the heads of the students, and brought it down into the center of the crowd. There was a big crush at the top there, and people were really mad at the cops, and it looked like it was really ready to blow up—everybody was ready for a nice big riot—when two professors, one was Wildavsky, intervened and started talking to the police captain.

There were a couple of kids who wanted to get in, and they started breaking windows and doors at the top of the steps.[15]

Larry Marks: I was in charge of the sound equipment before and during the sit-in, though I wasn't arrested. About five-thirty [in the morning of December 3], when the arrests were being made, Steve Weissman leaned out of a window and said, "Go get a picket line going," and that was how that started. During the sit-in I was picket captain on the first line, and after that I was in charge of bail. A female TA at the Subject A office was in charge of getting cars out to the jail. Dusty Miller and I and Dave Mandel were organizing the cars to follow the busses. Those cars were pulled over by the cops about halfway to Santa Rita. One guy was pulled over, and then another guy was pulled over, and then the busses speeded up. The pickup activities were conducted from the Subject A office. This was when Professor Hirsch, Professor Parkinson, and Professor Robinson became active.* The math department professors

---

*English professor Thomas Parkinson was the son of a San Francisco master plumber and union leader blacklisted in the great General Strike of the late thirties. Though Professor Parkinson became well known as a scholar, critic and poet, he did not lose his political sympathies. Students requested that he monitor their picketing of HUAC, and after the police washed the students down the steps of San Francisco's City Hall, he publicly commended the protesters for their peaceful and dignified behavior, and again for their peaceful picketing against ROTC. His openly expressed sympathies made him the subject of a right-wing broadside which called him a Stalinist and a homosexual—terms which at that time were all but synonymous.

On January 18, 1961, a deranged anti-

Communist (a former student of Parkinson's) walked into Dwinelle Hall carrying a sawed-off shotgun, intending to kill history professor Richard Drinnon, whom he believed to be a Communist. Instead, however, the lunatic stopped at the office of Professor Parkinson, where he shot both Parkinson and his graduate student Stephen Thomas, believing them to be Communists as well. He shot Parkinson first, and as the graduate student turned toward him in horror, the madman shot him because Thomas "looked at him in a haughty manner." Thomas was killed, and Parkinson only recovered after a delicate operation, though he carried sixty lead pellets in his head and jaw to his dying day. The police did a slapdash job of investigating the murder and the University

really stick out. They had met with the judge in his chambers earlier, and they got the bail bondsman and started working on the releases. Brian Mulloney set up microphones around noon after the sit-in. There were some police who came out of Sproul Hall and tried to grab the equipment. I was annoyed at that, because I was the one who was responsible for the equipment, I was the one who had taken it out. There were two PA systems operating. There was one on the steps of Sproul Hall, and they never got to that one, because it was so packed in. They made a good-sized jab for it, but they didn't make it. There was one at Bancroft and Telegraph. The microphones of that one were seized around noontime.[16]

Berkeley police officer William Radcliffe: They were singing and laughing, but I think they really were scared. You could feel some of the boys trembling as we carried them out. I don't think they were as brave as they acted.[17]

The last person to be arrested was Karen Taylor, a twenty-four-year-old senior in bacteriology, who said, as she was simultaneously hauled off by the police and interviewed by the *Oakland Tribune*, "This is only the beginning. The fight for freedom will continue."[18] By 4:45 PM on December 3, all that was left in Sproul Hall was a bunch of pooped-out cops and a lot of trash.

of California ignored the event entirely; not a single official word was heard on the case, nothing was said in defense of Parkinson's reputation, no praise for his excellence as a scholar, no regret over the deed. He was not even sent a condolence card. It was discovered later that efforts to say anything official in support of Professor Parkinson were blocked by Alex Sherriffs.

Parkinson was among that large percentage of the faculty which supported the goals but could not condone or accept the means of the Free Speech Movement. He headed the campus chapter of the American Association of University Professors, which came out in support of the students at an early point in the controversy, but the ambivalence created by the FSM's disruptive, confrontational methods kept him, as well as most of the other faculty, in a "wait and see" position until the intolerable presence of police on campus forced them to align themselves with one side or the other.

Professor Parkinson testified as an expert witness for the defense in the trial of Allen Ginsberg's *Howl*, and in the sixties defended the booksellers of Lenore Kandel's *The Love Book*. That he publicly expressed sympathy for the goals of the Free Speech Movement, and after the arrests actively supported the students and their cause, is a profound testimony to his physical and moral courage.

(This information has been drawn from a number of sources: an October 1992 conversation with his widow, Ariel Parkinson; a memorial eulogy by his longtime friend and associate Charles Muscatine; the 1962 book *Student*, by David Horowitz; and an account by Wayne Collins, Jr., of conversations with Professor Richard Drinnon.)

A strange, dark day. The University dragging its children down flights of stairs, to pose for mug shots in the basement, hauling them off to jail. Alameda County Sheriff's Department busses in caravan, taking students waving signs scribbled "FSM," flashing fingers in Churchill's "V" signal out slits of painted-over windows; muffled freedom songs, hoots of defiance from Black Marias sent by every adjoining police department; hundreds of cops cordoning off the administration building; thousands of curious students, faculty, locals; and newsmen by the score. Burton White, KPFA's star reporter and a constant presence at every rally or public announcement, was going berserk. Bancroft and Telegraph a parking lot for police vehicles. Graduate students picketing every University building. No classes; no teaching; just silence, confusion, outrage, disbelief, excitement. Many who hadn't gone wished they'd had a bit more courage. Many of the arrested, frightened and hungry, wished they were home again.

The group I was with was processed through into chilly barracks in Santa Rita, thirty-five miles south of Berkeley, near Pleasanton. We were pleased by the apt location: during the war, Santa Rita had been an internment camp for Japanese Americans. We felt that one injustice was reflected in another. Mario was put in solitary for making trouble about the ventilation system and for demanding telephone calls to lawyers. By early morning on the fourth, having each gotten a slice of bologna and a dot of yellow mustard between two pieces of white bread to sustain us, we were being processed out again.* Things at the jail were a mess, with hundreds of students being processed in even as hundreds more were being processed out. The cops at first had said that nobody would be released until we all were processed in, but the professors got municipal court judge Rupert Crittenden to tell them otherwise. Matters were somewhat delayed when the guards got things out of order and wanted us to sign for our confiscated property before we had received it. I refused, and promptly all those behind me also refused. The guards tossed me in solitary, where I sat for no more than twenty minutes before being joined by another guy who'd done the same thing. Jack managed to get us both out, and the exhausted, exasperated guards finally convinced us that it was OK, and not to make a federal case out of it for Christ's sweet sake. The main highway outside the gates was lined with parked cars for hundreds of yards in either direction, waiting to take us back to Berkeley.

---

*On December 4, 1964, the *Oakland Tribune* reported, "The students in the bull pens were fed 'bag lunches,' each containing two sandwiches, and cookies, and each one had a choice of milk or tea. Dinner was spaghetti and meatballs." But, by gum, all I remember is the bologna sandwich.

Tom Weller: I was among the last few to be released, and after a long afternoon of waiting, was thoroughly ready to go. Another late straggler was Miklos Nagy, a mad Hungarian campus hanger-on. Miklos hadn't even been in Sproul Hall, but was swept up by the cops anyway, probably for behaving in his usual hysterical Hungarian manner.

The previous waves of troops had redecorated the processing room with

Three University of California coeds smile at photographer through prison bars at the Oakland city jail today after their arrest at the Berkeley campus on trespassing charges. Women seized in the mass arrests were taken to the Oakland jail while men were transported to Santa Rita Prison Farm.

FSM COEDS IN JAIL. BERKELEY GAZETTE PHOTO.

"FSM" and "Free Speech" graffiti in various media. Miklos and I were the last two in the room. The guard brought out some buckets and sponges and said, "Alright, you two. Clean up these walls."

I started to do it, but Miklos began screaming and pounding his forehead with his fist. It was torture and against the Geneva Convention, he shouted, and furthermore he was going on a hunger strike and wished the Red Cross notified. I tried to get him to shut up—I just wanted to get out of there—but there was no hope. They threw us both in solitary.

"The Hole" was a telephone-booth-sized cell with a bare concrete floor with a drain in the middle and no furniture. But at least Miklos wasn't there. After letting us cool our heels for a while, just on general principles, they let us out and finally we got processed and released.[19]

Kate Coleman: The cops had been making raiding forays through our group to get at the leaders. When Mario and Suzanne were gone I took over the job. I had been loudly encouraging others to link arms and go limp and sing and make the cops' jobs hard for them, so they came after me next. They said, "Get her!" and climbed over other people to come at me. When they arrested me, they really hurt me—they twisted my arm up behind my back and then they threw me against the back of the elevator.

The women's search area in the campus police station was really just a closet. I'd thought that more of the action was going to be outside, where it would be cold, so I'd dressed more warmly than I really needed to. I was wearing tight pants and tight imitation patent-leather boots—I'd been in those same clothes since morning. When I took off my boots to be searched by the matron my feet smelled terrible—I was so embarrassed, it brought back all those stories about being hit by a car and having a hole in your panties—I wanted to look nice, and I was so humiliated at this men's locker room smell that was coming from my feet. I kept apologizing to the matron as she ran her hands under my clothes.

The women were at first packed into the Santa Rita women's drunk tank. There was one toilet right out in the open. We were all hungry, but got nothing to eat until eight hours later. None of us had been allowed to make a phone call. When Bettina joined us it catalyzed the group; we all cheered when we saw her, and she was let out to make a phone call for all of us. They'd let us keep our purses, and we went through them and pooled everything in a big pile in the middle of the floor: cigarettes, gum and candy, and shared it all out equally to everyone, even if it meant only half a stick of gum.

There were too many arrestees for Santa Rita, so they hauled all of us off to the San Leandro Armory, and herded the several hundred of us into the gymnasium. There we got to make phone calls to the central number that had been set up before the arrests. We were all over the blond wood floor, dancing and horsing around, and this really drove the guards crazy. The gym was a huge room with double doors at one end, and the basketball court had a line down the middle. The deputies lined up and pushed us back onto one side of the court, and made us stay on one side of the line. The bathroom was at the far end, and we had to ask permission to cross the line to go to it. Otherwise, we weren't even supposed to get close to the line, so it turned into a sort of game of "Mother, May I," where we would creep up close to the line until a guard would order us back, and we would dance around, coming closer and closer and then ask to go to the bathroom. We didn't take them very seriously; what were they going to do, arrest us? Finally, the guards relaxed and we wandered all over again; that was about when we finally got a Wonder Bread and bologna sandwich with a spot of mustard.[20]

Jeff Lustig: I ended up in the Oakland city jail, and played hearts all night with some graduate students. We played in the bathroom, where the light was on all night. There was this one kid who, around five o'clock, started kicking up a fuss—he wanted something to eat. "Hey, where's some food!" And he made more and more noise, and finally started saying, "I'm going to call my father and tell him that you're not feeding us!" and telling them what a big deal his father was. When they got around to handing out bologna sandwiches, there was one for everybody except him.[21]

Janis Zimdars: Being arrested was so bizarre—feeling pushed around by people who were not my intellectual or social equals—an uppity yet powerless feeling. This sounds so arrogant now, but it was the arrogance of young white middle-class naïveté. There was my real sympathy for the overextended staff at Santa Rita and for anyone who *had* to eat the god-awful food they handed out. I had absolutely no sense of humor—pity—when the mug shots were taken.

On arriving home I found my poor starving pet rat shaking the bars of his cage at me—how could I have forgotten? The abyss of disappointment in my mother's voice over the phone when I told her I had been arrested. Almost as bad as when I had answered truthfully when she inquired about my virginity—eventually she learned to quit asking. It took a long time to go to sleep, spacey as I was from lack of sleep and persistent wondering what we had accomplished.

Pam Mellin's parents were disgusted at her arrest, but her grandparents sent her a congratulations card and wrote that "Thank God, there was another Wobbly in the family to carry on the tradition." I envied that card, I can tell you.[22]

KATE COLEMAN. PHOTOGRAPHER UNKNOWN.

Mike Smith: This was the first time I was ever arrested—aside from juvenile things. As a result of my arrest an article in the *Chronicle* said I

was a member of the
Zeta Psi fraternity, and
the alumni at the na-
tional had an emergency
meeting to discuss
throwing me out, even
though I wasn't for-
mally a member of the
house—once you're a
member of a fraternity,
unless they kick you
out, you're a member.
The mayor of Pied-
mont, who was one of
the real red-hot alumni,
asked if I would meet
with him because he
wanted to find out just
what sort of an individ-
ual I was before he went
to the alumni meeting—
why somebody who
was a member of the

SANTA RITA COUNTY JAIL.

house could have fallen in with this den of Communists. It all boiled
down to he wanted to find out whether I was a Communist or just a
Communist dupe. He had some other alumni there, and I stood up and
said, "You're insulting my integrity. I'm leaving." The national didn't
do anything, because on a local level the people at the house went down
and said that what I did was my own business as far as the house was
concerned, and they didn't care about my involvement.[23]

Barry Jablon and Mike Abramovitch began setting up what later became Legal Central. Bail was originally set at $75 per offense, with $100
for resisting arrest (going limp was interpreted, for this purpose, as resisting arrest). Individual bail ranged from $166 to $276. By nine in the
morning professors managed to get Judge Crittenden to reduce the bail
to between $56 and $110 per demonstrator.* University students, professors, teaching assistants and Berkeley citizens had raised the bail,
some putting up their homes as surety. The money went through Jerry

---

*There's some confusion about both the
amounts of bail and what it was reduced
to, and when the bail was finally worked
out. Though the *California Monthly* states

that the bail was reduced by nine in the
evening ("Chronology," 62), that does not
jibe with either my recollection or what
other sources say.

OAKLAND TRIBUNE PHOTO, DECEMBER 4, 1964.

Barrish in Oakland, who was later to do all the bail bonding for the civil rights demonstrations and Vietnam protesters. Strange phenomenon: a bail bondsman with a strong social conscience. "Don't perish in jail: call Barrish for bail" was his slogan, and I carried one of his business cards with me all the time. Years later, Barrish gave it all up and became a documentary filmmaker.

Charles Muscatine: I met Charlie Sellers when we were in line in City Hall trying to post bail for the students, and we've been good friends ever since. Why was I posting bail? Because they were my students. Two-thirds of my students were involved. It was a personal thing.[24]

Associate Professor Sherwood Parker: My involvement with the faculty groups came late. I'd had contact with the students, but not with the faculty. The first real action I took—other than attending demonstrations, talking to and trying to convince individual faculty members that you were right, going to the Regents' vigil—the first real action I took on my own, was at the time of the sit-in I went into Sproul Hall and talked to people. I left Sproul Hall and talked to [professor of physics] Burton Moyer some more. After the arrests, [English professor] Henry

JEFF LUSTIG'S BAIL BOND RECEIPT FOR HIS ARREST ON
DECEMBER 3 IN SPROUL HALL. THE PREMIUM WAS $11, WHICH
IMPLIES A TOTAL BAIL OF $110. HE WAS BAILED OUT AT 2 AM,
BUT THAT TIME IS CROSSED OUT AND 9 AM WRITTEN IN. THE
BAIL WAS ARRANGED IN THE BERKELEY MUNICIPAL COURT
THROUGH THE ATLAS BAIL BOND AGENCY.

PREDAWN GATHERING OUTSIDE SPROUL HALL, DECEMBER 3, 1964.
PHOTOGRAPHER UNKNOWN.

Nash Smith had started a bail fund, and I started working with that. When that was completed, and we'd raised the ten or eleven thousand dollars, I spent my time talking with Judge Crittenden and driving back and forth to Santa Rita.

At the time the judge was having a very hard time determining even where the students were—he didn't know, no one knew. They were in perhaps five different places. Barrish was there trying to go through the police blotter so he could start writing bail bonds, large numbers of people were downstairs in the lobby and in the courtroom, there were people in the judge's chambers. I got a map from Alice Foley and took the cash we had and headed to Santa Rita, which is where most of the students were. We spent a couple of hours trying to get in. We parked on the shoulder—where the highway patrol were giving tickets to people; when I found that we couldn't get in I gave some of the money to a woman who was trying to bail her daughter out. Before I left Santa Rita the guard told me that they wouldn't release any of the demonstrators, even if they received a blanket bail bond, until the last person had been processed in.

I told Judge Crittenden what the guards had said, and he turned to one of the assistant district attorneys there and told him to call the sheriff and countermand that order. The district attorney looked unhappy, and said,

STUDENTS BEGIN MAKING PICKET SIGNS IN THE PREDAWN DARKNESS OUTSIDE SPROUL
HALL, DECEMBER 3, 1964. PHOTOGRAPHER UNKNOWN.

"Should we really do this? We've already waked him up twice tonight."
The judge insisted, and he called him up and the sheriff agreed to send out
a radio car to get the order for the immediate release of the students. By
now Henry Nash Smith had decided to spend all the money for a blanket
bail bond.* The process of writing individual bail bonds had broken
down—it had just taken too long, the court records were too chaotic,
they didn't know where people were, so they were going to write one
bond. In actual practice, the bond was never written, and the court order
was never delivered to Santa Rita. What happened is that they radioed the
order, and they began processing the students out. Ride Central had been
set up, and people signed up to bring the students home.

I drove Andrew Ross and Shannon Ferguson home and went over
to see if Joan Scheingold was OK. She was worried about suspension,
but I was sure that they wouldn't dare—if they tried it the explosion
would be incredible.

When that was all over, I started helping the students at Legal Central: we worked for nearly twenty-four hours straight organizing the
first defendants' meeting at Garfield Junior High.

*According to the *San Francisco Chronicle*, $83,710 was raised by the Berkeley faculty
members and agreed to by Crittenden as a blanket bail bond.

IBM PUNCHCARD HANDED OUT ON DECEMBER 3 AND 4. MANY WERE ACCOMPANIED BY
SIGNS SAYING, "I AM A STUDENT AT THE UNIVERSITY OF CALIFORNIA. PLEASE DO NOT
FOLD, SPINDLE OR MUTILATE ME."

The great change in faculty opinion occurred when the police came
on campus [December 3].* I learned then of the attempts at mediation,
and I learned of the attempts of Chancellor Strong to arrest Mario when
he reappeared on campus on October 5. The morning of the arrests,
about eleven o'clock, there was a meeting of the faculty of the physics
department, which concerned itself with sending a telegram to Governor Brown to halt the arrests—there were about forty-four names on it.
This was the first indication of a major reversal in the department's position. At a meeting a number of days before, there were many attacking
the students, and very few proponents; now [the department] was overwhelmingly against the arrests. When the faculty and department chairmen actually met with Mario and Steve Weissman, the general feeling
was one of surprise at how rational the students were.[25]

---

*"Beyond the loss of opportunities to
bring the protest to a stop, or to keep the
peace once it was established, the administration's errors conferred on the FSM
great moral advantage. Whatever the legal
merits, the use of police on campus un-
questionably turned almost the entire faculty against the administration. The
arrests of December 3 certified the moral
respectability of the movement; and, indeed, made the defense of the FSM and the
defense of the civil sanctity of the campus
nearly equivalent, at least for the time.
Not that the administrators had been un-
warned: after some 500 policemen had
been called to campus on October 2 (presumably to assist, if necessary, in freeing
the captured police car), a group of professors placed a black-bordered advertisement in the student newspaper, declaring
that 'This threat of force was wrong, and
. . . must never be repeated.' [*Daily Californian*, 20 October 1964. The advertisement was signed by nine professors,
including one departmental chairman.]
But even this unusual repudiation was not
heard" (Samuel Kaplan, "The Revolt of
an Elite: Sources of the FSM Victory,"
Graduate Student Journal, Spring 1965, 84).

STRIKING STUDENTS PICKETING BENEATH THE CAMPANILE. PHOTO BY BILL MENKEN.

STRIKE WHILE THE IRON IS HOT

PROCESSING OUT began at 2:00 AM on December 4, and ten hours later all the little hellions were on the loose and running around again. I got out of jail and back to campus just in time to set up the noon rally. All the arrested students were wearing large white "V's" on black arm bands, and boy were there a lot of them. It really impressed everyone. Standing at the top of the steps, I could see no end to the mass of people listening to Mario and Jack and Bettina explain what we had done and why we had done it and what we hoped to accomplish by it. We got a lot of support from people who hadn't paid us any mind until the arrests: the head of the state Building Services Union issued a statement in support of the FSM; assemblymen John Burton, Willie Brown and William Stanton spoke at the rally.

Pickets blocked campus entrances, encouraging students, professors and TAs to stay away from classes in protest over the demonstrators' arrests. Governor Brown's office in Sacramento was picketed by students from the Davis campus, and Brown actually went out of his office to talk to them.

The Graduate Coordinating Council met to discuss plans to implement the strike that was evidently already in progress. During the FSM the GCC had gathered under its umbrella a substantial number of the discontented, poorly paid and shabbily treated TAs, who tended to identify more with the undergraduates than with the faculty. TAs had no formal faculty affiliation and, as graduate students, they also lacked representation in the ASUC. TAs tended to dominate the GCC, and as they bore the brunt of the day-to-day teaching, it was easy for them to see to it that the strike was a success.

The strike was on, and continued until December 8. Perhaps one-half of all students did not attend class or had their classes canceled. The FSM and GCC together felt that a strike could be an effective tool to get long-term gains for students, to weaken the administration and

SUSAN STEIN

strengthen the faculty, as well as to increase the power of SLATE in representing student affairs with both the faculty and the administration.*

Sue Stein: In November, when the bans came out, the graduate students responded by setting up a whole bunch of tables that said things like "Comparative Literature Graduate Students." They didn't necessarily have any political significance; just an excuse for having a table up and having somebody sit there and violating University regulations.

The Graduate Coordinating Council had been formed just after the car. The first regular meeting of the GCC was held at the Physical Science Lecture Hall. There was a discussion going on between John Searle and Seymour Martin Lipset, and Searle absolutely dragged Lipset over the coals. It was the most amazing demolition of a man that I had ever seen. There were two other panelists: Myra Jehlin and David Rynin. Myra and David talked from the point of view of the students, and Lipset was arguing for Law and Order; that the students were unruly, and that they had no right to put pressure on the administration in that way; that there were legitimate channels. Searle was arguing that the channels weren't sufficient for redress of grievances, and that the students were pushed to the point of not having any other alternatives except to sit around the car and keep Jack from being arrested. Lipset kept saying that the students' real concern was in having tables up and being allowed to have protests generated on the campus,

---

*Even though SLATE was a banned organization, everyone knew perfectly well that it existed and was a real power among the students. Candidates for student body offices openly allied themselves with the organization, were voted for as members of SLATE and served as SLATE representatives.

not whether or not this particular guy was going to be arrested, so it was inconsistent with their aims. Of course, I agreed with what Searle was saying, but the reason he won that particular debate was because he's an extraordinarily witty speaker, and he was able to pick up every little imprecise thing that Lipset said, and turn it around to his own advantage.

It was the kind of meeting where a lot of people who were there were undecided; it was the beginning of the FSM and there were people who were there for the first time, really. They didn't know much about what was going on. It was the kind of meeting that brought a lot of people into the FSM or to the GCC. There were about three or four hundred people there, which at the time was an astonishing turnout. I thought I'd be the only one there.

At that time, I was an armchair participant. I wasn't quite ready to go out on the streets; I wasn't really sure that I wanted to spend my time fighting for these things, although I agreed with them from the start. I didn't have to be convinced that the students were right; I just had to be convinced that it was worth my time.

I started as a rank-and-file GCCer. I was elected from my department to be in the GCC, and gradually ended up in the GCC Executive Committee because I volunteered a lot. Sometimes it would meet every day, and sometimes every few days. The first mention of a strike was quite early in the [fall 1964] semester. It was suggested by the math department, who said that their faculty members had suggested that they have a strike, because the way things were shaping up, there would never be a solution, and we would ultimately have to have a strike in order to win anything. And, since the graduate students were the ones who really could effect a strike, since they were the teaching assistants and readers, it would have to come through the graduate students. When this was first suggested by the math graduate students, people kept thinking, "Oh, this was altogether too radical, we'll never get to that point, way in the future," but the idea was mulling around, and people were sort of talking about it. It was in the back of their minds. Then, when word got out to the administration that some graduate students were thinking of organizing a union, either under the auspices of the GCC or a separate union, the administration started getting really panicked. Right around the time that the tables were set up, Dean Elberg called a meeting of all the employed graduate students, and that meeting was so obviously one at which the administration was trying to subdue the graduate students. They started talking to us in terms of being "colleagues"! No dean has ever called me a "colleague" before or since! They were introducing all these faculty people by their first names—at the time nobody ever called Cheit *Earl*—Cheit got up and made a complete

STUDENT LETTERING PICKET SIGNS. PHOTO BY HOWARD HARAWITZ.

fool of himself by saying, "After this whole thing is over we'll have a big party together." Evidently there's a faculty Dixieland band, and he plays trombone or something. "After this is all over there'll be fellow-ship and good will among us, and we'll have this big band and it'll be on the dean's office, ha ha ha." Of course, people still go up to Earl Cheit and say, "What about that *band*? What about that *party* you promised us that never came off?"

But the graduate students were hip to this, and everybody was very, very hostile at that meeting, and they kept getting up and saying, "How come you never invited us to a meeting before?" The excuse was, "Well, we just want to get to know the graduate students." And people kept saying, "How come it's coincidental that you called us to a meeting to get to know us when you've heard rumors that we're organizing a union, and you've heard rumors that we might be thinking of a strike? In the midst of the FSM conflict, how come it's suddenly occurred to you to get to know your graduate students? Why haven't you done this before?"

We found that Dean Elberg and the faculty that were up there didn't know what was going on at *all*. They were totally misinformed, totally ignorant, and the meeting backfired on the dean's office. Instead of win-ning graduate students over to the administration, which was what it was intended to do, it turned out to solidify graduate student sentiment and make us much more militant.

Steve Weissman gave a superb presentation of what the advocacy is-sue was. It became the standard explanation. It was the first time I'd ever heard it publicly expounded that way, and it was the first time that these men on the faculty and from the dean's office had ever heard the *issues!*[1]

Bob Starobin: The meeting that Dean Elberg arranged was in Pauley Ballroom, where the faculty members of the CCPA were going to present their position to the TAs. This meeting was held just before the tables went up again.

We decided that we wanted equal time at this meeting and I went up to Elberg and demanded that we have equal time right after the faculty—Cheit and Rosovsky—presented their position. Elberg said he couldn't do it because it was not a debate, they were just presenting a position. We insisted, and he said that he'd have to ask the professors if it was OK, and finally he backed down and agreed that we'd be able to make a presentation "in the interest of free speech." So we chose Suzanne—or Suzanne volunteered, she was always volunteering—and Weissman. Suzanne gave a very bad presentation—she took a long time—and then Elberg tried to prevent Weissman from giving his presentation on the grounds that Suzanne had taken too long. I jumped up from the floor

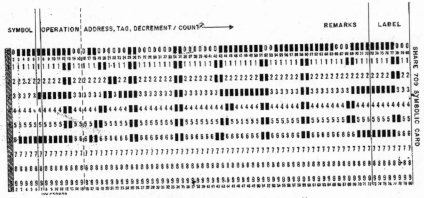

IBM CARD PUNCHED TO READ "STRIKE."

and went to the platform and started shouting that she hadn't taken all of our time, and that as a matter of fact the professors had talked for about an hour and Suzanne had only talked for about forty-five or fifty minutes, so there were actually about ten minutes left. Elberg got all shook and finally put it to a vote of the audience, who course voted to let Steve speak, and Steve managed to recoup some of the losses that Suzanne had caused by her bad presentation. That was really the turning point in the meeting, because every question from the floor to the professors just made them look sick. It became very obvious by the end of the meeting that they hadn't convinced any of the graduates of their position. Then of course later on the grads manned tables.[2]

Sue Stein: After these speakers, people spoke from the floor, making the point that they wanted the legality of their actions totally in the hands of the court and not in the hands of the University. People would get up and make eloquent statements about how they were not children anymore, and that they wished to be able to take the full consequences of their action, because they wanted to use the courts as a public forum for their political ideas. We wanted to be listened to, and if we were wrong, let the courts tell us so.

It really astonished the men at this meeting. Cheit finally got up, and he said, "You mean to say that you really would prefer to be put in the hands of the courts, knowing that the court might give you a much more severe penalty if you do something wrong? You mean that you would prefer that instead of having the kind, benevolent University take over and soothe the blows?" And people said, "Yes. That's precisely what we want. We're citizens and we want to have the same rights on the campus as off the campus. We don't want the University messing around; we don't need their paternalism. We can take care of ourselves."

They were astonished! Elberg and Cheit kept saying, "You really mean that?! You're joking! You don't realize that you're going to be worse off in the courts than in a faculty committee that judged whether or not some activity was wrong."

Then of course people got up and said, "Yes, but at least we have due process in courts, and the right of cross-examination; at least we can present our own evidence. At least it's not a kangaroo court. However more serious the penalty might be, we prefer the civil authorities."

DUSTY MILLER. PHOTO BY HELEN NESTOR.

They couldn't believe that we wanted to be subject to courts instead of University committees. They couldn't believe that we mistrusted the University, and that we couldn't accept a University finding as *necessarily* impartial.[3]

Brian Mulloney: On October 9, the word went out that graduate students were encouraged to start organizing something. A meeting was called by Bob Starobin and Skip Richheimer. It was decided by what was already the FSM Executive Committee that graduate students would have five representatives and two alternates. It went around the table: people stood up and made nominating speeches for themselves, said what they thought and what they proposed to do. I was elected an alternate.[4]

Bob Starobin: The GCC began as the result of a petition campaign started by Skip Richheimer and Henry May in the history department. They dittoed up petitions for grads and another for faculty, due by November 9, at which time we were going to have as big a meeting as possible. The meeting took place upstairs in Haviland Hall, with between one hundred and two hundred grads there. Ironically, the same room in

STRIKING ZOOLOGY TA.
PHOTO BY WALTER TSCHINKLE.

which it began was also where it met its demise.* Each department was represented by two delegates, and twenty-five departments were present. From among that number, we elected five delegates and two alternates. Those delegates were Skip Richheimer, Bob Starobin, Bob Kauffman, Charlie Vars and Myra Jehlin. The alternates were Brian Mulloney and Suzanne Goldberg. At the selection of the Steering Committee Suzanne was the only one who said she had enough time to serve. She got on more by default, because she wasn't the logical choice. Everyone knew that it would be a full-time job, and most of us couldn't be in continuous meetings and negotiations.

After the first meeting of the GCC, a more conservative group of graduates tried to start their own organization. It was led by Tom Calmar, from comparative literature; he was very anxious to get on the Executive Committee of GCC but lost. The only department where they had any strength was in sociology; there Hans Mueller was the main person. I wanted to meet these guys head on and attend their meetings, but Weissman wanted to ignore them and laugh them out of existence, which is what happened. Both of these guys were arrested and became real militant at the time of the strike. We managed to bring even the more moderate people along all the way.

The Sociology Club held a meeting in the Dynasty restaurant. Sociology was important because it was a big department. Davy Wellman, who was a radical, was president of the Sociology Club, but there were still problems because of Dick Roman and Hans Mueller. But members like Sam Farber, a tough radical, managed to bring the Sociology Club into the GCC structure. The same thing happened in the History Club, which had always been an academic thing that met every Friday afternoon, with a speaker, and they discussed academic problems. This

---

*After the FSM was over the teaching assistants went on to organize Local 1570 of the American Federation of Teachers (AFT), though by 1966 the local fell under the control of militants and disintegrated.

whole tradition had fallen apart by the spring of '64, and they had not elected any new officers since the last fall. So Richheimer and I decided to call a meeting of the club, and got ourselves elected co-chairmen, and so were pretty much in control of the whole situation in the history department, which was four hundred graduate students, and was also a key department in the humanities.

In most of the departments the clubs were the way of organizing the GCC. In those that didn't have clubs, they formed departmental organizations. In the Sociology Club we overcame the division and destroyed the Calmar-Mueller split.

Weissman wasn't involved in the first meetings. He was friendly with Skip Richheimer, and started coming to meetings of the GCC Executive Committee, and then within about a week of the first meeting, he became involved and started chairing. Weissman handled the potential split really well; he wasn't on the GCC Executive Committee, so he couldn't be on the FSM Executive Committee. But as a result of his being GCC chairman, he worked his way into the FSM Executive Committee. At that time, Brian Shannon was chairing the FSM meetings, but there was one meeting where Shannon lost control of the meeting and became personally involved in the debate, so people lost confidence in him as a chairman. That's when Weissman stepped in as FSM chairman. That's how he got on the FSM Executive Committee, and then was co-opted onto the Steering Committee.[5]

Sue Stein: After November 20, when the Regents and administration disregarded the findings of the Heyman Committee, and the four people were disciplined for actions of October, people were talking more and more openly about the need for a strike.

There was no question that it would have to come to that. We talked about the strike as the graduate student part of the FSM.

We had a long discussion and argument at which we discussed the history of this sort of strike and its possible repercussions. All the questions that could be raised were in fact raised and were in fact answered. The FSM Executive Committee was counting on the GCC having a strike, and it looked like the talk was going against it. Most of the questions were about whether we could have an effective strike. People felt that an ineffective strike would be worse than not having one at all.

Then there were a lot of people who felt that there were other things that we could do, and that it hadn't come to that. But that discussion turned into a history of what had happened, and showed that there were no channels open to us, or that they were channels that led nowhere.

The third category of questions concerned whether it would be wise to have a strike before we had formed the union, and whether we should form the union and let it call the strike.

The meeting was in 101 Cowell, which held about five hundred people. The room was packed. When the vote was taken, only two people in the entire room voted against it. At the same time, we set up a committee of people to look into very rapidly forming a union, to try to get the full prestige of a union behind the strike. The motion that was passed was that if police came on campus, or if there were arrests, that we would call a strike.

The Strike Committee, which was chaired by me and Brian, tried to find the most effective way of planning a strike and getting people out. People were in charge of publicizing the fact that we were going to have a strike, and organizing to make sure that people in every department would strike, and having people in every department go around to all the TAs and explain to them in advance, and personally, and stay for as long as it would take to explain why we wanted a strike and why every TA ought to. There was a lot of shit work that had to be done. We had signs ordered to be printed, we had people getting sticks and painting signs and posters, people were making reports and keeping tabulations. Getting a big coffee maker. Ordering a lot of donuts. Contacting the Red Cross. We finally decided that we would be able to pull off a strike that would be at least seventy-five percent effective. Preparations went on all day Tuesday [December 1]. We anticipated a strike, but if there was no strike at least we would have a lot of coffee and donuts. It's easier to call one off than to put one on.

The day that people went into Sproul Hall, we spent the rest of the afternoon preparing. We were busy doing that until two in the morning when we heard the cops were coming. Then we went home to sleep because we didn't know when we would get to sleep again.[6]

Bob Starobin: Benson Brown came on the Steering Committee from the GCC. He was an old *Root and Branch* guy. He was in the math department, and around November 9 he was part of the provisional Strike Committee, which consisted of Mulloney, Benson Brown and Skip Richheimer. They were to start propagating the idea of a strike. From that point on, Benson Brown became more and more important in the GCC organization because the Strike Committee would periodically report back to the GCC meetings on what the reaction to their propaganda was, and what the possibilities of a strike were. It was at that point that he began attending FSM Executive Committee meetings, and then when they reconstituted the Steering Committee, Brown was elected.[*]

---

*Benson Brown was elected along with Steve Weissman, Ron Anastasi and Marty Roysher.

Over Thanksgiving weekend there were meetings of the Graduate History Club, where I was doing my speaking. We were also having GCC meetings over Thanksgiving weekend, and there was great sentiment for action, for a sit-in. Everyone felt we had it in the bag, once the letters came in. There wasn't any serious split. The original Strike Committee was expanded; the people who were added

STUDENTS PICKETING CAMPUS BUILDINGS.
PHOTO BY WALTER TSCHINKLE.

to that were myself, Sue Stein, Bob Kauffman, Brian Turner and the Executive Committee of the GCC.* We weren't arrested because we felt that someone had to organize the strike, also the FSM Executive Committee made a decision that some people would stay out: Marty Roysher, Dusty Miller and Steve Weissman stayed out.

The mandate for the strike was that it was to follow the sit-in, in any event, and also in the event that cops were brought onto campus for any purpose. It was called for Thursday and Friday. The arrests took place over Wednesday night and Thursday morning.

So we were not prepared for the Thursday strike. For a little while, I was in favor of holding off until Friday, but the anarchic thing just began by itself, automatically. People just began without any organization from the FSM or anyone. Over the weekend we began organizing, and set up Strike Central, Picket Central and so on, but for the first two days it was anarchic.[7]

Brian Mulloney: The next meeting of the Strike Committee was for eight o'clock Thursday morning. I got called at six-thirty but said the hell with it and went back to sleep. Sue [Stein] and I were up on campus by

*Bob Starobin gives a slightly different chronology and makeup of the Strike Committee in his article "Graduate Students and the Free Speech Movement," where he says that the committee originally consisted of David Root, Benson Brown and Robert Richheimer, and expanded in early December to include Susan Stein, Fred Bauer, Robert Greenberg and himself, with Brian Mulloney coordinating the strike (25).

STUDENTS ON STRIKE IN FRONT OF SPROUL HALL. PHOTOGRAPHER UNKNOWN.

eight o'clock and at my office we had ten thousand leaflets that were supposed to be for the day before the strike; explaining what the issues were. They were fairly calm in tone, and were to be followed by a really vitriolic "Get out and get out now" leaflet the next day. So we borrowed several ditto machines and printed over them in ditto ink "Strike now!" and by eight-fifteen the TAs were out. Lines were up already. Lines had gone up by five-thirty. The thing got wildcatted—it was gone. There were people who were picketing empty buildings at six o'clock that morning. They were so pissed off about the cops and the arrests that the campus was in one huge ferment. By the time we got up there, the strike was *under way* whether we liked it or not. So we quickly tried to pull some control together and set up our strike headquarters. We got the name of one responsible person off each picket line by sending out a runner, and appointing that person captain for the day. By eleven-thirty that morning we knew where all the lines were except for one that was way the hell and gone down on Oxford Street. We had some sort of communication out to the lines so that they knew what was going on. We actually sent out food that day. We sent out donuts and coffee and sandwiches. Then what happened was we spent the rest of the day saying, "We need twenty-five pickets at Dwinelle Hall," and having people walk over where we suggested, and then finding out whether any people on any lines needed replacements, whether there was any trouble.[8]

At one o'clock on the third, as arrests were continuing in Sproul Hall, about a thousand professors, instructors and TAs met in Wheeler Auditorium, Professor Nathan Glazer presiding, and came down four-square on the side of the students. Henry F. May, chairman of the history department, introduced a resolution addressed to the president, the chancellor and the *Daily Californian*:

> In view of the desperate situation now confronting the University, every effort must be made to restore the unity of our campus community, and to end the series of provocation and reprisal which has resulted in disaster. With this purpose, the undersigned faculty members urge that the following actions be taken immediately:
>
> 1) That the new and liberalized rules for campus political action be declared in effect and enforced, pending their improvement,
>
> 2) That all pending campus actions against students for acts occurring before the present date be dropped,
>
> 3) That a committee selected by and responsible to the Academic Senate be established, to which students may appeal decisions of the Administration regarding penalties for violations relating to offenses arising from political action, and that the decisions of the committee are final.

Political science professor Herbert McClosky called for two additions to the resolution, requesting "retraction of the Regents' decision that the University could prosecute students for advocating illegal off-campus action" and demanding "that no student be prosecuted by the University for participating in any off-campus activity." The faculty overwhelmingly accepted both May's resolution and McClosky's additions and sent a telegram signed by 361 faculty members to Governor Brown, "strongly condemn[ing] the presence of the State Highway Patrol on the Berkeley Campus," and protesting the "exclusion of faculty members, including at least one member of our Committee on Academic Freedom, from Sproul Hall, at a time when the police were admitting newsmen and photographers."

> Punitive action taken against hundreds of students cannot help to solve our current problems, and will aggravate the already serious situation. Only prompt release of the arrested students offers any prospect of re-

storing the unity of campus life and of a return to normal academic functions.[9]

The faculty was plainly enraged at having the police on campus, as though this were some miserable banana republic with cops and students having it out on a regular basis. This was the first time in American history that the German academic tradition, barring civil authority from the University campus, had been disregarded. The outright rejection of the recommendations of the Heyman Committee and the contempt shown the faculty by the administration further alienated them. Touched in its *amour propre* the faculty allied itself not so much with the students as against the administration and Governor Brown. This was victory—in any negotiation including the students, the faculty and the administration, we now had the critical swing vote that we had lacked in October.

John Searle: Changes in faculty opinion in this period [October 2–November 20] can be described as a growing awareness of and agreement with the students' civil libertarian objectives, hostility to many of the tactics employed to achieve those objectives, and slowly accumulating irritation with the administration.

This irritation was in part due to the simple failure of the administration to solve the crisis, but also was partly the result of the near constant stream of false official statements. It was suggested by the authorities that the students were communists, in particular "Maoists and Castroites," that there was no Free Speech issue, that very few students were involved anyway, and that there were large numbers of off-campus agitators. Anyone on campus at the time could see that all this was false. Later, at the time of the strike, this sort of image protection reached new proportions when the authorities tried to pretend that the strike was a failure. At one point it was claimed that only thirty-nine classes were canceled on the entire campus (I know of several individual departments where more than thirty-nine classes were canceled) and that attendance always drops off slightly on Friday and was no worse than usual (this was said at a time when thousands of students were milling around the campus and there were picket lines at every major building.)*

In short, in a community dedicated to the search for truth, the official

---

*"On each of the three days, some 600 of 1200 TAs were on strike, while some 300 more were respecting the picket lines. In thirteen departments (Anthropology, Mathematics, History, Zoology, Social Science, Subject A, Political Science, Sociology, Economics, Philosophy, French, German and Slavic) with 500 TAs, 400

STRIKE AND WALKOUT. PHOTO BY HOWARD HARAWITZ.

lie does not sit well, and in its efforts to preserve its image with the larger public the administration was slowly undermining its moral authority with the faculty.

Another important factor in the steady shift of faculty opinion was that more and more of the best students, particularly the graduate students, were backing the FSM.[10]

Support for the FSM and the GCC strike was now widespread among both students and faculty, but was by no means universal. University Students for Law and Order (USLO), founded December 6, tried to break the strike. They planned an alternate rally for Monday the seventh, and sent teams of two faculty members and one student to talk to the living groups, telling the students that the legislature was going to take over the University and that they should return to classes.* They did well

---

were on strike, or 80 percent. In six departments of these thirteen (History, Anthropology, Sociology, Philosophy, Subject A, and Political Science) with 180 TAs, 175 participated in the strike, or 96 percent" (Starobin, "Graduate Students and FSM," 25–26).

*Kerr was bruiting this about as well, and an FSM leaflet published shortly after the strike maintains that "Kerr did not tell

them that State Senator George Miller, chairman of the Senate Finance Committee and the ranking member of the Senate Education Committee, has said that legislative appropriations will be kept '. . . entirely separate from political occurrences on and off the campus,' and that he resents the implications to the contrary which have been made by Kerr."

END CAL'S SHAME: GIVE FREE SPEECH NOW.
PHOTO BY GARY MORETTI.

with the living groups, and made inroads on the FSM position. But the organization didn't amount to much, and when its founder, Robert Dussault, resigned on the seventeenth of December the organization more or less dissolved.

Brian Mulloney: We were annoyed by continual forays of football players and freddies. We'd expected them to cause trouble, and that's why we had prepared in advance for Red Cross help. That sort of nonsense was going on all the time.

Sue Stein: Brian is exaggerating when he says "we," because very few football players were harassing *him*. *I* was the object of *much* harassment. These football players, while I was standing on the cement around Wheeler Oak, these huge men would kind of come lumbering up to me, and they would be taller than I was while I was standing on that cement wall, and they would kind of say, "Whaddayathinkyourdoing." And they would give me a rough time. A lot of them threatened me, they said, "Boy, if we ever . . . we're gonna follow you home and get you in some dark street somewhere." All sorts of threats levied at me. Then, of course, there was the time that people sat on my *feet*. That was because *Brian*, in his brilliant way, decided to take a little piss break or something. I don't know where you disappeared to for a few minutes.
Brian Mulloney: I think I went up to the math building for a few minutes. See what was going on at that end of the world.
Sue Stein: All I know is that I was standing there screaming, "We need so-and-so number of pickets at Cory Hall, does anybody know where Cory Hall is . . ." and there's this girl painting signs at the table and taking information and a can for contributions. The next thing I knew this female enclave was surrounded by these horrible-looking football types, who were threatening to smash us. They knocked over the table and started ripping up the signs. I was scared. I kept saying, "Has anybody seen Brian?" All these football people were sitting around in a

ring. Then this one big football player came and he sat down on my *feet*. He just sat down right in front of me, and looked up and said, "I'm havin' a sit-in." He was very heavy, and my toes were getting crushed, so I started wiggling my toes and my shoes and that ticked and annoyed him and he started yelling at me. Luckily at that moment, Dan Garrison happened to walk up, and he was all duded up in a suit—he was one step up from a TA, he was a Teaching Fellow—with an arm band that said, "Faculty," and it really worked! He came up and said, "Well, young lady, are you having any trouble here?" And I said, "Oh, Mr. Garrison!" So he started clearing off these guys. They really respond to authority! They didn't know it was just Dan Garrison who had been arrested shortly before.

He started playing the role of not being a friend of mine, but an impartial faculty member. He finally managed to chase away most of the guys who were sitting around, and the few who refused to leave, he engaged in this long conversation and tried to convince them that they were wrong. And he just chose coincidentally to talk right next to the place where the girls were painting signs. And either the guys were convinced—which I doubt—or they got bored with talking—which is more likely—and finally decided to go away.[11]

Mike Smith: I found out later from a friend of mine that was at the same house that I was in, that the fraternity presidents got together at the time of the strike and offered to send two thousand fraternity men down to break the strike, if the administration was willing. That's about the total number of fraternity men—they couldn't have gotten them all because most of them didn't care. Though there really was strong sentiment against the FSM. If they'd had the sanction of the administration, they could have got a couple of hundred rowdies and they would have thought nothing of attacking the strikers.[12]

Brian Mulloney: We found out over the weekend that the fraternity boys were hatching a plot to organize against us. Some really violent strikebreaking, organized gangs with clubs. We heard this through the grapevine, and then we got called by Harden Jones—Harden Jones called me in tears, and said there was going to be violence and the whole thing had to be called off, and I told him to get his ass in gear and get the dean of students to clamp down on the fraternities and the football team. I called the dean of students and called football coaches and all these people and told them that we had the people who were taking part in this thing identified—it was the crew team and the football team who were going to come down and defend Right and the American Way. We also called Mrs. Kerr—that was ghastly—telling her first that a danger of real vi-

LUDWIG, THE CAMPUS MASCOT, IGNORES THE
STRIKING STUDENTS.
PHOTO BY HOWARD HARAWITZ.

olence existed, and that if she wanted to save her husband's neck and avoid having a real riot on his hands instead of something that was just being played up in the press as one, she'd better get moving and use what leverage she had to get these things shut down. In the end she said that she saw no difference whatever between going on strike and physically assaulting people, which strikes me as an extraordinary dichotomy. She said, "If you need protection by police you should have thought about that beforehand when you were violating law and order, and if you get beaten up you deserve to." Or words to that effect.

We called the campus police, too, and were told to go shove it, in effect.

Sue Stein: So what happened was we got a brilliant idea, which is actually the one that worked to end that thing. It was Buddy [Stein]'s idea. We were all panicked and figured that these guys were going to come down and give us a hard time, so Buddy, who has a good newspaperman's sense of what's going to happen, says that we should call up a couple of people—like the coach of the football team—and say, "Hello, Coach so-and-so, this is John Jones from UPI. I understand that your football team is organizing to break up the strike that's going on the campus. Is there any truth to that rumor that we've heard from many sources?" And the guy said, "No, no, there's no truth to it at all." Buddy's the one that did all this. Then a few minutes later Buddy called up and said, "Hello! I'm Jane Smith from the AP and I understand that there's some football players that are organizing against the FSM strikers. Is there any truth to that rumor? We're wondering if we should send our man down to get some pictures of that little incident." And what evidently happened, was that word got through to the football guys, through the coach, who knew that bad publicity would do him no good.

I called Becky Tracy and she then got on the phone and called all her friends who were faculty wives, "Those people are going to be hurt and we've got to tell our husbands to do something about it!"

Brian Mulloney: The deans and coaches were up all that night collaring people and telling them not to go down, threatening them with the direst of results if they did. Also warning them that we were prepared for them, and that if they went down they would not be doing all the hurting, and that most of them would never play football again. One of the things that was in addition to the standard unions of the AF of L and CIO, there were a number of longshoremen and Wobblies out on the line, too. And they were not going to stand for any of this nonsense. I'm glad they stopped. This was Sunday night, over the weekend.[13]

NECKTIE PARTY

On the weekend of the strike, the campus was awash with rumors: the administration was determined to stop the strike at any cost; the National Guard was coming in; the Regents were going to expel thousands of students and fire hundreds of faculty members; the University would shut down; Chancellor Strong was in the hospital; faculty were meeting in secret; the department heads were meeting with Kerr and the Regents. The one thing that was certain was that under the quiet of the weekend campus was a foaming beehive of activity.

Some of these rumors proved, not surprisingly, to be true: various faculty contingents were in fact holding meetings—most notably the Two Hundred, who were largely sympathetic to the FSM goals, and the Council of Department Chairmen, who were not. Both groups had begun meeting as the arrests and strike disrupted the campus on December 3 and 4, the Two Hundred to forge motions to present at the Academic Senate meeting on Tuesday the eighth, and the department heads to work out a proposal to present to Clark Kerr. On Sunday, December 6, council chairman Robert A. Scalapino met with Kerr to work out an agreement, and Kerr announced that the department heads' proposal would be presented at a student-faculty-administration convocation at 11:00 AM on Monday in the Greek Theatre.

The FSM Steering Committee, Executive Committee and Strike Committee also met continuously over the weekend, and in a one-sided flow of information knew exactly what the administration was up to and took effective steps to counter it. We decided that Mario and Steve Weissman would walk up, from opposite sides of the stage, and converge on the microphone. We would also ask permission first, but would speak in any event.

Bob Starobin: The continuous Steering Committee meeting after the December sit-in and before the Greek Theatre events was at Bob Mac-

416

Laren's place on Bancroft Way directly across from Sproul Hall. This was over the weekend of December 6, after the sit-in, when the information was coming in about the departmental chairmen.

MacLaren has this completely kooky apartment, and the whole atmosphere was of counterintelligence—they were also on the phone with Governor Brown. The intelligence was terrific—they were finding out things that were happening between Scalapino and Kerr and the Regents while they were happening. Accurate information was slipping out of the departmental chairmen's meeting, mainly through economics department leaks. All this stuff coming in and we were figuring out what was going to happen. We had it completely figured out before Monday. There were a lot of wild ideas coming out, and I'm convinced that half of it was due to the physical environment—dinosaurs hanging down from the ceiling—and the guy himself is a complete kook! He couldn't stand any mess at all in his apartment, and he was constantly cleaning up. I was acting as liaison between the GCC Strike Committee and the Steering Committee.

At 3:00 PM Saturday, December 5, we got a report that Charlie Vars and Bob Weiman, who were both on the GCC Executive Committee, had made a trip to Governor Brown the day before, on Friday, and they had seen Moscowitz, the attorney general. These two graduate students were shocked at Moscowitz's ignorance on the question of advocacy, and they suggested that the Steering Committee push very hard on the question of amnesty for the eight hundred arrested students.*

Then we got a report by Marty Roysher on a meeting that took place between Steve Weissman, Myra Jehlin and professors of the economics department Allman and Gordon, on Friday night, concerning the proposals that would be before the Academic Senate. The professors were convinced that there could be a settlement, and were talking in these terms. Toward the end of the meeting, Professor Gordon shifted the topic away from the proposals before the Academic Senate, and started talking about an "elite group" and got very emotional, which is unlike him, and started saying that some action would come on Monday from this "elite group." That they were bludgeoning the administration. Who was in this "elite group"? Regent Roth was in this group, and it would probably make an offer of University amnesty to the students, and that the students would be supported in court. Weissman then asked Gordon, "Does the 'elite group' understand the position of the students?" and the answer was "yes." Steve then told him that the students would accept University amnesty, but would continue to press the administration on

---

*Bob Starobin is confusing the new attorney general, Thomas C. Lynch, with the former attorney general, Stanley Mosk, whom he had replaced in August 1964.

the issue of advocacy. Professor Gordon got quite mad, and said that the students were destroying democracy.

Bettina came in with the information that another proposal from this group was that six to ten FSM leaders would be suspended.

Gradually the composition of this "elite group" was revealed by Gordon: Professors Scalapino and Skitofsky, Regent Roth, and possibly Regent Coblantz. But there was no mention of Kerr being involved. Then Gordon said that we may never hear any more of this group ever again. The intrigue and counterintelligence got everyone at the Steering Committee very excited.

Then there was a phone call on Saturday morning from Paul Jacobs [director of the Institute for Industrial Relations], that Robert Hutchins, the famous educator, might be called in as the governor's observer.

Then Jacobs called Governor Brown directly. The Steering Committee had somehow managed to reach Governor Brown's son [Jerry], and Governor Brown's son had talked to his father and urged him to listen to what the students had to say about the situation. Brown's son had been on the Mississippi Summer Project, or had something to do with civil rights work the summer before, and somehow or another the Steering Committee approached him through that connection. Also, much of the talking to Governor Brown that morning was set up by Paul Jacobs. So the call to Governor Brown by the Steering Committee followed. On the call itself, they were trying to explain to Brown what the situation was. The one thing that Governor Brown said that sticks in my mind, was that he promised again and again that he would meet with the student leaders if they weren't satisfied with what Kerr had to say on Monday. Of course, we weren't satisfied with what Kerr had to say, and when it was mentioned to Brown he refused to meet with us. This conversation was taped and played back and then erased. There was a big debate over whether they should keep the tape, since making it in the first place was illegal.

Then Jacobs called us back after we talked to Brown. When Jacobs called us back, he said that Kerr was indeed involved in it, and in fact it was Kerr's group. This was contrary to what Professor Gordon had said the night before. Brown was also involved in it—it was Brown's role to sell the proposals of the "elite group" to the Regents. Jacobs said that the administration was trying very hard to reestablish order on the campus, and there might be a three-man mediation team brought in, consisting of Robert Hutchins, Supreme Court Justice Gibson, and somebody else, he didn't know who. Jacobs said that Kerr still did not understand what the issues were: he didn't understand the advocacy question for example. Then Charlie Vars, a grad in economics, called, and said that Kerr's faculty committee would take over the administration, and that they may have Strong's resignation already; that they would call for good faith by the students—that is, that the strike would have to be over by noon on Monday. But that the problem that Kerr's faculty committee was running into was with Chancellor Strong. We didn't understand the problem with Strong at that time.

Then Charlie Vars called back, and said that Attorney General Moskowitz's secretary had just called, and that Moskowitz was coming to Cal to handle the situation from University Hall.

Then we got news of the emergency meeting of the ASUC Senate, where they urged an end to the strike, and of a meeting of the Alumni Association, of which it was said again that they were "bludgeoning Kerr." We heard that they had come out with resolutions: one, that all students arrested be expelled; two, that the TAs on strike be fired; and three, that professors who supported us, including those who raised bail, should be dismissed.* Apparently the only one who dissented at the alumni meeting said that if the eight hundred students were expelled, "it might look bad for the University."

Then Bob Kauffman, a graduate in history, came in and he reported on negotiations with the "good faculty"—the Two Hundred. They had a package deal to offer: that the charges against the students be dropped; that the FSM would have to be willing to go along with the suspension of six to ten leaders, that the strike be called off on Monday. In return for this, the McClosky proposal would be adopted by the Academic Senate. Kauffman went on to say that Kerr could not speak for amnesty to the courts, but only for University amnesty, and that the face-saver for the administration would have to be some kind of discipline for the students. The content of the McClosky proposals was to be major changes in the advocacy rule, and to the chancellor's power over discipline of students in political cases. This was to be in exchange for disciplining of Mario, Art, Jackie and Brian Turner, plus some others.

Myra Jehlin came in to report on discussions with Henry Nash Smith.

By 11:00 PM Saturday, we had pieced together that there were in effect two groups contending for power. One group, headed by Kerr, the so-called elite group, was actually in control of the department chairmen. In other words, the department chairmen were just a front for this smaller group. They intended to act first, probably by Monday morning. Then there was the other group—the Two Hundred—leading lights being Searle, Henry Nash Smith, Sellers, Kornhauser, Zelnik,

*Here again we see the fine Italian hand of Alex Sherriffs, who was publicly all in favor of firing the striking TAs and made no bones about his opinion of faculty who supported the students.

Muscatine and Parkinson, who were working through the Academic Senate. They couldn't act before Tuesday.

On Sunday, a delegation of professors came in: Reginald Zelnik and Lawrence Levine, who were acting as intermediaries between the faculty Two Hundred and the FSM Steering Committee. We told them what we knew, which was really much more than they knew. Zelnik bolstered this by telling us that Scalapino was in Sacramento on Saturday. By early Sunday, we had pretty well pieced together what would happen on Monday morning in the Greek Theatre. Sunday night, Mario went to Joseph Tussman [chairman of the philosophy department] about being able to speak before the Academic Senate.

By Sunday night the GCC had found out exactly what the department chairmen would say, and what the actual progression would be on Monday. First the department chairmen would speak to the faculty and graduate students of each department, and then we would all troop up to the Greek Theatre and Kerr would say the same thing. We were quite well prepared for that. We were able to counter this fairly well in history, sociology and English. We reached most of the important departments and explained to them what would be said on Monday morning. The sociology grads gave the people in that department, like Nathan Glazer, a pretty hard time on Monday morning. They presented a fairly militant face—that they couldn't go along with these proposals, and that the proposals didn't meet the issue at all.

There was a meeting in the history department just as there were meetings in every other department, called by the department chairmen, and they managed to call about twenty-five or thirty of the couple of hundred graduate students. They had managed to call all the troublemakers, so we were all there. The meeting went something like this: it was in 101 Cal and Henry May was up on the stage; he was one of the spokesmen for the department chairmen. He had a piece of paper in his hand with everything that Kerr was going to tell us. And all the professors and students were out in the audience. Then the Kerr proposals were written up on the board, and they had a big discussion of what was going on. Naturally the faculty was split, Sellers and Stampp, Stocking and Levine with a fairly good position, and people like Sontag and Dean Barnes taking the other. So then I got up and tried to speak, and at first May didn't want me to, because he said it would take too long. A little bit later they let me speak, and I said in effect that the University was being run by the department chairmen, and that all semblance of faculty power had vanished, and that when governments were overthrown by military dictatorships all the faculty in this room would be shocked and horrified because they were all good liberals, but when it happened on this campus nobody says anything. That upset them very much and infuriated Henry May, who hasn't really talked to me since. Then a student, Richard Tyler, who had become quite conservative, got up and moved that the five proposals should be adopted by this meeting. It looked pretty bad, but Stampp got up and moved a substitute motion, that they only adopt point number one—University amnesty, which was the only good point in the whole thing. So of course, you vote on the substitute motion first, if that passes then it substitutes for the previous motion. So they voted on that, and it passed. Then they moved for adjournment. It left May looking pretty silly, because he'd only gotten one-fifth of the proposals through, and only the best one and the others had been in effect rejected. When I spoke against the substitute motion—I wanted them to reject all of them—that probably strengthened Stampp's hand, because I was identified with the lunatic fringe. Then, of course, everyone went up to the Greek Theatre.[1]

Departmental chairmen announced that all University classes held between nine in the morning and noon on December 7 were to be canceled, and that Kerr would address the University community in the Greek Theatre. The subject of his speech was a proposal to "inaugurate a new era of freedom under law," which had been unanimously approved by seventy-three department chairmen.[2] At eleven o'clock, sixteen thousand students, faculty members and staff gathered at the Greek Theatre to hear Clark Kerr, flanked by all the campus department heads, accept the proposal concerning free speech on campus that was presented him by Robert Scalapino for the Council of Department Chairmen, which said, in effect, that they would think about it. Acknowledging the gravity of his mistake in having tried to nail the student leaders, Kerr announced an amnesty in the disciplinary cases pending against Savio, Turner and the Goldbergs, and announced that students arrested in the sit-in would not face separate University disciplinary action.

John Searle: The failure of the chairmen's agreement involved a fairly subtle point that its makers apparently failed to grasp. The disciplinary proceedings against the leaders had indeed reopened the struggle, but once reopened it could not be stopped simply by suspending the discipline, for once reopened it focused everyone's attention on the principles left unsettled by the regents' compromise of November 20. Now, any attempt to solve the crisis without meeting those issues was bound to fail, and the chairmen were giving the students University amnesty at a time when that was no longer enough. Having ignited the fuel, one can't stop the fire by blowing out the match.

The administration . . . couldn't seem to grasp that it was both the case that the students fought so hard because they felt "alienated" and at the same time fought sincerely for free speech objectives. Thus in discussion with some members of the two hundred on the afternoon immediately after the Greek Theatre meeting, it became clear that a high official of the University simply did not understand the issue about advocacy. He had to go out in the hall and have the University lawyers explain it to him.[3]

It seemed to the administration that if the Scalapino proposals were used as a basis for negotiation, exams, winter rains and the spring break would reduce the FSM to a small group of activists that would pose little danger to the University. All Kerr had to do was keep things quiet for a little while.

The speakers were roundly booed, the faculty members were angered by the secretly arrived at *fait accompli*, and Kerr's written speech contained an unconscious element of self-mockery: the Greek Theatre, he observed, "has seen many great operatic and theatrical performances." People started laughing, and as they did so, Kerr stepped forward, looked up from the text of his speech and said, "I agree with you that this may seem a rather theatrical performance today—thanks to the audience, not to those of us up here."[4] The poor sap could never learn.

Having accepted the department chairmen's proposal, Kerr proceeded to read it to the assembly:

1. The University Community shall be governed by orderly and lawful procedures in the settlement of issues; and the full and free pursuit of educational activities on this campus shall be maintained.

2. The University Community shall abide by the new and liberalized political action rules and await the report of the Senate Committee on Academic Freedom.

3. The Departmental Chairmen believe that the acts of civil disobedience on December 2 and 3 were unwarranted and that they obstruct rational and fair consideration of the grievances brought forward by the students. [*Boos from the audience.*]

4. The cases of all students arrested in connection with the sit-in in Sproul Hall on December 2 and 3 are now before the Courts. The University will accept the Court's judgment in these cases as the full discipline for those offenses.

In the light of the cases now and prospectively before the courts, the University will not prosecute charges against any students for actions prior to December 2 and 3; but the University will invoke disciplinary actions for any violations henceforth.

5. All classes shall be conducted as scheduled.[5]

Before the meeting started, Mario had asked Kerr if he could speak. Kerr had fobbed him off on the department chairmen, who in turn passed the buck to Professor Scalapino. Scalapino told him that because the meeting was structured, he could not speak. Mario, ever aggressive, then picked a quarrel with Scalapino, contending that the department chairmen had no right to make any sort of public proposal that had not been approved by the Academic

CLARK KERR ADDRESSING STUDENTS AND FACULTY ASSEMBLED AT THE GREEK THEATRE ON DECEMBER 7, 1964. PHOTO BY AL SILBOWITZ.

Senate, and that by holding this meeting at all, they were forcing the Academic Senate to dance to the administration's tune. Professor Scalapino was scandalized by this allegation, but did not give in to Mario's demand to speak.

> *Bettina Aptheker:* Mario also told Scalapino, after permission to speak had been denied, that he would wait for the meeting to be adjourned and would then make an announcement about the FSM rejoinder. So they knew. I was with Mario when we went to talk to Scalapino.[6]

When Kerr finished, and Scalapino announced that the meeting was adjourned, Mario slowly walked toward the podium, intending to announce a rally in Sproul Plaza. He reached the microphone, placed both hands on it as if to collect his thoughts and at that moment was dived on by two campus policemen and dragged, in part by the necktie, back from the microphone and into a small room behind the stage. A few quick-thinking students made an effort to save him, but they were shoved aside or

MARIO SAVIO DRAGGED AWAY FROM THE PODIUM AS HE PREPARED TO ADDRESS THE
POST-MEETING CROWD IN THE GREEK THEATRE. PHOTO BY AL SILBOWITZ.

knocked down and held to the floor. There were no arrests. The crowd, of
course, was electrified, rising to its feet as one, many of them screaming
and crying out. The professors on the stage were paralyzed with shock.

Bob Starobin: When Mario was dragged off the stage, I ran up on the
stage like a lot of other people, and I ran into Henry May, and he said,
"I've never been so insulted by anyone in my life, about what you said
about the department chairmen being like a military junta in Latin
America." So I said, "Well, that's too bad." Later on I apologized to him,
but he hasn't really forgotten. May was so shook by what happened in
the Greek Theatre, because this just destroyed the department chairmen
and May's whole position of being the spokesman for them. He was on
TV and all the press conferences and everything. He was so upset that
he went home and had to stay in bed for three days. This is some indication of the impact that Mario's action had on some of the department chairmen. [Joseph] Tussman actually reversed his position,
though not because of what Mario did, but because he began to see the
issues.[7]

Mario Savio: I only half made the decision to speak on December 7. Half
the decision was made by Bettina. The night before, Steve Weissman
and I had decided that we would try to get to speak on the platform.

MARIO DRAGGED BY THE NECKTIE. NOTE THE PREPARED SPEECH CLENCHED IN HIS
HAND. PHOTO BY JEFF LEE.

Originally I was going to make a speech. We didn't know who to contact; we didn't know how this meeting was set up. I was up on that road just west of the Greek Theatre, and I saw Clark Kerr, walking along the road. I go up to him—I'd met him twice. October 2, and once before, when I was walking out of an Executive Committee meeting at Hillel and he was walking out of the YWCA.* I ran up behind him and said, "Hello, President Kerr"—I usually referred to him as "Clark" in speeches—"President Kerr, I understand you're going to make a speech. I think it would be appropriate for me to make a brief presentation after that speech. There is another side to this, after all." So he said, "I'm not sure that it would be appropriate. The meeting's been called by the department chairmen."

So I went up to the Greek Theatre, and went behind where the chairmen were starting to assemble. I asked one of them the same thing. And whereas Kerr had said, "I didn't call the meeting, the chairmen are in charge," the chairman said, "We're not in charge, Scalapino is in charge." And that was true. It was one of the problems. So I searched out Scalapino, and went through the same business all over again. He said, "Well, it would be inappropriate. This is a *faculty* meeting. Secondly, it's a structured meeting, not an open forum, so it would be inappropriate for you to speak." At that point Leggett said, "Well, *I'm* a

*Hillel on Bancroft Avenue was often used for Executive Committee meetings.

member of the faculty, and *I* want to speak." And he said that he didn't think it would be appropriate; but then he couldn't say it was a faculty meeting. So then I made it very clear to him that I'd be satisfied if I could make an announcement, but he was having none of this. So I went out and told the press what was going on. So then the press knew that I was going to try to speak at the meeting.

I said to 'Tina and Tom Miller, "I'm going to speak at this meeting." I said to Tom, "I'll run up on the stage and get the microphone, and you run interference with the faculty members on stage." That would have worked. But it really wouldn't have been the best way, and it certainly would have alienated some of the people who were assembled at the Greek Theatre. He says, "You ought to see if you can get people to call you to speak." I said, "Well, how am I going to do *that?*" And he says, "Well, why don't you walk up slowly?"

Those poor policemen. Inside I kept giving them all sorts of stuff: "You're abridging my rights! Arrest me or release me! You've got to let me out!" And I was trying to force the door open, and they were holding me back, I was making it clear that they were doing something that might get them into trouble, and they were a little confused, and they didn't know quite what to do. At the same time, quite a large group was assembling, and I could hear Alex Hoffman shouting, "Release him! I'm his lawyer!" and these policemen were really in a bad place. Finally, after the door had already been opened, they told me to calm down. They weren't bad guys. I talked to Tussman, and explained that I wanted to make a brief announcement, and he said OK. Then he said that if he had known that I wanted to speak he would have seen to it. Then I made the brief announcement. Sherry Stevenson's father gave me a new suit because my old one had been torn.[8]

The students began to chant, "We want Mario! We want Mario!" Chairman Beloof of the speech department came up to Kerr, who was standing mesmerized, and cried, "You have to let him speak!"* After considerable confusion Savio was released and allowed to address the wildly excited crowd. He announced a noon rally at Sproul Plaza, which I was at that instant furiously setting up, trying to get extra car batteries to power the bigger loudspeakers needed to handle the overload (I finally commandeered batteries out of cars and even hauled the battery out of the car that was used to transport the sound equipment). After the an-

*Hal Draper recounts that Beloof suddenly realized that this was the first time in his sixteen years on the Berkeley campus that he had ever spoken to the University president (*New Student Revolt*, 124).

AS MARIO WAS DRAGGED OFF THE STAGE, STUDENTS WHO TRIED TO HELP HIM WERE
HELD TO THE GROUND. OAKLAND TRIBUNE PHOTO BY RUSS REED.

nouncement of the rally, Mario said, echoing his speech to the crowd at
the end of the October demonstration around the car:

> Please leave here. Clear this disastrous scene, and get down to discussing
> the issues.[9]

The biggest crowd in the history of the Free Speech Movement
jammed Sproul Plaza to overflowing. Something like ten or twelve
thousand people heard Mario orate from the steps and, with a roar that
must have turned administrative bowels to water, rejected Kerr's proposals. Professor Beloof told the crowd that though he was one of the
department chairmen, he had never been told that Mario had asked to
speak, and that if he had been told, he would have wanted permission
granted. Professor Tussman told the students,

> I think at this point the University is in your hands and we have to trust
> to your judgment as you consider what ought to be done. . . . I leave
> the future of the University, which I assure you is now in your hands,

AFTER MARIO WAS RELEASED, AN IMMENSE CROWD GATHERED AT SPROUL HALL TO HEAR THE FSM POSITION PRESENTED. PHOTO BY HOWARD HARAWITZ.

with confidence that you care about the University, and that you will think about what you do, and do what you think is right.[10]

As if the gods weren't dealing bad enough cards to the administration already, student body elections were being held that day and the next, with heavy representation by SLATE candidates. Art Goldberg urged the crowd, "If you support FSM's goals, vote for the SLATE candidates."[11]

A telegram of support from Bertrand Russell was read aloud:

You have my full and earnest support. Warm greetings.

Russell also sent a telegram to Governor Brown:

Urgently appeal to you to halt University and police oppression of students at Berkeley Campus. Appalling restrictions upon their civil liberty. All who value individual liberty are supporting their cause.[12]

Mario had walked up onto a stage and, before he'd had any chance to speak, had been dragged down by the police. Coming as it did in the aftermath of the intense emotions created by mass arrests and a campuswide strike, this one relatively insignificant event did more to convert faculty and students to the FSM's cause than anything else. Later there were many accounts of professors who had been, up to that instant, hostile to the goals and means of the students, who were converted as was Saul of Tarsus when knocked off his horse by the Lord, from enemies of the FSM to, if not precisely friends, at least sympathizers. We all heard stories of older professors who had escaped Nazi terror and who, stunned by what the police had done before their very eyes, expressed shame and rage that they had condoned an administration which resorted to Storm Trooper tactics to prevent one student from speaking to a crowd. If there is one lightning-lit instant in the history of the FSM, this was it. Those poor dumb cops handed us victory on a silver platter.

It was announced that the strike would end at midnight, mainly to cut the Academic Senate some slack. Kerr's effort had failed.

WE WIN

Larry Marks: The faculty was speaking in some kind of foreign language that wasn't even understood by the faculty. The faculty during this whole thing were a bunch of lags; I didn't understand that, and Art didn't understand it. I have to admit that Jack and the Steering Committee *did* understand that, and that they knew that if you asked the faculty for something that they would say "no," but that if you went ahead and did it, they'd join you. This was frankly one of the major reasons that Art urged moderation, because he was too afraid of the faculty; he always was. The faculty always looked like they were going to fink out, but all you had to do was push them, and they'd go.[1]

Sherwood Parker: I had been a graduate student at Berkeley, and was away for five years on the faculty at the University of Chicago. Late Tuesday, the day before the police car, I arrived in Berkeley to teach.

In the crowd around the car I happened to meet a student I knew from Chicago. I was really amazed to find she was interested, because while she was in Chicago I considered her to be the most apolitical person I knew. She was slated to become one of the defendants.

Up to a few days before the arrests, I would say the physics department faculty was overwhelmingly against the students. This University is extremely hierarchical. Full professors only rarely ask the advice of associate professors, and so in turn down the line. Unless you have an unquestioned technical knowledge—they would ask me how to make a spark chamber pulser perhaps—but on political matters I would not be asked, except on one interesting ground: I was considered by many of the older faculty to know the students a lot better. If they wanted to find out the rumblings that were going on with the students, they might then ask me.

Burton Moyer, who was my professor when I was here as a graduate student and one of the five department chairmen who organized under Scalapino, is one of the kindest and best people; consequently, when I first spoke to him about it, very early in the game, I was really surprised to find how thoroughly he was against what was going on, and indeed he was never happy with anything all the way along, even though he did vote for the resolutions of December 8. He voted for them because he felt that nothing else would bring peace to the University.

Rumblings among the faculty I heard rather little of. The complaints that I heard were more directed against the administration for faculty grievances, for instance against the quarter system. Some of the more conservative people I know on the physics department faculty were very much against the administration, because they attempted to ram the quarter system down the throats of the faculty; not because of political actions. The people that were in favor of what the students were doing, for the most part, early in the game tended not to be too vocal at department meetings and such. Three or four days before the sit-ins of December 3 I took a straw poll, not by asking people but by observing comments they were making at the department meeting. And in terms of those who spoke up, the sentiment was overwhelmingly against the students. Partly this is because those who later proved to be in favor of the students weren't speaking much. I was one of the few that spoke, and was consistently trying to speak to the older people like Burt Moyer and Carl Helmholtz. But it was not looked upon too favorably by older faculty members. A while after all this occurred, one of the secretaries commented to Charley Ray, who works with me, that she certainly hoped I wouldn't be saying many more things like this, because she was worried since I didn't have tenure. One other full professor made the comment to me that he was very unhappy that I spoke at meetings. He felt that junior faculty members should be just that: junior. His exact words to me were that he just felt it was better to *do* what things you feel need doing, but that a young faculty member speaking in the senate creates a very bad impression. This was given in the sense of friendly, personal advice. He was the person who was largely responsible for getting me the faculty appointment out here. It was not as a superior ordering me to do anything. Indeed, he said that if your conscience makes you feel you must speak up, of course you do.

Basically, the Academic Senate meetings up to the time that coherent groups formed within the senate, namely the group of Two Hundred, and then the opposing group—the senate was just one long series of chaos. It was just painful to sit in and listen to the diversions and foul-ups due to Robert's Rules of Order. The impressions become vivid when Larry Levine brought his I think rather unfortunate motion up, and we saw it chopped to little pieces essentially on instructions from people that I suppose were responding to Clark Kerr—Arthur Ross and so on. This was after the vigil outside the Regents' meeting at University Hall—after the abortive sit-in.

DECEMBER 8, 1964, ACADEMIC SENATE MEETING
IN WHEELER AUDITORIUM.
PHOTOGRAPHER UNKNOWN.

I saw the resolution that Larry presented, and it seemed to me that it was going to invite all sorts of unnecessary attacks. It was not worded in such a manner as to state the principles clearly in a way that would make it hard to attack. It was so extreme against the administration as to invite unnecessary attacks. I decided I could not go about getting signatures, because I could not go along with the extreme tone. That resolution got chopped to pieces, not only on this basis, but by adroit use of parliamentary technique, which essentially found an error in it and defeated it on the grounds of the error. Larry Levine then tried to bring back a modified version, eliminating these technical errors, then the people—Ross—who were working on the chancellor's side chopped into *that* attempt, which I think would have passed even though it was not the greatest resolution. They used Robert's Rules of Order, saying, "It's too similar to a motion which has just been defeated, and you're not allowed to reintroduce motions." It was a real Donnybrook. The tactic that Ross used was to introduce a substitute motion, which completely emasculated the original motion, and got all the debate turned on the substitute motion, and we got tangled up in that. The substitute motion lost, the main motion lost, and the attempt to introduce it again was foiled on the grounds of similarity. The administration forces were never willing to debate something on its merits. They tried tactics of evasion, which left a very bad taste in my mouth.[2]

From the beginning, faculty opinion had been gradually shifting in favor of the goals of FSM. Late in the week before the Greek Theatre debacle, when the splendidly isolated department heads were devising their ill-fated proposals, the Two Hundred had also been busy, formulating resolutions to put before the Academic Senate meeting on Tuesday.

Charles Muscatine: The Free Speech Movement students had the ideas, and they had the action techniques, and with these they had the capacity to move people. On the other side was civil power. You've got the governor, you've got the Board of Regents, you've got the police; and that is one hell of a lot of power. Ultimately that power could smash the whole situation. The function of the faculty was to mediate between those two forces. The faculty felt the power of the ideas, and it felt the sympathy that those ideas generated—at least the liberal faculty felt that way. The liberals were also in a position to bring the whole University into a position where the power elite—the Regents and the governor—would not dare to use the means at their disposal. So, what happened as *we* see it, is that one of the greatest faculties in the world—twelve hundred people, most of whom were of substantial attainment and who commanded an enormous amount of respect—voted by a wide margin for a settlement which was by no means adverse to the student cause. That prevented the Regents and the governor from moving. Without taking any credit away from the students for the initiation and root motives—which were tremendously educational for the faculty—the faculty's act was an important factor in creating peace. Today, when you walk down Sproul Plaza and see all those tables, they're there under the exact same rules that were adopted on December 8, 1964.

When the Academic Senate passed its resolution, we were indescribably happy. We were so wrapped up in getting the Regents to back off that I don't think that we realized the depth of the revolution that had occurred. The students were ahead of the faculty by decades in their thinking about social questions and free speech. The faculty couldn't possibly have brought these changes about. Many of the faculty members were unfriendly or hostile; many of them were confused. A small group that was trying to organize the faculty made an important contribution. It took one hell of a lot of organizing, persuasion and managing of the academic bureaucracy to get those ideas into position. It also took the failure of the department chairmen's group.

When we were organizing the Two Hundred, we used the techniques that we had learned sixteen years before during the oath controversy. The oath controversy was three years of getting the faculty to position itself against the oath, so the whole technique was there in place. We'd learned how to maneuver a vote in the Academic Senate. When the free speech trouble started on campus, Charlie Sellers, Carl Schorske, John Searle, Howie Schachman of biochemistry and a few others drifted together and formed a group of twenty. The brilliance of the political thinking and historical insight came from Schorske, Henry Nash Smith and Sheldon Wolin—people who specialized in American history and American thought. I became the communications officer, and as it happened, I was the only one who had been intimately involved in the loyalty oath controversy and had experience in the technical art of organizing the faculty and getting it to do the things that it should do. I organized a telephone tree: twenty people each phoned two others who they thought would be sympathetic—that made sixty or so—and each one of those called two or three more, and we had the Two Hundred. We prepared our resolutions, and felt that we could present our ideas to the Academic Senate and get them passed.

At the crucial moment when we were trying to make peace, we knew about the group of chairmen's arrangement; we knew there was going to be a meeting at the Greek Theatre; we were confident that it was not going to work. We felt it would not be acceptable to the students and it certainly was not acceptable to many of us. I was horrified when Mario interrupted the proceedings, and I was even more horrified when they dragged him off the stage. I was never in favor of any kind of disruption or civil disorder. I was in favor of reasonable, rational discussion: all the sort of things that probably wouldn't have worked. I felt that civilization was breaking down. I was sort of scared. A different kind of scared from the loyalty oath; nothing in the loyalty oath controversy had anything to do with civil disorder. I prefer to work with reason, and with argument, and with political persuasion rather than with physical action.[3]

Ariel Parkinson: Problems created by the enforcement of a regulation prohibiting political activity—free speech—on the UC campus by an ill-advised and intransigent administration were resolved when the administration agreed to change the regulations to permit all political activity on campus consistent with respect to time, place and manner. What changed the position of the administration? How much help was the faculty?

The student position was that change was effected by united and overwhelming physical and ideological pressure from the students. The alternative to modification of the policy was destruction of the University. Faculty and administration capitulated because they had to. The helpful faculty members were a handful who fully and overtly supported the student position—both the goal of free speech on campus and the strategy of physical defiance and confrontation. With a few exceptions, faculty, Regents and administration were an opposing monolith, its members more or less guiltily engaged, like the power structure in the segregated South—where, in the civil rights movement, the student leaders had learned their tactics and earned their ribbons.

My understanding of the resolution is different: power in the University of California system, even more than power in America, is a bundle of sticks, and no agency holds all of them. The Board of Regents delegates to the Academic Senate of the University entire governance of the curriculum and all other academic matters. The senate is the governing board of the faculty and, to a great extent, since the University is an academy, of the students as well. The support of the Academic Senate was crucial to the ability of the administration to maintain its post–December 8 position on the free speech issue. If the initial position of the faculty "spokesmen" had prevailed, if the Academic Senate had voted to oppose the student demand for free speech and free political activity, there were several likely alternatives:

1. With delay upon delay, student patience snaps, crowd mania sets in; there is severe damage to the capital assets of the campus and a few injuries, probably inadvertent, to faculty and students. There is mass public dismay and anger, especially with the students, which results in a radical cut in state legislative financial support, and no free speech.

2. With continued student "intransigence," administrative patience snaps, faculty is split between a pro-student handful, and a law-and-order majority; with federal support, there is a quasi-military occupation of the campus, and People's Park occurs five years before its time. Since the stakes are much higher than at People's Park, the Establishment cannot afford to cede them. No free speech.

3. There is continued inconclusive violence, which resolves finally into minor adjustments—like setting up tables on the sidewalk, and ritual confrontation—like the protests against the Livermore Laboratory or the Vietnam War. Gradually, as disillusionment with the Vietnam War demonstrates that the students have been right, the issue is defused and regulations are changed to permit free speech on campus. The original objectors are already in their offices, brokerage houses, labs, board rooms, in their faculty clubs, or on the street.

Instead, the faculty split into two groups. Official executive power lay in the hands of the department chairmen, headed by Scalapino. The other, the rump group, sympathetic to the students, had already begun a strenuous, skilled, effective process of persuasion and negotiation. It included rapid enlistment of other faculty members through personal contact; mediation between students and administration; restraint of physical violence by the students; and a careful, systematic approach to breaching administration intransigence. The University is a huge bureaucracy, whose inertia, clumsiness and innate conservatism are part of its independence and integrity. In order to be "impersonal," free from arbitrary will, open to scrutiny, bureaucracies operate in a prescribed manner under a prescribed rule. The Two Hundred and their leaders knew the procedures, and therein lay their value. They talked the language. They pushed buttons and passed motions; they followed the track of incremental authority that required, or led, or permitted, the delegated executors of the University system, even against their better judgment, to change an unwise, unnecessary, unconstitutional, destructive rule.

Successful mediation, culminating in the December 8 resolution of the Academic Senate, did not just happen; it was not achieved by a re-laxed and gentlemanly effort. Hours on the telephone, passionate con-versation, typewriters clacking out endless and critically important—in a bureaucracy—memos. However "mild" the rump group's demeanor toward the students, it was not mild behind the scenes. "Savage" is a better word. However reproving the group's attitude toward individual student acts, support behind the scene for their moral and ideological position was unwavering and absolute.

The liberal faculty's successful exercise of its own bureaucratic le-verage on behalf of the student cause *at the least* accelerated the successful outcome of the issue by months, years, even decades. It is not surprising that historical accounts of the Free Speech Movement have, so far, ig-nored the key contributions of the faculty and cast its members largely as a negative force or as temporizers. As a fighter you know the enemy you are opposing and the ally who is at your side. The faculty who were successful advocates of the student cause were inside the enemy lines. They were speaking a dry language. They did not write dramatic edi-torials or pamphlets for the street. Their writing took the form of letters and memoranda: important, telling, and—for the students and public—out of sight.

In the Free Speech Movement, the students felt and managed a ground swell of wrath that broke into physical expression; they made a clear articulation of the basic issue; they exerted enormous pressure. By persuading a majority of the politically active faculty to coerce the administration to abrogate the offending rule, the liberal faculty brought the process which the students had begun and led to a successful and peaceful close.

Defiance breeds defiance. Physical force, just or unjust, does not al-ways attain its end. This time it did. The liberal faculty, operating dem-ocratically and through established channels of authority, were a major factor in that success.[4]

John Searle: On Friday, December 4, while the strike was still in full swing—with thousands of students milling around the campus, picket lines at all the buildings, and empty classrooms everywhere—a group of faculty members met to try to formulate a solution to the crisis. After several sessions and in an atmosphere of considerable tension two mo-tions for the Academic Senate meeting of the following Tuesday were formulated. Motion A dealt with the substantive issues, and eventually became the famous 824–115 resolution. Motion B called for the creation and election of an emergency executive committee to carry out motion A and do whatever else was necessary to solve the crisis. . . .

. . . [T]wo hundred professors gathered Sunday night to consider motions A and B. After several hours of intense discussion and some rewording of the resolutions, they were both accepted unanimously. . . . But the meeting did not conclude on an optimistic note, for at its end one of the [department] chairmen announced that they had reached an agreement with the authorities, and the terms of the agreement, when presented, were seen to be out of touch with the realities of the situation.[5]

The students got their mitts on the text, and five thousand copies of Motion A were printed and distributed on campus Monday morning. Many of those who attended Kerr's meeting at the Greek Theatre had already read the motion, or actually held the text in their hot little hands and compared it with what Kerr was saying, even as he was saying it. Motion A read:

PROPOSITIONS TO BE INTRODUCED BY THE COMMITTEE ON ACADEMIC FREEDOM AT THE DECEMBER 8th MEETING OF THE BERKELEY DIVISION OF THE ACADEMIC SENATE

In order to end the present crisis, to establish the confidence and trust essential to the restoration of normal University life, and to create a campus environment that encourages students to exercise free and responsible citizenship in the University and in the community at large, the Committee on Academic Freedom of the Berkeley Division of the Academic Senate moves the following propositions:

1. That there shall be no University disciplinary measures against members or organizations of the University community for activities prior to December 8 connected with the current controversy over political speech and activity.

2. That the time, place and manner of conducting political activity on the campus shall be subject to reasonable regulation to prevent interference with the normal functions of the University; that the regulations now in effect for this purpose shall remain in effect provisionally pending a future report of the Committee on Academic Freedom concerning the minimal regulations necessary.

3. That the content of speech or advocacy should not be restricted by the University. Off-campus student political activities shall not be subject to University regulation. On-campus advocacy or organization of such activities shall be subject only to such limitations as may be imposed under section 2.

4. That future disciplinary measures in the area of political activity shall be determined by a committee appointed by and responsible to the

TO THIS MEETING IS RESTRI...
THE Academic Senate, CONSISTING OF
regular INSTRUCTORS
Regular PROFESSORS
DEANS and DIRECTORS

NO VISITING PROFESSORS, LECTURERS,
TEACHING ASSISTANTS ARE NOT MEMBERS.

your colleagues at the door,
identify yourself by name and title.

ACCESS TO THE DECEMBER 8 ACADEMIC SENATE
MEETING WAS LIMITED TO MEMBERS OF THE
REGULAR FACULTY. PHOTOGRAPHER UNKNOWN.

Berkeley Division of the Academic Senate.

5. That the Division pledge unremitting effort to secure the adoption of the foregoing policies and call on all members of the University community to join with the faculty in its efforts to restore the University to its normal function.[6]

This may have been the first time that the elegant formula "time, place and manner" was used in the context of regulating speech. The phrase occurs in the Constitution (Article I, Section 4), but there it's talking about setting particulars for elections.

Brian Mulloney: The Committee of Two Hundred met on Sunday night, and decided that they were going to be able to pull the faculty together. After the meeting of the Two Hundred, a few of them came down [to talk with the Steering Committee]. Henry Nash Smith was among them, and Shinbroke was among them, and Strohman was there, and their object was to get us to call off the strike on Monday. First of all, we didn't have the authority to call off the strike without the GCC. We had a long conversation with them in which we convinced them that it was a bad idea to call off the strike. You don't call off the strike before you start negotiating, you call it off when you're in negotiations. They were told that the National Guard was going to be called in, that they were going to close down the University, people are out of jail now and there's nothing to be gained by going on. You'll harden public opinion against you. So, we finally told them no. The next day we had the strike, but Kerr had canceled classes and we had a hard time organizing. We were down to three picket lines that morning. After the Greek Theatre people were picketing in the rain. Later that day Henry Nash Smith called and apologized for having tried to get us to call off the strike. He said he had misjudged. That was really remarkable. The GCC voted to carry on the strike until Tuesday, at the time the Academic Senate meeting let out, at which time their actions would dictate whether to continue the strike.* We held a vigil of about ten thousand people outside the Academic Senate meeting.

Tuesday morning at about eleven we went to Dean Elberg and said who we were. The trouble was, the meeting was going to be packed with faculty members, and every student on campus was interested in the outcome. The problem of sorting the faculty from the general public and students was immense. You had twelve hundred faculty members trying to get into a room with a seating capacity of eleven hundred. So we offered, in addition to whatever the Academic Senate could muster in the way of sergeants at arms, to have FSM monitors there. Students were not to be allowed into the Academic Senate meeting, because if any students went in they couldn't get all the faculty in. So we said that in order to maintain law and order and all these things that they treasured so highly, we'd have a bunch of picket-line captains and monitors who were experienced at this sort of business, and who would be far better than any faculty member and better than any cop in the world at that point at keeping students out of there. You know damn well that if you get a faculty group or police group up there that people will just go straight through. We told him that the University had no power at all to control the students, you're incompetent to do that part—something that didn't please him too much—but of course we can do it, so we're offering our services. So we pushed him around a little bit, but he turned us down.

We did get an office for the GCC, and telephone lines, so that we'd have a place where he could contact us. We kept that for the next semester.[7]

On December 8, the Academic Senate came down solidly on the side of the FSM, just in time for Mario's twenty-second birthday. After three hours of debate it passed, unchanged, by a vote of 824–115, a "resolution unanimously approved at a meeting of approximately 200 faculty members on December 7," that is to say, Motion A.[8]

Professor Lewis Feuer introduced an amendment to the third section of the resolution, proposing that there be no restriction on "the content of speech or advocacy *on this campus provided that it is directed to no immediate act of force or violence.*"[9] This was the same old bugbear that had been hanging everything up all along, and by this time a lot more people understood the problems of prior restraint and advocacy. Intense debate followed, mostly centering on explanations of what prior restraint and advocacy actually meant, and why the students were so dead set on what

---

*This vote was reversed and the strike was called off at midnight on Monday.

VICTORY. PHOTO BY ROGER MINLOCK.

seemed to many faculty the incomprehensible demand that they be allowed to use the University as a staging ground for illegal activities. Whether the point was generally grasped or not, it at least became clear in the course of intense debate that this was the central problem; and that if Feuer's amendment were admitted, the entire gist of Motion A would be changed; and that the *very* powerful and *exceedingly* dangerous FSM would not accept it. Feuer's amendment was defeated 737–284. The Academic Senate and every professor there present were more than aware of the presence of some 10 percent of the student body standing right outside, listening to every word of the proceedings over loudspeakers. The students' cheers as Feuer's amendment failed and their football-game roar as the main motion passed must surely have elated some and terrified others. When the Academic Senate meeting adjourned, a path opened for the departing professors who, garlanded with acclaim and praise, walked hundreds of feet through solid walls of students.

To make certain that neither the students, the administration nor the general public could mistake the meaning of the Academic Senate, Joseph Tussman, chairman of the philosophy department, announced its meaning in clear words:

Anything that is illegal in the community at large is still illegal on campus. The question is: Should the University impose more restrictions on its students in the area of political activity than exist in the community at large? The Senate said: No.[10]

Nathan Glazer: The administration—President Kerr and Chancellor Strong—was absent and silent. . . . The students were barred from the meeting, but thousands were outside, and we could hear their roars of approval or disapproval as the debate went on. It was scarcely necessary to be reminded of the terrible power of the student movement, though two professors, both of whom supported the majority resolution, did remind us that chaos was at the door. I think there was a good deal of hysteria mixed in with the action of the Berkeley division of the academic senate [*sic*] that day. Afterward men who had been friends for years but had taken opposite sides approached each other with hesitation, and felt it necessary to reaffirm their friendship, so deeply had their emotions become involved.[11]

Martin Meyerson, later to become temporary chancellor until he was in turn unseated by events beyond his scope, remarked:

What we did in some ways rearranges the idea of what a University is for. It gives up the old idea of *in loco parentis*, and I think we realize that it's a two-way street. It used to be that a sheriff would call a dean to come down and pick up one of his undergraduates who was drunk and let him handle the punishment any way he thought best. But this kind of approach just isn't suitable for, say, a huge civil-rights demonstration. Of course, that means we can't ask to be a sanctuary from the local police, but, in practice, we were no longer a sanctuary anyway. I think academic people are apprehensive by nature. It is a big change, and the apprehension is certainly present. But I'm fairly optimistic.[12]

The FSM tried to get Governor Brown to grant amnesty to the arrested protesters, and the faculty made the same appeal to the court, but neither attempt bore any fruit.* Mario had just gotten back from an at-

*In January 1965, more than two hundred faculty members submitted a statement to the court, arguing for dismissal of the charges. The substance of the argument was that the "Supreme Court had recognized the justice of the sit-in technique in refusing to uphold the sit-in convictions of those whose cases have reached the court. . . . earlier the Court had emphasized that, 'The peaceful conduct for which petitioners were prosecuted was on behalf of a principle since embodied in the law of the land.' The principle contained in the *Hamm* case should be applied to the cases at hand" (quoted in Draper, *New Student Revolt*, 239–240).

VICTORIOUS STUDENTS LINKED HANDS AND SANG ON SPROUL HALL STEPS.
PHOTO BY ROGER MINLOCK.

tempt to see the governor, and in so many words accepted the sword of the vanquished and announced the end of the FSM:

> Our tactics caused the present success. . . . The Senate action was a direct attack on the doctrine of *in loco parentis*. . . . The FSM will now be a defense committee for 800 patriots.[13]

In the student elections held on Monday and Tuesday, candidates running on the banned SLATE platform swept all seven ASUC Senate positions. This is as close as the general student body ever got to expressing its opinion of the whole free speech controversy; I imagine that had the matter been put to the vote at other junctures, the consensus might have gone against us, but by now the tenor of the campus had permanently changed, enabling it to consider issues in ways that had been forbidden for almost thirty years. My generation was waking up.

After a raucous meeting, dancing in Edwards Field and tearful songs on Sproul Hall steps, the FSM dipped into its funds and threw a combination victory celebration and birthday party for Mario at Central. Red

442

Mountain wine flowed like water, rock 'n' roll rattled the windows, Mario's apartment was jammed to the gunnels with ecstatic, exhilarated victors.* As the celebration swirled around me, I curled up on a daybed in a corner of the dance floor and slept like a dead man.

JOYFUL STUDENTS DANCING IN EDWARDS FIELD.
PHOTO BY LOREN WEAVER.

Sue Stein: December 8, Tuesday night, we went to a party.

Brian Mulloney: That's right, we got drunk as skunks.

Sue Stein: Boy, did we get drunk! Wow!

Brian Mulloney: Yeah, just smashed. It was off at the old YPSL headquarters, and all the GCC were down there. It was after the December 8 open meeting, in which we discussed, "Shall we or shall we not continue the strike?" At that point it was decided unanimously they would all go back to classes. People were already pretty smashed. We collected $132 for a new suit for Mario Savio, passed all sorts of resolutions no one will ever remember, cheered various and sundry . . . it was a juvenile, raucous, glorious meeting. A final victory rally. Then we all repaired to the front of Sproul Hall steps where we linked arms and sang "We Shall Overcome," and then Mike Nagler and I went off and got about ten cases of beer and a lot of scotch and invited everybody over to the YPSL headquarters and the party was on. There were parties on all over the place.

Sue Stein: Steve Weissman was sitting in the corner saying, "Oh, this is terrible, oh, dear." He was so keyed up; and to have it just cut off at the end, and this looked like the end to everybody. Personally, Weissman felt that something was missing. He was all keyed up, and there was

---

*Red Mountain wine cost a dollar a gallon, and they threw in the jug for free; it turned your teeth black, and gave you a terrible headache.

nothing to be keyed up *to*. He was just all depressed, and Mario was walking around rubbing his hands saying, "But we don't really have a victory . . ." Stuff like that.

Then everybody suddenly realized that they had final exams coming up.*

---

*A group of graduate students, organized by James Petras, organized a tutorial program for the arrested students and anyone else whose studies had suffered because of the controversy. By finals time, several hundred students had been aided by the tutors. Some of the tutors, along with other students, went on to form the Free University of California, later the Free University of Berkeley (Starobin, "Graduate Students and FSM," 22). (Sue Stein and Brian Mulloney are quoted from their interview with Marston Schultz, January 20, 1966.)

WHISTLE WHILE YOU WORK

O<small>N</small> NOVEMBER 24, Dusty Miller and Dave Mandel had gotten together with Max Weiss and Deward Hastings at Fantasy Studios and recorded a 45 rpm record called *Joy to UC*, a selection of free speech carols parodying regular Christmas songs. On December 7, the Monday after the sit-in, the first part of Dusty Miller's massive recording project hit the streets and met with wild acclaim.

Dusty Miller: I'd heard that Mike Rossman was planning on putting out a musical—I'd heard that these guys were all pretty funny. So I got hold of Dan Paik and Kevin Langdon and Richard Schmorleitz, who'd been coming by my place, and Barry Jablon and his girlfriend,* who said, "Why not come over to my place." They were farting around with some Christmas carols—Joe LaPenta, Fançion Lewis, Ken Sanderson, Stevie Lipney and Julie Blake. I brought over a couple of gallons of wine and we sat down with four tape recorders and a couple of guitars, and divided up a whole bunch of Christmas songs. And everybody banged out their set of lyrics. We picked out the ones we wanted, and Barry said that he could do some arrangements into two-, three- and four-part harmony, and he would do a little guitar work. So we got together a few singers—I got hold of Leba Hurvitz (we needed a soprano, that's why I nailed her)—and the next day we all piled in the car and went over to Fantasy and recorded all this stuff.† I mimeographed off a bunch of song sheets and stuffed them into the jackets, and got a bunch of kids from Central to help glue the jackets together. Marion Syrek out there at his Vanguard Press had printed the jackets for us. It came out right after the big sit-in, and whoosh! it went like a bat out of hell. We unloaded about twelve or fourteen thousand.[1]

*This was either Kate Coleman or Karen Grassley.
†The "Free Speech Five Plus Four" were Susan Chesney, Stevie Lipney, Lee Felsenstein, Leba Hurvitz, Barry Jablon, Joe LaPenta, Dan Paik, Dustin Mark Miller and Dave Mandel, with guitar by Barry Jablon and Dave Mandel.

THE FREE SPEECH SINGERS ON SPROUL HALL STEPS. PHOTO BY HOWARD HARAWITZ.

Dusty later brought out another, not particularly successful, recording of events and sounds of the Free Speech Movement and, in 1967, a multicolored six-record album of songs and sounds of the early hippie era, upon which, accompanied by the roar and clank of a printing press, I sing the "International" to a strange, lyrical tune entirely unrelated to the martial thump of the original.

ARRAIGNMENT OF THE MASSES

DAVID STEIN: I had not gone into Sproul Hall during the sit-in there, for like Brad Cleaveland, I too was a nonstudent. I remember a long conversation with him at the time of the sit-in around the car in which he was attacking himself in disgust for not having scrounged up the $70 he needed for registration so that he could play a more central role in the events he had helped set off. The bit about "nonstudents" had hit him, too. My not being a student had been a result of quitting engineering in disgust when I had been informed that I could not repeat a midterm exam I had failed because I had just heard the news of Kennedy's assassination three minutes earlier. The pride of the engineers and this teacher was that they had all done just fine, being not in the least concerned with the political events outside. In any case, I had no love for engineering by then, and no skill in the mathematics required.

The night of the big bust, I, to keep myself free from temptation, had gone to San Francisco for dinner and jazz at the Jazz Workshop (Yousuf Lateef that night) with Beverly Allen. She later fed me for weeks when I had no other way to get a meal than to turn over a part of my FSM paid salary (yes, I got $125 a month and a mattress on the floor of Alex Hoffman's apartment to run that bloody office on Bancroft). At any rate, I had been having long conversations with a girl named Sue Kennedy, who was among the arrested. I wondered what had happened to her, and in my search was given an address on Dwight Way where she was supposed to be. It must have been about nine or nine-thirty in the morning, December 4, after the return from booking and all that, that I wandered into this place, where there was this bleary-eyed nineteen-year-old—the just-out-of-jail D. Goines—sitting behind a wooden desk with one or two phones on it. This same bleary-eyed youth looked up beseechingly and asked me if I could possibly watch the phone for a couple of hours while he got some sleep. I left that phone at Legal Central more than six months later, thank you! How sweet it was. Life was a dream. I would arrive at work there around seven-thirty

DAVID STEIN. PHOTOGRAPHER UNKNOWN.

or eight, and start in on the coffee and cigarettes.

We organized the defendants into twenty separate groups, each headed by a member of the "Council of Twenty," whose main task was to keep track of their fast-moving charges, and serve as leaders of a telephone tree; this meant that I only had to be in regular touch with the Twenty, rather than the full eight hundred. Oh! the lovely nights spent looking for stamps to mail out some urgent missive from Mal [Burnstein] to the eight hundred. We would head for the seedy side of Oakland along San Pablo to find small change around midnight on Sunday in order to feed the damned stamp machines in the Oakland Main P.O., which was the only place open at that ungodly hour. Carrying our hundreds of dimes or whatever was needed for stamps, we would then feed the machines continuously and force them to expel unending streams of stamps. The next morning, breakfast would be coffee, cigarettes, stamp glue and envelope glue. It still makes me deadly ill to remember the awful taste.

Mott Cannon, a man in his late fifties who worked in one of the University labs, lent me his antique VW transporter (a van with a 1.5:1 reduction gear on the rear axle, and a maximum speed of 43 mph with the pedal to the floor). This vehicle served me well during the trial, when I would start out at 6:30 or 7:00 AM to round up enough defendants to keep up a respectable appearance of seriousness in Crittenden's court and avoid having him serve bench warrants to force the whole eight hundred to appear daily in court. Playing sheriff in this absurd version of a paddy wagon was certainly one of the amusing little side shows. The transporter was also the vehicle of choice in making runs to San Francisco to pick up reams and reams of paper to feed the insatiable mimeograph machines.[1]

On December 6, the arrested demonstrators met with their army of lawyers at Garfield Junior High School.* The following morning, 768 people appeared at nine in the morning before municipal judge Rupert Crittenden in the Berkeley Community Theatre. Arraignment was postponed until December 14. There was a great deal of confusion about how many people had actually been arrested, and I imagine

FSM ATTORNEYS ROBERT TREUHAFT AND ALEX HOFFMAN. PHOTOGRAPHER UNKNOWN.

that if someone had not shown up, nothing would have happened. The police records were a mess, and the University's were no better. Some people had apparently been booked more than once, and had given a different name each time. The cops said that there had been 761 arrests, down from their original estimate of 801. The University said that 814 busts were made, with the following breakdown: 590 students, 135 non-students and 89 TAs, employees or unidentified.[2] (One of the "unidentified" was our attorney Bob Treuhaft, the first person arrested, whom Edwin Meese insisted on busting despite his credentials. The charges against him were eventually dropped, but his status as a defendant prevented him from representing us.) Names from all sources—newspapers, trial transcripts, FSM defendant lists—including those who died either before trial or before appeal (2) and those whose arrests were doubtful (19), as well as those against whom charges were dropped (6) or who had their cases separated (2), add up to 825.[†] The FSM kept track of 802 people in the succeeding years.

---

*Milton Nason was the organizer for the defense. Although we had more lawyers than Carter has pills, our main attorneys were Malcolm Burnstein, Richard M. Buxbaum, Henry M. Elson, Stanley P. Golde, Douglas J. Hill and Norman S. Leonard. Also participating in our defense were John Dunn, Ann Fagin Ginger, Siegfried Hesse, Howard Jewell, Larry Duga

and Spencer Strellis. Nearly forty lawyers were involved, all told.

†Liane Chu, Miklos Nagy, Gary Larson, Grover Krantz and Jonathan Golden were arrested when they went through an opening in a hedge on Barrows Lane to see what was going on. The police approached the small crowd that had gathered there and asked the ones in front for

One of the demonstrators, Lee Rhoades, had the misfortune to be arrested with a joint in his coat pocket, and the cops gleefully tromped all over him. Judge Martin N. Pulich set his bail at $3,300. He was the only one not freed on bail by the next day. This served to reinforce my terror of being arrested in connection with illegal drugs.

Lee claimed that neither the joint nor the coat was his; that his jacket had been taken from a coat rack at a café, and, assuming that his had been taken by mistake, he'd merely taken one that looked like his. Apparently the judge believed him, because he got off with a slap on the wrist: six months' probation and a fifty-dollar fine.

identification. They were then told to "come with me," taken into Sproul Hall and booked. Liane Chu (the former Miss Chinatown) was defendant Billy Clewlow's girlfriend, and during the 1964 spring semester Miklos Nagy had been a resident of the same rooming house as Billy Clewlow and Tom Weller. The other defendant against whom charges were dropped was Lance Gray.

WINDING DOWN

AFTER THE ACADEMIC Senate resolution on December 8, the rest of December was something of an anticlimax; a month of reaction and evaluation, of tying up loose ends. The fight wasn't over—there was still a Regents' meeting on the eighteenth to fret about—but in our hearts we knew the battle was ours.

ASUC president Charles Powell ruefully evaluated the ASUC Senate's role in the free speech controversy in unflattering but truthful terms:

> Overall, we've missed the boat. We have in many ways been inadequate in dealing with the free speech problem.[1]

Speaking of the original ban on political action on the Bancroft-Telegraph strip, Clark Kerr admitted in an interview with William Twombley of the *Los Angeles Times* on January 6 that

> he had made mistakes in judgment and tactics during the early stages of the uprising. When Kerr returned to the campus September 15 . . . he found that the day before Berkeley administrators had closed the traditional Sather Gate [*sic*] political area.
>
> "I thought that was a mistake and that we should return this area to the students," Kerr said, "but that was difficult. It had just been taken away—we could hardly turn around and hand it right back."

This remark, together with whiny accusations against the faculty for "actions against the statewide administration, the latest of which is the sentiment expressed for the FSM," aroused general displeasure.

In a February 1965 interview with A. H. Raskin for the *New York Times Magazine*, Kerr openly admitted failure:

We fumbled, we floundered, and the worst thing is I still don't know how we should have handled it. At any other University the administrators wouldn't have known how to handle it any better. . . .*

It was perfectly apparent that the decision [to ban the tables] was a mistake, both in the action itself and in the way it was done. There was no advance consultation with the students, the over-all University administration or anyone else. When a privilege had been extended as long as that had been, there should have been consultation—and especially against the background of an impending national election and intense student involvement in civil rights.[2]

It should be noted that Kerr not only never stopped covering his ass, he mulishly persevered in his use of the word "privilege," showing that he did not yet (and perhaps never would) grasp the idea that this was *not a matter of privilege*, and never had been. This was and had been from the

---

*Samuel Kaplan suggests that Kerr's inability to deal effectively with the demonstrators stemmed not only from his failure to understand the issues, but also from his "failure to comprehend the temper of the student body. . . . For example, President Kerr suggested over and over, almost from the start, that only a few 'hard core' students supported the movement. Similarly, he seemed to believe that the movement included enough Communists of one sort and another for him to remark on it on several occasions. Some observers have proposed that President Kerr and other administrators did not really believe what they were saying. The tactics they employed against the movement, however, make it seem plausible that they were convinced of the accuracy of what they said.

"The assumption that they believed what they said would account, for instance, for their efforts to eliminate a supposedly small hard-core that was the heart of the protest: destroy the core, and the movement would die. President Kerr has acknowledged himself that the university 'counted' on the discussions between the administration and the FSM leadership dur-

ing October and November 'to separate the well-intentioned students from the hard-core recalcitrants.' The same assumption would explain the decisions to summon police to campus on October 2 and again on December 3. Similarly, the attempts to identify the FSM as Communist or Communist-infiltrated could have been based on the assumption that since only a few students really cared about what FSM stood for, most would drop out once they learned the movement was Red. Or, again, the futile convocation assembled by President Kerr in the Greek Theatre on December 7 makes no sense if he knew that at least half the student body was actively hostile to his policies. On the other hand, if he believed that a widespread consensus still existed on campus against the FSM, then the convocation was the proper stroke to bring that consensus to bear.

"The administration's inability to obtain adequate information about the mood of the student body or the faculty was a symptom of a more general ailment that sometimes affects bureaucracies: a certain incapacity to deal with anything that is not routine." (Kaplan, "Revolt of an Elite," 85–86.)

get-go a straightforward constitutional issue, and even in defeat he simply could not get his head around the notion.*

Though the students and faculty accepted the Academic Senate's December 8 resolution as more or less the final word on the matter of free speech on the Berkeley campus, nothing was down in writing anywhere. Chancellor Strong was coming in for a great deal of flak—we were not even sure he was in charge anymore—and the administration had said nothing one way or the other about what could or could not be done, said or written by anybody. The students interpreted bureaucratic sloth and glue as intransigence and prepared themselves for more combat. The faculty did its level best to make sure that the resolution of December 8 was not undercut by other branches of the Academic Senate on other campuses, and did a splendid job of warding off reaction both in the academic community and among the general public. Just as had been the case in the loyalty oath controversy of 1950, in order for the efforts of the Academic Senate to stick, and for the disruptive controversy to end, it was essential that the faculty speak with one voice.

Sue Stein: It was unclear what the rules were on campus at that moment, it was unclear who the chief executive was, it was chaotic. The December 8 resolution didn't mean a thing to the people who worked at the University.

We were busy calling up people on the different campuses, trying to get them to help.

Brian Mulloney: In fact, a group of faculty members went that weekend to Los Angeles, Riverside and Santa Barbara. There were Academic Senate meetings all over the state to try and counteract the effect of the December 8 meeting, to try to cut the ground from under it. They fought this rather well; they sent people back to their own campuses—people who had graduated from those campuses, people who had contacts and who were professionally well respected, like Owen Chamberlain.

The big person who went down to L.A. was [Jacobus] ten Broek. They went down and argued on the floor of the Academic Senate

---

*In a conversation on May 14, 1992, Professor Peter Selz told me that he had recently spoken to Kerr, and that in his opinion Kerr *still* did not understand the constitutional issues that had been at stake in the Free Speech Movement. The only thing that Kerr had to say on the FSM era was that he was quite proud to have been the first victim of Reagan's term as California governor.

there, and at least blocked the really reactionary efforts that were
going on.

People operated at all levels: there were people who had just graduated from these other campuses who were calling their old professors
there and arguing for the point; and people with considerable standing
in the academic community were going down and doing things as the
opportunity arose. People were spread out pretty far; Kennedy and Wilson were at Cal Tech that weekend. They really put the line across. They
convinced the Cal Tech faculty, who were of course not directly involved, but who were nonetheless very prestigious, and that swung the
lead in the California system. Indirectly, but at the level of personal contacts that swung the University system. There was a very effective
speakers' bureau operating that week. Dan Garrison and Dave Rubin
and Bob Chase organized about thirty-six graduate students to go out
and speak in the surrounding community. By the time all was said and
done, they had over two hundred speakers at Rotary clubs, Kiwanis
clubs, things of this sort. Everywhere they could get an audience of over
two people, they'd go and speak.

Sue Stein: That whole week, we spent most of our time working with
that group of people who were spreading the word. Essentially, organizing labor for these faculty members; telling where they could buy
paper, how to organize people to collate reams and reams of data, and
periodically going to that place in Wheeler where they were collating
the stuff and sending it off to different campuses. Not only in California,
but we were sending ten or twenty to every campus that we had contact
with. We sent out an *enormous* number! Sixty, seventy thousand. About
a hundred thousand of those mimeographed blue things in all. We sent
out on the order of a million sheets of paper. In some departments there
was no paper left to run final exams off.[3]

On the ninth, the GCC organized the Union of University-Employed
Graduate Students, intending to affiliate itself with the AF of L. Math and
economics were best represented, and 250 TAs and research assistants
joined. Mike Abramovitch, of the math department, became the first
chairman.

On December 13, the administration indulged itself in a minor bit
of petty harassment, reneging at the last minute on its approval of
Wheeler Auditorium as a place for the arrested students and their legal
counsel to prepare for the arraignment that had been postponed until
December 14. An hour before the meeting was to start, Chancellor
Strong announced that "it is not proper to use University facilities for

the private counsel-client relationships," and the meeting had to be moved to the Berkeley Community Theatre.*

On December 14, the cases of those arrested in Sproul Hall were continued to January 5, giving everyone a chance to go home for the holidays. On the fifteenth, the ASUC approved a motion that the Regents accept the five-point Academic Senate proposal to end the controversy. That same day, James Farmer, the national director of the Congress of

---

*Dean Towle had approved the request to use Wheeler Auditorium on December 10; a "university spokesman" said that Towle had "not realize[d] the meeting would involve private client-counsel relationships" ("Chronology," 70). Although Strong was officially responsible for canceling the meeting, Arleigh Williams traces the real decision to Alex Sherriffs, lurking, as usual, in the shadows; Strong was, once again, just the fall guy.

Arleigh Williams: . . . The students had arranged for legal service and had gotten together on campus and asked for the use of Wheeler Auditorium, I think, so they could meet with the lawyers and get what was necessary for them to go before the court. We were denied that request by Alex. He was up at Leaky Lake. (This is getting sticky.) So as a result of that I had George Murphy, Tom Barnes, the whole office, doing their best to try to find a place so they could be helped. We tried everything under the sun.

Germaine LaBerge: Did you need a big auditorium?

Williams: We needed a big auditorium. We tried all of the religious organizations, all of the places around here that had some fairly good-sized auditorium. It was coming right down to the wire. Finally Tom Barnes, I think, got in touch with Charles Muscatine, and Charles Muscatine said, "I'll call you back." Finally he did call back. Charles Muscatine got in touch with the superintendent of the schools of Berkeley, and found out that the auditorium at Berkeley High was available. It was going to cost us some money. Alex was not going to let us have money of any kind, so I decided that it was time for me

to call Ed Strong. So I called Ed Strong and told him what the situation was and he said, "I'll take care of it. Go ahead and do it." So we did and we got them there.

LaBerge: At Berkeley High or Wheeler?

Williams: No, at the Berkeley Community Theatre. Then I called Ed and told him that it's all squared away. Charles Muscatine did the job for us; Alex was mad. But in the meantime, Alex was at Leaky Lake; that was his place where he makes his wine and what else. I don't know. As vice-chancellor of student affairs, he was up there when he should have been down here. The action here was getting on and getting stiffer and stiffer.

So that was it. That was Ed's response. Ed was supposed to be "ill" and Ed was not ill; I don't know just exactly what was going on over at their office. It was a sad commentary as far as I was concerned. I think I've got things in the correct sequence. I'm not sure about it.

LaBerge: Did you go to the meeting at the Berkeley Community Theatre?

Williams: No. I went to tell the students at Wheeler Hall where they had to go; I ran into Jackie Goldberg and asked her to let the others know that they had to go to the Community Theatre. She did and that was it.

LaBerge: Can you run by me again what this was for? This was for all students to get legal advice?

Williams: For the students to get legal advice—those who had been cited. . . .

LaBerge: Just to know that you had gone out and found them the place, you had somehow gotten money to pay for a place for them to get legal advice . . .

CORE DIRECTOR JAMES FARMER ADDRESSES
STUDENTS FROM BANCROFT AND TELEGRAPH,
DECEMBER 15, 1964. PHOTO BY HELEN NESTOR.

Racial Equality, addressed a noon rally of three thousand from Bancroft and Telegraph. He was introduced by Jacobus ten Broek, the celebrated, blind professor of political science. While praising the FSM and the role of students in the civil rights movement, Farmer remarked that he was not afraid to be labeled an outside agitator:

Every housewife knows the value of an agitator. It's the instrument inside the washing machine that bangs around and gets out all the dirt.

I applaud you and salute you. Wherever the battle for equal rights is fought the students of the University of California are in the forefront. Negroes must lend their support to you. This fight now is ours just as much as it is yours. If there had been no students, we would have had no Freedom Rides.

Are we to say now that the Bill of Rights includes Mississippi but not the University of California? I can understand the bigots of Mississippi because they are know-nothings. But we are not dealing with know-nothings at the University of California and I find it difficult to understand the curtailment of free speech and advocacy here.[4]

State Senator Hugh Burns, chairman of the State Senate Subcommittee on Un-American Activities (the "Baby HUAC" committee), had no kind words for the FSM, describing it in the December 17 *San Francisco Chronicle* as "a group of malcontents, silly kids and addle-headed

Williams: Ed Strong provided the money —his own personal check.
LaBerge: The students must have looked at that and known that you were here for them.

Williams: There was a comment or two.
LaBerge: Otherwise you would have been up at some lake also.
(Excerpted from Williams, *Dean of Students Arleigh Williams*, 98–99.)

teachers, egged on by Communist stooges."* Despite this, he said that his committee would not hold public hearings on the student revolt at Berkeley. Public hearings at this time would serve no useful purpose, making it "difficult for the University of California Board of Regents to solve the problem."[5] This was so plainly a load of cock that I'm surprised that anybody went for it, and perhaps nobody did; Burns didn't decline to investigate us out of the kindness of his heart; he declined to investigate us because he *couldn't*. The HUAC demonstrations had essentially pulled his teeth: what threat do you have over people who have no jobs, no money, no reputation to destroy? Precisely none, and these were the people that rose up against the innuendo and smears of HUAC and broke its back.†

Charges of "outside agitation" and "Communist subversion" rankled within the student body, and on December 16, Men's Residence Hall representative Mike Adams proposed in an ASUC meeting that these allegations should officially be refuted via a forty-page report prepared by eight poly-sci grads. The proposal was accepted, and two hundred dollars was appropriated for mimeograph paper.‡ Because it was to be an official ASUC publication, the *Graduate Political Scientists' Report* could be printed with official student mimeograph machines and ASUC supplies. However, somebody in the administration got to the ASUC with, probably, the usual dire warnings, and the ASUC Senate reneged on its approval. We went ahead anyway; ASUC support or no ASUC support we were still going to get it out, and we were going to use ASUC mimeograph machines, paper and supplies to get it out with. Especially as we wanted it done and on the streets by the Regents' meeting on the eighteenth, we figured we'd have to act fast, and decided to print it all at once, dividing up the stencils among seven mimeograph machines, going like blazes in separate campus departments and dormitories.

*In June of 1965, the Burns Report claimed that "apostles of class struggle" used the academic freedom of the university to camouflage themselves and take part in "Communist-front organizations." The report, formally known as the 12th Biennial Report of the Senate Fact-Finding Subcommittee on Un-American Activities, added that pro-Castro committees and former leaders of SLATE "are now running gigantic fronts for Communist movements . . . we wonder why any radicals—right, left or other sort—are tolerated."

†On Wednesday, March 3, 1965, Assembly Speaker Jesse M. Unruh (D-Inglewood) spoke before a capacity crowd in the Physical Sciences Lecture Hall, emphasizing that suggestions by Assemblyman Don Mulford that the state legislature investigate the FSM were not going to be followed up. Of course, at that exact moment the Filthy Speech Movement was erupting at the other end of the campus.
‡Mimeo paper was about forty-seven cents a ream, so this meant that we intended to print five thousand copies.

Somebody blew the whistle and all of a sudden the campus police started shutting them down. We were not entirely unprepared for this eventuality, and upon seeing the cops bearing down on him, the student in charge would remove the stencil and printed pages and run out the back way and get on the blower to Central, and a car would blast off and pick him up, stencil, paper and all, and take the whole works to another location that the cops didn't know about yet. We'd get a call like, "Unit One has just been shut down."

"OK. Head for Unit Twelve in the basement of Barrows Hall."

"Unit Six bailing out."

"A car is coming to pick you up and take you to Unit Thirteen in Stern Hall."

We got the report out with no real trouble, and had a lot of fun doing it, playing a particularly exciting game of "Can't-catch-me" and, of course, winning.

On December 18 the Board of Regents, eager to see an end to the embarrassing troubles of the fall, highly sensible of the animosity of both the faculty and student body and privately convinced that if the matter of freedom of speech were to come before the courts, they would lose, gave in.*

Berkeley students formed caravans, and in large numbers drove down to Los Angeles to attend the Regents' meeting. Not to be bullied, the Regents rejected the resolution of the Academic Senate, substituting one of their own, in which they asserted in guarded tones that they were the boss; that they loved the Constitution even more than anybody else did; that they did "not contemplate that advocacy or content of speech [on the Berkeley campus] shall be restricted beyond the purview of the First and Fourteenth Amendments to the Constitution"; and that they would "undertake a comprehensive review of University policies with the intent of providing maximum freedom on campus consistent with individual and group responsibility."[6] Which was all we wanted to hear.

Things were quiet during the Christmas recess, and we all took advantage of the respite to rest and recuperate. I brought Jack home for dinner a few times, and he and my dad, both being mathematicians, got on famously. My mother was just glad that I was alive and in one piece. My sisters and brothers were all agoggle.

---

*As was often the case, the FSM had a fly on the wall, and we knew what to expect of the Regents' meeting. Ron Anastasi told Marston Schultz, "Maurice Freedman was our contact at the Regents' informal gatherings at University House. He was the bartender there. He said that the Regents' legal advisor had said that their position was unconstitutional. Dean Kidner said that their position was weak. Strong looked nervous and Kerr looked very upset."

Reinstated in November as a full-time student, retroactive to September 30, I quit and received an honorable dismissal and a full refund of my tuition—seventy-five dollars—which I dumped into the FSM general funds.

Not counting the bail money for the people arrested in Sproul Hall, the fines imposed on the convicted students, or the legal costs, the whole expense incurred by the FSM was not much more than twenty thousand dollars, most of which was collected in the form of small change from the UC student body itself; I do not recollect that we got any large contributions from anybody. A twenty-dollar bill in the contribution can was a big deal. The bulk of the money went for mimeograph paper; next in line were telephones, sound equipment and rent.

Revenue continued to trickle in well after the FSM had disbanded. On the day that the FSM became an entity, one of the Steering Committee members had gone down to the Telegraph Avenue Co-op and taken out a single-share membership on the Movement's behalf, thus providing it with a Co-op identification number. The idea was that people could give the FSM Co-op number if they didn't have one themselves or instead of their own, and by that means make a painless contribution to the cause. At the end of every quarter, the Co-op paid a dividend to all its members in proportion to the amount of groceries they had bought. This was in the good old days when the Co-op was a healthy, well-managed operation, and the quarterly returns actually amounted to something. The Co-op rebates that came to the FSM after the trial was over and done with were turned over to the Campus Congress of Racial Equality. The idea of using a special Co-op number for various worthy causes persisted throughout the sixties, and if the Co-op hadn't fallen on evil times, self-destructing at last in 1989 through an almost inevitable escalation of rhetoric and left-wing infantile disorders, I wouldn't be surprised to hear that many of them were getting dividends still.

The Regents commissioned two reports on the FSM. One, from the right wing, was the Meyer Report, which laid out a detailed plan to wipe out the gains of the FSM. The other, the Byrne Report, from the Forbes Committee of the Regents, cut the tripes out of the Meyer Report, which was subsequently tabled forever and ever.

Another committee of the Regents, the Forbes Committee, which had been charged with an overall inquiry into the underlying causes of the FSM crisis, had set up an independent investigating commission under the Los Angeles lawyer Jerome C. Byrne. Byrne, with a budget of $75,000, had assembled a professional staff of experts on education and management, who carried on a three-month survey-in-depth. The

Byrne Commission report, dated May 7 [1965], came as a veritable bombshell. It was, in the words of the *S.F. Chronicle*, a "searing indictment of [the Regents] and the university administration . . . a striking rebuke both to present university policy and to the Regents' view of their own responsibilities. Equally remarkable was the report's relatively mild censure of the students." . . . There was an initial attempt to suppress its publication, but, with Byrne insisting, the Regents finally allowed it to be distributed (mimeographed). The *Los Angeles Times* was the only place where its text was made available to the general public, outside of an FSM pamphlet reprint; no university paper or publication gave its full contents to the campus community.[7]

Particularly considering its origins, the Byrne Report is simply astonishing. Consider these excerpts:

The crisis at Berkeley last fall has become known as the free speech controversy. It was that, but more fundamentally it was a crisis in government, caused by the failure of the President and Regents to develop a governmental structure at once acceptable to the governed and suited to the vastly increased complexity of the University.

The criticisms are rooted in one fundamental truth: *something* is seriously amiss in a system of government which induces a substantial fraction of the governed to violate the law and risk their careers in order to dramatize their dissatisfaction.

The events which have rocked the University of California in the past eight months are part of a continuing and inevitable conflict between the values of the academic world and those of the larger society. This conflict has always existed, and will continue to do so as long as the academic community continues to do its job.

A litmus test of leadership is the capacity to secure the willingness of others to follow in meeting a challenge or a crisis. On this score, the students were far more skillful—and, in the short run, successful—than the University. Even though the student protestants represented a great diversity of views and opinions, and against the fact that hours of debate preceded most of their decisions, the leadership was capable of decisive action rooted in genuine support from its constituency.

The University, too, displayed a consistent tendency to disorder its own principles and values.

While dedicated to the maintenance of a house for ideas and thought, it proved selective in determining whose ideas would gain admittance. While upholding the value of a continuing discourse in the academic community, it refused to engage in simple conversation with the membership of that community. While positioned as the defender of man's right to reason, it acted out of fear that a volatile public would react against the University if exposed to the reasoning of students. While championing the value of the individual and his responsibility for his own actions, it had sought to prevent the individual from suffering the consequences of his own self-determined actions in society. While postured to avoid prejudgement of facts, it sought to determine before the fact the legality or illegality of actions students would plan to take in the surrounding community. While responsible to and for itself, the University assumed it would be charged with responsibility for others, and in fear that the assumption would prove valid, established rules prohibiting others from acting on their own responsibility.[8]

Mario, suzanne goldberg, Marty Roysher and I were all together on New Year's Eve working on the "We Want a University" pamphlet, an outline of what the FSM felt lacking from UC as it stood, and a proposal for a "Free University of California" in which these faults would be remedied. Jack had gotten most of the writing done and was off somewhere with his girlfriend Phoebe Graubard, so, feeling like celebrating, the four of us went out and bought some cheap booze, and at midnight Suzanne fixed what she called Russian cocktails: a hideous concoction of one-third vodka (to this day I do not much care for vodka), one-third crème de cacao and one-third gin. We drank them out of eight-ounce tumblers, saluting each other and getting cheerier and sillier. Mario and Suzanne reached a point of friendliness that culminated in their going to it hammer and tongs right there on the floor, while Marty and I looked owlishly at each other and tried to hide our embarrassment. Eventually they retired, and Marty and I passed out in various attitudes, awakening the next morning with cricks in our necks. Mario and Suzanne hit it off, and eventually got married. New Year's Day was quiet, as always, but on the second the administration dropped the bombshell that Strong was out in the street.

If the Regents were wrong in conceiving of the protesting students as a monolithic machine, the students were equally mistaken in imagining that the governing bodies of the University, or its administration, were standing shoulder to shoulder. The Regents were quarreling among themselves, the administration was divided on the issues of faculty parking and the quarter system, Kerr and Strong were at swords' points, and Williams and Towle did not get along with Sherriffs, in a big way.

The Regents were particularly angered at the manner in which student discipline had been handled, believing that a firm hand at the helm from the very beginning would have averted the whole mess.* While they had capitulated on the substantive issues, they had rejected the proposal that student discipline be surrendered entirely to a committee of the Academic Senate. Carl Schorske, professor of history and a member of the Emergency Executive Committee elected to present the Academic Senate resolution to the Regents, told us that the Regents had absolute power and did not want to negotiate. He let us in on some of the problems that the Regents were experiencing internally, and said that the right wing was just barely under control, and that they would see the campus in ashes rather than give in. Schorske went on to tell us that Strong understood nothing of the controversy except as it affected himself. He said that Strong had a vested interest in creating disorder, and hoped to force the students to demonstrate, thereby splitting the students and faculty. Strong had split with Kerr, and allied himself with the right wing of the Regents. This faction wanted to shut down the University for the remainder of the semester if there was a continued strike and renewed demonstrations. Of this, Mario said, "We may have to shut down this University in order to save other universities." The threat of shutting down the University, however, was a potent argument for moderation, and made considerable headway in the living groups.[1]

Kerr was allied with the liberal faction of the Regents, and with the liberal faculty, who had never viewed him as an enemy. Once again, Kerr stood up to pressures from the Regents and others, and said that he was personally committed to the amnesty. In order to save face and still get out of the dreadful mess they were in, the administration needed a scapegoat to put all the blame on, and Strong, an unpopular guy with both factions, was elected.

Despite what must have been desperate internal upheavals, the administration kept reasonably closed ranks and did very little to tip off

---

*In his interview with Marston Schultz, Ron Anastasi recalled, "I knew a girl during the FSM whose family was close friends of the Carter family of the Board of Regents. Carter was over at dinner at her house, and she was there. Carter said he thought Strong was at fault in this whole matter and that now 'the thing to do is to get rid of Strong and the ringleaders of the FSM. Strong could have solved it very simply, but because he didn't it became very complicated. Why can't the rebels even look like gentlemen?' Apparently Carter believed the movement to be Communist-infiltrated. At one point he said, 'It's a typical Jewish trait to be a rebel.' [The girl] said that the Regents were also anti-Semitic. Carter said, 'The history of the students' response to the situation is that they will all break the same regulations and try to build to a larger and larger action.'"

ACTING CHANCELLOR
MARTIN MYERSON

MARTIN MEYERSON WAS APPOINTED ACTING
CHANCELLOR ON JANUARY 2, 1965. DAILY CAL
PHOTO. THE NAME IS MISSPELLED
IN THE CAPTION.

the students or faculty to their grave disagreements. We did discover that Kerr intended to send out a mass mailing to parents explaining the whole affair, but two things had gone wrong: first, one of the FSMers had gotten ahold of the IBM cards with the letter on it, thereby throwing a monkey wrench in the works; second, and more important, Strong's signature had been put on the letter without his permission, and when he found this out he refused to cooperate. So the letter was never sent. During the meeting over the cop car, the student negotiators had all noticed that Kerr seemed to have a condescending attitude toward Strong, "putting him down something terrible," in Mario's words, when he tried to participate in the negotiations.

As soon as their New Year's hangovers had died down to a dull roar, the Regents met in emergency session and replaced an allegedly ailing Chancellor Strong with a new broom. On January 2, 1965, Martin Meyerson, dean of the College of Environmental Design, was named acting chancellor of the University of California campus at Berkeley. Meyerson immediately called meetings with administration, faculty and the Steering Committee of the FSM, and on Sunday, January 3, announced provisional rules governing political activity:

> The Regents and President have asked me to issue provisions concerning the time, place and manner of political activity on the Berkeley campus. I shall do so as soon as I have had the opportunity to hear the

views of the Berkeley Division of the Academic Senate on the reports of its Committee on Academic Freedom, and the views of others, as they relate to the Regents' policies. Meanwhile, for political activity during this interim period, the following rules will cover those matters of greatest concern during the next few days:

1. OPEN DISCUSSION AREA: Until final plans can be developed for a suitable alternate discussion area, the Sproul Hall steps are available for temporary use for this purpose at the noon hour and between 4:00 and 6:00 PM. Suitable voice amplification will be provided by the University.

2. TABLES: Student organizations may set up tables in the following areas between 7:00 AM and 6:00 PM.

(a) At the Bancroft and Telegraph entrance.

(b) At the Golden Bear Restaurant area, east of the low concrete wall.

(c) At the North Gate and Tolman Hall areas, and between Kroeber Hall and the Law Building.

(d) Student organizations may receive donations, distribute literature, recruit members, and engage in the sale of such items as buttons, pins, and bumper stickers at the tables. Publications of a student organization may be sold at the tables.

(e) Posters or placards identifying the sponsors are to be attached to the tables and other posters may also be attached.

3. SPEAKER NOTIFICATION: The required advance notification for off-campus speakers is reduced to 48 hours; the Dean of Students Office will reduce or waive this requirement in those instances in which 48-hour notification is not feasible for reasons beyond the control of the sponsoring organizations.

Students should refer to the Office of the Dean of Students for necessary clarification.

The Emergency Executive Committee of the Berkeley Division of the Academic Senate concurs in these rules.[2]

Restrictions on content are conspicuous by their absence. No more faculty moderators, no more paid policemen at campus meetings. On the twelfth, Meyerson appointed sociology professor Neil Smelser as his special assistant in matters of student political activity, thus cutting Alex Sherriffs out of the circuit.[3]

The FSM held its first legal rally on Sproul Steps on January 4, 1965. Joan Baez sang, and speakers expressed *pro forma* dissatisfaction with everything that the administration was doing, out of habit if nothing else: we didn't like the proposals of the Committee on Academic Freedom; we didn't like Meyerson's provisions governing campus political activity; we especially didn't like the Regents and intended to sic our dog on them. But on the whole we were pretty damned pleased with ourselves, and let everybody know it. Interspersed with self-laudatory prose, the recognized spokesmen introduced the less conspicuous toilers in the field; we took our curtain calls one by one and then all together. I stood before the great crowd hailed as a hero, spoke my thanks and stood down. The play was over.

The Free Speech Movement had gained what it had sought, then folded in on itself and disappeared. We kept the organization's bureaucracy alive only long enough to deal with our debts and to keep track of the defendants. Gretchen Kittredge continued keeping the books and paying the bills as they trickled in, giving a final accounting to the Steering Committee before winding things up. David Stein kept the defendants' list up to date for two and a half years, until all the fines had been paid, all the probations completed and all the jail terms served, and then that was the end of it. To be sure, we severally continued to nip at the heels of the Establishment, but by late spring of 1965 the FSM had withered away and was no more.

> According to the best-known FSM leader, an intense, intellectually aggressive young man named Mario Savio, who was studying philosophy before he became involved in the controversy, "All that's left is the trial—legal and political defense—and making sure that the final rules on political activity are acceptable. Then, as far as the FSM goes, that's it; we disband."[4]

Of course, it was not quite as simple as that. Mario was particularly interested in creating a permanent heir to the FSM, one that could carry on its goals and ideals and protect them from encroachments by civil and administrative authorities.

> *Mario Savio:* I was always hoping the thing would end next week. There are organizations which, beginning with legitimate purposes, at one point having achieved those purposes end up existing in order to exist, and that's one thing the FSM wasn't going to do. But it seemed never to come. The bigger the machine we'd built got, the greater the problems that it seemed to unearth. I think that the Free Speech Movement ended December 8.[5]

> *Brian Mulloney:* I talked with as many people as possible about the idea of formally dissolving the FSM at that point. The job was done, you couldn't pick up the ball anymore. There were all these schmucks mak-

ing stupid remarks to the press and running that office. It should have folded on the first of January, instead of sometime in March.

Sue Stein: The faculty was fundamentally changed, in rather the fashion of the French Revolution where the bourgeoisie came in, dragged by the proletariat, but at one point the bourgeoisie dropped the proletariat. The faculty realized that their interests were different from the administration's interests, but also different from the students'. The faculty began solidifying power in the hands of the faculty, for the faculty interests. The faculty were brought into the whole FSM conflict through the students. They were dragged in kicking and screaming, but what happened was, finally they did get angry, and they realized that this was a time when they could get power. They realized that they *wanted* the power, which they hadn't realized before. Now, having been dragged in by the students, they began to realize that their interests were quite different from the students', and they dropped the students. The next revolution on this campus has to be for students to take power from the faculty, not for the students and faculty to take power from the administration.

Brian Mulloney: Of course, by that time I'll be a faculty member.[6]

The hardest part of winding up the FSM was terminating its main bureaucracy. While the Free Speech Movement was alive and kicking, the machinery flailed along at a frantic, anarchistic, but basically functional pace. As soon as the FSM became a mopping-up operation, Parkinson's Law kicked in and Central became a bureaucratic nightmare. By the middle of December, I was in favor of dynamiting the whole place. The files were a mess, the staff had become authoritarian and inefficient, and the whole thing was costing a lot of money that we needed for the defense. Not much was getting done and it was costing too much to do it. Ever since the episode with the stolen files, the workers at Central had greatly disliked me, and knowing that I was in favor of leaving not one stone standing upon the other and sowing the field with salt didn't help things along much. But something had to be done, and after considerable breast-beating and chaos, we resolved to take most of Central's functions away and create a new, efficient locus for communication and defense fundraising. This was the same as finding that you simply can't balance your checkbook, so you close the account and open a brand new one, vowing to balance the books religiously from then on. Of course, it didn't work.

The new miracle center would be called Nexus, which would leave the shit work to Central, which they got done pretty well, and take all the important things out of their hands. We set up Nexus at Ed Rosen-

UP AND DOWN . . . "The only way to appeal the rules is to get arrested," the administration told Jo Freeman. The sign at left will go up again as many times as police take it down until an arrest provides UCLC with a means of testing the interim Rules' constitutionality, she said yesterday.

JO FREEMAN AT HER SATHER GATE UCLC TABLE.
DAILY CAL PHOTO BY JOE MARSHALL.

feld's, which was in condemned housing at 1740 Sacramento. I didn't like the selection because it was too far away. At the time, none of us knew that the cure would prove to be worse than the disease. Ed Rosenfeld seemed a solid, dependable, intelligent guy. He'd been on the provisional Steering Committee.* Mario thought he was a pretty good guy, and Jack liked him and I liked him. So we set up Nexus, got us a couple of phones and file cabinets and set to work.

I turned out to be a terrible bureaucrat. I disliked the job, I didn't like living with Ed, who was a world-class slob, it rained all the time and I didn't like having to sleep on the couch in his cold, cheerless house. So I abdicated my post at Nexus, and most of the work was left to Rosenfeld, who became increasingly erratic and paranoid. Rosenfeld installed a loudspeaker system at the door, and refused to let anyone in if he feared that they were going to take away his telephones and files. He maintained that this precaution was to keep the East Bay Transit authorities from coming in. He'd been living there for about six months without paying rent.† Now we had *two* communications networks that didn't work. After more wailing and gnashing of teeth and endless meetings, we closed down Nexus and the old Central got its responsibilities back, doing no better than before.

The whole problem was resolved when we were notified that spec-

---

*A provisional Steering Committee was elected to make decisions in case the regular Steering Committee was unable to get out of jail. As it happened, the regular Steering Committee went through the revolving door of the legal system so fast that the provisional leadership never had a chance to do anything at all.

†This house was in a tract that had been purchased by the Bay Area Rapid Transit system for the construction of the high-speed light rail system BART. The houses had been condemned, but were rented out by BART in the interim. Apparently Rosenfeld was in arrears.

ulators had bought Mario's place and were going to tear down the building for a new apartment house. So we moved everything to the CORE office at Bancroft and Ellsworth, where Rosemary Feitis took over. The day we cleaned Central out and moved everything away, I found forty bucks in small change behind a bunch of books, and a hundred and fifty dollars in a cupboard; little caches of money were squirreled away here and there, amounting to almost a thousand dollars. Marilyn told me that it was her housekeeping money. Things had gotten out of hand, there.

In a last-ditch effort to get the ball rolling again, on Monday, May 10, 1965, Jo Freeman challenged the Interim Rules on Political Activity, which prohibited attaching posters to "structures . . . such as . . . Sather Gate," by setting up a University Civil Liberties Committee (UCLC) table at Sather Gate, and taping a sign to the gatepost. Jo pointed out that a VISTA table twenty feet away had done so, but that nobody was kicking about *them*. Jo said that she was trying for a test case, and intended to keep on violating the rules until they were changed or she was arrested or both. After a day or so, a campus policeman walked up and confiscated the sign. Jo put up another one, and he took it off. Jo pointed out that she had a pile of signs under her table, and the officer threw up his hands in disgust and walked away. On Thursday, May 13, Jo Freeman said it was "too cold," and moved to the Student Union steps. On Monday she was nowhere to be seen, and that was the end of that.

Looking back on the role the ASUC had played in the events of the last semester, undergrads felt that the ASUC had "dismally failed to represent them in any meaningful way," and that they needed an organization that would speak for their interests more than it bowed to the administration.[7] Early in 1965 we began to organize the Free Student Union (FSU), absorbing the feeble Undergraduate Association, which had formed more or less spontaneously right after the strike. The FSU was an expansion of the original SLATE concept, incorporating the machinery of the FSM and the triumph of the moment, and was intended to take over the student government via regular elections, appointments and a legitimate claim to real student representation. Months before this Dusty Miller had tried to form the FSU but was totally voted down. Mario and Dusty Miller were the main proponents, and together with the newly arrived Marvin Garson (Barbara Garson's husband), Tom Irwin and Bob Mundy, they began work on the theoretical aspects while Jack and I set up the machinery.

The FSU would have been the logical revolutionary progression, but it just didn't get off the ground. People were tired, and the real gung-ho movers and shakers went straight from the FSM into civil rights, not missing a beat. So much of the student energy was diverted first into civil rights and later the anti–Vietnam War movement that there was nothing left for the FSU. Personally, I wasn't the slightest bit interested in the FSU, because I was no longer a student. The FSM was, in small, a model of all revolutions. That it did not complete the full course was because it was superseded by other, more urgent causes, and for this I am thankful.

Marston Schultz: Jack didn't want to take any position in the FSU. He knew the problems that would be created if he did. Garson and he saw the problem: people were in need of organizing, and Jack felt the need to get this energy going somewhere, so he helped formulate the FSU. But I think that Jack and Goines and Garson sort of withdrew from the FSU right away. I don't think they wanted to be involved. They formulated the FSU so that they could terminate the FSM. The demise of the FSM was something that had been discussed for a long time, and Jack was one of the foremost proponents, and nobody had ever effectively done it.

The press had never accepted the death of the FSM, and the only way it was ever accepted was when they had a declaration that said, "Mario quits." Mario had quit the FSM, but that didn't mean that the FSM didn't exist anymore, so the next time they had a rally, Jack said, "We're dissolving the FSM and now we're going to have the FSU," and that officially terminated the FSM, which was needed.* The FSM had served its function and something more on an institutional idea was required.[8]

Lee Felsenstein: The Free Student Union, as I understood it, was what the FSM was to transmogrify itself into. It was to be our Stalinistic phase. I was inside the bureaucratic apparatus—trying to *be* the bureaucratic apparatus. I was one of the two or three "efficiency bureaucrats" that Michael Lerner later denounced as having ruined it all.

When I heard of the Free Student Union, I said to myself, "Aha! You're going to need *apparatchiks*, and here I am!" And of course, as was right, it didn't pan out.

Under the tutelage of Doug Keachie, in January I learned to use the IBM 026 key punches, to make punch cards, and to use the lister and sorter and the printer. This was not the mainframe, just the tabulating

*Savio stepped down as leader on Monday, April 26, 1965. The FSM formally dissolved itself at a noon rally on Thursday, April 28, 1965, at which the Free Student Union was proposed. The FSM Bancroft Avenue Central was shut down on Monday, March 29, 1965. The first general meeting of the FSU was on May 5, 1965, in Harmon Gymnasium.

FREE STUDENT UNION TABLE IN SPROUL PLAZA, 1965.
PHOTO © 1993 BY TED STRESHINSKY.

and sorting facilities. Basically, anybody who was going to use the computer had to enter their data on punch cards. So, as a public utility of the University there were rooms in Cory Hall with all the needful stuff—nobody gave a damn who used it. So what I did with those was work out a system that basically sorted people by areas of interest, major, useful skills, equipment and so on for the Free Student Union.

Thirty-two hundred students signed up, which looked pretty good. Memberships cost something like a quarter, and you got a union card. Nobody knew what to *do* with the union card; I certainly didn't, though my father was a union organizer. I actually told him quite proudly that I was a union organizer on campus, and he told me, "I couldn't give you any advice that would make any sense, so good luck." I would have liked for him to tell me exactly what to do, but by God nobody ever did.

We organized local meetings—that's what I did with the punch cards, sorted them out into rooms and times and so forth and everybody got sent their orders on where to go—and nobody obeyed the orders. I was there to work the machines, but nobody came. I remember going to several of the local meetings and finding *nobody there*. Nobody at all. It was a mass movement—a movement away from what we had planned. So we failed at being Stalinists. The failure of the programmatic structure of the Free Student Union was a triumph, really, of the masses. This was a grass roots rejection. Nobody organized the rejection, nobody spoke against the FSU; *they just didn't show up*. In a way, you might say that was one of our great victories.[9]

THE REVOLUTION WITHIN THE REVOLUTION

All men would be tyrants if they could.
—Daniel Defoe, *The Kentish Petition* (1712–1713)

I wish to persuade women to endeavor to acquire strength, both of mind and body, and to convince them that soft phrases, susceptibility of heart, delicacy of sentiment, and refinement of taste, are almost synonymous with epithets of weakness, and that those beings who are only the objects of pity and that kind of love . . . will soon become objects of contempt. . . .

I wish to show that the first object of laudable ambition is to obtain a character as a human being, regardless of sex.
—Mary Wollstonecraft, *A Vindication of the Rights of Women* (1792)*

ON JUNE 29, 1966, Betty Friedan formed the National Organization for Women (NOW). On September 7, 1968, at the Miss America Pageant in Atlantic City, New Jersey, Robin Morgan and members of the feminist organization WITCH (Women's International Terrorist Conspiracy from Hell) engaged in an act of guerrilla theater in which girdles, brassieres, spike heels, diapers, copies of *Cosmopolitan*, steno pads and dishtowels were tossed into a "freedom trash can." The event was reported in the *New York Post* as a "bra burning" and as such entered the realm of urban myth. Initially greeted with hoots of derision, the Women's Movement soon became a real threat to men's last, treasured bastion of inequality. The derision quickly turned to anger.

While the Women's Movement had not officially gotten off the ground in 1964, the sexual revolution was clearly under way. What was less clear was what the "sexual revolution" *was*, exactly. How come we suddenly took girls' sexual acquiescence so much for granted, when before it had been anything but? I mean, I lived through it; I should know, I guess.

Let's look at the basics. What boys want, at least in theory, is to get laid. As much as possible as quickly as possible by as many girls as pos-

---

*Wollstonecraft was responding to the English conservative and opponent of the French Revolution, Edmund Burke, who had written in his *Reflections on the Revolution in France*, "A woman is but an animal, and an animal not of the highest order." Mary Wollstonecraft married William Godwin in 1797 and died in childbed, giving birth to their daughter Mary Wollstonecraft, later Mary Wollstonecraft Shelley, author of *Frankenstein*.

sible. Any excuse will do, and we are restrained from wallowing in an abyss of carnal excess only at metaphorical gunpoint. It's hard-wired into our heads. Now, what *girls* want is no doubt something else again, but all that boys knew in the early 1960s was that right up until then they'd had the very devil of a time getting any, and all of a sudden things changed.

However, the deepest, surest conviction that boys have is that girls don't really, *really* want to do it. It was then, and remains today, an abiding article of faith among boys that as far as sex is concerned girls have to be tricked, cajoled, persuaded, conned or forced, and that they *never* give anything away for free. When you find a girl that seems to want to do it with few or no preliminaries and no strings attached, first you're suspicious. Then you go for it. But you never quite believe it. There's gotta be a catch. There's *always* a catch. In a sense, the early rumblings of the Women's Movement came as a relief. "Ah! *That's* what they want! At last we find out! *That's* what all this has been leading up to!"

> Did you take your Pill today?
> —Caption to a popular poster image of the pope, leaning forward and wagging an admonitory finger, circa 1965

I imagine that when the Pill first swam into the consciousness of my female schoolmates, their reaction was, "Hot diggidy-dog! Now we can at last be free of the fear of getting knocked up, and for once in our lives be on an even footing with the guys. Now *we* can do whatever we want and not have to pay for it, same as them." My recollection is that starting somewhere in the early sixties, the girls started to go for it like there was no tomorrow. This caught the boys, myself among them, quite by surprise, and it took us a few years to catch up. As the sixties wore on into the seventies, the girls who had at first found the sexual liberation granted by the Pill thrilling began to find being treated as an automatic sexual object somewhat burdensome. The boys, on the other hand, were in hog heaven. What it boiled down to, more or less, was that once again the girls had changed but the boys hadn't. By this time, of course, the ante had been upped, and just like anything else, the casual sexual climate had been easier to get into than it was to get out of. The girls found it difficult to switch from a general polymorphous promiscuity to something approaching moderation and serial monogamy, mainly because the boys wouldn't tolerate any change.

When the Pill became popular enough to permeate middle-class society, immediately the whole burden of contraception was transferred to the girl. Theretofore, it had grudgingly been borne by the boy who, as is attested by unwed mother statistics, shirked his responsibility often as not. For a variety of reasons, boys really hate condoms. By 1964, you didn't even have to ask; unless the girl was conspicuously a virgin, you assumed that she had made some appropriate provision against unwanted pregnancy. In the early sixties, we didn't even think about disease. There wasn't any.

> Girls say YES to boys who say NO to the draft!
> —Picket sign and slogan popular during the antiwar movement, 1965–1972

In keeping with the pervasive, unconscious sexism of the times, throughout the life of the Movement, the girls were the hewers of wood and drawers of water—gofers, the low (wo)man on the totem pole. The common perception of women in the FSM, civil rights and antiwar movements was that they were helpmeet, solace and reward. Renée Melody, my first FSM girlfriend, remembers what it was like:

> When I was helping at the original FSM Central, it was sort of the preliminary stages of the Women's Movement for me. I saw all these women who had no say in the strategy sessions—slaving to cook, slaving to type, slaving to wash dishes for the guys in the hope that one of them would lay one of his beams of light on her and actually acknowledge her existence. It seemed to me that the women threw themselves with a lot of zeal into a submissive position. It was bad enough that the men were asking them—I could understand that; the guys want to make use of you, fine—but why would the women voluntarily do it?
>
> I found that so disgusting that I refused to participate. The way we stopped seeing each other was you called me one night and you wanted me to type and I said, "Look, I got a D in typing. Typing is not my thing." And you said, "This is what I want you to do. Will you do this to help or not?" And I said, "I will do anything else, but I will not type." You were not going to ask a *man* to type; you were going to ask a *woman* to type. I was willing to help on the things that I knew how to help on, but if I was to be asked to type simply because I was a woman, I was not going to do it. That was over the line. If I'd been asked to answer the phone, to distribute leaflets—something that anybody could do—I would have done it. But not type.
>
> I had a giant crush on you, and I was more interested in being with you than being in the FSM, but I would not degrade myself. Even at that age, I would not degrade myself: if you didn't want to be with me, fine,

I wasn't going to lay down and die. If you wanted me to do that, it was just not going to happen. And that was the end of that.

There were one or two powerful women, like Bettina and Jackie, but then there were all these groupies that were hoping to have Mario in bed *just one night.* I thought it was disgusting and degrading, and I wasn't going to do it.

One afternoon when FSM Central was still up on the hill we decided to kiss 'em all off and go for a ride on that Honda 90—that was the high point for me. I remember the glares of the women—the slave women—as I walked out the door with you just to go and have fun. They hated me! They absolutely hated me! They hated me anyway, because I wouldn't cook and wash dishes. I was never good at cooking, I was never good at typing, and I wasn't going to pretend. I didn't have the consciousness yet that this was a feminist issue; I just knew it offended me, and I wasn't going to do it.[1]

Those like Bettina Aptheker, Jackie Goldberg and Sue Stein were perceived as anomalous. The National Organization for Women was no less a bombshell to the average college boy than to his girlfriend, and it took quite a while before the idea that there was cause for a separate movement actively promoting the rights of women began to percolate even as far as the highly politicized atmosphere of Berkeley. When it caught on, of course, it immediately confronted the baffled antagonism of their erstwhile harnessmates, the boys. The boys quite correctly perceived this revolution within the revolution as a serious threat to what had been for the preceding half-decade the biggest free lunch of all time, and greeted it with something less than loud hosannas.

I find it interesting that contemporaneous with the rise of the Women's Movement was a corresponding darkening of the sexual climate: sadomasochism and sexual fetishism, expressed in the most graphic forms in comix, popular literature, film and art, became trendy, acceptable, so commonplace as to be unworthy of comment. The shackles of sexual repression were metaphorically brought right out into the open as soon as they were challenged. In hip art, women were punished, humiliated, used as sexual objects even as the causes connected with women's liberation were given noisy lip-service in the same progressive sector.

As the Women's Movement gained momentum, sex became divorced from emotion, from any sort of commitment. It seemed as if men didn't want to think about it, about the permutations and resonances of what they were doing. And neither did the women.

He: Wanna fuck?
She: Your place or mine?
He: If you're gonna hassle, forget it!
—Joke current circa 1970

The Women's Movement was confused in the popular mind with women wanting to be like men, and a common image of the liberated woman was that of a man-hating bull-dyke, a castrating "women's libber" or a mannishly asexual competitor jockeying for position in the man's world.* Other efforts had unforeseen results: Robin Morgan and the 1968 Atlantic City "bra burners" somehow ended up creating the no-bra look. Not what they had in mind, I imagine.

As the swingin' sixties leached into the selfish seventies, the surviving shreds of middle-class sexual morality were court-martialed and blown from a cannon's mouth.

. . . the incident has all the swift compression of a dream and is seemingly free of all remorse and guilt; because there is no talk of her late husband or of his fiancée; because there is no rationalizing; because there is no talk at all. The zipless fuck is absolutely pure. It is free of ulterior motives. There is no power game. The man is not "taking" and the woman is not "giving." No one is attempting to cuckold a husband or humiliate a wife. No one is trying to prove anything or get anything out of anyone. The zipless fuck is the purest thing there is. And it is rarer than the unicorn. And I have never had one.
—Erica Jong, *Fear of Flying*, 1973

This bubble in the fabric of morality didn't last, of course. But the change back had little to do with either conventional morality or the Women's Movement. When dat ol' debbil HERPES an' dat *big* boogie **AIDS** come whoopin' down de pike, then you started seeing Willie putting on his overcoat. But he wasn't happy about it. No, Sir!

Got a stiffie?
Wear a Jiffie!
—Advertisement for Jiffie brand condoms, 1988

---

*"Men have always been expected to be helpful to women. The same is true now, but the mode of helpfulness has changed with changing sex roles. One example will suffice. In the past a man was expected to give his seat on a bus to a woman. Today it would be much more courteous for that man to give her his job" (P. J. O'Rourke, *Modern Manners*, 1983).

There's this riddle that was current in the mid to late sixties: A kid is being driven to a football game by his father, and on the way they get into an automobile accident. They're taken to the hospital and when the kid gets into surgery, the doctor says, "Oh, no! I can't operate on this boy; he's my son!"

What relationship was the doctor to the boy?

Answer: His mother.

This was a real riddle—one that stumped perfectly well-educated, hip, politically aware people. I remember feeling quite annoyed that I hadn't solved it, and miffed because, although I couldn't precisely put my finger on it, I felt that I had been tricked somehow.

It took me a long time to accept that women had a beef coming. I guess that the idea of the Women's Movement was, on every level, just too threatening to take in all at once. Even the meanest man was better, in his own eyes and that of society, than any woman. No matter how bad things were, there was always somebody you could be better than, kick around, give the shitty end of the stick. And she'd take it, because she believed it too. In the South, the social standing of the poorest white was still better than any Black man, and when that status quo was threatened, all hell broke loose. "If you're not better than a nigger, who are you better than?"

Woman is the Nigger of the World.
—John Lennon & Yoko Ono Plastic Ono Band, "Elephant's Memory," *Sometime In New York City*, Apple Records, 1972

So in the early sixties we broke all records standing up to HUAC and trying to improve the lot of the downtrodden Negro and jeopardizing our educational futures over the First Amendment and going to jail over the war in Vietnam and marching with the farmworkers and not eating grapes, but when the women who had constituted exactly one-half of the whole shebang turned their eyes to their own inequality and casually mentioned that they wanted a fair shake, we thought they had dropped down from Mars. No kidding. It really came as a surprise. Plus it made us mad.

Renée Melody: In a way I ended up turning over my ego to the Movement by marrying this guy just to get him out of the draft. It ended up setting the tone of the rest of my life. He got out of the draft with a psychiatric deferment, and had a choice of working for two years at the Saint Vincent De Paul's for seventy-five cents an hour, or getting married. We got married as sort of a *counter* counterculture thing. Nobody we knew was getting married. I got married with my arm in a sling from a motorcycle accident and my roommates as witnesses. I didn't even tell my family. Then he decided, "Well, now we're married. Now *I* want to have a baby." So when I broke out in hives and I had tunnel vision and no blood pressure, he asked the intern, "Well, could it be birth control pills? It probably could, couldn't it." The guy says, "Hey, I don't know; could be." So he goes home and throws my birth control pills away. I made an appointment for a diaphragm fitting and he essentially raped me one afternoon on July 10, 1968, at three-thirty in the afternoon. I had this incredible sense of my future coming at me and there was *nothing* I could do about it. After the first minute, I *knew* I was pregnant.[2]

. . . in the new code of laws which, I suppose it will be necessary for you to make, I desire you would remember the ladies, and be more generous to them than your ancestors. Do not put such unlimited power in the hands of husbands. Remember, all men would be tyrants if they could. If particular care and attention are not paid to the ladies, we are determined to foment a rebellion, and will not hold ourselves bound to obey the laws in which we have no voice of representation.
—Abigail Adams, from a letter to her husband, Samuel Adams, March 1776

THE FILTHY SPEECH MOVEMENT

WE'RE ASKING THAT THERE BE *NO* restrictions on the content of speech save those provided by the courts, and that's an enormous amount of freedom; and people can say things within that area of freedom that are not responsible. We've finally gotten into a position where we have to consider being responsible, because, y'know, now we've got the freedom within which to be responsible, and I'd like to say at this time I'm confident that the students, the faculty of the University of California will exercise their freedom with the same responsibility they've shown in winning their freedom.
—Mario Savio, rally on Sproul Hall steps, December 9, 1964

There have been two principal historical justifications for free speech, sometimes overlapping and sometimes in tension with each other. One theory sees free speech as an essential part of a free and just society that treats all its members as "responsible moral agents."

"Government insults its citizens, and denies their moral responsibility, when it decrees that they cannot be trusted to hear opinions that might persuade them to dangerous or offensive conduct."

The other . . . "instrumental" [theory] justifies free speech on the ground that it serves a greater good and creates a better country, helping to produce a better informed electorate or a more accountable government, for example.

"The 'instrumental' view of free speech holds that speech has value insofar as it serves a constructive, civilizing or decent purpose, and little or no value if it hurts or destroys it."
—Linda Greenhouse, "Two Visions of Free Speech"

Political speech has throughout history had an uphill battle with the state, as it potentially constitutes a threat to the welfare and stability of the state itself. Other forms of speech and expression, such as those that exceed the bounds set by polite society or which give offense to the sensibilities of private citizens, also threaten the political organism. These forms have in this century and the last been equally, if not upon occasion more severely, constrained. England and America, though by no means theocracies, are much governed by narrow Biblical references. Restrictions on the content of nonpolitical speech waxed throughout the nineteenth century—so much so that ordinary English words disappeared from dictionaries, and despite their common daily use by numberless citizens became not only illegal to print, but even to say in public.

Arriving at a useful definition of what is obscene or offensive is extraordinarily difficult, particularly in light of shifting degrees of tolerance from one cultural context to another. The test for criminality set out in the eleventh edition of the *Encyclopedia Britannica*, published in 1910, was "whether the exhibition or matter complained of tends to deprave and corrupt those whose minds are open to immoral influences and who are likely to visit the exhibition, or to see the matter published. If the exhibition or publication is calculated to have this effect, the motive of the publisher or exhibitor is immaterial. . . . The use of obscene or indecent language in public places is punishable as a misdemeanor at common law." Even casually examined, this means nothing at all, and is no more than a blank warrant to facilitate repression.

Obscenity was defined as "something offensive to modesty or decency, or expressing or suggesting unchaste or lustful ideas or being impure, indecent or lewd." Ordinary, ancient, English words that accurately described parts of the human body, words for daily physical activities and words concerned with the propagation of the species were prohibited, and we were compelled by prudery to wander in a fog of euphemism and Latin medical terms. Long passages of the classics were left untranslated (or stranger yet, translated from Greek into Latin); whole collections of ancient Greek vases and entire rooms of paintings from the buried cities of Pompeii and Herculaneum were locked away from the public gaze. A considerable confusion resulted from the collision of Victorian morality with "well-known and old-established works of widely recognized literary merit on the ground that they contain passages offensive to later notions of propriety. In the case of exhibitions of sculpture and pictures some difficulty is found in drawing the line between representations of the nude and works which fall within the definition [of obscenity] above stated. . . ."[1] Carried to extremes, nothing was sacred, including the Word of God itself: Thomas Bowdler, a sort of old-time Joe McCarthy of anti-obscenity, actually decided that the Bible was too raunchy for gentle ears and issued a sanitized version.* He also produced an expurgated version of Gibbon's *Decline and Fall of the Roman Empire* and in 1818 published *The Family Shakespeare* "in ten volumes, in which nothing is added to the original text; but those words and expressions are omitted which cannot with propriety be read aloud in a family." Algernon Charles Swinburne thought he was swell, saying in *Prose and Poetry* (1894) that "no man ever did better service to Shakespeare than the man who made it possible to put him into the hands of intelligent and imaginative children" and stigmatizing adverse talk about the expurgations as "nauseous and foolish cant."

It is difficult to portray human society while ignoring its most basic urges and biological needs, and artists and writers chafed under obscenity bans, challenging them repeatedly with varying degrees of success.

In February 1915, after having reviewed D. W. Griffith's film *The Birth of a Nation*, the Supreme Court declared that moving pictures were unsheltered by the First Amendment. (Of course, this was not too harsh a blow, because for all practical purposes the First Amendment did not at that time shelter any other form of speech or expression either.) It was not until 1952 that the Court, after thirty years of badgering by the ACLU, granted that protection to a motion picture: concerning the Marshall, Texas, ban on the film *Pinky*, Justice William O. Douglas wrote that the "evil of prior restraint . . . is present here in flagrant form. If a board of censors can tell the American people what it is in their best interests to see or to read or to hear, then thought is regimented, authority substituted for liberty, and the great purpose of the First Amendment to keep uncontrolled the freedom of expression defeated." It strains credulity that this statement was made at the height of the Communist witch hunts.

The 1964 Supreme Court decision on the film *The Lovers* established the further principle that "material dealing with sex in a manner that advocates ideas, or that has literary or scientific or artistic value or any other form of social importance, may not be branded as obscenity." For a while this meant that even the coarsest pornography carried a trans-

---

*Despite its many failings in the eyes of Victorian gentlefolk, the Old Testament nonetheless provided—if properly interpreted—a model for acceptable sexual activity, all other forms being against the law and punishable with the severest criminal penalties. Any reference to aberrant sexual behavior was necessarily veiled in the deepest euphemism and outright obfuscation. When I first heard the phrase, "the love that dare not speak its name," for example, I had absolutely no idea of what was being discussed.

parently fraudulent academic introduction giving the work the cachet of scholarly or literary value.[2] The first novel openly brought under the protection of the First Amendment was Henry Miller's *Tropic of Cancer*, in 1964.

The obscenity issue first came to the fore in Berkeley on Monday, November 11, 1964, when Jean Genet's *Un Chant d'Amour* was shown in Stiles Hall by SLATE.* On Wednesday, November 25, Dean Towle banned the movie from a campus film festival. This so annoyed Steve Weissman that he proposed setting up a projector in Sproul Plaza and showing the film on the wall of Sproul Hall, but the disciplinary action taken against four FSM leaders in that same week diverted his attention.

On Thursday, February 11, 1965, the exhibitor and U.S. distributor of the film, Saul Landau, was hailed before the Oakland Municipal Court, which reviewed the film for obscenity. He later tried to show it in Berkeley, but "the director of the special investigations bureau of the police department told him that 'it would be confiscated and all persons responsible arrested.'"†

Coincidentally, a seven-week series of public lectures on censorship and obscenity began on Wednesday, February 24, 1965, and continued throughout the succeeding uproar. It was well attended.

The Free Speech Movement's struggle for narrow political objectives coincided with a larger battle against restriction on all forms of expression. As far as the First Amendment was concerned, the Free Speech Movement had been on solid ground. The First Amendment had from its inception been construed as protecting political expression, but had not yet been found so elastic as to cover all forms of speech.‡ The argument that it was not fundamentally intended to protect *Webster's*

---

*"Set in a Paris prison and having no sound track, *Un Chant d'Amour* is the celebrated French author Jean Genet's only film. Reflecting his experience in prison, the film centers on an affair between two men living in separate cells" (Edward de Grazia and Roger K. Newman, *Banned Films* [New York: R. R. Bowker Company, 1982], 287).

†"After viewing the movie twice, Judge George W. Phillips, Jr., of the Alameda County Superior Court concluded it was obscene. On appeal the District Court of Appeals of California (three judges dissenting) affirmed the lower court's judg-

ment. A bare majority of the U.S. Supreme Court, without stating its reasons, affirmed the judgment condemning the film . . . as 'hard-core pornography.'" (Quotation here and above from de Grazia and Newman, 287–289.)

‡In the 1942 case *Chaplinsky* v *New Hampshire*, "the Supreme Court said that the First Amendment did not protect 'fighting words' which provoked immediate violence, and added that the First Amendment also did not apply to obscenity or private suits for libel" (Ronald Dworkin, "The Coming Battles over Free Speech," *New York Review of Books*, 11 June 1992).

SPEAKING . . . John Thomson, who started a furor when arrested for carrying an "obscene" sign last week, talking at Friday's rally at Sproul Hall.

JOHN THOMPSON. DAILY CAL PHOTO,
MARCH 8, 1965.

Third International Dictionary, James Joyce's *Ulysses* or the public performances of Lenny Bruce had been eroding throughout the previous decades, and one of the last challenges came from the University of California campus on March 3, 1965.* Following swiftly on the heels of the FSM's chaste victory, would-be poet John Thompson's almost unintentional assault on the remaining forms of censorship caught all of us by surprise.[3]

MARCH 3, 1965: THE DAY I BECAME FAMOUS FOR FIFTEEN MINUTES

I hitched out to Berkeley in the winter of '64–'65. I'd been living in New York City, first in my own cold-water flat up on East Third Street, and later with my friend David Rosenberg, in another tenement at 41 First Avenue. I was working part-time as a messenger for Airline Delivery Service, smoking a lot of pot, popping whites [Benzedrine], working briefly as a gaffer for Lenny Bruce, writing poetry and hanging out with my friends, most of whom were members of either the Student Non-violent Coordinating Committee's Lower East Side cadre (nicknamed the River Rats by the other SNCC chapters because we were so scruffy and militant) or the Progressive Labor Party [PL]. I wanted to

---

*The great cultural hero of the day was Lenny Bruce, the haunted, brilliant comedian and social gadfly whose shooting war with prudish authority had earned him a place in the adolescent pantheon. He was appearing at the hungry i in San Francisco, where Tom Weller, Karl Foytick and I resolved to see him in the flesh. During his act, which was far raunchier than his records, a drunk began to heckle from the audience and, when he became too big a pain in the ass, was unceremoniously tossed out into the street by the bouncer. I

guess that we three looked sympathetic, because after the act Lenny Bruce came up to us and asked us if we'd be willing to testify in court if the matter of the drunk came to that: every man's hand was against him, and in his terror of legal imbroglio he turned even to schoolboys for help. We shyly explained that we were underage and probably shouldn't even be here in the first place; that we would be glad to help if we could and that we sure had enjoyed the show and good luck.

do my part for The Revolution, but I was disorganized, depressed, painfully shy and mad at the world at that time. I was also a virgin, a condition that preyed on my mind most of my waking hours.

In the summer of '64 my friend Lou Pakula had hitched out to Berkeley with Peter Rosenberg, my roommate's little brother. When they came back, Lou told me that girls would come up to you on the street and ask if you had a place to stay, and more often than not, they'd take you in, feed you and fuck you. It sounded great to me, and I decided that if I didn't get a book of poetry published by my twenty-second birthday, I'd leave New York and go to Berkeley.

I had been writing stories since grammar school, and poetry ever since a friend had turned me on to Ginsberg's *Howl* a few years before. I tried submitting poems to literary magazines from time to time, but they were always rejected, often with harsh, snotty comments. Looking back on those poems I know that most of the rejections were deserved, but at the time *I knew those editors were jealous of the great talent they recognized in my poetry.* Anyway, the Pulitzer Committee didn't track me down and award me a prize, and a few weeks before my birthday I gave up on New York. I packed a borrowed knapsack, took my last paycheck, grabbed a bus to New Jersey, walked to a westbound freeway and started for Berkeley.

Since I'd been doing volunteer work for PL, I had the names and numbers of half a dozen politically active people in my pocket when I got to Berkeley. I looked up Denis Mosgofian and Brenda Goodman, a couple I'd met at a PL meeting in New York the year before. They let me stay at their house on Emerson Street in Berkeley, and in return I manned the table of the May Second Movement (M2M), a PL front group that was organizing Berkeley students to oppose the Vietnam War. Denis and Brenda helped to start the Berkeley chapter.

The atmosphere in Berkeley in the winter of '64–'65 can't really be described. Even an emotionally numbed-out and badly confused street poet and would-be author like myself could feel the winds of change blowing. Everyone in Berkeley, at least those with a leftist perspective, was giddy with a sense of power, with the knowledge that we *were actually making history.* I had friends that had gone down to Mississippi for Freedom Summer, and although I'd been invited to go along, I chickened out. When I thought about that, I was often consumed with self-loathing and disgust for my lack of courage. But here was a second chance to be part of something bigger than myself. Walking the streets in the days of the Free Speech Movement got you higher than a handfulla bennies.

On the flip side, there was also a chill of terror in the air. The Oakland police routinely murdered Black youths; several of the demonstrations I'd taken part in back in New York were bloodbaths, with the police smashing skulls while the media ignored us; people I knew (myself included) had been visited by the FBI, or endured random beatings at the hands of the police who were "searching" for drugs, or had their phones tapped, or were followed everywhere they went by men in suits and crew cuts. We had no illusions about the brutality of the system (or so we thought). In years to come, when we saw students being killed at Kent State, or the police murdering Black Panthers at will, we realized belatedly just how seriously the power structure took us, and what lengths they'd take to stop us. But we believed that since we were the sons and daughters of white, middle-class, educated people, the system's inherent contradictions would work in our favor and prevent anything really nasty from happening.

So I worked at the M2M table, walked picket lines and got politically involved. At the same time I was writing, smoking dope, trying to get laid, and hanging out with the street people who would soon be dubbed hippies by the press. I wanted to be a writer, but thought I had nothing to write about, so in my search for experience I took LSD, speed, downers and smoked pot, hitched all over the state of California, and later, had sex with any woman that would look twice at me. I remember at one point Denis Mosgofian told me that eventually I'd have to choose between politics and working for the greater good and my own self-destructive, drug-taking, pleasure-seeking, selfish nature. He hoped I'd do the right thing, and so did I, but by that time I knew in my heart that I'd rather have fun and work in the cultural revolution than put my nose to the grindstone and hang with the heavy politicos. When I left New York I'd vowed that I'd never work at another meaningless nine-to-five gig, and on one level, that's what the Revolution sounded like. I felt guilty about being so selfish, but I knew what I was capable of, and twenty-four hours a day on the barricades wasn't my style.

That, briefly, is the background to the events of March 3, 1965. I don't remember where I'd spent the night before, but that Wednesday was a cool, gloomy day. I wandered around campus, talked to friends, probably ate some pizza or a Chunky or two, and sat on the planter at Bancroft and Telegraph in front of the Student Union building. Once more I was thinking about my lack of experience. Nothing was happening in my life worth writing about (or so I thought), and what's a writer without a story to tell? Well, maybe if I got put in jail overnight, or for a few days, I'd have a story. With this half-baked idea in mind I borrowed a piece of lined notebook paper from a table manned by Dan Rosenthal.* I folded it in half and

---

*Chairman of Cal Conservatives for Political Action. The *Daily Cal* consistently got his name wrong, calling him "David" Rosenthal.

wrote FUCK on it with a red felt-tipped pen. Then I sat down on the planter to see what would happen.

Nothing. I was ignored. No big deal. I'm always ignored. Might as well go home and . . . A fraternity-looking guy—crew cut, arms like tree trunks, clear blank blue eyes—rushed at me and ripped the paper out of my hands. As he tore it up he raged at me. "What are you, some kind of degenerate? There are all kinds of chicks walking by here. My chick came by here a few minutes ago. What if one of them saw this?" Etc. He balled the paper up and threw it against my chest. "If you're still sittin' here when I get back I'm gonna break your neck," he said, and stormed off, fired up with righteous anger. Fred Sokolow, who was vice president of SLATE and had been sitting with Stephen Argent, who was selling [the student magazine] *Spider*, walked over and asked what had gone down. I told him, we laughed, and I borrowed another sheet of paper and made another sign.

The sun had come out, I sat with my sign. Mario Savio came by, did a double take and stopped. I knew him vaguely from seeing him around campus, but I was pretty much in awe of him. He was really doing something with his life, whereas I was a street poet who was wasting his life, too scared to get really involved, too scared to even "eat a peach," as T. S. Eliot might say. Mario pointed out that FUCK was a versatile word in the English language—it could be a noun, verb, adverb, adjective, gerund. I nodded and fixed the sign to read:

FUCK
(verb)

I sat there with the sign. Fred Sokolow, back at the *Spider* table, made a sign that said SHIT and held it up. I held up my sign. We flipped each other off, made faces, etc. I was getting bored. The frat guy hadn't come back, it was getting late, and I wasn't going to get arrested. I'd never go to jail, or write a book, or be a famous author. I was sitting there disgusted when a plainclothes cop appeared with the frat guy.

"What are you doing?" says the cop.

"Nothing," says I.

"What's this?" he asks, pointing at the placard.

"A sign."

"What's it say?"

"Can't you read?" If he thinks I'm going to say "fuck" to him, he's crazy.

The cop takes the sign and says, "You're under arrest."

I stand up. "What's the charge?"

He looks at me and says something like, "Don't be a wise guy," and grabs my elbow.

I'm marched down to the police station in the basement of Sproul Hall and put in a holding cell. There's a desk, a chair, and oddly enough, a pen, a pencil, and a writing pad of UC stationery. The window of the cell faces on Bancroft and it's open, though covered by a heavy mesh screen. Time passes. David Bills, one of my best friends, appears at the window.

"There's a big demonstration going on 'cause you got busted. This is what the FSM missed! There's a big crowd, and cops everywhere. Lots of people from the newspapers!"

After he leaves, I sit down at the table and write a "confession."

WHY I DID WHAT I DID.

My mother told me she would beat me to death if I didn't carry that "obscene" sign onto campus today. The priest said always to obey and love mother. I'm sorry if I caused you any trouble.

I'm laughing so hard by the time I finish the confession, I'm surprised no cops come over to see what's happening. I fold it up and palm it and wait, not really knowing what's going on outside. At last an officer comes to escort me to the Berkeley city jail. On the way out we're surrounded by a large, jeering crowd. I see Michael Klein, one of the people I know from M2M, in front of the crowd, and using my thumb, I flip the confession so it lands at his feet. He picks it up without the cop noticing and the next day the "confession" appears in the *Daily Californian*.

The cops driving me to the Berkeley jail play a "Mutt and Jeff" routine. One cop is very threatening, making remarks like, "You little punk. If we were alone, you'd be shitting my nightstick." The other one tries to restrain him and calm him down, but I'm taken in by the whole act and am pretty scared.

I stay in jail less than an hour before Denis Mosgofian bails me out and takes me back to the Emerson Street house. Denis and Brenda tell me what happened, and I tell them why I did it, and they kind of laugh, kind of cry. After all the work they put into the FSM, all it's taken is one moment of stupidity on my part, and the whole thing tumbles like a house of cards, etc. I decide I should look for lodgings elsewhere and I roam over to Michael Klein's house. He tells me that he's started the Fuck Defense Fund, or FDF for short, to raise money to pay for my bail and trial. I'm still in a daze, beginning to realize that my prank has gotten out of hand to say the least. Michael talks about raising money, and after agreeing to sit at the FDF table the next day, I go up to Telegraph Avenue. Somebody tells me there's a party at Art Goldberg's house, and I walk over with a few friends, smoking a joint on the way.

Goldberg greets me effusively and tells me what a great thing I've done. He tells me I've taken the struggle to the next logical step. It's fine to defend political speech, but what about artistic speech? Or meaningless speech? My poem (it was a poem? yeah, sure, that's what it was; it was a poem), he says, was an act of genius. And if it pissed people off so much the better, I was just showing up the inherent contradictions in the position they were assuming vis-à-vis blah, blah, blah, blah, and etc., etc., etc. Suddenly I'm not embarrassed at doing something dumb, I realize that I've dared to boldly go where no man has gone before and blah, blah, blah, blah. Blinded by Art's rhetoric and my own näiveté, I agree to address a rally in my behalf on Friday, March 5.

The newspapers (though they would not print the word in question, describing it only as "a four-letter word for sexual intercourse") had a great time making much of what they were pleased to announce as "the first offspring of the FSM." Kerr cleverly dubbed it "the Filthy Speech Movement," and although almost everyone from the FSM went out of their way to disavow any relationship, the goals of the Free Speech Movement and those of the Filthy Speech Movement became permanently wedded in the popular mind.*

As the FSM had attained its political ends, expanding First Amendment protections to more controversial forms of speech might look like a logical next step; but in fact the "filthy speech" issue created considerable division within the ranks of the Free Speech Movement's former activists. Some of us, though by no means all, were anxious to extend the ideals of the FSM beyond the relatively narrow confines of politics. Others were much alarmed at the unexpected barbarian horde to which we had inadvertently opened the gates. Indeed, most FSM veterans, prudish as dedicated politicos often are, were dismayed both by the personalities involved in the Filthy Speech Movement and by the media's gleeful confusion of the goals of the FSM with those of its apparent offspring. Stumbling all over itself to deny any connection, the FSM issued a statement on Monday, March 10, saying,

> Only in the recent controversy over "obscene" words can students be said not to have acted responsibly. The FSM did not initiate or support this controversy. We regret both that the students involved acted in an unfortunate manner and that the police and some administrators chose to escalate the issue and endanger campus peace rather than permit stu-

---

*The history of the Free Speech Movement presented in Don Pitcher and Michael Margolin's book, Berkeley Inside/Out will serve to illustrate this general confusion: "Many people in California found this new spirit of confrontation a threat, and those who opposed the FSM called it the 'Filthy Speech Movement'" [Berkeley, Calif.: Heyday Books, 1990], 142).

dent interest in the subject to wane. The problem is now in the courts, where it belongs. Any disciplinary action by the University will be directly contrary to the principles we supported last semester.[4]

Mario Savio: When the obscenity thing arose, I was in jail. I told the judge [at a hearing on the sit-in] he was a hypocrite, and he put me in jail for contempt.*

I was very dismayed; on the one hand, there were people who wanted to drop the whole thing as something we ought not to deal with. On the other hand, Jack presented the position that this was something we ought to defend as an abridgment of the content of speech. We shouldn't have been deciding what was or was not the content of speech any more than the administration. My position was that we should take a stand on the issue of due process. But somehow the issue seemed too abstract to people. People didn't want to associate themselves with the problem of obscenity.[5]

Ernest Besig, the Northern California director of the ACLU who had been in the forefront of FSM defense, uttered a printable "good grief," and announced that the issue "will be used to criticize and attack the free-speech policies of the administration." He hoped that students would demonstrate some degree of responsibility and "not make the administration's life more miserable."[6]

Art Goldberg was the exception among the radicals to the shunning of John Thompson's cause. Art was known as the "Marshmallow Maoist" because of his admiration for Peking political philosophy and simultaneous moderate opposition to FSM militancy; his espousal of the dirty-word cause, especially as he had been a high-profile spokesman for the FSM, was felt by most of us to be a trivialization of what we had fought for. Nonetheless, much of what Art had to say about freedom of speech was perfectly valid; if a person can be prosecuted on the basis of the content of speech, and especially if the grounds for prosecution are that the speech offends the listener, then speech is not free. This cut no ice with the politicos, however, and most of the students ignored the cause as well. A later Filthy Speech rally in lower Sproul Plaza drew precisely zero auditors.

Lee Felsenstein: My feeling on the Filthy Speech Movement was, "Oh, shit! These guys are ruining it for everybody!" I was actually one with

---

*Savio's contempt sentence was from Thursday, March 4, through Friday, March 5, 1965.

Charles McCabe in the *Chronicle* who said that these guys should be taken up a dark alley and have the shit beaten out of them. The professor who had hired me felt that what was going on with the Filthy Speech Movement was really getting to the core of what was necessary; that the people involved were on the correct path. It was making the next big step, the beginning of the cultural revolution. That was when the Haight-Ashbury started. We, the nice little children of Stalinists, had been very explicit about what we were excluding—excluding the personal, really; we intended to sacrifice ourselves, but we didn't succeed. That's when breakaway happened, that's when synergy, the unexpected, occurred. The revolutionaries had reached their limits, whereas the new crowd, the hippies, saw what needed to be done.

At the time I seethed with hatred about what these people were doing to tear down what we had done. Of course, I was wrong. We created so many opportunities to be wrong that we could really get ahead as a result. Our parents' generation was pretty much defined by the limbs they'd gotten out onto, and there they stayed, holding firm to the true faith. My parents were Stalinists—CP, both of them, my father was a section organizer—misused and finally discarded by the apparatus of the local party. What were we who were opposed to the Filthy Speech Movement to do? We were just kids; we got out on a limb and nobody much cared—we didn't have to defend it at all costs, we could try it on and then edge away from it and nobody noticed.[7]

Tom Weller: To me, the FSM's failure to stand up for John Thompson seemed like a betrayal at the time, and that Goldberg was the only guy who didn't wimp out.

As many people have pointed out, a schism was developing right about then between the conventional radicals and the "cultural revolutionaries"—those who thought that sex, drugs and rock 'n' roll would save the world. I was being strongly drawn in the latter direction, and so the "filthy speech" issue—as it seemed to represent personal freedom of behavior, sex, mores, etc.—seemed like the next progressive step.[8]

Jack Weinberg: My position on the obscenity issue was that while it was still going on I wanted it to stop. I tried to stop it. After it happened, my position was that this was a question of constitutional speech, and I made a speech to the Executive Committee to that effect. We fought for free speech, we didn't fight for *responsible* free speech. Therefore the same principle was at stake here.[9]

On Thursday, March 4, Letters and Science freshman David Bills was arrested as he sat beneath a sign advertising the Fuck Defense Fund.

NICHOLAS ZVEGINTZOV

GCC CAMPAIGN FLYER.

Oakland City College student Stephen Argent took his place and was immediately arrested. As officers led Argent and Bills into the basement of Sproul Hall, Michael Klein, a senior in engineering, followed. Once inside, Klein opened a copy of *Lady Chatterley's Lover*, which the courts had recently declared to be not obscene, and read from a paragraph concerning copulation. After reading the paragraph aloud twice, he too was arrested. As he was reading, Ed Rosenfeld held up a sign saying, "Support the fuck cause." He was arrested.

John Thompson: I spent Thursday in a dither. I had to address a rally, and worst of all, I had to make up the speech myself. I sweated, I wandered the streets in a daze. I couldn't think, or eat, and in fact, I was crapping my pants from nervousness. Finally I ran into a woman I knew named Jan. We spent the day together, and later she took me to her mother's house. Jan's mom, like most of the old-time lefties, was pissed at me, but she was a good sport. I told her I had to give a speech at the FDF rally the next day and she asked what I was going to say. I told her I had no idea. She said, "Well, they'll be expecting you to say fuck a whole lot, and you may get arrested again, so what you should say is everything but fuck. Say fornicate, say fooling around, say foreplay, or use all the euphemisms people use for fucking, that way you can make your point and point out how ridiculous the whole thing is." I saw the light. (Do I sound like I was easily impressionable? Eager to please? Spineless? Yes to all of the above.) With the premise of "saying while not saying" the f-word in mind, I wrote a brief speech and sweated out the rest of the night.

Noon Friday. There was a different rally scheduled for Sproul steps, and when Art Goldberg couldn't get them to give up their time, we had the FDF rally on the steps of the Student Union building. We had a large crowd, peppered with professors, plainclothes cops, uniformed police, FBI, newspaper people, TV stations, a stringer from *Time* magazine named Jann Wenner, etc. I gave my speech, using all the non-words and "clean" f-words. In addition, whenever I said a word starting with "f," I drew out the sound as though I just might say "fuck," but never actually said it. So in my speech I titillated the crowd with "ffffffffffflower," and "fffffffig," and the like, to its intense amusement and the growing disgust of the cops. My hands were shaking so badly that I could hardly read what I'd written. Dan Rosenthal announced that he had ordered one thousand "Fuck Communism" signs, and called for a test of law to "decide just where it [obscenity] becomes a public outrage."

More speeches followed, then we passed the hat to collect money. The rest of the day passed in a blur.

A table marked "Fuck Defense Fund" was set up and Oxford University business school graduate Nick Zvegintzov led the cheer,
"Give me an F!"
"F!"
"Give me a U!"
"U!"
"Give me a C!"
"C!"
"Give me a K!"
"K!"
"What does it spell?"
"FUCK!"
"What does it spell?"
"FUCK!"
Jim Prickett, another speaker at this rally, pointed to America's simmering involvement in Vietnam: "*That's* the obscenity!" Proto–hippie and campus oddball "Charlie Brown" Artman presented the laughing crowd with an analysis of obscenity:

The word [*fuck*] comes from Gaelic, where it meant "to sow in the ground," and it was, a few hundred years ago, a respectable word, and a respectable descriptive term for the sexual act. Since that time, it has been made into a dirty word that strikes fear (be it ever so subconscious) into the hearts of people that hear it.*

Pace Charlie: Paul Beale points out in the eighth edition of *A Dictionary of Slang and Unconventional English* (New York: Mac- millan, 1984) that in the seventh edition Eric Partridge "suggested that [the word *fuck*] is almost certainly cognate with the

The question is: is language generally considered to be obscene, obscene when it is not used in an obscene way? Corollary to this is the question: is language not generally considered to be obscene, not obscene if it is used in a suggestive way? "Pussy" is generally thought to be a nice clean word denoting a soft, warm, cuddly cat. It is known to most males to also denote sex with a female. When a candidate for the Ugly Man contest chooses to call himself "Pussy Galore" and proceeds to have buttons saying "I Like Pussy" hawked with cries of "Get your 'I Like Pussy' buttons here," is not this the height of obscenity, of hypocrisy, of filth and deceit?* What is considered obscene today, in another time and place may be considered pure and sacred. Exposing the female body in a bikini would have been considered obscene years ago.[10]

English department chairman Mark Schorer, who had written the introduction to the Grove Press edition of *Lady Chatterley's Lover*, felt a compulsion to explain to the students the difference between serious literature and a Bronx cheer:

> . . . if this language appears in a book, one can choose to read it or not to read it. This seems to me quite different from having that language or a single word from that language thrust upon one's attention in a public place. I do think that the whole business is unworthy of serious students and that it is going to make it more difficult for the faculty to protect what *are* your serious interests than would otherwise be the case. . . . I insist that there is a difference between reading and social conduct. One is a matter of private edification or indulgence; the other can easily become a public nuisance. There is a crucial difference between choosing to read what may be distasteful to others and imposing what is distasteful *on* others.[11]

Latin v. *pungere* and n. *pugil*, both ex a radical meaning 'to strike'; semantically, therefore, *fuck* links with **prick** . . . Transitive synonyms, many of them S. E. [Standard English], occur in Shakespeare (9), Fletcher (7), Urquhart (4), etc., etc.; intransitive in Urquhart (12), D'Urfey and Burns (6), Shakespeare (5), etc., etc." The *OED* (1987) does not agree that *fuck* was ever a respectable word or a respectable descriptive term for the sexual act, and it is possible that the word has always been more or less taboo.

*The "Ugly Man and Miss Beauty" contest was the lead-up to a big fraternity and sorority "Beauty and the Beast Ball." The Alpha Epsilon Pi candidate, Mark Hines, called himself "Pussy Galore," which referred to a character in the movie *Goldfinger*, one of the popular James Bond series of films. The *Daily Cal*, for reasons that transcended its casual orthography, insisted throughout on printing "Pussey Galore."

In fact, the "rally" that had refused to give up Sproul steps to the FDF crowd on March 5 was the final judging of the "Miss Beauty" contest, sponsored by Alpha Phi Omega—the judging was proceeding about a hundred feet away as Charlie spoke.

The crowd applauded Schorer and booed a speaker who tried to counter his argument. Despite the relative purity of the FDF speeches, pre-law senior Mark Van Loucks signed a police complaint against Thompson, Goldberg, James Prickett and Charles "Charlie Brown" Artman.

CHARLES "CHARLIE BROWN" ARTMAN.
PHOTOGRAPHER UNKNOWN.

John Thompson: Friday evening. I was back at the Goodman/Mosgofian residence. Denis and Brenda had gone off to dinner somewhere. At around 9:00 PM there was a knock on the door. I opened it to find a couple of peace officers—one city of Berkeley, one University. They asked if John Thompson was home, and like a dunce I said: "That's me."

"You're under arrest for public indecency," one of them said, and they cuffed me and drove me to Santa Rita Prison. They'd purposely waited until the Berkeley city jail was closed so that anyone who wanted to bail me out would have to make the long drive to Pleasanton. On the drive out the cops asked me questions, and I gave them the most outrageous answers I could think of. I said I was a secret agent of Peking, a visitor from another planet, an antiporn activist, etc. One of the cops later testified at my trial, adding to my already fantastic fabrications. I couldn't believe anyone would believe a word I said, but the cop was deadly serious, especially about my "admission" of being a Communist agent.

After I was booked, I spent the night in a holding tank with a couple of guys who'd gotten busted for driving under the influence and a biker who'd gotten busted swiping a TV set from his ex-girlfriend's apartment. Denis bailed me out the next morning and drove me back to Berkeley.

Art Goldberg was arrested twice that Friday, first at 2:00 PM on a complaint against what he had said on Thursday in connection with the

495

FOR THE CAUSE . . . Dennis Mosgovian solicits defense money for the non-student arrested Wednesday for allegedly "outraging public decency."

DENIS MOSGOFIAN AND MONA HUTCHIN. DAILY CAL PHOTO, MARCH 5, 1965.

spin-off arrests, from which he was released on $50 bail, and then again four hours later on Van Loucks' complaint against what he had said at the Friday rally. This time he was carted off to Santa Rita and held until 10:00 PM on $220 bail.

Another Cal student, Martin McCrea, swore out a complaint with the district attorney against Alpha Epsilon Pi, the fraternity selling, apparently with the administration's blessing, the "I Like Pussy" buttons to support their candidate in the "Ugly Man contest." "I'm not a Puritan," said McCrea, "I just feel the law should be applied equally to all groups."[12]

Arthur Ross, professor of business administration and chairman of the Emergency Executive Committee of the Academic Senate, said, "The faculty has done all it can to protect speakers, no matter what kind of jugheads they might be." He added that "obscene terms used for their own sake are not speech" and are not protected by the First Amendment.[13]

The activist challenge then shifted to another front. Jackie Goldberg, Rich and Sue Currier, Andy Magid, Sandor Fuchs, Alice Huberman, Steve DeCanio and Jim Prickett had together begun publishing a fortnightly magazine. Since there were eight editors, and a spider has eight legs, they decided to call it *Spider*, and the *ex post facto* title was a strained acronym for Sex, Politics, International Communism, Drugs, Extremism and Rock 'n' Roll.* It was printed by Deward Hastings on the Multi

*The "extremism" here referred to is a mocking parody of a campaign phrase used by United States Republican presidential candidate Barry Goldwater, considered a supreme example of a right-wing bad-guy by all members of the left: "Let me remind you that extremism in the defense of liberty is no vice. Let me fur-

496

2066 that had in bygone days printed *Root and Branch*. The first issue appeared on campus on March 1, 1965, and enjoyed modest sales—at two bits a copy—at tables set up at the edge of campus. That morning's *Daily Cal* gave it a short, pleasant, page nine review:

> Sex, Politics, International Communism, Drugs, Extremism and Rock and Roll are combined in "Spider," a magazine making its first appearance today.
>
> The sex figures in three prominent ways. There are dirty words in almost all the articles; there is a fascinating collage of sex ads from a girlie magazine, and there is a review of commercial sex films.
>
> To treat Adults Only films as if they were perfectly legitimate is an interesting idea, and seems perfectly valid. The criterion of excellence merely shifts to the quantity and quality of skin shown. I hope Richard Currier's "Saturday Night at the Nudies" will be a regular feature.[14]

Although the administration conceded that the magazine might not be legally obscene, on March 19 it was banned from sale or distribution on the campus.

Dean McConnell: I may say that, once the vice-president came in and said, "Have you read the literary magazine?" And I said, "No, I have not found that rewarding. I have not read it." He said, "I think you ought to read the current number." I said, "Why do you think so?" He said, "It's just been banned from the mails by the Postal Authorities." (*Laughter.*)[15]

Jackie Goldberg: When it hit the stands we saw all kinds of people—a couple of them we recognized from the D.A.'s office in Alameda County, reporters were buying them. The first copy of *Spider* was read by the Regents at their meeting; right after we heard this, about three days before the second issue was to come out, Rich Currier went up to Dean Williams' office and said, "Dean Williams, we heard that the Regents read this, does this mean that we can't sell it?" And Dean Williams told Rich that we would be informed *by letter* if there was to be any

ther remind you that moderation in the pursuit of justice is no virtue" (acceptance speech for the Republican presidential nomination, 16 July 1964). The phrase echoes Thomas Paine's "A thing moderately good is not so good as it ought to be. Moderation in temper is always a virtue; but moderation in principle is always a vice" (*Rights of Man*, part 1, 1792). Why we did not use these very phrases ourselves beats me all hollow. Perhaps it was because the territory had already been staked out. Mona Hutchin habitually wore a button that said, "I Am a Right-Wing Extremist," but then she could get away with it.

● MULTIVERSITY LOST
● THE ISSUE IS LAW AND ORDER
● INTERVIEW WITH KENNETH ANGER

SPIDER, VOL. I NO. III, APRIL 15, 1965.

discussion as to the suitability of the magazine, or whether it could be sold on campus, and that we didn't have to worry about anything happening in the way of a direct confrontation and so on.

So, the second issue comes out, and the next thing we know is that Dean Williams is down there telling us we have to quit selling. This happened early in the morning after we had moved our table onto the middle of campus. He threatened us with immediate suspension. At that moment, he had the power to suspend us *on the spot.*

He said, "The chancellor has called me and told me that you are not to be here. You're not to sell the magazine. I have to do this. If you don't leave, I can take disciplinary action against you, including the arrest of members of your group that are not students."

So, at that point, we asked if we could negotiate. At first it was just Sue Currier and I that went up to his office, where we explained that we had no desire to make this a confrontation, that we were under the understanding that anything would come by letter, and he apologized profusely that it wasn't being done this way, that he had direct instructions from the chancellor's office.

"Could we see the chancellor?" was our question.

He was very embarrassed, completely embarrassed by the whole situation. So he said, "I'll see what I can do about getting you in with the chancellor," would we please stop selling, and we told him that we wouldn't stop selling until we knew we were going to see the chancellor. So he said, "I'm not going to take any action against you until I can find out for you."

So we went out, and we continued selling. He called for us to come back in again. This time Rich came with us. Now there were three of us. Williams amiably, slowly, talked with us for most of the rest of the day, 'til around four o'clock. The same thing, getting to see the chancellor, following proper channels—it was very obvious that Williams was stalling for time, for us, so he wouldn't suspend anybody or arrest anybody. It was very, very obvious. We repeated the same conversation eighteen million times, and he didn't seem to get nervous or tired talking about it. He kept pleading with us to go home, we could see the chancellor that night, and "Don't make me do something I don't want to do, don't make it difficult for me." He knew that we weren't going to back down completely. Finally he invited the entire *Spider* staff in.

SPIDER, VOL. I NO. IV, MAY 3, 1965.

Mario comes flaming up, he's just gotta be in there; he was violently arguing with us that we didn't know what we were doing and that we were going to be hoodwinked. It was very insulting for him to assume that we didn't know how to handle things on our magazine. We let him in for a while and then we asked him to leave.

We talked. Van Houten and one of the administration lawyers were in there, and it's four-thirty, which is the time we usually took our table down anyway. He set up a meeting with the chancellor that evening, and Williams says, "Will you take the table down now?" Knowing full well that we were. And we said "Sure," and we went home. And nothing happened.

I blew my stack in the middle of the meeting with Meyerson. Meyerson's whole tone, his whole approach, was that we were eight kids trying to make trouble, to destroy the name of Cal. There wasn't even the slightest thought in his mind that the eight of us honestly wanted to put out a magazine of this type. We'd planned it for a semester and a half, we'd finally put in all the work and time, spent our own money financing the first issues, and this was beyond the farthest reaches of his thinking. We were just troublemakers.

After my tirade they wanted to caucus. Art and Mario wanted a con-

SPIDER SALESMAN AT BANCROFT AND TELEGRAPH. PHOTO BY DON KECHLEY.

frontation, but we thought that with the Graduate Student Union trying to get onto the ballot, that if we wanted a war it would be much better to go to war over an issue like that than *Spider* magazine.*

The student government was absolutely the most important thing in our meeting. We could not see the administration allowing the graduates in the ASUC, it would be too risky for them, because SLATE just wins every time the graduate students vote. That's why the graduate students were kicked out originally. We figured a confrontation on that was due any day, and that we would be taking the steam out of it by having a mock war just a few days before.

So we decided to play games. We pinpointed Meyerson to say that he was not objecting to content, but on our time of sale, our place of sale and our manner of sale. He'd agreed that content could not be regulated. We made him state that. So we got the thing into the special faculty committee that had been set up for exactly this sort of thing. We could very easily go to any committee and be clean on that, because we were selling the magazine in the same time, place and manner as the *Pelican* or any other magazine that was being sold.

He said, "The whole last semester was the students testing power,

*On March 1, 1965, undergraduates had voted 3,345–1,293 in favor of a constitutional amendment to restore ASUC membership to graduates. On March 25, the Regents voted unanimously to nullify the undergraduate vote. On April 5 and 6, a "Freedom Graduate Poll" sponsored by the GCC drew some 7,300 votes. A Student Judicial Committee overturned the results on April 8. On April 22 the Regents rescinded their ruling, and on the twenty-eighth the ASUC voted that graduates could immediately become members upon payment of a $3.25 fee. By April 29, only eleven grads had taken advantage of the offer. In student elections held on May 9, 1965, SLATE lost its ASUC majority.

and now I'm testing mine." We told him we weren't going to let him do that. We told him that it could go before a committee on the time, place and manner rules or he could look for *exactly* what he wanted to avoid—a confrontation. At which time, it went to the committee, which sold us out. It agreed with us, but still voted to support the chancellor. So we told Williams over that weekend that after the weekend we were going to sell the magazine anyway. Williams told the committee, and that committee lifted the ban before we sold the magazine the next time.

The main tactic we used with Dean Williams to help get him out of his spot was that we wanted to find some kind of a way to make a test case. It took him hours to find out what we meant by that. It meant nothing, really. They brought in lawyers to try and figure out how they would use the courts and how it had to go through which committees. That's what took most of the time. Williams called us after it was all over, and told us that it really meant an awful lot to him that it was resolved the way it was, and he was very grateful and respected us very greatly, and hoped that the magazine was very successful. I got the impression from him that if this had blown up in his face that he would not have been the next dean of students.* We kind of kept that in mind, too.[16]

During the *Spider* hoopla, Richard Schmorleitz, a senior in political science, wrote a play which he called a "satirical allegory on the use of language," entitled,

> *For*
> *Unlawful*
> *Carnal*
> *Knowledge*

—which went on sale on campus on Wednesday, March 12, 1965. This publication was banned on the ground that the arrangement of the title on the cover was obscene.

Esquire magazine did an article on *Spider* that catapulted the modest student publication into the public eye and did miracles for sales: the "fuck" edition sold ten thousand copies. After lengthy, absurd hearings, the administration then lifted the ban against *Spider* while continuing to ban the play. The whole confrontation made the administration look clumsy and foolish, and reinforced the idea that the principle of free speech required that the University not engage in censorship.

---

*Dean Katherine Towle retired on June 30, 1965, and Arleigh Williams was appointed Acting Dean of Students effective July 1.

SPIDER TABLE ON CAMPUS. PHOTO BY HOWARD HARAWITZ.

John Thompson: For the next month I hung around with the Filthy Seven, as we jokingly called ourselves, and made plans for the trial.* Michael Klein knew Kenneth Anger, the avant garde film maker, and Anger gave us his films for a benefit showing. Several of them had been declared obscene, but we weren't busted again. Art Goldberg somehow arranged a lawyer for us, but I said something in our first meeting that pissed the guy off, and he quit. Eventually we were represented by several lawyers, under the direction of future Oakland supervisor John George. We were tried in the Berkeley courthouse on Grove Street, Judge Floyd Talbot presiding. Stephen Argent, one of the Filthy Seven, lived nearby on Berkeley Way, and every morning we met at his house to smoke pot before going to the morning's session. We ate, or smoked, lunch at Stephen's too. We waived a jury trial, and endured the lying of the police and witnesses. For example my above-mentioned "confession" of being a foreign agent and the curious testimony of many frat boys and police who swore I said, "Fuck, fuck, fuck, fuck, fuck, fuck, fuck," etc., for the entire time on the mike. The police, by the way, had taped the whole rally, but my "speech" had mysteriously vanished from the tape, so the hearsay of the fraternity boys and police led to my conviction. As far as I know, I didn't do any time for the sign, which I *did* hold up, only for the speech I *didn't* give. At the trial we pretty much played it for laughs, figuring that the Supreme Court would overturn our expected conviction. They refused to hear our appeal, however, and a year later I spent thirty days in Greystone, the maximum security section of the Santa Rita "Rehabilitation" Center, where I got plenty to write about.

The obscenity trial itself turned into a farce. Deputy district attorney David Anderson, asking mathematics student Victoria DeGoff to testify to the meaning of "the word" in question got the reply, "Sexual intercourse."

"You do not find this offensive?"

"No."

Anderson was visibly nonplussed at this response.

In pronouncing his decision, Talbot said that John was "basically decent, but had the bad habit of being in the wrong place at the wrong time." John Thompson and Art Goldberg were the last people in America to serve time for an obscenity conviction.†

*Ten people were actually involved, of whom nine had been arrested.

†On June 9, 1990, E-C Records owner Charles Freeman was arrested for selling the album *As Nasty As They Wanna Be*, by the Miami-based rap group 2 Live Crew. The sale was to an adult undercover officer of the Dade County Sheriff's Department.

ROGER HEYNS

DAILY CAL PHOTO.

Acting on the recommendation of the Ad Hoc Faculty Committee on Obscenity, on April 22, 1965, Meyerson suspended three students and expelled one.

David Bills was suspended and convicted for sitting at a table on campus while holding a sign with the four-letter word on it.

Charles Artman was convicted of speaking obscene words at the March 5 campus rally.

Jim Prickett, who was a student at San Francisco State, nonetheless received a notice of expulsion from UC. When it was cheerfully brought to the attention of the authorities that he wasn't a student and that their punishment had no teeth, they ludicrously replied that since he wasn't a student, he couldn't *become* a student. He was convicted of speaking obscene words at the March 5 campus rally.

Michael Klein was suspended and convicted of speaking obscene words at a rally and reading aloud parts of *Lady Chatterley's Lover* in the Sproul Hall police station.

Ed Rosenfeld was convicted for exhibiting an obscene sign.

Dan Rosenthal was convicted of speaking obscene words at a rally.

Stephen Argent was convicted of exhibiting an obscene sign.

The group's label, Skywalker Records, had voluntarily placed the words, "Warning: Explicit Language Contained," on each album. Sales of the record were banned on the seventh of June by U.S. District Court Judge Jose Gonzalez, who said that the music "is an appeal to 'dirty' thoughts and the loins, not to the intellect and the mind." To that date, the album had sold 1.7 million copies nationwide. On October 3, 1990, an all-white jury found Freeman guilty of one count of selling obscene materials. It was the first conviction in the United States for selling an obscene musical work. Freeman did not do any time.

Nick Zvegintzov, who had led the F-U-C-K cheer, was brought before the disciplinary committee, and after the charges against him had been presented he stood and requested time for a rebuttal. The hearing officer told him that this was not a court of law and that he didn't get a rebuttal. He was suspended until the following semester, and although there was no direct evidence of official interference, the large grant that had enabled him to work in computer research disappeared. Shortly after this Nick received an offer from Carnegie-Mellon, quit UC in disgust and left Berkeley. Alone among those involved, Nick was not prosecuted at law.

Education grad Art Goldberg was expelled from Cal and given ninety days in jail.

John Thompson, convicted of displaying an obscene sign and of speaking obscene words at the March 5 rally, was given thirty days in jail. He was arrested twice later in that year, for shoplifting and for posting signs on telephone poles.*

One week after Thompson's arrest, the brouhaha led UC President Clark Kerr and Acting Chancellor Martin Meyerson to resign. Governor Brown, after lengthy talks with Kerr, announced, "I think it is a terrible shame that a few thoughtless troublemakers can hurt the reputation of the greatest University in the world and cause this brilliant president and hard-working chancellor to resign."[17]

Both Brown and the faculty wanted Kerr and Meyerson to rescind their resignations, and after a stormy meeting the Academic Senate passed a resolution to that effect. They both came back, but Meyerson was soon to be out in the street; his inability to handle the filthy-speech crisis had destroyed his chances of being named chancellor. Investigations by the *Daily Californian* revealed that the Regents had pressured Kerr to expel the Filthy Speech Movement leaders, and that both Kerr and Meyerson had refused to do so and had resigned in protest. Despite this, Meyerson expelled Art Goldberg on April 22. On July 1, Meyerson was replaced by the University of Michigan's vice president for academic affairs, Roger W. Heyns. Speaking for the new broom, on Friday, September 5, 1965, Acting Chancellor Earl F. Cheit issued new campus speech and organization rules, to which absolutely nobody paid the slightest attention.

---

*The shoplifting arrest was at the Telegraph Avenue Park and Shop on May 18, 1965. John Thompson and David Bills were arrested July 19, 1965, for posting signs illegally on a city street light. The posters were for a showing of the films of Kenneth Anger. Thompson and Bills were released on $22 bail each.

—Photo by Joe Marshall

EYES FRONT . . . Sedate beauty Carol Doda of "topless" fame and four companions ponder their decisions as they judge the Senior Sweetheart contest in Pauley Ballroom. The judges are l. to r. ASUC President-Eelect Jerry Goldstein, Louis Rice of the dean of students office, Miss Doda, Daily Californian Editor Justin Roberts, and clothing store owner Andre Godet.

CAROL DODA AND VARIOUS LUMINARIES. DAILY CAL PHOTO BY JOE MARSHALL.

Jackie Goldberg: Right after Art got thrown out of school I was invited to be Kerr and Meyerson's hostess at the seniors' ball. I didn't understand why they'd asked me, and when I went to see the administrator who'd done the actual inviting, he talked laughingly about the "Jackie Goldberg" who'd been so active in the Free Speech Movement, and wasn't it a shame. I told him that it was me, and he looked astonished—how could I be that person? They were very confused when they found out who they'd really asked.

I'd been waiting for them to ask me once more, and I wrote them this letter explaining to them that I felt that it was very insulting for them to think that I would want to represent them, at *any* function, after the despicable way that they allowed the events of this last year to occur, as well as being a party to them, and especially that I could be party in a representational way to a person who had expelled my brother.[18]

Announcing that "offenders must be disciplined and due process must have its place," Kerr decried the "continuing and destructive degradation of freedom into license," and the offenders were convicted and punished. But the long and the short of it was that somehow in this chaotic process the weight of rules and laws against "that word," which even in scholarly compendia of slang was written "f**k," and was not included at all in the *Oxford English Dictionary*, had crumbled away, and we were in the dawn of a new day, where you could say "fuck" if you wanted to—in print, on a sign, out loud or in a public speech. It was OK now.

Arrested in North Beach on April 22, 1965, for indecent exposure, the silicone pioneer Carol Doda not only saw the charges against her dismissed, but on May 19, 1965, was invited to help judge the Senior Sweetheart contest in Pauley Ballroom. Surrounding her, wearing what can only be called "shit-eating grins," were ASUC president-elect Jerry Goldstein, Louis Rice of the dean of students' office and *Daily Cal* editor Justin Roberts. Doda was definitely there in an official capacity, and her criminal record didn't seem to bother anyone.

But the hurrahing was not entirely over. On August 20, 1966, I attended a performance of Michael McClure's *The Beard*, which I found incomprehensible and dull. What was exciting was the Berkeley police busting McClure and the two actors, Richard Bright and Billie Dixon, right afterward for obscenity. The court dismissed the charges, and that may have been the last gasp of our local language guardians, at least for a while.

It was at about this time that I began to hear the term "Berserkeley" applied to our fair city. The hippie phenomenon, too, was getting off the ground, with its counterculture ideals and espousal of a muddled "back to nature" aesthetic.* I, for one, openly despised all

*The first notice of the hippies' birth was on September 6, 1965, in a *San Francisco Examiner* article about the Haight-Ashbury area of San Francisco. A NEW PARADISE FOR BEATNIKS was the headline. Reporter Michael Fallon coined a twist on the old term "hipster" to describe them.

HERE? . . . Carol Doda, North Beach's sensational topless swimmer, will make her campus debut Tuesday as one of the judges in the annual Senior Sweetheart Contest.

CAROL DODA. DAILY CAL PHOTO, MAY 14, 1965.

that "peace, love and good vibes" shit, and thought hippies were obnoxious wimps. The consequences of revolution are not always pleasing to the revolutionaries.

Except in the significant area of recreational and psychoactive drugs, by the mid-1970s the state had largely abandoned its role as protector of the public mores.

Government bears the same relationship to its citizens that a shepherd bears to his sheep: in return for sustenance and protection, the sheep are shorn of their wool and upon occasion eaten. Government is the natural enemy of freedom. The Constitution, and in particular, the first ten amendments to it, are the protection of the people against their government, making the relationship between the shepherd and the sheep a little less unequal. However, these protections are themselves guaranteed by nothing but the constant vigilance and struggle of the people themselves against their own government.

I believe that the First Amendment is absolute and indivisible; that despite two hundred years of legislative temporizing, it means exactly what it says; and that the distinctions among various forms of speech are false. The notion that political speech is protected by the First Amendment but obscene speech falls outside its limits, or that there exists some valid distinction between private and commercial speech, is a pernicious legalism that should be destroyed. It is designed not so much to protect us from ourselves, as to weaken us so that the government will be stronger and better able to exploit us at its leisure.

The First Amendment is designed to protect political speech.

All forms of speech become political when they are restricted or forbidden.

Therefore, all forms of speech are protected by the First Amendment.

A BODY IN MOTION TENDS TO REMAIN IN MOTION

W<small>E WERE SO SCARED</small> of offending each other with our roles so un-defined that each kept bowing to the other in an utterly foolish sort of dance. He had never sat at a table with a white woman, and since that situation is within the heart of the mess of the South, it was not some-thing done easily. I had been trying to talk with him for weeks without success and now realized that in some extraordinary paradox he would never think of us as equal until I ordered him to. I begged him to sit down; he wouldn't; I *told* him to sit down. He did, in great confusion. Somehow or other, everything was all right after that.

We could have stayed at home and gone to the beach. . . . Few northern Negroes even came. We came. Don't we earn some recogni-tion, if not praise?
—Sally Belfrage, white Student Non-violent Coordinating Committee volunteer, Summer 1964

By January 1965, the FSM had come full circle, and its activists merged imperceptibly with the revived civil rights movement. Jack and I bor-rowed his girlfriend Phoebe's piece-of-junk, fugitive-from-the-scrap-yard, two-tone car and drove to Los Angeles in the rain to be present at a statewide Congress of Racial Equality convention. It was heavy-duty politics. Bill Bradley of San Francisco CORE introduced a motion to re-strict the rights of campus-based CORE chapters—a move aimed at the Berkeley Campus CORE group. It was part of a new development to-ward nationalism in CORE (which we didn't understand at the time) and it was all mixed up with some controversy over the handling of a state-wide CORE campaign aimed at Bank of America.

Our group attended in force. We were gearing up for the Jack Lon-don Square demonstrations and getting ready to jump back into civil rights activism with all four feet. We arrived with typewriters and mimeo machines and immediately set up a working office at the con-vention site. We impressed everyone with our level of organization and

MARCHING . . . Three hundred fifty persons marched to Oakland yesterday after a sympathy rally. The ranks of marchers swelled as the group neared Oakland and observers claimed nearly 1000 persons were in the final group. Another picture is on page 3.

CONGRESS OF RACIAL EQUALITY MARCH FROM BERKELEY TO OAKLAND.
DAILY CAL PHOTO, MARCH 10, 1965.

chutzpa and we won on our issue of representation for campus chapters. We also played a large role in the proceedings of the convention. As a result, the major statewide leaders of CORE hated us from then on.

Jack and I stayed with some L.A. CORE girls who were neither impressed by our credentials as genuine radicals and purple-heart demonstrators nor bowled over by our personal charms. They were nice enough to us, but did not put out.

That winter I became heavily involved in civil rights marches, demonstrations and picketing. After getting arrested at Sproul Hall, I went on to get arrested about once a week for a period of time. I rang up fourteen arrests, all told, if you count the times I was picked up for no particular reason and cut loose again without being charged. Without missing a beat, I went from tending to my own affairs to tending just about anybody's. After participating in the FSM, the civil rights movement, the anti–Vietnam War movement and the farmworkers' movement, I at last realized that there are two kinds of fights: there's fighting your own fight and there's fighting somebody else's fight. And fighting somebody else's fight is a bad idea. He has to fight for himself, or it doesn't count, and it will have to be done all over again sometime.

In 1854, a conference of Negroes declared: "It is emphatically our battle; no one else can fight it for us. . . . Our relations to the Anti-Slavery movement must be and are changed. Instead of depending upon it we must lead it."[1] In June of 1966 Stokely Carmichael and John Hulett of the Student Non-violent Coordinating Committee created the Black Panther party in Lowndes County, Alabama; right after this, SNCC threw out all the white people. Having had enough of passive resistance, their stated goal was Black Power. Shortly after this I first heard Black people refer to white people as "honkeys." In the same spirit, on July 5, 1967, CORE dropped the word "multiracial" from descriptions of its membership. This made the white civil rights activists real unhappy: "After all we've *done* for them!" Swear to God, I actually heard people say it.

But tough shit, it was the only way to go; if you have an organization in which there are skilled, educated, experienced white kids, bursting with vitamins and enthusiasm, and unskilled, uneducated, inexperienced Black people, who all their lives have feared and deferred to whites, there is a natural tendency to let the people who can do the work well, and who *want* to do the work, do it. So you have a white typist, and a white bookkeeper, and all the skilled office and coordinating jobs get done by the white kids and the Black people *don't learn anything*, except maybe to defer to white kids; the white kids, willy-nilly, gravitate into positions of authority and power and the people for whom all this is, in theory, undertaken don't get any experience doing what they really must learn to do. Took me a while to figure this out.

At any rate, before all this happened we white kids did our level best to assist in the burgeoning civil rights movement. Charity begins at home, and the first object of our attentions was the nation's highest volume restaurant, good old Spenger's Fish Grotto down on Fourth Street. My well-honed skills as a firebrand and song leader fit right in. We cooled Spenger's right smart, and went on to the much tougher nut, the restaurants of Oakland's trying-hard-to-be-snazzy-but-not-quite-making-it Jack London Square. The foot of Broadway soon rang with civil rights songs and the cheery clangor of the Paddy Wagon. These bastions of Oakland's cherished Jim Crow heritage occupied our undivided energies every Friday and Saturday night for months. The harassment cut badly into their trade, and one after the other, they saw that the better part of valor was to cave in and hire a Negro or two in some conspicuous position.

One particularly memorable technique was the use of a sailboat that, piloted by Gene Novak, slowly sailed back and forth under the eyes of the bayside diners, bearing a banner blazoned with the words "Freedom Now." The first evening it was brought into play, I was busted by the Oakland cops for no reason that anybody could figure, and almost as soon as I was bailed out, the charges were dropped.

Jack trusted me to try my fledgling wings as a civil rights organizer, and under his tutelage I devised the bizarre plan of "instant demonstrations." With the FSM phone tree at my disposal, I could get hold of anywhere from a few dozen to a few thousand demonstrators at the drop of a hat, and for a while did just that: an "instant demonstration," though planned, was unannounced; all of a sudden, demonstrators would descend, "like a wolf on the fold," on some luckless bastard whose restaurant or business we had targeted. Whooping and hollering, chanting and singing, waving picket signs and making a tremendous fuss, this civil rights bolt from the blue may or may not have furthered the cause much, but it did serve to confuse and terrify our targets and bothered the sand out of the cops, who never knew which way to jump. Instant picketing was called off by CORE on March 11, 1965, because "the police gave in." This is baloney, of course. The real reason was that if nobody knew when or where the confrontation was going to occur, the newsmen didn't come, the cops didn't come, and nobody paid any real attention.

As with the FSM, the time I spent marching, singing, rallying, hell-raising and getting busted on behalf of our dusky brethren is a complete blur. Where did I live? What did I eat? Whom did I sleep with? I have no clear idea. Fragments of memory, like shards of glass, flashbulbs illuminating a darkened museum, are all I have. Vignettes, snapshots with no dates, pieces of conversation, scraps of paper inscribed with enigmatic notes. Nothing comes together clearly. But I do remember having one hell of a good time.

QUIS CUSTODIET IPSOS CUSTODES?

The FBI BEGAN to take an active interest in me and my affairs. One late afternoon, while I was sleeping my few hours between whatever I'd been doing all night and whatever I was going to start doing all night again, I was awakened by a firm knock on the door. The kind that says, "You don't know me, but I work for a government agency or maybe I'm a bill collector or a process server." Not a timid knock, not the knock of a door-to-door salesman, nor yet the knock of a person handing out religious tracts for the Seventh Day Adventists. The kind of knock that has some beef behind it; maybe a gun. A professional knock. A knock that someone who knocks on a *lot* of doors has learned to make. It was an FBI man, dressed in funeral black.

"David Goines?"

"No, I'm sorry but he's not in. Perhaps I could relay a message?"

"Yes. Here's my card. Ask him to call me, would you?"

I was flattered that they wanted to talk to me, and apprehensive for the same reason. I did not call him.

On March 21, 1987, I wrote the FBI and requested that under the Freedom of Information Act they send me copies of whatever they might have gathered about me and my activities. They dicked around for an astonishingly long time, jumping through hoops of their own devising and sending me incomprehensible progress reports at apparently random intervals. On August 2, 1988, I waited in line at the post office and was rewarded for my pains with a fat packet from the U.S. Department of Justice. One hundred nineteen pages of information had been reviewed, of which eighty-nine were released. A truly amazing percentage of the eighty-nine released pages were blacked out.* The covering

---

As phrased by the poet Juvenal (*Satires* VI.347), "Quis custodiet ipsos custodes?" asks the eternal question, "Who shall guard the guards themselves?"

*I am given to understand that the blacked-out portions either give information about somebody else or compromise the FBI's sources.

document went on to inform me that "during the review of material pertinent to the subject of your request, documents were located that contain information furnished by other government agency(ies)," and that I would be advised by the FBI "as to the releasability of this information following our consultation with the other agency(ies)." The much-delayed material turned out to be four pages of communications from the 115th Military Intelligence Group, U.S. Army. They revealed that David Lance Goines had "stated substantially that he was against our economic system which he believed to be anti-democratic, and had no intention of pledging loyalty to any cause, ideal or group, especially the U.S." Sounds right to me.

This peek into the inner workings of the FBI has done nothing to inspire my confidence in it as anything more than a weary, clumsy, regulation-ridden bureaucracy, trying desperately to follow its own rules, starting at phantoms, convinced that everything had a traceable tie to organized Communism and pitifully grateful for the slightest courtesy.

Of course I had hoped for a dramatic tale of thud and blunder, me figuring largely, consuming vast stores of the government's energies and detailing my every move as of consuming interest to its minions. Well, no such luck. My vanity was not to be catered to this time.

So it seems that the intimidating visit was no more than a weary gumshoe futilely trying to substantiate Malcolm Burnstein's loud public complaint to the United States attorney Cecil Poole that the civil rights of six demonstrators, Mark Comfort, David Friedman, Michael Parker, Cyril Joseph Symmons, Sharon Stern and me, had been violated on February 12, 1965, when we were arrested by the Oakland police during the Jack London Square demonstrations at the Sea Wolf restaurant. Big deal.

Through one of their special agents on campus, the FBI had been aware of me from October 1, 1964, on. But clearly I was no great threat to the national security. They appear to have kept pro forma tabs on me throughout 1965, but after that they probably had to apportion limited manpower to the much graver problems that beset the rest of the decade, and drop the small fry. *Sic transit gloria mundi.**

The event that so concerned Mr. Hoover's myrmidons was actually fairly important to the history of the Bay Area civil rights movement. The FSM had interfered with the momentum of the civil rights move-

---

*"So passes the glory of this world" (Thomas à Kempis [1340–1471], *Imitatio Christi*, chapter 3, section vi).

ment, draining the activists and their energies to its First Amendment cause. After the FSM was over, interest had waned, and it proved difficult to get a good turnout for the picket lines at Oakland's Jack London Square.

One of the earliest of these demonstrations was at the Sea Wolf restaurant. Our February 12 demonstration had only a few picketers (the FBI report says not more than 125), but we made up for our small numbers by singing and hollering at the top of our lungs. The police, helpless in the face of our noisy, obnoxious exercise of First Amendment rights, lashed out with characteristic hasty stupidity and busted Sharon Stern for profanity. I was right behind her in the line and, equally characteristically, got into a shouting match with the arresting cop, who just as promptly arrested me for interfering with an officer in the discharge of his duties. Mike Parker was right behind me, and like dominoes, David Friedman and Cyril Symmons got busted too. One big advantage of Jack London Square, as far as the cops were concerned, was that it was only a few blocks from the jail. This cut two ways, as they were to discover. The demonstration moved, in part, to that location also. Out in front of the jail, Mark Comfort tried the official patience too far—he said, "Damn cops"—and joined us in the clink, charged likewise with profanity, disturbing the peace and interfering with an officer. Hot dog!

As usual, clumsy official zeal had handed us the card we needed, and with Malcolm Burnstein turning this into a full-scale shooting war, succeeding demonstrations revived to their pre-FSM levels and numbered their participants in the hundreds and thousands.

The importance of these civil rights arrests was threefold: First, it gave Campus CORE the much needed boost into the public eye that let us get the Bay Area civil rights movement ball rolling again. Second, it forced the FBI to take active, high-profile cognizance of what Mal characterized, as quoted in my FBI file, as "continual harassment of peaceful pickets on the part of the Police Department,"

at a time when the FBI was particularly sensitive to any allegation that it was neglecting its duties to protect citizens in the exercise of their Constitutional Rights.

One of the reasons that the FBI took quick notice of Mal's complaint was that he made it

in the midst of a demonstration in the lobby of the Federal Building with a crowd of demonstrators, radio, TV and newspapermen surrounding them [Mal Burnstein and United States attorney Cecil Poole]. In view of the delicate nature of the situation because the demonstrations giving rise to this case are continuing on a weekly basis . . . This office feels that if we do not follow through on these allegations it will give these people ammunition to attact [sic] the FBI's handling of civil rights investigations.[1]

Sweet are the uses of adversity.

Third in importance, and not entirely to our liking, was that the Oakland police really cleaned up their act, refusing to be provoked or make any arrests unless substantial, applicable laws were actually broken.

Charges against us for these arrests were dismissed on May 7, 1965.

BOGALUSA

Often, the young face the prospect of death with more courage and acceptance than the old, for they have more vigor to do it with, little empty time to reflect and less of the past to lose.
—Richard Adams, *Maia* (1984)

FRESH FROM OUR triumphs in the Jack London Square civil rights demonstrations, in early July of 1965 Jack Weinberg and I took it into our heads to hitchhike to Bogalusa, Louisiana, to help with the emerging civil rights movement. Later on, this kind of ad hoc response was strongly discouraged, mainly because of the incredible trouble that a person ignorant of the ways of the South and unwilling to submit to strict discipline within the Movement could get himself into. Jack and I did indeed manage to get ourselves into a lot of trouble, without even knowing what kind of trouble we were in. This wasn't the same as the student protests.

Everyone knew that civil rights workers in the South were putting themselves in some danger. A few had already been killed, and there was a good chance that a couple of western white boys would find themselves in an uncomfortable situation if they didn't watch their step. However, I had absolutely no fear and not a lick of sense; the danger was what made it attractive.

The Bogalusa civil rights movement had come right out and proclaimed a policy of armed self-defense, which heated things up a bit beyond what they were elsewhere. We were members of Campus CORE, and Louisiana had fallen to the Congress of Racial Equality's share in the division of territory among the various American civil rights organizations. We were experienced, enthusiastic CORE members who were going to live forever, so we went to help.

There was a serious labor dispute at the Zellerbach paper mill, the town's main employer. Since Zellerbach was a San Francisco–based company, the civil rights movement in the Bay Area saw the presence of the paper factory in Bogalusa as a good pressure point to get some results on a national level. Added to this was a big civil rights campaign by CORE to use the strike as a springboard for campaigns in the toughest nut to crack, the troglodyte state of Louisiana.

It was a union problem as much as a race problem; and it was as much a school desegregation fight as anything else. Into the bargain, the Black union-leadership was challenging the established church leadership, using this particular struggle for a crowbar. Black leaders in the Baptist church had formed the Deacons for Defense and Justice, who had publicly announced that they would give as good as they got. It was a lot of trouble among the local folks who were basically having it out with each other. The whole thing was turning into a giant, terrible, dangerous mess and we blithely tripped into the middle of it, providing in the process a great deal of entertainment for a great many folks. We departed the South having failed to get ourselves killed or even hurt. As it was, the worst thing that happened to me was I caught a head cold from falling asleep on the floor in front of a fan.

On the day we left Berkeley, Jack and I took my cardboard suitcase and filled it with a few changes of socks and underwear, and some emergency tins of sardines and a box of crackers, and hung our thumbs out on University Avenue in midmorning. We took little money, trusting that God would provide, which as usual He did. Hitchhiking is an act of faith anyway, and asking a little bit more is not unreasonable. By evening we had made it to Needles, which was about right, as we wanted to cross the desert by night. Things went fairly well until we got into the red dirt of Flagstaff, Arizona.

It was the Glorious Fourth, and our last ride warned us urgently that we should not put out the thumb within the city limits, or we would find ourselves guests of the state on vagrancy charges. We took the advice to heart, and walked a few miles through the summer heat, jeering cowboys, and wretched Indians staggering and grunting in the last extremities of festive intoxication. At the outskirts of town we met up with a pallid, emaciated boy who told us that he had that very day been cut loose from the county jail, and the only reason we hadn't been arrested was that it was the Fourth of July and the jails had been emptied to make room for all the drunks and brawlers. He had been sentenced to thirty days for hitchhiking, and was released early on the condition that he shake the dust of Arizona from off his feet and not be seen again. He was doing his best to cooperate. We were grateful that providence had led us to make our trip through Flagstaff on this particular day.

The three of us kept company for a short while, but it is more than twice as hard for three men together to get a ride as two, which is hard enough. So we parted ways about twenty miles out of town. Still finding it hard to get a lift, Jack and I split up, with the intention of meeting again in Bogalusa. I was first in line, and soon got a ride from a fellow whom I persuaded to stop and pick up my buddy. One short-hop lift after another led us into the more hospitable, if empty, state of New Mexico.

Standing in the middle of the flat, hot New Mexico desert, with the only sign of human habitation an Indian trading post about a mile away, we got a lift in a pickup with an Indian family, Mom and Pop in the cab with two small babies, and a handful of older kids in the back. We rode with them for about a hundred miles, through a brief pitchforks-and-hammer-handles rainstorm.

At the farther outskirts of Amarillo, Texas, right across the road from a huge arrow stuck in the ground and covered with flashing lights advertising Indian curios, we sat for fourteen hours without a ride. There was nothing else in any direction as far as the eye could see but this big arrow. I grew mighty tired of that arrow after a while. After a night of fruitless effort the sun came up like a brass hammer, and before it was a hand's breadth above the horizon the temperature felt like 90 degrees in the shade, and there wasn't any shade. We finally got a lift from a farmer who was going from town to his place, which was only about five miles down the road, then a short hop with a station wagon full of kids and a father who wanted gas money in return for a lift, but it broke the spell and we got along all right from then on.

Our last ride in Texas was with a kid who had just been mustered out of the army and was going home in his brand-spanking-new, fire-engine-red Ford Fairlane. The road in Texas was four lanes wide, straight as a die and flat as a billiard table. We were doing ninety miles an hour, which is the only way to drive across Texas. It was nighttime and hot; that muggy summer heat that you don't find anywhere but in the South. At two o'clock in the morning we got into Louisiana, and with no warning this magnificent Texas road dropped about four inches and turned into a pig trail, bang! just like that. At that moment, we should have reflected that perhaps Bogalusa, Louisiana, was not where we belonged. We pulled into a gas station, and the kid at the pump told us that we shouldn't be together, us two funny-looking white northern-type guys and this Black kid whose car it was, or we might get into some kind of trouble, he said. So we thanked our ride and Jack and I went to the Shreveport Greyhound station about 3:00 AM feeling strange and scared. Shreveport didn't seem to have much in the way of night life, except for police cruisers. They eyed us and we tried to look innocent, or at least too small-fry to bother with. It's a good thing that we made it through Shreveport, because the mayor and chief of police had just that year constructed a small-scale concentration camp specifically for the anticipated flood of civil rights workers. It curdles my blood to think of it.

The only advantage of Louisiana over Texas was that I could understand Black people when they talked. In Texas they sounded like they had a mouthful of mush, and I couldn't make out a single word. In Louisiana they all made sense again, because the Black population of Oakland is from Louisiana, mostly. The Oakland Negroes were the only Black people I had ever heard, and I thought all Black folks would talk the same way, but I was wrong.

We bought bus tickets to Bogalusa, and when the bus pulled in there at about nine or ten in the morning, the first goddamn thing we did was almost get ourselves killed for real. In deep South towns there were, at that time, two bus stops: there was one place where the colored folks got on and off the bus, and a different place where white folks got on and off the bus. Anybody raised in the South, or who had spent so much as five minutes there, knew this perfectly well. Well, we would never have thought of such a thing, so we got off at the first place the bus stopped, which was the wrong one, thereby announcing to all who cared to see, which was everybody, that we were from Out of The Area, and sufficiently ignorant of the Ways of The South that you could safely bet that we were Outside Agitators, which, of course, we were.

Just where the bus let us off was a grocery with a screen door, the kind that has an advertisement printed on tin set across the door at an angle, to keep people from punching in the screen when they come in or leave. Usually the sign advertises soda pop or chewing tobacco or something that people buy a lot of. This one was for some kind of soft drink that I had never heard of, but I wasn't surprised, as I had seen that southern people drank staggering quantities of soda from dawn to dusk, and of brands that were to be found nowhere else, seemingly. A big bottle of pop was only a dime, too. Soda pop was somewhat exotic where I came from. Here it seemed to be a staple.

We walked into the store's dimness, intending to ask after the whereabouts of the part of town we were looking for, but the proprietor fixed us with his reptilian gaze and scared us off. We figured that he was the wrong sort of person to ask directions of, and we were probably right.

Right across the street was a Bill Up's gas station, so we figured we'd go there instead to ask after the street where Robert Hicks lived. Robert Hicks was the head of CORE in that area and an unpopular fellow with the Klan. We might just as well have asked where the local Congress of Racial Equality headquarters was and been done with it. What we didn't know was that this particular Bill Up's gas station was the headquarters of the Ku Klux Klan in Bogalusa, which was the center of the Klan in

Louisiana, which was the heart of the Klan in the whole damned South. What we didn't know would fill a book. So we went in and asked directions, and they said they didn't know. We thought that was kind of funny, not knowing where a fairly important street was in this small town.

So we went to the phone booth, and called Mike Jones at the CORE headquarters, and he said,

"Where are you?"

"At Bill Up's gas station, right across the street from where the bus let us off."

Well, Mike knew where we were, and just how much trouble we were in, and he told us to sit tight, and not go anywhere, and not get in any car with anybody unless he was in it, too. So in about two shakes, three big cars came roaring down the street and pulled up alongside the phone booth where we were and Mike Jones grabbed us and we all took off without even coming to a complete halt, really. Inside were lots of Black men, and they all had guns. Mike told us where we had been, and we felt that we'd had a narrow escape, but we didn't really understand just how narrow that escape was. We were still just having fun. This ignorance is probably what saved my hide a million times. Anybody who knew what he was doing wouldn't have done the things I did, or if he did would have been so apprehensive and tight that he would have gotten seriously killed.

Here we were in the middle of the dog fight that was the town of Bogalusa. Boy Howdy! The whole town smelled of sulfur, from the paper mill. And it was hot and humid all the time. Every day at two in the afternoon it rained, but the rain didn't cool things off a bit. It was like an alien planet.

In order to drive down the road that led to the Hicks' house, you had to flash your lights in a certain code, or you would, at the least, be buying some new tires; at the worst, you could get bad lead poisoning. Black workmen repairing a roof on that street had guns sticking out of the back pockets of their coveralls.

Jack and I were split up and shared around, as two of the few white people who were willing to have high profiles in those parts. We got together every night at the church, where we were set in the choir, a place of honor. I loved to sing, and even knew many of the songs and learned the rest right quick. Many of these folks had never heard a white person sing, and claimed that I was an asset to the choir and wouldn't I like to stay on. Jack had a voice like a frog, but they liked his singing too, which made me suspect their praises a bit.

One evening after service, a buxom, light-skinned girl of about sixteen shyly asked if I were English. I told her no, I was as American as anybody; maybe more so, since I was about an eighth each of American Indian and Black African with the remaining chunk a real melting-pot slumgullion of English and Irish and Europeans and Chinese and Jews and whoever else had got into each other's britches for the last four-five hundred years around here. Why do you ask? She went on to tell me that the way I talked was so clear and precise that everyone had thought that I must be from England, because nobody had ever heard any talk like that, ever. She asked me to come to her house and have Sunday dinner with her family, and I said I would, but by Sunday we were gone. Probably just as well, as I imagine that her father would not have taken kindly to his pretty daughter being romanced by any not-around-for-long northern boy, no matter if he *was* a member of CORE.

Later that week there was a big march, all through the downtown area, beginning at the Union Hall and circling around to end at the Baptist Church. There were a couple hundred people in the march, and many more than that on the sidelines. The folks on the sidelines were hostile and silent. The marchers were frightened and sang quavery civil rights songs, huddling close together in the rain.

The marchers were almost all Black locals, making the handful of white participants stand out like neon signs. Two toughs jumped among the marchers and beat on a tall, weedy white kid, who fell to the ground in the approved nonviolence protective posture, but got hurt badly anyhow. The bullies ran off, and the cops made no move to pursue them.

Along about the middle of the march, there was a commotion close behind where I was. Someone had thrown a rock into the group of marchers, and a young girl had been struck by it. She was taken to a nearby car for first aid. A hostile man from the sidelines pursued her right into it, seemingly intent on doing her more mischief. Inside the car was an armed member of the Deacons for Defense. The deacon inside the car shot the man in the chest. It made a sound like a firecracker going off. This woke up the police, and the marchers too. The deacon was arrested, but released on bail that same night. The wounded man lived.

We finished up that march much sobered, and the church service was something to remember for the heartfelt singing and passionate oratory, the hoarse, rhythmic preaching flowing seamlessly into the choir's response and back out again. I want to tell you! That music made the hair stand up on the back of my neck. It reached out and grabbed me and shook me and *made* me move, *made* me stand up and yell and holler and lose myself. Before this night, the church music had been good, but this was glorious. What with tinny piano, electric guitar, drums, shouting and "dancing before God," it didn't seem like church music—it was too amazingly good, it took me away. I realized, right there, right then, that music was powerful stuff: this music was *not entertainment*; this music made you *do* things—go out and risk your life, for one.* Contrasted to this elemental force, the popular fluff that I had been confusing with real music was abruptly revealed for what it was, and I kind of lost my taste for it.

The general opinion was that the shooting would surely find some kind of repercussions, so we all were on the alert. There was a fear that somebody who didn't wish us well would try and burn the Union Hall if we didn't watch out for it. In the summer of 1964, twenty southern Negro churches and meeting places had been firebombed; these fears were not groundless. I took a stint at guard duty that night in the Union Hall, and since nobody expected me to defend it with hard words or my fists, I was handed a mean-looking revolver that evidently had seen a lot of use; the butt was wrapped in friction tape, all the bluing was worn off, and the six shiny bullets in the cylinder winked at me in a nasty, seductive way. We spent the night telling stories and drinking coffee with homemade whiskey in it, and along about three o'clock we were relieved by some other folks who would stand guard on the hall until dawn.

Next morning, we were taken to a woman's house for a big outdoor breakfast. Big, friendly Black women standing behind food set out on boards up on trestles. Red-and-white checked tablecloths, big smiles in the bright, muggy morning sunshine. Most of the food was unfamiliar to me, grits and catfish and things that I hadn't ever eaten, but it was good and I was hungry. I asked for my coffee black, which was how I ordinarily drank it, and the woman goggled at me as though I had asked for it to be poured into my naked hands. When I drank it I understood, as it was half chicory and had been boiled to make it stronger. But instead of admitting that it would indeed be better with a pint of hot milk, which is how they all drank theirs, I pretended that I liked it and drank it down. It wound my spring for a week.

The second march was a few days later. Louisiana state troopers had been called up, seemingly every one in the state. Half of them carried

---

*To give you an idea of what kind of music I'm talking about, you should listen to the gospel music of Roebuck Staple and his four children. A good sampling is on the Charley label's *The Staple Singers "Pray On"* compact disk (CD Charley 220). Sam Cooke and the Soul Stirrers' album *In the Beginning* (Ace CDCHD 280) will similarly raise up a dead man.

riot guns and the other half carbines, and they lined both sides of the march, one every three or four feet. They carried the guns in their hands with the barrels pointed in the air.

James Farmer, head of national CORE, came into town to lead the march. He was sweating and scared. Before we set out, we were asked to march quietly and not to sing. I believe that every white person in town was there to watch, and things were mighty tense. As we marched, everything was as silent as a funeral; there wasn't a sound from either side. About halfway along, someone among the spectators set off a firecracker. At the noise, the troopers swung around and pointed their riot guns and carbines at the watching crowd. It was an amazing sight.

After that march, Jack and I were told that we had to get out, as we were more of a liability than a help, and the white folks in the civil rights cause, there in Bogalusa, had become prime targets for the Klan, and it wasn't going to help anybody with anything if we got ourselves killed; so thanks a whole bunch and these guys here are going to get you out of town safely.

Later we learned that we had also become a bone of contention among our hosts, the Hicks family, the local CORE organization and the preacher who was the nominal leader of the Deacons for Defense and Justice. It is possible that we were hustled out for fear that our presence would help the wrong side in a faction fight.

There was also the matter of our FSM trial in Berkeley. A court hearing was coming up that we were supposed to be back for in person. We argued that it wouldn't be necessary—that we could be represented without being there in the body, but our lawyer, Mal Burnstein, said that if we didn't come back, Edwin Meese, the assistant district attorney, would issue an order for our arrest, and you may be sure that the Bogalusa sheriff would lurch around in a red-eyed passion to get at us. And God alone could help us if we landed in a Bogalusa jail.

Since there was no chance in hell that our hosts would hand us over to the authorities, there was some good reason to fear that the whole thing would resolve itself into a pointless shoot-out. So we agreed to leave.

We got a ride with James Farmer's entourage; some of them were FBI men. We went out of there three cars in a row and us in the middle at one hundred miles an hour, with our escorts prepared to shoot at anybody who tried to pass or interfere with us, and we didn't stop or slow down 'til we got to the airport in New Orleans.

First time I ever was in an airplane was flying back to San Francisco courtesy of some Berkeley lawyers who didn't want us to hitchhike home again. I saw America and the Grand Canyon from the air, and from our eagle's vantage, a circular rainbow. As always, I was profoundly relieved to be back in Berkeley again, where things made sense, and I felt safe.

We got back to Berkeley just in time to be sentenced for our FSM arrests.

PEOPLE ARRESTED IN SPROUL HALL
ON
DECEMBER 3, 1964

Some defendants were charged in two counts with violation of Penal Code §§602(o) (trespassing) and 409 (unlawful assembly); most were charged in three counts with violation of Penal Code §§602(o), 409, and 148 (resisting arrest). All were acquitted of violation of Penal Code §409. Thus, those charged in two counts were convicted and punished on one count. With the exception of Mona Hutchin, those charged with three counts were convicted and punished on two counts, and the punishments tabulated here are the total of the two separate punishments. Where no period of probation is indicated, the defendant rejected the conditions of the summary court probation. Juveniles received probation from juvenile court.

Each listing indicates whether the defendant participated in the appeal; the number of counts charged and whether the defendant pleaded *nolo* (no contest) or opted for stipulation or a court trial; and the sentence. Italicized names were considered by the court to be FSM leaders.

This list is compiled from contemporary newspaper reports, court records, the Byrne Report and the official FSM defendants' list, current February 15, 1965. A few names of people were listed as having been arrested in Sproul Hall or having entered pleas in newspaper accounts only (*Oakland Tribune, Berkeley Gazette*), and do not appear elsewhere in the court record. Some people were listed twice or even three times by combinations of first, middle and last names; some garbled names appear along with correctly reported names; some names don't seem to belong to anybody; some belong to real people whom I do not believe were actually arrested; and some names of people whom I am reasonably sure were arrested seem to have been omitted entirely from both newspaper and other official reports. In every version of the defendants' names, spelling variations plague the text.

I would appreciate corrections from participants.

Mark Aaronson: 3 counts, nolo; 1 year probation, $75 fine

Manuel G. Abascal: appeal; 3 counts, trial; 1 year probation, $150 fine, 10 days suspended

Joan Abbey: 3 counts, nolo; 1 year probation, $75 fine

Eileen Adams: appeal; 3 counts, stipulation; 1 year probation, $150 fine, 10 days suspended

Mary Jane Adams: appeal; 3 counts, stipulation; 1 year probation, $150 fine, 10 days suspended

Mary Kathleen Adams: appeal; 3 counts, stipulation; 1 year probation, $150 fine, 10 days suspended

Richard Mark Adelman: 3 counts, stipulation; 1 year probation, $150 fine, 10 days suspended

Margot S. Adler: appeal; 3 counts, trial; 1 year probation, $150 fine, 10 days suspended

Dunbar Aitkins: appeal; 2 counts, stipulation; $150 fine or 15 days in jail

Charlene Akers: appeal; 3 counts, stipulation; $250 fine or 25 days in jail

Mark Huxley Akin: appeal; 3 counts, stipulation; 1 year probation, $50 fine

Richard P. Albers: 3 counts, stipulation; 1 year probation, $150 fine, 10 days suspended

Lynne Alexander: appeal; 3 counts, stipulation; 1 year probation, $150 fine, 10 days suspended

Richard Alexander: appeal; 3 counts, trial; 1 year probation, $150 fine, 10 days suspended

Roberta Alexander: appeal; 3 counts, stipulation; $250 fine or 25 days in jail

Brian Allen: 3 counts, nolo; 1 year probation, $75 fine

Anya Allister: appeal; 3 counts, stipulation; $250 fine or 25 days in jail

Richard D. Ambro: appeal; 2 counts, stipulation; 1 year probation, $50 fine

Louise Ames: 2 counts, nolo; 6 months probation, $25 fine

Ronald Anastasi: appeal; 3 counts, trial; 2 years probation, $200 fine, 30 days suspended

THE SLAMMER

AFTER MUCH uproar and delay, the bringing to justice of the whole eight hundred some-odd who were arrested in Sproul Hall had finally gotten off the ground in early March, 1965. The main disagreements revolved around whether we were to be tried collectively or as individuals. The opening statement was made by the district attorney, J. Frank Coakley, who wanted blood.*

Mario instantly got himself into hot water by making a comment to Judge Crittenden about "shameless hypocrisy" that netted him two days in stony-lonesome for contempt.

The prosecution, headed by Lowell Jensen, wanted for the sake of convenience to try us as a body, and this was vigorously opposed by the FSM leaders as well as by some of the more radical defense lawyers, who naturally wanted to gum everything up as much as possible. This position was not shared by everyone.

Jack Weinberg: Some of our lawyers saw themselves in the role of Officers of the Court. They convinced the other lawyers that it was a violation of ethics to cooperate in an effort to obstruct justice and bring the Alameda County system of criminal justice to a grinding, screeching halt. These lawyers made their living every day within the Alameda County courts and wanted to maintain cozy relations. One lawyer, Stanley Golde (who had been Crittenden's law partner before Crittenden had been called to the bench), stood out as a ringleader. Mal Burnstein, because of his Movement credentials, was given the unpleasant job of fronting for the effort to get the defendants to give up their rights

---

*Both Coakley and the then assistant prosecutor, Edwin Meese III, later disgraced their offices and came in for public censure. Some years after the FSM trial, Coakley was indicted and convicted of fraud and removed from office. Meese, who came from Oakland and had graduated from law school in Berkeley, tumbled from grace and resigned from office in 1987 when, as attorney general under President Reagan, he came under criminal investigation connected with his financial peccadilloes.

Ardeth Anderson: 3 counts, nolo; 1 year probation, $75 fine

Michael Anker: 3 counts, nolo; 1 year probation, $75 fine

Bettina Aptheker: appeal; 3 counts, trial; 45 days in jail

Shirley Ann Arimoto: 3 counts, nolo; 1 year probation, $75 fine

Linda J. Artel: appeal; 3 counts, stipulation; 1 year probation, $150 fine, 10 days suspended

Charles Artman: appeal; 3 counts, stipulation; $250 fine or 25 days in jail

Roger Asay: appeal; 3 counts, stipulation; $250 fine or 25 days in jail

Peter Aschenbrenner: 3 counts, stipulation; 1 year probation, $150 fine, 10 days suspended

Gail Ashkenas: appeal; 3 counts, trial; 1 year probation, $150 fine, 10 days suspended

June Nikki Atkin: appeal; 3 counts, stipulation; 1 year probation, $150 fine, 10 days suspended

Donald O. Auclair: 3 counts, stipulation; $250 fine or 25 days in jail

Robert Avakian: 3 counts, nolo; 1 year probation, $75 fine

Richard Avery: appeal; 2 counts, stipulation; 1 year probation, $50 fine

Nancy Ruth Axelrod: appeal; 3 counts, trial; 1 year probation, $150 fine, 10 days suspended

David Bacon: juvenile

Kenneth Baker: appeal; 3 counts, stipulation; 1 year probation, $150 fine, 10 days suspended

Frank Bancroft: appeal; 2 counts, stipulation; $100 fine or 10 days in jail

Michael Barglow: appeal; 3 counts, trial; 1 year probation, $150 fine, 10 days suspended

Raymond Barglow: 3 counts, nolo; 1 year probation, $75 fine

Dan Barki: appeal; 3 counts, stipulation; 1 year probation, $150 fine, 10 days suspended

Larry Lee Barnes: appeal; 3 counts, stipulation; $250 fine or 25 days in jail

Linda S. Barnes: appeal; 3 counts, trial; 1 year probation, $150 fine, 10 days suspended

Iris Baron: appeal; 3 counts, trial; 1 year probation, $150 fine, 10 days suspended

Richard Baron: 3 counts, stipulation; 1 year probation, $150 fine, 10 days suspended

Kenneth Barter: appeal; 3 counts, stipulation; $250 fine or 25 days in jail

Deborah Bartlett: appeal; 3 counts, stipulation; 1 year probation, $150 fine, 10 days suspended

Carrol J. Baum: 3 counts, nolo; 1 year probation, $75 fine

Dennis E. Bearden: appeal; 3 counts, stipulation; 1 year probation, $150 fine, 10 days suspended

Richard Beasley: appeal; 3 counts, stipulation; 1 year probation, $150 fine, 10 days suspended

Robert Bekes: appeal; 2 counts, stipulation; 1 year probation, $50 fine

Bruce R. Bell: appeal; 3 counts, stipulation; 1 year probation, $150 fine, 10 days suspended

James Allen Berberich: $250 fine or 25 days in jail (newspaper listing only)

Darwin K. Berg: appeal; 3 counts, stipulation; $250 fine or 25 days in jail

Peter Bergman: appeal; 2 counts, stipulation; 1 year probation, $50 fine

Carl Bergren: appeal; 3 counts, trial; 1 year probation, $150 fine, 10 days suspended

Gordon S. Bergsten: appeal; 2 counts, stipulation; 1 year probation, $50 fine

Madelon Berkowitz: appeal; 3 counts, stipulation; 1 year probation, $150 fine

Linda Berris: 2 counts, nolo; 6 months probation

Joann Biasotti: appeal; 3 counts, stipulation; 1 year probation, $150 fine, 10 days suspended

David Bills: appeal; 2 counts, stipulation; 1 year probation, $50 fine

Edward Bingham: appeal; 3 counts, stipulation; 1 year probation, $150 fine, 10 days suspended

John Bishop: appeal; 3 counts, trial; 1 year probation, $150 fine, 10 days suspended

Allen Black: appeal; 3 counts, stipulation; 1 year probation, $150 fine, 10 days suspended

Victoria Blickman: appeal; 3 counts, stipulation; 1 year probation, $150 fine, 10 days suspended

to a jury trial. The tactic was to insist that we were not a group, but that each defendant would have to meet individually with a lawyer and make an individual decision. The lawyers would argue that all but a hard core were waiving a jury trial, and any of the rank-and-file defendants who didn't go along were going to get time in jail. The lawyers talked to the defendants one by one and got the waivers. Those of us who believed in collective activity wanted a meeting of defendants where the issue would be debated and a vote taken. The lawyers did not permit this. I think some of them felt their main duty was to protect the "innocents" from their radical leaders. Radical leaders like me came away feeling that the lawyers' committee and the judge were in cahoots—but we had to go along with the jury waiver so as not to split the defendants.

As a result of the jury waiver, we defendants lost our whole bargaining position. Jury trials for eight hundred are difficult to carry out; a mass show-trial is easy.

Peter Franck had strong feelings that lawyers were not supposed to impose their will on Movement defendants, but that the Movement was supposed to make basic policy and the lawyers were supposed to come up with legal tactics based on this policy. This ideological dispute between Peter Franck and Mal Burnstein resulted in bad blood between them, and they didn't speak for seven years.[1]

It must also be considered that none of the FSM lawyers were getting a red cent for their services. As it stood, Malcolm Burnstein was putting in months of unpaid time while trying to earn some kind of a living on his other cases. The prospect of jury trials, each one of which would have required massive legal activity, perhaps subtly influenced the Movement lawyers to stump for a collective judge trial. This still does not answer the question of why we did not propose a "stalking horse" trial, in which a small number of defendants or even only one would be tried and we would agree to accept that verdict as applying to us all.

Perhaps the reason was that Meese and Jensen gave us to understand that, come what may, the leaders were going to be singled out and given exemplary sentences. This forced us to depart from the usual civil rights tactic of pleading guilty in return for a token punishment and led to a threat on the part of the defense of a demand for eight hundred jury trials, which was countered by the prosecution's threat that if the cases were not consolidated, reactionary Southern California judges would be dragged out of retirement and brought up to Berkeley by the cartload. Basically, with Mal giving no more than lukewarm support for individual trials, the confused defendants dropped the whole idea.

Yet another aspect of the controversy surrounding whether or not we

Elizabeth Blum: appeal; 2 counts, stipulation; 1 year probation, $50 fine

Joseph Blum: appeal; 2 counts, stipulation; $100 fine or 10 days in jail

Kenneth D. Blum: appeal; 3 counts, stipulation; 1 year probation, $150 fine, 10 days suspended

Karen Bolliger: 3 counts, stipulation; 1 year probation, $150 fine, 10 days suspended

John A. Bollinger: appeal; 3 counts, stipulation; 1 year probation, $150 fine, 10 days suspended

John Eric Bond: 2 counts, nolo; 6 months probation

Abraham Bookstein: appeal; 3 counts, stipulation; $250 fine or 25 days in jail

Roberta Boone: 3 counts, stipulation; 1 year probation

Charles Bordin: appeal; 3 counts, stipulation; $250 fine or 25 days in jail

Jacqueline Boris: 3 counts, stipulation; 1 year probation, $150 fine, 10 days suspended

Joseph Botkin: appeal; 3 counts, trial; 1 year probation, $200 fine, 10 days suspended

Thomas J. Bouchard, Jr.: appeal; 3 counts, stipulation; $250 fine or 25 days in jail

Judy Bowman: appeal; 3 counts, stipulation; 1 year probation, $150 fine, 10 days suspended

Thomas Boyden: 2 counts, nolo; 6 months probation, $25 fine

Barbara Bozman: appeal, 3 counts, stipulation; $250 fine or 25 days in jail

Della Bradford: appeal; 3 counts, trial; 1 year probation, $150 fine, 10 days suspended

Ann Bradsher: appeal; 3 counts, stipulation; 1 year probation, $150 fine, 10 days suspended

Victoria Brady: 3 counts, stipulation; 1 year probation, $150 fine, 10 days suspended

David John Brannam: appeal; 3 counts, trial; 1 year probation, $200 fine, 10 days suspended

Barbara Bridges: appeal; 3 counts, stipulation; $250 fine or 25 days in jail

Glenn Brineiro: appeal; 3 counts, stipulation; 1 year probation, $150 fine, 10 days suspended

Bob Brister: appeal; 3 counts, stipulation; 1 year probation, $150 fine, 10 days suspended

Richard Broadhead: appeal; 3 counts, stipulation; $250 fine or 25 days in jail

Joel Brodsky: appeal; 3 counts, trial; $250 fine or 25 days in jail

Anthony Brown: 2 counts, nolo; $50 fine or 5 days in jail

Lana D. Brown: appeal; 3 counts, stipulation; 1 year probation, $150 fine, 10 days suspended

Steven Browne: appeal; 3 counts, stipulation; 1 year probation, $150 fine, 10 days suspended

Jean Brownlee: appeal; 3 counts, stipulation; $250 fine or 25 days in jail

Fred Bruderlin, Jr.: appeal; 3 counts, stipulation; 1 year probation

Jeremy Bruenn: appeal; 3 counts, stipulation; $250 fine or 25 days in jail

Frederic Brunke: appeal; 2 counts, stipulation; 1 year probation, $50 fine

Wendell Brunner: appeal; 3 counts, stipulation; $250 fine or 25 days in jail

James Buschell: 3 counts, nolo; 1 year probation, $75 fine

Alan Butler: appeal; 3 counts, trial; $250 fine or 25 days in jail

Marilyn Buttrey: appeal; 2 counts, stipulation; 1 year probation, $50 fine

Richard Byers: 3 counts, trial; 1 year probation, $150 fine, 10 days suspended

Michael Byxbe: 3 counts, stipulation; 1 year probation, $150 fine, 10 days suspended

Paul Cahill: newspaper listing only

Martha Callaghan: appeal; 3 counts, stipulation; 1 year probation, $150 fine, 10 days suspended

Tom Calmar: newspaper listing only

Lawrence Calmus: appeal; 3 counts, stipulation; 1 year probation, $150 fine, 10 days suspended

Ellen Calvin: 3 counts, nolo; 1 year probation, $75 fine

Ludwig Caminita III: 2 counts, nolo; 6 months probation, $25 fine

Annette Cammer: defendants' list only

James G. Carr: 3 counts, stipulation; 1 year probation

were to demand individual jury trials or settle for a mass trial was perhaps the most influential on the eventual decision. This was a group of eight hundred transients who were in Berkeley for only the short time that was required to get a University degree; that accomplished, they would scatter to the four corners of the earth, with no intention of ever returning. Therefore, most of them did not have years to spend awaiting trial, appearing for various legal events from time to time, and at last wading through a lengthy affair culminating in a jail term or fine when they were supposed to be forging careers, marriages and families. Thus, for most of the defendants, the prospect of a quick mass trial would, win or lose, get the whole thing out of the way so that they could leave this preparatory part of their lives when it was time to do so. Most of the defendants who appealed their convictions were also those who planned to stick around for a few years. The defendants who did not appeal generally planned to take their medicine right now in one big cod-liver-oil gulp and move on.

It may also be that the force of tradition played a role: the only real precedents for trials of social activists had been set by Communists and labor organizers in the twenties and thirties, and they usually tried to get a mass trial to reinforce the concepts of solidarity and collective action and responsibility. Though not overtly influencing our decision, as we more or less rejected much of what had gone before, this may have been at the back of the minds of the Movement attorneys, subtly influencing their decision-making process. This uniform lack of interest in the paths that our elders had trodden before us perplexed and irritated the members of the Old Left.* We were a movement not following a line, but in search of a line. We never found it.

---

*"The new radicalism is different from the old radicalism of the 1930s. The arguments of the pre-war Left no longer seem relevant to the lives of the post-war adolescents who never experienced the Great Depression, except for a vague memory, perhaps, that their families used to be poor. The impotence of the Left in the face of the Cold War and McCarthyism, sealed by the death of the Progressive Party, and, overseas, the revelations about Stalin, and the quashing of the Hungarian Revolution, discredited the only alternative that the Left had to offer to what was wrong with America. Furthermore, the class theory of Marxism seemed foreign, and the manipulative tactics of the Communist Party and of the conflicting Trotskyist factions repulsive, to a genera- tion born into a seemingly amorphous middle-class society in which the psychic distance, at least, between men of different socio-economic classes was broken down, so that what once was viewed as a struggle against an alien exploiting class (against whom any means of attack might be acceptable), was felt as a conflict with an enemy whom we recognized not so much by the fact that he is so different from us, as by the fact that he is so much like ourselves. . . . The means used by the Old Left seemed to reveal its lack of comprehension of the ends it was supposedly fighting for" (Gerald Rosenfield, "Generational Revolt and the Free Speech Movement," *Liberation*, December 1965, 14–15).

Elspeth Jane Casagrande: appeal; 3 counts, stipulation; 1 year probation, $150 fine, 10 days suspended

Norma J. Cash: appeal; 3 counts, stipulation; $250 fine or 25 days in jail

Donald L. Castleberry: appeal; 3 counts, stipulation; 1 year probation, $150 fine, 10 days suspended

Marie Celestre: juvenile

Ira Chaleff: 3 counts, nolo; 1 year probation, $75 fine

Donald T. Chambers: defendants' list only

Merle C. Chambers: 3 counts, nolo; 1 year probation, $75 fine

Terry Chambers: appeal; 3 counts, trial; 1 year probation, $150 fine, 10 days suspended

Wendy Chapnick: appeal; 3 counts, stipulation; 1 year probation, $150 fine, 10 days suspended

Everett W. Chard: 3 counts, trial; 1 year probation, $150 fine, 10 days suspended

Hollis Chenery: 2 counts, stipulation; $100 fine or 10 days in jail

William Christensen: appeal; 3 counts, stipulation; $250 fine or 25 days in jail

Liane Chu: charges dropped

Trudy L. Chudner: 3 counts, nolo; 1 year probation, $50 fine

Gary R. Church: 3 counts, nolo; 1 year probation, $75 fine

Mario Cicconi: appeal; 3 counts, stipulation; 1 year probation, $150 fine, 10 days suspended

Robert C. Cirese: appeal; 3 counts, stipulation; 1 year probation, $150 fine, 10 days suspended

Carl William Clewlow, Jr.: appeal; 2 counts, stipulation; 1 year probation, $50 fine

Martin J. Cohen: 3 counts, stipulation; 1 year probation, $150 fine, 10 days suspended

Michelle Cohen: appeal; 3 counts, stipulation; 1 year probation, $150 fine, 10 days suspended

Andra C. Cohn: appeal; 3 counts, stipulation; 1 year probation

William R. Coit: appeal; 2 counts, stipulation; $100 fine or 10 days in jail

James E. Colby: appeal; 2 counts, stipulation; 1 year probation, $75 fine

Richard H. Colby: 3 counts, nolo; $100 fine or 10 days in jail

Mary Cole: appeal; 3 counts, trial; 1 year probation, $150 fine, 10 days suspended

Hilbert J. Coleman: appeal; 3 counts, stipulation; 1 year probation, $150 fine, 10 days suspended

Kate Coleman: appeal; 3 counts, trial; 1 year probation, $150 fine

Bryson Collins: 3 counts, nolo; 1 year probation, $75 fine

Randall Collins: appeal; 3 counts, stipulation; 1 year probation, $150 fine, 10 days suspended

William A. Collins: appeal; 3 counts, trial; 2 years probation, $150 fine, 10 days suspended

Richard H. Colton: appeal; 2 counts, stipulation; 1 year probation, $50 fine

William E. Cook: appeal; 2 counts, stipulation; $100 fine or 10 days in jail

Winton W. Cooley: 3 counts, trial; 1 year probation, $200 fine, 10 days suspended

Stephanie Coontz: appeal; 3 counts, trial; 2 years probation, $150 fine, 10 days suspended

Lee Gordon Cooper: 3 counts, nolo; 1 year probation, $75 fine

Paul M. Coopersmith: appeal; 3 counts, stipulation; 1 year probation, $150 fine, 10 days suspended

Jane Corey: appeal; 3 counts, stipulation; 1 year probation, $150 fine, 10 days suspended

Ann Lauraette Cornett: appeal; 2 counts, stipulation; 1 year probation, $50 fine

Michael E. Cortes: appeal; 3 counts, stipulation; 1 year probation, $150 fine, 10 days suspended

Joseph C. Cotham: appeal; 2 counts, stipulation; $100 fine or 10 days in jail

Alan R. Cotler: 2 counts, stipulation; 1 year probation, $50 fine

James L. Cowan: appeal; 2 counts, stipulation; $100 fine or 10 days in jail

Richard A. Cowan: appeal; 3 counts, stipulation; $250 fine or 25 days in jail

Stephen Crafts: 2 counts, stipulation; 1 year probation, $50 fine

William E. Crawford: appeal; 3 counts, stipulation; $250 fine or 25 days in jail

Eileen Lindsey Crocker: appeal; 3 counts, stipulation; $250 fine or 25 days in jail

A January 10, 1965, letter to the FSM defendants from the lawyers' committee outlines the early stages of figuring out how we were going to be tried:

Dear Defendant,

Those of you who were at the last meeting will recognize much of the material in this letter; the rest of you will need it in order to arrive at a decision concerning your plea, which must soon be entered.

First, some general points. On January 5, the Court granted us a three-week continuance for the purpose of entering pleas. Starting January 26, unless the court changes its order, you must appear personally to enter a plea. The cases are set in groups of 50 each morning and afternoon from January 26 until all pleas are entered. You will be notified of when your group is to appear. Failure to attend a court session when you have been ordered to attend may result in a bench warrant for your arrest. Consult with a lawyer who is now being assigned to your group if you have any special problems regarding attending court.

Everything from here on in this letter is to be treated as strictly confidential. The lawyers' research committee has given us a report, which indicates that there are numerous possible legal and constitutional defenses to each of the charges against you. These possible defenses are both interesting and respectable, and range from questions of the proper interpretation of the statutes under which you are charged, to the argument that the 1st Amendment rights of assembly, petition, and speech protected your right to be in Sproul Hall at the time, and under the circumstances, in question. *You must understand, however, that all of the lawyers agree that under the political circumstances of this case, the chances of winning on any of these questions is remote, certainly under 50%.*

There are now strong indications that if all or most of you plead no contest to the trespass charge, the district attorney will dismiss the other charge or charges. If that happens, there are further indications that sentencing would be as follows:

For all but the "leaders" there would be no jail time; there might be a fine of up to $50, and there would probably be a term of court probation of up to six months. Court probation means that you need not report to anyone, but you can, if you have broken the law while on probation and [sic] be sentenced on the original conviction.

For "leaders" (an unknown number of people probably not to exceed 20) there may be up to 30 days in jail, or fines of over $50, and possibly a period of probation which may well be longer than six months.

The no contest plea to one charge with dismissal of the other two may be available only if most defendants accept it; on the other hand, it may be offered if a majority accept it, and the rest of the defendants

Eunice Cunningham: 2 counts, stipulation; 1 year probation, $50 fine

Forest W. Curo: appeal; 3 counts, stipulation; 1 year probation, $100 fine, 10 days suspended

Craig Currier: 2 counts, stipulation; 1 year probation, $50 fine

Glenn W. Cushman: 2 counts, nolo; 6 months probation, $25 fine

Agnes M. Cyr: appeal; 3 counts, stipulation; $250 fine or 25 days in jail

Dee Ann Darney: appeal; 3 counts, stipulation; 1 year probation, $150 fine, 10 days suspended

Alan L. Davenport: appeal; 3 counts, stipulation; 1 year probation, $150 fine, 10 days suspended

Mary S. Davenport: 3 counts, trial; 1 year probation, $150 fine, 10 days suspended

Russ Davidson: appeal; 2 counts, stipulation; 1 year probation, $50 fine

Ruth Daryn Davidson: 3 counts, nolo; 1 year probation, $75 fine

Susan Davis: 3 counts, nolo; 1 year probation, $75 fine

Sylvia M. Dawkins: 3 counts, trial; 1 year probation, $150 fine, 10 days suspended

Walter Wedige Dayton: appeal; 3 counts, trial; 1 year probation, $200 fine, 10 days suspended

Thomas E. Dean: appeal; 3 counts, stipulation; 1 year probation, $150 fine, 10 days suspended

Stephen DeCanio: 3 counts, trial; 2 years probation, 60 days in jail

William G. Deck: appeal; 2 counts, stipulation; 1 year probation, $50 fine

Ralph Deitch: appeal; 3 counts, stipulation; 1 year probation, $150 fine, 10 days suspended

Rafaella DelBourgo: appeal; 2 counts, stipulation; 1 year probation, $50 fine

Rob Dempewolf: 2 counts, stipulation; 1 year probation, $50 fine

Thomas N. Dennis: appeal; 3 counts, trial; 1 year probation, $150 fine, 10 days suspended

Donald L. Denny: appeal; 3 counts, stipulation; $250 fine or 25 days in jail

John B. Derrick: 2 counts, stipulation; $100 fine or 10 days in jail

J. Mark Desmet: appeal; 3 counts, stipulation; 1 year probation, $150 fine, 10 days suspended

Christine DeVault: appeal; 3 counts, stipulation; 1 year probation, $150 fine, 10 days suspended

Frederic Deyo: 2 counts, stipulation; 1 year probation, $50 fine

Richard G. Dillon: 3 counts, stipulation; 1 year probation, $150 fine, 10 days suspended

Mark Dinaburg: juvenile

Natasha Doner: appeal; 3 counts, stipulation; 1 year probation, $150 fine, 10 days suspended

Ellen A. Doughty: appeal; 3 counts, stipulation; 1 year probation, $150 fine, 10 days suspended

Richard Drogin: appeal; 3 counts, stipulation; $250 fine or 25 days in jail

Susan C. Druding: appeal; 3 counts, trial; 1 year probation, $150 fine, 10 days suspended

Michael S. Duke: appeal; 3 counts, trial; $250 fine or 25 days in jail

Richard F. Dunbar: appeal; 3 counts, stipulation; 1 year probation, $150 fine, 10 days suspended

Sharryn I. Dunbar: appeal; 3 counts, stipulation; $250 fine or 25 days in jail

Daniel Early: appeal; 3 counts, stipulation; 1 year probation, $150 fine, 10 days suspended

Marilyn Eden: appeal; 3 counts, stipulation; $250 fine or 25 days in jail

Robert Eden: appeal; 2 counts, stipulation; $100 fine or 10 days in jail

John J. Edminster: appeal; 3 counts, stipulation; $250 fine or 25 days in jail

Robert Eichberg: 3 counts, nolo; 1 year probation, $75 fine

Michael Eisen: appeal; 3 counts, trial; 2 years probation, $100 fine (Penal Code §602[o]), 1 year probation, $100 fine, 10 days suspended (Penal Code §148)

Oren Eisenberg: 3 counts, stipulation; 1 year probation, $150 fine, 10 days suspended

Diana Eisenstein: appeal; 3 counts, trial; $250 fine or 25 days in jail

agree to a single, court trial (which will be explained to you later on). This plea may be available to the defendants only up to January 26.

The alternatives to the possible no contest plea are roughly as follows:

1. People may plead guilty to all charges against them. This plea can't be changed later, and sentencing is at the sole discretion of the court.

2. a. A not guilty plea may be entered, and a trial held. This plea can be changed at any time before trial. A trial may be either by jury or by the judge (a court trial). Many of our lawyers have felt that most judges, being subject to continuing political pressure, would be less likely to acquit you than would a jury.

b. As you know, you are charged in groups of ten, and the indications are that trials would normally be in those groups—meaning 80 separate trials. Each jury trial would likely take two weeks, on the average, and the experience in the San Francisco sit-in cases was that the defendants were ordered to be present throughout the trial. That would, in addition to a serious drain on your time, tie up the Berkeley court for a considerable period of time, undoubtedly further creating public pressure against our case. The lawyers' predictions on the result of such trials are, as stated above, that most of you would be convicted. Many unknown judges would be used in such trials, and we could, frankly, expect considerably more harsh sentences than are now being offered—probably jail for the majority of convicted defendants, maybe even 30 days or more.

c. It may be possible to obtain a single trial for all defendants—either a judge or jury trial. This might be done by agreeing to admit some facts such as that all defendants were present in Sproul Hall, that they heard an order to disperse, and that those charged with resisting arrest went limp. It might not, on the other hand, be necessary to admit more than identity. You would probably not all need to be present at all stages of such a trial, saving your time; and only one court would be used, saving the public time and expense as well. In addition, your lawyers feel that we have the best chance of winning a single trial. The difficulty is, that we have no right to such a trial, but the court and district attorney's office must agree to it. Preliminary indications are that the district attorney's office will not agree to a single jury trial. They are afraid that a jury might, in the circumstances of a single trial, acquit you all. That attitude on the part of the district attorney's office may change if enough public pressure is brought to bear on the issue, pointing out that we are willing to simplify matters and not clog the courts—but we can in no way promise that this will happen, and, as I stated above, the no contest offer may not be open past January 26.

Patricia S. Eliet: appeal; 3 counts, stipulation; $250 fine or 25 days in jail

Wallace D. Ellinger: appeal; 3 counts, stipulation; 1 year probation, $150 fine, 10 days suspended

Barbara Elliott: 3 counts, stipulation; 1 year probation, $150 fine, 10 days suspended

Michael S. Entin: 3 counts, nolo; 1 year probation, $75 fine

Kenneth A. Epstein: 2 counts, nolo; 6 months probation, $25 fine

Marney Erenberg: appeal; 3 counts, stipulation; 1 year probation, $150 fine, 10 days suspended

Alan N. Eschelman: appeal; 3 counts, stipulation; 1 year probation, $150 fine, 10 days suspended

Suzi Evalenko: 3 counts, nolo; 1 year probation, $75 fine

Michael L. Evanson: appeal; 3 counts, trial; $250 fine or 25 days in jail

Judy A. Fagerholm: appeal; 3 counts, trial; 1 year probation, $200 fine

Jan Faigen: newspaper listing only

Dennis Fast: appeal; 3 counts, stipulation; 1 year probation, $150 fine, 10 days suspended

Rosemary Feitis: appeal; 3 counts, stipulation; $250 fine or 25 days in jail

Eric J. Feldman: appeal; 2 counts, stipulation; $100 fine or 10 days in jail

Gary William Feller: appeal; 3 counts, trial; 1 year probation, $150 fine, 10 days suspended

Lee Felsenstein: appeal; 3 counts, stipulation; 1 year probation, $150 fine, 10 days suspended

Shannon R. Ferguson: appeal; 3 counts, stipulation; 1 year probation, $150 fine, 10 days suspended

Geoffrey E. Fernald: 3 counts, nolo; 1 year probation, $75 fine

Ethan Figen: appeal; 3 counts, stipulation; 1 year probation, $150 fine, 10 days suspended

Amy Jo Fillin: 3 counts, trial; 1 year probation, $150 fine, 10 days suspended

Richard Fink: appeal; 3 counts, trial; 1 year probation, $150 fine, 10 days suspended

Charles P. Fischer: appeal; 2 counts, stipulation; 1 year probation, $50 fine

Ralph Fisher: appeal; 3 counts, stipulation; 1 year probation, $150 fine, 10 days suspended

Rebecca Fisher: 3 counts, nolo; 1 year probation, $50 fine

Irving S. Fishman: appeal; 3 counts, stipulation; 1 year probation, $150 fine, 10 days suspended

Thomas Fiske: appeal; 3 counts, stipulation; 1 year probation, $150 fine, 10 days suspended

Elena Flemming: appeal; 3 counts, stipulation; $250 fine or 25 days in jail

Anthony E. Ford: appeal; 3 counts, stipulation; 1 year probation, $150 fine, 10 days suspended

Phillip R. Forester: appeal; 3 counts, stipulation; 1 year probation, $150 fine, 10 days suspended

David Lewis Frank: appeal; 3 counts, stipulation; 1 year probation, $150 fine, 10 days suspended

Katherine Simon Frank: appeal; 3 counts, stipulation; $250 fine or 25 days in jail

Peter J. Franke: 3 counts, stipulation; 2 years probation, $150 fine, 10 days suspended

Joan Franklin: 3 counts, trial; 1 year probation, $150 fine, 10 days suspended

Ira Freed: appeal; 3 counts, stipulation; 1 year probation, $150 fine, 10 days suspended

Jane Freedman: appeal; 2 counts, stipulation; $100 fine or 10 days in jail

Warren Freedman: appeal; 3 counts, stipulation; $250 fine or 25 days in jail

Jo Freeman: appeal; 3 counts, stipulation; $250 fine or 25 days in jail

Mark Freudenthal: 2 counts, nolo; 6 months probation, $25 fine

Marion Friedland: appeal; 2 counts, stipulation; 1 year probation, $50 fine

Ellen Friedman: appeal; 2 counts, stipulation; $100 fine or 10 days in jail

Sandor Fuchs: appeal; 3 counts, trial; 2 years probation, 30 days in jail

Stephen L. Gabow: 3 counts, stipulation; 1 year probation, $150 fine, 10 days suspended

Gail Gardner: appeal; 3 counts, stipulation; 1 year probation, $150 fine, 10 days suspended

d. The district attorney's office appears to be willing to agree to a single court trial, being certain that the judge would not feel himself politically able to acquit you of all charges. We think that this is a realistic assessment of the situation; a single court trial may be possible if all, or a majority, of you chose it. Undoubtedly, the district attorney's office will not consent to a mass court trial unless almost all defendants chose either that or a no contest plea. A single court trial, even if quite probably resulting in conviction on the trespass charge, has several advantages: it might well be that the judge can and will acquit on the resisting charge; it gives us a forum to state our entire case and reason for being in Sproul Hall; it enables us to raise all of our legal questions at the trial and, more important, on appeal and, in all likelihood, since the trial will be before Judge Crittenden, and since this kind of a trial does not clog the courts and thereby create a new wave of hostility against us, sentences should be close to what [we] are now likely [to get] on a no contest plea.

Much of the above is necessarily fluid and somewhat ambiguous—we hope you will understand that we are as definite as the situation allows. You are now being assigned to lawyers who will be able to answer your questions concerning the above.

You must decide on a plea as an individual, but the lawyers recognize that you may wish to discuss with your fellow defendants these questions; and we further recognize that other considerations than those of a strictly legal nature apply to this case. The nature of the issues that took you into Sproul Hall, the unity of the defendants, etc. are all issues which you must consider. Likewise, some of you have individual problems which must be considered in planning your plea.

When you see the lawyer assigned to advise your group, please feel free to ask all the questions you care to. Do not, on the other hand, expect the lawyer to tell you what to do—that would place an enormous burden upon us, and it is not really properly our function.

We are pleased to serve you, and to join with you.

PLEASE NOTIFY US OF ANY CHANGE OF ADDRESS. We must be able to keep in contact with you.

If you have any questions which your lawyer cannot answer, or if you violently object to the lawyer assigned to you, please call me.

Very truly yours,
Malcolm Burnstein

On March 10, 1965, after months of wrangling, the defendants were offered a choice of nolo (chosen by 101 defendants), stipulation (500 de-

Frank Garfield: appeal; 3 counts, stipulation; 1 year probation, $150 fine, 10 days suspended

Jonathan Garlock: appeal; 3 counts, trial; 1 year probation, $150 fine, 10 days suspended

Susan Garlock: appeal; 3 counts, trial; 1 year probation, $150 fine, 10 days suspended

Daniel Garrison: 2 counts, stipulation; 1 year probation, $50 fine

Barbara Garson: appeal; 3 counts, trial; $300 fine or 30 days in jail

Marvin T. Garson: appeal; 3 counts, trial; $300 fine or 30 days in jail

Gary Geller: $150 fine (newspaper listing only)

David R. Geneson: appeal; 3 counts, stipulation; 1 year probation, $150 fine, 10 days suspended

Donna B. Germain: appeal; 3 counts, trial; $250 fine or 25 days in jail

Pamela Gerould: appeal; 3 counts, trial; 2 years probation, $150 fine

Dorrie S. Gilden: 3 counts, stipulation; 1 year probation, $150 fine, 10 days suspended

Stephen Gillers: appeal; 3 counts, stipulation; 1 year probation, $150 fine, 10 days suspended

Lynne Gilroy: 3 counts, stipulation; 1 year probation, $150 fine, 10 days suspended

Jeann (Dianne) Gimian: 2 counts, nolo; 6 months probation, $25 fine

Jerry Ginsburg: appeal; 3 counts, trial; 1 year probation, $150 fine, 10 days suspended

Evan S. Gladstone: appeal; 2 counts, stipulation; 1 year probation, $50 fine

Lenny Glaser: newspaper listing only

Philip Gleason: appeal; 3 counts, stipulation; $250 fine or 25 days in jail

Barry Glick: appeal; 3 counts, stipulation; 1 year probation, $150 fine, 10 days suspended

Diane Schott Glick: 3 counts, nolo; 1 year probation, $75 fine

Robert L. Goddard: appeal; 3 counts, stipulation; 1 year probation, $150 fine, 10 days suspended

John Goertzel: appeal; 3 counts, trial; 1 year probation, $150 fine, 10 days suspended

Dolores M. Goff: appeal; 3 counts, stipulation; 1 year probation, $150 fine, 10 days suspended

Joseph R. Goglio, Jr.: 3 counts, stipulation; 1 year probation, $150 fine, 10 days suspended

David L. Goines: appeal; 3 counts, trial; 60 days in jail

Arthur Goldberg: appeal; 3 counts, trial; 120 days in jail

Devora Goldberg: appeal; 3 counts, trial; 1 year probation, $150 fine

Jacqueline Goldberg: 3 counts, stipulation; 2 years probation, $400 fine or 40 days in jail

Suzanne Goldberg: appeal; 3 counts, trial; 45 days in jail

Lee Frances Goldblatt: appeal; 3 counts, trial; $250 fine or 25 days in jail

Jonathan Golden: charges dropped

Renee Goldsmith: appeal; 3 counts, stipulation; 1 year probation, $150 fine, 10 days suspended

Jeanne Golson: appeal; 3 counts, stipulation; 1 year probation, $150 fine, 10 days suspended

Laurel Gonsalves: 3 counts, trial; 1 year probation, $150 fine, 10 days suspended

Brenda J. Goodman: appeal; 3 counts, trial; 2 years probation, $200 fine, 10 days suspended

Jerrold R. Goodwin: appeal; 3 counts, trial; $250 fine or 25 days in jail

Barry Gordon: appeal; 3 counts, stipulation; 1 year probation, $150 fine, 10 days suspended

Jeffrey A. Gordon: 2 counts, nolo; 6 months probation, $25 fine

Helaine Grabowski: appeal; 3 counts, stipulation; 1 year probation, $150 fine, 10 days suspended

Phillip Grant: appeal; 3 counts, stipulation; 1 year probation, $150 fine, 10 days suspended

Elizabeth Gravalos: appeal; 3 counts, trial; 1 year probation, $150 fine

Lance Gray: charges dropped

Alexander Green: 3 counts, nolo; 1 year probation, $75 fine

Douglas Green: 3 counts, trial; 1 year probation, $150 fine, 10 days suspended

David Greenberg: appeal; 3 counts, stipulation; 1 year probation, $150 fine, 10 days suspended

fendants) or a collective trial before a judge (155 defendants).* There were to be no individual jury trials, though one defendant, the San Francisco schoolteacher Howard Jeter, held out for a jury trial, got it, and was—as I recollect—cut loose because of a hung jury. If a person pleaded nolo, they stood the best chance of getting a light sentence; stipulation of the charges carried a greater risk, and a trial was the most risky of all. Along with the other hard-liners, I opted for a trial.

In return for making the task of the state even marginally possible, the majority of defendants were to be cut loose with probation, a fine and a suspended sentence. Appeals brought before the California Supreme Court by Larry Duga and Peter Franck had been rejected on June 14, and sentencing began on the nineteenth of July. Before he began sentencing, Judge Crittenden asked every defendant to write him a letter explaining in their own words why they had done what they did. Though most of these letters have been lost, mine, through some miracle, was preserved in a photocopy.† I wrote my explanation out on lined notebook paper right there in the courtroom and handed it in as court adjourned, as though I had taken a test in a classroom. Some of the garbled syntax and all of the snottiness is explained by this.

Literacy Test

In the fall semester of 1964, I had been involved in the University for one year as a major in Classics. I had come to the University with the intention of learning how to think, how to communicate, and how best to exist with my fellow-man, whom I did not like very much. Having become, however, rather quickly disenchanted with the concept of the University being an ideal bastion of learning, I fell back in my stud-

---

*The plea of *guilty* is an admission that the accused is justly charged and that a trial is not necessary. If you're guilty as sin and everybody knows it, you plead guilty and hope that this shred of cooperation gets you a lighter sentence, which it usually does. *Nolo contendere* is a plea made by the defendant in a criminal action, equivalent to an admission of guilt and subjecting them to punishment, but leaving open the possibility to deny the alleged facts in other proceedings, such as a related civil case. To *stipulate* is to agree mutually concerning conduct or evidence during legal proceedings. What this meant in this par-

ticular case was we agreed that, yes, we had been there and yes, we had resisted arrest, but we still wanted a trial with a chance of getting off. Those of us who opted for a court trial said that we were *not guilty* and made the state prove that we had been there and that we had indeed resisted arrest. In return for making more trouble, we stood a chance of getting a harsher punishment if convicted.
†If anybody knows where these letters are, Katherine Simon Frank is looking for them and can be contacted through me, care of the publisher.

Robert D. Greenberg: appeal; 3 counts, trial; 1 year probation, $150 fine, 10 days suspended

George Greenleaf: appeal; 3 counts, trial; 1 year probation, $150 fine, 10 days suspended

Brent Greenslade: appeal; 3 counts, stipulation; 1 year probation, $150 fine, 10 days suspended

John D. Gregory: appeal; 3 counts, stipulation; $250 fine or 25 days in jail

Roberta Gregory: appeal; 3 counts, stipulation; $250 fine or 25 days in jail

Lilly Grenz: appeal; 3 counts, stipulation; 1 year probation, $150 fine, 10 days suspended

David Gross: appeal; 2 counts, stipulation; 1 year probation, $50 fine

Anne Groves: appeal; 3 counts, stipulation; $250 fine or 25 days in jail

Joseph Gustin: 3 counts, nolo; 1 year probation

Les R. Haber: appeal; 3 counts, stipulation; 1 year probation, $150 fine, 10 days suspended

Peter Haberfield: appeal; 3 counts, stipulation; 1 year probation, $150 fine, 10 days suspended

Conn M. Hallinan: appeal; 3 counts, stipulation; $250 fine or 25 days in jail

Matthew Hallinan: appeal; 3 counts, trial; $300 fine or 30 days in jail

Patrick Hallinan: defendants' list only

Peggy Hallum: appeal; 3 counts, stipulation; 1 year probation, $150 fine, 10 days suspended

Marc Halpern: 2 counts, stipulation; 1 year probation, $50 fine

Michael Halpern: appeal; 3 counts, stipulation; 1 year probation, $150 fine, 10 days suspended

Ann E. Halterman: 3 counts, stipulation; 1 year probation, $150 fine, 10 days suspended

Margaret Ham: appeal; 2 counts, stipulation; 1 year probation, $50 fine

Steve Hamilton: appeal; 3 counts, trial; $250 fine or 25 days in jail

Larrie L. Hamlin: appeal; 3 counts, stipulation; $250 fine or 25 days in jail

Dale Hannaford: appeal; 3 counts, stipulation; 1 year probation, $150 fine, 10 days suspended

Ilene M. Hanover: 3 counts, nolo; 1 year probation, $75 fine

Mark Hardin: appeal; 3 counts, trial; 1 year probation, $150 fine, 10 days suspended

Ronald Hargreaves: 2 counts, stipulation; 1 year probation, $50 fine

Gordon Harrington: appeal; 3 counts, trial; $250 fine or 25 days in jail

Halli Harris: appeal; 3 counts, stipulation; 1 year probation, $150 fine, 10 days suspended

Joseph Amos Harris: appeal; 3 counts, stipulation; 1 year probation, $150 fine, 10 days suspended

Sandra Harris: 3 counts, stipulation; 1 year probation, $150 fine, 10 days suspended

Victoria Hasser: 2 counts, stipulation; 6 months probation

Carol E. Hatch: appeal; 3 counts, stipulation; $250 fine or 25 days in jail

Eva Havas: appeal; 2 counts, stipulation; 1 year probation, $50 fine

John Roger Hawkins: 3 counts, nolo; 1 year probation, $75 fine

Susan Hawley: appeal; 3 counts, trial; 1 year probation, $150 fine

Judith Hechler: 2 counts, nolo; 6 months probation, $25 fine

Stephen Hechler: appeal; 3 counts, stipulation; 1 year probation, $150 fine, 10 days suspended

Sulamith Heins: 3 counts, nolo; 1 year probation, $75 fine

Barbara Henderson: 3 counts, stipulation; 1 year probation, $150 fine, 10 days suspended

Herbert Henryson III: 3 counts, trial; 6 months probation

James Herberich: appeal; 3 counts, stipulation; 1 year probation, $150 fine, 10 days suspended

Luis Hernandez: appeal; 3 counts, stipulation; 1 year probation, $150 fine, 10 days suspended

Richard T. Hersk: 3 counts, nolo; 1 year probation, $25 fine

Karen Hickey: appeal; 3 counts, stipulation; 1 year probation, $150 fine, 10 days suspended

ies and began to study things which pleased me. I had found my professors stuffy and narrow, or classes too large and the courses infinitely
pedantic. Notable exceptions to this general pattern only lent greater
weight to my flight from formal education. I found the dynamism my
professors lacked in the political world of the University community,
and (without knowing too much about what I was doing or why) went
to work for SLATE and the SLATE *Supplement*. In this I found a way to vent
my frustration at the University, and to learn something about how to
better the situation which, I felt, was no better than a memory exercise,
or perhaps a complete ruse. The *Supplement* provided a realistic basis for
reform, was intimately tied up with the affairs of the school, and provided a forum for those such as myself who felt a need for learning and
not dictation. Having developed a vested interest in my own bullshit, I
participated in the protest against the University regulations which I felt
unjustly forbade the sale of the *Supplement*, and was indefinitely suspended from the University on September 30 for having manned a SLATE
table, advocated direct political action, and soliciting funds and
membership.

This marked the beginning of my involvement in what came to be
known as the Free Speech Movement. I participated, more through outrage than analysis, in the September sit-in, and in the holding of the
police car. Concurrent with my suspension I lost my job with the University Library, and became a free agent, capable of carrying on full-
time work for the Movement. My commitment to the FSM increased
with my involvement, and soon my activities and influence in the FSM
were of no small proportion. I printed and supervised the distribution
of some 1.5 million leaflets, was head-monitor, set up the first central,
nexus and legal office, was a member of the x-com, and de-facto member of the steering committee, [engaged in] sabotage and set-up rallies
and sit-ins, and the like.

I felt that to keep silence or to remain inactive was to speak against
the Movement; that the concept of Freedom of speech exists only insofar as it is used, and will die with disuse; that I had a responsibility
extending far beyond that of my own sphere of existence to insure the
success of the Movement in that education—to be called that at all—
must be pragmatic as well as theoretical. One of the basic responsibilities
of a citizen is to be a political man, and if [he is to develop] the right to
learn and understand politics, he must be exposed to, explore and either
accept or reject, through his own thought processes, divergent political
and social opinions; that he must act on his beliefs, and that unless he
does, he is unworthy of citizenship. If the University purports to be a
place where the whole man is educated, how could it stifle political

Shelagh Hickey: appeal; 3 counts, trial; 1 year probation, $150 fine, 10 days suspended

James Hicks: appeal; 3 counts, stipulation; $250 fine or 25 days in jail

Julie Ann Hightower: appeal; 2 counts, stipulation; 1 year probation, $50 fine

Louis N. Hiken: appeal; 3 counts, trial; 1 year probation, $150 fine, 10 days suspended

Geoffrey A. Hirsch: appeal; 3 counts, trial; 1 year probation, $150 fine

Robert Hirschfeld: appeal; 2 counts, stipulation; 1 year probation, $50 fine

Henry Hitz: appeal; 3 counts, stipulation; 1 year probation, $150 fine, 10 days suspended

Charles Hixson: appeal; 3 counts, stipulation; 1 year probation, $150 fine, 10 days suspended

George Holbrook: 3 counts, stipulation; 6 months probation

Fred Hollander: appeal; 3 counts, stipulation; $250 fine or 25 days in jail

Lynne Hollander: appeal; 3 counts, stipulation; $300 fine or 30 days in jail

Dennis G. Holt: appeal; 3 counts, stipulation; 1 year probation, $150 fine, 10 days suspended

Pam Horner: newspaper listing only

James N. Houillion: appeal; 3 counts, trial; 1 year probation, $150 fine, 10 days suspended

Constance J. Howard: 2 counts, nolo; 6 months probation, $25 fine

Michael Howard: juvenile

Alice Huberman: appeal; 3 counts, stipulation; $250 fine or 25 days in jail

Jaime L. Huberman: appeal; 3 counts, stipulation; $250 fine or 25 days in jail

Marsha Hudson: appeal; 3 counts, trial; 1 year probation, $150 fine, 10 days suspended

Natalie Huebsch: 3 counts, nolo; 1 year probation, $75 fine

Mary A. Hughes: appeal; 3 counts, stipulation; $250 fine or 25 days in jail

Richard B. Hunter: appeal; 3 counts, stipulation; 1 year probation, $150 fine, 10 days suspended

John W. Huntington: appeal; 2 counts, stipulation; 1 year probation, $50 fine

Mona Hutchin: 3 counts, trial; 1 year probation, $50 fine

Patricia Iiyama: appeal; 3 counts, trial; $300 fine or 30 days in jail

Susan Imhoff: appeal; 3 counts, stipulation; 1 year probation, $150 fine, 10 days suspended

Peter B. Irlenborn: appeal; 3 counts, stipulation; $250 fine or 25 days in jail

Margaret Irving: 3 counts, nolo; 1 year probation, $50 fine

Peter O. Israel: appeal; 3 counts, stipulation; 1 year probation, $150 fine, 10 days in jail

Janet Jackson: appeal; 3 counts, stipulation; $250 fine or 25 days in jail

Alan Jacobs: appeal; 2 counts, stipulation; $100 fine or 10 days in jail

Marna Jacobsen: appeal; 3 counts, stipulation; 1 year probation, $150 fine, 10 days suspended

Ethyl Jacoff: 2 counts, stipulation; 1 year probation, $25 fine

Sherryl Jaffee: appeal; 2 counts, stipulation; 1 year probation, $50 fine

David R. James: appeal; 3 counts, stipulation; $250 fine or 25 days in jail

Michael James: appeal; 3 counts, trial; $250 fine or 25 days in jail

Peter K. Janke: appeal; 3 counts, trial; 1 year probation, $150 fine, 10 days suspended

Nicholas Jankowski: appeal; 3 counts, stipulation; 2 years probation, $150 fine, 10 days suspended

Dave Jessups: newspaper listing only

Howard P. Jeter: jury trial

Elsa P. Johnson: appeal; 3 counts, stipulation; $250 fine or 25 days in jail

Sylvia Kalitinsky: appeal; 3 counts, stipulation; $250 fine or 25 days in jail

Annette Kammer: 3 counts, nolo; 1 year probation, $75 fine

Phillip Kamornick: appeal; 3 counts, trial; $250 fine or 25 days in jail

Elliott Kanter: appeal; 3 counts, stipulation; 1 year probation, $150 fine, 10 days suspended

Paul Kapiloff: appeal; 3 counts, trial; 1 year probation, $150 fine, 10 days suspended

Daniel Kashinsky: appeal; 3 counts, stipulation; 1 year probation

Harold Kasinsky: appeal; 2 counts, stipulation; $100 fine or 10 days in jail

expression, and still hope to produce a responsible citizenry? If it did not, in fact, hope to produce citizens and men, but only eunuchs and servile, conceptionless bags of information, then it was evil, and merited destruction. If it could, however, be repaired, then I hoped to contribute to the betterment of my University, my society, and—indirectly—myself.

When I saw that all our attempts to negotiate our inalienable rights with the Institution were to no avail, that the officials of the University sought only to deceive and trick us and not treat us like men, that they ignored our petition for redress, that they scorned our repeated attempts at meaningful negotiation, we resolved to force them to listen or die. And not only to listen, but to act, that in their act they would find our requests reasonable, and return to us our rights as citizens and students.

Here we became the dog in the manger—if we can't have a university, you (the officials) can't either. We decided to so tie-up the "normal functioning of the University" that we would have to be heard.

When we marched into Sproul Hall, we went with the intention to stay as long as possible, the only way out of the place to be quite oblique, i.e.—via some prison.

The possibility of arrest was constantly present, and when it became real I decided to go limp, that is, to refuse to assist the arresting officer in his removal of my person from its place of petition. Going limp would materially slow down the process of arrest, and make even more clear to those outside and inside what we were asking, by causing the time of our stay to be extended and to give all a greater opportunity to analyze our action.

I was, in Sproul Hall, fourth floor captain and song leader. I teased the arresting officers about their actions and [made] remarks to keep up the spirit of myself and others, I continued in the FSM until I felt my usefulness exhausted, and am now on the executive board of CORE.

David L. Goines

I don't know what Judge Crittenden made of all this, or if he even read it. A few of the more inflammatory phrases are circled or checked and the letter is initialed by, I presume, whoever read it before passing it on to the judge. I doubt that it had any effect on my sentence.

Fines were from $25 to as high as $400, a formidable sum for most.* Almost half of the sentences were one year's probation, a $150 fine and a ten-day suspended jail sentence. Rather than pay fines that they

---

*To give you some idea of just how formidable these fines were, my total income from my job as a page in the library, upon which I lived for my freshman year and the summer of 1964, was $960 after taxes.

Robert L. Kass: appeal; 2 counts, stipulation; $100 fine or 10 days in jail

Paula Katz: appeal; 3 counts, stipulation; 1 year probation, $150 fine, 10 days suspended

Denise Kaufman: appeal; 3 counts, stipulation; $250 fine or 25 days in jail

Carolyn Kausek: appeal; 3 counts, stipulation; 1 year probation, $150 fine, 10 days suspended

Daniel Keig: appeal; 3 counts, trial; 1 year probation, $150 fine, 10 days suspended

Linda Kaye Kennedy: appeal; 3 counts, stipulation; 1 year probation, $150 fine, 10 days suspended

Susan Kennedy: appeal; 3 counts, stipulation; 1 year probation, $150 fine, 10 days suspended

Diane Kepner: appeal; 3 counts, trial; $250 fine or 25 days in jail

Gordon Kepner: appeal; 3 counts, trial; $250 fine or 25 days in jail

Virginia Kerber: newspaper listing only

Andrew Kerr III: 3 counts, nolo; 1 year probation, $75 fine

Alexander Kershaw: appeal; 3 counts, trial; $300 fine or 30 days

Frederick Kettering: 3 counts, stipulation; 1 year probation, $150 fine, 10 days suspended

Charles Keyser, Jr.: 3 counts, nolo; 1 year probation, $75 fine

Robert Keyston: 3 counts, nolo; 5-day work order, 1 year probation, $50 fine

Ina S. Kilstein: appeal; 3 counts, stipulation; 1 year probation, $150 fine, 10 days suspended

John P. Kimball: appeal; 2 counts, stipulation; 1 year probation, $50 fine

Kathleen Kimball: appeal; 2 counts, stipulation; 1 year probation, $50 fine

Jonathan King: appeal; 3 counts, stipulation; 1 year probation, $150 fine, 10 days suspended

Daniel Kirchner: appeal; 3 counts, stipulation; $250 fine or 25 days in jail

Kenneth Kirkland: appeal; 3 counts, stipulation; 1 year probation, $150 fine

Bruce Kirmmse: appeal; 2 counts, stipulation; 1 year probation, $50 fine

Bonnie Klapper: appeal; 2 counts, stipulation; 1 year probation, $50 fine

Margaret Klein: appeal; 3 counts, stipulation; 1 year probation, $150 fine, 10 days suspended

Michael Klein: appeal; 2 counts, stipulation; $100 fine or 10 days in jail

Karen Kline: appeal; 2 counts, stipulation; $100 fine or 10 days in jail

William Knight: appeal; 3 counts, trial; 1 year probation, $150 fine, 10 days suspended

Larry Knop: appeal; 2 counts, stipulation; $100 fine or 10 days in jail

Jonathan Knowles: appeal; 3 counts, stipulation; $250 fine or 25 days in jail

Judith Knowlton: appeal; 3 counts, stipulation; 1 year probation, $150 fine, 10 days suspended

Michael Kogan: appeal; 3 counts, stipulation; $250 fine or 25 days in jail

David Kolodney: appeal; 3 counts, stipulation; $250 fine or 25 days in jail

Gary A. Kopp: 3 counts, nolo; 7 days probation, $50 fine

Gerald Korshak: appeal; 3 counts, stipulation; $250 fine or 25 days in jail

Davic Kosingsky: newspaper listing only (?Daniel Kashinsky)

Irene Kovacs: appeal; 3 counts, stipulation; 1 year probation, $150 fine, 10 days suspended

Kris L. Kraft: appeal; 2 counts, stipulation; $100 fine or 10 days in jail

Dana Kramer: appeal; 3 counts, stipulation; 1 year probation, $150 fine, 10 days suspended

Fredrica Kramer: appeal; 3 counts, trial; 1 year probation, $150 fine, 10 days suspended

Ivan Kramer: appeal; 2 counts, stipulation; $100 fine or 10 days in jail

Grover Krantz: charges dropped

Michael Kroll: appeal; 3 counts, trial; 1 year probation, $150 fine, 10 days suspended

Robert Kroll: appeal; 3 counts, stipulation; 1 year probation, $150 fine, 10 days suspended

Peter Kroopnick: appeal; 3 counts, trial; 1 year probation, $150 fine, 10 days suspended

Jack Kurzweil: newspaper listing; one version of defendants' list

William Lakeland: appeal; 2 counts, stipulation; 1 year probation, $50 fine

FSM DEFENDANTS IN CONVERSATION OUTSIDE THE MAKESHIFT COURTROOM AT THE
BERKELEY VETERANS' HALL. PHOTO © 1993 BY TED STRESHINSKY.

couldn't afford, a few dozen others chose to serve ten to thirty days. As
a sop to the prosecution, who couldn't conscience letting the leaders and
spokesmen go scot-free, about a dozen of us got actual sentences, varying in length from 30 days to 120 days. Jack Weinberg, Art Goldberg
and Mario Savio got 120 days each, Mike Rossman got 90 days in jail,
Brian Turner, Steve DeCanio and I got 60 days, Suzanne and Bettina 45.
Sandor Fuchs and Sid Stapleton got 30 days, and Ron Anastasi was
given a 30-day suspended sentence and a $200 fine. By July 23, more
than one hundred students had been sentenced and at least half of them
refused the terms of probation.

Probation would have pulled our claws, as it was a promise that you
wouldn't get into any mischief for that whole time. If you did get in
trouble, they could lock you up for as long as a year. Not a good deal.
I had no intention of staying out of Dutch, so that option was roundly
rejected by me and all the other gung-ho activists. Ultimately, 203 defendants rejected probation.

Some defendants received extended payment plans, half a dozen
failed to appear and bench warrants were issued for their arrests, and two
had been killed in accidents. Jackie Goldberg wanted to get out of
Berkeley and forget what had been for her a series of extraordinarily
painful episodes. She had been accepted at the University of Chicago
and was to begin classes with the fall term. What she wanted was to get

Robert Lander: 3 counts, stipulation; 1 year probation, $150 fine, 10 days suspended

Louise Landes: newspaper listing only

Joseph LaPenta: appeal; 3 counts, trial; $250 fine or 25 days in jail

Barbara Lapham: juvenile

Joseph LaPointe: 3 counts, trial; 1 year probation, $250 fine

Gary Larson: charges dropped

Frank Laszlo: appeal; 3 counts, stipulation; 1 year probation, $150 fine, 10 days suspended

Donna Launer: 3 counts, nolo; 1 year probation, $25 fine

Patricia A. Lawrence: appeal; 3 counts, stipulation; 1 year probation, $150 fine, 10 days suspended

Sallie Leary: appeal; 2 counts, stipulation; $100 fine or 10 days in jail

Harvey Lehtman: appeal; 3 counts, stipulation; 1 year probation, $150 fine, 10 days suspended

Ronald Leiter: appeal; 3 counts, stipulation; 1 year probation, $150 fine, 10 days suspended

Kenneth W. Leonard: appeal; 3 counts, stipulation; 1 year probation, $150 fine, 10 days suspended

Stephen Leonard: appeal; 3 counts, stipulation; 1 year probation, $150 fine, 10 days suspended

Lewis J. Lester: appeal; 3 counts, stipulation; $350 fine or 35 days in jail

Lowell Levant: appeal; 3 counts, trial; 1 year probation, $150 fine, 10 days suspended

John W. Levenson: appeal; 3 counts, stipulation; $250 fine or 25 days in jail

Linda J. Leventhal: appeal; 3 counts, trial; 1 year probation, $150 fine, 10 days suspended

Louise Levi: 3 counts, stipulation; 1 year probation, $150 fine, 10 days suspended

Emily Levin: 2 counts, stipulation; 1 year probation, $50 fine

Anita S. Levine: appeal; 3 counts, trial; $250 fine or 25 days in jail

Theresa Leviten: 3 counts, nolo; 1 year probation, $50 fine

Esther Levy: appeal; 2 counts, stipulation; 1 year probation, $50 fine

Claude R. Lhospital: appeal; 3 counts, trial; $250 fine or 25 days in jail

Margaret C. Lima: appeal; 3 counts, trial; $250 fine or 25 days in jail

Sheila Linder: 2 counts, nolo; 6 months probation

Daniel Lindheim: appeal; 2 counts, stipulation; 1 year probation, $50 fine

William P. Lindo: appeal; 2 counts, stipulation; 1 year probation, $50 fine

Jerome F. Lindsey: 3 counts, stipulation; 1 year probation, $150 fine, 10 days suspended

Elizabeth Linsky: 3 counts, nolo; $100 fine or 10 days in jail

Leonard Lipner: appeal; 3 counts, trial; 1 year probation, $150 fine, 10 days suspended

Steven Marc Lipson: appeal; 3 counts, stipulation; 1 year probation, $150 fine, 10 days suspended

Ronald D. Lipsy: 3 counts, nolo; 1 year probation, $75 fine

Peter Lipton: appeal; 2 counts, stipulation; $100 fine or 10 days in jail

Albert Bernard Litewka: appeal; 3 counts, stipulation; $250 fine or 25 days in jail

Jack Paul Litewka: appeal; 3 counts, trial; 1 year probation, $150 fine, 10 days suspended

Mary Jones Lloyd: appeal; 3 counts, stipulation; 1 year probation, $150 fine, 10 days suspended

Jeanne L. Longfellow: newspaper listing only

Michael Lorette: 2 counts, stipulation; 1 year probation, $50 fine

Michael G. Lorimer: appeal; 3 counts, stipulation; 1 year probation, $150 fine, 10 days suspended

Cheryl Loskutoff: 3 counts, nolo; 1 year probation, $75 fine

Douglas Loskutoff: appeal; 3 counts, stipulation; $250 fine or 25 days in jail

Donald F. Lowe: 2 counts, stipulation; 1 year probation, $50 fine

Ann Lowery: 3 counts, trial; 1 year probation

Paul Luben: appeal; 2 counts, stipulation; 1 year probation, $50 fine

Russell J. Ludeke: appeal; 3 counts, stipulation; 1 year probation, $150 fine, 10 days suspended

R. Jeffrey Lustig: appeal; 3 counts, stipulation; $250 fine or 25 days in jail

it all over with, get out of politics forever, leave Berkeley and never come back. She pleaded *nolo contendere* and was convicted. Through her lawyer, Stanley Golde, she told Crittenden that she wanted jail time to be served immediately, no fine and no probation. When Crittenden heard this, he turned red as a turkey cock, recessed the courtroom and demanded to see Golde in his chambers. He was furious, thinking that because Jackie wanted jail, everyone following her would want to do the same thing, and this would mess up his plans for sentencing in a big way. He refused Jackie's request, and instead levied on her the highest fine of any defendant—$400—two years' probation and the choice of forty days to be served right now or forty days suspended. Forty point-less days would keep her out of Chicago, so she took the suspended sentence and probation, shook the dust of Berkeley from off her feet and spent the next two years struggling to pay the fine.

As soon as sentencing began, the matter of an appeal came up. Judge Crittenden wanted to set new bail for those who intended to appeal. The alternative was to go to jail immediately. A group of defendants calling itself "Operation Fight Back" petitioned Judge Crittenden to carry over the bail posted before the trial, release the defendants on their own recognizance or set a nominal bail of $25. This Crittenden refused to do. Appeal bail was set at $550 for most demonstrators convicted of both trespassing and resisting arrest; this meant either posting the whole sum, which was impossible, or kissing almost $35,000 good-bye by paying 10 percent to a bail bondsman. This in addition to all the bail money we'd had to come up with to get out of jail in the first place. As a sub-stitute for appeal bail, 110 University professors offered to take formal custody of those defendants released on their own recognizance, but the judge would not accept this.

On Friday, July 30, I was selected as the guinea pig in an effort to reduce the appeal bail, which we maintained was excessive and illegal. I was taken into custody, the attorneys for both sides went to it like cats and dogs for an hour in Crittenden's chambers, and the request for re-duction in bail was denied. In the afternoon session Judge Crittenden compromised and instituted a ten-day grace period for sentenced defen-dants to file notices of appeal, at which time they would either have to post bail or be sent to jail. During this time the old bail would continue in effect. As a consequence I was ordered released from custody. I was in the Berkeley jail long enough to sample the luncheon cuisine, and out again in time for dinner with friends.

Crittenden got the flu and went on vacation. Judge Floyd Talbot took his place, and our attorneys tried again, bringing before him motions to

Stephen Jon Lustig: appeal; 3 counts, stipulation; 1 year probation, $150 fine, 10 days suspended

Rolf Hasso Lutz: deceased before appeal (motorcycle accident); 3 counts, trial; 1 year probation, $75 fine

Glenn A. Lyons: appeal; 3 counts, trial; 1 year probation, $150 fine, 10 days suspended

Robert B. MacLaren: appeal; 3 counts, trial; 1 year probation, $150 fine, 10 days suspended

Alys Mainhart: 3 counts, stipulation; 1 year probation, $150 fine, 10 days suspended

Edward Malbin: appeal; 3 counts, stipulation; 1 year probation, $150 fine, 10 days suspended

Thomas Mallard: 3 counts, nolo; 6 months probation

William Maraskin: newspaper listing only

Michael Marcus: appeal; 3 counts, trial; 2 years probation, $200 fine, 10 days suspended

Michela M. Marcus: appeal; 2 counts, stipulation; 1 year probation

Louis Margetti: appeal; 3 counts, stipulation; 1 year probation, $150 fine, 10 days suspended

Brian Mark: appeal; 3 counts, stipulation; 1 year probation, $150 fine, 10 days suspended

Karen Mark: 3 counts, nolo; 1 year probation, $75 fine

Landis F. Markley: appeal; 3 counts, stipulation; 1 year probation, $150 fine, 10 days suspended

Philip N. Marsh: appeal; 3 counts, stipulation; 1 year probation, $150 fine, 10 days suspended

Lawrence F. Marshik: 3 counts, stipulation; 1 year probation, $150 fine, 10 days suspended

Clarke Mason: appeal; 2 counts, stipulation; $100 fine or 10 days in jail

Martha E. Masterson: appeal; 2 counts, stipulation; 1 year probation, $50 fine

Peter D. Matteson: appeal; 3 counts, trial; $250 fine or 25 days in jail

Susan Hester Mattox: 2 counts, stipulation; 1 year probation, $50 fine

Robert S. McClintock: 3 counts, nolo; 1 year probation, $75 fine

John F. McDaniel: appeal; 3 counts, stipulation; 1 year probation, $150 fine, 10 days suspended

Walter B. McGah: appeal; 3 counts, stipulation; 2 years probation, $150 fine, 10 days suspended

Margaret McKean: 2 counts, nolo; 6 months probation, $25 fine

Sandy McKean: appeal; 2 counts, stipulation; 1 year probation, $50 fine

Douglas E. McLaughlin: appeal; 3 counts, stipulation; 1 year probation, $150 fine, 10 days suspended

Pamela Mellin: appeal; 3 counts, trial; 2 years probation

Paula H. Mellon: 2 counts, nolo; 6 months probation, $25 fine

David J. Melnick: appeal; 3 counts, stipulation; $250 fine or 25 days in jail

Ralph Mendershausen: appeal; 3 counts, trial; 1 year probation, $150 fine, 10 days suspended

Elizabeth B. Merrill: appeal; 3 counts, stipulation; 1 year probation, $150 fine, 10 days suspended

John Arthur Meyer: appeal; 2 counts, stipulation; 1 year probation, $50 fine

Richard R. Meyer: appeal; 3 counts, trial; 2 years probation, $150 fine, 10 days suspended

Richard Meyers: appeal; 3 counts, stipulation; 1 year probation, $150 fine, 10 days suspended

Helen C. Michen: 3 counts, stipulation; 1 year probation

Dustin Miller: newspaper listing only; probably not arrested in Sproul Hall

Evelyn Miller: appeal; 3 counts, stipulation; $250 fine or 25 days in jail

Richard Miller: appeal; 3 counts, stipulation; 1 year probation, $150 fine, 10 days suspended

Tom Miller: probably arrested

Wendy Miller: appeal; 3 counts, trial; 1 year probation, $150 fine, 10 days suspended

William Miller: appeal; 3 counts, stipulation; 1 year probation, $150 fine, 10 days suspended

John O. Milligan: appeal; 2 counts, stipulation; $100 fine or 10 days in jail

reduce or altogether eliminate the bail required for defendants to remain at liberty pending appeal of their convictions. Our attorney, Francis Heisler, argued that if the $550 appeal bond stood, it was tantamount to depriving us of our right to appeal; in addition to the $300,000 appeal bail, the legal costs of the appeals would be between $10,000 and $15,000. Deputy district attorney Lowell Jensen replied that the size of the appeal bonds was "up to the good judgment of the trial court," that on one sentencing day 47 percent of the defendants had failed to appear, and that eighty bench warrants were outstanding for defendants who hadn't showed up when they were supposed to.[2] Judge Talbot denied the motion to reduce bail.

On August 12, Talbot sentenced seventy more defendants and recessed the court until September 13.

On Friday, August 13, six of us—John Levinson, Jack Weinberg, Dunbar Aitkins, Anita Levine, Nicholas Zvegintzov and I—went to jail rather than post appeal bond. David Melnick, David James, Barbara Bridges, Barbara Garson and Lewis Lester went to jail rather than put up appeal bail during the next week, bringing the total to eleven. All of the 561 other defendants who chose to appeal put up either the whole bail or the bail bond. Not many of them were helped by the FSM's defense fund, which was flat broke.

Peter Franck thinks that we went to jail intentionally to keep the appeal alive by a few people refusing to post bond. Mal Burnstein thinks that with the appeal going, figuring it would lose, some of us decided to serve time now instead of later. This would certainly have helped to keep the matter in the minds of the troops, if nothing else, and we could always ask for a stay of execution of the balance of the sentence pending the outcome of the appeal. Since it was only a misdemeanor charge, there would have been no problem breaking off the sentence with a stay of execution at any time. We could always serve the balance sometime down the pike.

Jack Weinberg: At the end of the trial, we were informed that the leaders would get some jail time and that probation was going to be part of everyone's sentence. For me and others, a central goal of the FSM had been a struggle to involve students in civil rights activism in the face of a University administration pressure to cut it off. Now we were faced with sentences that would put eight hundred of the most committed student activists on probation.

I (and others) saw accepting probation as something like a promise not to participate in demonstrations during the probation period, and in

Marilyn Milligan: appeal; 3 counts, trial; $250 fine or 25 days in jail

Carolyn Millstein: appeal; 3 counts, trial; 1 year probation, $150 fine, 10 days suspended

Jerry Millstein: appeal; 3 counts, trial; 1 year probation, $150 fine, 10 days suspended

Mary A. Minch: 3 counts, nolo; 1 year probation, $75 fine

David Minkus: appeal; 3 counts, stipulation; $250 fine or 25 days in jail

Dorian Mintzer: 3 counts, nolo; 1 year probation, $75 fine

Charles C. Mitchell: appeal; 3 counts, stipulation; $250 fine or 25 days in jail

Ronald L. Mock: appeal; 2 counts, stipulation; 1 year probation, $50 fine

James Donald Moon: appeal; 3 counts, stipulation; 1 year probation, $150 fine, 10 days suspended

Stanley A. Moore: appeal; 3 counts, stipulation; 1 year probation, $150 fine, 10 days suspended

Marc O. Morris: appeal; 3 counts, stipulation; 1 year probation, $150 fine, 10 days suspended

Ronald D. Morrison: appeal; 3 counts, trial; $250 fine or 25 days in jail

Judy Morshead: appeal; 3 counts, stipulation; 1 year probation, $150 fine, 10 days suspended

Elfreda L. Mortenson: appeal; 3 counts, stipulation; 1 year probation, $150 fine, 10 days suspended

Michael A. Mosher: 2 counts, nolo; 6 months probation, $25 fine

Robert Moule: appeal; 3 counts, stipulation; 1 year probation, $150 fine, 10 days suspended

Hans Mueller: newspaper listing only

Hanna Muldavin: appeal; 3 counts, stipulation; 1 year probation, $150 fine, 10 days suspended

Peter Muldavin: appeal; 3 counts, stipulation; 1 year probation, $150 fine, 10 days suspended

Rodney G. Mullen: appeal; 3 counts, trial; 1 year probation, $150 fine, 10 days suspended

Richard A. Muller: 3 counts, nolo; 1 year probation, $75 fine

Laura Mura: defendants' list only

William Muraskin: 3 counts, nolo; 1 year probation, $75 fine

Craig W. Murphy: appeal; 3 counts, stipulation; $250 fine or 25 days in jail

Stephan T. Murphy: appeal; 3 counts, trial; 1 year probation, $150 fine, 10 days suspended

Carol Muryama: appeal; 2 counts, stipulation; 1 year probation, $50 fine

Miklos Nagy: charges dropped

Richard H. Nanas: appeal; 3 counts, stipulation; 1 year probation, $150 fine, 10 days suspended

Margaret Neidorf: appeal; 3 counts, trial; $250 fine or 25 days in jail

Mary Elizabeth Nelbach: appeal; 3 counts, trial; 1 year probation, $150 fine, 10 days suspended

Mary Louise Nelson: appeal; 3 counts, stipulation; $250 fine or 25 days in jail

Victoria L. Nelson: appeal; 2 counts, stipulation; 1 year probation, $50 fine

Steven D. Nickerson: appeal; 3 counts, stipulation; 1 year probation, $150 fine, 10 days in jail

David H. Noble: appeal; 3 counts, stipulation; 1 year probation, $150 fine, 10 days suspended

James Normandin: 3 counts, nolo; 1 year probation, $75 fine

Robert Novick: appeal; 2 counts, stipulation; 2 years probation, $50 fine

Carole Nusinow: appeal; 3 counts, trial; 1 year probation, $150 fine, 10 days suspended

Norman Lee Oleson: appeal; 3 counts, stipulation; 1 year probation, $150 fine, 10 days suspended

Michael Olive: appeal; 3 counts, stipulation; $250 fine or 25 days in jail

Robert W. Oliver: appeal; 3 counts, stipulation; 1 year probation, $50 fine

Edwin J. Oliviera: appeal; 2 counts, stipulation; 1 year probation, $50 fine

Madeline Ollson: juvenile

Nora Jean Opler: appeal; 3 counts, stipulation; $250 fine or 25 days in jail

Eleanor Osgood: appeal; 3 counts, stipulation; 1 year probation, $150 fine, 10 days suspended

UC's Warning on Fraternity Bias

By James Benet

University of California fraternities and sororities were sharply warned by several university regents yesterday about their racial practices.

"I think fraternities, including my own, do practice discrimination," said Regent Fred Dutton, Los Angeles and Washington attorney.

"I intend to make an issue of it, if during the rush period in the next two months they don't take a look in good faith at people from minority groups.

FREE CHOICE

"They don't have to choose them—I support their right of free choice of associates—but they should really take a look and select people on an individual basis," Dutton declared.

UC President Clark Kerr said the University's policy of requiring non-discrimination pledges from living groups is not merely legalistic, and that the administration can and will actively oversee their practices.

Dutton failed an an attempt to have the Regents put off their decision on a plan to allow student living groups give their houses to the University, and then lease them back, so that gifts and bequests for the houses will be deductible for income tax purposes.

NEW PROGRAM

Regents William Coblentz, Mrs. Edward Heller, and Norton Simon supported Dutton's request for delay, but the Regents voted to go ahead after they were told that one Berkeley fraternity will close unless the plan is promptly approved.

Under the program, living groups may use the University name for fund-raising purposes.

Dutton objected.

"Are not great political issues as important educationally as living quarters? Yet the board refuses to allow the University name to students involved in them.

David Goines, with toothbrush, was prepared for his 60-day sentence

Appeal Bond 'Too High'

Jail for Six UC Sit-Ins

By Don Wegars

Six convicted University of California sit-in demonstrators chose yesterday to go to jail instead of paying what they considered exorbitant bail to appeal their convictions.

high, the defendants are being denied "for financial reasons" their Constitutional right of appeal.

He said the first phase alone of the appeal process will cost about $15,000.

Coincidently, it was announced out of court that an

ters in his behalf. But Levenson said he still was unable to afford the bond.

The court ordered the same bond reduction for 29-year-old Robert MacLaren, who posted the $200. Judge Talbott said he had been, "very

A Welcome For UC's Ludwig

Ludwig, the University of California's amphibious mascot, may yet find a way out of troubled waters.

The German shorthair, who has lent his name to the fountain across the plaza from Sproul Hall, will move with his master, John Littleford, to Alameda this fall.

And Alameda is a city which takes a dim view of leash-less German shorthairs, regardless of their celebrity.

The University—from administration to student body—has been in something of a flap since the announcement of the dog's departure was made some ten days ago.

It was revealed yesterday that Luwig has been offer3d the use of the fountain in front of the new Alameda irst National Bank at 2424 Santa Clara avenue.

Bank president Russell Spillman suggested, at any rate, that Ludwig try out the fountain. Then "if you find it satisfactory," he wrote in a letter to the dog, "we would be most happy to make it available for your recreation."

Forrest Tregea, executive director of the Associated Students of the University of California, thanked Spillman for the offer, but suggested that the bank fountain be made free of "beatniks, radicals, subversives, communists and troublemakers."

These people, said Tregea, have had Ludwig "very troubled" during his si-year tenure at Cal.

"DAVID GOINES, WITH TOOTHBRUSH, WAS PREPARED FOR HIS 60–DAY SENTENCE."
SF CHRONICLE, AUGUST 14, 1965.

Daniel F. Paik: appeal; 3 counts, stipulation; $250 fine or 25 days in jail

Michael Papo: appeal; 3 counts, trial; 1 year probation, $150 fine, 10 days suspended

David C. Parke: appeal; 3 counts, stipulation; 1 year probation, $150 fine, 10 days suspended

Peter R. Paskin: 3 counts, nolo; 1 year probation, $75 fine

Eugene Patterson: appeal; 3 counts, stipulation; 1 year probation, $150 fine, 10 days suspended

Sandra Patton: 3 counts, stipulation; 1 year probation, $150 fine, 10 days suspended

Alan R. Paulson: appeal; 2 counts, stipulation; 1 year probation, $50 fine

Dennis Peacocke: appeal; 3 counts, trial; 1 year probation, $150 fine, 10 days suspended

Terry Peacocke: appeal; 2 counts, stipulation; 1 year probation, $50 fine

Judith Peters: appeal; 3 counts, stipulation; 1 year probation, $150 fine, 10 days suspended

Susan B. Peterson: appeal; 3 counts, stipulation; 1 year probation, $150 fine, 10 days suspended

Merrilyn Phillips: appeal; 2 counts, stipulation; 1 year probation, $50 fine

Ronn Pickard: appeal; 3 counts, trial; $250 fine or 25 days in jail

Thomas Pierce: appeal; 3 counts, stipulation; 1 year probation, $150 fine, 10 days suspended

Bohdan Pilacinski: appeal; 3 counts, stipulation; 1 year probation, $150 fine, 10 days suspended

Harold M. Pinsker: appeal; 3 counts, stipulation; 1 year probation, $150 fine, 10 days suspended

Stephen Plagemann: appeal; 3 counts, stipulation; 1 year probation, $150 fine, 10 days suspended

Martha Platt: appeal; 2 counts, stipulation; 1 year probation, $50 fine

Patricia Power: appeal; 3 counts, stipulation; 1 year probation, $150 fine, 10 days suspended

Haley Lynne Pyle: appeal; 2 counts, stipulation; 1 year probation, $50 fine

Jack N. Radey: juvenile

Judith J. Radu: appeal; 2 counts, stipulation; 1 year probation, $50 fine

Faith Rafkind: 2 counts, stipulation; 1 year probation, $50 fine

Michael Raugh: appeal; 3 counts, stipulation; $250 fine or 25 days in jail

Eric Rawlins: 3 counts, stipulation; 1 year probation, $150 fine, 10 days suspended

Martin Rechsteiner: 2 counts, stipulation; 1 year probation, $50 fine

Craig Reece: appeal; 3 counts, stipulation; $250 fine or 25 days in jail

Richard Reichbart: appeal; 2 counts, stipulation; 1 year probation, $50 fine

John Reinsch: appeal; 3 counts, stipulation; $250 fine or 25 days in jail

Tanga Reske: appeal; 3 counts, stipulation; $250 fine or 25 days in jail

Norman Rhett: appeal; 2 counts, stipulation; 1 year probation, $50 fine

Lee Rhoades, Jr.: 2 counts, nolo; 6 months probation, $50 fine

Barbara Rice: appeal; 2 counts, stipulation; $100 fine or 10 days in jail

Walter Rice: 3 counts, nolo; 1 year probation, $75 fine

David H. Richardson: appeal; 3 counts, stipulation; $250 fine or 25 days in jail

Allan Rooks Robbins: 2 counts, stipulation; 1 year probation, $50 fine

John Roberts: appeal; 3 counts, stipulation; $250 fine or 25 days in jail

Judy Robinson: 2 counts, stipulation; 1 year probation, $50 fine

Steven Robman: appeal; 3 counts, trial; 1 year probation, $150 fine, 10 days suspended

Martin H. Rock: 3 counts, nolo; 1 year probation, $75 fine

Carl Rodriguez: appeal; 3 counts, stipulation; 1 year probation, $150 fine, 10 days suspended

Janet Rogers: appeal; 3 counts, stipulation; 1 year probation

Hal Rosen: 2 counts, stipulation; 1 year probation, $50 fine

Edward J. Rosenfeld: appeal; 3 counts, trial; $250 fine or 25 days in jail

Larry Rosenzweig: appeal; 2 counts, stipulation; 1 year probation, $50 fine

the world of student politics, one year is a long, long time. To indicate our intention of continuing with demonstrations, several of us—including you [David Goines] and me—informed the judge we would not accept probation. I think we also refused appeal bail as a way of expressing displeasure at how the whole thing had been handled. Those who refused probation had time added to their sentences. As it turned out, no machinery was ever set up to revoke anyone's probation. However, I believe that if the leaders had gone along with probation, the authorities might have used

VIETNAM DAY COMMITTEE ORGANIZER JERRY RUBIN. PHOTO BY HOWARD HARAWITZ.

it to try and halt later demonstrations.

Going to jail at the end of the trial was our choice—a sort of demonstration. It may have been partly motivated by a feeling that we activists had lost control to the lawyers during the trial, that we had been forced—in solidarity with the other defendants—to go along with a farce. At the end of the trial, we were again free to act and preferred jail to the lawyers' charade. I think it was our way of saying, "The struggle goes on." It may also have been a way of sending a message to the majority of sit-inners who would have to do no jail time—a message that jail was nothing to be feared and that probation should not discourage them from participating in future demonstrations. After serving one month, bail was posted and we were released. In 1967, everyone with time to serve came to jail.[3]

So, on the day of the trial when we knew who was going to get what, I put my toothbrush in my pocket (giving the news photographers a swell picture as I kissed my girlfriend Patti Iiyama good-bye), and in considerable excitement mingled with only the mildest of fore-

Richard Rosenzweig: appeal; 2 counts, stipulation; $100 fine or 10 days in jail

Leonard Rosi: appeal; 3 counts, stipulation; 1 year probation, $150 fine, 10 days suspended

Andrew B. Ross: appeal; 2 counts, stipulation; 1 year probation, $50 fine

Deborah Rossman: appeal; 3 counts, trial; 1 year probation, $150 fine, 10 days suspended

Michael Rossman: appeal; 3 counts, trial; 2 years probation, 90 days in jail

Cydny E. Rothe: appeal; 3 counts, stipulation; 1 year probation, $150 fine, 10 days suspended

Netta Rovelli: 3 counts, nolo; 1 year probation, $75 fine

Carolyn C. Rubin: appeal; 3 counts, stipulation; 1 year probation, $150 fine, 10 days suspended

James K. Ryan: 3 counts, stipulation; 1 year probation, $150 fine, 10 days suspended

Mara Sabinson: appeal; 3 counts, trial; 1 year probation, $150 fine, 10 days suspended

Donald Stone Sade: 3 counts, nolo; 1 year probation, $75 fine

Earl C. Salo: 3 counts, nolo; 1 year probation, $75 fine

Kenneth Salzberg: appeal; 2 counts, stipulation; 1 year probation, $50 fine

Barbara A. Samuels: appeal; 3 counts, stipulation; $250 fine or 25 days in jail

Jim Samuels: appeal; 3 counts, stipulation; $250 fine or 25 days in jail

Peter A. Sanders: appeal; 3 counts, stipulation; 1 year probation, $150 fine, 10 days suspended

Leland Sandifur: appeal; 3 counts, stipulation; 1 year probation, $150 fine, 10 days suspended

Ruth Sapiro: appeal; 3 counts, stipulation; $250 fine or 25 days in jail

Paul Russell Sapp: appeal; 2 counts, stipulation; 1 year probation, $50 fine

Steven Saslow: appeal; 3 counts, trial; 1 year probation, $150 fine, 10 days suspended

William Satterthwaite: appeal; 3 counts, trial; 1 year probation, $150 fine, 10 days suspended

Richard A. Saunders: appeal; 3 counts, trial; $250 fine or 25 days in jail

Mario Savio: appeal; 3 counts, trial; 120 days in jail

Joan Scheingold: appeal; 3 counts, stipulation; 1 year probation, $150 fine, 10 days suspended

Rebecca Schiffrin: appeal; 3 counts, stipulation; 1 year probation, $150 fine, 10 days suspended

Emile Dan Schimenti: appeal; 3 counts, stipulation; 1 year probation, $150 fine, 10 days suspended

Michael Schlesinger: 3 counts, nolo; 1 year probation, $75 fine

Richard Schmorleitz: appeal; 3 counts, trial; 2 years probation, $150 fine, 10 days suspended

Maxine Schoenbrun: 3 counts, nolo; $150 fine or 15 days in jail

Katura N. Schoene: 3 counts, stipulation; 1 year probation

Judith Schorer: appeal; 3 counts, stipulation; $250 fine or 25 days in jail

Michael Schreiber: 3 counts, trial; $250 fine or 25 days in jail

Marston A. Schultz: appeal; 3 counts, stipulation; $250 fine or 25 days in jail

Uriel Schumm: appeal; 3 counts, stipulation; 1 year probation, $150 fine, 10 days suspended

Judith Schwartz: 3 counts, nolo; 1 year probation, $75 fine

George C. Seay, Jr.: appeal; 2 counts, stipulation; 1 year probation, $50 fine

Diana Elizabeth Senf: appeal; 3 counts, trial; 1 year probation, $150 fine, 10 days suspended

Anne Shapiro: appeal; 3 counts, stipulation; $250 fine or 25 days in jail

Dana Rae Shapiro: appeal; 3 counts, trial; $250 fine or 25 days in jail

Lawrence M. Shapiro: appeal; 3 counts, trial; 1 year probation, $150 fine, 10 days suspended

Marsha Shapiro: appeal; 3 counts, stipulation; $250 fine or 25 days in jail

Ruth Shapiro: defendants' list only

Kate M. Shattuck: appeal; 3 counts, trial; 1 year probation, $150 fine, 10 days suspended

Richard J. Shavitz: 3 counts, stipulation; 1 year probation, $150 fine, 10 days suspended

Photographs by Steve Somerstein

BODIES ON THE GEARS . . . A demonstrator protesting the war in Vietnam stands aside as the "war machine" roars by. Vietnam Day Committee spokesman says they will stop the troop trains in future. **(More pictures on Page 4.)**

VDC ORGANIZED BERKELEY TROOP TRAIN PROTESTS OF AUGUST 12, 1965.
DAILY CAL PHOTO BY STEVE SOMERSTEIN.

boding, was bundled off to the holding tank in the Berkeley city jail. We joked and sang, and approached it as a gloomy lark. I was proud that I had been given one of the more severe sentences. It made me feel that I was important and really was getting to them.

Just before we began our jail terms, the Black folks of Watts decided to go hog wild, violating the most basic rule of survival, which is "Don't shit where you eat." They set out to blow up, burn down, loot and pillage their entire section of Los Angeles. National guardsmen moved in, and four people were killed. In Chicago, Black rioters trashed a fire station and rioted for the second consecutive night.

The Vietnam War had attracted our attentions, as well, and kept them firmly focused. Berkeley campus protests on May 21, 1965— called "Vietnam Day"—kicked off the massive, unremitting student resistance to the Vietnam War. On the tenth of August, two hundred Vietnam Day Committee (VDC) protesters invaded the Berkeley City Council chambers, demanding that the council deny the Santa Fe railroad's permit to carry troops through Berkeley to the Oakland army base. The city voted unanimously against the proposal. Two days later, Jerry Rubin led a demonstration of some five hundred anti–Vietnam

Robert J. Shaw: 3 counts, stipulation; 1 year probation, $150 fine, 10 days suspended

Michael A. Shea: appeal; 3 counts, trial; 2 years probation, $150 fine, 10 days suspended

Michael Sheats: 3 counts, nolo; 1 year probation, $75 fine

Mark Shechner: appeal; 3 counts, trial; 1 year probation, $150 fine, 10 days suspended

Dennis Sheldrick: appeal; 2 counts, stipulation; 1 year probation, $50 fine

Mary Jane Sheppard: appeal; 3 counts, stipulation; 1 year probation, $150 fine, 10 days suspended

Mary E. Shippee: appeal; 3 counts, stipulation; 1 year probation, $150 fine, 10 days suspended

Michael Shodell: appeal; 2 counts, stipulation; $100 fine or 10 days in jail

David Glenn Showers: appeal; 3 counts, trial; 2 years probation, $150 fine, 10 days suspended

Beth Susan Shub: appeal; 3 counts, stipulation; $250 fine or 25 days in jail

Michael Ira Shub: appeal; 3 counts, stipulation; $250 fine or 25 days in jail

Jeff Shurin: 3 counts, nolo; 1 year probation

Ilene Siegel: appeal; 3 counts, stipulation; $250 fine or 25 days in jail

Leni Siegel: appeal; 3 counts, stipulation; 1 year probation, $150 fine, 10 days suspended

Edward Jose Silveira: appeal; 3 counts, stipulation; 1 year probation, $150 fine, 10 days suspended

Ann-Judith Silverman: 3 counts, stipulation; 1 year probation, $150 fine, 10 days suspended

Barbara R. Silverman: appeal; 3 counts, stipulation; $250 fine or 25 days in jail

Barry M. Silverman: appeal; 3 counts, stipulation; $250 fine or 25 days in jail

Murray Silverstein: appeal; 3 counts, stipulation; 1 year probation, $150 fine, 10 days suspended

Tedi Siminowski: appeal; 3 counts, trial; $250 fine or 25 days in jail

Keith J. Simons: appeal; 3 counts, stipulation; $250 fine or 25 days in jail

Durward Skiles: appeal; 3 counts, trial; 1 year probation, $150 fine, 10 days suspended

Marsha Skolnick: 3 counts, nolo; 1 year probation, $75 fine

Samuel P. Slatkin: juvenile

David P. Smith: appeal; 3 counts, stipulation; 1 year probation, $150 fine, 10 days suspended

Garwood Smith: appeal; 3 counts, stipulation; $250 fine or 25 days in jail

James Curtis Smith: appeal; 3 counts, stipulation; $250 fine or 25 days in jail

Jerry S. Smith: 3 counts, nolo; 1 year probation, $75 fine

Jon Rogers Smith: appeal; 3 counts, trial; $250 fine or 25 days in jail

Linda Frances Smith: appeal; 3 counts, trial; $250 fine or 25 days in jail

Michael James Smith: appeal; 3 counts, stipulation; $250 fine or 25 days in jail

Michael Reid Smith: appeal; 3 counts, stipulation; 1 year probation, $150 fine, 10 days suspended

Sharon F. Smith: appeal; 3 counts, stipulation; 1 year probation, $150 fine, 10 days suspended

Valerie A. Smith: 2 counts, stipulation; 1 year probation, $50 fine

Hershel Snodgrass: appeal; 3 counts, stipulation; $250 fine or 25 days in jail

Andrea Snow: appeal; 3 counts, stipulation; 1 year probation, $150 fine, 10 days suspended

Russell Snyder: appeal; 2 counts, stipulation; $100 fine or 10 days in jail

Suzanne Sobel: appeal; 3 counts, stipulation; 1 year probation, $150 fine, 10 days suspended

Fred Sokolow: appeal; 3 counts, stipulation; $250 fine or 25 days in jail

Kathleen Wilson Sokolow: appeal; 3 counts, trial; 1 year probation, $150 fine

Stephen A. Sokolow: appeal; 3 counts, stipulation; $100 fine or 10 days in jail

Earl C. Solo: newspaper listing only

Susan Sonnenshein: appeal; 3 counts, stipulation; 1 year probation, $150 fine, 10 days suspended

Leonard Sosna: appeal; 3 counts, stipulation; 1 year probation, $150 fine, 10 days suspended

William G. Stanton: appeal; 2 counts, stipulation; 1 year probation

War protesters to the Santa Fe railroad station, where they sat on the tracks, boarded the train, pulled the emergency stop cord, leafleted conscripts and kicked off seven years of progressively violent protest against the U.S. government's stupid, wasteful effort to interfere in the internal affairs of the pocket-handkerchief-sized nation of Vietnam.

The lid was coming off, all over. Things were going to get a *whole* lot worse by the end of the decade.

We spent the night in the Berkeley jail, and early next morning were loaded into a bus with barred windows and a wire-meshed-off driver and delivered over to the tender mercies of the county sheriff's department. It wasn't quite as much fun as when we had gone to Santa Rita the first time, in a huge, disorganized, hollering mass. This time there were only a few of us, and we knew that we were not popular with the authorities. Jack and I, along with the others of our lot and a dozen or so common criminals, were processed through, our clothing and property taken from us (I got to keep my toothbrush), and issued the baggy Navy-surplus blue jeans and work shirts of prisoners. The shoes were also Navy issue, big black clodhoppers that immediately gave me blisters.

First to the barber, a Black trusty who plainly did what he did reluctantly, but who had been told to cut our hair right straight off, and did. He apologized, in a gruff way, even as he scalped. Next to the delousing room, where we were liberally dusted with DDT powder (bend over and spread your cheeks). That was followed by a hot shower. When we were clean and shiny and bug-free, the resident doctor gave us a once-over-lightly, took a blood sample and sent us on our way. Then to the commissary, where cigarettes, candy, toothbrushes and toothpaste, underwear and socks, letter-writing materials and stamps were made available for those who had the wherewithal in their pockets when processed in. No state or federal tax was charged, which made smokes mighty cheap (I think they were about twelve cents a pack). Money could be placed into your account by outside people, too. I was, of course, completely broke, but good old Ernie Karsten had put ten dollars in my account. You could go to the commissary twice a week. I fell into the A–H category, so I went on Mondays and Thursdays.

I found out that in lieu of cash, cigarettes were money. L&Ms were at the bottom of the heap, and Pall Malls, which is what I smoked anyway, were the most sought after. The most you were permitted to buy in one week was a carton of smokes and five candy bars. Candy was dandy, but tobacco was what made the world go around. Those who had no money in their accounts made do with one ounce of dry, flaky,

Elizabeth Stapleton: appeal; 3 counts, trial; $350 fine or 35 days in jail

Sydney R. Stapleton: appeal; 3 counts, stipulation; 30 days in jail

Bernard L. Stein: appeal; 2 counts, stipulation; $100 fine or 10 days in jail

Julie Stein: 3 counts, nolo; 1 year probation, $75 fine

Alan B. Steinberg: appeal; 3 counts, trial; 1 year probation, $150 fine, 10 days suspended

Karen Steiner: appeal; 2 counts, stipulation; 1 year probation, $50 fine

Marylee Stephenson: 3 counts, nolo; 1 year probation, $50 fine

John R. Stering: appeal; 3 counts, stipulation; $250 fine or 25 days in jail

Lee Charles Stern: 3 counts, nolo; 1 year probation, $75 fine

Sharon Stern: probably arrested

Michael R. Stevens: appeal; 3 counts, trial; 1 year probation, $150 fine, 10 days suspended

Price Stiffler, Jr.: appeal; 2 counts, stipulation; 1 year probation, $50 fine

Peter Stine: appeal; 3 counts, stipulation; 1 year probation, $150 fine, 10 days suspended

Eugene Stromberg: appeal; 3 counts, trial; 1 year probation, $150 fine, 10 days suspended

Elizabeth Sucher: 3 counts, nolo; 1 year probation, $75 fine

Gary I. Sugarman: appeal; 3 counts, stipulation; 2 years probation, $150 fine, 10 days suspended

Thomas C. Sullivan: appeal; 3 counts, stipulation; $250 fine or 25 days in jail

Frank Summers: appeal; 3 counts, stipulation; 1 year probation, $150 fine, 10 days suspended

Terry Norman Sumner: deceased before trial (canoeing accident on the Colorado River)

Mark H. Switzer: 3 counts, nolo; 1 year probation, $75 fine

Stephen Tabachnick: 3 counts, nolo; 1 year probation, $75 fine

Penelope Taft: appeal; 3 counts, stipulation; $250 fine or 25 days in jail

Mae Takagi: appeal; 3 counts, stipulation; $250 fine or 25 days in jail

Jan Tangen: appeal; 3 counts, stipulation; 1 year probation, $150 fine, 10 days suspended

Barbara Tapper: 3 counts, nolo; 1 year probation, $75 fine

John I. Taylor: 3 counts, nolo; 1 year probation, $50 fine

Karen Taylor: 3 counts, nolo; 1 year probation, $75 fine

Lynne Taylor: 3 counts, stipulation; 1 year probation, $150 fine, 10 days suspended

Damon Tempey: appeal; 3 counts, stipulation; $250 fine or 25 days in jail

Marvin Tener: appeal; 3 counts, stipulation; 1 year probation, $150 fine, 10 days suspended

Paul Terwilliger: appeal; 3 counts, stipulation; 1 year probation, $150 fine, 10 days suspended

Lois Thomas: appeal; 3 counts, trial; $250 fine or 25 days in jail

Adrienne H. Thon: appeal; 3 counts, stipulation; $250 fine or 25 days in jail

Keith Thoreen: appeal; 3 counts, trial; 1 year probation, $150 fine, 10 days suspended

Carol Tout: appeal; 3 counts, stipulation; $250 fine or 25 days in jail

Robert E. Treuhaft: separated and case dismissed

Sue Trupin: appeal; 3 counts, trial; $250 fine or 25 days in jail

Brian J. Turner: appeal; 3 counts, stipulation; 2 years probation, 60 days in jail

William Turner: appeal; 3 counts, stipulation; 1 year probation, $150 fine, 10 days suspended

David A. Tussman: 2 counts, stipulation; 6 months probation

Albert L. Upton: appeal; 3 counts, trial; 1 year probation, $150 fine, 10 days suspended

Michael F. Urmann: appeal; 3 counts, stipulation; 1 year probation, $150 fine, 10 days suspended

John Van Eps: appeal; 3 counts, stipulation; 1 year probation, $150 fine, 10 days suspended

Carolyn Lee Vaughn: 3 counts, stipulation; 1 year probation, $150 fine, 10 days suspended

soapy-tasting, state-issue tobacco every Monday, or did odd services for wealthier inmates to earn a smoke here and there. There wasn't much to do, nor much possible in the way of conspicuous consumption or show, so the smallest service or distinction was sought after and carried a premium. Pall Mall wrappers were used for crafts, and woven into the shape of picture frames and other decorative gifts. Clothes were laboriously "ironed" in the sun with weights, and lined, warm denim coats and newer shirts were bartered for cigarettes. I paid one pack a week for a cup of coffee in the morning, made with grounds stolen from the mess and boiled with a "stinger"—an appallingly dangerous device made of a length of wire and a plug; it heats water by simply running a live current through it. That coffee was the only good stuff there was to drink, the mess hall coffee being made from water recirculated through the grounds of what had already been used by the officers. There wasn't ever enough good coffee to go around.

One of our attorneys, Larry Duga, stuffed a handful of Marsh Wheeling stogies into my pocket when we were closeted in the privileged lawyer-client cubicles. The guards shook me down after the conference, of course, but they were looking for weapons or drugs, not cigars. I gave the cigars away judiciously, earning the genuine gratitude of a few key inmates. I gave two to the big Black guy who had said, when a white cracker-type was harassing Jack, "Boy, I got six weeks of good time, and I'm willing to spend it all on you." Nobody even looked cross-eyed at us after that.

The deal was that if you minded your affairs, and worked at one of the jobs available to inmates, you got "good time," which is the reduction of your sentence by as much as one-fourth. The longer your sentence, and the shorter you get, the more you are held hostage to your good time.* Near the end of nine months of a one-year sentence, people get awfully good, and quiet. You could also get ten days off your sentence for every time you gave blood. Lots of people gave blood. Jack maintains that we both did so, but if I did, I have no recollection of it. I got out after thirty days, having served only half my sentence, and when I returned in 1967 to serve the balance of my sentence, there was some question of whether or not my good time should be counted from the stretch I served before, or whether I was out that time. Since I served exactly thirty days in 1967, I guess I didn't get it.

The men's part of the jail was made up of five compounds of bar-

---

*People near the end of their sentences are "short"; that is, they have only a short portion of their term to serve.

Esther R. Veedell: appeal; 3 counts, stipulation; 1 year probation, $150 fine, 10 days suspended

Brian Viani: appeal; 3 counts, stipulation; 1 year probation, $150 fine, 10 days suspended

Julia Vinograd: 2 counts, nolo; 6 months probation

Robert Vogel: appeal; 3 counts, stipulation; $250 fine or 25 days in jail

John Von Golwyn: appeal; 3 counts, stipulation; $250 fine or 25 days in jail

Dale Vree: 3 counts, nolo; 1 year probation, $75 fine

David R. Wald: appeal; 3 counts, stipulation; $250 fine or 25 days in jail

Hazel D. Wald: appeal; 3 counts, stipulation; $250 fine or 25 days in jail

Jack T. Waldron: appeal; 3 counts, stipulation; $250 fine or 25 days in jail

Hyale Wall: appeal; 3 counts, stipulation; 1 year probation, $150 fine, 10 days suspended

Marlin Wallach: appeal; 3 counts, trial; 2 years probation, $150 fine, 10 days suspended

Carolyn Walsh: appeal; 3 counts, stipulation; $250 fine or 25 days in jail

Jeffrey Walter: 2 counts, stipulation; 1 year probation, $50 fine

Virginia Kerber Walter: appeal; 3 counts, trial; 1 year probation, $150 fine, 10 days suspended

Alfred W. Walters: appeal; 3 counts, stipulation; 1 year probation, $150 fine, 10 days suspended

Phillip Michael Warren: appeal; 3 counts, stipulation; $250 fine or 25 days in jail

Myrna Wask: newspaper listing only

Donna Watson: appeal; 3 counts, stipulation; 1 year probation, $150 fine, 10 days suspended

William T. Webb: 2 counts, nolo; 6 months probation, $25 fine

Stephen Wedgley: 3 counts, nolo; 1 year probation, $75 fine

Ellen Wedum: appeal; 3 counts, stipulation; 1 year probation, $150 fine, 10 days suspended

James Weil: appeal; 3 counts, stipulation; 1 year probation, $150 fine, 10 days suspended

Jack Weinberg: appeal; 3 counts, trial; 120 days in jail

Michael Weinberger: appeal; 3 counts, stipulation; 1 year probation, $150 fine, 10 days suspended

Judith Weitman: 3 counts, nolo; 1 year probation, $75 fine

Alice Weldon: appeal; 2 counts, stipulation; $100 fine or 10 days in jail

Thomas W. Weller: appeal; 3 counts, stipulation; 1 year probation, $150 fine, 10 days suspended

Julie Wellings: appeal; 3 counts, stipulation; 1 year probation, $150 fine, 10 days suspended

David T. Wellman: appeal; 2 counts, stipulation; $100 fine or 10 days in jail

Andrew Wells: appeal; 3 counts, stipulation; 1 year probation, $150 fine, 10 days suspended

Benjamin Franklin Wells III: appeal; 3 counts, stipulation; $250 fine or 25 days in jail

Carolyn Wells: 3 counts, stipulation; 1 year probation, $150 fine, 10 days suspended

Marjorie Wennerberg: appeal; 3 counts, trial; $250 fine or 25 days in jail

Sumner L. West: appeal; 3 counts, stipulation; $250 fine or 25 days in jail

Lorace White: appeal; 3 counts, stipulation; 1 year probation, $150 fine, 10 days suspended

Lynda G. White: appeal; 2 counts, stipulation; 1 year probation, $50 fine

Ruth Eleanor White: 3 counts, nolo; 1 year probation, $75 fine

Sara Wickland: appeal; 3 counts, stipulation; 1 year probation, $150 fine, 10 days suspended

Diane Wiczai: appeal; 3 counts, stipulation; 1 year probation, $150 fine, 10 days suspended

Louis Wiczai, Jr.: appeal; 3 counts, stipulation; 1 year probation, $150 fine, 10 days suspended

Peter Wiesner: appeal; 2 counts, stipulation; 1 year probation, $50 fine

Anthony Wilde: appeal; 3 counts, trial; 2 years probation, $300 fine, 20 days suspended

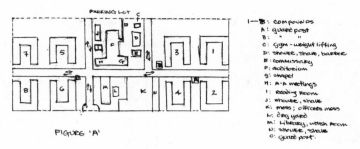

FIGURE 'A'

The whole surmounted, like candles on a cake, by machine gun towers – a memory of things past, as they seem not to be in use – although they are in good repair.

"THE WHOLE SURMOUNTED, LIKE CANDLES ON A CAKE, BY MACHINE GUN TOWERS—A MEMORY OF THINGS PAST, AS THEY SEEM NOT TO BE IN USE—ALTHOUGH THEY ARE IN GOOD REPAIR." I-8: COMPOUNDS; A: GUARDPOST; B: GUARDPOST; C: GYM-WEIGHTLIFTING; D: SHOWER, SHAVE, BARBER; E: COMMISSARY; F: AUDITORIUM; G: CHAPEL; H: AA MEETINGS; I: READING ROOM; J: SHOWER, SHAVE; K: MESS, OFFICERS' MESS; L: DRY YARD; M: LIBRARY, READING ROOM; N: SHOWER, SHAVE; O: GUARD POST. MAP OF SANTA RITA SENT BY THE AUTHOR IN A 1967 LETTER TO ALICE WATERS.

racks, each of which was self-contained and could be separately locked up. Each compound contained three separate barracks arranged in the shape of an asphalt U painted for basketball, the mouth of the U pointed inward toward the main street, the whole enclosed by a twelve-foot wire-mesh fence topped with barbed wire. Each barracks held twenty to forty men, and the whole population was about seven hundred. Peak occupancy was in the late summer, when as many as twelve hundred men were there, dwindling to as few as three hundred in the winter.

More or less in the center of the prison compound was a mess hall, a chapel and auditorium complex, the library, laundry room and dry-yard. Off the main street were three side streets, on which were shower rooms, the commissary and a small gym. The administration building and maximum security area were on the far west side of the compound, and the fire station and firemen's barracks were to the northeast. High-security Greystone and the small women's barracks were on the other side of the administrative area. Inside the compound were two guard towers. Prisoners were required to walk between white lines painted along the edges of the street and the gutter, keeping the center of the road clear. Running was not allowed.

The streets were lined with sad roses and stringy cactus. The plots around the booking office and administrative area were maintained by old-timers who manicured the grass and shrubs, but never managed to make them look less than moth-eaten.

The barracks were lit by sunlight during the day, and by two rows

Lyle Willis: appeal; 2 counts, stipulation; 1 year probation, $50 fine

Jeanne Wilson: appeal; 3 counts, stipulation; $250 fine or 25 days in jail

Seth Wingate: appeal; 3 counts, stipulation; $250 fine or 25 days in jail

Robert Winter: appeal; 3 counts, stipulation; 1 year probation, $150 fine, 10 days suspended

Susan Winthrop: appeal; 3 counts, stipulation; 1 year probation, $150 fine, 10 days suspended

David Wirt: 3 counts, nolo; 1 year probation, $75 fine

Stephen Wirtz: appeal; 2 counts, stipulation; $100 fine or 10 days in jail

Alan Wofsy: appeal; 3 counts, stipulation; 1 year probation, $150 fine, 10 days suspended

Goldye Wolf: appeal; 3 counts, stipulation; 1 year probation, $150 fine, 10 days suspended

Robert C. Wolfson: appeal; 3 counts, stipulation; $200 fine or 20 days in jail

Jonathan Woodner: appeal; 3 counts, stipulation; 1 year probation, $150 fine, 10 days suspended

Myrna Belle Wosk: 3 counts, nolo; 1 year probation, $75 fine

Warren Yee: 3 counts, nolo; 1 year probation, $75 fine

Florence Yellin: appeal; 3 counts, trial; 1 year probation, $150 fine, 10 days suspended

Ronald Kent Yoder: 2 counts, stipulation; 1 year probation, $50 fine

Barbara Zahm: appeal; 3 counts, stipulation; 1 year probation, $150 fine, 10 days suspended

Malcolm Zaretsky: appeal; 2 counts, stipulation; $100 fine or 10 days in jail

Ronald Zeiger: appeal; 3 counts, stipulation; 1 year probation, $150 fine, 10 days suspended

Janis Anne Zimdars: appeal; 3 counts, stipulation; 1 year probation, $150 fine, 10 days suspended

Laurel Zimmerman: appeal; 3 counts, stipulation; $250 fine or 25 days in jail

Matthew Zion: appeal; 3 counts, stipulation; $250 fine or 25 days in jail

Nicholas Zvegintzov: appeal; 3 counts, trial; $250 fine or 25 days in jail

Madeline Zysman: appeal; 3 counts, stipulation; 1 year probation, $150 fine, 10 days suspended

TOTAL 825

of eight naked bulbs in early morning and late evening. Three blue lamps spaced evenly along the ceiling burned all night.

The white-clad messmen lived in Barracks 6, the detail office and "white collar" workers in 2, and the firemen off to one side in 9. The prison hierarchy accommodated hard-core homosexuals without seeming to discriminate against them. They were put in an entirely different barracks in a separate part of the compound. The fire department was commonly understood to be staffed by homosexuals, further segregating them from the common run of inmate by their clothes as well as by their schedules. They wore khaki instead of blue, worked in three daily shifts and ate on a different timetable.

We FSMers were split up among the barracks, perhaps to forestall our organizing a prison union or something equally terrifying to the authorities, and I found myself all alone in a big dormitory with twenty malefactors, mostly Black. The single cots were spaced about three feet apart. Each prisoner was issued a thin cotton mattress, too-short top and bottom sheets, a pillow and pillow case and one dark green military blanket. Whenever you were reassigned anywhere, or were moved for trial, you bundled all this stuff up and took it with you. When things got crowded, the space could hold twice as many in bunk beds. We got counted eight times a day, and guards in pairs came through the barracks two times in each night to do a head count. If anyone was in the can, the guards would have a spaz attack and get all excited and give the guy a hard time, waking everyone up in the process. There were, of course, no private stalls or individual toilets. I had trouble squatting there in front of God and everybody trying to take a shit, and was constipated for the first couple of days. But nature worked her wonders with my bowels and soon everything was copacetic. I got used to it as just another part of the already alien life of being in jail.

The first night I was there, a poor old Black guy with the DTs raved and mumbled up and down the floor between the cots all night long, keeping everyone awake. People yelled at him and told him to shut the fuck up, but of course he didn't.

As it turned out, we were considered heroes by the Black prisoners and curiosities by the white ones, the Hispanics keeping to themselves as usual. Except for a few FSM defendants, there were no Asians. I was given no trouble, and came into a good share of polite concern from my fellows, most of whom were interested in us as exotic visitors to their world of petty screw-ups and ne'er-do-wells. We all were approached by the curious, and at any free moment one or another of us would be seen in conversation with some denizen of the underworld, being asked mostly plain questions about civil rights or left-wing pussy. Nobody, not even the guards, so much as pretended that we belonged there.

I wrote letters for the illiterate (genuine illiteracy came as a surprise to me), earning the sobriquet "professor" in my barracks, and something of a name for generosity because I didn't charge. Letters were restricted to two sheets of lined paper, written on the lines and on one side only, and were handed over unsealed at mail call. Incoming mail was similarly restricted, and delivered opened. Although you could write to the outside as much as you wanted, you could only receive one letter per week from any given person, and only one letter a day no matter what. Although I can't imagine that the authorities did more than give letters a once-over-lightly, the knowledge that big, grubby paws and prying eyes were involved in every postal transaction had a distinct chilling effect on the degree of literary intimacy indulged in between Patti and me. We also were forbidden to write anything about the internal affairs of the jail, or to comment on the prison system. Made for rather dull reading, I'm afraid. After a while we figured out that the guards could care less about the number of letters we got or what they said. In one letter I sent to Alice Waters when I was serving the balance of my time in 1967, I included a highly detailed plan of the entire prison, just to see if it would go through or not, and all that happened was that it was stamped just like all the others:

> LETTERS NOT TO EXCEED TWO PAGES
> USE ONLY ONE SIDE OF PAPER
> LIMIT ONE LETTER PER WEEK
> **SANTA RITA**
> **REHABILITATION CENTER**

In addition to letters from my friends, I got two from people I'd never heard of, one of whom sent me a dollar and warm encouragement.

It was sobering to encounter a type that I had not suspected existed: the institutional man. The old fellow was about sixty-five, and looked twenty years younger. He had first been arrested for armed robbery in 1917, and had been sentenced to thirty years. As soon as he got out, just before World War II, he did it again. He was currently doing some easy time for a misdemeanor smash and grab. In all, he hadn't spent six months on the outside since he was a lad, and although he talked a good fight, he clearly had no more notion of women or the ways of the world than would a child. He had been institutionalized. He couldn't survive away from the comfortable, familiar, *orderly* environment of prison. He had no concept of money, or of going to a store and buying clothes, or such ordinary things. When he got out, he was confused by the choices, paralyzed by the noise and frightened by the odd-looking, strange-smelling, curiously bumpy other half of the human race. So he would promptly do something to save himself, to get back in where he belonged. Prison had been kind to him; he had the smooth face of a man who has lived his life without care, without stress, without women. As chaste as a monk, as careless as a child, as innocent as a moron. He *liked* it in Santa Rita. Prison took care of him, gave him clothing and food, provided entertainment, kept bad people away from him, sheltered him, and ordered his entire life, from his getting up to his lying down. A contented man. The difference between Hell and Heaven is no difference; you are in Hell if you don't like where you are and what is going on, and in Heaven if you do. Same place, different attitudes.

Halfway through our stay, Jack and I were roused out of bed at 2:00 AM to make it to an arraignment in downtown Oakland for another civil rights trial. There we were kept in the top-floor courthouse jail, called the "Top of the Mark" in humorous reference to the elegant San Francisco restaurant. By getting into just the right spot in the dayroom, we could see the University campanile. After arraignment, it was up again in the wee hours and back to the comparatively pleasant Santa Rita. At least there you could get outside, get some air, exercise, see and do different things. Some prisoners spent months in the lifeless, echoing holding cells, turning paler and sadder as the days crawled by.

I read the library dry. Prison libraries are odd—lots of detective books and murder mysteries, but no sex stuff. I wasn't bored, but I was lonely and horny as the devil. "Sleeping alone isn't so bad, it's sleeping alone in the presence of thirty others who are themselves sleeping alone. Community loneliness."[4]

It was not much fun being surrounded by criminals, either. I was on my best behavior all the time.

I was put onto a road gang, doing the make-work that jails need to keep people from getting antsy and causing trouble. We cut weeds alongside of the internal roads and fences, and spent some time reducing the fire hazard of man-tall dry grass and brush surrounding the ghost town of abandoned buildings. In addition to having been a temporary holding barracks for Japanese on their way to less pleasant desert lodgings, Santa Rita had been a big military hospital. The end of the war had made the whole complex useless except for a small part of it that turned out to be good to keep petty criminals in. The deputy in charge of our gang was an intelligent man who seemed genuinely interested in what

I had done and why I had done it. Not too conspicuously, so as to avoid censure from his superiors and my fellows, we had long talks as I threatened weeds or tidied the verge of roads. I worked hard in the summer heat, getting a second-degree sunburn on the tops of my ears; having been covered up by hair for years, they hadn't seen much of the light of day, and were as tender as babies' feet.

If you strayed too far from the paths of righteousness, or had a bad reputation, or were a hard case, you went to Greystone. Greystone was a large, cinder block, tin-roofed enclosure, filled with tiers of mesh cages. You got one of your own, or if you were unlucky, you got roommates. Limited access to the library, limited visitor privileges. Not much to do but smoke and beat off. The guards patrolled from catwalks above, and the lights were never turned down. Bad news. Occasional maniac yells drifted over, reminding the general run of the population to keep their noses clean.

Greystone was also used as a holding tank for prisoners awaiting trial. The place was so dreadful that it functioned as a lever to persuade them to cop a plea, if only to get out and be transported to a regular prison, where things were believed to be much better. An unfortunate who had no money for bail, and whose trial had been set for sometime in the indefinite future, could wait in this purgatory for six to ten months, or even longer. That the machineries of justice ground slow was no great matter unless you happened to be in jail waiting for them to grind.

But as bad as it was, there was worse. You fuck up good, you go to the Hole. The Hole was solitary confinement: no privileges, no tobacco, restricted diet until you cleaned up your act, the misery enhanced by the shrieks and din of others in your same boat. Mucho bad news. In each case, the offender also lost a portion of his good time, or if the transgression was of sufficient gravity, all of it, in which case, lacking any leverage over him, the prison authorities consigned him to spend the rest of his sentence in the Hole or Greystone.

The mess hall was a large, dreary, bus-station-like room with rows of green linoleum-topped tables and long, green-painted metal benches. The ceiling was supported by high pillars, and the monotony of the walls relieved by murals done at one time or another by several unskillful hands, their lower portions protected and obscured by plywood panels.

The food was plentiful and nourishing, but dull. Pitchers of weak, tepid coffee with milk already in it and weak, greasy tea with sugar and lemon already in it on every table; on really hot days—hotter than the hinges of hell, like 105 degrees or hotter—we got watered-down Tang, which caused fist fights in the mess hall, the greedy ones getting most of it and the ones who couldn't or wouldn't quarrel over it not getting any. Every day of the week had its own predictable menu, except for holidays with their traditional meals. You could always tell what day of the week it was by what you were eating. We were informed that it was exactly the same food as served in the army. The trick of preparation is to combine first-class ingredients with third-rate cooks. Easy. Do everything by the numbers: not good, but not bad, either. The bread was baked in the prison bakery, and came out exactly like Wonder Bread. I don't know how they did it. The women's food was the same as the men's, except that the women's Tuesday hot dogs were served to them cut into short segments.*

Up at six in the morning, awakened by KSFO, a San Francisco talk and easy-listening station. After a brief interval, a vintage air-raid siren, and then a verbal command over the loudspeaker. The speakers stayed on all day, until lights out. In addition to the lovely music, we heard occasional announcements, ball games and names called for visitors on Sunday. The easy-listening music was mitigated by the complex, close harmony of Black streetcorner quartets; I'd never heard singing quite like it—studied, clearly derived from a musical tradition of which I had been ignorant. I didn't so much like it as I was confused and entertained by it; the sound was not, strictly speaking, melodious to my ear—lots of discordant minors and contra-tenor descants. The singing was extemporized within a framework of existing musical idiom, but the idiom was alien to me.†

Every barracks had a trusty who was spared the hard work in the sun, and who stayed in or about the barracks all the time that the general population was elsewhere. These men lazily polished the already slick red-painted concrete floors, or cleaned the head, or cleaned windows, confabulating under the central quadrangle eaves most of the time and making little pretense of busting their hump. Usually older Black men, serving six months to a year, they were often ex-cons who knew the ropes and were doing easy time, and had no intention of making things hard on themselves or others. They were noncommissioned officers, as

---

*My understanding was that the women's food was the same as the men's, but Patti Iiyama remembers from her stay in 1967 that it was exceedingly dull, with beets playing a prominent part in every meal, morning, noon and night. She has not touched a beet since.

†The interested reader can get some idea of what this a capella singing was like by listening to the group Take 6, *Doo Be Doo Wop Bop!* (Reprise 9 25670-2) and *So Much 2 Say* (Reprise 9 25892-2).

it were, passing along the rules and discipline of the guards, and providing a lubricant for the more gritty aspects of the prison machinery.
They knew exactly who was doing what and where, and this kept most
people in line. You could break the rules within limits, but no further.
When some mysterious line was crossed, and everyone knew just exactly where it was, you were no longer allowed to get away with whatever petty scam or infraction you were pulling, and an ignored warning
meant an abrupt, harsh yank on the leash.

Each morning, the shower-room trusty distributed razors, carefully
gathered and counted twice; woe betide him if he came up short in the
count when he brought them back to the guard. You could shave every
day if you wished, and were required to shave at least once a week. Radicals who valued their beards took care to stay out of Santa Rita.

Breakfast at six-thirty, report to your work party at eight, make it to
work by nine. If it's your day to go to the commissary, you go after
breakfast or before the evening meal. If you don't feel well, or don't feel
like working, you go to the doctor and make up some exotic bullshit
and get a lay-in slip. But not working is so much more boring than
working that most people don't try to get off. Knock off work to wash
up and get to lunch by noon and back to work at one. Off work by four-
fifteen and back by five, with supper at six, mail call at seven-thirty and
lights out at ten. No playing cards or gambling, so most inmates played
dominoes—a noisy game that I never got the hang of—checkers, back-
gammon or chess. An old con in my barracks lay in wait for me over
the chessboard and hustled me pretty bad; I was easy meat for him, what
with my college-boy intellectual pretensions and all. You can get damn
good at chess if you have fifteen or twenty years to practice in, and you
apply yourself.

Saturday a dull day off, and no mail call. On Saturday night, half the
compound went to see a movie while the other half was locked in, and
Sunday the other half got to go. If you weren't in somebody's bad
books, that is. If you were "in-bads" with the guards, you got to sit in
the bull pen while everyone else went to see the film. The women prisoners got to see the movie from the balcony. The balcony was curtained
off until just before the film started, but there was always enough time
for waves and blown kisses to pass between us. One evening when my
compound, number 5, went to the movie, there was a "shakedown."
While everyone was out, the guards went through everything, looking
for contraband and excess commissary items. A fair amount of stuff
came up missing, including one guy's pet sparrow hawk, which he had
raised from a chick. The next day there was a foul-up in commissary,

so many of us didn't have smokes. This led to a general rebellion, breaking up of furniture, light bulbs and windows after lights out, and after one (non-FSM) prisoner got up a petition, everything was returned except the bird, which had flown away, glad to be out of prison, too.

Sunday was visitor day. In order to get a visitor, you had to put them on a written list that you submitted beforehand. If somebody showed up that wasn't on the list, too bad. Sunday visits were limited to fifteen minutes, and each visitor could only see a prisoner once per Sunday. My family visited me, Mother glowing with embarrassment at simply being in a jail, Father half-proud that I was there for my beliefs. With the exception of babes in arms, kids had to stay in the car, as no one under eighteen was admitted to the visiting area. A few of the FSMers' friends were turned away at the gate because they were dressed in blue jeans and blue work shirts, same as the inmates. The guards feared that this resemblance would gum up the works, and that somebody might disappear without permission. Tom Weller drove Patti Iiyama out every Sunday to visit me, bright as a button and dressed up fit to kill—a brilliant butterfly among drab hens and crows, exciting wonder and envy among the inmates. Most visitors were inmates' long-suffering mothers or wives, and they looked as you would expect the mothers and wives of piss-ant criminals to look. Kind of weary and downtrodden and gone to seed. Patti and I sat separated from one another by the six-foot-wide visiting table, inarticulate with lust. My stock went up a good deal after that first Sunday.

I did nothing to attract the adverse attention of the authorities, so after thirty surprisingly long days I found myself being processed out. In addition to my musty clothes, I was given all the letters that had been sent me above the quota of the one per day that prisoners were allowed to receive.

The whole business of being in jail was worth it for the brilliant joy of freedom when I got outside. I was released on a bright summer morning, filled with apprehension every minute that they would take me back again. Waiting for me in the parking lot were Steve Lustig, David Stein and Patti. Dressed in a tight-bodiced red-and-white checked dress with a full skirt, she was so beautiful that it took my breath. We went first to the Caffè Mediterraneum for a decent cup of coffee, and then straight to bed. That time of getting under cool clean sheets in the middle of the day and making sweet love is a perfect memory.

BETTINA APTHEKER (ARROW R.) AND MARIO SAVIO (ARROW L.) WERE IN THE FORE OF THE MARCH
Just as they came up to the courthouse, David Goines was led outside by deputy sheriffs

"DON'T WORRY, IT'S ONLY GOINES!" DEFENDANTS MARCHING FROM THE UC CAMPUS
TO THE COURTHOUSE. SF EXAMINER PHOTO, JULY 30, 1965.

THE CAR

DURING THE FSM trial, the cops for once knew exactly where I was, so I was twice arrested for gone-to-warrant traffic tickets, once by the Berkeley police and, on the twenty-ninth of July, by the Oakland cops. On each occasion I was back on the street within hours, but the sensation created by seeing me dragged out of the courtroom by huge goons provided everyone with much needed righteous wrath and general good cheer.

On the twenty-ninth, deputy sheriffs led me out of the courtroom just as a thousand or so students marching from campus arrived across the street to begin a rally in Constitution Park (later Ho Chi Minh Park and later yet Provo Park), immediately across the street. Fifty or so demonstrators raced over to surround the car, à la Jack Weinberg, but before much of anything could be organized the Berkeley cops moved in and formed a cordon around the car, which barreled out of there as though the devil himself were on its heels. Mario was giving a speech about the appeal bail, and as he saw what was happening yelled out, "Don't worry! It's only Goines!"

At the Oakland-Berkeley line I was transferred to an Oakland squad car, then to the city jail, and was out again by the time they'd finished the paperwork.

The reason for these arrests was simple. I piloted four wheels with the same deep concern for the rules of the road and abundance of common sense that I had displayed on two. The previous summer, I'd managed to have five motorcycle and scooter accidents, breaking a leg, a finger, wrecking Jon Petrie's Vespa and vaulting myself and my roommate Tom Weller over a car. In late December of 1964, I had been given an Austin Mini Cooper by Benson Brown and his incredibly beautiful wife, Megan. Benson had accepted a teaching position in Vancouver, Canada, and decided that rather than sell his car he would give it to me. It was, in fact, not a great idea at all, but I was delighted. I had no driver's license, nor did I trouble myself to get insurance. I named the car Freiheit after the refrain from a German-language Spanish Civil War song, "Die Thälmann-Kolonne."*

The Austin Mini Cooper is in reality a racing car. It weighs only half a ton, with a transversely mounted 1200cc four-cylinder engine, and front-wheel drive. It has tiny fat wheels, 5.95 inches by 10 inches, and is only half a foot off the ground. It corners like it's on rails, and has a top speed of 130 miles per hour, although acceleration above seventy is painfully slow. Benson's was red with double white racing stripes down the middle from front to back, and the muffler was shot. I was a reckless speeder in Peugeot and Volkswagen, and to have a car that actually went like stink was a dream come true, except for the general public, the police, and my passengers.

I drove this rocket-powered roller skate like a damned fool, and began to accumulate a great many parking tickets, speeding tickets and every kind of moving violation. My way of dealing with them was to put them under the passenger-side visor and forget about them. When too many had built up, and they began falling into the lap of the hapless, terrified passenger, I threw them away. If I picked up a cop behind me, I would accelerate and try to escape. I got away about half the time, and it became a regular game of fox and hare between me and the police, with no particular malice on either side.

Only once did a cop display anger, and I marvel that I wasn't arrested on the spot. I had sent a driver to the San Francisco airport instead of the Oakland airport, where the people to be picked up were actually arriving. Rather than send someone else to the correct airport, or go myself, I thought that it would be a grand idea to catch the first group on their way and redirect them. With David Stein as a passenger, I took off down Telegraph Avenue like a bat out of hell, and definitely went

---

*Spaniens Himmel breitet seine Sterne
  Über unsre Schützengräben aus.
  Und der Morgen grüßt schon aus der
    Ferne,
  Bald geht es zum neuen Kampf hinaus.

  Die Heimat ist weit,
  Doch wir sind bereit.
  Wir kämpfen und siegen für dich:
  Freiheit!

Spanish heavens spread their stars
Above our trenches.
And the morning that already greets us
  from afar
Will shortly see another battle.

Our homeland is far away,
But we are ready.
We fight and conquer for thee:
Freedom!

Text by Karl Ernst, music by Peter Daniel; this music is to be found on the Folkways album *Songs of the Spanish Civil War* (FH 5436), sung by Ernst Busch and Chorus.

up onto the sidewalk to go around traffic at least once.* Somewhere near Haste I picked up a cop, and decided to race him to the Oakland line, figuring that he would have to stop there and give up the chase. Near Ashby I remembered the "in hot pursuit" clause, and pulled over on the far side of the intersection. The policeman jumped out of his car and pointed his revolver in my face and told me to get out. I explained that the driver's side door didn't work, and that I would have to get out on the passenger side, if that would be OK. I got out, and gave him the usual song and dance about having left my driver's license in my other pants, and he let me go, but David Stein had to drive the rest of the way.

David Stein: During the Jack London Square–protest phase there was the time when you and I and at least four others crowded into Freiheit, heading for Oakland, only to get stopped by a cop and given a series of tickets for basically vehicular deficiencies. We had not proceeded two blocks after unctuously accepting his reprimand, when the same zealous minion of the law proceeded to stop us all over again and write out a virtually identical second ticket. We managed to get both of them thrown out because here we finally had a prima facie case of harassment.[1]

On the matter of the traffic offenses, I at last was hailed up before Rupert J. Crittenden, the same judge who had been on the bench for the FSM trial. In this I was represented by Stanley Golde and Spence Strellis. Golde, the moderate who had championed the position that the FSM defendants should have a collective judge trial, had also been the partner of Judge Crittenden before he was called to the bench, and the trial was brief. I was found guilty of some astronomical number of misdemeanors, all of which had gone to warrant and grown to an incalculable sum of money due in fines. I was told by the judge that it would be seventy-five dollars or ten days.

Smartass that I was, I started to say, "Your Honor, I'll take the money, as I have all the time I need." But my attorney shushed me violently and said that I would pay the fine, Your Honor. He then paid it himself. The judge amended the sentence so that, as a condition of my reprieve, I was to sell the car and agree not to drive again for ten years. I agreed. I walked out of the courtroom a free man. This was as great a miscarriage of justice as I have ever witnessed, not that I am complaining, mind you.

---

*Telegraph Avenue was at this time a two-way street.

I held to my end of the bargain, and didn't drive, to speak of, or try to get a driver's license until I was twenty-nine years old. In return for four hundred bucks, I transferred the car to my pal David Stein, who fixed the muffler and, after straightening things out with the local gendarmes, drove it until he in turn sold it to a couple of kids from Moraga. It was wrecked in an accident four years later. Unfortunately, Judge Crittenden did not live to witness my rehabilitation, as he died of cancer in 1968.

BETTER LIVING THROUGH CHEMISTRY

If you remember the sixties, you weren't there.
—Robin Williams (attributed)

I̶T MAY SEEM strange, but the sixties were not an unremitting orgy of sex, drugs and rock 'n' roll. Not the first half, at least. Although I was a dreadful little hoodlum in high school, neither I nor any of my dreadful little hoodlum friends had so much as heard of marijuana. Our aspirations rose no higher than beer and cigarettes. My first year at Cal was distinguished by nothing at all in the way of either dope or sex, and I didn't like early sixties rock 'n' roll. When Karl Foytick, Tom Weller and I became roommates in the summer of 1964, we collectively decided to burst the bourgeois bonds and buy some dope and get whacked. Karl looked the most beatniky, so he was elected to score some marijuana from the friendly Black guy on the corner, though it turned out that the only credential you actually needed was a five-dollar bill. That evening the three of us, with some considerable to-do and ceremony, solemnly smoked what was either the lowest grade of weed in the land, or oregano. Maybe you had to get used to it, but I was unimpressed. Tom fell asleep. Karl claimed to be high and giggled a lot. This was really avant garde, believe it or not. Before and during the Free Speech Movement I knew of only two incidents concerning drugs, both of them bad. Lennie Glaser was all but destroyed by his jail term from a marijuana bust, and Lee Rhoads accidentally had a roach on him in the Sproul Hall sit-in and reaped a peck of trouble for it. The pharmacopoeia consumed by freewheeling Filthy Speech Movement pioneer John Thompson was news to me, and I didn't want to have anything to do with it. My post-FSM experimentation with drugs was limited by my fear of being arrested on a nonpolitical charge. I wouldn't touch marijuana, or even stay around a place where it was being used—and I was a real self-righteous pain in the ass about it, too. I was quite sure that if the cops ever got me on a drug charge they would lock me up and throw away the key. In that suspicion I was probably one hundred percent correct. Lysergic acid diethylamide-25, on the other hand, derived in part from the humble

ergot fungus (responsible, we are told, for some mighty peculiar behavior during the Middle Ages), was perfectly legal.

Augustus Owsley Stanley III, a Cal student and the grandson of the
United States senator from Kentucky, combined a genuine natural talent
with a few tricks from a chemistry-major girlfriend, dropped out of UC
and set up his first LSD factory in north Berkeley. He was "the world's
greatest acid manufacturer, bar none," according to Tom Wolfe in *The
Electric Kool-Aid Acid Test*, and I must say that I agree. Nobody else,
either then or since, seemed capable of rendering the same delightful,
fantastic, paranoia-free trip. The high was wonderful, but the best thing
about LSD was the immense, crystalline calm of the following day. I have
often wished that there was a drug that gave no more than the serenity
of the day after a session with acid.

In the summer of 1965 Tom Weller, Patti Iiyama and I scored some
acid and decided to take it—first time trip for all of us—as a trio. We
dropped the pretty, triangular purple pills and sat still and waited with
some excitement for what might happen. The 250-microgram Owsley
LSD was a pure, inexpensive (indeed, in this case free) substance; the high
began mildly, and we weren't really sure when we left the ordinary
world and floated into the realm of synaesthesia and hallucination. In
time, I had—as do so many who take LSD—a marvelous insight into the
nature and arcane workings of the universe, and decided to write it
down before it misted away. But the thought was so important that it
couldn't be written in an ordinary way, and I decided to calligraph it on
a lovely sheet of paper. I began, and realized that the initial capital had
to be beautifully illuminated, such was the gravity of my thought. I began designing a brilliant letter, after the Book of Kells, and as the sun
rose I'd almost gotten a good enough design, but I had forgotten what
I was going to say.

THE TYRANT'S FOE, THE PEOPLE'S FRIEND

By MIDWINTER OF 1965, although active in the civil rights movement, I wasn't much involved in student politics, and began to feel an urge to work. I had gotten printing experience, after a fashion, by running first FSM and later civil rights leaflets on a mimeograph machine. I sounded out Marion Syrek, who had moved his Vanguard Press storefront print shop to 5935 Grove, just over the Oakland line, about the chances of employment. He told me to drop by and we'd see what could be done. Late one afternoon, I dropped into what was by then called the Berkeley Free Press (despite its Oakland address) and he agreed to give me a tryout on his old black 11″×14″ Multilith 1250. He explained the basic principle, showed me how to turn it on, how to turn it off, where to put the ink and the paper, and where the finished printed pieces came out. Then he left. There I was, man against machine. That night, the rich, spicy smell of printer's ink became part of my life. When Marion returned, and my memory is that it wasn't until the next morning, I was still there, surrounded by heaps of grubby, useless paper and in the last extremity of misery. I suppose that he was impressed enough by the stick-to-itiveness, as it surely wasn't my printing skill, to offer me work on an occasional basis, and more important, to teach me how to print. Marion was a trim, smallish, balding Trotskyist in his early fifties. The antics of the new crop of radicals were barely tolerable to him, though most of the time his wry, fatalistic sense of humor carried him past the more difficult parts.

That January was a month of bright, hazy winter days, and the long walk to and from Marion's shop gave me some much needed time to myself; time to think. I liked working on the press, and called every day that I wasn't otherwise committed, asking,

"Any work today?"

Usually, Marion didn't really need me, but I would show up anyhow, hoping to get a crack at the Multi, or just sweep up.

THE AUTHOR AT BERKELEY FREE PRESS, 1966. PHOTOGRAPHER UNKNOWN.

Phil Roos, Deward Hastings and Dunbar Aitkins had bought an old 14″×20″ Multilith 2066 some years before to print the student quarterly *Root and Branch*. An offshoot of SLATE, it had provided a forum for, among others, the unsuccessful congressional candidate Robert Scheer, one of the main figures in both the HUAC and Cuba demonstrations. The press had come to Berkeley from Reed College, and was stored for a time in Aryay Linsky and Jerry Miller's apartment, from thence to Dunbar's basement.

Before and during the FSM, Dunbar Aitkins published an on-again, off-again science journal called *Particle* in a basement in one of those old, archetypically Berkeley brown shingles that stood where People's Park is today.

Tom Weller: There in the basement Deward printed the *FSM Newsletter*. One day Dunbar and I and some others were there, and a little old man came down the stairs. It was the landlord.

In a heavy Middle-European accent, he told Dunbar, "You gotta get out of my place. I don't want no Communist papers here." It was more in sorrow than in anger. "You told me you was printing your science papers. You didn't tell me you was printing no Communist papers. You gotta get out."

We were stunned. There was an uncomfortable silence, and he left. Maybe if any of us there had been big politicos we would have answered with a ringing defense of freedom of the press. But we were just the rank and file. Besides, you had to figure maybe the old guy had good reasons for not liking Communists.[1]

As a result of this eviction, I helped move the press to the basement of Lewin's Metaphysical Books on Ashby and College, which Mike Bennett had briefly owned as "The Bookshelf" until tangles with the FBI caused his eviction. The press stayed in the basement, though, and there Deward ran off some FSM material in early December. By early 1965, the opera-

WINTER 1962 ISSUE OF ROOT AND BRANCH.

tion was going great guns, and Deward had managed to create quite a fire hazard under the floor of the bookstore. In this mare's nest he was assisted by Bennett, who was still living in the loft above the store with his girlfriend, Laurel Benedetti. I would come by and help out, usually in the small hours of the morning after finishing whatever civil rights work I had been doing. We would breakfast on coffee and hot, fresh donuts from Dream Fluff across the street.

Deward Hastings and Marion Syrek merged into the Berkeley Free Press, actually in Berkeley this time, in mid-1965, and moved all the equipment to a Grove and Virginia apartment building that had just been bought by Phil Roos. The building had four storefronts, and the one at 1705 had for many years been Linefelter's shoe repair shop, which had gone vacant with the owner's death. The shoe shop became a print shop. Next door, at 1703, was a beauty salon run by ancient ladies who were not pleased to have us as neighbors. Within a few months they packed it in, and the Free University of Berkeley (FUB) made its headquarters on the premises of this former temple to antique pulchritude.

Marion was in charge, and we tried to run the shop along approved socialist lines, with meetings and votes and so on, not to mention a con-

The contents of this package have been
prepared by a responsible chemist as pure
as contemporary laboratory procedures
can make them. No adulterant or
speed has been added. Buffering
quantity this mixture are commercial but-
ting compounds or specified vitamins in
minimum daily requirement or equivalent
amounts.

VISIONARY COMPANY

Quantity_____

Dosage_____

Contents_____

_____

Buffer_____

_____

LSD LABEL PRINTED AT BERKELEY FREE PRESS,
MID-1965. THE ORIGINAL IS 3″ WIDE, PURPLE
INK ON A TEXTURED MAGENTA PAPER.

fused Maoist affair called "criticism and self-criticism," but it really didn't work terribly well, and we all toiled incredibly hard for almost nothing. The place was going full-bore twenty-four hours a day, seven days a week, beatniks and Commies pouring in and out and the cops giving us a wide berth. Between the print shop and the almost daily demonstrations and rallies, I was working for social change full steam.

I took the hero Alexei Stakhanov for my model: the (perhaps fictional) Russian revolutionary coal miner who, on August 31, 1935, drilled 102 tons of coal in six hours, fourteen times the norm for his shift, and who lived only for the glory of the Soviet. My motto, consciously echoing the horse in Orwell's *Animal Farm*, was "I will work harder."

In late summer of 1965, the press went through its first serious spasm of political and personal disagreements. I suppose that Marion Syrek got sick of dealing with the band of lunatics who largely comprised the available work force. There was no love lost between Deward and Marion, and Marion may simply have wearied of dealing with him. Syrek moved his old black Multilith to a small shopfront on Telegraph Avenue beyond the Co-op, and set up a new Trotskyist press, to better serve the causes to which he was sympathetic and, I am sure, to avoid dealing with all of us.

After a brief hiatus, Deward took over as boss and the propaganda mill started grinding again. Our productivity was not high, but our ignorance and enthusiasm were without bounds. Jack made a brief stab at learning the printing trade, but was a hopeless mechanical illiterate, and gave it up. I was moving back toward my basic anarchist leanings, and for no real reason, gave him a hard time about his politics. It made him feel bad, as he thought that I expected him to have all the answers, and he didn't have them. Jack and I lost touch after that, he still involved with radical politics, and I gradually moving away from activist politics of any kind.

Adding to the difficulties of a short-handed print shop trying to stay open all day and all night, Deward conceived the genuinely insane notion of "watch and watch," valid I suppose in time of war on board a military vessel, but to impose four hours on and four hours off on printers, for God's sake, was merely demented. As a measure of my youth and enthusiasm, I actually went along with it. All this time, I was being paid a theoretical wage of $25 a week, which I often did not get. We soon reached an advanced state of exhaustion, accompanied by the irritability and clumsiness of severe sleep deprivation. This was a time when I would often stay on the job for interminable stretches; the longest being five entire days without sleep. I did that at least twice, and two or three days of solid work were a commonplace.

THE SHOP HAD been on the rocks ever since Marion quit, and Deward's stewardship came to an end right around Christmas. Once again, Phil Roos put the place up for grabs to whosoever would take it and run it as a radical organ for social change. In January of 1966, Leo Bach took over the Berkeley Free Press. Leo was a solid old lefty who had a small Christmas card imprinting business in his garage. The Berkeley Free Press was not operating at the moment, and in the absence of the usual left-wing printer, Leo had taken on a monster order for a leaflet written by Marvin Garson. I printed a quarter of a million copies of that sucker if I printed one. I'd started printing in Leo's garage, and then we moved, quite nearly printing as we went, back to the shop on Grove Street.

On one side, the leaflet had a picture of two Vietnamese babies who had been burned by napalm. On the other, the text began: "If you met the father of these children, what would you say to him?" John Seltz intended to bomb the leaflet over the Rose Bowl game on January 1, 1966, and everything was in the plane and ready to go, when the airplane had a flat tire on the runway in Pasadena. They couldn't get it fixed in time. Frank Bardacke, who had helped with the wording and concept, was stoned on acid, watching the game in a room full of people, waiting for the whole stadium to erupt. But nothing happened. No 250,000 leaflets falling like a malevolent snowstorm; no national TV coverage. No nothin'. UCLA beat Michigan 14–12. What an anticlimax.

John, not one to give in to the slings and arrows of outrageous fortune, got another plane, painted out its identification numbers, and bombed the whole Bay Area instead. Not nearly the impact, of course, but better than nothing.

Seltz hand-picked a crew for his next adventure. The Army was using a tract of land in Tilden Park for training dogs. John made up large, official looking signs that said:

WARNING: WAR DOGS KEEP CHILDREN AND FOOD AWAY

People kicked up an enormous fuss, and in three days the Army folded up its tents and stole away into the night. Fantastic success. Except that one of his handpicked guys was a *Life* magazine reporter, and the entire event was chronicled, in loving detail for all the world to see, in a weekly magazine with national and international circulation.

Hearing that a Veterans of Foreign Wars (VFW) pro–Vietnam War rally was scheduled, John Seltz and Tom Andre stole in the night before and painted antiwar slogans all over the walls. When they got back,

FRANK BARDACKE SPEAKING AT THE "MASKORCION AND YELLOW SUBMARINE" DEMONSTRATION, DECEMBER 7, 1966. PHOTO BY HOWARD HARAWITZ.

when it was just too late to do anything about it, Tom realized that he had left his wallet, full of identification, on one of the benches in the hall.

John had equipped his pickup truck with yellow flashing lights, and built a big mock bomb that he mounted in the bed, sticking out beyond the cab. On the sides and back the words DANGER! NAPALM! were painted in bright red. With this rig, he would follow the trucks transporting napalm from Dow Chemical to the Port of Oakland, along their freeway route through the populous areas of the North Bay. Mostly, he was just a pain in the gizmo; the truckers ignored him, and the highway patrol gave him millions of tickets. He made a lot of motorists nervous, and got some newspaper coverage.

One particular night, there must have been a new driver, because when John picked him up, lights flashing, this dummy figured that he was an official escort, sent because he might get lost or take the wrong road. Nearing Berkeley, the driver managed to attract John's attention, and indicated that he would follow him, as he didn't know the approved path to the munitions dump. John could hardly believe it. He pulled around in front, and slowed to a crawl. The truck kept right on his tail. John took the Ashby exit and, intending to lure it to Bancroft and Telegraph, drew this huge truck full of napalm right to the intersection of Telegraph and Ashby, where, making a left turn, it got stuck. A fucking miracle. The Jabberwock, customarily jammed to the gills with left-wingers and antiwar activists, was but a block away. John telephoned there, Berkeley Free Press, my house, Mike Bennett's, Marvin Garson's, Frank Bardacke's—everywhere. To no avail. Nobody, but nobody, was around that night. The biggest goddamn fish that he would ever, ever catch in his whole life was going to get away, and there was nothing to be done about it. Good old John Seltz; what a hard-luck guy he was. He fled his traffic tickets and moved to rural Oregon.

NEW BROOM

L<small>EO BACH</small> didn't know much about printing, but he actually paid me once a week. We had no further half-baked Maoist criticism and self-criticism sessions. The shop became a cheerful, if no more efficient, place. He bought lunch regularly, which was all I ever ate. I lived on an Oscar burger, fries, one or two packs of Pall Malls and about a gallon of black coffee every day. Although Leo was good to the workers, he was sloppy with supplies and suppliers. He always bought the cheapest, hard to run, paper at a schlock house in San Francisco called King Paper ("Where Cash is King"). The crap they sold was mill rejects, roll ends, train-wreck salvage and stuff that had been miscut or ordered by mistake by other printers. It was the kind of paper that the instant you try to get it through the press, it tries to turn back into a tree. Leo put off paying bills and taxes as long as he could. Not a good plan.

Leo hired Mike Bennett on as a pressman, and the three of us worked, basically, the same hours that I had worked before. If I got off at nine o'clock at night I considered it a holiday. Mike Bennett had a brilliant sense of humor and, although it was marred by a too-great attraction to firearms, Dexedrine and liquor, a charming personality. Mike liked jazz, and introduced me to the radio station KJAZ and the pre-hippie Haight-Ashbury world of smoky jazz clubs.

We three weren't enough, really, and Leo found a bearded introvert named Steve Fox to pad out the crew. He had a German shepherd named "Man" (spelled for no clear reason *Ghmanne*) and lived on a houseboat and kept unsavory company. The name "Man" was a bit of black humor that I, at the time, did not appreciate; Steve was a Jew, and the guards at the Nazi concentration camps were reputed to have said to their dogs when they wanted to sic them on a Jew, "Man, kill that dog."

It became obvious that mere blather wasn't going to take care of the bookkeeping, either, and Leo lucked out in finding Sweet Joann Wyler to keep the sheriff and creditors at bay. Before Leo's tenure we had ignored bookkeeping as a bourgeois affectation.

The old Multilith 2066 had disappeared along with Deward, and two Multilith 1250s couldn't handle the load. We needed a bigger machine, and in the middle of summer Leo got one for us. For six thousand bucks, fronted by the enduring idealist Phil Roos, we became the proud owners of an 18″×24″ Solna ATF Chief 24, serial number 824. Built in 1954 without much consideration for operator safety or ease of adjustment, it was and still is a royal pain in the neck to run, much less get work of any quality out of. It was delivered through the front window, and in the process of setting it down and leveling it one of the workers cut his hand to the bone. None of us had the faintest idea of how to run it, and the old fart sent by American Type Founders took one look at this wild-haired bunch of hippies and decided that we weren't worth very much of his time. He gave us the minimum instruction, and ungraciously at that. From there on out, it was a matter of developing theories and notions about how to make it work. Near the end of the year, we found that the vanes in the vacuum pump were cracked; that had made feeding a matter of chance and luck more than skill. The feeder was poorly designed anyway, and even when it was perfectly adjusted it wasn't perfect. What a pile of used food Leo had been suckered into. There was no instruction manual, and when we ordered one from the factory in Solna, Sweden, it failed to arrive. The manual finally came in 1970, postmarked 1966. It was for the wrong press. By then we'd figured out how to run it as well as such a press could be run, and had found a decent Swede mechanic named Svend Pedersen who would bail us out when things got really bad.

IF YOU CAN'T SAY SOMETHING NICE . . .

W$_E$ DIDN'T JUST print pure political stuff, boring old leaflets and portraits of Marx and Lenin. Lots of people out there wanted things printed that nobody else would print for love or money. Jefferson Poland, a ban-the-bomb activist from the early sixties, had gone on to found the Sexual Freedom League, and petitioned the court to change his legal name to Jefferson Fuck Poland.* I don't think the court allowed it, although on what grounds I can't imagine. Anyhow, that's what he called himself and was called by others thereafter, so it doesn't much matter if the court gave its august stamp or not. Other printers wouldn't take his money, usually citing the delicate sensibilities of the bindery girls, so we got all his trade. I designed the League's letterhead; chaste as ice, really, it was a 20-percent screen of Albrecht Dürer's *Adam and Eve* (the one where Eve is tempting Adam with the fruit of the tree of knowledge of good and evil), printed in sepia on cream stock.

The Sexual Freedom League held weekly orgies, to which we were all cordially invited, though Leo was the only one who attended. Aside from the ready availability of plenty of sweet young things—none of whom, as far as I could determine, were to be counted among the Sexual Freedom League's membership—the kind of women who liked dipping themselves in Wesson Oil and fucking hordes of total strangers really

---

*The Sexual Freedom League was founded as an affiliate of the New York City League for Sexual Freedom. As reported in the *Daily Cal*, July 16, 1965, the Sexual Freedom League's positions were summarized thus: We believe everyone has the right to manufacture, buy, sell, possess any kind of book, picture, statue, moving picture, etc. We demand repeal of harsh penalties for sexual relations with consenting persons under 18. We oppose college regulations and curfews which restrict the sexual and personal rights of students. Freedom of choice should be carefully respected in having or not having children, birth control methods and family planning. All laws and regulations which seek to restrict or deny such freedom should be repealed. Prostitution should be legalized. The discrimination present in our society against homosexuals should be abolished.

FREEDOM . . . Jefferson Polland, a member of the contro-versial "Sexual Freedom League" sits at his Telegraph Ban-croft table in hopes of educating the public to his way of thinking.

JEFFERSON POLAND AT THE SEXUAL FREEDOM LEAGUE TABLE. DAILY CAL PHOTO BY JEFF LEE.

didn't appeal to me all that strongly. One in particular was warm for my form. Unfortunately for her, I found her deeply frightening; a leftover beatnik, lots of black eye-makeup and beads and bangles. Unusually tall, shaped like the Venus of Willendorf, huge dugs surmounting ample hams, a delicately unpleasant smell masked by patchouli oil. No. But really, I've got to print tonight. Thanks a lot for asking, though.

"Well, as long as you're not *hungry*." Nudge, nudge; wink, wink. Yuck.

JFP had opened the floodgates, and we printed quite a bit of pornography, mostly real rock-bottom trash. One guy, who smelled so bad that nobody would go near him but Leo, came in with a manuscript and a wad of hundred-dollar bills that would choke a horse, and asked us to print his book for him. It was called *Red*, a pitiful collection of dreary fantasies, typed on an IBM Selectric in a rambling monotone. Awful dreck, but every week he brought in more pages, and more century notes to back them up. He always wore a long, filthy black overcoat. We finally finished the thing, and bound it, and delivered his precious book to the poor old bum. Leo wished that it would go on forever. The rest of us pitied and despised "Red," as we called him, and were just as glad to see him go.

That mainstream printers shied away from pornography made some sense, but they also declined the work tendered by religious eccentrics.

NAKED PROTEST

—Photo by Konstantin Berlandt

"IT WAS HOT . . . and unusual in that it was also sultry." The atmosphere was right for a protest. The sky and the water were blue. Three Sexual Freedom Leaguers waded in and stripped off their clothes. Several hundred spectators waited half an hour in anticipation. And they weren't disappointed. Eventually Shirley Einsiedel (left), Jefferson Poland, and Ina Saslow emerged stark naked. One little boy shouted, "Man, this is living!" For complete story see page 10.

SEXUAL FREEDOM LEAGUE DEMONSTRATION, UC CAMPUS, AUGUST 26, 1965.
DAILY CAL PHOTO BY KONSTANTIN BERLANDT.

We handled huge quantities of printing for Meher Baba, Krishnamurti, and this or that evanescent Holy Man. Mike was printing a flier for Meher Baba on the Multi, and I a poster for same on the Chief. Thousands upon thousands of portraits of the wet-eyed, mustachioed Svengali eventually got to me, and I began chanting the text, in time with the press, in my best East Indian accent, "I was Rama, I was Krishna, I was this one, I was that one, and now I am MEHER BABA!" Mike, joining in the chant, cracked up laughing, and Leo was stuck with the two of us being overwhelmed by the giggles. Later, the more viable cults bought their own presses.

LIE DOWN WITH DOGS, RISE UP WITH FLEAS

Under Marion Syrek, the Berkeley Free Press had been (nominally) a union shop with a union bug. When he left, he took his union affiliation with him, and for a while we were nonunion. In order to print mainstream political materials, like for the Democratic party, we needed a union label. As long as we were a tiny, radical print shop, nobody gave a good goddamn what we did or printed, but if we wanted the plums, we needed that label. So, in January 1967, we organized into the Oakland Printing Pressmen and Assistants Union, Local 125. It came to me as a great surprise that the workers' shield and bulwark against capitalism was run by a bunch of slimeballs who made the Mafia look like a benevolent society.

Steve went alone to our first union meeting, and that happened to be the annual election. He noticed that there was only one name for each slot, and felt that this was not right. So he up and volunteered to run for union president, arguing that it was not in the best interests of a democracy to have but one guy running for each office like the way they do it in Russia for example. Right after his little speech, two big guys came up to him and told him to get the fuck out and never come back. He immediately understood their simple argument, and obliged. The union thugs further made it clear that this invitation extended to the entire shop. Thereafter, the union fined each of us one dollar every paycheck for not attending the monthly meeting.

As I found out more about the union, and its management, I grew to hate it and them. In the late 1940s, a small outfit on University Avenue called Berkeley Mimeograph wanted to join the union for much the same reasons that had inspired us. The union refused to let them in because the owner, Ernie Gray, and all the employees were Black. In 1967, when it was cool to be Black, the OPP&AU approached Ernie Gray with the idea of organizing Berkeley Mimeo into the union. When he refused, saying that he had gotten along without them when he needed them and they could get along without him when they needed him, the union threw up a picket line around his shop. It didn't last, because even the reddest among us could see the injustice. After this, my relationship with the union representative who came around from time to time grew cooler yet. Leo was courteous, because he was management, but the rest of us wouldn't even talk to the guy or be commonly polite.

It turned out that we might as well have saved ourselves the trouble of seeking the liberal trade. Every chance they got, they screwed us. The radicals never stiffed us, and the crazies always honored their commitments to the letter. Even a few right-wing types who had dealt with us by accident paid right on the barrelhead. The most liberal group of all, called the Committee for Liberal Representation, skipped out on a two-thousand dollar printing bill accumulated during the unsuccessful Scheer for Congress campaign. They were a bunch of whiny opportunists who genuinely despised the working man and used him when they could, discarding him like used Kleenex when it suited their convenience. I went from merely despising liberals to hating them. I'd give up my front seat in Hell to see that they collectively paid what they owed the press—with interest.

In only one instance did we get out of a liberal con man what was due us. The owner of the Omnivore restaurant, on Shattuck near the Oakland line, came on with a "friend of the Movement, Peace, Love and Good Vibes" spiel and got us to print him up menus, business cards, stationery and envelopes, the whole shooting match, with no money down and a considerable discount because he was such a nice guy and a swell liberal fellow. Well, he never paid. Months went by, and all our entreaties for payment were turned aside with bland excuses. One Sunday evening, all sitting around and wondering what to do for dinner, we resolved to give the Omnivore our trade. Six of us ordered lavishly, wine and hors d'oeuvres . . . the works. When the tab, about seventy-five dollars, was presented, Leo put his own bill for printing right on top of it. The waitress, confused and angry, stalked off to the owner, who threatened and fulminated, but to no avail. We smugly told him that we were now even-Steven, and he could put his dinner check in his pipe and smoke it. Everybody was pleased with the trade except him. That's the only time I recollect that we got any satisfaction out of a deadbeat.

BOMBS AND GUNS

JACK WEINBERG: A few years after the FSM things began to change. Civil rights went into decline for various reasons and the locus of activism for "white radicals" shifted to the Vietnam War. This changed the dynamic. The early civil rights movement had a very optimistic, positive spirit. Our side was morally right, we were on the side of history, we had no doubt we would win—it was a cause worth dying for. In contrast, after 1967, the apparent inability of the anti–Vietnam War movement to affect events made its activists feel impotent. Many began to turn to "radical politics" as an end in itself and not just as a means.[1]

Despite enjoyable interludes—mostly in the form of the rapidly warming sexual climate—things in general were moving toward the truly unpleasant late sixties. At the press, we started getting bomb threats. When we called the police, they sent a man out, and as he walked in the door the telephone rang; he answered it and it was, by God, a bomb threat. That made them sit up and snort. The telephone company put an official tap on our line, which, as far as I know, is there to this day. We taped up all the windows and stole a dozen fire extinguishers, which we then arranged conspicuously on Leo's desk. He just about passed out when he saw them the next morning, knowing they were all hot.

We started carrying guns, and I bought a nasty little .38 Colt Cobra from Mike for a hundred bucks. By way of overkill, I also kept a sawed-off Winchester pump twelve-gauge shotgun leaning against the wall near the big press. While emptying it for cleaning one evening, I accidentally hit the trigger and almost blew Earl "The Great Humbead" Crabb's head off. Six inches above his head was a hole the size of a watermelon in the back door. We were a lot more careful with firearms after that.

Early one Sunday morning, Leo is there alone, and this young kid, about fourteen, comes in the door. He reaches into his coat and pulls out a big black automatic pistol and starts talking crazy about Commies and waving it around. Leo's sweating blood, but keeps the kid talking, humoring him along, and gradually edges the desk drawer open, where he keeps the nine-millimeter Browning. Just before Leo gets his hand on his own pistol, the kid kind of wanders over close enough to him, and Leo snaps his arm out and grabs the kid and gets the gun away. The fucking thing's a toy. Leo almost shot a kid carrying a toy gun. Leo shits a brick.

A big guy who represented himself as a contractor came in the shop wanting a business card. He was a loud talker, and started to rant and rave about how he remodels buildings—*ugly* buildings. How he likes to destroy ugly buildings like this one. How he doesn't much like hippies or Commies and ugly buildings. This is an ugly building and he'd like to see it go. By this time he had four guns aimed right at him, only he didn't know it. This was just after a series of bomb threats, you understand. As soon as he leaves, we call the cops and they have him in about a minute. Turns out that he is a bona fide contractor who specializes in remodeling ugly buildings. No real threat. We have become a little paranoid, but not much. Even paranoids have enemies.

At one-thirty in the morning of April 9, 1966, we were startled by the sound of an explosion. It sounded distant, but big. In seconds, the phone rang and it was Pam Mellin asking if we had heard that the Vietnam Day Committee headquarters had been bombed. Jesus H. Christ. We jumped into Leo's car and went over to 2407 Fulton where the headquarters were, and the street was full of fire engines and ambulances and cops. Red lights flashing all over the place and the whole front of the building just plain gone.

All the VDC leaders had been there having a meeting in the living room. They had just adjourned, and gotten up and walked together into the kitchen to get some eats, and the room followed them out. One minute earlier and everyone would have been jam. That would have changed things a lot. Danny Kowalski was still in the attic. The cops found him, sound asleep. At first they thought he was dead. He'd slept through the whole thing and could hardly believe it.

The VDC bombing occurred one day after the *Oakland Tribune* printed an article about a VDC fundraiser in UC's Harmon Gymnasium, which was represented as a drugged-out wild sex orgy. The Jefferson Airplane had played, and many people were stoned on acid (which was still legal), but the only concrete evidence of an actual orgy was one used condom on the floor of the balcony.

Tit for tat, on June 27, 1967, someone blew up the Berkeley draft board office at Allston Way and Grove. The little old ladies who worked there were unhurt, as the two homemade bombs had gone off in the small hours of the morning, but so terrified that they refused to return to the trenches. The office was closed, and Berkeley's draft matters transferred to Oakland.

Leo and I were targeted by the ultra-right-wing weekly *Tocsin*. They'd had a hard-on for me ever since the early FSM, and we were finally granted the honor of a photo on the front page. Leo and I were standing and talking at an anti–Vietnam War demonstration, and were identified as known Communists and tools of the Kremlin subsidized by Moscow Gold. Though we were amused, we also understood that those photos were there to identify us to the crazies on the right. Nothing ever came of it.

THE *BERKELEY BARB*

THE SAME month that saw the FSM defendants off to Stony Lonesome also witnessed the first big Vietnam protest. On August 12, 1965, hundreds of demonstrators blocked the Berkeley right-of-way of Southern Pacific, preventing the passage of troop trains. Disgusted with the media's handling of this and earlier events, Max Scherr founded a People's Newspaper. The *Berkeley Barb* picked up where Paul Krassner's Greenwich Village–based *Realist* had left off. Getting news to print was no problem, nor was getting ads to pay for the paper. The sexual revolution had spawned sex advertising. In no time, the *Barb* was a freewheeling forum for every kind of sexual service, desire or inclination imaginable (and some that exceeded the bounds of intelligibility), and was half sex ads, half radical politics. By 1969 the circulation had reached 90,000, far more than the conservative *Berkeley Daily Gazette*, the editorial tenor of which ran so counter to the mood of the community it purported to serve that it was almost a joke.

Max Scherr was something of a tightwad, and in 1969 the staff went out on strike for higher wages, better working conditions, more political reporting and less sleazy sex advertising. Max wouldn't talk turkey, so the whole crowd started the *Tribe* at 1708A Grove, across the street from the press. That location didn't suit, so in a month they moved the whole kit and caboodle into the vacated laundromat next to the press at 1701 Grove. Deprived of its dedicated workforce, the *Barb* limped along in guilty splendor, becoming a sex rag with no more than a tip of the old chapeau to the correct causes. When Max died of cancer in 1973, the *Barb* became nothing but a sex advertiser. In 1978 the *Barb* spun off the sex stuff to the *Spectator*, a weekly tabloid completely free of politics. Although the *Spectator* prospered, the *Barb*'s circulation dropped below 3,000, and the last issue was published on July 3, 1980.

MAX SCHERR (RIGHT), 1969. PHOTO BY BOB GILL.

Tom Weller: Max Scherr was running a beer and wine bar called the Steppenwolf when I met him. It was the kind of place where your elbows stuck to the tabletops. When the radical/hippie community started to feel the need for its own newspaper, Max joined some mostly Co-op types who had formed a committee to talk about it. And talk. And talk. Finally Max got disgusted and said he could start his own paper in a week and the hell with you all. So he did.

The *Barb* was a perfect reflection of its owner. Max always wore a filthy gray cap and a scraggly beard. The paper was a sloppy, smudgy designer's nightmare, and the ink was so cheap that reading it turned your fingers black. Max addressed the radical agenda with all the taste and intelligence of the *National Inquirer.* I recall one headline that shrieked, INFANT RIPPED FROM MOTHER'S ARMS BY NARCS!

Max's stinginess was legendary. He could always be seen hawking the paper himself at major events—it pained him to give up all those nickel commissions. The paper for a long time was run out of his big, old, incredibly untidy house, kitchen piled high with dirty coffee cups. Anytime anybody asked for anything—like pencils or paper clips—he whined about how they were trying to bankrupt a poor old man.

Whining, in fact, was his normal mode of expression. One time I was sitting on the bench in front of Peet's Coffee and Max wandered up and joined me. "Well," he said bitterly, "I see you already got the good end of the bench."

During a dirty-laundry-exposing divorce trial years later it turned out that Max had been salting away the considerable profits from the paper in a Swiss bank account.[1]

LET SLEEPING DOGS LIE

I PARTICIPATED in a few marches and demonstrations, and did the obligatory public incineration of the draft card. Most of my time, though, was spent behind a printing press. The revolution ran on paper and ink and the Berkeley Free Press was where it all came from. The antiwar and civil rights movements kept us running at full capacity.

In response to the difficulties of addressing the nonstudent, nonactivist population (preaching to the saved was fun, but what we wanted was to win some souls from Satan), we came up with a clever technique. What piece of paper will no one throw away, will people actually pass along to someone else, regardless of political inclination? You got it. Money, banknotes, the old mazoola, scratch, gelt, yenom. We ordered up dozens of rubber stamps saying "Get out of Vietnam," and simply stamped both sides of every bill that went through our hands. The idea caught on, and it was the unusual Dead President that wasn't the grudging bearer of this message. As a further protest, it was common to see ordinary American-flag postage stamps affixed upside down, as a symbol of distress.

In the middle of summer 1966, I drew the unwelcome attentions of the government when, quite gratuitously, I sent a letter to my draft board that began:

Gentlemen: Please remove my name from your mailing list, as I am no longer interested in your organization.

And continued in much the same vein for several pages. I really don't know why I did this. It seems unreasonable in retrospect, but this was about the time that I was doing my best to win the "all-time most civil rights arrests" award, and getting busted for possession of a smart mouth and failure to kiss ass was more or less my style.

I had registered for the draft when I turned eighteen, and had gone to the Oakland draft board for a preliminary physical. The result was that I was classified 4-F, because of my poor eyesight. As a student, I hadn't bothered to get reclassified 2-S, figuring that a 4-F was good enough. Of course, the Army can draft anybody, anytime, for any reason, but the need for half-blind rabble-rousers is so limited that I felt myself safe.

I guess that the letter was the last straw, or perhaps it merely drew me to their attention, but a month or so later I received the official communication that turns the blood to icewater:

> Greetings from the President of the United States. You have been selected . . .

Drafted. Reclassified 1-A and drafted, sure as God made little green apples. Shit, oh dear.

My draft physical (which I passed with flying colors, even though I couldn't count my fingers at arm's length without my glasses on) ended with an intelligence test. The Army Alpha is cleverly designed, consisting of four sets of basic questions, increasing in difficulty and contrived to show just about everything that the Army wants to know about how well educated you are and where your intellectual strengths might lie. The four types of questions concern mathematics, diagrams of exploded boxes that indicate spatial conceptualization, word skills, and comparison of objects or ideas—the "A shoe is to a foot as a glove is to a: 1) hand 2) arm 3) head 4) leg" kind. There are twenty-five of each kind of question, making a hundred questions all told. I believe that there is a time limit of an hour. I got them all correct but one, further arousing the mistrust of the sergeant in charge.

After the test, the group of conscripts was asked to sit at school desks and write a short essay. I am not at all sure what we were asked to write about, perhaps it was the Army, or patriotism, or America. I took the opportunity to vomit out a Niagara of vitriol, revealing in excessive detail my feelings about the war, the Army, the draft, the president and the government in general. I was still writing long after everyone else had gone. The same suspicious sergeant took the thick sheaf of papers from me, and said that they would be contacting me in the near future.

Sure enough, Army Intelligence called me up in about a week, wanting to chat. On the advice of my attorney, Art Wells, we met in his office. They would ask questions, and as soon as I would climb up on the soapbox, Art would shut me up.

I had recently finished reading C. Northcote Parkinson's humorous but deadly accurate book analyzing the nature of bureaucracies, *Parkinson's Law*, wherein he gives useful advice about how to get things from them when they wish to obstruct and, more important, how to avoid giving them something when you don't want to. In this case, the thing they wanted that I didn't want to give them was me. Basically, his advice was: Write the bureaucracy a letter, and time the response. This reveals the period in which the letter will sit on somebody's desk, along with your file. When the letter has been answered, the file will be returned to its proper place. Next, write them another letter, and if the time for a response is just about the same, you have discovered the period of time that your file is moving around within the office. Now, start writing letters within the period of response. Subject matter is unimportant, as they must respond to everything, without regard to content. Since your file now is kept in constant motion and never gets back into the filing cabinet where it belongs, but is always in transition from one department to another, *sooner or later, they will lose it!* When you stop getting replies, stop writing immediately, and you will essentially have ceased to exist, as far as they are concerned. I did just that. I wrote letters like,

Dear Sirs:
As I am not the sole surviving son of a veteran killed, wounded or missing in action, I request a deferment for this reason.
Thank you for your attention to this matter.

Dear Sirs:
As I am not currently the sole support of my family, I request a deferment for this reason.
Thank you for your attention to this matter.

Dear Sirs,
As I am not currently enrolled in an accredited four-year college or university, I request a deferment for this reason.
Thank you for your attention to this matter.

Dear Sirs,
As I am not an ordained minister of the Gospel, Catholic priest, or rabbi, I request a deferment for this reason.
Thank you for your attention to this matter.

And so on and so forth, *ad nauseam*.
My correspondent was a seriously dumb young woman named

Debby Dirt or something like that, with big, loopy, subliterate hand-writing—the kind that has little circles over the lowercase *i*'s, and happy faces in them if she is cheerful or wants to seem so. This poor child was the officer in charge of my case, and had a hell of a time figuring what I was up to.

Dr. Jerry Rosenfield wrote a letter to the draft board that stated, in essence, that I would make one damned piss-poor soldier, that inducting me into the armed services would be to court a resounding failure, that they had better try it on somebody else. I do not remember that there was a response.

Sure enough, after some time of this, they lost my file, and I heard nothing whatever from them until late 1972. By then the war was over, and my ass was saved. The file had, apparently, fallen (or been pushed) down behind a filing cabinet. I guess now with everything on computers, this trick won't work anymore. But it might!

Paul Richards: Years later I asked Aubry Grossman, a left-wing lawyer who defended many of the draft resisters, "Aubry, you know, I went against the draft, and I fought for years, and all of a sudden they stopped coming after me. Why?" He said, "Well, in late '68 or early '69, a decision was made within government circles to stop prosecuting war resisters. Basically it was because the judges' kids were not going, either." There was a crescendo of resistance within the bowels of the system. Tons of conscientious objector forms; legal appeals that the government had to fight at great cost; the system was breaking down. That's how you got your file lost. You know what that means? It means that we owe our lives to the peace movement.[1]

Tom Weller got drafted too, but took a different tack. When the rank of dewy-cheeked boys was asked to stand forward, thereby indicating that they were entering the armed services of their own free will and volition, it was the fashion not to do so. So much so, that at least at the Bay Area draft boards, the draftees were told in advance that if they did not wish to stand forward, a second officer would come in and deal with them later. Tom did not stand forward, but explained that he would be glad to, that he had no objections whatever to the Vietnam conflict, or war or fighting in the Army, but as long as he was being deprived of his liberty and happiness, with a chance at the brass ring of death thrown in for nothing, all he wanted was to be given a jury trial, and to be represented by a lawyer. This stopped them cold in their tracks. The ACLU jumped on the case with cries of glee, and really got their claws in. The case went before the U.S. Supreme Court, generating mountains of briefs and a whole shelf of handsomely bound books, stamped in gold on the cover and spine *The People of the United States* v *Thomas William Weller.* Tom's lawyers were the big guns, running rings around the wimpy U.S. attorney's office. Just when things were getting really interesting, the war ended and the case fell into desuetude.

Tom Weller: My draft case was a legal masterpiece. I got Peter Franck in on the deal at the outset. He planned a campaign that would push all the right buttons, plug all the loopholes. Most draft cases, after all, were the haphazard result of some poor bozo just standing up for his beliefs as best he knew how. Mine was a well-oiled machine.

Insofar as there was a legal crux to the case, beyond just a desire to a) avoid the draft and b) screw the bastards, it was the question of due process in the draft board procedure. The system had been set up during World War I to give the draft some kind of decent human face. The theory was that your friends and neighbors—a local bunch of plain folks constituted as the draft board—would review cases on an informal, nonadversarial basis, with an eye to preventing hardship and injustice. This was probably a good idea, and worked fine as long as there was a political consensus.

Clearly, as soon as you start demanding a lawyer, a transcript, *habeas corpus, e pluribus unum,* or whatever, the whole thing is up the spout.

So we peppered these poor folks for years with letters, demands, appearances, objections and whatnot. By the time they finally told me to shut up and go to war, there was an apparent mountain of denied rights and procedural errors, all carefully engineered by Peter to overcome the specific problems or omissions that had defeated previous objectors.

When the time came to take that final nonstep forward, everything had been politely arranged in advance between my lawyers and the government's. The patriotic lads who had taken that step into their country's service were herded off by a sergeant, who remarked, "You goddamn monkeys get your fucking asses through that door, right now!" The officer said to me, the traitorous hippie shirker, "Please come this way, Sir." It hardly seemed fair, I thought. I was taken to be interviewed by the FBI man, a kindly, pipe-smoking gent who could have had a career playing Santa Claus.

Some weeks later I got a letter from Cecil Poole, the then U.S. attorney, asking me to come down at such-and-such a time to be arrested. All very civilized. Later, when the case came before the court of appeals, Poole was *amicus curiae* on my behalf, and bought us all lunch.

The case went to the federal court, then up to the Supreme Court, then back down to the court of appeals, apparently just because everybody was tired of doing it in the usual order.

The United States of America v *Thomas William Weller* sounded like a mismatch, and it was. They didn't have a chance.

The American Civil Liberties Union sent out its big guns. I remember when my attorney entered the courtroom. He had flowing silver hair and, for Christ's sake, a cape. It couldn't have been more impressive if he'd ridden in on a white horse.

The U.S. attorney was a skinny kid in a Penney's corduroy coat. He approached with tiny eyes agleam. Clasping the great man's hand, he said in a tremulous voice, "I've always dreamed of meeting you, Sir." I took this for a good sign.

The court of appeals took the case under consideration, and finally they mislaid it. Or something. They never made any decision. Can they do that? I don't know, but that's what they did.[2]

FRUITS AND NUTS

The state of California's deep sympathy with the plight of the migrant laborer in the mid-sixties was amply illustrated by a remark, reputedly made on the senate floor by the Honorable George Murphy when legislation to mitigate their lot was proposed, that (and I paraphrase) "Mexicans are more suited to stoop labor and the short hoe because they are built closer to the ground."* The whole matter of the bracero program and migrant laborers was far from resolved, and the dipshits in high places weren't making things easier for anybody.

On September 16, 1965, the United Farm Workers under Cesar Chavez voted to strike the Central Valley grape growers. The farmworkers urged a boycott of table grapes, and good radicals did not eat them. Even now I have a little trouble looking a bunch of grapes in the eye. Welch's grape jelly, Gallo wine and Coors beer were also not fare for good radicals. Somehow, food had developed political leanings. Later on, everything from whales to milk became political bones of contention. This was just the start of it.

In the summer of 1966, Mike Bennett and I decided to drive to Delano, down near Bakersfield, and see what was shaking with Cesar Chavez's people and the strike against DiGiorgio Fruit, one of the big growers. We had volunteered to take boxes of food and clothing to the strike headquarters. Mike thought that the DiGiorgio men all drove white pickups, and he worried about every white pickup truck that we

---

*Although it is generally agreed that this is just the sort of colorful remark that Senator Murphy commonly came out with, I cannot find the citation. The closest I've been able to come is the observation of an Imperial Valley grower, anonymously quoted in the *New York Times Magazine* on September 15, 1974, that "Those people were made to suffer; some of them even enjoy the work. God made the Mexicans with stubby legs and greasy hair. So, you see, they can lean low and tolerate the sun in the fields. Chavez made those people think they're something better." I thank Connie Reyes of the Berkeley Public Library for research assistance in this matter.

CHILDREN PICKING PLUMS, MONTEREY, CALIFORNIA, 1958.
PHOTO BY HARVEY RICHARDS.

saw. Even for the times, Mike was overly paranoid. We dropped off the charity, which was received much as charity often is, and, instead of hanging around—we felt somewhat out of place, being rather Anglo and all—we headed back. While we were still in town, we found that we were both flat. This came to light when I asked Mike to loan me two bits for smokes, and he said he didn't have two bits. We were completely broke, except for a glove compartment full of his mother's Blue Chip Stamp books. We cashed them in for ten dollars at the Blue Chip Stamp Redemption Center, and bought gas and cigarettes, and drove home again.

When we returned, we got a call that stevedores were refusing to cross a farmworkers' grape-strike picket on the San Francisco waterfront, but that there weren't many people on the line and they needed reinforcements. The picket was "informational," which meant that it had no clout or union sanction, or anything that the longshoremen's union had to honor, but they were all a bunch of old lefties and sympathetic to the cause, so even a feeble token line was good enough for them.

When Mike and I arrived, a thin, dyspeptic lawyer for United Fruit

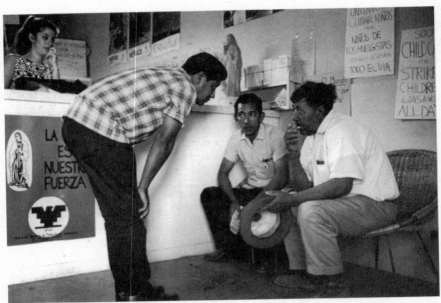

CESAR CHAVEZ (LEFT) AT THE FARM LABOR OFFICE, DELANO, CALIFORNIA.
PHOTO © 1993 BY TED STRESHINSKY.

was reading the riot act through a bullhorn, and people were leaving the line right and left. We thumbed our noses at him and picked up signs and started walking. He told us that we were unlawfully obstructing the unloading of his company's goods and that if we didn't disperse immediately we would be arrested. We flipped him the bird. A police captain came up to us and asked us politely if we were going to leave, and we said no. I was kind of surprised that he was so polite, until I looked around and saw about a hundred longshoremen with the tools of their trade in hand, muttering among themselves and mocking the lawyer. The captain said that he was really sorry, but that this guy had a court order and that if we wouldn't go, he would have to arrest us, if we didn't mind, Sir. We stayed put. We were arrested by the captain, a lieutenant and two sergeants. They treated us like we were made out of glass, helping us gently into the paddy wagon, and asking us if we were, for God's sake, comfortable. As I was being assisted in, one cop actually told me to watch my step. We were not handcuffed. San Francisco was a strong union town, and there was no way in hell that they were going to brutalize us or even harm a hair on our heads with half the membership of the International Longshoremen's Union and two of the Hallinan brothers standing around. The Hallinans gave the notion of "fighting Irish" new meaning. Butch and Kayo Hallinan were left-wing attorneys, their dad was an old-time labor lawyer, and they all loved a good fight. The

606

boys were former Golden Gloves champs. No shit, they really did love a good fight. Plus there were four more brothers somewhere else just in case. The cops did not want to give anybody any excuses. We were taken downtown, and treated in the station like they were booking the pope—the cops even gave us cigarettes, when we told them we were out. Mike and I found this so excruciatingly funny that we laughed ourselves into near hysterics in the drunk tank and had to be separated like naughty schoolboys. The cops just couldn't stand it, us laughing like hyenas and disturbing the honest drunks and pimps. John Leggett saw us languishing amongst the winos and went our bail, whereupon we were bailed out as fast as the machineries of justice could turn, which was Pretty Damn Quick. We called my dad from the jail, and went to his office on Mission Street to get him to buy us lunch, sitting around the rest of the afternoon shooting the breeze.

This was my fourteenth and last arrest. I had been convicted and did time for the FSM bust, and had gotten a slap on the wrist for flouting the traffic codes. Nothing at all happened as a result of the other charges. I was often arraigned, or dragged from one cell to be transported into another jurisdiction for further processing, but I got no time, fines, lectures, harsh words or nasty looks. The fix was in, somewhere, somehow. I don't know why I was the darling of so many highly placed big guns, but I'm sure glad that I was. It may have been no more than that I was doing what they would have liked to do, had they had absolutely nothing to lose. But they did, and so I was their vicarious Peck's Bad Boy. I was as cheerful as a cricket, afraid of nothing, and filled with piss and vinegar. I took my charmed life for granted. I had no good sense. I *never* looked before I leaped. This amorphous, anonymous group of elders saw to it that as little harm came to me as a result of my impudent rascality as could be arranged, and without a moment's reflection I took it as no more than my rightful due.

MUTATIS MUTANDIS

B Y THE SPRING OF 1967, it had become obvious that Leo wasn't making it. The liberals weren't paying their bills, nobody was extending credit, nothing was working out. Not thinking quite fast enough on my feet, I had accidentally been nailed by a process server, and we were on C.O.D. with all the suppliers that would still deal with us. Dodging creditors and the tax man, despairing in his heart of making it, Leo took off to Reno with his last couple of grand in a futile bid to win enough at the tables to keep the shop afloat. The predictable happened, and he returned, mighty blue, with his tail between his legs and two thousand dollars lighter. I was out of work again.

About this time, Bill Buckman showed up on the doorstep. Bill had devoted considerable energies to the "Scheer for Congress" cause. So much, indeed, that he had been late to work and groggy too many times at Mike Roberts Color, and gotten himself fired. Bill had been around the Berkeley Free Press quite a few times, bringing in leaflets and campaign materials that he had designed and laid out. Now he came in looking for work, and Leo told him how it was with the finances. The shop was going bust, and there was no work for anyone. Bill talked it over with his wife, Shirley, and borrowed twenty-five hundred dollars on his life insurance. With this money, he set the shop up again, striking a new deal with the eternal sugar daddy, Phil Roos. Bill's first act in office was to change the name of the press. Not only because by now the name "Berkeley Free Press" was suspected by every Bay Area supplier, but because the word "Free" seemed to imply that we didn't charge for our work. Of course, we often did not charge, but that was more by accident than by design. So, in May of 1967, without much fanfare, the radical "Berkeley Free Press" became the bourgeois "Berkeley Graphic Arts." The clientele didn't change to speak of, but we did start getting

Mutatis mutandis: the necessary changes having been made.

a slightly greater volume of work from nonpolitical sources. The best stuff was psychedelic dance posters, but most of that went to Levon Mosgofian's T. Lautrec Litho in San Francisco.

Bill hung on as a commercial printer until the winter of 1970, when the realities of trying to print competitively with ancient machines and modestly skilled workers caught up with him, too. In 1971, I took the shop over as a design studio and specialty publishing operation, renaming it "Saint Hieronymus Press," which it remains to this day.

THE SECOND JAIL TERM AT SANTA RITA

OUR LAST APPEALS finally failed, and on June 21, 1967, I went into Santa Rita to serve the balance of my FSM sentence. Defendants who had refused probation got ten to thirty days, and defendants who either could not or would not pay their fines received short sentences of varying length, usually one day for each ten bucks. Although there couldn't have been more than twenty-five of us all told, things in the outside world were much less pleasant than they had been in 1965, and the authorities had much better reason to fear a unified, highly politicized bloc of inmates. So we were split up as before. Mario, Marvin Garson, Jeff Lustig and Steven Saslow worked in the bakery from four in the morning, so I didn't see much of them except on Saturday. I hoed weeds, picked tomatoes and cultivated sugar beets.

Michael Rossman was a garbageman. The slops he gathered were cooked up and shipped off to the hog farm. Jack was put to work on the hog farm, dirty and smelly, but he claimed that he sort of liked it because you were pretty much left on your own out there. The guards didn't like the place, and came around as little as they could. After a while, he wearied of the pigs, or they of him, and he was transferred to a crew of old, easygoing cons who were in charge of roofing. Jack did well at the job until he decided that he wanted to get a good tan and left off his straw hat all afternoon. He got heatstroke, and after a few days' recuperation in the barracks, was transferred to an office job for the remainder of his stay, where he discovered that the county of Alameda turned quite a tidy profit off the sugar beets and tomatoes cultivated by the prisoners.

Jeff Lustig: I didn't have to go in, unlike you guys who had to go. I could have paid my fine, but I figured that it was better for the state to pay for my keep than for me to pay the state. When we went in and the bars clanged shut behind us at the Berkeley jail, I remember tapping you on the shoulder and saying, "I feel liberated, David." That was the end of the semester when we had lots of political activity on campus, I'd finished my MA thesis, and I'd broken up, gone back together and broken up again with Suzy. For me a month in jail would be like a month's vacation. All I had to do was sleep and eat starchy food and work. I didn't have to think about anything. I may have been one of the people for whom jail was truly rehabilitative.

When I was in line being processed in at Santa Rita, your high school buddy Kenny Bailey was there and he asked me what I could do, and I said, "Housepainting," and he said not to tell them that. Housepainting meant being out in the hot July sun fixing those barracks or hoeing weeds. "Tell them that you worked as a baker. That's a good job." I told Kenny that I didn't know anything at all about baking, but he said, "So what, neither did any of the guys in the bakery. There's a guy in charge and he tells you what to do and you do it." So I told them that I was a baker, and got in.

There was this huge Hawaiian guy, Augustino, I think his name was—arms like cannonballs—who was the head of one of the invisible gangs that the place was full of. Kenny said that when Mario came in this guy was going to choose him out. I asked him why, and he said that it was just the way it was: he was the leader of a gang and Mario was the leader of a gang and they had to sort it out. Nothing personal. If you tripped me up in the dining hall, the guy above me in my gang would punch you out and then the guy above you in your gang would beat him up and so on until it got up to the leaders, who would square off and see who was top dog. It's just the way it was.*

I told him that we were different, that we weren't a fighting gang,

---

*Since the FSMers were not in any proper sense criminals, we had no understanding of the prison subculture, and mostly weren't even aware of it. We were outsiders and everyone treated us that way. The underlying principle of prison is that a lone individual is exceedingly vulnerable, and in order to survive must be allied in some manner with a larger group. Usually the gangs are organized by race. In most jails, the gangs form an unstable tripod of white, Black and Hispanic, constantly vying among themselves for power. The Hispanics have traditionally been the best organized, retaining the cohesive family and neighborhood structure of the outside. The gangs form a sort of uneasy prison union, which in return for privilege and power keeps things on an even keel. Sooner or later, anyone who breaks the law for a living is going to end up in jail. Once in jail, he is in the hands of the gangs. Thus it behooves those on the outside to cooperate with those on the inside, to such an extent that, as the phrase has it, "The inside controls the outside." In order to make the prison work at all, the guards must seek the cooperation of these organized inmates. In addition, the outside influences the guards, who often provide a conduit between the outside and the inside. Key inmates can be extraordinarily powerful. Not too much of this goes on at the lowly level of the county jail, but there is enough.

JEFF LUSTIG'S DETAIL OFFICE ASSIGNMENT ORDER, SANTA RITA COUNTY JAIL, 6-22-67.

or even a gang at all. We were just a bunch of guys who had done something together and so we were serving time together. He didn't get it. That's when I decided to get as many of our guys on the bakery crew as possible. Each of the two crews had eleven guys, so if it came to a fight three or four out of eleven had a lot better odds than four or five guys in a group of forty hacking weeds. We were successful, too. When Mario was being processed in, I gestured to him through the chain-link fence and whispered, "Bakery!" Mario got on the other crew; Garson was on mine; and I forget the others.

When I was in Cuba—I had gone there in 1963 with Bob Mates to test the travel ban—tensions had built up and led to trouble between the Black members of our organization and the white ones. It eventually led to a fistfight, because one guy attacked another guy, and his friends stood by him and the other guy's friends stood by *him* until it was a mess. I don't think that much would have come of it if we hadn't talked the friction up and made a big, inevitable deal out of it. So I kept my mouth shut about what Bailey had said. But I really needed to talk to somebody about it. Steven Saslow was a nerdy kind of guy, who unlike the rest of us made no pretense of being a tough guy in the prison environment. He was just himself. Every day he walked up and down the compound for exercise; people made fun of him, but it didn't bother him. In the bakery, he asked a guy for the core from a roll of paper towels, and some honey, and with that he made a *microscope!* He put a nick in his finger and let all the guys look at the blood under the microscope; these big Black guys crowding around, wanting to look at their own blood, too. Everybody was knocked out, and he became a sort of pet, a guy that the others liked and respected. But he did it by just being himself. He was the only one who had the courage to do that. I finally walked up and down with him, and told him about what Kenny had said, and he agreed that the best course was to say nothing, and not get everybody inflamed and defensive and alarmed, because that would be the surest way to make something happen. When Mario got in, the first night he was writing letters for guys in his barracks, and became very popular. I knew then that there would be no trouble, and was glad that I'd kept quiet.

Brian Turner managed to get his arm broken for misunderstanding the rules in a game of five-to-life football. He caught the football and ran with it, scoring a goal. Members of the opposing team came up to him and told him, "Don't do that again." The next time the ball came his way, he caught it and ran with it. They tackled him, beat the shit out of him and broke his arm. He got his arm splinted, and was thrown in solitary for making trouble.

I fell in with a Black guy who taught me how to use the weight room. Every afternoon we would talk, and he would ask me questions like, "What's the difference between protesting and complaining?" If I could have come up with a two-sentence answer to that, it would have been something.[1]

There was an attempted escape in the laundry truck, and Steven Saslow had a chance to go but turned it down. It would have been foolish to earn another year or two in jail to get out of a few weeks of easy time. The escapee was caught within hours, anyway.

Just as before, the eternal radio played songs that almost nobody liked. The Black and Hispanic inmates disliked the Beatles, and there were more of them than anybody else, so just to irritate the greatest number of inmates, the guards made sure that we heard lots of Beatles music, which was OK by us FSM kids. Their "Lovely Rita, Meter Maid" sounded over the scratchy intercom more like "Santa Rita Meter Maid," and we were amused to sing it that way. A popular tune of the day was the 5th Dimension's obnoxious, insipid *Up, up and away in my beautiful, my beauuuut-iiiii-fuuul ba-loooooon*, of which I grew heartily sick. If ever I hear it, I'm invisibly transported back to that hot, dreary jail.

Although I wanted a calligraphy pen and ink, and tried to get a copy of my own book, *An Introduction to the Elements of Calligraphy*, in, none of it was approved. Books could come directly from a publisher to an inmate, but somehow Saint Hieronymus Press failed to qualify and the book sent me ended up in my property and was given me when I got out. My Rapidograph had been confiscated with the explanation that it would make somebody a good hypodermic. I was offended, but then I didn't know much. When I got out, I sent the prison library a copy of my calligraphy manual. I'd gotten much better at chess, and played Jeff Lustig endlessly. Together we studied openings out of the one chess

ALICE WATERS. FRENCH GOVERNMENT PHOTO.

book in the prison library, though it never got much beyond the queen's pawn.

I met some Hell's Angels, and was surprised to find them literate, intelligent and perfectly pleasant. Nice boys, just a little wild. I also found that my high school hoodlum buddy, Kenny Bailey, and his pugnacious Irish brother-in-law were in residence. Kenny was carrying a .22 slug in him from an unsuccessful robbery attempt, and had already spent four years in prison. Both had been convicted of yet another stupid misdemeanor in a long, tiresome string of dumb-ass crimes, and were doing their easy time as a vacation of sorts from their normal lives. Mean existences crowded with no money, no prospects, daytime TV, alcoholism, drugs, dirty diapers and nagging wives. As soon as they got out, they had another warehouse burglary planned. Boy, was I lucky to get away from those two when I did.

Patti, Bettina and Rosemary were also serving their sentences then.* In February of 1967, Bettina had married Jack Kurzweil. When it came time to serve her time, she was six months along with child. The kid was off to a good start as a lefty; whilst still *in utero*, it did forty-five days with its mother. Bettina insisted on serving her sentence, as the alternative of probation precluded activism for two years. Despite assurances that she was given adequate medical care, and that she got protein every day, we all worried about her.

Patti Iiyama: In the women's barracks there wasn't much to do. There wasn't any exercise yard and only a tiny garden area; one lucky woman

---

*"Today, the Glorious Fourth, we had chicken for lunch, and another dreadful movie this evening. Last movie we saw the girls through the curtain—Rosebean [Rosemary Feitis] looked chipper, 'Tina as big as a bus, Patti was astonishingly little- girl-like in her blues. I think Pam Mellin is in, but I'm not at all certain of that. They all looked healthy and more or less cheerful" (letter from the author to Alice Waters, 4 July 1967).

got to work in it, even though it didn't need much care. We starched and ironed our clothes, and mended, cooked and washed. We were very clean and neat. We wore shapeless one-piece blue dresses that buttoned up the front. They had white collars, but it was not a blouse, only part of the dress. The sizes were limited, and nothing was small enough for me, so I looked like an orphan. We had two changes of dresses: one brand-new that we were supposed to wear on visitors' day, and one all ratty and worn out that we were to wear for everyday. I reversed the order and so did all the other FSMers.

When I went in, only one other FSMer—Anita Levine—was there, and she'd been in for a few days all alone. We were together for a while and then Rosemary and Bettina came in. Anita got out before I did; she only had twenty-five days. I got one or two days good time off my sentence. The other women there were mostly prostitutes and bad-check writers. They all used drugs, and came into jail on purpose to escape their pimps and fatten up and get off drugs for a while. One woman wrote a bad check on purpose just to get into jail for a rest and regular food; it was better than the outside, and it was safe. One woman got real sick and the guards wouldn't do anything about it, and we made a big fuss and threatened to call our lawyers, and they finally got her to a hospital.[2]

The only high point, if it can be called that, was when Professor Searle, Dale Greenmeyer and Brian O'Brien planned a "solidarity picket" for Sunday, July 2, at the entrance to Santa Rita. When we found out about this, and the likelihood that all visiting would be canceled if it happened, we did our sincere and level best to tell them not to do it if they wanted to see us in one piece again. Fortunately, they seemed to have gotten the picture.

In 1966, when Robert Scheer ran for Congress, the Berkeley Free Press did much of his campaign printing. The "Scheer for Congress" liaison was the lovely, delightful Alice Louise Waters, whose task it was to bring the copy or camera-ready art to the press, oversee its production and return the finished goods to campaign headquarters. I set my sights straight at her, and not long after meeting, we began living together. Driven to Santa Rita by David Stein, she visited me faithfully every weekend.

David Stein: I remember vividly the several Sundays in which it was my duty to borrow a car, usually Ashoke Kerr's improbable '52 Chevy convertible known affectionately as Rosinante, and drive Alice Waters to visit you. I would also visit Michael Rossman, and Mario and Suzanne. Then after our return from Santa Rita, Alice and I would have a late lunch/early dinner on the little porch of your apartment on Grove Street, the one next to the red-headed Gail O'Connor, Mal Burnstein's lover, and downstairs from the shrink from the Free Clinic, Dr. Hippocrates, who did so much to help other recipients of "Greetings" letters to evade their civic irresponsibility.*

After a while, the disparity between the number of visitors that the FSMers got (lots) and the number that most of the other prisoners got (none) started to make for trouble. Since every visitor was separate, and you got your name called out over the intercom each time, it made things even more obvious. We heard rumors that the old visiting-list system, which had been discontinued since my last stay at Santa Rita, was going to be reinstated "because of abuses by the demonstrators," so we wrote our friends and asked them to stay away, and maybe only one or two come for each of us. I told Alice that I only wanted to see her, and that all others could cool their heels in the car.

Alice and David Stein picked me up at eight-thirty in the morning, July 21, to take me home again.

In the late 1960s, the final disposition of the FSM defendants' cases was taken over by Berkeley judge George Brun, who cleared up the ragtag and bobtail and took care that those who had been minors at the time of the arrests and wanted to have their records sealed had an opportunity to do so.

---

*I believe that Dr. Hippocrates was actually Eugene Schoenfield, who did not live upstairs from me. Dr. Jerry Rosenfield lived upstairs from me, and wrote a letter that was instrumental in saving my butt from Vietnam. Neal Blumenfeld was a psychiatrist who was sometimes referred to as "Psychiatrist to the FSM." These three may have been mixed together in David Stein's memory. The quotation above is taken from letters he wrote me in 1990.

POST HOC

S UE STEIN: The FSM spread all over the place. These guys would go in and say to their administrators, "On the one hand . . ." They would come in wearing their nice suits, saying, "We're civilized people, of course, and we don't wanna have to do a thing like the thing that happened at Berkeley, we're not that type of student body here, and of course it wouldn't work . . ." And then they would say from the other side of their mouth, "*But,* unless you come across with those things, we're gonna have to take off our Brooks Brothers suits and put on sloppy clothing so that we don't have to worry about the police messing it up! And we're gonna go the whole route. Of course, you realize we don't wanna do this, 'cause we're civilized." And they managed to get a *tremendous* amount out of their universities.[1]

A logical though unanticipated result of the Free Speech Movement was to alter the demographics and escalate the radicalism of the Berkeley campus. Conservative students went elsewhere, and students from all over the United States who were interested in social protest selected Cal above all others. The influx of kids looking for a cause contributed mightily to the dramatically changing shape of Berkeley through the rest of the century.*

This was not the only result, as Greil Marcus pointed out in a com-

---

Post hoc: after this.

*Reports of increasing radicalism at Cal led conservative parents to send their children to college elsewhere, and even as the campus population increased from 18,728 in 1959 to 25,454 in 1966 the percentage of students from white, Anglo-Saxon, Protestant backgrounds declined. Between 1959 and 1966 the number of students from Protestant families dropped from 55 to 39 percent, while those from Catholic families rose from 11 to 18 percent; those from Jewish families remained steady, and those reporting themselves to be from nonreligious backgrounds increased from 6 to 27 percent. By 1965, students were coming from new social groups: 31 percent of Cal students had at least one foreign-born parent (statistics from Rorabaugh, 34).

mencement address to the graduating class of the history department at
UC Berkeley in 1988:

> In that same year [1964] . . . an event took place that I want to turn to
> today. That was the Free Speech Movement: a few students, then several
> thousand students, insisting that the limits the University administra-
> tion had placed on their advocacy of social change were wrong. This
> event had far-reaching consequences, though not even the most far-
> seeing of those who were part of the event could have imagined the
> most concrete, perhaps the most important, of its consequences. Today,
> thanks to the commercial hook of media anniversaries, there are plenty
> of books in the stores highlighting the Free Speech Movement as the
> spark for the decade of protest called "The Sixties"—but this may just
> be gush.
>
> More vitally, the Free Speech Movement was very likely the crucial
> factor in Ronald Reagan's election as governor of California in 1966—
> and thus, if one follows the line, his election as president of the United
> States fourteen years after that. In 1980, Ronald Reagan, calling for "Na-
> tional Renewal," and setting himself against the chaos of the previous
> two decades as the embodiment of traditional values, was still running
> against the Free Speech Movement. Edwin Meese, who as an assistant
> district attorney of Alameda County led the prosecution of Free Speech
> Movement demonstrators, who insured that sentences would be stiff (in
> some cases, as much as six months for occupying a campus building),*
> is today attorney general of the United States; it was that prosecution
> that brought him to the attention of Ronald Reagan.

Clark Kerr was fired after Ronald Reagan beat out Pat Brown for
California governor. In January 1967, at the first Regents' meeting attended by Reagan, the Regents voted 14–8 to give Kerr the gate. But
in 1980, when UC took over the California School for the Deaf and
Blind, Kerr got a whole campus named after him. I find it highly poetic
that the blind and deaf students were hornswoggled out of their school
under the pretext of earthquake safety, and that the emptied grounds
were named after a man who behaved throughout the Free Speech
Movement as though his students were also blind and deaf and could
easily be tricked and manipulated. The new school for the blind and deaf
is located on land that is no less seismically frisky.

---

*Actually, the worst anybody got was 120
days, which was still pretty damn stiff
considering that first-offense trespassing
usually got something like a $25 fine at the
outside.

CLARK KERR AT THE MOMENT HE IS FIRED BY RONALD REAGAN.
PHOTO © 1993 BY TED STRESHINSKY.

Caught in the crossfire among the waffling, inaccessible Clark Kerr, the vindictive, slightly cuckoo Alex Sherriffs and the more fanatical, intransigent activists (such as myself), Arleigh Williams preserved a gentle humanity and a genuine concern for the welfare of the students in his charge. This endeared him even further to those who already knew him, and created a climate of trust that ameliorated some of the harsher episodes that the sixties had in store for us all.

Mike Rossman, a member of the FSM Steering Committee, had been taught to fish by Arleigh Williams in the late 1940s. These sorts of ties are not obliterated even in the heat of the moment.

Tom Weller: Arleigh Williams was a famous football star at Cal and ended his days there as an administrator. Everybody always called him "Arleigh"—students, administrators, everybody. He was just one of those kinds of people—it wouldn't occur to you to call him anything else. Since he was liked by everybody, administration and FSM alike, he often served as a go-between and mediator.[2]

Arleigh Williams: I had many conversations someplace between [September] 30 and October 2 [1964], where I made a real appeal to give me the opportunity to put this [free speech] issue into the Academic Senate. I felt that the principle was on the side of the students, and that this body was

619

going to be able to lend its support to bring about a change in rules and regulations. Students were arguing on the basis of principles involved in the First Amendment; students were arguing on principles involved in the Fourteenth Amendment. You could always argue, too, that the University had the duty and responsibility to devise rules and regulations to be able to administer itself. But these rules and regulations cannot abrogate the freedoms which are guaranteed to us by the Constitution.

I think we could have involved many, many faculty who were interested in this and could have prepared a statement which would have brought it to the floor of the senate. I felt at that time that this was something that the University itself, all of the components of its personality, would be interested [in]. I couldn't sell this deal at that time. I wish I could've. I believe that we would have been able to put this in an appropriate arena, and as a consequence we would've gained the same things that ultimately came out of this, without the conflict which was exercised in the process. I proposed it many times. In fact, we made many proposals in the process of trying to solve it. We were trying to do what was possible to structure something appropriate to debate and to order, as I feel that order must be maintained. This was not a society where doors were closed. There were feelings that doors were closed, and they're not. I don't think that anyone can ever argue that this is so. Sometimes you meet opposition, this is quite true, but the presentation of ideas is, I feel, one of the great strengths of this University. Ideas are always examined and when they have real power behind them, they become a way of life. Sometimes there's much debate.

I think others would have argued, "Oh, we can't do this." Some felt the faculty had abrogated its responsibility and did so during the loyalty oath, and others were fearful that they wouldn't get their promotions if they did something like this. I'm not hypothesizing at this moment; these are statements which were given to me at the time. I argued to the contrary. As you know from a historical standpoint, my argument didn't carry much water at that time, and didn't have success in bringing this about. I will never get over feeling that I wish I would've been powerful enough to have gotten it to where I think it should have been. I think, too, we'd have made progress just as fast as we've made it now, maybe even faster. Perhaps at the moment it appeared that it would have been much, much slower. Well, this is all water under the bridge. It didn't come about that way, and now [1966] we are still in the process of recovery.

We have to wait a few years to determine what's going to happen. The University has built-in inventory processes. It examines itself constantly. I think any university worth its salt, or any individual worth his salt, must do this. You can't be satisfied with the pattern of operation which is very convenient. That stifles progress; it doesn't enhance or encourage progress in any way.

Without regard to whether it contributed to the nation as a whole, I think this is a positive thing which has come out of all this battle. I hope that as a result of it, we're going to become a greater University than we ever were before. People feel quite the contrary at the moment, but this is one of the difficult things, because so many of us are in the front-line trenches, constantly defending the University, defending students, and trying to interpret what this place is and what a university should be. We have to go out and point out the necessity of understanding that the University isn't an institution that supports the status quo. If it supports the status quo, it fails. The University is a place where ideas germinate and bloom, and have an effect to shift the society. So give us time, I think we'll recover. We'll recover some of the lost souls who've lost faith in the University; they'll be back.[3]

Looking back, the shadowy figure of Vice-Chancellor Alex Sherriffs emerges, Queeg-like, as the villain of the melodrama: it was he who twice suppressed the memo from Cunningham making it clear that legally there was no reason to interfere with campus political activity, and it was he who, in the physical absence of Kerr, initiated the restrictions on partisan politics in the Bancroft-Telegraph strip, falsely implying Kerr's authority in the matter. Sherriffs was a frustrated crowd-pleaser who wanted his students to love him. He taught a ludicrous, pandering psychology course for which he was sharply criticized in the *SLATE Supplement*. This particularly stung him in his pride, and, combined with his pathological terror of Communism, may have sent him 'round the bend. Throughout the Free Speech Movement, Sherriffs suppressed crucial information, interfered with Deans Williams and Towle in their efforts to communicate with Chancellor Strong, and at every juncture obstructed conciliation. It was Sherriffs who, after the administration had essentially gained the victory, threw the entire matter into chaos by demanding—through the right wing of the Regents—the heads of Mario, Art, Jackie and Brian over the vigorous protests of Arleigh Williams. Sherriffs was behind the initiation of police action on campus in the sit-in of December 2 and 3, and in a last, spiteful spasm, it was he who denied the arrested students the use of Wheeler Auditorium to confer with their lawyers. After the hoopla was over, Sherriffs spewed blame in every direction, particularly at Katherine Towle, who had opposed him at every turn throughout.

Jackie Goldberg: The only thing Dean Towle did, and she did a gorgeous job, was she raked Alex Sherriffs over the coals for two and a half hours in her last official meeting—the administrators' meeting—as dean of students. It was scathing: about his total irresponsibility, his complete paranoia, how he hated students, how he was absolutely not the person to be involved in their affairs at all. She cited case after case after case.* That's one test of Heyns, the new chancellor. If he gets rid of Sherriffs, we've got a chance on this campus. I don't think it'll take long at all, because Williams hates Sherriffs, too.[4]

Alex Sherriffs was removed from his position at the request of Chancellor Heyns as soon as Heyns took office; soon after he was hired as Ronald Reagan's chief aide for higher education.† It is entirely fitting that Alex Sherriffs ended up working for the "genial sociopath" Ronald Reagan, sworn enemy of the Free Speech Movement and all it represented.[5]

Would it all have happened without Alex Sherriffs touching the match to the powder keg? Kerr, Towle and Arleigh Williams were in favor of leaving the Bancroft-Telegraph area strictly alone, and vigorously resisted outside pressures to clamp down on student organizing for off-campus issues. But I think it would have happened anyway, sooner or later. The civil rights movement and the FSM offended adult nostalgia for a time that never was and never would be. The pressures were building both for increased activism and increased repression, and if the civil rights movement hadn't set it off, the Vietnam War protests would have. Cal Berkeley is the most likely place in either event. The personalities involved would have been different, though there would likely have been even more representation by highly skilled, veteran civil rights activists. The administration would largely have been the same faces with the same attitudes; the faculty would have been in the identical man-in-the-middle position. The specific characters from the student community would have been replaced by other, similar people—the flavors would have been different, but the dish would still have been served up piping hot. The time was right.

---

*"Vice-Chancellor Alex C. Sherriffs attacked the Free Speech Movement, lost his job, and joined Governor Ronald Reagan's staff. Dean of Students Katherine A. Towle . . . quietly, vehemently, and unsuccessfully opposed Sherriffs' policies" (Rorabaugh, photo insert following page 50).

†"Sherriffs went to Regents meetings, appeared to instruct Reagan how to vote, and insisted on attending the executive sessions as the governor's representative. When some Regents protested, Reagan got angry, and the Regents decided to protect their budget by allowing Sherriffs to continue to attend the closed sessions" (Rorabaugh, 158).

As for me? Standing on that chair with *SLATE Supplement*s in my hand and in consequence getting thrown out of Cal was the single luckiest thing that happened to me in my life. I was on the wrong track, trying to do things that I was not well suited for; the FSM freed me to go where I ought to go. From my days in the Free Speech Movement I keep the fondest of memories and an almost fanatical love for the First Amendment. As long as this nation has a free press, freedom of speech, freedom of assembly and the ACLU to defend these rights, all else will follow. That's worth fighting for, and that's what the FSM, perhaps the purest political movement in this nation's history, was all about.

In addition, I learned that the only way to get power is to *take* it. Nobody is going to give it to you willingly, no matter how nicely you ask. The law changes to recognize shifts in political strength; it does not promote those shifts. Had we stayed within legal avenues—avenues defined by our adversaries—we would never have gotten anything in the free speech, civil rights or antiwar movements. There is no redress of grievance for those whose only remedy is the law.

> Let me give you a word on the philosophy of reforms. The whole history of the progress of human liberty shows that all concessions yet made to her august claims have been born of struggle. . . . If there is no struggle there is no progress. Those who profess to favor freedom and yet depreciate agitation, are men who want crops without ploughing up the ground. They want rain without thunder and lightning. They want the ocean without the awful roar of its many waters. The struggle may be a moral one; or it may be a physical one; or it may be both moral and physical, but it must be a struggle. Power concedes nothing without a demand. It never did and it never will.
> —Frederick Douglass, letter to a white abolitionist, 1849

POSTSCRIPT

Lᴵᴋᴇ ᴛʜᴇ ʙᴏᴜʀʙᴏɴs, the University administration has "learned nothing, and forgotten nothing."* A monument to free speech erected on the Berkeley campus in 1992 in approximately the spot where Jack sat in a police car for thirty-two hours was only grudgingly allowed, and on it any direct reference to the Free Speech Movement was absolutely prohibited.

---

*"Ils n'ont rien appris, ni rien oublié" (Charles Maurice de Tallyrand-Périgord [1754–1838]).

ENDNOTES

For complete information on interviews and correspondence, see "Bibliography & Sources."

Quotation of Clark Kerr preceding "Bright Youth Passes . . ." is from Jay Stevens, *Storming Heaven: LSD and the American Dream* (New York: Atlantic Monthly Press, 1987), ix; Roger Sandall is quoted from W. J. Rorabaugh, *Berkeley at War: The 1960s* (New York: Oxford University Press, 1989), 20.

DUCK AND COVER

1. Mike Benton, *The Comic Book in America* (Dallas: Taylor Publishing, 1989), 41.

2. I direct the interested reader to Bruno Bettelheim's *The Uses of Enchantment: The Meaning and Importance of Fairy Tales* (New York: Vintage, 1977).

3. Benton, 45.

4. Maurice Horn, *Sex in the Comics* (New York: Chelsea House, 1985), 134.

5. Benton, 115.

6. Joe Sasfy, liner notes to the digitally remastered CD album *The Rock 'n' Roll Era, 1958: Still Rockin'*, Time-Life 2RNR21.

QUI TACET CONSENTIT

1. Thomas Jefferson, letter to William Stevens Smith, 13 November 1787.

2. A history of the First Amendment and its continuing struggles with state and federal authority can be found in Robert J. Wagman, *The First Amendment Book* (New York: Scripps Howard, 1991).

3. I refer the interested reader to John Peter Zenger's *Brief Narrative of Case and Trial* (1736), considered by the Grolier Club of New York City to be among the one hundred most influential American books. See also Isaiah Thomas, *The History of Printing in America* (New York: Weathervane Books, 1970), and for a discussion of the history of freedom of the press in America, Leonard W. Levy, *Freedom of the Press from Zenger to Jefferson* (New York: Bobbs-Merrill, 1966).

4. Levy, xxv.

5. Levy, 378.

6. American Civil Liberties Union, *ACLU Briefing Paper*, no. 1, 1992.

7. American Civil Liberties Union, 1984–1985 annual report.

8. Steven Heller, "Cold War Design: Battling the Red Menace," *Print*, May/June 1992, 99.

TOWN AND GOWN

1. In the main, this history of Berkeley is drawn from Don Pitcher and Malcolm Margolin, *Berkeley Inside/Out* (Berkeley, Calif.: Heyday Books, 1990).

2. Steven Warshaw, *The Trouble in Berkeley* (Berkeley, Calif.: Diablo Press, 1965), 15.

FIAT LUX

1. Quotations of Bob Gill are from written and verbal communications to the author, 16 November 1990 and 22 April 1992.

I HAVE HERE IN MY HAND A LIST . . .

1. Heller, 95.

2. Heller, 94.

3. Heller, 94.

4. Heller, 94–95.

5. Heller, 97.

THE YEAR OF THE OATH

1. David P. Gardner, *The California Oath Controversy* (Berkeley and Los Angeles: University of California Press, 1967), 25.

2. Gardner, 26.

3. George Stewart, *The Year of the Oath* (Garden City, N.Y.: Doubleday, 1950), 145.

4. Gardner, 30, 132.

5. Gardner, 230.

6. Quotations of Charles Muscatine are from an interview by the author, 21 October 1992.

7. In addition to the works by Gardner and Stewart cited above, see William B. Hyland, *The Cold War: 50 Years of Conflict* (New York: Random House, 1992).

THE ADMINISTRATOR

(Epigraph) Clark Kerr is quoted from Mark Kitchell's film *Berkeley in the Sixties*, 1989.

1. Quoted in Pitcher and Margolin, 69.

2. *Look* magazine, 23 February 1965, 31.

3. Howard Zinn, *A People's History of the United States* (New York: Harper and Row, 1980), 256–258.

4. Hal Draper, *Behind the Battle of Berkeley: The Mind of Clark Kerr*, Independent Socialist Club publication, 4 October 1964, 3.

5. Clark Kerr, *The Uses of the University* (Cambridge, Mass.: Harvard University Press, 1963), 115.

6. Kerr, *Uses*, 68.

7. Kerr, *Uses*, 33.

8. Kerr is chief author with joint authors J. T. Dunlop, Frederick Harbison and C. A. Meyers (Cambridge, Mass.: Harvard University Press, 1960). A later Oxford paperback (1964) is considerably less blunt, lacking the frankness of the Harvard work. I owe this synopsis to Hal Draper's *Mind of Clark Kerr*.

9. This and succeeding quotes are from Kerr, *Industrialism and Industrial Man*, as quoted in Draper, *Mind of Clark Kerr*, 10–11, 13.

MAN IN THE MIDDLE

1. Kerr, *Uses*, 40, 29.

2. Rorabaugh, 12.

3. Rorabaugh, 13.

4. Interview by the author.

5. Rorabaugh, 15.

6. John Searle, "The Faculty Resolution," in Michael V. Miller and Susan Gilmore, eds., *Revolution at Berkeley: The Crisis in American Education* (New York: Dial, 1965), 93.

IN LOCO PARENTIS

1. *Look*, 23 February 1965, 30.

2. Quotations of Renée Melody are from an interview by the author, 20 October 1992.

3. Sheldon Wolin and John Schaar, quoted in Irving Howe, "Berkeley and Beyond," introduction to Miller and Gilmore, xvii.

4. Howe, "Berkeley and Beyond," xvii.

5. John F. Boler "Behind the Protests at Berkeley," in Miller and Gilmore, 112; reprinted from *Commonweal*, February 1965.

SLATE

1. Robert Starobin, "Graduate Students and the Free Speech Movement," *Graduate Student Journal*, Spring 1965, 17.

2. Interview of Paul Richards by the author, 29 August 1992.

3. Quoted from the 1989 film *Berkeley in the Sixties*.

4. Personal correspondence.

5. Max Heirich and Sam Kaplan, "Yesterday's Discord," *California Monthly* 75, no. 5 (February 1965): 28.

6. Heirich and Kaplan, 28.

7. Heirich and Kaplan, 28.

8. Brown's and Kerr's speeches are quoted in David Horowitz, *Student* (New York: Ballantine, 1962), 125.

9. Sue Louchard (sociology graduate), undated SLATE leaflet probably printed in early fall semester, 1961.

10. Quotations of Tom Weller are from correspondence with the author, August 1990.

11. Personal correspondence.

CIVIL RIGHTS

1. Personal correspondence.

2. Interview by the author.

3. From an interview of Tom Miller and Gretchen Kittredge by Marston Schultz, taped 31 July 1965.

FREEDOM SUMMER

1. From an interview of Mario Savio and Suzanne Goldberg by Marston Schultz and Burton White, taped in 1965.

2. Correspondence with the author, 1986–1987.

BONE OF CONTENTION

(Epigraph) John Searle is quoted from "The Faculty Resolution," 94.

1. Personal correspondence.

2. From a taped NBC news report about the FSM and events that led up to it, broadcast early in January 1965. Art's speech was probably made before October 1964.

3. Interview of Arleigh Williams by Marston Schultz, taped 24 February 1966.

4. Warshaw, 17.

QUESTION AUTHORITY

(Epigraph) Clark Kerr is quoted from the 1989 film *Berkeley in the Sixties*.

1. "Chronology of Events: Three Months of Crisis," *California Monthly* 75, no. 5 (February 1965): 36.

2. "Chronology," 36.

3. Interview by the author.

4. Schultz interview.

5. "Chronology," 36.

6. "Chronology," 36.

7. "Chronology," 36–37.

8. "Chronology," 37.

9. "Chronology," 37.

10. This information is largely from a telephone interview of Jackie Goldberg by the author during the week of 8 October 1990.

11. "Chronology," 37.

12. "Chronology," 37.

13. Interview of Jackie Goldberg by Marston Schultz, taped 27 July 1965.

14. Schultz interview.

15. "Chronology," 37.

16. "Chronology," 37.

17. "Chronology," 38.

18. Schultz interview.

19. "Chronology," 38.

20. "Chronology," 38.

21. Schultz interview.

22. "Chronology," 38.

23. Schultz interview.

24. Arleigh Williams, *Dean of Students Arleigh Williams: The Free Speech Movement and the Six Years' War, 1964–1970*, interviews conducted by Germaine LaBerge, 1988 and 1989, Bancroft Library Regional Oral History Office, University of California, Berkeley, 1990, 228–232.

REBEL WITH A CAUSE AT LAST

1. Interview by the author.

2. Schultz interview.

3. Schultz interview.

4. "Chronology," 38.

5. Schultz interview.

6. "Chronology," 38.

7. Schultz interview.

8. Schultz interview.

9. *Dean of Students*, 228–232.

10. Interview of Larry Marks by Marston Schultz, taped 23 July 1965.

11. Schultz interview.

THE FIRST SIT-IN

(Epigraph) Mario Savio is quoted from the *California Monthly* "Chronology," 39.

1. Contemporary KPFA tape.

2. Contemporary KPFA tape.

3. Contemporary KPFA tape.

4. Personal correspondence.

5. Schultz interview.

JACK WEINBERG AND THE POLICE CAR

1. Schultz interview.

2. Schultz interview.

3. Personal correspondence.

4. Contemporary KPFA tape.

5. "Chronology," 41.

6. "Chronology," 41.

7. Schultz interview.

8. Schultz interview.

9. Contemporary KPFA tape.

10. "Chronology," 41.

11. Schultz interview.

THE SIMPLE JOYS OF NONFATAL COMBAT

1. "Chronology," 41.

2. Schultz interview.

3. Schultz interview.

4. Schultz interview.

5. Schultz interview.

6. Interview of Robert Starobin by Marston Schultz, taped 23 July 1965.

7. Contemporary KPFA tape.

8. Schultz interview.

9. Schultz interview.

10. Interview by the author.

Near Riot

1. Contemporary KPFA tape.
2. Contemporary KPFA tape.
3. Contemporary KPFA tape.
4. Schultz interview.
5. Interview of Brian Shannon by Marston Schultz, taped 16 January 1966.
6. Interview of Mike Smith by Marston Schultz, taped 17 January 1966.

Jack Goes to the Can

(Epigraph) Jack Weinberg is quoted from the *Oakland Tribune*, 2 October 1964.

1. Contemporary KPFA tape.
2. Personal correspondence.

The Wee Small Hours

1. Schultz interview.
2. Interview of Jeff Lustig by the author, 15 June 1992.
3. Personal correspondence.

The Captured Cop Car: Day Two

1. "Chronology," 41.
2. Warshaw, 23.
3. "Chronology," 42.
4. "Chronology," 42.
5. *Oakland Tribune*, 2 October 1964.

A Chat with Dad

1. Interview of Warren Goines by the author, 14 June 1987.

Better a Live Dog Than a Dead Lion

1. Schultz interview.
2. Schultz interview.
3. Schultz interview.
4. Schultz interview.
5. Schultz interview.
6. Schultz interview.
7. From interviews of Sam Slatkin by Marston Schultz, taped 23 July 1965 and 19 January 1966.
8. Contemporary KPFA tape.
9. From the interview of David Goines and Patti Iiyama by Marston Schultz, taped 20 July 1965.
10. Contemporary KPFA tape.
11. Schultz interview.

12. Interview of Jack Weinberg by Marston Schultz, taped in early 1965.
13. Schultz interview.
14. Contemporary KPFA tape.
15. Contemporary KPFA tape.

The Free Speech Movement

(Epigraph) Mario Savio is quoted from contemporary KPFA tapes.

1. "Chronology," 44.
2. *Tractus Logico-Philosophicus*, 1921.
3. Schultz interview.
4. Schultz interview.
5. Schultz interview.
6. Schultz interview.
7. Schultz interview.
8. Schultz interview.
9. Schultz interview.
10. Interview of Mona Hutchin by Marston Schultz, taped 19 October 1965.
11. From interviews of Andy Wells by Marston Schultz, taped 17 October 1965 and 7 January 1966.

Hello, Central

1. Schultz interview.
2. Personal correspondence.
3. Interview of Lee Felsenstein by the author, 28 May 1991.
4. Personal correspondence.
5. Luke 6:38.

We Are the Children Our Parents Warned Us Against

1. A. H. Raskin, "The Berkeley Affair: Mr. Kerr vs. Mr. Savio & Co.," in Miller and Gilmore, 81; reprinted from *New York Times Magazine*, 14 February 1965.

Why We Had the Bulge on Them

1. Samuel Kaplan, "The Revolt of an Elite: Sources of the FSM Victory," *Graduate Student Journal*, Spring 1965, 87.

Reactions

1. "Chronology," 44, 47.
2. "Chronology," 44.
3. "Chronology," 44.
4. Starobin, "Graduate Students and FSM," 17–18.

5. Schultz interview.

6. "Chronology," 44.

RED-BAITING

1. "Chronology," 45.

2. "Chronology," 48.

3. Bettina Aptheker, correspondence with the author, 27 August 1990.

HOT AIR

1. "Chronology," 45.

2. "Chronology," 45.

3. Hal Draper, *Berkeley: The New Student Revolt* (New York: Grove Press, 1965), 135.

4. Interview by the author.

5. "Chronology," 46–47.

6. "Chronology," 45.

7. "Chronology," 46.

8. "Chronology," 48.

9. Schultz interview.

10. Telephone interview of Jackie Goldberg by the author, 24 April 1992.

11. Schultz interview.

12. "Chronology," 48.

13. "Chronology," 48–49.

14. "Chronology," 50.

15. "Chronology," 50.

16. All quotations are from "Chronology," 51.

17. "Chronology," 51–52.

18. "Chronology," 52.

19. Schultz interview.

20. Schultz interview.

21. Schultz interview.

22. "Chronology," 51.

23. "Chronology," 51.

24. Schultz interview.

25. From an interview of Brian Mulloney and Sue Stein by Marston Schultz, taped 20 January 1966.

26. Schultz interview.

INTERNAL COMBUSTION

1. This and the Tigar–Savio exchange above, Schultz interview.

2. Schultz interview.

3. Schultz interview.

4. Personal correspondence.

5. Schultz interview.

6. Schultz interview.

7. Schultz interview.

8. Schultz interview.

9. Schultz interview.

10. "Chronology," 52.

11. Schultz interview.

12. Interview of Ron Anastasi by Marston Schultz, taped in 1965.

13. Schultz interview.

14. Interview of Marilyn Noble by Marston Schultz, taped 20 September 1965.

15. Schultz interview.

16. Schultz interview.

17. Schultz interview.

18. Schultz interview.

19. Schultz interview.

20. Schultz interview.

21. Schultz interview.

22. Personal correspondence.

23. "Faculty Resolution," 96.

DIRECT ACTION

1. "Chronology," 53.

2. "Chronology," 53.

3. Rorabaugh, 29.

4. Schultz interview.

5. "Chronology," 53.

6. Starobin, "Graduate Students and FSM," 20.

7. Schultz interview.

8. "Chronology," 54.

9. Draper, *New Student Revolt*, 35–37.

10. "Chronology," 54.

11. "Chronology," 55.

12. "Chronology," 56.

13. "Chronology," 56.

14. "Chronology," 56.

CHILDREN'S CRUSADE

1. "Chronology," 55.

2. Schultz interview.

3. "Chronology," 57.

4. "Chronology," 57.

5. Schultz interview.

LOOK BEFORE YOU TAKE THE GREAT LEAP FORWARD

1. Draper, *New Student Revolt*, 92.

2. Schultz interview.

3. Schultz interview.
4. Schultz interview.
5. Schultz interview.
6. Interview of Steve Weissman by Marston Schultz, taped in 1965.
7. Schultz interview.

DEUS EX MACHINA
1. "Chronology," 58.
2. "Chronology," 58.
3. "Faculty Resolution," 97.
4. Schultz interview.
5. The speeches are transcribed from tapes made by Marston Schultz of KQED radio "Profile" interviews broadcast after 20 November 1964 but before the sit-in of 3 December.
6. Schultz interview.
7. Schultz interview.
8. Schultz interview.
9. Schultz interview.

THE BIG SIT-IN
1. Contemporary KPFA tape.
2. *San Francisco Examiner*, 3 December 1964.
3. Schultz interview.
4. Personal correspondence.
5. Interview of Kate Coleman by the author, 6 October 1990.
6. Contemporary KPFA tape.
7. Brown's speeches are quoted from Warshaw, 76 and 90.
8. Schultz interview.
9. Schultz interview.
10. Schultz interview.
11. Schultz interview.
12. Schultz interview.
13. Schultz interview.
14. Schultz interview. Unfortunately, most of this tape was recorded with a low battery and is unintelligible.
15. Schultz interview.
16. Schultz interview.
17. *Oakland Tribune*, 3 December 1964.
18. *Oakland Tribune*, 3 December 1964.
19. Personal correspondence.
20. Interview by the author.
21. Interview by the author.

22. Correspondence from Janis Zimdars to the author, 7 May 1991.
23. Schultz interview.
24. Interview by the author.
25. Interview of Sherwood Parker by Marston Schultz, taped in 1965.

STRIKE WHILE THE IRON IS HOT
1. Schultz interview.
2. Schultz interview.
3. Schultz interview.
4. Schultz interview.
5. Schultz interview.
6. Schultz interview.
7. Schultz interview.
8. Schultz interview.
9. All quotations are from "Chronology," 63.
10. "Faculty Resolution," 96–97.
11. Schultz interview.
12. Schultz interview.
13. Schultz interview.

NECKTIE PARTY
1. Schultz interview.
2. "Chronology," 65.
3. "Faculty Resolution," 102.
4. Quoted in Searle, "Faculty Resolution," 101.
5. "Chronology," 67.
6. Personal correspondence.
7. Schultz interview.
8. Schultz interview.
9. "Chronology," 67.
10. Draper, *New Student Revolt*, 124–125.
11. "Chronology," 68.
12. "Chronology," 68.

WE WIN
1. Schultz interview.
2. Schultz interview.
3. Interview by the author.
4. Personal communication to the author from Ariel Parkinson, widow of Professor Thomas Parkinson, 21 October 1992.
5. "Faculty Resolution," 99–100.
6. FSM leaflet handed out 7 December 1964.

7. Schultz interview.

8. "Chronology," 68.

9. "Chronology," 68.

10. "Chronology," 68.

11. Nathan Glazer, "What Happened at Berkeley," in Miller and Gilmore, 177–178; reprinted from *Commentary*, March 1965.

12. Quoted in Calvin Trillin, "Letter from Berkeley," in Miller and Gilmore, 267; reprinted from *New Yorker*, 3 March 1965.

13. "Chronology," 68.

WHISTLE WHILE YOU WORK

1. Interview of Dusty Miller by Marston Schultz, taped 31 July 1965.

ARRAIGNMENT OF THE MASSES

1. Quotations of David Stein are from correspondence to the author, 27 April and 23 July 1990.

2. "Chronology," 66.

WINDING DOWN

1. "Chronology," 69.

2. "The Berkeley Affair," 86, 90.

3. Schultz interview.

4. Compiled from reports in "Free Speech and the Negro Revolution," *News and Letters Pamphlet*, July 1965, and the *Daily Californian*, 16 December 1964.

5. "Chronology," 72.

6. "Chronology," 73.

7. Draper, *New Student Revolt*, 151–152.

8. Excerpted from the FSM reprint of the Byrne Report to the Forbes Committee of the Board of Regents, 15 May 1965.

HAPPY NEW YEAR

1. Information compiled from Mario Savio's interview with Marston Schultz.

2. "Chronology," 74.

3. Draper, *New Student Revolt*, 137.

4. Trillin, 257.

5. Schultz interview.

6. Schultz interview.

7. "Chronology," 72.

8. Marston Schultz, during his interview of Sam Slatkin and Larry Marks, 23 July 1965.

9. Interview by the author.

THE REVOLUTION WITHIN THE REVOLUTION

1. Interview by the author.

2. Interview by the author.

THE FILTHY SPEECH MOVEMENT

(Epigraph) Mario's speech is transcribed from a contemporary KPFA tape; Linda Greenhouse's "Two Visions" (quoting Ronald Dworkin) appeared in the *New York Times*, 24 June 1992.

1. *Encyclopedia Britannica*, 11th ed., s.v. "obscenity."

2. For an exhaustive treatment of censorship and the movies, see Edward de Grazia and Roger K. Newman, *Banned Films* (New York: R. R. Bowker, 1982).

3. This account of the Filthy Speech Movement is largely from a personal interview with John Thompson, a.k.a. J. Poet, 26 September 1990, and personal correspondence from Thompson, 11 October 1990. All quotations from Thompson are from this interview and correspondence. I have also drawn from an account of the Filthy Speech Movement by Brian Hill, *East Bay Express*, 1 October 1990. See also contemporary issues of the *Daily Californian*, *Life*, *Time* and *Newsweek*.

4. *Daily Californian*, 11 March 1965.

5. Schultz interview.

6. *Daily Californian*, 4 and 5 March 1965.

7. Interview by the author.

8. Personal correspondence.

9. Schultz interview.

10. Excerpted from a 6 March 1964 handout by Charles Artman, recapitulating his speech of the previous day.

11. Draper, *New Student Revolt*, 141–142.

12. *Daily Californian*, 9 March 1965.

13. *Daily Californian*, 8 March 1965.

14. Tom Collins, review article, *Daily Californian*, 1 March 1965.

15. From an introductory speech deliv-

STUDENTS SITTING IN SPROUL HALL, SEPTEMBER 30, 1964. PHOTOGRAPHER UNKNOWN.

ered to an assemblage of college deans in 1966, taped by Marston Schultz.

16. Schultz interview.

17. *Daily Californian*, 10 March 1965.

18. From the interview by Marston Schultz and a telephone interview by the author, 22 April 1992.

A BODY IN MOTION TENDS TO REMAIN IN MOTION

(Epigraph) Sally Belfrage is quoted from the review by Eleanor Holmes Norton of *Freedom Summer*, in *New Politics* 4, no. 3 (Summer 1965): 83–84.

1. Quoted in Zinn, 180.

QUIS CUSTODIET IPSOS CUSTODES?

1. All quotations are from the FBI's file on David Goines.

THE SLAMMER

1. Personal correspondence.

2. *Oakland Tribune*, 13 August 1965.

3. Personal correspondence.

4. From correspondence of David Goines to Alice Waters, June and July 1967.

THE CAR

1. Personal correspondence.

THE TYRANT'S FOE, THE PEOPLE'S FRIEND

1. Personal correspondence.

BOMBS AND GUNS

1. Personal correspondence.

The *Berkeley Barb*

1. Personal correspondence.

Let Sleeping Dogs Lie

1. Interview by the author.
2. Personal correspondence.

The Second Jail Term at Santa Rita

1. Correspondence to the author, 1991.
2. Interview by the author.
3. Interview of Patti Iiyama by the author, 15 June 1992.

Post Hoc

1. Schultz interview.
2. Personal correspondence.
3. Schultz interview.
4. Schultz interview.
5. The quote is from Ian Shoales, *San Francisco Examiner*, 24 March 1991.

The closing quotation of Frederick Douglass is from Philip Foner, ed., *The Life and Writings of Frederick Douglass* (New York: International Publishers, 1975).

BIBLIOGRAPHY & SOURCES

As SELF-APPOINTED FSM HISTORIAN, throughout 1965 and into 1966 Marston Schultz taped interviews with people who had been active in the Free Speech Movement. He'd originally intended to "write the definitive book on the FSM, and make a film," but what with one thing and another, he never got around to it. So he salted the recordings and photographs away under his bed, and the temperate climate of San Francisco preserved them against the possibility that they might someday be of interest. Learning that I was working on a history of the FSM, in 1991 he made them available to me. I have transcribed and edited those that I found useful, and added the material to this history of the FSM and subsequent events.

The interviews were made at 1⅞" per second on quarter-inch reel-to-reel tape. The interviews are with Dunbar Aitkins, Ron Anastasi, Bettina Aptheker, Gene Bardack, Brad Cleaveland, Joel Geier, David Goines, Jackie Goldberg, Suzanne Goldberg, (Steve?) Heist, Walt Herbert, Mona Hutchin, Patti Iiyama, Bob Kauffman, Gretchen Kittredge, David Kolodny, Eric Lavine, Larry Marks, University Dean McConnell, Dusty Miller, Tom Miller, Brian Mulloney, Marilyn Noble, Sherwood Parker, Bill Porter, Paul Potter, Arthur Ross, Michael Rossman, Mario Savio, Alan Searcy, Brian Shannon, Sam Slatkin, Mike Smith, Hershel Snodgrass, Bob Starobin, Sue Stein, Jack Weinberg, Steve Weissman, Andy Wells, Arleigh Williams and University Dean Williamson. Although I have listened to all the recordings, I have not directly quoted all the people interviewed. Marston often carefully noted the day and time, but sometimes forgot to mention the month and year. Sometimes no date was mentioned. Therefore, some interview dates are approximate. Interviews from which I have quoted include:

Ron Anastasi: 1965
David Goines and Patty Iiyama: July 19, 20 and 23, 1965

Jackie Goldberg: July 27, 1965
Mona Hutchin: October 19, 1965
Larry Marks: July 23, 1965
Dusty Miller: July 31, 1965
Tom Miller and Gretchen Kittredge: July 31, 1965
Brian Mulloney and Sue Stein: January 20, 1966
Marilyn Noble: September 20, 1965
Sherwood Parker: 1965
Mario Savio and Suzanne Goldberg: 1965, shortly after Mario and
    Suzanne were married. The interview was conducted with the
    assistance of Burton White of KPFA.
Brian Shannon: January 16, 1966
Sam Slatkin: July 23, 1965, and January 19, 1966
Mike Smith: January 17, 1966
Bob Starobin: July 23, 1965
Jack Weinberg: Early 1965
Steve Weissman: 1965
Andy Wells: October 17, 1965, and January 7, 1966
Arleigh Williams: February 24, 1966

Of particular interest are KPFA recordings of the events of Thursday
and Friday, October 1 and 2, 1964. The KPFA field recordings were made
by Burton White, Jerry Farrell, Mike Eisen, John Whiting, Al Silbowitz,
Scott Keach and Dave Bacon, under the direction of Burton White.

Marston told me that the FSM paid radio station KPFA $300 to preserve
their tapes of FSM events rather than record over them. He believes these
tapes are stored in a KPFA archive in Los Angeles. The KPFA tapes from
which I have quoted are duplicates or tapes made for public distribution.

In 1965 Marston taped Academic Senate meetings, ASUC meetings,
chancellor's meetings, events at the *Spider* table, rallies, *Spider* hearings,
Executive Committee meetings, FSU meetings and speeches. Most of
the 1965 meetings and events had to do with the Free Student Union
and the Filthy Speech Movement.

Interviews conducted and correspondence received by me include:

Bettina Aptheker: Personal correspondence, August 27, 1990
Kate Coleman: Interview, October 6, 1990
Stephanie Coontz: Personal correspondence, March 17, 1989
Janis Zimdars Dolphin: Personal correspondence, May 7, 1991
Lee Felsenstein: Interview, May 28, 1991
Bob Gill: Personal correspondence, November 16, 1990, and April
    24, 1992

Warren Goines: Interview, June 14, 1987
Jackie Goldberg: Interviews, October 8, 1990, and April 24, 1992
Patti Iiyama: Interview, June 15, 1992
Jeff Lustig: Personal correspondence, 1991; conversations, 1992
Renée Melody: Interview, October 20, 1992
Charles Muscatine: Interviews, October 3 and 21, 1992
Ariel Parkinson: Personal correspondence, October 1 and 21, 1992
Paul Richards: Interview, August 30, 1992
David Stein: Personal correspondence, April 27 and July 23, 1990
John Thompson: Interview, September 26, 1990; personal
    correspondence, October 11, 1990
Tom Weller: Personal correspondence, August 1990
Jack Weinberg: Personal correspondence, February 16, 1986,
    March 15, 1987, May 10, 1987, and August 18, 1987

I have not transcribed any of the interviews literally. A literal transcript of spoken conversation is almost unintelligible. Most speech is full of digressions, half-completed remarks, meaningless interjections and repetitions. With varying degrees of success, Marston and I tried to keep our subjects on the track, returning them repeatedly to the topics that interested us. Usually, I have taken all the parts of an interview that relate to a particular event and have put them together; then I've taken the relevant sections and inserted them into the greater narrative.

Though I have swapped parts around and deleted what I felt to be irrelevant portions of interviews, I have made a sincere effort not to alter the sense or substance of what has been said.

I thank Alice Waters for the loan of the letters I wrote her while I was serving my second term at Santa Rita. Thanks to Steven Warshaw of Diablo Press for making his archive of FSM photos available to me. I also thank David Stein for preserving the defendants' list all these years and making it available to me.

This book was edited by the able and tolerant Jane Whitley, who saved me from many an egregious error. I also thank the following for additional editorial assistance: James Michael Bennett, Wayne Collins, Jr., Sal Glynn, Edie Sei Ichioka, R. Jeffrey Lustig, Courtney Leigh Murphree, Charles Muscatine, Kinde Nebeker and Richard Seibert.

I thank the following for design assistance: Patricia Curtan, Edie Sei Ichioka and Richard Siebert.

Because many names have been transcribed verbatim from contemporary tapes and newspaper accounts, there may be some misspellings or misinterpretations. In addition, even contemporary sources spell names in a variety of ways. My own name is misspelled in several accounts and newspaper reports, for example. I've tried to get names right, but in the absence of agreement among authorities, it seems a hopeless task.

In compiling quotations, background information and the chronology of the FSM I have made extensive use of a number of books, pamphlets and magazine and newspaper articles, including:

American Civil Liberties Union. ACLU annual report, 1984–1985.
————. *ACLU Briefing Paper*, no. 1 (1992).
Aptheker, Bettina. *FSM: The Free Speech Movement at Berkeley, An Historical Narrative.* With an interpretive essay by Robert Kauffman and Michael Folsom. San Francisco: W. E. B. Du Bois Clubs of America, 1965.
Belfrage, Sally. *Freedom Summer.* New York: Viking, 1965.
Benton, Mike. *The Comic Book in America.* Dallas: Taylor Publishing, 1989.
Boler, John F. "Behind the Protests at Berkeley." In *Revolution at Berkeley*, 107–115. *See* Miller and Gilmore. Reprinted from *Commonweal*, February 1965.
"Chronology of Events: Three Months of Crisis." *California Monthly* 75, no. 5 (January 1965): 35–74.
The Daily Californian. September 1964 through May 1965.
de Grazia, Edward, and Roger K. Newman. *Banned Films.* New York: R. R. Bowker, 1982.
Draper, Hal. *Behind the Battle at Berkeley: The Mind of Clark Kerr.* Independent Socialist Club publication, 4 October 1964.
————. *Berkeley: The New Student Revolt.* New York: Grove, 1965.
Foner, Philip, ed. *The Life and Writings of Frederick Douglass.* New York: International Publishers, 1975.
Glazer, Nathan. "What Happened at Berkeley." In *Revolution at Berkeley*, 160–181. *See* Miller and Gilmore. Reprinted from *Commentary*, March 1965.
Gardner, David P. *The California Oath Controversy.* Berkeley and Los Angeles: University of California Press, 1967.
Gitlin, Todd. *The Sixties: Years of Hope, Days of Rage.* New York: Bantam, 1987.
Heirich, Max, and Sam Kaplan. "Yesterday's Discord." *California Monthly* 75, no. 5 (February 1965): 20–32.
Heller, Steven. "Cold War Design: Battling the Red Menace." *Print*, May/June 1992.

Horn, Maurice. *Sex in the Comics*. New York: Chelsea House, 1985.

Horowitz, David. *Student*. New York: Ballantine, 1962.

Hyland, William B. *The Cold War: 50 Years of Conflict*. Garden City, N.Y.: Random House, 1992.

Kaplan, Samuel. "The Revolt of an Elite: Sources of the FSM Victory." *Graduate Spring Journal*, Spring 1965.

Kerr, Clark. *The Uses of the University*. Cambridge, Mass.: Harvard University Press, 1960.

Kerr, Clark, et al. *Industrialism and Industrial Man*. Cambridge, Mass.: Harvard University Press, 1963.

Kitchell, Mark. *Berkeley in the Sixties*. Documentary film, 1989.

Levy, Leonard W. *Freedom of the Press from Zenger to Jefferson*. New York: Bobbs-Merrill, 1966.

Lipset, Seymour Martin, and Sheldon Wolin, eds. *The Berkeley Student Revolt: Facts and Interpretations*. New York: Anchor, 1965.

Miller, Michael V., and Susan Gilmore, eds. *Revolution at Berkeley: The Crisis in American Education*. With an introduction by Irving Howe. New York: Dial, 1965.

Pitcher, Don, and Malcolm Margolin. *Berkeley Inside/Out*. Berkeley, Calif.: Heyday Books, 1989.

Raskin, A. H. "The Berkeley Affair: Mr. Kerr vs. Mr. Savio & Co." In *Revolution at Berkeley*, 78–91. See Miller and Gilmore. Reprinted from *New York Times Magazine*, 14 February 1965.

Rorabaugh, W. J. *Berkeley at War: The 1960s*. New York: Oxford University Press, 1989.

Searle, John. "The Faculty Resolution." In *Revolution at Berkeley*, 92–104. See Miller and Gilmore.

Starobin, Robert. "Graduate Students and the Free Speech Movement." *Graduate Spring Journal*, Spring 1965.

Stern, Jane and Michael. *Sixties People*. New York: Knopf, 1990.

Stevens, Jay. *Storming Heaven: LSD and the American Dream*. New York: Atlantic Monthly Press, 1987.

Stewart, George. *The Year of the Oath*. Garden City, N.Y.: Doubleday, 1950.

Thomas, Isaiah. *The History of Printing in America*. New York: Weathervane Books, 1970.

Trillin, Calvin. "Letter from Berkeley." In *Revolution at Berkeley*, 253–284. See Miller and Gilmore. Reprinted from *New Yorker*, 3 March 1965.

Wagman, Robert J. *The First Amendment Book*. New York: Scripps Howard, 1991.

Warshaw, Steven. *The Trouble in Berkeley*. Berkeley, Calif.: Diablo Press, 1965.

Williams, Arleigh. *Dean of Students Arleigh Williams: The Free Speech Movement and the Six Years' War, 1964–1970*. Interviews conducted by Germaine LaBerge, 1988 and 1989. Bancroft Library Regional Oral History Office, University of California, Berkeley, 1990.

Witness 2, no. 2/3 (Summer/Fall 1988). Special issue, "The Sixties."

Zinn, Howard. *A People's History of the United States*. New York: Harper and Row, 1980.

In addition to material on the FSM per se, I have used various reference works in compiling the larger chronology:

Adams, Cecil. *The Straight Dope*. New York: Ballantine, 1986.

Branch, Taylor. *Parting the Waters*. New York: Simon and Schuster, 1988.

Coontz, Stephanie. *The Way We Never Were*. New York: Basic Books, 1992.

Daniel, Clifton, ed. *Chronicle of the Twentieth Century*. Chronicle Publications, 1989.

Grun, Bernard. *The Timetables of History*. New York: Simon and Schuster, 1982.

Halberstam, David. *Summer of '49*. New York: Avon, 1989.

Hoffman, Mark S. *World Almanac*. Pharos Books, 1987; 1990.

Johnson, Otto, ed. *Information Please Almanac*. Boston: Houghton Mifflin, 1987.

Wright, John W., ed. *The Universal Almanac, 1991*. Andrews and McMeel, 1991.

Additional information was provided by a number of library reference services, magazines and newspapers. These include:

Alameda County Law Library Reference Service
Berkeley Public Library Reference Service
The Daily Californian
Life magazine (Fall 1989, special issue: "The 60s")
Los Angeles Times
National Public Radio broadcasts
New York Times
Oakland Public Library Reference Service
People magazine (Fall 1989, special issue: "The '60s")

San Francisco Chronicle
San Francisco Examiner
San Francisco News Call Bulletin
San Francisco Public Library Reference Service
San Jose Mercury News
This Fabulous Century (Calendar for the year 1990, Time-Life Books)

For granting permission on the following materials, I am grateful to: the Bancroft Library, for permission to quote from the oral history interviews with Arleigh Williams conducted by Germaine LaBerge in 1988 and 1989 and memo dated July 22, 1964; *California Monthly*, for permission to quote from that publication, Volume 75, no. 5 (February 1965); Oxford University Press, for permission to quote from *Berkeley at War: The 1960s* by W. J. Rorabaugh; John Searle, for permission to quote from his "The Faculty Resolution," included in *Revolution at Berkeley*, edited by Michael V. Miller and Susan Gilmore; and Special Rider Music, for permission to reprint "The Times They Are A-Changin'," words and music by Bob Dylan, copyright © 1963, 1964 by Warner Bros. Inc., copyright renewed by Special Rider Music, all rights reserved, international copyright secured.

I am grateful for access to a transcript of the FSM trial, contemporary newspaper clippings and commentary on the FSM preserved in the Alexander Meiklejohn Civil Liberties Institute, Box 673, Berkeley, California, 94701.

Thanks to Tom Weller for the loan of his archive of FSM leaflets, pamphlets, newspaper clippings and related material, as well as material relating to subsequent events.

In addition, I have sought and gotten valuable opinions, advice and recollections from many participants in the events of the time, including: Bettina Aptheker, Frank Bardacke, Malcolm Burnstein, Kate Coleman, Wayne Collins, Jr., Stephanie Coontz, Janis Zimdars Dolphin, Zette Emmons, Lee Felsenstein, Peter Franck, Kathie Simon Frank, Dennis Galloway, Bob Gill, Warren Goines, Art Goldberg, Jackie Goldberg, Terence Hallinan, Patti Iiyama, Michael Jones, Jeff Lustig, Gretchen Kittredge Mackler, Robert Mates, Charles Muscatine, Doris Muscatine, Ariel Parkinson, Janet Peoples, Roger Plumb, Michael Rossman, Mario Savio, Marston Schultz, Peter Selz, David Stein, John Thompson, Alice Waters, Jack Weinberg, and Tom Weller.

The photographs in this book are from a number of sources, the most important being a box of miscellaneous photos and negatives that the indefatigable Marston Schultz had accumulated and stored in a fruit crate under his capacious bed. Every reasonable effort has been made to contact photographers whose work is reproduced in this book. Though sometimes the name of the photographer was not known with absolute certainty, I have nevertheless made an informed guess, and credited accordingly. In some cases the photograph could not be credited, and I have written "photographer unknown." The author and publisher would be much obliged if photographers whose work is incorrectly credited, or not credited at all, would contact us so that things may be made right in future editions. Photographers whose work is used and publications from which photographs have been reproduced include the following:

Berkeley Gazette
Konstantin Berlandt
Bob Bryant
California Monthly
Daily Californian
Ron Enfield
Paul Fusco
Dennis Galloway
Elsa Garcia
Bob Gill
Carol Gill
W. C. Goines
Howard Harawitz
Don Kechley
Robert R. Krones
Jeff Lee
Life
David Linn
Look
Steve Marcus
Joe Marshall

Bill Menken
Roger Minlock
Gary Moretti
Richard Muller
Helen Nestor
Oakland Tribune
Anna Belle O'Brien
Russ Reed
Harvey Richards
Michael Rossman
San Francisco Chronicle
San Francisco Examiner
San Francisco News Call Bulletin
Steve Somerstein
Ted Streshinsky
The Trouble in Berkeley
Walter Tschinkel
Douglas Wachter
Loren Weaver
Lonnie Wilson
Marshall Windmiller

To all of you who participated in the Free Speech Movement: In writing this history of the FSM, I've tried to cover everything of importance as fairly and fully as possible, given the limitations of my own memory, the memories of others and contemporary reference sources. However, I know there are errors, both of commission and omission, that can be corrected if I find out about them. If you find a mistake, or see that a name is misspelled, or somebody who was a defendant is not mentioned, or somebody who was not a defendant is listed as having been arrested, or any event is not as you remember it, please contact me, and I will make an effort to fix things in a future edition, should there be one.

APPENDIX I

FSM PROFILE

This information is drawn from *Dean of Students Arleigh Williams: The Free Speech Movement and the Six Years' War, 1964–1970*, interviews conducted by Germaine LaBerge, 1988 and 1989, Bancroft Library Regional Oral History Office, University of California, Berkeley, 1990, pages 257–274.

Arleigh Williams concluded that the students arrested represented the most dedicated element of the Free Speech Movement, and that these students "seem to be only moderately deviant from University norms."

Of the 735 current and former students arrested in Sproul Hall, 688 were currently registered; 141 were graduates and 547 undergraduates (71 freshmen, 135 sophomores, 160 juniors, 176 seniors, 4 students with limited status and one of unknown status).

Of the undergraduates, 313 were male, 234 female; 109 of the graduates were male, 32 female. Of the 47 students not registered, 30 were male and 17 female.

The age distribution of current and former students was

```
16 . . . . . . . 1
17 . . . . . . . 6
18 . . . . . . 90
19 . . . . . 136
20 . . . . . 118
21 . . . . . 135
22 . . . . . . 79
23 . . . . . . 49
24 . . . . . . 44
25+ . . . . . 77
```

The average age was 21.

The arrested students were drawn from sixty different major fields. The largest percentage of FSM students (32.17 percent) were from the social sciences. Language and literature students comprised the next largest group (4.81 percent).

Though the grades of the students show a heavier than normal concentration at the two ends of the grade scale, particularly at the lower end, almost one-fourth of the undergraduates and one-third of the graduates had at one time excelled in academic pursuits. Of the graduate students, 33.4 percent had graduated with honors and/or been elected to Phi Beta Kappa.

Of the 688 currently registered students, 419 (60.81 percent) had attended one or more institutions of higher learning before coming to Berkeley. "So," Williams points out, "most of the students were well acquainted with the system of higher education the administration of which they were criticizing."

Most of the students were single. Relatively few (11 percent) lived in University-approved housing, with less than 1 percent (5 students) living in fraternities or sororities.

Most of the students were from the Bay Area, though a higher than average representation of students were from East Coast states, especially New York (10.23 percent).

Only twelve of the FSM students had had conduct violations reported before the arrests. Of these, nine violations were directly related to the Free Speech Movement. Two others concerned arrests for possession of drugs, and one student had been dismissed from Brandeis for "unbecoming" conduct.

About 30 percent of the students worked part-time.

APPENDIX II

A GUIDE TO CONTEMPORARY COMMITTEES, ORGANIZATIONS & TERMINOLOGY

AAUP: Pronounced as separate letters. American Association of University Professors. Favored the goals of the FSM.

Academic Senate: The whole body of regular faculty in the UC system. Throughout the text the Berkeley Academic Senate is called the Academic Senate, but it actually is a branch of the larger statewide body.

ACLU: Pronounced as separate letters. American Civil Liberties Union. Founded in 1920 by Roger Baldwin; focus on First Amendment issues. In 1964 the Northern California chapter was independent of the national, having fallen out over the issue of Japanese internments during World War II: the Northern California chapter had wanted to fight them, and the national organization had not.

Acts for Peace: Late 1950s and early 1960s ban-the-bomb group.

Ad Hoc Academic Senate Committee on Student Suspensions: See *Heyman Committee*.

Ad Hoc Committee for March 23: Loose coalition of UC campus political organizations to showcase protests at the March 23, 1962, Charter Day speech given by President John F. Kennedy at the UC campus.

Ad Hoc Committee to End Discrimination: Headed by Tracy Sims and Michael Myerson; organized the 1964 Sheraton-Palace, Cadillac, Auto Row, Mel's Drive-in and *Oakland Tribune* demonstrations. SLATE and Du Bois Club influence.

Ad Hoc Faculty Committee on Obscenity: Faculty committee established by Chancellor Martin Meyerson to deal with the Filthy Speech Movement.

AFT: Pronounced as separate letters. American Federation of Teachers. Democratic party liberal.

American Friends Service Committee: Quaker organization involved in just about every important cause from ban-

the-bomb and civil rights issues to anti–Vietnam War protests.

anarchism: Romantic nineteenth-century movement based, as are most branches of Socialism and Communism, upon a belief in the ultimate perfectibility of Man. Pierre Joseph Proudhon (1809–1865) formulated the early anticlerical, anticapitalist philosophy brought to maturity by the moderate theorist Pyotr Alekseyevich Kropotkin (1842–1921). Mikhail Alexsandrovitch Bakunin (1814–1876) represented the left wing, dedicated to violence and destruction. In the 1960s, remnants of classical anarchism persisted in the principle of "speeding up the dialectic" by creating trouble *ex nihilo* in order to make people angry with the System and Establishment. Hippies and Yippies represented a firm allegiance to the ideals of anarchism. The Weather Underground and instigators of events surrounding People's Park were more illustrative of Bakunin's slogan, "The passion for destruction is also a creative passion."

Association of California State College Professors: Sympathetic to the FSM from an early point.

ASUC: Pronounced as separate letters, or "A-Suck" by the disgruntled. Associated Students of the University of California. Campus undergraduate student government. Known as the "sandbox," it was a powerless organization ignored by both the students and the administration.

Bancroft and Telegraph: After late 1950s campus expansion, the center of student political activity.

Ban the Bomb: Watchword of the CND, and an epithet often applied to peace activists.

BASCAHUAC: "Ba-ska-hew-ak." Bay Area Student Committee Against (for the Abolition of) the House Un-American Activities Committee. An ad hoc committee organized in 1960 specifically to bring down HUAC by, among other

644

things, showing annotated versions of the propaganda film *Operation Abolition*.

Beatnik: Term coined by Herb Caen, April 2, 1958. The more-show-than-go descendants of the Beats. As an epithet, it replaced "bohemian" and was in turn replaced in 1965 by "hippie"; it was applied to any political dissident or nonconformist.

Women: long, straight black or blonde hair, heavy black eye-makeup, black leotard top, wraparound wool skirt, black tights or stockings, sandals, heavy silver jewelry, modern dance (Jules Feiffer cartoons). Men: black beret, sunglasses, trim goatee and mustache, black turtleneck sweater, tight slacks, sandals without socks, poetry, bongo drums (Maynard G. Krebs of "Dobie Gillis").

Beats: *Je pisse sur tout d'un grand hauteur.* Antipolitical. "Living in the rubble of a once-confident Old Left, they didn't want to change society so much as to sidestep it" (Todd Gitlin, *The Sixties*, 51). Jack Kerouac, Allen Ginsberg, Neal Cassady, Gary Snyder, William Burroughs *inter alia*. San Francisco's North Beach and New York's Greenwich Village.

Berkeley Barb: Newspaper founded in 1965 by Max Scherr to provide a forum for the Movement and changing sexual mores. The politics were taken over by the *Tribe* in 1969 and the sex by the *Spectator* in 1978.

Berkeley Free Press: Incorporating Vanguard Press and the *Root and Branch* printing equipment, the Berkeley Free Press was the Movement printer in the Bay Area from 1965 to 1967.

Berkeley Young Democratic Club: Moderate Democratic group.

Black: With the emergence around 1966 of the Black Power movement, the appellation "Black" began to replace "Negro" as the accepted usage. See the footnote in the chapter "Civil Rights."

Black Muslim: Adherent to the late 1950s Black Separatist movement of Elijah Mohammed. Malcolm X broke with Elijah Mohammed and was shortly thereafter assassinated.

Black Panther party: Created in 1966 out of SNCC by Stokely Carmichael and

John Hulett in Lowndes County, Alabama; the beginning of the Black Power movement. At the same time, the Oakland-based Black Panther party was formed by cultural nationalists Huey Newton and Bobby Seale, calling for armed self-defense.

CAL: "Cal." Conservatives at Large. Conservative student group. Usually referred to by its full name.

California Students for Goldwater: Conservative campus organization favoring Barry Goldwater as the 1964 Republican candidate for president over moderates Scranton, Lodge and Rockefeller. Member of the United Front.

CCPA: Pronounced as separate letters. Study Committee on Campus Political Activity, or Campus Committee on Political Activity; also known as the Williams Committee. Student-faculty-administration committee formed to discuss and negotiate rules for political activity on campus. Dissolved November 9, 1964.

CCR: Pronounced as separate letters. California College Republicans. Moderate-conservative campus organization. Member of the United Front.

CDC: Pronounced as separate letters. California Democratic Council. Statewide Democratic party organization.

Central: FSM communications center. Although there were dozens of Centrals formed for every purpose, the main Central at 2536 College was the nerve center.

Chancellor's Committee on Student Conduct: Student disciplinary committee proposed by the administration to review student suspensions of September 30, 1964, in lieu of the nonexistent Faculty Committee on Student Conduct. Rejected by the FSM.

Christian Crusade Against Communism: One-man anti-Communist crusade.

Christian Fellowship for Social Justice: Late 1950s and early 1960s peace group.

CIPA: Pronounced as separate letters. Committee for Independent Political Action. Participant in the United Front.

Cited Students Association (Club, Organization): FSM suborganization made up of the seventy-five students cited by UC deans on November 9, 1964, for resumption of banned political activity.

Citizens for Chessman: Ad hoc organization opposed to capital punishment organized around the cause of Caryl Chessman, who was executed on May 2, 1960.

CNA: Pronounced as separate letters. Committee for Nonviolent Action. Antiwar organization conceived as a vehicle for radicals. Compare SANE.

CND: Pronounced as separate letters. Committee for Nuclear Disarmament. Pacifist group of British origin, founded 1958. Originator of the peace symbol.

CNVA: Pronounced as separate letters. Committee for Non-Violent Action. Pacifist group attempting to thwart atomic bomb testing in 1958 and 1959.

Committee for Liberal Representation: New Left political fundraising organization.

Committee on Academic Freedom: Subcommittee of the Berkeley division of the Academic Senate. In favor of the goals of the FSM.

Conservatives at Large: Conservative UC organization.

Conservatives for an Open Campus: Conservative UC organization.

CORE: "Core." Congress of Racial Equality. Major national left-of-center civil rights organization. Integrated, activist, militant, nonviolent. Founded in Chicago, 1942, by James Farmer. At Berkeley, a strong ISC influence. Member of the United Front.

Council of Departmental Chairmen: Group of UC department chairmen who worked out the proposals made in the Greek Theatre. Chaired by Robert Scalapino.

counterculture: Late sixties and early seventies youth culture, consciously acting in contradiction to the perceived cultural ideals of their parents' generation.

CP: Pronounced as separate letters. Communist party. Often called simply "the Party."

CPUSA: Pronounced as separate letters. Communist Party of the United States of America. "If it's raining in Moscow,

they're carrying umbrellas in New York." Soviet apologists who nonetheless were moderates close to the Democratic party politically.

Daily Californian: UC Berkeley campus daily newspaper. Throughout the FSM hostile to the students' goals and sucking up to the administration.

Deacons for Defense and Justice: Louisiana Black self-defense organization loosely affiliated with CORE. Its policy of armed self-defense was an inspiration for Huey Newton's 1966 Black Panthers.

democratic centralism: "A communistic system or principle of hierarchic organization that seeks to combine democratic participation of the rank-and-file in the discussion of policy and the election of officers and of delegates to the next higher unit with strict obedience by the members and lower bodies to the decisions of the higher units and with absolute authority residing in fact at the apex of the hierarchic structure and strict discipline being enforced" (Webster's Third New International Dictionary). Within limits, the FSM was a democratic centralist organization relying on a substructure of participatory democracy.

Democratic Socialist Club: Subfaction of YPSL. Politically, between YPSL and the YDS. Social Democrats. Member of United Front.

Du Bois Club: W. E. B. Du Bois Club. Named after American educator, sociologist and co-founder of the NAACP, W. E. B. Du Bois (1868–1963); often referred to as "Da Boys" club. West Coast origins, dominated by CP red-diaper babies. Shortly after Du Bois' death, taken over by the CP, reorganized and renamed "Young Workers' Liberation League." Member of the United Front.

Executive Committee: "Ex Com." Large group composed of representatives of all campus organizations; formed general policy and elected the FSM Steering Committee. Originally (October 5, 1964) consisted of two representatives from each of the eighteen United Front organizations. Expanded on Thursday, October 8, to include seven representatives of the newly formed Independent Students Association and in the week of October 11 to include seven representatives from the newly formed GCC. Campus religious groups received representation as did the eighty students who worked to put out the Rossman Report. By the middle of October, the FSM Executive Committee consisted of fifty-six members.

Faculty Committee on Student Conduct: Nonexistent student disciplinary committee agreed upon in the October 2 pact to review the student suspensions of September 30, 1964. See *Chancellor's Committee on Student Conduct.*

FBI: Pronounced as separate letters, or "Fee-bees" by campus radicals. Federal Bureau of Investigation.

FDF: Pronounced as separate letters. Fuck Defense Fund. Organized during the Filthy Speech Movement.

Fellowship of Reconciliation: Ban-the-bomb group.

Filthy Seven: Defendants in the Filthy Speech Movement. There were actually nine of them.

Filthy Speech Movement: Originated March 3, 1965, by John Thompson; center of the UC campus obscenity issue.

FLN: The Algerian Front Libération National.

flower child: Youthful member of the hippie counterculture. Vague, wimpy drug consumer.

For Unlawful Carnal Knowledge: Banned play produced during the Filthy Speech Movement.

freddy: Fraternity boy.

Freedom Riders: Participants in 1961 interracial attempts to implement Supreme Court decisions banning segregation in bus terminals.

Freedom Summer: Civil rights activism—specifically, voter registration in Mississippi—during the summer of 1964. The interested reader is referred to Sally Belfrage's *Freedom Summer* (New York: Viking, 1965).

FSM: Pronounced as separate letters. Free Speech Movement.

FSU: Pronounced as separate letters. Free Student Union. Short-lived successor to the FSM.

FUB: "Fub." Free University of Berkeley.

Established in emulation of FUNY (Free University of New York) in the spring of 1965 by Jeff Lustig, Bob Mates and Stew Albert.

FUC: "Fuck." Free University of California. Sproul Hall sit-in predecessor of the Free University of Berkeley (FUB).

FUNY: "Funny." Free University of New York. Founded in early 1965 by Alan Krebs. Possibly influenced by FUC; influential on FUB.

GCC: Pronounced as separate letters. Graduate Coordinating Council. Formed as the graduate arm of the FSM. Organized strike to follow the Sproul Hall sit-in and arrests.

Group for Academic Freedom: Organizing body consisting of nonsigners of UC's anti-Communist loyalty oath.

GSA: Pronounced as separate letters. Graduate Student Association. Formed to represent UC graduate students after their removal from the ASUC. The organization had withered away by 1964, and was replaced by the GCC.

HCUA: See HUAC.

Heyman Committee: Ad Hoc Academic Senate Committee on Student Suspensions. Appointed by the Academic Senate to make recommendations about the fate of the students suspended on September 30, 1964. Chaired by Ira Michael Heyman.

Hillel Foundation: Located on upper Bancroft, often used for FSM Executive Committee meetings.

hippie: Term coined in 1965 and used to describe the denizens of the Haight-Ashbury district of San Francisco. Broadly, the youthful adherents of the 1960s counterculture. Vaguely left, but essentially apolitical and anarchistic, influenced more by the peace movement, Eastern mysticism and dope than by any political agenda. "Peace, love and good vibes."

HUAC: "Hew-ak." House Un-American Activities Committee. According to W. J. Rorabaugh, "In the forties newspaper headline writers had abbreviated the House Un-American Activities Committee as HUAC. When leftists attacked the committee by calling it 'hew-ack,' the committee responded by changing its name to the House Committee on Un-American Activities and calling itself, in committee publications, HCUA. The press and the public, however, continued to use HUAC, and only the most slavish followers of the committee, such as Berkeley's anti-communist periodical, *Tocsin*, adopted the cumbersome HCUA designation" (*Berkeley at War*, 188).

Hyde Park area: At UC, area designated for "free speech" (subject to campus restrictions). So-called after Speaker's Corner in London's Hyde Park, home to soapbox orators since the late nineteenth century.

Independents: FSM Executive Committee members elected to represent students who were not members of any campus political organization.

Inter-Faith Council: Coalition of campus religious organizations. Generally much involved in liberal issues. Member of the United Front.

Inter-Faith Staff Workers and Student Leaders: Campus religious organization favoring the goals of the FSM.

ISC: Pronounced as separate letters. Independent Socialist Club. Revolutionary Marxist-Socialists, differentiating themselves from the reformists, such as YPSL or the Social Democrats. Participatory bottom-up Socialists. Highly influential in Campus CORE. Member of the United Front.

IWW: Pronounced as separate letters, or "Wobblies." Industrial Workers of the World. Old-line anarcho-syndicalists, World War I antiwar and activist union organizers; founded in 1905 by Eugene Debs and Big Bill Heywood. An archaism by 1964.

John Birch Society: Ultraconservative organization established by Robert Welch in 1958.

Kerr Directives: Rules limiting campus political activity issued October 22, 1959, to replace and clarify Gordon Sproul's outdated Rule 17.

KPFA: Listener-sponsored left-liberal, counterculture radio, founded in 1949. 94.1 FM.

liberals: People who considered themselves, politically, on the side of the angels, but who did not favor confrontational, activist political tactics. Clark Kerr and Governor Brown were both classic liberals, opposed to the bracero program, in favor of civil rights legislation, opposed to Proposition 14, opposed to the loyalty oath and so on. What they did not like was trouble, especially trouble that made trouble for them. The troublemakers were *radicals*.

Lower Sproul Plaza: See *Student Union Plaza*.

M2M: Pronounced as separate letters. May Second Movement. Named after a spring 1964 New York City antiwar demonstration. Progressive Labor leadership. Member of the United Front.

Maoist: The epitome of Stalinist political thought. Maoists broke with the CP because it was not hard-line enough.

Mississippi Freedom Democrats: Civil rights challenge to the mainstream Democratic party in the 1964 presidential election.

Mississippi Summer Project: 1964–1965 civil rights activity aimed primarily at voter registration, bringing white civil rights workers into the South.

Mount Madonna Park: First significant large-scale nonsectarian gathering of student groups since the 1930s. Anti-HUAC. Concerned with civil rights, student rights, ban-the-bomb issues.

the Movement: Political and cultural expression of the counterculture, originating politically in the peace and civil rights movements, and culturally with the beatniks. In short, anybody opposed to the status quo.

Movement Against Political Suspensions: MAPS students were suspended for "speaking over an illegal microphone" as a part of campus Vietnam War protests. This led to a student strike in December 1966.

NAACP: "N, double-A, C, P." National Association for the Advancement of Colored People, founded 1909.

New Left: Late 1950s origins in attacks on the CP for its orthodoxy and irrelevance. Its left-liberal adherents expressed themselves in *Ramparts* magazine. Fond ideologically of C. Wright Mills. Initially non-Marxist; matters of concern to the working class were no concern of theirs.

Newman Hall: Catholic-sponsored off-campus meeting place for student political events.

Nexus: Abortive FSM communications center.

No on 14: Campaign against California's controversial "Fair Housing" proposition, appearing on the fall 1964 ballot.

Old Left: An "alphabet soup of tiny self-fissuring sects" (Gitlin, 76), the Old Left suffered political defeat and moral collapse in the 1950s. Eclipsed by the New Left.

Operation Fight Back: Group of FSM defendants who tried to get appeal bail reduced or eliminated.

participatory democracy: In the case of the FSM, decision making by consensus, subject to a vote only when consensus could not be reached. The FSM had no authority to enforce its decisions, and could only function by the consent and cooperation of its student base, which needed to understand, agree with and support its platform and goals.

Particle Berkeley: Science club; member of the United Front. Dunbar Aitkins' quarterly science journal, *Particle,* was printed on the old *Root and Branch* offset press, which in mid-1965 went to the Berkeley Free Press.

the Party: The Communist party.

Peace Strike: 1930s Spanish Civil War (Republican) organization.

Phee Gees: Phi Gamma Delta fraternity. Anti-FSM.

PLM: Pronounced as single letters. Progressive Labor Movement. "More Catholic than the pope," ultraleft CP turned Maoist. Later the Progressive Labor Party (PLP). Arranged 1963 and 1964 visits to Cuba in violation of the State Department travel ban. The trips were sponsored by Federación Estudiantil Universitio (FEU).

Port Huron Convention: Old SDS (Michael Harrington) clashes with New SDS (Tom Hayden) in 1962, resulting in the Port Huron Statement, the New Left manifesto.

progressive: "Most communist language had little relevance to the sixties, but one word that did survive was *progressive,* which communists had adopted during the Henry Wallace presidential campaign in 1948. It is significant that when Robert Scheer ran for congress in 1966, he did not run as a *progressive.* Scheer needed to build a political coalition that included both *progressives* and left-liberals, i.e., domestic supporters of leftist ideals who abhorred communism. Thus, Scheer called himself a *radical* democrat" (Rorabaugh, 188).

radical: The term preferred by the New Left. See *progressive.*

Ramparts: Small-circulation liberal Catholic quarterly modified to become the official organ of the New Left.

Regents: Titular owners of the University of California.

Root and Branch: New Left political journal founded in 1959 by UC graduate students Phil Roos, Robert Scheer, Maurice Zeitlin and David Horowitz, *inter alia.*

Rossman Report: Report compiled by UC students on the administration's restriction of student political activity and expression; edited by mathematics graduate Michael Rossman.

ROTC: Pronounced as separate letters, or "Rot-see" by the disaffected. Reserve Officers' Training Corps (or Course). Compulsory military training for UC undergraduate males until 1962.

Rule 11: Created by President Gordon Sproul in 1936. Required University presidential approval of off-campus speakers.

Rule 17: Issued by President Sproul in 1937 in response to student political activity; replacing Rule 11, it also forbade fund-raising for off-campus issues.

SAE: Pronounced as separate letters. Sigma Alpha Epsilon fraternity. Anti-FSM.

sally: Sorority girl.

SANE: "Sane." National Committee for a Sane Nuclear Policy. 1957 ban-the-bomb organization directed by William Sloane Coffin. Pro–Democratic party. Conceived as a vehicle for liberals. Compare CNA.

Sather Gate: Before late 1950s campus expansion, the entrance to the UC campus and site of student rallies and protests.

SCAL: "Scal." Student Committee on Agricultural Labor. Anti–bracero program organization. Ken Cloke, a mover and shaker in early 1960s SLATE, was chairman.

SCLC: Pronounced as separate letters. Southern Christian Leadership Conference. Southern clergymen led by Martin Luther King, Jr.

SCLU: Pronounced as separate letters. Student Civil Liberties Union. Member of the United Front. Concerned with overturning the Kerr Directives.

SDS: Pronounced as separate letters. Students for a Democratic Society. Premier national leftist nonsectarian youth group, formed at the University of Michigan in June 1962 from the ashes of the SP suborganization League for Industrial Democracy (LID). The Port Huron Statement contained its basic principles, and defined much succeeding New Left activity. In Berkeley, largely made up of graduate student emigrés and preempted by SLATE. Activist, militant and confrontational. In 1969 disintegrated into the Weather Underground. Member of the United Front.

Sexual Freedom League: West Coast affiliate of the New York City League for Sexual Freedom. Established in Berkeley in the summer of 1965 by Jefferson Fuck Poland.

SLATE: "Slate." Pseudo-acronym, humorously called by members "Student League Accused of Trying to Exist." Umbrella group for student protest at UC. Offspring of TASC. Conceived as a student political party, it actually succeeded briefly in taking over the ASUC. Far and away the largest student organization, with several hundred active members. Member of the United Front.

SNCC: "Snick." Friends of the Student Non-violent Coordinating Committee. Founded by Black college students in 1960 and headed by Stokely Carmichael. Impatient with Martin Luther King's non-violence and reformism; became the 1966 Black Power movement. Member of the United Front.

Social Democrats: Worse than liberals, providing a Left cover for the State Department. *New Leader* magazine. Ferocious anti-Communism led them to support every form of foreign government that was in accord with U.S. policy. Supportive of loyalty oaths at home. Conservative faculty member Lewis Feuer, who called the FSM "a melange of narcotics, sexual perversion, collegiate Castroism, and campus Maoism," did so in a *New Leader* article, "Rebellion at Berkeley" (December 21, 1964).

Social Problems Club: Held antiwar rallies at UC during the 1930s.

SP: Pronounced as separate letters. Socialist Party. Reformist socialists, supporting Democratic party politics. Most members were actually registered Democrats.

Spartacist League: Self-proclaimed as following in the footsteps of Karl Leibknecht and Rosa Luxembourg, the heads of the newly founded Communist party in Germany circa 1919. Named after the Roman slave rebellion in 73–71 BC, the Spartacist League was not, strictly speaking, related to the earlier movement except in name. An early 1960s SWP splinter group that considered the SWP revisionist.

Spider: Campus literary magazine involved in the Filthy Speech Movement. The title was a strained acronym for Sex, Politics, International Communism, Drugs, Extremism and Rock 'n' Roll.

Sproul Hall: Center of UC Berkeley bureaucracy. Site of FSM sit-ins.

Sproul Plaza: Site of captured police car and FSM rallies.

SPU: Pronounced as separate letters. Student Peace Union. American Friends Service Committee spin-off, 1959. Controlled by the left wing of YPSL. At loggerheads with SANE, in that they were for unilateral disarmament. Opposed to the Democratic party.

SRE: Pronounced as separate letters. Students for Racial Equality. Collected food and clothing for the striking miners of Harlan, Kentucky, in 1961.

Stalinist: "Oh, you may be a friend of Max Schachtman, / Leon Trotsky and you may agree, / Oh, you may see some promise in old Norman Thomas, / But you ain't no comrade to me." (Sung to the tune of "Show Me the Way to Go Home." Max Schachtman was Leon Trotsky's secretary, and the center of a Trotskyist splinter group.)

By the late 1950s, Stalinists largely defined themselves as anti-Trotskyites. The reverse was also true. By 1964 nobody called himself a Stalinist.

Steering Committee: Small group

elected by the FSM Executive Committee to make rapid decisions on a day-to-day basis.

Stiles Hall: Off-campus meeting place for campus political organizations, especially SLATE.

Students for Cal: Post-sit-in, anti-FSM organization. Widely ignored.

Students for Civil Liberties: Anti-HUAC organization.

Students for Fair Housing: CORE affiliate. Member of the United Front.

Student Union building: Seat of UC student government. Kitty-corner from Sproul Hall.

Student Union Plaza: Out-of-the-way plaza behind the Student Union building; rejected by the FSM as an alternative Hyde Park area when the tables were banned from Bancroft and Telegraph. Also called Lower Sproul Plaza.

SWP: Pronounced as single letters. Socialist Workers Party. The official Trotskyists—keepers of the flame, inheritors of the mantle. Until the early 1970s, the Sherman-Williams Paint company had a huge neon sign over its Emeryville factory, easily legible from San Francisco, on which an animated paint can poured red paint over a globe of the earth, with the slogan, SWP COVERS THE EARTH. Everybody thought this was hilarious.

TA: Pronounced as separate letters. Teaching assistant.

TASC: "Task." Toward an Active Student Community. The student reform movement of the late 1950s and early 1960s, concerned with fair housing, birth control information and the peace movement. At Berkeley, reformed in 1958 as SLATE.

Technocracy: "A movement flourishing in the early 1930s and advocating replacement of the capitalist price system of industrial production and distribution by a system of control by technicians aiming primarily at production to the limit of industrial capacity" (*Webster's Third New International Dictionary*). Tech-weenies with nerd-pacs; by the 1960s almost extinct.

The Tribe: 1969 spin-off of the *Barb*. Berkeley organ of the Movement.

Trotskyist: Adherents to the anti-Stalinist line. Leon Trotsky was banished from Russia in 1929 and assassinated on Stalin's orders in 1940. Trotskyists, sometimes called "Trots," stood for Workers' Democracy, as opposed to Russian-style bureaucratic control.

Trotskyite: Unfriendly term used by Stalinists. The phrase "Trotskyite Wrecker" was often on the lips of Stalinists. I know that these distinctions sound weird, but at the time they were important.

the Two Hundred: Faculty members of the Academic Senate who hammered out a proposal to end the free speech controversy. Favored the goals of the FSM. The proposal was put before the Academic Senate on December 8 and passed by a wide margin.

UCLC: Pronounced as separate letters. University Civil Liberties Committee. Young Democrat affiliate. Jo Freeman, chairman.

UFW: Pronounced as separate letters. United Farm Workers. Began as AWOC (Agricultural Workers Organizing Committee)—older Filipino—which merged in the early 1960s with Cesar Chavez's NFW (National Farmworkers Union)—younger Mexican—to form the UFW. The organization came to liberal attention with a boycott of nonunion table grapes.

Undergraduate Association: Short-lived predecessor to the FSU; its first meeting was on December 7, 1964.

Union of University-Employed Graduate Students: GCC descendant that became the short-lived local 1570 of the AFT.

United Front: Umbrella organization of fall 1964 UC campus political groups. Nonsectarian. Originally consisting of Cal Students for Goldwater, CCR, CIPA, CORE, W. E. B. Du Bois Club, ISC, M2M, Particle Berkeley, SCLU, SDS, SLATE, SNCC, Students for Fair Housing, USI, Women for Peace, YD, YPSL, YR, YSA. Later joined by the Inter-faith Council, Democratic Socialist Club, and the University Society of Libertarians.

University Society of Libertarians: Member of the United Front.

USI: Pronounced as separate letters. University Society of Individuals (Individualists). Libertarian conservative group. Member of the United Front.

USLO: Pronounced as separate letters.

University Students for Law and Order. Short-lived anti-FSM organization formed after the sit-in.

Vanguard Press: Predecessor to the Berkeley Free Press.

VDC: Pronounced as separate letters. Vietnam Day Committee. Originated in a teach-in on the UC campus on May 21–22, 1965, organized by Jerry Rubin. Activist, confrontational, antiwar.

Weathermen: Terrorist SDS splinter group formed in Chicago in June 1969. Later the Weather Underground.

Weather Underground: Terrorist SDS splinter group.

Wesley (Wesleyan) Foundation: Politically aware youth organization of the Methodist Church. Across from the UC campus at Dana and Bancroft.

Westminister House: Located at Bancroft and College; used for FSM Executive Committee meetings.

Wobblies: See IWW.

Women for Peace: Antiwar, ban-the-bomb group. CP-oriented. Member of the United Front.

Women Mobilized for Berkeley: Liberal Berkeley boosters *cum* civil rights organization, participating in remedial educational projects for disadvantaged Berkeley residents. Dissociated itself from CORE when downtown picketing began.

Women Strike for Peace: Organized by Washington, D.C., professional women to protest resumption of A-bomb tests on November 1, 1961.

Women's International League for Peace and Freedom: Ban-the-bomb organization, later involved in partisan politics and antiwar activism.

YAF: Pronounced as separate letters. Young Americans for Freedom. Right-wing, anti-Communist, anti-peacenik group organized in 1960 by William F. Buckley.

YD: Pronounced as separate letters. Young Democrats. Leftish-liberal Democrat organization. Member of the United Front.

"Yellow Submarine": Beatles' song which to some extent became the anthem of anarchistic, or at least anti-old-style-left-wing-politics youth in the late 1960s. Preceding a UC student strike in December 1966, there was a meeting between the Graduate Student Association and the undergrads, at the end of which the grads sang "Solidarity Forever" and the undergrads responded with "Yellow Submarine." "Yellow Submarine" became the theme of the strike. The leaflet calling the strike, written by Frank Bardacke and Marvin Garson and printed at the Berkeley Free Press, sported a yellow submarine and contained a black mask to be worn during a "Maskoertion" protest, in order to prevent the administration from singling out participants.

Yippies: Youth International Party. The name "Yippies" came first and the explanation "Youth International Party" second. Founded in 1967 by Abbie Hoffman, Jerry Rubin, Paul Krassner and Dick Gregory. Apotheosis of 1960s counterculture, an anarchistic blend of drugs, politics, sex and music.

YPSL: "Yip-sl." Young People's Socialist League. Right-wing social democrat youth group of the Socialist party, less its Trotskyist members; more important as a forum than as an activist organization. Norman Thomas followers; anti-Communist. Member of the United Front.

YR: Pronounced as separate letters. Young Republicans. Conservative. Member of the United Front.

YSA: Pronounced as separate letters. Young Socialist Alliance. Youth arm of the Trotskyist SWP. *Spider* magazine quipped, "The YSA supports only those countries that jail its members." Member of the United Front.

Hal Draper, in his post-FSM book, *Berkeley: The New Student Revolt*, estimates that "A membership count of these clubs would show perhaps 200–300 members in all, but their influence extends pretty strongly to another few hundred, and in more diluted form to perhaps a thousand; from this point it would shade off rapidly" (166).

DRAMATIS PERSONAE

Mike Abramovitch: GCC; Legal Central; first chairman of the Union of University-Employed Graduate Students. Embroiled in the coup attempt of November 9.

Mike Adams: Men's Residence Hall representative to the ASUC. Favored publication of the *Graduate Political Scientists' Report* on the FSM, to refute charges of "Communist subversion."

Dunbar Aitkins: Particle Berkeley; publisher of *Particle*; Engineering Central.

Stew Albert: Co-founder of the Free University of Berkeley.

Ron Anastasi: Psychology undergrad. Independent representative to the Executive Committee; Regents' meeting representative. Co-organizer of the Steering Committee reorganization of November 8; elected to the Steering Committee in the reorganization of November 8. Important in the general organization of the FSM's various committees and subcommittees.

David Anderson: Deputy district attorney prosecuting the Filthy Speech trial.

Glenn Anderson: Lieutenant governor; member of the Board of Regents.

Henry Anderson: UC researcher into the bracero program; author of the suppressed "Harvest of Loneliness."

Tom Andre: Anti–Vietnam War activist.

Kenneth Anger: Ford Fellow; avant-garde filmmaker (*Scorpio Rising, Inauguration of the Pleasure Dome, Fireworks*). Aided participants in the Filthy Speech Movement.

Bettina Aptheker: Undergraduate in history. FSM theoretician; CPUSA; Du Bois Club; CCPA negotiator. Moderate, highly influential member of the Steering Committee. Worked on FSM trial newsletter, *The Defendant*. Daughter of Herbert Aptheker, CPUSA theoretician.

Stephen Argent: *Spider* magazine staff; arrested in the Filthy Speech Movement.

David Armor: SLATE; ASUC president, 1959–1960.

Charlie Brown Artman: Proto-hippie and campus oddball; arrested in the Filthy Speech Movement.

Judge Axelrod: San Francisco judge for HUAC protesters.

Leo Bach: Berkeley Free Press owner, 1966–1968.

Sam Bader: FSM Central staff.

Joan Baez: Radical folksinger who lent her name and active support to the FSM. Boyfriend Ira Sandperl.

Roger Baldwin: Founder of the ACLU, 1920.

Frank Bardacke: "Bar-da-kee." Chairman of the Ad Hoc Committee for March 23; SLATE; anti–Vietnam War activist. In Africa during the FSM. With Marvin Garson, author of the "napalmed babies" leaflet intended for the 1966 Rose Bowl. Author of People's Park leaflet, "Free in the Parks."

Thomas Barnes: Assistant dean. Spoke to the demonstrators in Sproul Hall, September 30, 1964.

Jerry Barrish: "Don't perish in jail: call Barrish for bail." FSM, civil rights and anti–Vietnam War bail bondsman.

George Batzli: GCC alternate representative to the FSM Executive Committee.

Fred Bauer: GCC Strike Committee.

Mike Bennett: Owner of the Bookshelf, where the FSM press operated in late 1965 and early 1966. Anti–Vietnam War activist; Berkeley Free Press printer.

Jack Berman: Attorney for HUAC protesters.

Ernest Besig: Director of the Northern California ACLU. Represented the suspended students before the Heyman Committee.

David Bills: Arrested in the Filthy Speech Movement.

Julie Blake: Independent representative to the Executive Committee. Participated in November 8 Steering Committee reorganization; wrote free speech carols for the *Joy to UC* recording.

Neal Blumenfeld: "Psychiatrist to the FSM."

Carl Blumstein: Bacteriology student. Production manager of *Root and Branch*; production staff of SLATE *Supplement.* Co-author of November 1961 SLATE pamphlet, *The Big Myth?*

Earl Bolton: Vice president of administration.

Philip Brody Boyd: Member of the Board of Regents; director of Security First National Bank; director of Citizens National Trust and Savings Bank; president of Deep Canyon Properties.

Marsha Bratten: Winner of 1964 Robert Gordon and Ida W. Sproul Awards; CCPA appointee.

Mark Bravo: SNCC; cited and suspended September 30, 1964.

Richard Bright: Actor arrested in 1966 on obscenity charges, for his performance in Michael McClure's *The Beard.*

Benson Brown: GCC; GCC Strike Committee; *Root and Branch.* Elected to the Steering Committee in November 8 reorganization; resigned over the issue of the abortive sit-in; replaced by Bob Starobin. Gave an automobile to David Goines. Wife Megan.

Doug Brown: SLATE *Supplement* editorial staff.

Edmund G. Brown: Governor of California, 1959–1966; member of the Board of Regents.

Willie Brown: Active on behalf of jailed civil rights demonstrators; supportive of FSM defendants; active in California politics.

George Brun: Berkeley municipal judge who made the final disposition of the FSM cases.

Bill Buckman: Founder of Berkeley Graphic Arts, successor to the Berkeley Free Press, 1968–1970.

Jim Burnette: Involved with Jo Freeman and Dick Roman in the November 9 coup attempt.

Hugh Burns: Democrat California state senator from Fresno; chairman of the State Senate Subcommittee on Un-American Activities ("Baby HUAC").

Malcolm Burnstein: Represented the suspended students in the CCPA; represented FSM defendants; represented Jack London Square defendants.

Richard M. Buxbaum: FSM attorney.

Jerome C. Byrne: Los Angeles lawyer commissioned by the Forbes Committee to prepare a report on the causes of the FSM.

Paul Cahill: United Front; Young Republicans; president of University Society of Individuals. Member of the October 2 negotiating team.

Tom Calmar: Comparative literature grad. Attempted to create a conservative graduate student organization in competition with the GCC. Later became active in the FSM.

John Canaday: Member of the Board of Regents; vice president of Lockheed Aircraft; vice president of the California Manufacturing Association.

Stokely Carmichael: SNCC; co-founder of the Black Panthers.

Edward Carter: Chairman of the Board of Regents; president of Broadway-Hale stores; director of Emporium Capwell, Northrop Corporation, Pacific Mutual Life, Western Bancorporation, United California Bank, Pacific Telephone and Telegraph, Southern California Edison. Trustee of the Irvine Foundation.

Richard Casey: Freshman philosophy student; in October 1959 withdrew from Cal and forfeited his Regents' Scholarship rather than enroll in ROTC.

Keith Chamberlain: Graduate intern, Presbyterian Campus Ministry, Westminister House. Sympathetic to the goals of the FSM from the beginning, and helpful to the individuals within it.

Owen Chamberlain: Professor of physics and Nobel Laureate; pro-FSM after the Academic Senate resolution.

Dorothy Chandler: Member of the Board of Regents; vice president and director of the Times-Mirror Company.

Merrill F. Chandler: University of California police lieutenant; arrested Jack Weinberg on October 1, 1964.

James Chaney: Civil rights worker assassinated June 22, 1964.

Cesar Chavez: Leader of United Farm Workers.

Earl Cheit: Professor of business administration and author of the Cheit proposal,

in the CCPA. Replaced Meyerson as chancellor.

Milton Chernin: Dean of the School of Social Welfare; CCPA appointee.

Susan Chesney: One of the "Free Speech Five Plus Four" performers of FSM free speech carols.

Brad Cleaveland: Author of the "open, fierce and thoroughgoing rebellion" letter in the 1964 SLATE *Supplement*.

Ken Cloke: 1958 SLATE co-organizer; 1961 SLATE representative-at-large to the ASUC Executive Committee.

J. Frank Coakley: District attorney of Alameda County.

Warren Coates: Young Republicans; United Front.

William Coblentz: Member of the Board of Regents; San Francisco attorney. Northern California ACLU; director of the Bay Area Urban League, the California Business Advisory Council, Advance Materials and Processes, Hollister Land Company, Kimball Manufacturing. Participant in the "elite group."

Hilbert Coleman: CORE; one of the very few Black participants in the FSM.

Kate Coleman: SLATE; Independent representative to the Executive Committee; Command Central.

Wayne Collins, Sr.: ACLU lawyer; together with Ernest Besig, represented the suspended students before the Heyman Committee.

Mark Comfort: Arrested in Jack London Square civil rights protest.

Stephanie Coontz: SLATE; Du Bois Club; United Front organizer; Executive Committee. Leafleter; with Patti Iiyama, discoverer of the coup attempt of November 9. Cited student on November 9.

Jim Creighton: 1960 ROTC protester; picketed while in uniform and received a punitive F in the course.

Rupert J. Crittenden: Primary judge trying the FSM defendants.

Thomas Cunningham: University counsel; twice informed Alex Sherriffs of the probable illegality of suppressing student First Amendment rights. Supposed author of a letter to the Regents proposing legislation unfavorable to the FSM's goals.

Rich Currier: Editorial board of *Root and Branch*; co-editor of *Spider* magazine. Wife Sue Currier.

Sue Currier: SLATE *Supplement* editorial staff; co-editor of *Spider* magazine. Husband Rich Currier.

Wendy Dannette: FSM Central staff.

W. Thomas Davis: Member of the Board of Regents; president of the Alumni Association; president of Blue Goose Growers and of its parent company, Western Fruit Growers Sales Corporation.

Donald Dean: FSM Central staff.

Steve DeCanio: Served time for Sheraton-Palace; co-editor of *Spider* magazine.

Victoria DeGoff: Friendly witness in the Filthy Speech trial.

Bob Dietrich: Engineering Central.

Shirley Dietrich: FSM Central staff.

Billie Dixon: Actress arrested on obscenity charges for her performance in Michael McClure's *The Beard*, 1966.

Hal Draper: Independent Socialist Club; author of *Behind the Battle of Berkeley: The Mind of Clark Kerr* (October 1964) and *Berkeley: The New Student Revolt* (1965). Rented mimeograph machine to the FSM.

Larry Duga: FSM attorney.

John J. Dunn: FSM attorney.

Robert Dussault: Strikebreaker and anti-FSM founder of the USLO.

Frederick Dutton: Member of the Board of Regents; U.S. assistant secretary of state for congressional relations. Attorney for Southern Counties Gas until 1957; in 1958 served as chairman of the Brown for Governor Committee, then as executive secretary to Governor Brown.

Gerald Dworkin: Editorial staff of *Root and Branch*.

Mike Eisen: UCLC; FSM Press Committee.

Sanford Elberg: Dean of the graduate division. Informed students sitting in at Sproul Hall on September 30 that the cited students had been suspended. Attempted to placate TAs and research assistants to prevent union organizing and GCC strike.

Henry M. Elson: FSM attorney.

Medgar Evers: NAACP field secretary assassinated June 12, 1963, in Jackson, Mississippi.

Sam Farber: Sociology Club; organizer of the GCC.

James Farmer: Founder and national director of the Congress of Racial Equality. Addressed a noon rally of three thousand from Bancroft and Telegraph on December 15, 1964.

Rosemary Feitis: Central; ran FSM Central when it was on Bancroft.

Lee Felsenstein: Engineering Central; "Free Speech Five Plus Four" carol performer; FSU organizer.

Lewis Feuer: Conservative faculty member; fundamentally opposed the goals of the FSM.

James Fisher: Assistant chaplain, Newman Hall Catholic Student Center. Calmed crowd on the night of October 1–2, averting a riot. General spiritual adviser during the FSM to those who needed it.

William Forbes: Member of the Board of Regents; executive assistant to the president of CBS; Young and Rubicam; president of the Southern California Music Company; director of Bell Brand Foods, Ltd. Former president of UCLA Alumni Association.

Steve Fox: Berkeley Free Press printer.

Peter Franck: SLATE co-founder; FSM and antiwar attorney.

Kathie Frank: Staff of *The Defendant*, FSM trial newsletter.

Jo Freeman: United Front; Young Democrats; October 2 negotiating team. Outspoken critic of FSM leadership; engaged in separate negotiations with Kerr and organized the November 7–9 coup attempt. Chairman of UCLC and activist protester of the Interim Rules on Political Activity.

Joe Freeman: SLATE Supplement editorial staff.

William Fretter: Dean of the College of Letters and Science; CCPA appointee.

David Friedman: ISC; CORE; United Front organizer. Arrested in Jack London Square protests.

Sandor Fuchs: "Fewks." SLATE chairman, 1964–1965; United Front organizer; co-editor of *Spider* magazine. Cited and suspended September 30; member of the October 2 negotiating team. Embroiled in November 9 attempted coup.

Joseph Garbarino: Professor of business administration; CCPA appointee.

Victor Garlin: Editorial staff of *Root and Branch*.

Betty Garmon: Chairman of Campus Friends of SNCC, 1963–1964.

Dan Garrison: Teaching Fellow; GCC; Strike Committee. Organized speakers after the Academic Senate resolution.

Barbara Garson: YSA; CORE; United Front organizer; co-editor of FSM *Newsletter*. Husband Marvin Garson.

Marvin Garson: YSA; Free Student Union organizer; anti–Vietnam War activist. Active before the FSM in campus politics; latecomer to the FSM. Author of *The Regents*; with Frank Bardacke, author of the "napalmed babies" leaflet. Wife Barbara Garson.

Joel Geier: ISC; United Front organizer.

John George: Attorney representing the Filthy Speech Movement defendants.

Bob Gill: Peace movement; anti-HUAC activist; early student movement and co-founder of TASC at San Jose State. YPSL; SDS; BASCAHUAC. FSM photographer.

Steve Gillers: Co-editor of FSM *Newsletter*.

Ann Fagin Ginger: FSM attorney.

Lenny Glaser: Proto-hippie social activist; a constant presence at Bancroft and Telegraph before the FSM began. Advocate of the legalization of marijuana.

Nathan Glazer: UC faculty member; with Seymour Martin Lipset, one of the instigators of the Jo Freeman coup attempt of November 9. Politically moderate; believed his role in the FSM was that of go-between. His services were not appreciated by the activist students. During the arrests, organized a pro-student faculty meeting.

Art Goldberg: Education grad. Youth Action Union; SLATE chairman, 1963–1964; SLATE Supplement advertising and sales. FSM moderate; Steering Committee. Participated in Sheraton-Palace, *Oakland Tribune* arrests; suspended September 30. Embroiled in November 9 attempted coup; not reelected to Steering Committee after November 8 reorganization, but reinstated a week later. Arrested in the Filthy Speech Movement; expelled. Jackie Goldberg's brother.

Jackie Goldberg: Women for Peace; United Front organizer and spokesman;

Delta Phi Epsilon pledge mother; FSM moderate. Member of the October 2 negotiating team; Steering Committee; co-editor of *Spider* magazine. Not reelected to the Steering Committee after the November 8 reorganization; recipient of November disciplinary letter. Brother Art Goldberg.

Suzanne Goldberg: Philosophy graduate student. SNCC; initially FSM secretary and GCC alternate representative to the Executive Committee; later on the Steering Committee. FSM hard-line radical. Girlfriend of Jack Weinberg in the early part of the FSM, later the girlfriend and in 1965 the wife of Mario Savio.

Lee Goldblatt: FSM bookkeeper.

Stanley P. Golde: FSM attorney. Former law partner of Judge Crittenden; law partner of Spence Strellis.

Jerry Goldstein: ASUC vice president, 1964–1965.

Barry Goldwater: Right-wing Republican candidate for U.S. president, 1964. Defeated by Lyndon Johnson with the greatest plurality in American history.

Cyril Wolfe Gonick: Editorial staff of *Root and Branch*.

Andrew Goodman: Civil rights worker assassinated June 22, 1964.

Brenda Goodman: Progressive Labor; M2M. Housed and helped John Thompson; lived with Denis Mosgofian.

Robert A. Gordon: Professor of economics; member of the Heyman Committee.

Robert Greenberg: GCC Strike Committee.

Dale Greenmeyer: Co-planner of the Santa Rita solidarity picket.

Cornelius Haggerty: Member of the Board of Regents; president of the Building and Construction Trades Department, AFL-CIO.

Mason Haire: Professor of psychology and research psychologist in the Institute of Industrial Relations; member of the Heyman Committee.

Irving Hall: HUAC protester; co-producer of "In Search of Truth," a rebuttal to *Operation Abolition*; secretary-treasurer of BASCAHUAC.

Vincent Hallinan: 1952 presidential candidate for the Progressive party; San Francisco left-wing lawyer. Defended waterfront labor leader Harry Bridges. Patriarch of the formidable Hallinan tribe: Daniel; Conn "Ringo"; Matthew "Dynamite" (Du Bois Club co-founder); Patrick "Butch" (1958 SLATE co-organizer); Terence "Kayo" (Du Bois Club co-founder).

Deward Hastings: SLATE; Engineering Central; free speech carols. Central initially at Deward's apartment. Ran the FSM printing press; in 1965 merged with Marion Syrek to form the Berkeley Free Press.

Donald Hatch: SNCC; cited and suspended September 30.

Catherine (Mrs. Randolph A.) Hearst: Member of the Board of Regents.

Elinor (Mrs. Edward) Heller: Member of the Board of Regents; board member of the World Affairs Council of Northern California, San Francisco Symphony Association, League of Women Voters.

Siegfried Hesse: FSM attorney.

Ira Michael Heyman: Professor of law. Chairman of the Ad Hoc Academic Senate Committee on Student Suspensions (the Heyman Committee) created by the Academic Senate to hear the cases of the eight students suspended September 30, 1964. Neither the findings nor the recommendations of this committee pleased the administration.

James Hicks: Head of the Bogalusa Deacons for Defense and Justice.

Douglas J. Hill: FSM attorney.

Mo Hirsch: Professor of mathematics. Steadfastly pro-FSM, and a damned fine musician.

Alex Hoffman: FSM attorney.

Lynn Hollander: Editorial production of the Rossman Report.

J. Edgar Hoover: Head of the Federal Bureau of Investigation. Sworn enemy of everyone to the left of Attila the Hun. Insane, vindictive and incompetent.

Pam Horner: CCR; moderate Republican; United Front. From around October 10, briefly a member of the Steering Committee.

David Horowitz: Anti-HUAC activist; co-founder of *Root and Branch*. Author of *Student*.

Alice Huberman: Co-editor of *Spider* magazine.

John Hulett: SNCC; co-founder of the Black Panther party of Lowndes County.

Gary Hunt: FSM liaison with other campuses.

Leba Hurvitz: Singer on the "Free Speech Five Plus Four" recording, *Joy to UC*.

Robert Hurwitt: English grad; GCC Executive Board (1965).

Mona Hutchin: Vice president of the University Society of Individuals; United Front organizer; Regents' meeting representative. Elected to the Steering Committee in the reorganization of November 8. In 1965 challenged the "men only" rule on riding the running boards of cable cars.

Patti Iiyama: English major. SLATE; Friends of SNCC; SLATE ASUC senator (1962–63, 1963–64); United Front; Executive Committee. Leafleter; with Stephanie Coontz, unveiler of the coup attempt of November 9. Suspended 1966 for participation in Movement Against Political Suspensions (MAPS); suspended 1967 for Stop the Draft Week.

Carl Irving: *Oakland Tribune* reporter; drew Sherriffs' attention to political activity in the Bancroft-Telegraph area.

Tom Irwin: Press Central; printing and media liaison; Engineering Central. Rossman Report production; Free Student Union organizer.

Peter Israel: FSM leafleter.

Barry Jablon: Command Central; Legal Central; "Free Speech Five Plus Four" carol performer. His apartment on Ridge was the location of the meeting on Monday morning, November 9, before the tables went back up.

Paul Jacobs: Director of the Institute for Industrial Relations; labor organizer.

Myra Jehlin: GCC representative to the Executive Committee; panelist in the Physical Science Lecture Hall debates.

Lowell Jensen: Head of the FSM prosecution.

Dave Jessup: Involved with Jo Freeman in the November 9 attempted coup.

Howard Jewel: FSM attorney.

Mike Jones: CORE; Bogalusa civil rights activist with the Deacons for Defense and Justice.

Sanford Kadish: Professor of law. Proposed a modification of the Cheit proposal in the CCPA; the Kadish proposal was accepted by students and faculty, but rejected by the administration.

Eli Katz: Acting assistant German professor during the academic year 1963–1964. Confirmed by both the German department and the Senate Committee on Privilege and Tenure for a permanent job, but denied the position by Strong and Kerr because of his supposed involvement in Communist political activity some years earlier.

Bob Kauffman: History grad. Fair Play for Cuba Committee; Du Bois Club; GCC delegate to the Executive Committee; GCC Strike Committee. Co-organizer of the Steering Committee reorganization of November 8.

Laurence Kennedy: Member of the Board of Regents; former district attorney of Shasta County; member of the law firm of Carr and Kennedy, among whose clients were Pacific Telephone and PG&E.

Clark Kerr: UC's first chancellor, 1952–1958; president of the UC system, 1958–1967.

Frank Kidner: Dean of educational relations; administration representative on the CCPA.

Ann Kilby: Involved with Jo Freeman in the November 9 coup attempt.

Jon King: SLATE *Supplement* advertising and sales.

Gretchen Kittredge: FSM bookkeeper. Boyfriend Tom Miller.

Michael Klein: Ph.D. candidate in English; M2M. Arrested in Filthy Speech Movement.

William F. Knowland: Former California senator; owner and editor-in-chief of the *Oakland Tribune*; California manager of the Goldwater for President campaign.

Tom Knowles: FSM Press Committee.

Leo Koch: Cal alumnus; assistant professor of biology dismissed in April 1960 from his position at the University of Illinois for advocating "free love." Spoke on the UC campus May 11, 1961.

David Kolodny: Independent representative to the Executive Committee.

William Kornhauser: UC professor; member of the Two Hundred.

Danny Kowalski: VDC activist.

Alan Krebs: Founder of the Free University of New York, model for the Free University of Berkeley.

Saul Landau: Exhibitor and U.S. distributor of Jean Genet's *Un Chant d'Amour*.

Kevin Langdon: Co-writer of free speech carols.

Joe LaPenta: "Free Speech Five Plus Four" carol performer.

John Leggett: UC sociology professor. Acted as go-between on October 1 and 2, 1964.

Norman S. Leonard: FSM attorney.

Lewis Lester: ISC; Du Bois Club; United Front organizer. With Patti Iiyama and Stephanie Coontz, discoverer of the coup attempt of November 9.

Eric Levine: Student on the October 2 negotiating team.

Laurence Levine: Professor of history; pro-FSM. With Charles Sellers, set up the Two Hundred.

Fançion Lewis: Free speech carols; Peter Franck's legal secretary. She could type 120 words a minute letter-perfect and talk on the phone at the same time. She'd stop typing and that little IBM ball would keep on whizzing around for another 30 seconds. Most amazing thing I ever saw.

Aryay Linsky: SLATE chairman in 1959.

Betty Linsky: Independent representative to the Executive Committee. Participated in the November 8 Steering Committee reorganization; Sexual Freedom League.

Stevie Lipney: SLATE; carol performer in the "Free Speech Five Plus Four."

Seymour Martin Lipset: UC professor of sociology. Relatively hostile to the means of the FSM; not clear on the constitutional issues. Believed his role in the FSM should be that of go-between; faculty negotiator, October 1 and 2, 1964. Lipset seems to have been the mainspring behind the attempted coup of November 9, enlisting most notably Jo Freeman as well as an unclear number of others. With Sheldon Wolin, editor of *The Berkeley Student Revolt: Facts and Interpretations* (1965).

Albert Litewka: Free Speech Defense Fund; staff of FSM trial newsletter, *The Defender*.

Jeff Lustig: Political science undergrad. Cuba visit in 1964; co-founder, Free University of Berkeley.

Bob MacLaren: GCC.

Andy Magid: Co-editor of *Spider* magazine.

Colonel Malloy: UC Berkeley ROTC commander.

Dave Mandel: "Free Speech Five Plus Four" carol performer.

Irving L. Markovitz: Editorial staff of *Root and Branch*.

Ruth Markovitz: Editorial staff of *Root and Branch*.

Larry Marks: United Front organizer; co-organizer of the November 8 Steering Committee reorganization; FSM ham radio network.

Robert Mates: Cuba visitor in 1964; Free University of Berkeley co-founder.

Henry May: Chairman of the history department. Introduced liberal resolution adopted at the general faculty meeting in Wheeler Hall on December 3. Spokesman for the department chairmen before the meeting in the Greek Theatre.

Herbert McClosky: Professor of political science. Introduced pro–free speech amendments to Henry May's resolution at the December 3 general faculty meeting.

Michael McClure: Playwright arrested on obscenity charges for the 1966 production of *The Beard*.

Martin McCrea: Participant in the Filthy Speech Movement. Signed a complaint against Alpha Epsilon Pi fraternity for "selling obscene materials and using obscene language in a public place."

Donald McLaughlin: Member of the Board of Regents; chairman of Homestead Mining Company; director of United Nuclear Corporation, International Nickel Company, Bunker Hill Company, Cerro Corporation, San-Luis Mining Company, Western Airlines, Wells Fargo Bank.

Edwin Meese III: Alameda County assistant prosecutor responsible for the Sproul Hall arrests as well as the prosecution of the defendants. This brought him to the favorable attention of Ronald Reagan.

Robert Meisenbach: The only 1960

HUAC protester to be tried on a felony count. He was found not guilty.

Pam Mellin: Worked in the dean's office; typed FSM leaflets. Roommate Janis Zimdars.

Renée Melody: FSM participant.

Theodore Meyer: Member of the Board of Regents; president of Mechanics' Institute; member of the law firm Brobeck, Phleger and Harrison; director of Broadway-Hale stores, Newhall Land and Farming Company.

Martin Meyerson: Dean of the College of Environmental Design. Briefly on the CCPA; appointed UC Berkeley acting chancellor January 2, 1965; dropped the ball during the Filthy Speech Movement. Not confirmed as chancellor on June 30, 1965.

Dustin "Dusty" Mark Miller: Participated in the United Front vigil, spoke from the car on October 1–2. Independent representative to FSM Executive Committee; co-organizer of the Steering Committee reorganization of November 8; not reelected to the Steering Committee after the reorganization. "Free Speech Five Plus Four" carol performer. Free Student Union organizer.

Frank Miller: Business and finance officer of the Berkeley campus.

Jerry Miller: Chemistry student. *SLATE Supplement* managing editor; co-author of November 1961 SLATE pamphlet, *The Big Myth?*

Mike Miller: Chairman of Chessman Committee; chairman of Northern California SNCC; TASC; SLATE co-founder; co-author of November 1961 SLATE pamphlet, *The Big Myth?*

Tom Miller: CORE; United Front organizer; hard-liner in the October 2 negotiating team; active early in the FSM. Girlfriend Gretchen Kittredge.

Frederick L. Moore: ROTC protester; hunger strike on Sproul Hall steps, October 1959. Withdrew from UC.

Denis Mosgofian: Progressive Labor; M2M. Housed and helped John Thompson; lived with Brenda Goodman.

Samuel Mosher: Member of the Board of Regents; chairman of Signal Oil and Gas Company; vice president of American Independent Oil Company; chairman of Flying Tiger Lines.

Philip E. Mower: UC policeman; knocked down, bitten, and had his shoes removed during the scuffle at Sproul Hall doors, October 1, 1964.

Burton Moyer: Professor of physics.

Hans Mueller: Sociology grad. With Tom Calmar, attempted to create a conservative competitor to the GCC. Later became an FSM activist.

Roger Muldavin: Engineering Central.

Brian Mulloney: Zoology TA. GCC representative to the Executive Committee; Engineering Central; co-organizer of the Steering Committee reorganization of November 8. With Sue Stein, co-chair of the GCC Strike Committee.

Bob Mundy: FSM Central staff; loudspeaker detail; Free Student Union organizer.

George Murphy: California senator; loudmouthed right-winger.

George S. Murphy: A "little dean"; cited students in violation of University rules.

Charles Muscatine: Came to UC in 1948; tenured professor of English in 1960. One of the faculty members who refused to sign the loyalty oath; was dismissed and reinstated. Member of the Two Hundred.

Michael Myerson: SLATE co-founder; chairman of SLATE in 1961; co-chairman of the Ad Hoc Committee to End Discrimination. Sheraton-Palace, Mel's and Cadillac, *Tribune* pickets.

Milt Nason: FSM attorney and defense organizer.

Manuel Nestle: Editorial staff of *Root and Branch*.

Marilyn Noble: FSM housemother at Central.

Gene Novak: CORE activist.

JoDean Nudd: FSM liaison with other UC campuses.

Brian O'Brien: Co-planner of solidarity picket at Santa Rita.

Dan Paik: FSM activist; "Free Speech Five Plus Four" carol performer.

Karen Pally: FSM financial manager.

Mike Parker: Grad student in political science. ISC; arrested in Jack London Square protests.

Sherwood Parker: Associate professor

of physics; active in bailing the FSMers out of jail.

Thomas Parkinson: Professor of English; victim of an anti-Communist assassination attempt. Generally pro-FSM; favored a universal amnesty after the Academic Senate resolution. Authority on the Beat Generation.

Peter Paskin: FSM activist.

Edwin Pauley: Member of the Board of Regents; chairman of Pauley Petroleum Company; director of Western Airlines, First National Bank and Trust Company.

William Petersen: Faculty negotiator on October 1 and 2, 1964.

Jim Petras: Organized tutorial program for the arrested students; early anti–Vietnam War organizer.

Jon Petrie: Business manager for the *SLATE Supplement to the General Catalog.* Before the FSM, roommate of Tom Weller and David Goines.

Kathy "Kitty" Piper: FSM Central staff; kept a log of petitions, documents, posters and leaflets.

Steve Plagemann: *SLATE Supplement* editorial staff.

Jefferson Fuck Poland: Peace activist; founder of the Sexual Freedom League in Berkeley, summer 1965.

Cecil Poole: United States district attorney.

Charles Powell: ASUC president; winner of the 1964 Robert Gordon and Ida W. Sproul Awards; CCPA appointee. Generally antagonistic to the means, though not so much the ends, of the FSM.

Richard E. Powell: Professor of chemistry and chairman of the chemistry department; member of the Heyman Committee.

Jim Prickett: Co-editor of *Spider* magazine.

Martin N. Pulich: Trial judge for the case of Lee Rhoades.

Max Rafferty: Member of the Board of Regents; state superintendent of education.

Ronald Wilson Reagan: Sports announcer and actor; president of the Screen Actors Guild, 1947–1952, and again in 1959. Elected governor of California in 1966 and in 1970. President of the United

States 1980–1988. Much of a mind with J. Edgar, though considerably taller.

Lee Rhoades: FSM defendant charged with possession of marijuana. Marijuana charges dropped.

Louis Rice: A "little dean"; with Dean Murphy, involved in the citing of students on November 9.

Paul Richards: Civil rights activist; president of W. E. B. Du Bois Club, 1963. His father, Harvey Richards, was an important Movement photographer and filmmaker.

Robert "Skip" Richheimer: History grad. GCC organizer; GCC delegate to the FSM Executive Committee; GCC Strike Committee.

Ron Rohman: *SLATE Supplement* editorial staff.

Dick Roman: Young Democrats; United Front; early but nonparticipating member of the Steering Committee. Involved with Jo Freeman in the attempted coup of November 9. General obstructionist.

Robin Room: Sociology grad. SLATE; GCC Executive Board (1965).

Joan Roos: *SLATE Supplement* editorial staff. Husband Phil Roos.

Phil Roos: Co-founder of TASC; co-founder of *Root and Branch*; editor of the *SLATE Supplement.* Financially supported the Berkeley Free Press. Wife Joan Roos.

David Root: GCC Strike Committee.

Ed Rosenfeld: Nexus; arrested in the Filthy Speech Movement.

Jerry Rosenfield: Anti–Vietnam War protester and assistant to those wishing to avoid the draft.

Dan Rosenthal: Young Americans for Freedom; Cal Students for Goldwater; United Front. Hurt student cause during the October 2 negotiations and in the attempted coup of November 9. Arrested in the Filthy Speech Movement.

Henry Rosovsky: Professor of economics and history; chairman of the Center for Japanese and Korean Studies; CCPA appointee. With Glazer, Schorske, Tussman and Smelser, participated in an October 2, 1964, meeting of professors with administrators, presenting Chancellor Strong and Vice-Chancellor Lincoln Constance with a compromise solution drawn up by Glazer. Strong rejected the compromise.

Arthur Ross: Professor of industrial relations; chairman of the CCPA. Though the students at first felt he was a possible avenue to useful negotiation, he was more than anything on the side of the administration, and was later felt by the protesters to have suckered and betrayed them.

Michael Rossman: Mathematics graduate. Caryl Chessman protests; United Front organizer; Executive Committee; FSM's "moral philosopher." Assembler of the work of eighty students on the subject of political repression at Berkeley, 1958–1964: *Administrative Pressures and Student Political Activity at the University of California: A Preliminary Report* became known as the Rossman Report. Elected to the Steering Committee after the November 8 reorganization; Regents' meeting representative.

William Roth: Member of the Board of Regents; director of Matson Navigation, Crown Zellerbach, Pacific Intermountain Express, United States Leasing Corporation. Participant in the "elite group."

Martin Roysher: FSM mailings; elected to the Steering Committee in the reorganization of November 8; set up and ran Command Central during the sit-in.

Jerry Rubin: Sociology undergrad. SLATE; Cuba visit in 1964; Yippies; anti–Vietnam War activist.

Bertrand Russell: British mathematician and philosopher; profound pacifist and antiwar activist. Co-founded the Committee for Nuclear Disarmament in 1958; in 1961 was sent to prison for civil disobedience and activity with the Committee of 100, an influential, militant antiwar organization. His public support of the FSM was significant among liberal faculty.

Dave Rynin: SLATE; GCC; panelist in Physical Science Lecture Hall debate.

Ken Sanderson: Co-writer of free speech carols for *Joy to UC* recording.

Mario Savio: Philosophy undergraduate. Mississippi Summer Project (1964); Campus Friends of SNCC chairman; hard-liner in the October 2 negotiating team; FSM spokesman. Activist-oriented. Steering Committee; CCPA negotiator; Regents' meeting representative. Recipient of No-

vember disciplinary letter. Married Suzanne Goldberg in 1965.

Robert A. Scalapino: Faculty negotiator October 1 and 2, 1964. Participant in the "elite group"; chairman of the Council of Departmental Chairmen.

Robert Scheer: Co-founder of *Root and Branch*; 1966 congressional candidate.

Serena Turan Scheer: Editorial staff of *Root and Branch*.

Max Scherr: *Berkeley Barb* founder.

Richard Schmorleitz: Political science undergrad. Press Committee; free speech carols; Filthy Speech Movement. Author of *For Unlawful Carnal Knowledge*.

Eugene Schoenfield: "Dr. Hippocrates"; hip headshrinker for the free clinic.

Mark Schorer: English department chairman; wrote introduction to the Grove Press edition of *Lady Chatterley's Lover*.

Carl Schorske: Professor of history.

Marston Schultz: SLATE *Supplement* editorial and production staff; Rossman Report production. FSM historian; gathered interviews and photographs throughout 1965 and early 1966.

Ludwig von Schwarenberg: Canine campus mascot; fountain in Sproul Plaza was named after him in 1963.

Sue Schwartz: Involved with Jo Freeman in the November 9 coup attempt.

Michael Schwerner: Civil rights worker assassinated June 22, 1964.

William Scranton: Unsuccessful presidential contender in the 1964 Republican National Convention at the Cow Palace, San Francisco.

Alan Searcy: UC Berkeley vice-chancellor for academic affairs; CCPA appointee.

John Searle: UC philosophy professor vocally sympathetic to the FSM; member of the Two Hundred. Co-planner of the Santa Rita solidarity picket.

Charles Sellers: UC professor of history; pro-FSM. With Laurence Levine, set up the Two Hundred.

John Seltz: Anti–Vietnam War activist.

Philip Selznick: Chairman of the sociology department; chairman of the Center for the Study of Law and Society.

Pete Sessions: SLATE *Supplement* editorial staff.

Brian Shannon: YSA. Chaired early FSM meetings; chaired Independents' meeting.

Dana Shapiro: Staff of FSM trial newsletter, *The Defendant*.

Alex Sherriffs: Psychology professor; vice-chancellor in charge of student affairs; rabid anti-Communist. Fired by Chancellor Heyns in August 1965; went to work for Ronald Reagan.

Cyril Simmons: Arrested in Jack London Square civil rights protests.

Norton Simon: Member of the Board of Regents; president of Hunt Foods; director of McCall Corporation, Northern Pacific Railway, Wheeling Steel.

Tracy Sims: Co-chairman of the Ad Hoc Committee to End Discrimination. *Tribune* pickets, protests at Cadillac, Sheraton-Palace and Mel's Drive-in.

Sam Slatkin: "Cited Students Club"; FSM Central staff.

Henry Nash Smith: Professor of English; former chairman of the Academic Freedom Committee of the Academic Senate; member of the Two Hundred. Started a bail fund as the students were being arrested in Sproul Hall.

Mike Smith: Former San Quentin guard; member of Zeta Psi fraternity. Active in the FSM; organized the Greek pro-FSM petition. Cited on November 9 and elected to the Executive Committee.

Herschel Snodgrass: Physics grad; GCC Executive Board (1965).

Fred Sokolow: Participant in the Filthy Speech Movement; *Spider* magazine.

Al Solomonow: SLATE *Supplement* editorial staff.

Larry Spence: FSM public relations.

Karen Spencer: Command Central.

Nina Spitzer: Early student spokesman; FSM press secretary.

Robert Gordon Sproul: UC president, 1930–1958.

Elizabeth Gardner Stapleton: YSA; cited and suspended September 30. Husband Sid Stapleton.

Sid Stapleton: YSA; FSM Steering Committee theoretician. Withdrew late in the FSM because of other obligations. Wife Beth Stapleton.

Bob Starobin: History grad. Editorial staff of *Root and Branch*; GCC organizer;

GCC delegate to the Executive Committee; Strike Committee. Author of "Graduate Students and the Free Speech Movement" (*Graduate Student Journal*, Spring 1965).

Buddy Stein: M.A. candidate in English literature. GCC; Strike Committee. Wife Susan Stein.

David Stein: FSM Legal Central. Kept track of the 802 defendants until all sentences were served and fines paid.

Sue Stein: Comparative literature student. GCC; with Brian Mulloney, co-chair of Strike Committee. Husband Buddy Stein.

Walter Stein: GCC; with Bob Starobin, wrote the graduate students' reply to the deans after the November 9 resumption of activism.

Sharon Stern: FSM finances; arrested in Jack London Square demonstrations.

Sherry Stevens: FSM secretary; kept minutes of Executive and Steering Committee meetings.

Spence Strellis: FSM attorney; partner of Stanley Golde.

Edward W. Strong: UC chancellor, 1961–1965.

John Sutake: "Soo-take." FSM Central staff.

Wilmont Sweeney: Berkeley's first Black city councilman, elected 1961.

Marion Syrek: Printed the first runs of the free speech carols covers at his Oakland Vanguard Press; later merged with Deward Hastings to form the Berkeley Free Press. Returned to Vanguard in late 1965.

Floyd Talbot: Judge in the case of the Filthy Speech Movement; judge in the Free Speech Movement.

Jessie W. Tapp: Member of the Board of Regents; president of the State Board of Agriculture; chairman of Bank of America.

Karen Taylor: Last person arrested in Sproul Hall, December 3, 1964.

Jacobus ten Broek: Celebrated blind professor of political science; sided with the students throughout the FSM. Introduced James Farmer at Bancroft and Telegraph on December 15, 1964.

John Thompson: Instigator of the Filthy Speech Movement.

Adrienne Thon: FSM bookkeeper.

Fritjof Thygesson: Founder of TASC.

Mike Tigar: 1961 SLATE candidate for ASUC president; KPFA announcer. Boalt Hall law student; editor of Boalt Hall *Law Review*. FSM moderate.

Edward C. Tolman: UC professor of psychology; led the faculty protest against the loyalty oath. Tolman Hall named in his honor.

Katherine A. Towle: "Tole." Former Marine Corps colonel; dean of students, 1959–1965. Early spokesman for the administration position; CCPA appointee; hostile to Alex Sherriffs. More than anyone else in the administration, Dean Towle was caught between two fires, and was much troubled in her conscience by what she was required to do.

Forrest Tregea: "Tre-gay." UC Berkeley superintendent of buildings and grounds; intensely hostile to the demonstrators.

Robert Treuhaft: FSM attorney; husband of author Jessica Mitford (*The American Way of Death*).

Brian Turner: SNCC; GCC Strike Committee; FSM moderate. Embroiled in attempted coup of November 9 and in consequence voted off the Steering Committee. Recipient of November disciplinary letter.

Joseph Tussman: Chairman of the philosophy department. Publicly announced the December 8 Academic Senate resolution supporting the goals of the FSM.

Lloyd Ulman: Professor of economics and industrial relations; director of the Institute of Industrial Relations; member of the Heyman Committee.

Jesse Unruh: Member of the Board of Regents; Speaker of the Assembly; Democrat.

Brian Van Arkadie: Editorial staff of *Root and Branch*.

Peter Van Houten: One of the "little deans"; cited students violating University regulations.

Charlie Vars: Economics grad. GCC Executive Committee; GCC delegate to the FSM Executive Committee. Made visits to Governor Brown and Attorney General Moscowitz.

Theodore Vermeulen: Professor of chemical engineering; CCPA appointee.

Sherry Waldren: Worked in Kerr's office; intercepted letters from Kerr and Cunningham which were believed to indicate false dealings on the part of the administration.

James Walker: Psychology student; co-author of November 1961 SLATE pamphlet, *The Big Myth?*

Alice Waters: Scheer for Congress liaison.

Bob Weiman: GCC Executive Committee.

Jack Weinberg: Mississippi Summer Project (1964); chairman of Campus CORE; FSM tactician; Steering Committee. Activist-oriented; arrested and held in police car. Labeled a "nonstudent" by the administration and the press, he had graduated with a degree in mathematics the year before. In the early stages of the FSM, boyfriend of Suzanne Goldberg.

Max Weiss: Free speech carols.

Steve Weissman: SDS; GCC organizer and chairman; Regents' meeting representative. When Brian Shannon lost control of an FSM meeting, Weissman replaced him as FSM chairman, whence he became a late but highly influential member of the Steering Committee, particularly important in bringing grads to the FSM cause and as a liaison with faculty.

Tom Weller: Roommate of Jon Petrie, through whom he became involved with the *SLATE Supplement*. Press Central; loudspeaker detail; draft resister; roommate of David Goines.

Davy Wellman: President of the Sociology Club and GCC organizer.

Andy Wells: Executive Committee; co-organizer of the November 8 Steering Committee reorganization.

Jan Wenner: *SLATE Supplement* editorial staff; stringer for *Time*.

Burton White: HUAC protester; co-producer of "In Search of Truth," the rebuttal to *Operation Abolition*; chairman of BASCAHUAC. KPFA reporter constantly present at FSM activities.

Aaron Wildavsky: Political science student.

Arleigh Williams: Dean of men; chairman of the Committee on Campus Political Activity (the Williams Committee). Arleigh Williams graduated from Cal in 1935, where he had been an outstanding football halfback. He taught at Richmond

High and returned to Cal in 1957 as director of activities for the ASUC until his appointment in 1959 as dean of men. He succeeded Katherine Towle as dean of students when she retired in 1965.

Robley Williams: Professor of virology; CCPA appointee.

Ed Wilson: With Mario Savio, SNCC co-chair.

Bob Wolfson: CORE; United Front organizer; aggressive member of the October 2 negotiating team.

Sheldon Wolin: UC professor; member of the Two Hundred. With Seymour Martin Lipset, editor of *The Berkeley Student Revolt: Facts and Interpretations* (1965).

Joann Wyler: Berkeley Free Press bookkeeper.

Bob Wyman: GCC alternate representative to the FSM Executive Committee.

Maurice Zeitlin: SLATE; Fair Play for Cuba; co-founder of *Root and Branch*.

Reginald Zelnik: Acting assistant professor of history; member of the Two Hundred.

Janis Zimdars: FSM participant. Roommate Pam Mellin.

Nick Zvegintzov: Ford Fellow; business administration Ph.D. candidate; in early 1965 acting chairman of the GCC. Arrested in the Filthy Speech Movement.

The information about the Regents is from a pamphlet published by Marvin Garson in 1964, *The Regents*.

APPENDIX IV

CHRONOLOGY OF THE FREE SPEECH MOVEMENT WITHIN THE LARGER CONTEXT OF SURROUNDING HISTORICAL EVENTS

A short history of the twentieth century:

Aughts: Money
Teens: Fight
Twenties: Drink
Thirties: Starve
Forties: Fight
Fifties: Buy
Sixties: Dope
Seventies: Sex
Eighties: Money
Nineties: Crazy

1920: Roger Baldwin founds the ACLU.

Armistice Day, 1932: Students passing out antiwar leaflets at the Army-Navy game played in UC's Memorial Stadium are "rudely dispersed."

1933: Students selling the newspaper of the Social Problems Club are attacked outside Sather Gate with homemade tear-gas bombs. One student is hospitalized with burns.

April 1933: An antimilitarism rally at Sather Gate sponsored by the Social Problems Club is dispersed by the police.

1934: Against the wishes of UC president Gordon Sproul, the Social Problems Club conducts the straw poll which reveals that students are opposed to compulsory ROTC 2–1.

October 1934: Five UCLA students—one of them the president of the student body—are suspended for protesting involuntary ROTC.

November 5, 1934: A sympathy strike for the UCLA students is called at Sather Gate. Eggs and vegetables are thrown at the speakers. Senior fraternity men act as "undercover agents" to gather information for the American Legion on campus radicalism.

March 20, 1935: Eighteen students distributing leaflets for the Anti-War Week Committee are arrested for violating Berkeley's ordinance requiring a five-dollar permit for any group distributing pamphlets.

April 10, 1935: Charges against the pamphleteers are dropped and the ordinance changed.

April 12, 1935: One-quarter of the student body of UC Berkeley attends a one-hour Sather Gate rally against "War and Fascism."

1936: The ASUC sponsors a speech by Socialist Norman Thomas on the UC campus. Rule 11, requiring University presidential approval of off-campus speakers, appears two weeks later. Thenceforth, nonapproved speakers address crowds from outside Sather Gate.

1937: At a Harmon Gymnasium peace rally, 4,500 students unanimously approve resolutions against compulsory ROTC.

1937: Peace Strike planners suggest sending medical aid to Spain. Gordon Sproul announces Rule 17, which expands restrictions of Rule 11, forbidding fund-raising for off-campus groups.

1938: Martin Dies (D-Tex.) becomes the chairman of the newly formed House Un-American Activities Committee.

September 1, 1939: Germany invades Poland. World War II gets off the ground.

1940: The world population is 2.3 billion. The United States population is 132.2 million (5.3 percent of world population). California population is 6.9 million (5.2 percent of U.S. population).

April 22, 1941: A peace strike rally at UC Berkeley attracts 2,000 students.

April 24, 1941: A Sather Gate peace strike rally attracting 3,000 students will be the last campus protest of any significance until the loyalty oath controversy.

December 7, 1941: The United States enters World War II.

February 19, 1942: Executive Order 9066, signed by President Roosevelt, requires the incarceration of 120,000 people of Japanese ancestry.

June 12, 1942: UC Regents require all University employees to sign a California loyalty oath.

666

March 24, 1944: The spiritualist medium Mrs. Helen Duncan, together with two other women and one man, are charged with witchcraft—specifically, with taking money to raise the spirits of the dead—under the English Witchcraft Act of 1735. On April 4, they are found guilty and actually imprisoned, a prosecution which calls forth caustic comments from Prime Minister Winston Churchill. The Act is not completely repealed until April 21, 1951.

September 8, 1944: Remote-controlled supersonic V-2 rockets are directed at London and Antwerp from the German base in Peenemünde.

December 18, 1944: All Japanese relocation units are to be closed by the end of 1945.

1945: Women's suffrage becomes law in France.

1945: The Federal Communications Commission (FCC) allocates broadcast television frequencies. The four networks—the National Broadcasting Company (NBC), the Columbia Broadcasting System (CBS), the American Broadcasting Company (ABC) and the DuMont network—broadcast only a few hours weekdays and Sundays, and not at all on Saturdays. The slim fare soon includes shows like the "Gillette Cavalcade of Sports," "Small Fry" and "Kraft Television Theater."

1945: Marvin Camras develops magnetic recording tape, an offshoot of his 1938 wire recorder. In the process, he develops stereo recording, in which RCA is not the slightest bit interested.

1945: Karl von Frisch presents the theory of the honeybee's dance language.

January 1945: President Franklin Delano Roosevelt begins his fourth term of office.

January 25, 1945: Grand Rapids, Michigan, fluoridates its municipal water supply.

January 27, 1945: Soviet troops sweeping through Poland discover 5,000 prisoners in the Auschwitz concentration camp.

February 20, 1945: A minimum wage of 55 cents an hour is ordered for textile workers.

March 12, 1945: "In spite of everything I still believe that people are good at heart."

The fourteen-year-hold diarist Anne Frank dies in Bergen-Belsen concentration camp.

April 18, 1945: Bergen-Belsen concentration camp is liberated by the Allies.

May 2, 1945: Berlin falls to the Allies, and the "Peace" rose is named at the Pacific Rose Society in Pasadena.

May 8, 1945: War in the European theater comes to an end.

Mid-1945: German typography completes the transition from black letter to Roman serif and sans serif faces.

July 5, 1945: President Truman orders the Navy to take over Goodyear rubber plants in Akron, Ohio, to halt a strike.

July 10, 1945: In the coal, utility and dairy industries, 19,000 are on strike.

July 16, 1945: An atomic device, produced at Los Alamos, New Mexico, is exploded at Alamogordo, New Mexico.

July 28, 1945: Lost in the fog, a B-52 bomber crashes into the 78th and 79th floors of the Empire State Building, killing thirteen people.

July 31, 1945: The USS *Indianapolis* is sunk in combat after delivering the atomic bomb to the U.S. base on Tinian.

August 1945: After deposing the Japanese-installed Emperor Bao Dai, Ho Chi Minh proclaims the Democratic Republic of Vietnam, and restores universal suffrage.

August 6, 1945: Delivered by the superfortress *Enola Gay*, the twenty-kiloton uranium atomic bomb "Fat Man" destroys Hiroshima, a thriving city of 343,000. The explosion and ensuing fire kill 66,000 people immediately and injure 69,000. Including deaths from exposure to radiation, the eventual toll is 157,071.

August 9, 1945: The plutonium atomic bomb "Little Boy" detonates above Nagasaki, home to 250,000 people. An estimated 39,000 die instantly, 25,000 are injured and 40 percent of the city is damaged or destroyed.

August 14, 1945: Japan unconditionally surrenders.

August 18, 1945: Nationwide 35-mph speed limit is repealed.

September 2, 1945: World War II ends. American dead: 405,399.

September 5, 1945: H. Corvin Hinshaw and William H. Feldman of the Mayo

Clinic report the first successful use of streptomycin in treating tuberculosis in humans.

September 15, 1945: In Mittersill, Austria, the twelve-tone composer Anton Webern pays the ultimate price for his tobacco habit when, taking a break from his labors, he steps out on his balcony for a smoke; unable to understand the shouted command of an American soldier, he is shot dead for violation of curfew.

September 17, 1945: Strikes force the closing of Ford Motor plants. In Detroit, 77,000 workers are out of work due to strikes, and an additional 210,000 are jobless due to cancellation of war contracts. The strike ends on February 27, 1946, with a raise of 18 cents per hour.

October 1945: *Life* magazine reports that "A 'hot rod'. . . is an automobile stripped for speed and pepped up for power until it can travel 90 to 125 mph. Most hot rods are roadsters."

October 5, 1945: Transcontinental telephone service is disrupted for six hours in a demonstration of strength by Bell Telephone employees.

November 21, 1945: Nationwide strike shuts down General Motors plants; 180,000 workers out. The strike ends on March 13, 1946, with a pay raise of 18 cents an hour.

1946: In the U.S., the incidence of infectious syphilis cases peaks at 76 per 100,000.

1946: The Dutch painter Han van Meegeren is accused by the restored Dutch government of having sold pictures by Jan Vermeer to Goering during the war. In defense, he claims to have painted them himself, including a celebrated and expertly authenticated imitation of *The Supper at Emmaus* as well as a hitherto unsuspected forgery of Dirck van Baburen's *The Procuress*. Challenged, van Meegeren is able to prove himself the author of the whole group of pictures by painting a similar work while in prison.

1946: Joseph Stalin brutally disbands the Ukrainian Catholic Church.

1946: Dr. Benjamin Spock's *The Common Sense Book of Baby and Child Care* is published by Pocket Books.

1946: Tide detergent, the "New Washing Miracle" with "Oceans of Suds," is intro-

duced as a product that works even better than soap, particularly with the new synthetic fabrics.

1946: Women in Italy are ensured the right to vote.

1946: Truman creates the Atomic Energy Commission (AEC) to regulate the fledgling nuclear power industry.

1946: The experimental Stout 46 is the first car with a fiberglass body.

1946: Radio broadcaster Mel Allen travels with the Yankees to every game and does the first live broadcasts of away games. Until now, away games have been done by local sports announcers using the Western Union ticker and recreating as best they could the sounds and sights of the ballpark.

1946: UC Regents forbid students to engage in any unauthorized activity that conveys the impression that they represent the University. Postwar student enrollment triples.

January 1, 1946: Emperor Hirohito publicly denies his divinity. He is retained as a national symbol, but no longer has any political power.

January 10, 1946: United Nations assembly opens in London.

January 16, 1946: In Chicago, 200,000 packing plant workers go out on strike.

January 19, 1946: In Pittsburgh, 800,000 steel workers go out on strike. In addition, General Electric is on strike, taxi drivers in Washington, D.C., are on strike and coffin makers have walked off the job.

February 14, 1946: ENIAC (Electronic Numerical Integrator and Calculator), the first all-electronic computer, is created by J. Presper Eckert and John W. Maunchly after concepts developed between 1937 and 1942 by John Vincent Atanasoff. ENIAC is 100 feet long and 10 feet high and requires 18,000 vacuum tubes.

Spring 1946: A Bedouin shepherd boy, idly tossing stones along the cliffs of the Dead Sea, discovers the Qumran caves in which are preserved jars housing fragile leather scrolls. They are revealed to be an Essene copy of the Old Testament, dating from the first century BC.

March 20, 1946: The last War Relocation Center, at Tule Lake, California, closes. All incarcerated people of Japanese ancestry have been relocated to normal outside communities.

April 1, 1946: In Pittsburgh, 400,000 soft coal workers strike. The strike is resolved May 29 with a raise of $1.85 per day.

April 10, 1946: For the first time ever in Japan, women exercise the right to vote. Thirty-eight women are elected to the Diet.

April 17, 1946: Equipment under the trade name "Faximile" is first demonstrated publicly. The machine broadcasts printed matter over frequency modulation and a receiving set picks it up and prints it onto a roll of specially treated paper at a constant speed.

May 12, 1946: AT&T announces car radio-telephone service in St. Louis.

May 23, 1946: Despite government seizures, rail unions go out on strike. The U.S. lifts control of railroads on May 29.

June 3, 1946: The Supreme Court rules segregation in public transportation unconstitutional.

June 14, 1946: New York shipping is paralyzed as 200,000 dock workers go out on strike.

July 1, 1946: The U.S. begins peacetime testing of atomic devices by detonating a bomb on the Bikini atoll in the Marshall Islands.

July 5, 1946: In a fashion show at the Piscine Molitor, Paris, Louis Réard introduces the bikini, modeled by Micheline Bernardini. The explosive sexual impact of the scanty garment is thought equal to that of the atomic tests at the Bikini atoll.

July 7, 1946: Mother Frances Xavier Cabrini (1850–1917), founder of the order of the Sacred Heart, is made the first American saint.

September 6, 1946: Maritime strikes paralyze U.S. shipping on all coasts.

September 22, 1946: Secretary of State Henry A. Wallace is removed from office by President Truman for criticizing U.S. anti-Communism.

October 2, 1946: At a medical symposium at the University of Buffalo, Dr. William Rienkoff announces a possible link between cigarette smoking and cancer.

October 22, 1946: In Astoria, Queens, New York, the xerography process is invented by Chester F. Carlson.

November 21, 1946: Some 400,000 of John L. Lewis' United Mine Workers go out on strike. On December 4, Lewis is fined $10,000 and the UMW $3.5 million for contempt. Lewis calls off the strike on December 7, but on March 7, 1947, the Supreme Court upholds the fine. The next day, Lewis declares that "only a totalitarian regime can prevent strikes," and on March 31, calls another walkout in sympathy with miners killed in the Centralia explosion.

1947: Ground is broken for the original Levittown, a development of 17,500 houses in a former Long Island potato field. The four-and-a-half-room, two-bedroom, Cape Cod–style houses with unfinished attics are mass-produced in a reverse assembly-line process called "site fabrication." The houses cost $6,990. Suburbia comes into existence.

1947: The biggest single year of population growth in U.S. history, with births at 3.9 million, places the estimated 1947 population total at 143.4 million. Hello, baby boom. California has 9.8 million residents, a rise since 1940 of 42.1 percent. Hello, Sunshine State.

1947: The symbolism of pink for girls and blue for boys completes its evolution. At the beginning of the century, the convention was quite the opposite: "There has been a great diversity of opinion on the subject, but the generally accepted rule is pink for the boy and blue for the girl. The reason is that pink being a more decided and stronger color is more suitable for the boy; while blue, which is more delicate and dainty, is prettier for the girl" (*The Infants' Department*, June 1918).

1947: The stored computer program concept is invented by John von Neuman.

1947: Willard F. Libby et al. find Carbon 14 useful for dating of archaeological data.

1947: Kevin Tuohy develops and begins manufacture of corneal (contact) lenses, making them of clear plastic instead of glass.

1947: R. J. Reynolds Company, of Louisville, Kentucky, introduces aluminum foil.

1947: British designer Kenneth Wood markets the Robot Kenwood Chef, the first food processor.

1947: Thor Heyerdahl sails on the raft *Kon-Tiki* from Peru to Polynesia in 101 days to prove his theory of prehistoric migration.

1947: Grey whales are protected by international treaty. Right whales have been protected since 1935.

1947: One of the publishers who has depended on sales of comic books to kids via well-meaning adults is Max C. Gaines, who in 1933 invented the comic book medium, and whose *Picture Stories from the Bible* debuted in 1942. Gaines' company, Educational Comics, has tried a variety of "picture stories" without much success. In 1947, his son, William M. Gaines, inherits his father's firm, changing the name to Entertaining Comics (EC) and publishing a series of wild and grisly war comics (*Frontline Combat, Two-Fisted Tales*), crime comics (*Crime SuspenStories*), horror comics (*Witches' Cauldron, Tales from the Crypt*) and humor comics (*Mad*, in 1952), which are eagerly bought by kids rather than their parents.

February 1, 1947: Edwin H. Land invents the Polaroid Land Camera, which takes self-developing "instant" photographs.

March 22, 1947: With Executive Order 9835, President Truman announces a new security program to "search out any infiltration of disloyal persons" in federal posts. The House reports that nine alleged Communists have been fired from government jobs since July 1946. Between Truman's launching of this security program and December of 1952, 6.6 million people are investigated. Not a single case of espionage is discovered, though 500 people are dismissed for "questionable loyalty."

April 7, 1947: In a nationwide telephone strike, 350,000 walk out; 230,000 of the strikers are women.

April 11, 1947: Playing for the Brooklyn Dodgers, Jackie Robinson breaks the color barrier in major league baseball.

May 4, 1947: In a daring daylight attack, Zionist guerrillas blast their way through the walls of the prison fortress in Acre, Palestine, freeing 251 prisoners.

June 23, 1947: The U.S. Senate passes the Taft-Hartley Labor Act over a presidential veto, 68–25. The act will make unions liable for breach of contract damages in the wake of disputes; outlaw the closed shop; require a 60-day cooling-off period for strikes; grant the government an 80-day injunction against strikes that threaten the public safety; forbid political contributions from unions; and force labor leaders to take non-Communist oaths.

June 24, 1947: Kenneth Arnold of Boise, Idaho, makes the first reported sighting of a flying saucer near Mt. Rainier, Washington. Widespread faith in visitors from outer space is traceable to one man, pulp-magazine editor Ray Palmer. Palmer's 1940s publications *Amazing Stories* and *Fantastic Adventures* are the vehicle for the "true" stories of Richard Shaver, a Pennsylvanian plagued by a race of aliens called Deros. As thousands of readers begin writing in with their own testimonials about the Deros, circulation doubles and space invaders go big time.

June 28, 1947: The last trolley car in Manhattan, New York, is retired as the city completes its transition to diesel busses. By the end of World War I, about 25,000 miles of trolley track crisscrossed U.S. cities.

July 9, 1947: Colonel F. A. Blanchard becomes the first woman to be appointed a regular Army officer.

July 26, 1947: Congress authorizes legislation creating the Central Intelligence Agency (CIA), Allen Dulles, founding bureaucrat. The National Security Council is created by the National Security Act. The NSC is chaired by the president; members include the vice president and secretaries of state and defense. The chairman of the Joint Chiefs of Staff is the military adviser; the CIA director is the intelligence adviser. The NSC advises the president on integration of domestic, foreign and military policies relating to national security.

August 15, 1947: Britain grants independence to India and Pakistan.

August 20, 1947: Truman predicts that the U.S. will end the fiscal year with a $4.7 billion surplus.

September 12, 1947: An eight-day steel strike in Pittsburgh ends with a wage hike of 15 cents per hour.

September 30, 1947: The first televised World Series baseball game, New York

Yankees vs. Brooklyn Dodgers, is broadcast from New York City on the DuMont network to five cities. The game is sponsored by Gillette razors and an estimated 3 million people watch, mostly in taverns. America has an estimated total of 325,000 sets, one-half of which are in the New York area.

October 3, 1947: The 200-inch Mount Palomar telescope mirror is completed. First light is June 3, 1948, and the first photographic plate is exposed on November 13, 1949.

October 17, 1947: Flying the Bell X-1 rocket-powered aircraft *Glamorous Glennis*, Chuck Yeager breaks the sound barrier.

October 23, 1947: Actor Ronald Reagan, president of the Screen Actors Guild, testifies before the House Un-American Activities Committee that though the guild is not controlled by leftists, "There has been a small clique which has consistently opposed the politics of the guild board. . . . That small clique has been suspected of more or less following the tactics we associate with the Communist party." Actor Robert Taylor testifies against other stars, and HUAC declares that it will produce "at least 79" subversives in the coming days. Lauren Bacall, Humphrey Bogart, Danny Kaye and Gene Kelly arrive in Washington for an anti-HUAC protest.

November 25, 1947: The American Motion Picture Association votes to bar ten professionals who were held in contempt of the House Un-American Activities Committee. It furthermore resolves to refuse jobs to Communists.

1948: The word "teenager" enters common speech.

1948: The West Coast inventor Frank Morrison, capitalizing on the postwar fascination with UFOs, begins manufacturing "Morrison's Flyin' Saucer," the original plastic frisbee. The toy is named after the Frisbee Pie Company, founded in Bridgeport, Connecticut, in 1871. Yale College students in nearby New Haven had discovered in 1903 that the tins in which these pies were baked and shipped made excellent flying toys.

1948: Peter Goldmark of CBS invents the microgroove system of recording. The long-playing record, or LP, places 224–300 grooves per inch on a vinylite 10- or 12-inch disk. It plays at 33⅓ rpm, making possible 23 minutes of recorded music.

1948: Dr. Roy Plunkett's Teflon is introduced for industrial applications.

1948: DuPont chemist Earl Tupper introduces versatile polyethylene kitchen containers and a way to market them through home-sale parties. Tupperware sales top $25 million by 1954.

1948: Like every other human that has inhabited the planet, Swiss mountaineer George de Mestral notices that thistles and cockleburrs stick to his clothes. The difference is that Mestral goes on to invent Velcro. By the late 1950s, textile looms turn out 60 million yards of the nylon fastening material each year.

1948: Cadillac introduces the tail fin, a styling detail inspired by the P-38 fighter aircraft. This year's Cadillac is yours for only $2,833.

1948: The flying-wing bomber design is conceived by Northrop Corporation founder Jack Northrop; the design is scrapped by the government in favor of more conventional bomber designs. A contributing factor is the crash of the YB-49 prototype bomber, which kills Air Force test pilot Glen Edwards. The Mojave Desert Air Force base that now bears his name has become a focus of advanced flight testing research.

1948: George Gamow and Ralph Alpher's *The Origin of Chemical Elements* proposes the "Big Bang" theory of the origin of the universe.

1948: The term "Celsius" replaces "centigrade" in scientific terminology.

1948: Norbert Wiener's *Cybernetics* is published.

1948: A scientific basis is established for the use of dental floss: it discourages the formation of plaque and tartar, formerly thought to protect teeth from decay.

1948: Dow Chemical introduces latex paint.

1948: Cadillac offers the Hydra-Matic automatic transmission. Goodrich introduces tubeless tires; Daimler features electric windows.

1948: Americans buy 135 million paperback books.

January 1948: Dr. Alfred Charles Kinsey of the University of Indiana, world's foremost authority on the gall wasp, publishes *Sexual Behavior in the Human Male.*

January 12, 1948: In a unanimous decision, the Supreme Court orders the state of Oklahoma to admit 28-year-old Ada Lois Sipuel, a Negro woman, to the University of Oklahoma Law School. By law, the state could build a separate institution for her, but the Court observes that as sole student she would "not receive much of a law education."

January 30, 1948: Mohandas K. Gandhi is assassinated in New Delhi by a Hindu fanatic.

March 8, 1948: In response to a suit brought by the atheist Madalyn Murray O'Hair, the Supreme Court rules religious instruction in public schools unconstitutional.

March 15, 1948: Two hundred thousand miners strike for better pensions.

March 28, 1948: Composer Dmitri Shostakovich is forced to give up his chair at the Moscow Conservatory of Music.

March 29, 1948: The U.S. Supreme Court voids a New York state law barring sale of books of lust, crime and bloodshed.

April 1, 1948: The United States starts flying supplies to Berlin to thwart a Soviet attempt to squeeze the Allies out.

April 7, 1948: In New York, the United Nations' World Health Organization (WHO) begins work.

April 22, 1948: The Zionist Haganah seizes the port of Haifa; Arabs agree to evacuate.

May 14, 1948: The Free State of Israel is proclaimed in Tel Aviv as British troops evacuate Palestine.

May 28, 1948: A seventeen-day strike against Chrysler Corporation ends with wage increase of 13 cents per hour, raising the base pay to $1.63 per hour.

June 20, 1948: The "Ed Sullivan Show" makes its TV debut.

June 24, 1948: President Truman signs into law an act requiring men aged 19 through 25 to register for the military draft.

June 30, 1948: John Bardeen, William Shockley and Walter Brittan announce their invention of the transistor.

July 7, 1948: Putting on a major league uniform for the first time in his 23-year baseball career, Negro League legend Satchel Paige signs to pitch for the Cleveland Indians. During the summer, he treats 48,000 Cleveland fans to his famous "hesitation pitch," the legality of which is hotly debated.

July 26, 1948: The U.S. military is officially desegregated as President Truman signs Executive Order 9981, requiring "equality of treatment and opportunity for all persons in the armed services without regard to race, color, religion or national origin." The order is to be executed "as rapidly as possible."

August 3, 1948: Whittaker Chambers tells HUAC of a Red "underground" in federal posts, implicating former State Department official Alger Hiss.

September 22, 1948: Truman denounces spy inquiries in Congress, accusing HUAC of being more un-American than those it investigates.

September 30, 1948: HUAC urges the ousting of Attorney General Tom Clark if he fails to prosecute alleged spies.

October 1948: HUAC implicates Charlie Chaplin.

October 24, 1948: Bernard Baruch tells a Senate committee, "We are in a cold war which is getting warmer."

November 1948: After 48 dry years, Kansas repeals Prohibition.

1949: Simone de Beauvoir's *The Second Sex* is published.

1949: Nash Motors installs seat belts in 40,000 of its 1949 models. Citing consumer resistance, the company discontinues the experiment in the next model year.

1949: Chrysler's key-turn starter replaces the starting button.

1949: Volkswagen exports Dr. Porsche's 1939 Beetle to the U.S.

1949: Beer is sold in cans.

1949: Murphy's Law, commonly quoted as "If it can go wrong, it will," is formulated by Captain Edward A. Murphy at Edwards Air Force Base. The original quote and its source are not discovered until January 13, 1977, when Jack Smith, a columnist with the *Los Angeles Times*, reveals that he has gotten a letter from

George E. Nichols of the Jet Propulsion Laboratory in Pasadena, stating that Nichols knows not only the origin of the law but the true identity of Murphy. According to the Nichols letter, "The event that led to the naming of the law occurred in 1949 at Edwards Air Force Base . . . during Air Force Project MX981. . . . The law was named after Captain Ed Murphy, a development engineer from Wright Field (Ohio) Aircraft Lab. Frustration with a strap transducer that was malfunctioning due to an error in wiring the strain gauge bridges caused him to remark [of the technician who had wired the bridges at the lab], 'If there is any way to do it wrong, he will.' I assigned the name Murphy's Law to that statement and the associated variations."

1949: The FCC repents its generosity, deciding that television is hogging too much of the broadcast spectrum (each TV channel requires a bandwidth 600 times wider than an individual radio station), and reassigns the original Channel One band (44 to 50 MHz) for use by people with mobile radios.

1949: Neptune's moon Nereid is discovered.

1949: George Orwell's bleak vision of a totalitarian future, *1984*, is published. He began writing the book in 1948, reversing the last two digits to set the time of the book's title.

1949: The apartheid program is established in South Africa.

January 10, 1949: RCA-Victor introduces the seven-inch 45 rpm record.

Spring 1949: Advertisements in the *New York Times* push baseball as the reason to buy a set: "Batter Up! Imperial offers you a Box Seat. RCA Victor Television. $375. Installation and home owner policy $55. 52-square-inch screen." The GE set—"So Bright! So Clear! So Easy on the Eyes!"—is $725.

March 2, 1949: A B-50 bomber, *Lucky Lady II*, flies nonstop around the world. The flight takes 94 hours, 1 minute, and involves four midair refuelings. This demonstrates that the United States can drop an atomic bomb anywhere, anytime, on anybody.

March 25, 1949: UC Regents decide unanimously that, effective June 24, all faculty and employees must sign an anti-Communist oath in addition to the oath of constitutional loyalty required of all state employees.

April 1949: A Chicago federal jury convicts General Motors of conspiring with Standard Oil and Firestone to replace electric transportation with busses and to monopolize sale of busses. GM is fined $5,000.

April 6, 1949: Truman says that he won't hesitate to use the A-bomb again, if necessary.

April 15, 1949, 3:00 PM: Berkeley's listener-supported radio station KPFA, 94.1 megacycles, broadcasts the first of its non-commercially funded programs.

April 16, 1949: American and British planes start arriving on an average of one every 61.8 seconds to bring 13,000 tons of supplies every day to blockaded Berlin. By the end of September, there have been 277,264 flights into Berlin.

April 17, 1949: The Republic of Ireland gains its independence from Great Britain. The six northern counties remain British.

May 1949: The V-8 engine design, creation of a General Motors group headed by Charles "Boss" Kettering, makes its appearance in the Oldsmobile 88 and Cadillac.

May 12, 1949: Soviets lift the Berlin blockade. An exodus of East Berliners turns from a trickle to a flood, and by the year's end, over 125,000 have sneaked across city lines.

June 23, 1949: The first woman graduates from Harvard Medical School.

August 1949: Led by Edward C. Tolman, 157 UC employees refuse to sign the anti-Communist loyalty oath. By July 1950, all but 36 will have signed.

August 25, 1949: In New York, RCA announces the invention of a system for broadcasting color television.

September 3, 1949: Australian John Cade publishes results of the first clinical trials of lithium on mental patients.

September 23, 1949: The Russians demonstrate that they have the atomic bomb.

October 1, 1949: The People's Republic

of China is formally proclaimed, and Mao Tse-tung is elected chairman.

October 1, 1949: Pittsburgh Steel strike begins; 500,000 walk off the job.

October 7, 1949: Mrs. Iva Toguri D'Aquino, a.k.a. "Tokyo Rose" of Japanese wartime broadcast notoriety, is sentenced in San Francisco to a $10,000 fine and seven to ten years in prison for treason. She is paroled in 1956.

October 9, 1949: Harvard Law School begins admitting women.

October 12, 1949: Eugenie Anderson gets a post in Denmark as the first U.S. woman ambassador.

October 14, 1949: Eleven leaders of the U.S. Communist party are convicted, after a nine-month trial in New York City, of advocating violent overthrow of the U.S. government. On October 21, federal judge Harold R. Medina sentences ten Communist defendants to five years in prison each, and the eleventh, a war veteran, to three years. The Supreme Court upholds the convictions on June 4, 1951. Seven surrender July 2, 1951; of the other four, hunted as fugitives, one, Gus Hall, is captured October 8, 1951, and given three additional years. Robert G. Thompson is captured August 27, 1953. Five defense lawyers, cited for contempt during the trial, receive sentences ranging from one to six months on April 24, 1952.

October 17, 1949: Northwest Airlines becomes the first in the U.S. to serve alcoholic beverages in flight.

December 21, 1949: New York's Museum of Modern Art shows 200 works by Paul Klee.

December 26, 1949: Albert Einstein publishes his new "generalized theory of gravitation." Just as the theory of relativity united space, time, matter and energy in one all-encompassing theory, the unified field theory attempts to unite gravitation and electromagnetism in one set of equations.

"Things are more like they are now than they ever were before."
—Dwight David Eisenhower

1950: World population is 2.5 billion (an increase of 10.9 percent over 1940). United States population is 151.3 million (an increase of 13 percent over 1940 and 6.2 percent of world population). California population is 10.5 million (an increase of 42 percent over 1940 and 6.9 percent of U.S. population). U.S. literacy rate is 96.8 percent.

1950: Americans buy 330 Volkswagens.

1950: Cadillac places tenth and eleventh in the 24-hour Le Mans auto race.

1950: The 100-inch-wheelbase, 2,576-pound Nash Rambler is the first modern compact car to sell in high volume: about 58,000 units.

1950: There are 1.5 million TV sets in the U.S.

1950: Of Negro women aged 15 to 44, 70 percent live with a husband.

1950: The Northgate Shopping Center, the nation's first shopping mall, opens in a suburb of Seattle, Washington.

1950: Arnold Neustadter invents the indispensable office tool: the Rolodex rotary file.

1950: Embarrassed at having insufficient money to pay a dinner bill, Francis Xavier McNamara invents the Diner's Club multipurpose credit card.

1950: "We are sworn that no boy or girl, approaching the maelstrom of deviation, need make that crossing alone, afraid, or in the dark ever again." The Mattachine Society, founded in 1950 in Los Angeles (1953 in San Francisco), is the first successful homosexual organization in the U.S.

January 14, 1950: The United States recalls all consular officials from Communist China after the American consulate general is seized in Peking.

January 17, 1950: Masked bandits rob Brinks' Boston express office of $2,775,395.12.

January 25, 1950: Alger Hiss is convicted and sentenced to five years in prison for perjury in denying that he had passed top government secrets to Whittaker Chambers, a onetime agent for the Communists.

February 5, 1950: A month-old soft coal strike spreads to 400,000 miners in six states.

February 7, 1950: In Wheeling, West Virginia, Senator Joe McCarthy (R-Wis.) tells the Republican Women's Club, "While I cannot take the time to name all of the men in the State Department who have been named as members of the Communist party and members of a spy ring, I have here in my hand a list of 205 that were known to the Secretary of State as being members of the Communist party, and who nevertheless are still working and shaping the policy of the State Department." He offers no further proof and shows no one the list.

February 8, 1950: In Salt Lake City, Utah, Senator Joseph McCarthy claims he has a list of 57 Communists working in the State Department.

February 28, 1950: The French Assembly curbs sales of Coca-Cola.

March 1950: The Cadillac four-door sedan offers a curved, one-piece windshield.

March 5, 1950: Children are reported to spend 27 hours a week watching TV—as much time as they spend in school.

March 15, 1950: Stalin and Mao sign a mutual defense treaty.

March 17, 1950: The heaviest known element, californium, is discovered at the University of California, Berkeley.

March 26, 1950: McCarthy names ex–State Department adviser Owen Lattimore as a Soviet spy.

March 30, 1950: Truman denounces Senator Joseph McCarthy as a saboteur of U.S. foreign policy.

April 10, 1950: In San Francisco, Harry Bridges is given a sentence of five years for concealing his Communist affiliation at his naturalization hearing.

May 12, 1950: The American Bowling Congress ends its 34-year-old rule that limits membership to white males.

May 25, 1950: In New York, the Brooklyn-Battery Tunnel, the longest in the United States, is opened.

June 17, 1950: In Chicago, Richard G. Laoler performs the first human kidney transplant.

June 25, 1950: North Korean Communist forces invade South Korea. The United Nations' Korean police action begins.

June 30, 1950: U.S. forces arrive in Korea.

July 1, 1950: Japan is allowed to return to its own currency and regain control of its economic affairs.

August 1950: Thirty-six nonsigners of the UC loyalty oath are fired.

August 1, 1950: Guam becomes a U.S. territory.

August 12, 1950: A 438-page guide on civilian defense against atomic bomb attack is released by the Department of Defense and the Atomic Energy Commission. Among other things, citizens are warned not to beget offspring for two or three months following exposure to atomic radiation so as not to pass on chromosomal aberrations.

September 23, 1950: Overriding Truman's veto, Congress passes the Mundt Bill, which requires Communist organizations to identify their officers and to prove how they spend funds. The president says that this is like trying to get thieves to register with the sheriff.

October 1950: In an article entitled "Computing Machinery and Intelligence," appearing in the publication *Mind*, British mathematician and founding father of Artificial Intelligence (AI), Alan M. Turing (1912–1954), develops the Turing test, the first and indeed last word on the subject: if a computer can perform in such a way that an expert cannot distinguish its performance from that of a human who has a given cognitive ability, then the computer also has that ability. Expressed colloquially: if it looks like a duck, and walks like a duck, and quacks like a duck, then it's a duck.

November 1, 1950: Assassination attempt on President Truman by Puerto Rican nationalists.

November 2, 1950: Playwright and philosopher George Bernard Shaw dies, providing in his will that the income from his estate be used for 21 years on the design and dissemination of a new alphabet for the English language, to be based on "Oxford" or "BBC" pronunciation. The heirs compromise on £8,300 to be set aside for the alphabet and for the publication, using it, of Shaw's play *Androcles and the Lion*.

November 18, 1950: Roman Catholic bishops protest sex education in public schools.

December 1, 1950: There are 2,200 drive-in movie theaters in the U.S., twice as many as last year.

1951: "Disc jockey Alan Freed began calling his Cleveland radio show 'Moondog's

Rock and Roll Dance Party.' The music that Freed played is known in the record business as rhythm and blues, or R&B, a term devised in 1949 to refer to music made and consumed primarily by Black Americans. R&B had been thriving for years, though most white adults seemed all but unaware of it, content with the pop music mainstream represented by the major labels Columbia, Decca, RCA and Mercury.

"Freed's audience was young and, more important, racially mixed. For white teenagers, R&B was new, fascinating and illicit. The fact that their parents were somewhat threatened by this music only added to its appeal. By 1954, Freed's show had helped transform the sexual colloquialism 'rock 'n' roll' into a ubiquitous musical noun and, thus, to grant R&B an aura of acceptability." (Liner notes to *Roots of Rock, 1945–1956*, Time-Life, 1992.)

Jackie Brenston's "Rocket 88," by the Delta Kings, launches the Sun Recording Co., Memphis, and is considered by some the first recorded rock 'n' roll song. Or maybe the first is "It's Too Soon to Know," by the Orioles (It's a Natural Recording Co., Baltimore).

1951: The first exhibit of Abstract Expressionist art is held in an East Ninth Street gallery in Manhattan; featured are works by Jackson Pollock, Mark Rothko and William de Kooning, *inter alia*.

1951: British film censors introduce the "X certificate" classification for movies deemed unsuitable for minors.

1951: The maximum monthly Social Security payment is about $30. There are approximately 40 workers for each recipient of Social Security benefits.

1951: In *Dennis v United States*, at the height of the postwar "Red Scare," the Supreme Court upholds the conviction of eleven American Communist leaders under the Smith Act of 1940, which made it a crime to belong to organizations teaching or advocating the violent overthrow of the government. The "clear and present danger" doctrine can be disregarded, the Court holds, "if the gravity of the 'evil,' discounted by its improbability, justifies such invasion of free speech as is necessary to avoid the evil." Over 100 Communists

are indicted as a result, effectively destroying the Communist Party of the United States of America as a political force.

1951: Ford Motor Company adopts the automatic transmission.

1951: In response to a classroom assignment, David A. Huffman develops the data compression scheme known as Huffman encoding, which finds the most efficient method of representing numbers, letters or other symbols using a binary code.

January 1951: Chrysler Corporation launches the hydraulic fluid and piston device, power steering, that puts forth 65 percent of the muscle needed to steer its big cars. It costs $184.20 extra. The device was invented by Francis W. Davis over a 25-year period.

February 26, 1951: The Twenty-second Amendment is added to the Constitution, limiting the president to two terms of office.

March 29, 1951: Julius Rosenberg, his wife, Ethel, and Morton Sobell are found guilty of conspiracy to commit wartime espionage; specifically, the communication of atomic secrets to the Russians. The Rosenbergs are sentenced to death, and Sobell to thirty years. Appeals are denied. David Greenglass, brother of Ethel and a state witness, receives fifteen years in prison.

April 11, 1951: Modigliani show opens in New York's Museum of Modern Art.

May 2, 1951: The Radio Corporation of America broadcasts color television programs from the top of the Empire State Building. Unlike color programs from the competing CBS system, which require special converters, the RCA pictures are received by black-and-white sets in the New York area. There are 15 million TV sets in the U.S.

May 23, 1951: One month after students in Farmville, Virginia, have walked out of segregated R. R. Moton High School, demanding better Negro schools, NAACP attorneys file suit for completely integrated schools. Consolidated with four similar suits, it reaches the U.S. Supreme Court as part of *Brown v Board of Education of Topeka*.

July 9, 1951: Dashiell Hammett receives a

six-month jail sentence for withholding names of contributors to the Communist-leader bail-bond fund.

September 4, 1951: Transcontinental television is inaugurated with President Truman's address at the Japanese Peace Treaty Conference in San Francisco.

November 10, 1951: Coast-to-coast direct dial telephone service, without the assistance of an operator, becomes available.

December 4–14, 1951: The worst air pollution ever recorded, a London miasma of coal fumes combined with dense fog, kills between 3,000 and 4,000 people.

1952: "What is good for the country is good for General Motors, and what is good for General Motors is good for the country." Charles E. Wilson, to the Senate Armed Forces Committee.

1952: In a letter to HUAC summarizing her position on the hearings, Lillian Hellman states, "To hurt innocent people whom I knew many years ago in order to save myself is, to me, inhuman and indecent and dishonorable. I cannot and will not cut my conscience to suit this year's fashions."

1952: General Motors introduces the four-barrel carburetor in the Cadillac and Oldsmobile.

1952: Power steering appears on regular-production autos.

1952: The Radar Range, the world's first microwave oven, is introduced by Dr. Perry Spencer, an engineer at Raytheon.

1952: "Bandstand," hosted by Bob Horn, later "American Bandstand" (1956), hosted by Dick Clark, debuts on WFIL-TV in Philadelphia.

1952: UC President Gordon Sproul creates the position of chancellor, and appoints professor of industrial relations Clark Kerr to the post.

1952: Citing the wartime emergency of the Korean police action, President Truman seizes steel plants to keep them operating despite a strike. In *Youngstown Sheet and Tube Co.* v *Sawyer*, the Supreme Court holds that his action is an unconstitutional usurpation of executive authority. Only an act of Congress, not the president's inherent executive powers or military powers as commander in chief, can justify such a sizable confiscation of property, despite the wartime emergency.

February 29, 1952: New York City puts up four "Walk/Don't Walk" signs in Times Square. The city also installs three-color traffic lights, with amber signals between the green and red, to help reduce accidents.

April 3, 1952: British mathematician Alan M. Turing is tried and convicted of "gross indecency with a male person" and is put on probation on the condition that he "submit for treatment by a duly qualified medical practitioner at Manchester Royal Academy." The "treatment" is, essentially, to be a medical experiment calculated to cure him of the disorder of homosexuality. The regimen, a series of injections of the female hormone estrogen, lasts for one year, renders him impotent and causes him to grow pronounced breasts.

April 15, 1952: The Franklin National Bank, New York, issues a bank credit card.

April 22, 1952: One million Americans view a televised Nevada A-bomb test.

April 30, 1952: Despite a ruling restoring mills to government control, 600,000 steel workers walk off the job.

May 2, 1952: First jetliner passenger service opens with a British DeHavilland Comet flying from London to Johannesburg.

May 29, 1952: Greece, the birthplace of democracy, grants the vote to women.

May 30, 1952: The Vatican bans André Gide.

July 10, 1952: Michael Ventris announces that he has successfully deciphered Linear B inscriptions from Crete. The script is a form of Greek.

July 14, 1952: General Motors announces an optional air-conditioning unit for 1953 models.

July 21, 1952: California has its second greatest recorded earthquake, rocking 100,000 square miles and killing eleven.

August 19, 1952: In New York, the United Nations drafts a convention on women's rights.

August 30, 1952: Although there is some reason to believe that the Carl Zeiss Optical Company built and patented the geodesic dome in Germany during the 1920s, R. Buckminster Fuller patents the assemblage of triangular trusses that grows stronger as it grows larger; in the wake of his invention, thousands of domes spring up all over the world.

October 3, 1952: First video recording on magnetic tape.

October 17, 1952: The California Supreme Court rules that UC employees cannot be required to sign an anti-Communist loyalty oath. In November UC offers nonsigners their jobs back, but not their back pay.

October 20, 1952: Soft coal mines are struck to protest a U.S. order cutting 40 cents from a $1.90-per-day pay raise.

October 23, 1952: New York City dismisses eight teachers for alleged Communist activities.

November 13, 1952: Harvard's Paul Zoll is the first to use electric shock to treat cardiac arrest.

November 21, 1952: The U.S. Bureau of Engraving and Printing issues the first two-color postage stamp. The stamp is printed by the rotary gravure process.

November 25, 1952: *The Mousetrap,* a play by Agatha Christie, opens in the Ambassadors Theatre (capacity 433), London.

Mid-December 1952: After fourteen years of searching the western Indian Ocean for a second specimen of *Latimeria chalumnae,* the not-so-missing link between the extinct lobe-finned fishes and other vertebrates, British ichthyologist James Leonard Brierly Smith is notified by Captain Eric Hunt that Ahmed Hussein, a fisherman from the island of Anjouan, has caught one and he had better come and get his coelacanth before the French grab it. Subsequently, coelacanths are taken in plenty from the Comores archipelago, which is apparently the home of this notable fish.

December 15, 1952: Twenty-six-year-old Christine Jorgenson, *née* George Jorgenson, emerges as a woman after a stay in a Copenhagen hospital, two thousand hormone injections and six surgical operations.

1953: Mazel discovers Cave Cougnac, near Gourdon, France, containing prehistoric paintings.

1953: W. LeGross Clark proves the Piltdown Man to have been a hoax.

1953: The National Weather Service begins using women's names to identify hurricanes in the Atlantic. Hurricanes and typhoons in the eastern North Pacific are also identified by women's names.

1953: Michelin introduces the radial tire.

January 3, 1953: Samuel Beckett's *Waiting for Godot* makes its Paris debut.

February 1, 1953: Storms and high tides breach Holland's dikes, leading to widespread destruction and at least 1,500 deaths.

March 26, 1953: The Mau-Mau, or "Hidden Ones," of Kenya's Kikuyu tribe, form to force the small number of land-controlling Britons from Kenya and to regain ancestral lands from the government. The rebellion climaxes in sporadic violence, with the murder of 71 and wounding of 100 fellow Kikuyus who have remained loyal to the colonial government.

April 1953: *TV Guide* makes its debut.

April 8, 1953: Jomo Kenyatta, tribal leader of the Kikuyu, is found guilty of organizing the Mau-Mau rebellion.

April 12, 1953: Dr. Jonas Salk announces that a cure for poliomyelitis has been found.

April 25, 1953: The double-helix nature of deoxyribonucleic acid (DNA) is discovered by F. H. Crick and James D. Watson.

May 1953: In Pittsburgh, Pennsylvania, Dr. Jonas Salk inoculates a test group of 700 children against polio. In the spring of 1954, more than a million children are inoculated in a larger field trial financed by the March of Dimes. Within the next half-dozen years, the Salk vaccine reduces the incidence of polio in the U.S. by 95 percent.

May 1953: Hollywood introduces 3-D movies. Titles include *House of Wax* and *Bwana Devils.*

May 29, 1953, 11:30 AM: Edmund Percival Hillary and Tenzing Norgay reach the 29,002-foot peak of Mount Everest.

June 19, 1953: Ethel and Julius Rosenberg are executed at Sing-Sing prison, Ossining, New York.

June 21, 1953: Martial law is declared in

East Berlin as citizens strike and riot in protest against Soviet work quotas.

July 26, 1953: Korean armistice signed. American dead: 33,746.

October 1953: Hugh M. Hefner produces the first issue of *Playboy* magazine, featuring Marilyn Monroe in the altogether. The magazine is a significant departure from other girlie publications, emphasizing writing by well-known authors, a coherent social philosophy, plenty of cheerful, friendly, wholesome, and above all, *busty* "girl next door" models, and a full-color centerfold "Playmate of the Month." The magazine's symbol is a rabbit.

November 3, 1953: First coast-to-coast color television broadcast.

December 3, 1953: University of Iowa researchers announce that they have achieved the first human pregnancy using deep-frozen sperm.

December 12, 1953: Jomo Kenyatta is sentenced to seven years in prison for his role in Kenya's 1953 Mau-Mau rebellion.

1954: The official use of torture, characterized by Jean-Paul Sartre as the "plague of the twentieth century," appears among liberal democratic states with France's Fourth Republic's suppression of the Algerian revolt.

1954: Dr. Alfred Charles Kinsey, of the University of Indiana, publishes the companion volume to his 1948 book about what makes men tick with his *Sexual Behavior in the Human Female*.

1954: Known chemical elements at the time of Christ: 9; around AD 1500, 12; around 1900, 84; in 1954, 100.

1954: The U.S. has 6 percent of the world's population, 60 percent of the automobiles, 58 percent of the telephones, 45 percent of the radio sets and 34 percent of the railroads.

1954: U.S. newspapers number 1,798, publishing 59 million copies daily.

1954: The Swiss designer Adrian Frutiger, working in Paris at the Deberny & Peignot foundry, creates the visually programmed library of 21 sans serif fonts named *Univers*. All 21 fonts have the same *x*-height and ascender and descender lengths, and the size and weight of the uppercase is close to that of the lowercase.

1954: A method of phototypesetting, developed during the war by two telephone engineers, E. K. Hunter and J. R. C. August, is exhibited as the "Lumitype Machine" in Paris, and in the U.S. as the "Photon."

1954: TV dinner introduced by Swanson. The first dinner is turkey with dressing, mashed potatoes and peas.

1954: Psychiatrist Frederic Wertham condemns comic books in *Seduction of the Innocent*; the Comics Code Authority is instituted.

1954: "Sh-Boom," by the Chords, ushers in the rock 'n' roll era.

1954: "Under God" is added to the Pledge of Allegiance.

1954: A measles vaccine is developed by Enders and Peebles.

1954: Forty-five rpm "doughnut disks" outsell seventy-eights.

1954: Using Arthur Korn's turn-of-the-century observation that certain compounds under certain conditions give off electrons when struck by light, scientists at Bell Laboratories produce a solar cell.

January 8, 1954: To celebrate his nineteenth birthday, Elvis Presley brings his guitar to a Memphis studio and pays $4 to make his own recordings of "Casual Love" and "I'll Never Stand in Your Way."

January 21, 1954: The *Nautilus*, the first atomic-powered submarine, is launched at Groton, Connecticut.

February 15, 1954: A French bathyscaphe descends to 13,284 feet in the Atlantic.

March 1, 1954: The hydrogen bomb exploded by the United States today at its mid-Pacific proving grounds is believed to be 600 times more powerful than the one dropped on Hiroshima, which released the equivalent of 20,000 tons of TNT.

March 1, 1954: Five U.S. congressmen are wounded when Puerto Rican terrorists open fire in the House chamber.

March 12, 1954: Declaring "We are not a nation of fearful men," newsman Edward R. Murrow takes on Senator Joseph McCarthy via CBS television.

March 13, 1954: The Atomic Energy

Commission (AEC) awards a Pittsburgh contract for the first nuclear power plant, designed to produce 60,000 kilowatts.

March 31, 1954: Leica, the originator of the 35mm camera, introduces a new 35mm rangefinder that offers a number of unique features: single-window range and viewfinder; bayonet thread lock allowing a quick change of lenses; a lever instead of a knob for advancing the film; shutter speeds of 1/10 second to 1/1000 of a second; and an optional built-in exposure meter.

April 1, 1954: Westinghouse Electric Corporation, the only company with a color TV actually on the market, reduces the suggested retail price of its 12-inch color TV sets from $1,295 to $1,100. So far 30 sets have been sold.

April 18, 1954: U.S. oil companies introduce premium-grade gas, hailed as the greatest gasoline innovation since tetraethyl lead in the 1920s.

April 22–June 17, 1954: Senator Joseph R. McCarthy leads televised investigations into what he maintains is Communist influence in the U.S. Army.

May 6, 1954: In Oxford, England, Roger Bannister runs one mile in 3 minutes, 59.4 seconds.

May 7, 1954: Dien Bien Phu, a French military outpost in northwest Vietnam, falls to Ho Chi Minh's Vietminh army.

May 13, 1954: Ike authorizes construction of the Saint Lawrence Seaway between Montreal and Lake Erie.

May 17, 1954: The Supreme Court, in *Brown* v *Board of Education of Topeka*, unanimously bans racial segregation in public schools as a violation of the Fourteenth Amendment clause guaranteeing equal protection of the law. The "separate but equal" doctrine of *Plessy* v *Ferguson* (1896), already limited in a series of cases dating back to *Missouri ex rel Gaines* v *Canada* (1938), is overruled. "Separate educational facilities are inherently unequal," the Court holds. As a result of this decision, the white authorities in Farmville, Prince Edward County, Virginia, close the entire public school system for five years rather than compromise the practice of racial segregation.

May 24, 1954: International Business Ma-

chines (IBM) announces that it will lease "electronic brains" specifically designed for business use. The system consists of a central arithmetical and logic unit that processes data from a bank of cathode-ray memory tubes. Information is fed to the machine from reels of magnetic tape, each capable of storing all the numbers in the Manhattan telephone directory. Thirty of the devices have already been ordered. The typical installation will cost $25,000 per month.

June 7, 1954: Alan M. Turing kills himself by eating an apple dipped in cyanide.

June 14, 1954: Americans take part in a nationwide civil defense test in preparation for possible atomic attack.

July 12, 1954: Ike proposes an interstate highway system for general use and for national defense in the event of atomic war.

July 14, 1954: Princeton University makes a computer available for rental by private industry.

July 31, 1954: A six-year research program reveals that the eye-burning smog (smoke plus fog) that afflicts the Los Angeles area is caused by the chemical action of sunlight on auto exhaust fumes and industrial emissions, producing ozone. The origin of the destructive pollutant has been a mystery until now.

August 17, 1954: The pope allows U.S. clergy to deliver the sacraments in English.

August 27, 1954: Two U.S. icebreakers complete the first trip through the Northwest Passage, Atlantic to Pacific.

September 17, 1954: India outlaws bigamy.

October 1954: James Dean stars in *Rebel Without a Cause*, directed by Nicholas Ray. Dean, killed in an auto accident on September 30, 1955 (the day after his film *Giant* is finished), becomes the symbol of alienated American youth.

October 7, 1954: In Poughkeepsie, IBM displays an all-transistor calculator needing only 5 percent of the power of comparable vacuum tube devices.

October 11, 1954: The U.S. Civil Service has fired 2,600 since August under the Communist Control Act.

October 21, 1954: President Eisenhower offers South Vietnam economic aid.

Late fall 1954: Bill Haley and the Comets' "Shake, Rattle and Roll" makes the charts.

December 2, 1954: The U.S. Senate votes 67–22 to condemn Senator Joseph McCarthy for contempt of a Senate elections subcommittee, abuse of its members and insults to the Senate during its investigations of charges against him brought by the Department of the Army growing out of his investigation of alleged subversive activities.

December 16, 1954: The television industry announces that its profits exceed those of radio.

1955: Ultra High Frequency (UHF) waves are produced.

1955: Clair Patterson and his colleagues at the California Institute of Technology determine the age of the solar system (4.5 billion years) by dating meteorites.

1955: Franz Kafka's *The Trial* is published.

1955: New York artists Jasper Johns, Robert Rauschenberg and others pioneer Pop art.

1955: Birth-control pioneers Margaret Sanger and Katherine Dexter McCormick commission the development of an effective birth control pill.

1955: In Ocean Beach, California, surfer and beach bum Jack O'Neill invents the wet suit.

1955: In Chicago, Ray A. Kroc opens his first hamburger stand.

1955: Congress authorizes the use of the phrase "In God We Trust" on money.

1955–1958: The incidence of reported syphilis cases reaches a low of 4 per 100,000.

January 5, 1955: DuPont introduces "Fantastique," a tricot knit fabric made of polyester yarn. Dacron garments are easily laundered, fast-drying, wrinkle-resistant and require no ironing.

January 31, 1955: In New York, RCA demonstrates its music synthesizer.

February 12, 1955: President Eisenhower agrees to send military advisers to train the South Vietnamese army.

June 11, 1955: Eighty die at Le Mans racetrack when a three-car crash sends a fiery Mercedes racer into the grandstand. In consequence, Mercedes retires from auto racing.

July 11, 1955: U.S. Air Force Academy opens.

July 13, 1955: Ruth Ellis, sentenced to death for the murder of her unfaithful lover, is the last woman in England to die by hanging.

July 18, 1955: The 160-acre Disneyland amusement park opens in Anaheim, California.

August 12, 1955: Minimum wage is increased to $1 per hour.

October 1955: Named after the poem "Songs of Bilitis" by Pierre de Louys, the lesbian organization Daughters of Bilitis is founded in San Francisco.

October 4, 1955: In Atlanta, Georgia, Bell Telephone uses the light of the sun to power a telephone call.

November 19, 1955: British academic C. Northcote Parkinson, writing for *The Economist*, elucidates the principle that "work expands so as to fill the time available for its completion." Its two axioms are "An official wants to multiply subordinates, not rivals," and "Officials make work for each other." Parkinson's Second Law is "Expenditure rises to meet income." Parkinson's Third Law is "Expansion means complexity and complexity, decay; or to put it even more plainly—the more complex, the sooner dead."

November 25, 1955: The Interstate Commerce Commission (ICC) orders an end to segregation on trains and busses crossing state lines by January 10, 1956.

December 1955: *The Man with the Golden Arm*, starring Frank Sinatra, though banned in Maryland, becomes the first film since 1934 to be shown without the Motion Picture Association of America (MPAA) seal of approval. In 1934, the MPAA, under strong public and religious pressure, decided to refuse a seal of approval to any films that "portray addiction to narcotics." This prohibition had been enforced with only one exception: *To the Ends of the Earth*, a 1948 film that lauded the Federal Bureau of Narcotics.

December 1, 1955: Rosa Parks refuses to give her bus seat to a white man in Montgomery, Alabama. She is arrested, fined and jailed.

December 5, 1955: In Montgomery, Alabama, a bus boycott begins under the leadership of the Reverend Martin Luther King, Jr.

December 5, 1955: The American Federation of Labor and the Congress of Industrial Organizations, America's two largest unions, merge into the AFL-CIO, with George Meany as president and Walter Reuther vice president. Membership is estimated at 15 million.

December 26, 1955: RKO sells its film library for TV distribution.

1956: *Invasion of the Body Snatchers*, directed by Don Siegel, is thought by many to be a metaphor for Communist infiltration.

1956: After noticing that teenagers tend to play the same forty or so songs over and over on jukeboxes, radio station manager Todd Stortz develops a new format called Top 40. With its frenetic mix of hits, fast-talking disc jockeys (DJs) and repetitious station jingles, the Top 40 format sweeps the nation.

1956: The percentage of white-collar workers in the U.S. surpasses that of blue-collar workers.

1956: Drag racing in hot rods becomes popular.

1956: Undergraduate men at UC Berkeley vote 2–1 to make ROTC voluntary.

January 12, 1956: The FBI solves the Boston Brinks robbery of January 17, 1950. Eight men are charged, but not a penny of the loot is found.

February 24–25, 1956: In a series of secret speeches, Soviet premier Nikita Khrushchev denounces Josef Stalin's brutal rule.

March 1956: UC professors dismissed over the loyalty oath receive back pay.

March 17, 1956: The IRS closes the leftist journal *Daily Worker* for tax evasion.

April 14, 1956: In Chicago, AMPEX displays a device to record TV shows on magnetic tape.

April 24, 1956: The Supreme Court upholds a lower court ban on intrastate bus segregation; in the South, Negroes are no longer required to sit in the back of the bus.

April 27, 1956: Heavyweight champion Rocky Marciano retires from professional boxing, entirely undefeated in a career that lasted from 1947 to 1956. He has a record of 49 wins (43 by KO) and no losses or draws.

May 16, 1956: "The Great Panty Raid" involves thousands of students surging around UC Berkeley sororities and dorms. The police are called out, firemen are injured. A judge awards the injured sororities $4,500 in damages to repay the cost of lost underwear.

June 30, 1956: U.S. steel workers strike; 650,000 walk out.

July 13, 1956: Seven Hungarian student defectors land a hijacked airliner in West Germany.

September 9, 1956: Elvis Presley appears on the "Ed Sullivan Show," singing "Hound Dog" and "Love Me Tender" to 54 million viewers, an estimated 82.6 percent of the total television audience. Because of his "deeply disturbing" stage manner (i.e., pelvic gyrations), the camera shows him only from the waist up during the performance.

September 28, 1956: Transatlantic telephone cable goes into operation, spanning the 2,250 miles between Newfoundland and Scotland.

September 30, 1956: The Algerian Front Libération National (FLN) places its first bombs in European cafés.

October 23, 1956: Anti-Soviet demonstrations turn into a full-scale rebellion as Hungarians in Budapest battle police, troops and tanks.

November 4, 1956: The Hungarian rebellion is crushed, with 20,000 dead and 150,000 wounded. After fierce street battles, 200,000 more flee abroad.

1957: Code-A-Phone introduces the automatic telephone answering machine.

1957: Gordon Gould conceives the idea of the Laser (Light Amplification by the Stimulated Emission of Radiation).

1957: Minnesota Mining and Manufacturing (3M) begins the commercial manufacture of video tape.

1957: The New York Giants baseball club moves to San Francisco and the Brooklyn Dodgers move to Los Angeles.

1957: "A man named Geisel who called himself Seuss wrote a very nice book, but what was the use? No publisher liked it, they turned it down flat. 'Who on earth wants to read of a cat in a hat? The pictures are odd, the rhymes even worse,' said the publishers, panning each line of each verse" (*Chronicle of the Twentieth Century*, 808).

1957: Jack Kerouac publishes *On the Road*. The "new barbarians," as the Beat Generation is called, congregate in New York's Greenwich Village and San Francisco's North Beach, which become the centers of the bohemian life.

1957: *The Bridge on the River Kwai*, starring Alec Guinness, has a screenplay by blacklisted writers Carl Forman and Michael Wilson, though it is credited to Pierre Boullé, who speaks no English.

1957: UC students protest compulsory ROTC. TASC forms.

1957: Roger Revelle and Hans E. Suess of the Scripps Institution of Oceanography observe in an article in *Tellus* that humanity is performing a "great geophysical experiment," not in a laboratory, but on our own planet. The outcome of the experiment should become clear within a few decades, but it essentially began at the start of the Industrial Revolution: since then human beings have increased the atmospheric content of carbon dioxide by about 25 percent through burning fossil fuels and clearing forests.

1957: Edouard Hoffman of the HAAS type foundry of Switzerland, in collaboration with Max Miedinger, decides to refine and update the popular nineteenth-century *Akzidenz Grotesque* fonts. The new sans serif, with an even larger *x*-height than *Univers*, is first released as *New Haas Grotesque*. When this design is produced in Germany by D. Stempel AG in 1961, the face is renamed *Helvetica*, after the traditional name for Switzerland.

January 13, 1957: The Wham-O company introduces the frisbee, under the name "Morrison's Flyin' Saucer," to selected West Coast stores.

February 1957: At the Amundsen-Scott South Pole Station, the United States establishes a permanent base for the International Geophysical Year (1957–1958).

March 6, 1957: Ghana becomes the first Black African territory to win its independence from European colonial powers.

March 25, 1957: The European Common Market Treaty is signed in Rome.

March 26, 1957: San Francisco police raid City Lights Bookstore, seize copies of Allen Ginsberg's *Howl and Other Poems*, and arrest Lawrence Ferlinghetti on the charge of selling pornography. *Howl* is similarly confiscated as obscene by customs collector Chester MacPhee.

May 4, 1957: Disc jockey Alan Freed, coiner of the phrase "rock 'n' roll," hosts the first prime-time TV network special on rock 'n' roll music.

June 12, 1957: In Tocca, Georgia, the 364-pound Paul Anderson, America's 1956 Olympic weightlifting champion, raises the greatest weight ever lifted by a human being: 6,270 pounds in a back lift (weight raised off trestles).

June 14, 1957: In Paris, Paul Gauguin's *Still Life with Apples* sells for $255,000, the highest price ever paid for a work of modern art.

June 24, 1957: The Supreme Court declares that obscenity is not a form of speech protected by the First Amendment.

July 16, 1957: Under police guard, the first Negro family moves into the planned community of Levittown.

August 14, 1957: The *New York Times* reports the growing problem of juvenile delinquency.

September 24, 1957: Eisenhower sends federal troops to Little Rock, Arkansas, to quell mobs and enforce school integration.

October 1957: A liberalized version of Rule 17 permits off-campus groups composed entirely of UC students to use campus facilities for programs of special interest to the student body.

October 4, 1957: Russia launches *Sputnik I*, the first earth-orbiting satellite.

October 20, 1957: The last American commercial network radio comedy show, "The Stan Freberg Show," goes off the air.

November 5, 1957: Women are admitted to sit in the British House of Lords.

November 14, 1957: Queen Elizabeth abolishes presentation at court for debutantes.

November 30, 1957: The remains of Captain Bligh's *Bounty* are found off Pitcairn Island.

December 1957: Rock 'n' roll star Jerry Lee Lewis bigamously marries Myra Gale Brown, the barely thirteen-year-old daughter of his first cousin and bass player, J. W. Brown. (Her birthday is the day of the wedding.) During his subsequent tour of England, public attention is focused disapprovingly on the nuptials, and his career is destroyed.

1958: The stereophonic long-playing record is introduced.

1958: Clark Kerr becomes UC president. TASC reorganizes as SLATE.

1958: William J. Lederer and Eugene Burdick publish *The Ugly American*, a fictionalized account of diplomatic affairs in Southeast Asia.

1958: In a controversial "long weekend" proposal, President Eisenhower orders some federal holidays to be observed on Mondays.

1958: Bondi, Gold and Hoyle propound the steady state theory of the universe.

1958: The Japanese export cars Toyopet Crown and Fuji-Go appear at the Los Angeles Import Car Show and are received with indifference. Toyota sells 288 cars in America this year.

1958: The drug thalidomide, prescribed in Europe and Britain for morning sickness, is linked to major birth deformities. About 7,000 children have been born with flipperlike arms and legs, as well as other gross deformities, because their mothers took the drug during pregnancy. The drug was kept off the U.S. market because Dr. Frances Kelsey, a medical officer with the Food and Drug Administration (FDA) had suspicions about its safety.

1958: In response to a problem that physicians explicitly categorize as female, U.S. tranquilizer consumption reaches 462,000 pounds, up from essentially zero in 1955.

1958: Premier Imre Nagy, the inspiration for the Hungarian rebellion, is hanged by the Soviets and buried face down in an unmarked grave.

January 24, 1958: Sir John Cockcroft of Britain and Lewis Strauss of the United States announce that they have created nuclear fusion.

January 31, 1958: The Van Allen radiation belt is discovered by *Explorer I*, the first U.S. earth satellite.

February 21, 1958: In response to Bertrand Russell's request for a symbol for the Campaign for Nuclear Disarmament (CND), British graphic designer Gerald Holtom incorporates the wigwag signals for "N" and "D" into a circle, thus creating the peace symbol.

March 11, 1958: In South Carolina, six people are injured as a B-47 accidentally drops an unarmed atomic bomb on a farm house.

March 24, 1958: Elvis Presley is inducted into the United States Army. Shorn of his locks, he is now just plain U.S. 53310761, and his pay has dropped to $83.20 per month.

May 3, 1958: Chairman Mao demands a "great leap forward" of the Chinese people. Peasants are shifted from fields to backyard steel furnaces, and millions of farmers are to be deployed into "people's communes," in which all private property is abolished. In addition, every Chinese citizen is asked to kill ten houseflies every day.

May 15, 1958: A retrospective performance of the works of John Cage is held in New York.

June 16, 1958: The Supreme Court bans denial of passports to suspected Communists, such as Paul Robeson, who after a seven-year struggle finally gets one. Robeson was denied a passport after a visit to Russia in 1952.

June 28, 1958: Edson Arantes do Nascimento scores three goals against France and two against Sweden to secure for Brazil the World Cup and himself the title, "Pele, King of Soccer."

Summer 1958: Jack S. Kirby, working for Texas Instruments, develops the integrated circuit, made out of a single slice of germanium. This, the first computer chip, is 0.040 inches high by 0.062 inches wide. All the functions of the mighty ENIAC can now be put on a panel the size of a playing card.

August 1958: Wham-O introduces the

hula hoop. The hoop is native to Australia; when J. Russell and D. Reynolds import it into the U.S., it catches on explosively.

October 4, 1958: British Overseas Airways Corporation introduces jet airliner passenger service over the Atlantic.

December 1958: The ASUC Executive Committee asks the UC administration to restore the Sather Gate tradition of free speech.

December 6, 1958: The world's largest oil tanker, capacity one million barrels, is launched in Kure, Japan.

December 10, 1958: Domestic jet airliner passenger service, New York to Miami, is offered by National Airlines.

1959: Louis B. "Creaky" Leakey discovers the skull of "Nutcracker Man" (from approximately 600,000 BC) in Tanganyika. Mary Leakey finds the skull of Australopithecus in Tanzania.

1959: The founders of the Mattel Toy Company, Ruth and Elliot Handler, notice that their daughter Barbie prefers teenage cutout dolls to burpers and cooers, and commission Jack Ryans—former husband of Zsa Zsa Gabor and designer of the Sparrow and Hawk missiles for Raytheon—to design the Barbie doll. In 1961, Barbie Handler's brother Ken becomes the prototype for Barbie's boyfriend.

1959: Number one nonfiction book is Pat Boone's *'Twixt Twelve and Twenty.*

1959: U.S. Postmaster General Arthur Summerfield bans D. H. Lawrence's *Lady Chatterley's Lover* from the mails on the grounds of obscenity. The ruling will be reversed in 1960 by the Circuit Court of Appeals.

1959: UC president Clark Kerr grants Edward Tolman an honorary degree. UC campus population jumps by 7,000 between 1959 and 1964.

1959: A decline in federal funding for syphilis control is generally thought to be responsible for a rise in the incidence of reported cases, now at 12 per 100,000.

1959: Hank Ballard records "The Twist," the B side of "Teardrops on Your Letter." Ernest Evans, a.k.a. Chubby Checker, records a cover version that by 1961 shoots up to number one, initiating a dance craze that the promotional material for the film

Hey, Let's Twist characterizes as "obscene, exciting, erotic, wild, athletic, silly, frenetic, animal, frenzied, relaxing—and a wonderful way to unleash hostilities." Like the sixties themselves.

1959: Featuring front-wheel drive and a transversely mounted 850cc engine, the Austin/Morris Mini 850, designed by Alec Issigonis, goes on sale in England.

1959: Selling 131,078 units, the compact Lark automobile saves Studebaker's bacon.

1959: The Nikon F 35mm instant-return single-lens reflex camera is introduced.

1959: Tranquilizer consumption reaches 1.15 million pounds.

January 1, 1959: Cuban president Fulgencio Batista indicates his resignation by fleeing the island, and Fidel Castro, a good left-handed pitcher almost drafted by the New York Yankees, takes over.

January 3, 1959: Alaska becomes the 49th state.

January 4, 1959: The Soviet *Lunik* rocket and satellite passes the moon, sending back signals from 343,750 miles out.

February 3, 1959: "The day the music died." A light plane carrying rock 'n' roll singers Buddy Holly, J. P. "Big Bopper" Richardson and Richie Valens crashes near Mason City, Iowa, killing all three and sending millions of teenaged fans into mourning.

March 18, 1959: Hawaii becomes the 50th state.

April 7, 1959: By referendum, Oklahoma ends 51 years of Prohibition.

April 25, 1959: Consummating Jacques Cartier's 1533 dream, the Saint Lawrence Seaway opens, linking the Atlantic Ocean and the Great Lakes, thus allowing oceangoing ships to reach the Midwest.

April 27, 1959: At UC Berkeley, graduate students are disassociated from the ASUC.

May 15, 1959: It is announced by the International Whaling Commission that the catch of blue whales has dropped from 82.1 percent of the whaling fishery in 1931–32 to 4.6 percent in 1957. The largest mammal on earth could be extinct in five years unless stringent controls are put on the whaling industry.

May 15, 1959: At UC Berkeley, SLATE

candidate David Armor becomes ASUC president.

May 20, 1959: Japanese-Americans regain the citizenship lost during World War II.

June 29, 1959: The motion picture of D. H. Lawrence's book *Lady Chatterley's Lover,* ruled obscene in the state of New York, is found upon appeal to the U.S. Supreme Court to be a form of speech protected under the First and Fourteenth Amendments.

August 1959: The design journal *Communication Arts* is the first magazine to be printed by offset lithography rather than letterpress.

August 9, 1959: After eight centuries of operation, Les Halles, the central wholesale market on Paris' Right Bank, is to be removed in the interest of efficiency.

August 15, 1959: A fallout shelter has been tested at Princeton, New Jersey. Cooking by candlelight, reading by flashlight, the Powner family has survived two weeks in their $1,195 pre-fab shelter and liked it. "I got to know my children better," says Mrs. Powner.

September 22, 1959: Freshman Richard Casey withdraws from UC, forfeiting a Regents' Scholarship, rather than enroll in ROTC.

October 7, 1959, 6:30 AM: *Lunik III* transmits photographic images of the dark side of the moon.

October 19, 1959: Faked emotions, rigged questions and phony games of chance emerge in a congressional investigation of Dan Enright's popular CBS television shows. These practices apparently ran smoothly for years until a Tennessee preacher said he "had been fed an answer" on "The $64,000 Question."

October 19, 1959: At UC Berkeley, Frederick L. Moore, Jr., begins a hunger strike to protest compulsory ROTC.

October 22, 1959: Kerr issues directives governing campus political activity. Protest ensues on all UC campuses.

December 19, 1959: In Houston, Texas, the reputed last Civil War veteran, Walter Williams, dies at the age of 117.

1960: World population is 3 billion (an increase of 17 percent over 1950). United States population is 179.3 million (an increase of 16 percent over 1950 and 5.9 percent of world population). California population is 15.7 million (an increase of 33 percent over 1950 and 8.6 percent of U.S. population).

1960: Americans own 85 million television sets.

1960: Americans discard 400,000 tons of plastic.

1960: The first transistor radio, a bone-white Sony not much larger than a cigarette pack, with a gold circular speaker disk in front, is sold through Sears. Any teenager able to scrape together $16.50 for the cheapest two-by-four-inch Silvertone has the power to secede from the adult world at any time.

1960: Alfred Hitchcock's film *Psycho* stimulates sales of transparent shower curtains.

1960: The first working model of a laser is produced by T. H. Maiman.

1960: The first fully automated photocopier, the Haloid Xerox 914, becomes available. With exclusive patent rights, Xerox copiers are the only plain-paper copiers on the market. The device was invented by Bob Gundlach, who joined the Haloid Company in 1952.

1960: Wilson Greatbatch develops the surgically implantable pacemaker, replacing the external pacemaker developed by Paul Zoll.

1960: Kerr's *Industrialism and Industrial Man* is published. Kerr names a new campus building in Edward Tolman's honor.

1960: The city of Berkeley, California, population 111,268, has 94 gasoline and oil service stations.

1960: Despite a trend among American automakers to produce ever larger cars, compact cars, like the Chevrolet Corvair (250,007 units sold this year), gain in popularity.

1960: The first Playboy Key Club opens in Chicago.

1960: Wentworth and Flexner publish the *Dictionary of American Slang,* creating thereby quite a ruckus, as the reference work includes many of the words the *Oxford English Dictionary* rather prudishly left out.

1960: The design firm of Chermayeff & Geismar design the first truly abstract logo. Made for the Chase Manhattan Bank, it is a fragmented octagon, often referred to as the Beveled Bagel.

1960s: Aided by the lowering of automobile roofs, Jackie Kennedy's forsaking of her pillbox for her bouffant, JFK's handsome hatless head, the decreasing amount of time spent at the mercy of the elements and youthful rejection of parental fashions, the hat (excepting the baseball cap) wanes as a significant aspect of American fashion.

January 5, 1960: The French newspaper *Le Monde* publishes a Red Cross report on torture in Algeria.

February 1, 1960: Sit-ins begin when four Negro college students in Greensboro, North Carolina, refuse to move from a Woolworth lunch counter. By September 1961, more than 70,000 people will have participated in civil rights sit-ins.

February 17, 1960: Ike approves CIA training of Cuban exiles to overthrow Castro's Cuban government.

March 29, 1960: The *New York Times* publishes a full-page advertisement titled "Heed Their Rising Voices," describing the treatment of protesting Negro schoolchildren by the Alabama police. The advertisement contains some errors in fact. L. B. Sullivan, a Montgomery city commissioner in charge of police, claims that the advertisement will be understood to be critical of him, sues the *Times* in an Alabama court, and wins a $500,000 settlement. In 1964, in *New York Times* v *Sullivan,* the Supreme Court will rule that a public official cannot win a libel verdict against the press unless it is proved not only that some statement was false and damaging, but that the statement was made with "actual malice"—that journalists were not just careless or negligent in researching their story but published it either knowing that it was false or in "reckless disregard" of whether it was false or not.

April 21, 1960: The government of Brazil packs its bags and moves to Brasilia, a brand new city on a central plateau 600 miles from the coast, designed by architect Oscar Niemeyer.

April 27, 1960: In yet another move

against teenage "jungle music," Congress investigates payola, the practice of playing records in return for recording industry bribes, in which American Bandstand's Dick Clark and disc jockey Alan Freed are implicated.

May 1960: HUAC subpoenas eighteen-year-old UC student Douglas Wachter.

May 1, 1960: Francis Gary Powers, shot down in his U-2 spy plane over Russia, neglects to take his poison suicide capsule, thereby causing an enormous political imbroglio.

May 9, 1960: The FDA approves Enovid and Norlutin as oral contraceptives; within six years one out of five American women of childbearing age has a prescription. A month's supply costs about $10.

May 13, 1960: Police hose HUAC protesters down San Francisco City Hall steps. Hundreds of UC students participate, and thirty-one are arrested.

June 20, 1960: The bottle-nosed dolphin is believed, because of its large brain, to have an intelligence at least equal and perhaps superior to that of man, according to marine scientist John C. Lilly.

June 21, 1960: In Zurich, the German Armin Hary runs 100 meters in 10 seconds flat.

July 29–31, 1960: Mount Madonna conference forms anti-HUAC coalition.

September 7, 1960: The American primitive painter Grandma Moses celebrates her 100th birthday.

October 25, 1960: The Bulova watch company, of Jackson Heights, New York, introduces the Accutron, a wristwatch with an electronic power source and a vibrating tuning fork as a source of regulation.

1961: Hamburger aficionado Ray Kroc likes what he sees at the McDonald Brothers hamburger stand in San Bernardino, California, franchises the business and eventually buys it.

1961: Julia Child publishes *Mastering the Art of French Cooking*.

1961: Three percent of the nation's passenger cars come equipped with seat belts.

1961: As an advertising gimmick, Howard Gossage persuades Rainier Ale to offer sweatshirts with the portraits and names of Bach, Beethoven or Brahms, thereby establishing the trend of imprinted sweatshirts and T-shirts. This is not the first time anyone has printed something on a T-shirt, but it did signal the beginning of a major fashion trend. The first printed T-shirts were from a shop in Ann Arbor, Michigan, in 1933, and sported University of Michigan insignia.

1961: Chux disposable diapers are suggested by Consumers Union as a "Best Buy Christmas Gift" for the infant who "has everything." Disposable diapers account for one percent of the market this year.

1961: 3M and Revere, with Dr. Peter Goldmark of CBS laboratories, develop the M-2 stereo cartridge system with automatic cartridge changing, which uses special ⅛-inch-wide magnetic tape that provides high-fidelity stereo at low speeds. By 1966, the tape is used in designing the cassette system, thus opening the door to cassette tape decks, car stereos, and portable cassette players.

1961: Joseph F. Engelberger and George C. Devol build their first robot, which is delivered to a General Motors plant. The Unimate is a hydraulic-powered robot that runs a die-casting machine. To "learn" its task, the robot is led painstakingly through the process so it can make a digital magnetic recording of what it does as it goes.

1961: The Motown Record Corporation of Detroit produces its first major hits.

1961: John Howard Griffin publishes *Black Like Me*, an account of his adventures disguised as a Black man, in which he portrays the plight of the American Negro.

1961: The UC Berkeley campus expands one block south to Bancroft and Telegraph.

1961: The U.S. ban on the works of novelist Henry Miller (*Tropic of Cancer*, 1934, *The Colossus of Maroussi*, 1941) is lifted.

1961: Inspired by reading a 1960 newspaper account of two Portuguese students who had been arrested and imprisoned by their government for having raised a toast "to Freedom," London attorney Peter Benenson founds Amnesty International as a private association dedicated to ministering to the lot of political prisoners, or "prisoners of conscience."

1961: *Webster's Third International Dictionary* is published. It describes the language as it is currently being spoken, and consequently excites a rage rarely seen in response to a reference book. Wilson Follett, in a long piece in the *Atlantic Monthly*, calls it "A very great calamity . . . a dismaying assortment of the questionable, the perverse, the unworthy, and the downright outrageous . . . a scandal and a disaster."

January 3, 1961: The United States severs all diplomatic and consular relations with Cuba.

February 24, 1961: In the Olduvai Gorge, Tanganyika, the Leakeys unearth the bones of an eleven-year-old child, a representative of Australopithecus Africanus and the oldest member of the human race yet known to science.

March 1, 1961: President Kennedy announces the formation of a U.S. Peace Corps to aid developing nations.

April 3, 1961: The Twenty-third Amendment gives residents of the District of Columbia the vote.

April 12, 1961: The Russian Major Yuri Alekseyevich Gagarin becomes the first human to orbit the earth.

April 17, 1961: Cuba is unsuccessfully invaded by an estimated 1,200 anti-Castro exiles backed by the United States. "Bay of Pigs" protests on U.S. college campuses.

May 1, 1961: A National Airlines flight, en route from Miami to Key West, Florida, is skyjacked to Havana, Cuba.

May 4, 1961: Black Muslim leader Malcolm X is denied permission to speak on the UC Berkeley campus.

June 10, 1961: SLATE loses on-campus status.

August 13, 1961: East Germans erect the 29-mile Berlin Wall between East and West Berlin to halt the flood of refugees.

September 10, 1961: Police in Carlsbad, California, eject sidewalk surfers from clogged beach drives. Police report that surfers with boogie boards on roller-skate wheels are taking over parking-lot ramps leading to the beach. The craze sweeps San Diego County, where the miniature surfboards on discarded or pirated roller-skate wheels turn the hills leading to the beaches into asphalt waters. By 1962, any piece of wood will do, and "terra surfing" is booming across the country. Custom-made boards can be had for as little as $1.49, and kids as far away as Wisconsin are singing "Sidewalk Surfing" with Jan and Dean. Soon the California Medical Association issues an alert on skateboarding, calling it a "new medical menace," and almost before the sport is born it goes into a swift decline. It isn't until the mid-1970s and the introduction of polyurethane wheels by college student Frank Namowsty that skateboarding really catches on.

September 28, 1961: Singer Bob Dylan performs at Gerde's Folk City Café in Greenwich Village.

October 10, 1961: Joseph Heller's *Catch-22* is published.

November 14, 1961: The 700 American military advisers in South Vietnam will be joined by an additional 200 Air Force instructors. It is proposed that the number of military advisers be increased to 16,000 over the next two years.

November 15, 1961: The Metropolitan Museum of Modern Art buys Rembrandt's *Aristotle Contemplating the Bust of Homer* for $2.3 million. Museum attendance begins a steady rise.

December 22, 1961: James Davis becomes the first American soldier to be killed in Vietnam when he and three Vietnamese soldiers are ambushed west of Saigon.

December 31, 1961: The theory of continental drift, first proposed by German Alfred Wagner in 1912 and amplified in 1958 by S. Warren Carey, is given a lift by Princeton University geologist Harry Hess. He proposes the idea of "plate tectonics," in which the continents float on huge plates of the heavier rock that make up the earth's crust.

1962: New York AM radio station WMCA begins calling its disc jockeys "the WMCA good guys." The phrase is printed on thousands of mustard-yellow sweatshirts with a stylized "happy face" drawn on the back. The garment is worn all over the city. WMCA drops the logo in 1971

when its format switches from rock to talk.

1962: The Ford Motor Company designs tiny cars to compete with the German Volkswagen, but Henry Ford publicly drops the idea as "un-American."

1962: Rachel Carson's *Silent Spring* launches the environmentalist movement.

1962: Overrepresentation of rural districts in state legislatures, which has effectively disenfranchised millions of urban voters, leads the Supreme Court to abandon its traditional noninterference in drawing legislative boundaries. The Court, in *Baker* v *Carr*, rules that Tennessee citizens deprived of full representation by "arbitrary and capricious" malapportionment are denied equal protection under the Fourteenth Amendment.

1962: Random House publishes Helen Gurley Brown's *Sex and the Single Girl*.

1962: New Balance introduces the Trackster, the first modern running shoe.

1962–1963: Telephone prefixes are abandoned. The Marvellettes' 1961 rock 'n' roll song "BEachwood 4-5789" becomes (in theory) the prosaic "234–5789," and Elizabeth Taylor's 1960 film *Butterfield 8*, the uninspiring *288*.

January 1962: Despite their successes in the Liverpool music scene, the Beatles are rejected by Decca, a major British recording studio. After a hard day's night, manager Brian Epstein and his four protegés (John Lennon, George Harrison, Paul McCartney and drummer Pete Best—later replaced by Ringo Starr) decide to produce their first album themselves.

March 1962: An unauthorized rally at UC Berkeley, protesting resumption of atmospheric atomic bomb testing by the United States, is dispersed by police at the behest of the dean of students' office.

March 23, 1962: Edward W. Strong becomes chancellor. Campuswide demonstrations protest President John F. Kennedy's speech at Charter Day ceremonies.

May 1962: UC president Clark Kerr persuades the Regents to make ROTC voluntary, effective June 29.

July 11, 1962: At 7:35 PM, EDT, Americans

see their first live television pictures from Europe when signals from France are transmitted via the Telstar communications satellite.

July 26, 1962: The House passes a bill for equal pay regardless of sex.

August–November 1962: Cuban missile crisis. Perceiving that the USSR proposes to build missile bases in Cuba, President Kennedy orders a Cuban quarantine, which is lifted after the Russians back down. The world is inches from nuclear war. Sponsored by the YSA, 1,500 UC Berkeley students attend a noon-to-midnight protest. SLATE holds a rally at Wheeler Oak to protest the American blockade.

September 25, 1962: Because of his race, James Meredith is denied admission to the University of Mississippi by Governor Ross Barnett. A U.S. court of appeals finds Barnett guilty of civil contempt and threatens him with arrest and fines. U.S. marshalls and 3,000 soldiers suppress riots when Meredith arrives on campus to begin classes.

December 5, 1962: In London, heavy smog kills 55 people.

December 14, 1962: The *Mariner 2* spacecraft gives mankind its first close-up view of another planet as it flies within 21,000 miles of Venus and beams back data across 36 million miles of space.

December 29, 1962: The Kennedy administration meets Fidel Castro's ransom demands of $62 million plus pharmaceuticals and medical supplies for the return of the Bay of Pigs prisoners in Cuba. According to Cuba, almost nothing is actually delivered.

1963: More than 15,000 U.S. troops are in Vietnam.

1963: A "credibility gap" becomes apparent between official government versions of events and what is reported in the media concerning events in Cuba, Vietnam and the civil rights movement.

1963: Betty Friedan publishes *The Feminine Mystique*. American men are about to undergo a shakeup.

1963: UC president Clark Kerr attempts to repeal the campus ban on Communist speakers. In June the Regents agree;

groups now must present "balanced programs." Albert J. "Mickey" Lima is the first American Communist to speak on the UC campus since the ban was imposed in 1951. Kerr's *Uses of the University* is published.

1963: Reversing its 1942 *Betts* v *Brady* decision, the Supreme Court in *Gideon* v *Wainwright* holds that the Sixth Amendment guarantees access to qualified counsel, which is "fundamental to a fair trial." Gideon is entitled to a retrial because Florida failed to provide him with an attorney. After this decision, states are required to furnish public defenders for indigent defendants in felony cases.

1963: Jessica Mitford publishes *The American Way of Death*. The funeral industry undergoes a shakeup.

1963: The 47th annual San Francisco Bay to Breakers race, 7.5 miles, draws 25 runners.

1963: Renewed worldwide interest in Art Nouveau.

1963: Andy Warhol, Robert Rauschenberg, Jasper Johns, Claus Oldenberg and other artists are represented in New York's Guggenheim Museum show of Pop art, featuring paintings of soup cans, comic-strip-style canvasses, inflatable sculpture, etc.

1963: The pop-top beer can is introduced.

1963–1964: UC chapter of CORE pickets downtown Berkeley businesses.

January 7, 1963: U.S. first-class postage is raised to five cents.

March 21, 1963: "The Rock," the federal prison at Alcatraz in the middle of San Francisco Bay, becomes a hollow, echoing shell as the last 27 prisoners are removed. No one has ever successfully escaped from it.

March 25, 1963: Davey Moore dies of injuries sustained in a featherweight bout with Sugar Ramos.

Good Friday, 1963: Pope John XXIII interrupts the service at Saint Peter's to order that a reference to "perfidious Jews" be stricken from the liturgy.

May 2, 1963: Five hundred are arrested in a Birmingham, Alabama, civil rights march; police disperse crowds with dogs and firehoses.

May 6, 1963: One thousand are arrested in a Birmingham civil rights march.

May 18, 1963: In an effort to reestablish order in Alabama, President Kennedy sends federal troops to the racially divided area.

May 31, 1963: Mississippi police jail 600 Negro children.

June 10, 1963: In Saigon, the Buddhist monk Ngo Quang Duc burns himself to death to protest religious persecution by the Catholic Diem government.

June 12, 1963, 8:00 PM: After a ten-week period in which there are 758 racial demonstrations and 14,733 arrests in 186 American cities, President Kennedy declares in a nationally televised speech, "We are confronted primarily with a moral issue. It is as old as the Scriptures and is as clear as the American Constitution. The heart of the question is whether all Americans are to be afforded equal rights and equal opportunities, whether we are going to treat our fellow Americans as we want to be treated."

June 12, 1963, midnight: Medgar Evers, the NAACP's Mississippi field secretary, is assassinated from ambush in Jackson, Mississippi.

June 17, 1963: The Supreme Court rules, 8–1, that no locality may require recitation of the Lord's Prayer or Bible verses in public schools.

June 18, 1963: In Alabama, 450 Negroes are arrested for defying injunctions against sit-ins.

June 19, 1963: Valentina Tereshkova, the first woman space traveler, is sent into orbit.

June 20, 1963: In South Africa, it is reported that one out of every 236 in the total population is in prison.

July 1, 1963: Nationwide postal zip codes are introduced, to the displeasure of those who feel that everything is being depersonalized.

Summer 1963: In response to the actions of Alabama and Mississippi Freedom Riders, the Interstate Commerce Commission issues a ruling banning overt segregation in all places and vehicles used in public interstate transportation, requiring that signs be posted saying, "Seating on this vehicle or in this station must be regardless of race, creed, color, religion or national origin."

August 28, 1963: The Reverend Dr. Martin Luther King, Jr., addresses a crowd of 200,000 demonstrating in Washington, D.C., in support of Negro demands for equal rights: "I have a dream that this nation will rise up and live out the true meaning of its creed. 'We hold these truths to be self-evident: that all men are created equal.' We will not be satisfied until justice runs down like waters and righteousness like a mighty stream. And if America is to become a great nation, this must become true. And when *this* happens . . . we will be able to speed up that day when *all* God's children, Black men and White men, Jews and Gentiles, Protestants and Catholics, will be able to join hands and sing in the words of the old Negro spiritual, 'Free at last! Free at last! Thank God Almighty, we are free at last!' "

August 30, 1963: A diplomatic "hot line" goes into operation between Moscow and Washington. The line is to be used only by heads of government, and then only in the event of emergency.

October 26, 1963: The science journal *Nature* reports that Smithsonian astronomer Gerald Hawkins has successfully demonstrated astronomical alignments at Stonehenge. The stones had suggested an astronomical observatory to the English scholar Dr. W. Stukely as early as 1740— American astronomer Samuel Langley and English astronomer J. N. Lockyer proposed similar hypotheses in 1889 and 1894—but the theory has been proved by Hawkins' computer simulations, which demonstrate that the stones mark not only the most northerly (midsummer) sunrise, but also other midsummer and midwinter sunrise and sunset positions. Hawkins and, independently, the English researcher C. A. Newham have further demonstrated that special sighting stones also allowed observations of the moon's motions, including its northernmost and southernmost positions of rising and setting. The observatory belongs to the oldest part of Stonehenge, dating from about 2600 BC. Larger, later stones (placed as recently as 2000 to 1500 BC) reveal no intelligible alignments, though the erection of 30- to 50-ton stones, transported from 30 kilometers away, and 5-ton stones transported more than 380 kilometers over both sea and land, demonstrates an extraordinary engineering capacity.

October 29, 1963: Madame Nhu speaks at UC Berkeley's Harmon Gym and is picketed.

November 1963: Mel's Drive-in in San Francisco is picketed by civil rights activists; 111 are arrested. Mel's in Berkeley is picketed on November 8.

November 18, 1963: Commercial push-button telephone service is inaugurated.

November 21, 1963: Campus CORE announces plans to picket downtown Berkeley businesses during Christmas.

November 22, 1963: President John Fitzgerald Kennedy is assassinated by sniper fire in Dallas, Texas.

November 24, 1963: Kennedy's accused assassin, Lee Harvey Oswald, is shot dead while in prison by Jack Ruby, a Dallas nightclub owner. The event is broadcast on national television.

December 7, 1963: During the Army-Navy game, instant replay is used for the first time in a TV sports broadcast.

December 19, 1963: Publisher Ralph Ginsburg is sentenced by the Federal District Court to five years in jail and a $42,000 fine on a 28-count federal indictment for distributing obscene materials through the mails. The prosecution testified that the publications would disturb mental patients and were dangerous to the community, especially to young persons. The publications were *Eros*, a newsletter titled *Liaison*, and a book titled *The Housewife's Handbook on Selective Promiscuity*. After lengthy Supreme Court appeals (*Ginsburg* v *United States*), he begins an eight-month prison sentence on February 17, 1972.

Dissenting Supreme Court justice Hugo Black writes that "the federal government is without any power whatever under the Constitution to put any type of burden on speech and the expression of ideas of any kind." A further dissent is expressed by Justice Potter Stewart: "If the Constitution means anything, it means that a man cannot be sent to prison for distributing publications which offend a judge's aesthetic sensibilities, mine or any others. Censorship represents a society's lack of confidence in itself. It is a hallmark of an authoritarian regime."

The court's liberal members prevail on that very same day in another obscenity case, when they reverse the Massachusetts ban on John Cleland's *Memoirs of a Woman of Pleasure*, commonly known as *Fanny Hill*, outlawed since 1821.

1964: UC Berkeley freshman class enrollment increases by 37 percent. Acting assistant professor Eli Katz is denied promotion.

1964: In line with the Supreme Court's *Baker* v *Carr* decision, all states reapportion their legislatures in conformance with the "one man, one vote" doctrine of *Reynolds* v *Sims*.

1964: Three hundred contestants participate in the Boston Marathon.

1964: Romantic and grandiose plans to turn the Amazon into a cornucopia of large farms, mines and hydroelectric plants initiate systematic deforestation of the Amazon river basin.

1964: New York's sumptuous Pennsylvania Station (designed by McKim, Mead and White to resemble the baths of Caracalla) is demolished to make way for urban renewal in the form of the Madison Square Garden complex. As a consequence, historic preservation becomes a popular cause rather than a hobby of the odd curmudgeon.

1964: The Bulfontein case exposes the routine use of police torture in South Africa.

1964: The U.S. Bureau of the Census determines that California has become America's most populous state, surpassing New York. California also leads the nation in both personal income and expenditures.

1964: First sperm banks open in Tokyo and Iowa City.

1964: The Supreme Court upholds Title II of the Civil Rights Act of 1964, outlawing private discrimination in public accommodations, as a legitimate exertion of federal power over interstate commerce. In *Heart of Atlanta Motel, Inc.* v *United States*, the Court holds that Congress has "ample power" to forbid racial discrimination in facilities that affect commerce by serving interstate travelers. The Heart of Atlanta Motel is located on two interstate highways, so the Court can sidestep the *Civil Rights Cases* (1833) protection of private discrimination to overrule it.

January 15, 1964: In Los Angeles, the Whisky-a-Go-Go disco opens.

January 18, 1964: General Luther L. Terry, himself a smoker and U.S. Surgeon General, issues a report on smoking and health which concludes that smoking is a "health hazard of sufficient importance in the United States to warrant appropriate legal action."

January 23, 1964: The Twenty-fourth Amendment is adopted, ending the poll tax.

February 1964: UC Berkeley's Campus CORE pickets and holds shop-ins at Lucky. A picket line is established at the Sheraton-Palace in San Francisco, protesting discriminatory hiring practices.

March 1964: Sheraton-Palace pickets draw 1,000 demonstrators; 810 are arrested, of which 100 are UC students.

March 3, 1964: Some 464,000 Negro and Puerto Rican students boycott public schools in desegregation protests.

March 13, 1964: Kitty Genovese, 28, is stabbed to death in full view of 37 of her Queens, New York, neighbors, who do not come to her aid and who do nothing to prevent the assault. Her screams attract attention, and as lights are turned on, her assailant flees. When the lights are turned off, he returns to finish the job.

March 16, 1964: Auto Row demonstrations begin, to continue through the summer. Of 100 arrests, 20 are from UC.

March 27, 1964: An earthquake hits Anchorage, Alaska, killing 60 to 100 people.

April 4, 1964: The Beatles occupy the top five positions on the *Billboard* "Hot 100" chart:

1. "Can't Buy Me Love"
2. "Twist and Shout"
3. "She Loves You"
4. "I Want To Hold Your Hand"
5. "Please Please Me"

In addition, they hold numbers 16, 44, 49, 69, 78, 84 and 88.

April 7, 1964: With the System/360 family of computers, International Business Machines (IBM) introduces upward and downward compatibility, thus allowing data processing operations to grow from the smallest machine to the largest without rewriting vital programs.

May 1964: California's state legislature makes palmistry and fortune-telling for profit legal by local option.

May 4, 1964: In New York, the Pulitzer committee decides that no fiction, music or drama is worthy of prizes this year.

Summer 1964: UC activists organize anti-Goldwater demonstrations at the Republican National Convention in San Francisco. "No on 14" campaign. Mario Savio (SNCC) and Jack Weinberg (CORE), among others, participate in "Freedom Summer" civil rights activity in the South.

June 2, 1964: Rudi Gernreich, a bathing suit mischief-maker since the early fifties, introduces the topless swimsuit.

June 16, 1964: Comedian Lenny Bruce goes on trial in New York on charges of obscenity.

June 16, 1964: Carol Doda, the siliconed pioneer, dances topless at San Francisco's Condor Club. Getting one silicone injection each week for twenty weeks, she increases her bust size from 36 C to 44 DD.

June 20, 1964: Mount Zion Methodist Church, in the small, rural Negro community of Longdale, Neshoba County, Mississippi, is the first of twenty Southern Negro churches to be firebombed during the summer of 1964.

June 22, 1964: On their way to investigate the burning of a rural Negro church, three civil rights workers, Michael Schwerner, Andrew Goodman and James Chaney, are arrested by Deputy Sheriff Cecil Price in Neshoba County, Mississippi, held in jail until after dark and then turned over by Price to the Ku Klux Klan. Six weeks later, on August 4, the FBI finds their bodies buried in an earth-fill dam near Philadelphia, Mississippi. On October 20, 21 white men are arrested and convicted by an all-white federal jury of conspiracy in the slayings.

June 24, 1964: The Federal Trade Commission announces that health warnings will be required on all cigarette packages: "Caution: Cigarette smoking may be hazardous to your health."

July 2, 1964: Nullifying a vast network of Jim Crow laws, Lyndon Baines Johnson signs the Civil Rights Act.

July 22, 1964: UC Vice-Chancellor Alex Sherriffs brings up the issue of political activity in the Bancroft-Telegraph area at the "bicycle meeting."

July 29, 1964: The University administration resolves to end political organizing on UC property.

August 2, 1964: The U.S. destroyers *Maddox* and *C. Turner Joy* are believed to have been attacked by North Vietnamese torpedo boats in the Gulf of Tonkin. Later analysis reveals that the ships' radar was malfunctioning, and there was no attack.

August 7, 1964: The U.S. Congress passes the Gulf of Tonkin Resolution, giving the President power to "take all necessary measures to repel any armed attack against the forces of the U.S. and to prevent further aggression." This is as close as the United States gets to a declaration of war in Vietnam.

September 1964: Edward T. Kores, Jr., of Westbrook, Connecticut, attends his first day of classes only to have the high school superintendent suspend him on the grounds that his bangs are too similar to those sported by the Beatles; the superintendent tells Kores that he may return to school if he brushes his bangs back.

September 1, 1964: As ruled by the UC Regents in the spring of 1959, all sororities and fraternities must remove any charter requirements for membership based on race, religion or national origin by this date.

September 4–18, 1964: Picketing of the *Oakland Tribune* is announced and organized from the Bancroft-Telegraph area.

September 10, 1964: The SLATE *Supplement to the General Catalog* includes a letter calling for "open, fierce and thoroughgoing rebellion."

September 16, 1964: All student organizations receive letters from Dean of Students Katherine A. Towle that, effective September 21, political activity will no longer be permitted on the 26-by-90-foot strip of University property at Bancroft and Telegraph. Student political organizations meet at Bancroft and Telegraph to discuss restrictions on organizing activity.

September 17, 1964: The United Front forms and meets with Dean Towle to protest the new policy.

September 18, 1964: The United Front petitions the dean of students for the use of the Bancroft-Telegraph area, pledging that student groups will police themselves and not interfere with traffic.

September 20, 1964: The United Front resolves to protest the politics ban with vigils, pickets, rallies and civil disobedience.

September 21, 1964: Dean Towle accepts most student proposals, but stands firm on the issue of advocacy and solicitation of funds. All-night vigil on Sproul Hall steps.

September 22, 1964: The ASUC requests the Regents to allow free political and social action up to the posts traditionally accepted as the entrance to the campus.

September 23, 1964: Chancellor Strong emphasizes UC's "Open Forum" policy and reiterates the University's stance against the mounting of social and political action from the campus.

September 25, 1964: President Kerr condemns the student demonstrations.

September 27, 1964: The United Front announces plans to picket the next day's University Meeting, set up tables at Sather Gate and hold a rally in front of Wheeler Hall.

September 28, 1964: Chancellor Strong announces a substantial concession—that campaign literature advocating "yes" or "no" votes on propositions and candidates may now be distributed at Bancroft-Telegraph and eight other campus locations. Pickets march to University Meeting. Mario Savio and Art Goldberg are cited by Dean Williams.

September 29, 1964: Tables are set up at Bancroft-Telegraph and Sather Gate. Student names taken.

September 30, 1964: SNCC and CORE set up tables at Sather Gate. Five students—Mark Bravo, Brian Turner, Donald Hatch, Elizabeth Stapleton and David Goines—are requested to appear at 3:00 PM before Dean Williams for disciplinary action. Five hundred students sign a petition of complicity and accompany the cited students to Dean Williams' office. Williams refuses to see all of them, and asks the five, plus three leaders—Art Goldberg, Sandor Fuchs and Mario Savio—to see him. None of the eight appears in his office. Students remain in Sproul Hall, and at midnight Chancellor Strong announces that the eight have been indefinitely suspended. Students remain until 3:00 AM.

October 1964: Announcements just before Thanksgiving that cranberries are carcinogenic nearly destroy the industry. Some years later, the tests from which these findings result are shown to be flawed; the revised scientific opinion is that cranberries are perfectly OK.

October 1, 1964: At noon, Jack Weinberg is arrested at a CORE table in front of Sproul Hall. Students sit down around the police car to which he is carried, preventing its departure. Demonstrators speak from the top of the car. Five hundred students sit in at Sproul Hall. At 6:15 PM, demonstrators and police battle for control of Sproul Hall doors, demonstrators prevailing. Anti-demonstrators converge on Sproul Plaza, and a fire engine races through campus. Potentially violent confrontation between demonstrators and fraternity boys averted. Demonstrators remain around police car all night.

October 2, 1964: A crowd of 7,000 occupies the area between Sproul Hall and the Student Union. Some 500 police arrive by 5:30 PM. Demonstration spokesmen meet with Kerr and Strong and sign an agreement, the "pact of October 2," ending the demonstration at 7:30 PM.

October 3–4, 1964: The Free Speech Movement forms.

October 5, 1964: Protesters hold a noon rally on Sproul Hall steps. Chancellor Strong announces appointments to the Campus Committee on Political Action (CCPA). FSM Central established. The Independent Students Association is formed to represent nonaligned students.

October 6, 1964: FSM rejects Strong's appointments.

October 7, 1964: First meeting of the CCPA. Protesters declare the CCPA illegally constituted.

October 8, 1964: The FSM Executive Committee and Steering Committee are fully formed. The ACLU announces its intention to intervene on behalf of the suspended students. Arleigh Williams receives a pro-FSM petition from fraternities and sororities. Heyman Committee formed to review suspensions.

October 11, 1964: FSM meets with Strong concerning the CCPA. The Graduate Coordinating Committee (GCC) forms.

October 12, 1964: Reinstatement of suspended students is urged by 88 faculty members.

October 13, 1964: The Academic Senate passes motions in favor of maximum freedom and peace and order. FSM requests meeting with the Regents. The CCPA holds first public hearing; FSM sympathizers reject the committee as illegally constituted. FSM begins negotiations with vice president of administration Earl Bolton over composition of the CCPA.

October 14, 1964: The FSM threatens massive demonstrations within forty-eight hours if the administration fails to modify the CCPA. Professor Arthur Ross meets with FSM and agrees to discuss modifications of the October 2 agreement with the administration.

October 15, 1964: The CCPA is modified. Regents refuse to meet with FSM.

October 25, 1964: The Heyman Committee advises that the eight suspended students be reinstated during its investigation.

October 26, 1964: Strong refuses the Heyman Committee's request.

October 26, 1964: The English rock group the Rolling Stones arrives in America, driving another wedge into the already widening generation gap.

October 28, 1964: Dean Towle reemphasizes that advocacy of direct action is not permitted.

November 2, 1964: FSM threatens direct action.

November 3, 1964: The Heyman Committee completes its hearings.

November 4, 1964: FSM pickets on Sproul Hall Steps.

November 5, 1964: The Cunningham letters are made public.

November 7, 1964: The CCPA reaches an impasse over advocacy of illegal acts. Steering Committee reorganized.

November 8, 1964: FSM announces that it

intends to lift its self-imposed moratorium on political activity on Monday, November 9. Internal split and attempted coup.

November 9, 1964: Internal split resolved. Coup fails. FSM resumes on-campus activism. Tables are set up, and about 75 demonstrators' names are taken. GCC hints at a strike. The CCPA is dissolved.

November 10, 1964: Some 200 GCC protesters continue defiance of University regulations. Participants in the November 9 demonstration are sent notices to appear at the dean's office for disciplinary action. No one appears.

November 11, 1964: Jean Genet's *Un Chant d'Amour* is shown in Stiles Hall by SLATE.

November 12, 1964: The report of the disbanded CCPA is released, recommending that advocacy of legal off-campus activity be permitted.

November 13, 1964: The Heyman Committee recommends that the suspended students be reinstated. Professor Ira Heyman addresses the report to the Academic Senate instead of Chancellor Strong.

November 16, 1964: Tables again appear on the steps of Sproul Hall. FSM circulates a petition in support of its stand on advocacy of illegal off-campus acts, to be presented to the Regents' meeting on Friday, November 20.

November 17, 1964: Tables on Sproul Hall steps. No official action is taken; FSM announces that the tables will stay until they have become legal.

November 18, 1964: Sanford Elberg, dean of the graduate division, calls a meeting of all University teaching assistants.

November 19, 1964: The California Democratic Council supports FSM goals.

November 20, 1964: FSM holds a rally, march to the Regents' meeting at University Hall, and vigil. FSM representatives are admitted to the meeting but not allowed to speak.

November 20, 1964: The Vatican approves exoneration of the Jews of guilt for the crucifixion of Jesus.

November 23, 1964: FSM rally on Sproul Hall steps. Abortive sit-in.

November 23, 1964: The Vatican abol-ishes Latin as the official language of the Roman Catholic liturgy.

November 24, 1964: Chancellor Strong accedes to all FSM demands except the issue of advocacy. The FSM considers itself defeated.

November 25, 1964: Dean Towle bans *Un Chant d'Amour* from campus.

November 28, 1964: Disciplinary letters for actions subsequent to September 30 arrive at the residences of Mario Savio, Art Goldberg, Jackie Goldberg and Brian Turner. A number of campus organizations are charged with violating campus regulations.

November 30, 1964: Strong rejects FSM demands that disciplinary action be dropped. FSM threatens direct action. GCC announces a plan for a strike. Free speech rally at UCLA. Kerr repeats allegations of Communist outside agitators in FSM.

December 1, 1964: FSM issues an ultimatum, threatens direct action if administration does not meet its demands within 24 hours. GCC announces a strike for Friday, December 4.

December 2, 1964: Demonstrators pack four floors of Sproul Hall.

December 3, 1964: At 3:00 AM Chancellor Strong requests that the demonstrators end their sit-in. At 3:45 AM Governor Brown orders arrests. Twelve hours later, some 800 protesters have been arrested. At 1:00 PM, as the arrests continue, 800 professors meet in Wheeler, passing resolutions favoring political freedom and amnesty and condemning the use of police on campus. Governor Brown is picketed by Davis students. Pickets attempt to block campus entrances. GCC meets to implement the strike.

December 4, 1964: FSM rally attracts some 5,000 students. Strike continues.

December 6, 1964: Kerr announces a special University meeting on December 7. Strong is hospitalized with gall bladder pains. The arrestees meet with their lawyers at Garfield Junior High.

December 7, 1964: Sproul Hall demonstrators appear for arraignment. At 11:00 AM, 16,000 students and faculty gather in the Greek Theatre to hear an address by Clark Kerr. Amnesty for all actions prior to December 3 is declared. Mario Savio attempts to speak, but is dragged off stage by police. Savio is released and announces a rally in front of Sproul Hall, at which 10,000 students reject Kerr's political proposals. A moratorium on the strike is to begin at midnight. The faculty Two Hundred meet. The Undergraduate Association holds its first meeting.

December 8, 1964: The Academic Senate meets and adopts the FSM platform. SLATE candidates sweep all seven ASUC Senate positions.

December 9, 1964: The Union of University-Employed Graduate Students forms.

December 12, 1964: Kenya becomes an independent state, with Jomo Kenyatta as prime minister and president.

December 13, 1964: Chancellor Strong denies the use of Wheeler Auditorium for a pre-court client-counsel meeting; the meeting is moved to Berkeley Community Theatre.

December 14, 1964: The cases of arrested demonstrators are continued to January 5.

December 15, 1964: Introduced by Professor Jacobus ten Broek, James Farmer, national director of CORE, addresses a crowd of 3,000 from city property.

December 18, 1964: The Regents do not ratify the Academic Senate resolutions, but state that they "do not contemplate that advocacy or content of speech shall be restricted beyond the First and Fourteenth Amendments to the Constitution."

December 28, 1964: The Committee on Academic Freedom of the Berkeley division of the Academic Senate releases its recommendations concerning political activity.

December 31, 1964: Chancellor Strong announces that the recommendations will go into effect on Monday, January 4.

Mid-1960s: Urban Renewal in Sacramento, Oakland, San Francisco and other major U.S. cities—largely the razing of tracts of slum housing and decayed businesses—leads to widespread homelessness among America's urban poor.

1965: Birth rates and population growth rates begin to fall in North and South America, Europe and Australasia. Birth rates in sub-Saharan Africa are notably unaffected.

1965: The U.S. Mint phases out 90-percent-silver coins, replacing the dime and quarter with a cupronickel-clad copper sandwich containing no silver, and the half-dollar with a debased coin containing only 40 percent silver.

1965: Berkeley Free Press founded.

1965: The elementary primer, *Fun With Dick and Jane,* from which American children since 1931 have learned to read ("See Spot. See Spot run. Run, Spot, run!") is dropped from the general curriculum. The text has provided young students with grist for their fledgling intellectual mills as well as an unrelentingly white, middle-class view of society.

1965: Toyota introduces the Toyota Corona to the American market.

1965: Specifically targeting the Chevrolet Corvair, consumer advocate Ralph Nader publishes *Unsafe at Any Speed*, a virulent criticism of American automobile manufacturers.

1965: In Chicago, there are 2.5 workers for each person receiving some sort of public assistance.

1965: Panty hose are first manufactured.

1965: Skateboards are first commercially manufactured.

1965: Wu Han, historian and vice-mayor of Peking, writes an historical drama, *Hai Jui Dismissed from Office,* presenting an old story in a new wrapper. In concert with Mao Tse-tung, the "Gang of Four"—Chiang Ching (Mao's wife), Chang Chun-chiao, Yao Wen-yuan and Wang Hung-wen—write an article criticizing the play. Ensuing disputes over ideological purity usher in the Cultural Revolution, whose militant arm is the Red Guard. In the following decade, much of China's historical and cultural heritage is destroyed and some 5 percent of the population is executed, imprisoned or put to forced labor.

1965: Rembrandt's *Titus* is sold at Christie's, London, for 760,000 guineas ($2,128,000).

1965: "Op art"—nonobjective art directed at creating optical illusions based on the use of color, form and perspective in unusual ways—becomes the rage.

1965: Leroy "Satchel" Paige, approximately 60 years old, pitches three scoreless innings for the Kansas City Athletics.

January 2, 1965: Chancellor Strong is replaced by acting chancellor Martin Meyerson.

January 3, 1965: Meyerson issues campus regulations concerning political activity on the UC campus. All significant FSM points are granted.

January 4, 1965: The FSM holds its first legal rally on the steps of Sproul Hall at noon.

February 10, 1965: Martin Luther King and 770 others are arrested in Selma, Alabama, as Negroes picket a county courthouse demanding an end to discriminatory voting requirements.

February 11, 1965: Saul Landau goes before Oakland Municipal Court for distribution of *Un Chant d'Amour*.

February 12, 1965: Civil rights arrests at Oakland's Jack London Square.

February 21, 1965: Black nationalist Malcolm X is fatally shot during a Harlem rally in New York City.

February 24, 1965: A seven-week series of lectures on obscenity and censorship begins on the UC campus.

March 1, 1965: *Spider* magazine appears on campus. Undergraduates vote 3,345–1,293 for a constitutional amendment to restore ASUC membership to graduates.

March 3, 1965: John Thompson is arrested on campus for "outraging the public decency" by displaying an obscene sign.

March 4, 1965: David Bills, Stephen Argent, Michael Klein and Ed Rosenfeld are arrested in the "Filthy Speech" controversy.

March 4, 1965: Augustus Owsley Stanley III mixes his first commercial batch of LSD.

March 5, 1965: Art Goldberg, John Thompson and others hold a "filthy speech" rally. Mark Van Loucks signs complaints against Goldberg, Thompson, James Prickett and Charles Artman. Goldberg and Thompson arrested.

March 8, 1965: Martin McCrea signs a complaint against the Alpha Epsilon Pi fraternity for "selling obscene materials and using obscene language in a public place."

March 8, 1965: First U.S. ground units arrive in Vietnam.

March 9, 1965: President Clark Kerr and acting chancellor Martin Meyerson resign.

March 10, 1965: FSM defendants are offered the choice of nolo, stipulation or trial.

March 11, 1965: Civil rights activist Reverend James Reeb dies of a beating administered by whites in Selma, Alabama.

March 12, 1965: *For Unlawful Carnal Knowledge* goes on sale and is banned. A special ad hoc committee set up to hold hearings on the issue of obscenity on campus has its first meeting. By a nearly unanimous vote, the Academic Senate urges University president Clark Kerr and acting chancellor Martin Meyerson to stay at their posts.

March 13, 1965: President Kerr and acting chancellor Meyerson withdraw their resignations at the Board of Regents' meeting, "pending further discussions."

March 19, 1965: *Spider* banned. *Spider* editors meet with Meyerson.

March 21–25, 1965: An Alabama civil rights march led by the Reverend Dr. Martin Luther King, Jr., starts with 3,200 and swells to 25,000. The marchers are guarded along the way by 4,000 troops dispatched by President Johnson.

March 22, 1965: Standing on Sproul Hall steps, Richard Krech attempts to burn his draft card, but the wind keeps blowing it out, so he tears it up.

March 23, 1965: Fifteen Vietnam War protesters are arrested at the Oakland Army Terminal.

March 25, 1965: Viola Luizzo is shot to death in Alabama while transporting Freedom Marchers.

March 25, 1965: The Regents vote unanimously to nullify the undergraduate vote allowing grads back into the ASUC.

March 29, 1965: FSM Central shuts down.

April 1, 1965: *Spider* magazine goes on sale legally at Ludwig's Fountain under a new set of administration rules for selling literature on campus.

April 5–6, 1965: A "Freedom Graduate

Poll" sponsored by the GCC draws some 7,300 votes. On April 22, the Regents rescind their ban of grads from the ASUC. The ASUC Senate announces on April 28 that the grads may become members of the ASUC upon payment of a $3.25 membership fee; by April 29, only eleven grads have joined.

April 17, 1965: Marching outside the White House, 15,000 protesters demand an end to U.S. intervention in Vietnam.

April 22, 1965: Carol Doda and 22 other topless dancers are arrested in San Francisco's North Beach nightclubs for indecent exposure.

April 22, 1965: Art Goldberg is expelled from UC for his part in the Filthy Speech Movement and Michael Klein, Nicholas Zvegintzov and David A. Bills are suspended until the following semester.

April 26, 1965: Mario Savio steps down as FSM leader.

April 28, 1965: The FSM formally dissolves itself. The FSU is proposed.

April 29, 1965: Commissioner of education Frances Keppel orders all public schools desegregated by the fall of 1967.

May 5, 1965: First general meeting of the FSU.

May 9, 1965: SLATE loses its ASUC majority.

May 11, 1965: John Thompson, Art Goldberg and seven others are found guilty on various charges of obscenity in Berkeley Municipal Court. Thompson and Goldberg become the last people in America to serve time for an obscenity conviction.

May 15, 1965: Sit-ins halt the Armed Forces Day parade on Fifth Avenue in New York.

May 21, 1965: Vietnam Day, conducted from noon May 21 until 6:00 PM May 22 on the Berkeley campus, kicks off the massive, unremitting student resistance to the Vietnam War.

May 24, 1965: The U.S. Supreme Court voids a law curbing Communist propaganda in the mails.

June 1965: Artist Bill Ham puts on the first psychedelic light and rock 'n' roll show, with the Charlatans, at the Red Dog Saloon in Virginia City.

June 7, 1965: In *Griswold* the U.S. Supreme Court establishes the fundamental right to contraception. Speaking for the court, William O. Douglas says, "The right to privacy is not found in the letter of the Constitution, but in its penumbra."

June 14, 1965: In Jackson, Mississippi, 472 are arrested in a civil rights march.

Mid-1965: Prosecutions are begun against 380 men refusing to be inducted into the armed services.

Mid-1965: Jefferson Fuck Poland founds the Sexual Freedom League.

July 1965: CORE activists Weinberg and Goines go to Bogalusa.

July 1, 1965: Acting chancellor Martin Meyerson is replaced by Roger W. Heyns. Earl F. Cheit is appointed acting chancellor until the beginning of the academic year.

July 15, 1965: *Mariner 4* sends back the first close-up photos of Mars.

July 28, 1965: Sentencing of FSM defendants begins.

August 9, 1965: In Washington, D.C., 350 antiwar protesters are arrested.

August 10, 1965: Six days of riots begin in Watts, a predominantly Negro area of Los Angeles. National guardsmen are called in and 34 people are killed, 1,000 injured and 4,000 arrested. Fire damage is estimated at $175 million. In Chicago, in the second consecutive night of civil disorder, Negro rioters destroy a fire station. In response, Marvin Jackmon coins the phrase "Burn, baby, burn."

August 10, 1965: VDC protesters demand that the city of Berkeley deny Santa Fe's permit to carry troops through Berkeley to the Oakland army base. Berkeley refuses.

August 12, 1965: Jerry Rubin heads an antiwar demonstration with 500 protesters at the Santa Fe railroad station.

August 13, 1965: Jail terms begin for those FSM defendants who do not post appeal bond.

August 13, 1965: The counterculture newspaper *Berkeley Barb* is founded.

August 20, 1965: Vice-chancellor Alex Sherriffs is fired.

August 26, 1965: President Johnson declares by executive order that men married after midnight tonight are no longer exempt from the draft. Students carrying less than 12 units are liable to be drafted. Single male students can expect to receive an induction notice within 21 days of graduation.

September 5, 1965: Acting Chancellor Cheit issues campus speech and organization rules.

September 6, 1965: The first notice of the hippies' birth appears in a *San Francisco Examiner* article about the Haight-Ashbury area of San Francisco. A NEW PARADISE FOR BEATNIKS is the headline.

September 9, 1965: Sandy Koufax of the Los Angeles Dodgers pitches a perfect game. This is his fourth no-hitter in four years.

September 16, 1965: The United Farm Workers under Cesar Chavez vote to strike the Central Valley grape growers.

November 9–10, 1965: When a relay switch in Ontario malfunctions, the entire northeast U.S. and parts of Canada lose electrical power. The blackout affects some 30 million people. In popular myth, nine months later there is a marked increase in the birth rate.

November 15, 1965: The Supreme Court voids a law requiring Communists to register with the government.

December 1965: U.S. forces in Vietnam reach 385,300, not including 60,000 men in the U.S. fleet and 33,000 stationed in Thailand.

December 3, 1965: The National Council of Churches asks the United States to halt bombings of North Vietnam.

December 10, 1965: Bill Graham promotes his first rock concert at the Fillmore Auditorium.

December 10, 1965: Hemlines rise to six inches above the knee, as the miniskirt, attributed to London designer Mary Quant, makes its fashion debut.

1966: In *South Carolina* v *Katzenbach*, the Supreme Court upholds federal intervention in voting rights. South Carolina has sued the attorney general, contending that the 1965 Voting Rights Act encroaches on the reserved powers of the states, treats the states unequally and violates separation of powers. Chief Justice Warren rules that the Fifteenth Amendment gives Congress broad powers to "use any rational means to effectuate the constitutional prohibition of racial discrimination in voting." After this decision, Southern Negroes register and vote in massive numbers.

1966: Roughly equal proportions of men and women entering college—about 5 percent—plan to pursue mathematics majors; 10 percent of college freshmen plan to major in the sciences and mathematics; 20 percent are interested in a teaching career; and 65 percent of students cite "getting a general education" as their reason for going to college.

January 17, 1966: An American B-52 accidentally drops a hydrogen bomb over the Atlantic Ocean near Almeria, Spain. It is recovered by minisubs on March 17.

March 1, 1966: The Russians report that a space probe has crashed on Venus, marking the first human contact with another planet.

March 15, 1966: Negro teenagers riot in Watts. Two are killed and at least twenty-five injured.

March 21, 1966: In the *Fanny Hill* case, Supreme Court justice William Brennan states that "a book cannot be proscribed unless it is found to be utterly without redeeming social value. This is so even though the book is found to possess the requisite prurient appeal and to be patently offensive. Each of the . . . federal constitutional criteria are to be applied independently; the social value of the book can neither be weighed against nor canceled by its prurient appeal or patent offensiveness."

April 9, 1966: The Vatican abolishes the *Index librorum prohibitorum*, its list of banned books.

April 9, 1966: VDC headquarters bombed.

April 14, 1966: In Switzerland, the Sandoz Corporation suspends distribution of LSD.

April 18, 1966: Masters and Johnson's *Human Sexual Response* is published.

April 21, 1966: Dr. Michael de Bakey implants an artificial heart in a human at Houston Hospital. The plastic device functions and the patient lives.

May 12, 1966: University of Chicago students seize the administration building.

May 13, 1966: In New York, students take over the administration building at City College.

May 15, 1966: Eight thousand antiwar activists circle the White House for two hours.

Summer 1966: Stokely Carmichael and John Hulett of SNCC create the Black Panther party in Lowndes County, Alabama. Having had enough of passive resistance, their stated goal is Black Power.

June 4, 1966: In the largest political ad ever published, 6,400 sign a *New York Times* appeal against the Vietnam War.

June 6, 1966: Civil rights activist James Meredith is shot in the back as he marches in Mississippi.

June 13, 1966: Expanding on *Gideon v Wainwright* (1963) and *Escobido v Illinois* (1964), in the case of *Miranda v Arizona* the Supreme Court sets forth stringent interrogation procedures for criminal suspects, to protect their Fifth Amendment freedom from self-incrimination. Ernesto Miranda's confession to kidnapping and rape, obtained without counsel and without his having been advised of his right to silence, is ruled inadmissible as evidence. The decision obliges police to advise suspects of their rights upon taking them into custody. Shortly afterward, policemen begin carrying printed "Miranda cards," from which they read the warnings stating, in effect, "You are under arrest. You have the right to remain silent. Anything you say can and will be used against you. You have the right to an attorney. If you cannot afford an attorney, one will be appointed for you."

June 25, 1966: James Meredith rejoins civil rights marchers on U.S. Highway 51 near Jackson, Mississippi.

June 29, 1966: Betty Friedan begins forming the National Organization for Women (NOW).

July 1, 1966: Medicare, a government program to pay part of the medical expenses of citizens over 65, begins.

July 15, 1966: In Chicago, troops quell race riots; 2 dead, 57 hurt.

July 31, 1966: Severe racial unrest and rioting in Chicago, New York and Cleveland.

August 10, 1966: The U.S. Treasury halts printing of two-dollar bills.

August 20, 1966: Berkeley police arrest Michael McClure, Richard Bright and Billie Dixon on obscenity charges for a performance of McClure's play, *The Beard*. The case is not brought to trial.

August 27, 1966: Iowa polls show that 54 percent think that the U.S. role in Vietnam is a mistake.

August 29, 1966: The Beatles play Candlestick Park in what will be their last public concert.

September 23, 1966: Minimum wage is increased to $1.60 per hour.

October 6, 1966: The U.S. government declares LSD-25 "dangerous and illegal."

November 15, 1966: San Francisco police arrest a clerk at the Psychedelic Shop in the Haight-Ashbury for selling *The Love Book*, Lenore Kandel's book of erotic poems.

December 1966: At the University of California, Berkeley, 5,000 students boycott classes to protest the suspension of participants in anti–Vietnam War rallies.

1967: Meister Brau, Inc., of Chicago introduces Meister Brau Lite, a reduced calorie beer; women are targeted as the primary consumers. The beer, promoted as a diet drink, is not notably successful.

1967: Microwave ovens become small enough to be commercially practical, and are widely introduced.

January 6, 1967: *Time* magazine chooses the 25-year-old-and-younger generation as its Man of the Year.

January 15, 1967: The Green Bay Packers play the Kansas City Chiefs in Los Angeles for football's Superbowl I.

February 10, 1967: The Twenty-fifth Amendment, fixing the line of executive succession, becomes part of the U.S. Constitution.

February 15, 1967: Twenty-five hundred women storm the Pentagon, demanding that the U.S. "Drop Rusk and McNamara, not the Bomb."

April 4, 1967: United Fruit panics in response to a hoax initiated in the *Berkeley Barb*, announcing that a friend of Barry Melton, the drummer for the rock band

Country Joe and the Fish, has discovered an amazing new psychedelic drug, "mellow yellow": banana peels, dried, baked, scraped, then smoked. The FDA announces a study of the possible hallucinogenic effects of smoking dried banana peel.

April 5, 1967: The Diggers, the Straight Theatre, the *Oracle* newspaper, the Church of One and the Family Dog form the "Council of the Summer of Love."

April 25, 1967: The nation's first abortion legalization law, signed by Colorado governor John Arthur Love, permits therapeutic abortion for cases in which a three-doctor board of an accredited state hospital agree unanimously.

April 30, 1967: Saying "I ain't got no quarrel with them Viet Congs," heavyweight champion Muhammad Ali (né Cassius Clay) refuses the draft and is stripped of his title.

May 18, 1967: Tennessee governor Buford Ellington repeals the "Monkey Law" upheld in the 1925 Scopes trial.

Summer 1967: Health officials announce that San Francisco's venereal disease rate is six times higher than in 1964.

June 12, 1967: The U.S. Supreme Court rules that states cannot ban interracial marriages.

June 21, 1967: The Summer of Love officially arrives.

June 21, 1967: All FSM defendants with time to serve go to jail.

June 22, 1967: Police captain Dan Kiely announces that as many as 300 hippies a day are arriving in the Haight-Ashbury district of San Francisco. The total arriving in the Bay Area during the Summer of Love is estimated to be as high as 100,000.

June 27, 1967: The Berkeley draft board office is bombed.

July 1967: The University of California buys a tract of land in the block above Telegraph between Haste and Dwight.

July 5, 1967: The Congress of Racial Equality (CORE) drops the word "multiracial" from descriptions of its membership.

July 16, 1967: In Newark, New Jersey, the death toll in four days of racial rioting hits 26; 1,500 are injured; 1,000 are arrested.

July 23, 1967: Racial violence erupts in Detroit; 7,000 national guardsmen aid police after a night of rioting. Similar outbreaks occur in New York City's Spanish Harlem; Rochester, New York; Birmingham, Alabama; and New Britain, Connecticut.

August 1, 1967: Stokely Carmichael, H. Rapp Brown and Adam Clayton Powell call for a Black revolution in America.

September 15, 1967: The Polish sprinter Ewa Klobukowska, entering a meet as a woman, is banned from competition for failing to pass a chromosome test.

October 2, 1967: Thurgood Marshall is sworn in as the first Black U.S. Supreme Court justice.

October 3, 1967: Robert Crumb's underground comic magazine *Zap #0* hits Bay Area newsstands. This is the first of the underground "comix" and the legitimate successor to the banned *Mad* and *Tales from the Crypt*.

October 16, 1967: "Stop the Draft" week begins in Oakland.

October 18, 1967: Dr. James L. Goddard, commissioner of the Food and Drug Administration, equates the dangers of marijuana use with those of alcohol and calls for the removal of criminal penalties.

October 21, 1967: An antiwar rally at the Lincoln Memorial draws 50,000 demonstrators. The rally turns violent, and some 250 protesters are arrested, including novelist Norman Mailer.

October 27, 1967: Catholic priest Philip Berrigan and two accomplices pour blood over Selective Service files in Baltimore, Maryland.

November 1967: The University of California begins demolition of the housing above Telegraph between Haste and Dwight.

November 9, 1967: The first issue of *Rolling Stone* is published in San Francisco by 21-year-old Jann Wenner.

December 2, 1967: The first human heart transplant operation is performed on Louis Washkansky, 55, at the Groote Schuur Hospital, Cape Town, South Africa, by a team of 30 headed by Dr. Christiaan Bernard. Washkansky lives until December 31, 1967.

December 3, 1967: Last run of the Twentieth Century Limited.

December 30, 1967: Protesters attempt to shut down armed forces induction centers in New York; 546 are arrested. Among those taken into custody are beatnik poet Allen Ginsberg and pediatrician Dr. Benjamin Spock.

1968: Put into effect and guided by psychiatrist Aaron Stern, an elasticized film rating system replaces the Hays Office Production Code. The code originated in 1934 as a Hollywood answer to the Catholic Legion of Decency, as well as to forestall government regulation. The system is eventually modified to give films a rating of "G" (general audiences), "PG" (parental guidance suggested for children under thirteen), "R" (restricted: under seventeen not admitted), or "X" (adults only). Failure to copyright the rating system allows pornographic filmmakers to run riot with the "X" rating, thereby rendering it useless to mainstream film distributors.

1968: The Chemical Bank of New York introduces a single queue winding back and forth between stanchions, feeding customers first come, first serve to the next available teller.

1968: Halyville, Alabama, population 5,000, is the first community to designate the telephone numbers 9-1-1 for all emergency calls.

1968: Color television sets outsell black and white.

1968: The American consumption of California table wines outstrips that of dessert wines.

1968: The San Francisco Bay to Breakers race attracts 800 runners.

1968: China Airlines bans tobacco smoking on all flights.

1968: Believing that World War II is still on, and honoring his oath never to surrender or give up the fight, Sergeant Shoichi Yokoi of the Japanese Imperial Army is discovered by hunters in the jungle of Guam.

January 1968: The Chemical Bank of New York introduces the automatic teller.

January 18, 1968: At a White House dinner, entertainer Eartha Kitt speaks out against the Vietnam War, thereby displeasing her hosts.

January 30, 1968: The Viet Cong launch the Tet offensive.

April 1968: *The Long Short Cut*, by Andrew Garve, published by Harper and Row, is set into type completely by electronic methods of composition.

April 4, 1968: The Reverend Dr. Martin Luther King, Jr., is assassinated in Memphis, Tennessee.

April 9, 1968: The assassination of Rev. King touches off riots in major cities. Chicago, Baltimore, Washington and Cincinnati are hit the hardest.

April 15, 1968: The Houston Astros beat the New York Mets, 1–0, in 24 innings of play.

April 19, 1968: The first indisputable attainment of the North Pole over the sea ice is made by American Ralph Plaisted and three companions after a 42-day trek in four snowmobiles.

April 23, 1968: At Columbia, 300 protesting students barricade the office of the college dean.

April 25, 1968: Columbia University closes as protests grow.

April 26, 1968: Two hundred thousand New York college and high school students cut classes in antiwar protests.

May 3, 1968: Students riot at the Sorbonne, Paris; 500 are arrested.

May 20, 1968: France is near paralysis as millions of workers occupy factories, mines, schools and offices.

May 30, 1968: France is totally immobilized by protesters and a general strike. De Gaulle raises the minimum wage by 35 percent.

June 3, 1968: Pop artist Andy Warhol is shot by Valerie Solanas, the founder of SCUM (Society for Cutting Up Men), because he has declined to film her *SCUM Manifesto*. Solanas had sold the rights to Olympia Press for $500, and Warhol, in turn, had purchased the movie rights.

June 4, 1968: The evening he wins the California Democratic primary, Robert F. Kennedy is assassinated at the Hotel Ambassador, Los Angeles.

June 28–July 3, 1968: Sparked by expressions of sympathy with French students, rioting begins in Berkeley. Citywide dusk-to-dawn curfew.

Mid-1968: Prosecutions are initiated against 3,005 men who have refused to be inducted into the armed services.

August 26, 1968: The National Student Association announces that there have been 221 major protests in U.S. colleges since the start of the year.

August 29, 1968: The Democratic National Convention is disrupted by battles between antiwar demonstrators and Chicago police.

September 7, 1968: At the Miss America Pageant in Atlantic City, New Jersey, Robin Morgan and members of the feminist organization WITCH (Women's International Terrorist Conspiracy from Hell) engage in an act of guerrilla theater in which they crown a sheep as Miss America, set off stink bombs and unfurl a banner—seen on television worldwide—that proclaims a startling new phrase: WOMEN'S LIBERATION. Later in the day, girdles, brassieres, spike heels, diapers, copies of *Cosmopolitan*, steno pads and dish towels are tossed into a "freedom trash can." The latter event is reported in the *New York Post* as a "bra burning."

September 30, 1968: In Mexico City, troops evacuate the campus of the National University after clashes between police and students. Deaths are put at 49 as the troops fire on students.

October 18, 1968: Tommie Smith (first place, 200-meter dash) and John Carlos (third place, 200-meter dash) are suspended for raising their fists in the Black Power salute while receiving their Olympic medals.

October 23, 1968: Berkeley students seize an administrative building on campus.

November 4, 1968: Police battle West Berlin students protesting disbarment of their defense attorney; 150 injured.

November 7, 1968: In Prague, crowds burn the Soviet flag and battle police. Students occupy university buildings to support progressive reform.

November 12, 1968: The Supreme Court voids an Arkansas law banning the teaching of evolution in public schools.

November 14, 1968: In New Haven, Connecticut, Yale University announces plans to go coed.

November 17, 1968: With one minute left in the game, and the outcome in doubt, NBC television switches millions of sports fans from the Jets vs. Raiders football game to a rerun of the movie *Heidi*. Becoming aware of viewer displeasure, NBC later says it is sorry, and that it won't happen again.

December 1968: The last housing in the tract above Telegraph Avenue between Haste and Dwight is demolished. UC leaves the land vacant and it becomes a muddy parking lot.

December 3, 1968: Astroturf is patented by the Monsanto Company. The artificial, grasslike playing surface is first used in Houston's indoor sports stadium, the Astrodome.

December 16, 1968: Spain rescinds its 1492 law expelling Jews. The first Spanish synagogue built in 600 years is dedicated in Madrid.

1969: Issuance of American currency in denominations larger than $100 is discontinued.

1969: The heroes of the motion picture *Easy Rider* epitomize the long-haired rebelliousness of young men. All the things long hair is thought to stand for—disrespect for authority, drugs, uncleanliness, overt sexuality and, as the movie claims, freedom—cause violent visceral reactions among those portrayed as ignorant Southern crackers, culminating in the murder of the film's heroes.

January 7, 1969: California governor Ronald Reagan asks the legislature to "drive criminal anarchists and latter-day Fascists" off college campuses.

January 10, 1969: The 141-year-old *Saturday Evening Post* ceases publication.

January 14, 1969: Morton Sobell is released from prison.

January 19, 1969: Cuban skyjackings become epidemic. There have been seven this month so far, and Cuban maps are now standard issue to all commercial U.S. pilots.

January 22, 1969: The Third World Liberation Front (TWLF) begins a student strike at UC Berkeley. Wheeler Hall is gutted by arson.

January 28, 1969: The Union Oil Company's platform A, about five miles offshore Santa Barbara, blows out, spewing thousands of gallons of oil into the ocean every hour. The leak is located and plugged on February 8.

February 13, 1969: Campus unrest at the University of Wisconsin brings in 900 national guardsmen; 500 national guardsmen are called in at the University of North Carolina to quell students battling police over Black rights.

February 27, 1969: The University of Rome is closed as thousands of students and leftists protest Nixon's arrival.

March 1969: Judy Carne, an actress in the television comedy series "Laugh-In," visits New York's "21" Club wearing a tunic-topped pantsuit. When she is denied entry because of a policy against women in pants, she takes her pants off, checks them in at the cloakroom and enters the dining room wearing only the tunic, which is barely long enough to be considered a micro-miniskirt. The "21" Club changes its policy the next day.

April 1969: American forces in Vietnam reach a peak of 543,400.

April 3, 1969: U.S. battle deaths in Vietnam total 33,641, equaling the number of U.S. soldiers killed in battle in the Korean Conflict.

April 4, 1969: Dr. Denton A. Cooley of Saint Luke's Episcopal Hospital in Houston implants an artificial heart in Haskell Karp, 47. Karp dies on April 8.

April 4, 1969: CBS kills the "Smothers Brothers Show" as "too controversial." The show has often lampooned President Nixon and criticized the Vietnam War.

April 5, 1969: Thousands march down the Avenue of the Americas in protest of the Vietnam War.

April 19, 1969: Cornell University president James Perkins cancels his Parents' Day address, "The Stability of the University," as 100 Black students seize the student union and campus radio station.

April 20, 1969: In response to an article in the *Berkeley Barb*, hundreds of people appear at UC's vacant lot above Telegraph,

between Haste and Dwight, where they plant flowers, grass and trees. The site is soon called "People's Park."

April 24, 1969: Antiwar demonstrators protest in 40 major cities as American B-52 bombers launch their biggest attack to date.

May 1969: Antiwar, civil rights and self-determination activists seize the Columbia, Queens, Berkeley and Cornell campuses.

May 1969: In the Oakland induction center, where draftees report from all of Northern California, 2,400 of 4,400 men ordered to report for induction do not show up.

May 14, 1969: Canada legalizes abortion and homosexuality in an omnibus criminal code bill.

May 15, 1969: UC fences People's Park and riots ensue. Police fire on the crowds, killing one man and blinding another. When governor of California Ronald Reagan is told that the blood is on his hands, he replies, "Fine. I'll wash it off with Boraxo." Berkeley is under military occupation for the next two weeks.

May 16, 1969: The Russian exploratory spacecraft *Venera 5* lands on Venus and returns atmospheric data.

May 18, 1969: The first live color-TV images of the earth from space are relayed by the *Apollo 10* spacecraft.

May 19, 1969: Two federal antimarijuana laws are invalidated in a unanimous Supreme Court decision to overturn the conviction of drug guru Timothy Leary. Leary had been convicted of failing to notify authorities that he had marijuana in his possession and failing to purchase a tax stamp; the Court ruled that both laws violated Fifth Amendment protection against self-incrimination.

May 22, 1969: The Canadian government offers to allow American military deserters to settle in Canada.

June 1969: A faction of Students for a Democratic Society (SDS) members, fed up with what they perceive as gutless leadership, come to the national SDS convention in Chicago with a position paper titled "You Don't Need a Weatherman to Know Which Way the Wind Blows." The title is adopted from Bob Dylan's apocalyptic song, "Subterranean Homesick Blues." After a violent faction fight, the bunch that comes away from the convention with the membership roster and the bank account call themselves the Weathermen. Soon to become the Weather Underground, they espouse violent revolution and terrorism in a desire to become the *ne plus ultra* of the New Left.

June 27, 1969: A routine police raid on the Stonewall Inn, a homosexual bar in Greenwich Village whose clientele runs mainly to drag queens, sparks the beginnings of the gay rights movement. The customers resist arrest, throwing beer cans and cobblestones and using a parking meter as a battering ram to get at police holed up inside the bar. Eventually, the crowd sets the bar on fire; rioting goes on all night and for three days thereafter in neighborhood streets and alleys.

July 8, 1969: Withdrawal of U.S. combat troops from Vietnam begins with the departure of 84 of the 543,400 still stationed there.

July 15, 1969: The polluted and oil-slicked lower portion of the 80-mile-long Cuyahoga River, which bisects Cleveland as it flows into Lake Erie, catches fire.

July 16–24, 1969: Neil Armstrong and Edwin Aldrin, Jr., are the first men to land and walk on the moon.

August 1969: Multiple-exposure photographs of Paula Kelly, the taxi-dancing star of *Sweet Charity*, mark the first appearance of pubic hair in *Playboy*'s pages.

August 15, 1969: Near the small town of Bethel, New York, 400,000 people arrive at Yasgur's farm for the Woodstock music festival.

Fall 1969: The first node of the ARPANET (Advanced Research Projects Agency Network) computer network is installed at the University of California at Los Angeles. ARPANET is a product of military concern over the durability of the U.S. communication network.

September 8, 1969: The children's educational program "Sesame Street" makes its public television debut.

October 18, 1969: The U.S. government, heeding the results of laboratory experiments linking food additives to cancer, requires the removal of cyclamates from the market and limits use of monosodium glutamate. Steps are also taken to ban use of the insecticide DDT.

November 3, 1969: The census places New York's population at 7,964,200.

November 9, 1969: Led by Richard Oakes, a Mohawk, and Grace Thorpe, a Sac and Fox (and the daughter of Jim Thorpe), 78 American Indians land on Alcatraz Island in San Francisco Bay. They occupy "the Rock" for eighteen months.

November 15, 1969: A quarter of a million antiwar protesters, characterized by Vice President Spiro Agnew as an "effete corps of intellectual snobs" and by the sympathetic press as "nattering nabobs of negativity," gather peacefully in Washington, D.C.

November 25, 1969: Nixon renounces germ warfare and orders the destruction of stockpiles of weapons.

Late 1969: Some 33,960 men are delinquent in reporting for induction into the armed services.

Late 1960s: The most ecologically abused of the Great Lakes, Lake Erie, is pronounced dead.

Late 1960s to early 1970s: Due to the fashion for long, unkempt hair among young men, tonsorial trade declines drastically, and barbers go broke all over the U.S.

1970: Population of the world is 3.6 billion (an increase of 18 percent over 1960). Population of the United States is 203.3 million (an increase of 12 percent over 1960 and 5.5 percent of world population). Population of California is 19.9 million (an increase of 22 percent over 1960 and 10.1 percent of U.S. population). World population growth peaks at 2 percent.

1970: In the U.S., 448 universities are closed or on strike.

1970: Hospital care costs in the U.S. reach an average of $81 per patient per day, and $644.28 per average patient stay.

1970: The U.S. Mint removes all silver from the half-dollar coin, and resumes production of the dollar coin, which is a similarly debased cupronickel sandwich. (*Silver* dollars were minted from 1794 to 1935.)

1970: Drilling on a USSR "superdeep" research well begins on the Kola Peninsula, through the Baltic continental shield. By December 1, 1984, the well reaches a depth of 12,000 meters, eclipsing the previous record holder, the U.S. Bertha Rogers natural gas well of 9,674 meters. An eventual depth of 15,000 meters is planned by 1989–90. The temperature of the earth at 11,000 meters is already 392 degrees Fahrenheit.

1970: Violating the "men only" regulation, a woman disguised as a man runs in San Francisco's Bay to Breakers race.

1970: The price of gold on the free market falls below the official price of $35 an ounce.

1970: The Public Health Smoking Act requires all cigarette packages and all cigarette advertising to carry health warnings. It furthermore bans tobacco ads on American radio and television.

1970: Risking mutiny, the British Admiralty ends the 300-year-old naval tradition of the daily issue of grog.

February 13, 1970: GM is reported to be redesigning automobile engines to run on unleaded gasoline.

March 12, 1970: Terrorist bombs damage three New York buildings.

March 18, 1970: The U.S. mail service is paralyzed by its first postal strike.

March 22, 1970: A terrorist bomb injures fifteen at the Electric Circus, a popular East Village nightclub. The New York police have responded to 2,246 bomb scares in the last three weeks.

March 28, 1970: An explosion in a Greenwich Village townhouse kills three members of the Weather Underground. An investigation determines that the house contained 57 sticks of dynamite, as well as blasting caps, several homemade pipe bombs and other explosives.

Another massive explosion in a Manhattan apartment kills one man and seriously injures another. In the debris, police discover live bombs, guns, a picture of Malcolm X and Black Panther party literature.

April 4, 1970: Jack Weinberg, author of the phrase, "Don't trust anyone over 30," turns 30 himself. This is front page news

in the *San Francisco Chronicle* and the *New York Times*.

April 14, 1970: Canon and Texas Instruments jointly introduce the pocket electronic calculator, retailing for $400.

April 15, 1970: Fifteen western European nations accuse Greece of torturing prisoners.

April 29, 1970: Seven are shot in student rioting at Ohio State.

April 30, 1970: Millions of Americans march and participate in rallies to mark the nation's first celebration of Earth Day.

April 30, 1970: The Ohio National Guard disperses students with tear gas and shotguns; 73 are hurt and 100 arrested.

May 1, 1970: Police use tear gas to disperse a rally of 12,000 Black Panther supporters.

May 4, 1970: Four Kent State students, protesting the U.S. incursion into Cambodia, are shot dead by national guardsmen. Eight others are wounded. This only days after California governor Ronald Reagan is quoted as saying, regarding disruptive student demonstrations, "If it takes a bloodbath, then let's get it over with."

May 15, 1970: Two are killed and twelve wounded as police open fire on the women's dorm at Jackson State, Mississippi.

May 17, 1970: Thor Heyerdahl and a multinational crew of seven set sail from Morocco in a frail papyrus boat, the *Ra II*, in an effort to prove that ancient Egyptians could have reached the New World.

May 28, 1970: Maoist-oriented students battle Paris police in the second day of rioting.

June 1970: Fearing disruption, the administration refuses the 3,100-person graduating class of UC Berkeley a graduation ceremony.

June 3, 1970: Hars Gorbind Khorana of the University of Wisconsin synthesizes the first artificial gene.

June 25, 1970: A New York judge orders McSorley's Saloon to serve women. On August 10, the first female quaffer to enter the 116-year-old bar is Lucy Komisar, vice president of NOW.

June 26, 1970: In Paris, Jean-Paul Sartre and Simone de Beauvoir are arrested for their role in a Maoist weekly.

June 27, 1970: Four are killed and one hundred hurt in rioting between Belfast Protestants and Catholics.

June 28, 1970: Thousands of homosexuals march from Greenwich Village to Central Park in a demonstration protesting laws discriminating against and punishing homosexuality.

July 1, 1970: New York State's liberal abortion law goes into effect; 147 abortions are performed and 1,263 further applications received for the $300–$500 operation in New York City alone.

July 6, 1970: California passes the Family Law Act, introducing the "no fault" divorce.

July 7, 1970: Forty-seven are shot in rioting in Asbury Park, New Jersey.

July 9, 1970: The U.S. Justice Department sues Mississippi to force fall school integration.

July 12, 1970: A little less than two months after leaving Morocco, the *Ra II* sails into Bridgetown Harbor, Barbados.

July 29, 1970: Cesar Chavez of the United Farm Workers signs contracts with 26 grape growers.

August 14, 1970: The FCC orders TV to give prime time to critics of the Vietnam War.

September 1, 1970: The first computer chess tournament opens in New York.

October 8, 1970: The top New York State lottery prize reaches one million dollars.

November 12, 1970: In Buffalo, New York, scientists report synthesizing a living cell.

December 4, 1970: Six Weathermen are arrested in New York for attempting to blow up a bank.

December 15, 1970: The Food and Drug Administration orders the recall of one million cans of tuna believed to be contaminated with mercury.

1971: Fifteen nodes of ARPANET are operating across the country.

1971: War loans and indebtedness incurred as a result of the American Civil War (1861–1865) are finally paid off.

1971: Walter Tracy's *Times Europa* is the last newspaper typeface to be designed specifically for hot-metal setting.

1971: Women are allowed to participate in the San Francisco Bay to Breakers race.

1971: "Conceptual" art becomes the major new craze in America.

1971: Ted Hoff invents the microprocessor, the Intel 4004 "computer on a chip." It is 0.110 by 0.150 inch in size.

January 6, 1971: At the University of California, Berkeley, researchers announce the first synthetic production of growth hormones.

January 23, 1971: In New Haven, Connecticut, a tanker goes aground, spilling 385,000 gallons of oil onto Long Island Sound.

February 1971: The clear-bubble umbrella is introduced, allowing one to see as well as keep dry in the rain.

February 7, 1971: Women are accorded the right to vote in Swiss national elections, though suffrage is not extended to all elections in all cantons.

February 10, 1971: At 6:00 AM, a 6.6 magnitude quake hits the Los Angeles area, killing 51 and injuring 880. Property damage is estimated at $1 billion.

February 28, 1971: The male electorate of Liechtenstein refuses the vote to women.

March 1, 1971: A bomb explodes in the Senate wing of the Capitol, causing damage throughout the building, but no injuries.

April 20, 1971: The Supreme Court unanimously rules that bussing of students may be ordered to achieve racial desegregation.

April 24, 1971: An antiwar rally on Capitol Hill draws 200,000 demonstrators, among them 700 Vietnam vets who toss away their war medals in protest.

April 25, 1971: The New Jersey Turnpike is blocked for four hours by 1,000 war protesters; 100 are arrested.

May 3, 1971: Police and military units arrest approximately 12,614 people as antiwar militants disrupt government business in Washington, D.C.

June 30, 1971: The Supreme Court overrules Justice Department efforts to prevent the *New York Times* from printing the Pentagon Papers, documents revealing government duplicity in the Vietnam conflict. The government bases its plea on the grounds of national security, but in a brief *per curiam* opinion, the Supreme Court observes that the government has not met the "heavy burden of showing justification" for "prior restraint" on freedom of the press. The government thus fails in its first attempt in American history to restrain a newspaper from publishing information.

June 30, 1971: The Twenty-sixth Amendment to the U.S. Constitution gives eighteen-year-olds the vote.

July 2, 1971: Oregon enacts highway-litter legislation.

August 15, 1971: President Nixon begins a sweeping economic program calling for a 90-day wage, price and rent freeze. He also frees the dollar for devaluation against other currencies by cutting its tie with gold.

August 28, 1971: Chez Panisse restaurant opens in Berkeley.

September 16, 1971: *Look* magazine ceases publication.

September 25, 1971: Title II of the Emergency Detention (McCarran) Act, empowering the attorney general to put any person deemed a threat to the national security into concentration camps without hearing or trial, is repealed.

September 28, 1971: After a fifteen-year confinement as a seeker of political asylum in a U.S. embassy, Cardinal Mindszenty accepts exile in Rome.

October 12, 1971: The House of Representatives passes, 354–23, a constitutional amendment banning legal discrimination against women because of their sex. The Equal Rights Amendment has been bandied back and forth between House and Senate for decades, passing in the one only to be killed in the other; on March 22, 1972, however, the Senate will finally confirm the House measure, 84–8, and send it on to the states for ratification. The ERA reads: "Equality of rights under the law shall not be denied or abridged by the United States or by any State on account of sex."

October 28, 1971: Britain joins the European Common Market.

November 3, 1971: The U.S. proposes to deny passports to those who refuse to take an oath of allegiance.

November 10, 1971: In Belfast, two women are tarred and feathered for dating British soldiers.

November 19, 1971: In Tokyo, 1,785 are arrested for demonstrating against U.S. bases in Okinawa.

November 26, 1971: London outlaws caning of students as punishment in schools.

December 18, 1971: President Nixon raises the price of gold from $35 an ounce to $38 an ounce, thereby devaluing the U.S. dollar by 8.57 percent in an attempt to make American goods more competitive on the world market.

December 26, 1971: A band of Vietnam veterans seize the Statue of Liberty in an antiwar statement.

December 28, 1971: The Justice Department sues Mississippi officials for ignoring ballots cast by Black voters.

1972: Title IX of the Civil Rights Bill prohibits discrimination in school athletics on the basis of gender.

1972: The Crayola "flesh" crayon is renamed "peach."

1972: The Boston Marathon attracts 1,230 contestants.

1972: Lithium is found to aid in treating manic depression.

1972: The FCC ban on radio and television advertising of menstrual products is lifted.

1972: Expanding on its 1963 *Gideon* v *Wainwright* decision, the Supreme Court rules in *Argersinger* v *Hamlin* that an accused person is entitled to representation by an attorney in all cases that might result in imprisonment.

1972: As Beetle number 15,007,034 rolls off the assembly line, Volkswagen breaks the production record held since 1927 by the Model T Ford.

1972: Richard "Lucky" Leakey and Glynn Isaac discover a 2.5-million-year-old human skull in northern Kenya.

1972: Lovelock and Margulis propose the Gaia hypothesis.

1972: The Dow-Jones index for industrial stocks closes above the 1,000 mark.

February 6, 1972: In response to hijackings and terrorist incidents, random searches of luggage are initiated at Kennedy International Airport.

February 18, 1972: The California Supreme Court voids the death penalty.

February 21, 1972: Nixon arrives in Peking for an eight-day visit to China.

March 24, 1972: Britain suspends the provincial government and parliament of Northern Ireland and establishes direct rule.

April 1–13, 1972: Major league baseball strike.

April 3, 1972: Charlie Chaplin returns to the U.S. after a twenty-year absence.

April 28, 1972: In Oxford, England, five colleges break tradition and decide to admit women for the 1973 term.

April 30, 1972: Five nuns are arrested in New York for an antiwar protest in Saint Patrick's Cathedral.

May 8, 1972: In Berkeley, protesters tear down the fence around People's Park.

May 15, 1972: The U.S. returns control of Okinawa to Japan.

May 16, 1972: Alabama governor George Wallace is shot while campaigning for president.

May 21, 1972: Michelangelo's *Pietà* is smashed by a hammer-wielding madman. ("*Pietà!*" Oh, my God! I thought you said "*Piñata!*")

May 22, 1972: In the first visit of a U.S. president to Moscow, Nixon arrives for a week of summit talks with Kremlin leaders.

June 14, 1972: The Environmental Protection Agency announces a near-total ban on agricultural and other use of the pesticide DDT.

June 17, 1972: Five soon-to-be-famous burglars are apprehended by police as they attempt to bug Democratic National Committee headquarters in the Watergate apartment complex, Washington, D.C.

June 29, 1972: The Supreme Court rules the death penalty unconstitutional.

August 10, 1972: A great daylight fireball, in substance either a large meteoroid or small asteroid, grazes the earth's atmosphere over western North America; it descends over Utah and Idaho, reaches perigee over Montana (the only place where loud sonic booms are actually heard), and then ascends over Alberta and escapes back into space. Fireballs of such magnitude and duration are exceedingly rare. Another might have been the Great Fiery Meteor seen over Europe on August 18, 1783.

August 11, 1972: The last U.S. combat troops leave Vietnam.

August 29, 1972: In reaction to hijackings and bombings, Trans World Airlines and American Airlines begin inspection of passengers' baggage before boarding.

September 4, 1972: At the Olympic games in Munich, Mark Andrew Spitz takes seven gold medals (100-meter freestyle, 200-meter freestyle, 100-meter butterfly, 200-meter butterfly, 400-meter freestyle relay, 800-meter freestyle relay and 400-meter medley relay), bringing his career total to nine. In 1968, he took a silver in the 100-meter butterfly, a bronze in the 100-meter freestyle, and golds in the 400-meter freestyle relay and 800-meter freestyle relay. In his six-year career, he sets a total of twenty-six world records.

September 5, 1972: Eleven Israeli athletes at the Olympics are killed after eight members of an Arab terrorist group invade the Olympic Village.

December 1972: Targeting heroin at the street level, President Nixon declares a "War on Drugs."

December 7–19, 1972: Sixth and last lunar landing.

December 17, 1972: The U.S. birthrate falls below zero growth. The average family now has 2.08 children; the zero-growth rate is 2.1 per family.

December 29, 1972: *Life* magazine ceases publication.

1973: Thirty-seven nodes of the ARPANET computer network are operating nationwide.

1973: Federal Express ("When it absolutely, positively, has to be there overnight") begins overnight delivery service to all points in the United States.

1973: A New York criminal court judge rules the motion picture *Deep Throat* "indisputably and irredeemably obscene."

1973: In a landmark decision, the U.S. Supreme Court in *Miller* v *California* lays down "basic guidelines" for the "trier of the fact" of obscenity:

(a) Whether "the average person, applying contemporary community standards" would find that the work, taken as a whole, appeals to the prurient interest.

(b) Whether the work depicts or describes, in a patently offensive way, sexual conduct specifically defined by the applicable state law.

(c) Whether the work, taken as a whole, lacks serious literary, artistic, political or scientific value.

January 5, 1973: At all 531 U.S. airports, boarding passengers will now be subject to a thorough inspection.

January 11, 1973: The American League allows a tenth player, the "designated hitter," to bat in place of the pitcher.

January 22, 1973: The Supreme Court rules 7–2 in *Roe* v *Wade* that a state may not prevent a woman from having an abortion during the first three months of pregnancy, invalidating abortion laws in Texas and Georgia and, by implication, overturning restrictive abortion laws in 44 other states. The Court holds that such laws are an unconstitutional invasion of privacy. Only in the last trimester of pregnancy, when the fetus achieves viability outside the womb, might states regulate abortion—except when the life or health of the mother is at stake.

January 23, 1973: Nixon announces that in 60 days the last of the non-combat personnel remaining in Vietnam will be withdrawn.

January 27, 1973: The military draft is discontinued, and American armed forces become all-volunteer.

March 4, 1973: The rings of Saturn are discovered to be composed of large chunks of solid matter.

March 29, 1973: The last American troops leave Vietnam. American dead: 58,151.

It is estimated that the cost of each documented Viet Cong kill was between $250,000 and $325,000. The total estimated cost of the war is equal to 32 years of Vietnam's GNP.

SONGBOOK

SONGS OF, BY, AND FOR THE F.S.M.

LABOR
DONATED

SUGGESTED
DONATION 25

INTRODUCTION

Throughout the free speech controversy it has been evident
that the administration has assumed that the students would act as
individuals who could be easily frightened away by a token exercise
of authority. They expected that we would act with the same regard
for precedent and pecking order that they had. The record has
shown that we have acted more commendably.

From the beginning we have acted as a group, a community which
would suffer no individual to be singled out for punishment for
what all had done or should have done. Every action taken by the
students has been a mass action. We have never turned our backs
and hoped that the problem would go away if we ignored it. That
course was consistently taken by the Administration, and their
problems did not go away, but increased. Finally, they admitted
defeat on December 3rd by calling in hundreds of policemen to drag
the problems off to jail.

The press has been almost uniformly unfavorable to us, to say
the least. But there are among us many people who know from
the examples of the IWW and the CIO that a good song lasts far
longer and has a wider circulation than any editorial.

And so the songs were written, for the most part individually
by students caught up in the movement. The subjects are many,and
more songs are constantly being written. "The Twelve Days of
Semester" and the "Lament of a Minor Dean" as well as the page
of Christmas Carols were written as part of a songwriting
project by Joe La Penta, Ken Sanderson, Dusty Miller and Barry
Jablon. The carols have been recorded on a 45-RPM record entitled
"Joy to U.C.". They deal with the original demonstrations of
October 1st-2nd. "Free Speech"was written about the Sproul Hall
sit-in of December 2nd-3rd by Malvina Reynolds, grand old gal
of topical songs. "Womb with a View" concerns the maddening
paternalism that is Administration policy, and "Join the FSM"
is a general recruiting type song. Both were written by Dan Paik,
one of the arrested students.

The distortions of the press are handled by Genevieve Hailey
in "President Kerr". Dave Mandel wrote "Battle of Berkeley Talking
Blues" which satirizes the events surrounding the October demonstrations. "Put My Name Down" was written by myself for Nov. 9th
when the FSM again set up more tables and gave the Deans more
names than they could handle. This is also the subject of Dan
Paik's "Man Goin' Round Takin' Names","Hey, Mister Newsman" by
Richard Kampf addresses itself to those journalists who pay
more attention to unconventional dress than to the issues
involved. "An Age Old Tale" by Paul Gilbert will, as its mame
implies, be good for a few more ages, as it describes the general
situation in its poetic verses. Richard Schmorleitz, press
secretary of the FSM, found time from his duties to write
"I Walked out in the Streets of Berkeley" along with Dan Paik.
"Times are Getting Hard" by Kitty Piper and "I Don't Want Your
Kind Protection" by Peter Krug were written in off moments at
FSM Central, our main office. There are more, for which I
do not have space to mention.

These, then, are our songs, and they constitute a powerful
weapon. No amount of sanctimonious speeches can stop them,
no number of frantically summoned policemen can sapture and
imprison them. Sing them loud and sing them often. You will
be helping to fight the battle for Constitutional rights.

Lee Felsenstein

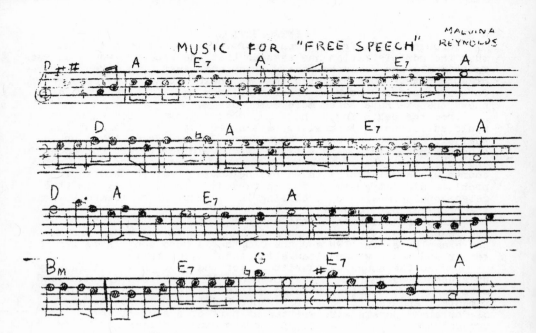

MUSIC FOR "FREE SPEECH"
MALVINA REYNOLDS

MUSIC FOR "AN AGE OLD TALE" PAUL GILBERT
(ALL CHORDS ARE MODAL)

FREE SPEECH

Words and music by
Malvina Reynolds

How'd you like to be a cop arresting students?
How'd you like to be a copper clubbing brains?
They're the most illegal law
That the students ever saw,
And they shove the Constitution down the drains.

Free speech, it's in the Bill of Rights,
Free speech is our pride,
And we'll fight until we win,
And get our liberty again,
And if we go to Santa Rita
We'll sing "Freedom! Freedom!"
As we ride.

Well, a cop's idea of order is a nightstick.
His persuasion is a heavy left and right,
When that freedom cry goes up,
He reacts like Pavlov's pup,
And starts beating every picketer in sight.
CHORUS
Well, we got an education in the classroom
Where we used the text book and the old slide rule,
But when police made a call
On the kids in Sproul Hall,
Well, we learned some things we never learned in school.
CHORUS
Well, we know what's going on outside the campus,
And we're citizens who mean to have our say,
And we'll keep on speaking free,
And we'll call 'em as we see,
Even though they take our loudspeakers away.
CHORUS
Let the students and professors run the college,
Mr. Kerr can tend the I.B.M. machines,
Let them know that our U.C.
Is no robot factory,
But a place to learn what justice really means.
CHORUS

copyright 1964 by
Schroder Music Company
2027 Parker Street
Berkeley, Calif., 94704

I WALKED OUT IN BERKELY   by Richard
                                       Schmorleitz
tune: Streets of Laredo   and Dan Paik
                              copyright 1964 by
                              Fantasy/ Galaxy Records.

As I was out walking one morning in Berkeley,
As I walked out in Berkeley one day,
I spied an old man all sad and dejected
His hands they were shaking, his hair it was gray.

"I see by your books,boy, that you are a student"
These words he did say as I tried to go by,
"Come sit down beside me and hear my sad story"
 He then shook his head and he gave a deep sigh.

"It is here on the campus that I am the Chancellor
I push the buttons and run the whole show,
These are my children but now they're ungrateful
They think they are adults, they think they are grown.

"Can you hear them shouting and screaming and singing?
They think they're so smart and they think they're so strong
They want to make speeches but never say nice things,
But they're only students so they're in the wrong."

They stopped my cop car and kept making speeches,
Those beatniks and communists sat in my hall.
We can do without them, they always cause trouble,
This school'd look its best with no students at all.

It was then that I left him to go to my classes
But I heard some voices and noticed a crowd.
I left off my studies and listened to their side,
I gathered my books and sat down on the ground.

I wish he had been there to watch and to listen,
To hear what all of those students did say.
It wasn't a final or even a midterm
But we showed we'd learned something at Berkeley that day.

(Repeat first verse)

IT BELONGS TO THE UNIVERSITY   copyright 1964
words:Joe La Penta   Cireco Music co.,
Music: Twelve Days of Christmas   BMI

On the first of semester the dean said to me,
"It belongs to The University."
On the second of semester the dean said to me,
"No bumper stickers, it belongs to The University"
3rd:"Don't ask for members"
4th:"Don't collect money"
5th:"NO CIV-IL RIGHTS!"
6th:"No organizing"
7th:"No   :mounting action"
8th:"No demonstrations"
9th:"You'll be suspended"
10th:"We'll call out troopers"
11th:"Maybe we'll bargain"
12th:"Our word is law!"

        THE LAMENT OF A MINOR DEAN
words:Joe La Penta
music:"Oh, what a Beautiful Morning"

There are five thousand reds in the Plaza.
There are five thousand reds in the Plaza;
The mike is so loud and its drawing a crowd,
And I'm sure that our rules say it's just not allowed.
        (chorus):

Oh, this will look bad in the papers,
This will look bad in the press.
Call out the troopers from Oakland,
They'll get us out of this mess.

There holding a car in the Plaza,
Theyre holding a car in the Plaza,
They're standing on top and they're flaunting a cop,
It's out of control and it's just got to stop;

(chorus)

The Regents are in Sacramento,
Oh, the Regents are in Sacramento.
The president's gone and I can't carry on,
How can I make decisions with no brass around?

(chorus)

It's open revolt on the campus,
It's open revolt on the campus;
We're crawling with reds 'neath our desks and our beds,
And I wish that the Chancellor would call out the feds!

(chorus)

AN AGE OLD TALE
                words and music by Paul Gilbert
                Copyright 1964 Fantasy/Galaxy Records

The concrete sidewalks ache from   crushing foot steps
The torrid asphalt moans in the raging sun
The streets bear the stamp of weary wanderers
Toiling down a road they've just begun.

The barren aged minds fall faint and fallow
The dim lit homes of fear lie barred and bare
The fountains of their dreams stagnate like   swamplands
Polluted and abandoned without care.

The tyrants tongue is cloaked with righteous anger
The bigot's boast is cloaked with cunning snares
The gambler gains his place with posted policemen
And the coward yields to all in sheer despair.

Oh the colors on the canvas sadly murmur
With bloody crimsons flowing to the ground
And the mad maimed mouths in mutilated anger
Frantic try to form a warning sound.

The stranglingvenomed vine with craft is creeping
Clinging to the pillars of the past
    ..Through shaded windows flickering lights keep seeping
The fertile fields outside just out of grasp.

But the blaring horns m and timely trumpets muted
Cannot forever lose their magic spell
And soon in wonderous beauty human heart strings
Will stir in speech and song to freedom's knell.

                JOIN THE FSM
                    tune: Which Side Are You On (Aunt Molly
                    Jackson); words: Dan Paik
                    Copyright 1964 Fantasy/Galaxy Records

I am a Berkeley student, as brave as I can be,
And they have kicked me out of school, because I would be free.
        Join the FSM, come join the FSM.

I went to Mr. Kerr, and here's the words he said,
Dan Paik I just can't teach you sir, 'cause youre a Rooshian red

Now I read my Constitution, here's what it says to me,
There's many got to fight and die, because they would be free.

Now if you want your freedom, step in and march along,
We'll all be glad to have you, we're many thousand strong.

The men who fought for freedom, here's what I hear from them
If you want to keep your liberty, better join the FSM.

<u>WOMB WITH A VIEW</u>
words and music by Dan Paik
copyright 1964 by Fantasy/Galaxy
Records.

```
     E  EEEE   E  EE   E    E
I said to my mama, I'm going down town
            E  E  E   E  EE D D C
She said looky here son, why do you put me down?
      E   E EEE    E   E  E   E   E
I'll send you to a place where they love you like me
     E   E  EE    E E CC C CC
Gonna send you to Berkeley to the University.
         G   A  C  EE  EE    E EF E
Chorus: Where its warm (pretty pretty, and oh so warm) 2X
G  G  G   G  G  G GFF F   G
People there love you like a mama would do
 C  C   C   D# E CC   G G  A  B C
And it's oooo pretty pretty, its a womb with a view.
```

So I packed up my clothes, put on my hat,
I asked a policeman where is Berkeley at,
He said, "That's in California where the livin' is fine,
With lots of pretty women you can ball all the time. (chorus)

I walked up to Mr. Kerr with my hat in my hand,
I says, "Sir, won't you let me be a college man?"
He looked me in the eye, he patted my head
He changed my diaper and here's what he said, (chorus)

I had me a penny, a nickel and a dime
Figured that I'd have me one big ol' time,
Walkin' on the campus and what do I see
But a thousand policemen and they all agree, (chorus)

Then I says to Mr. Kerr, "What you think of that?"
He says to me, "Boy, gimme my coat and hat,
I don't like it round here, they treat me unkind,
I'm goin to D.C. where they treat me fine, (chorus)

note: the printed letters represent notes of the melody.
The tune is rock and roll and should be jazzy.
```

```

PUT MY NAME DOWN
words: Lee Felsenstein
music: Hard Travellin' by Woody Guthrie

Chorus:
I'm going to put my name down, brother, where do I sign?
          Sometimes you have to lay your body on the line,
          We're going to make this campus free
          And keep it safe for democracy
          I'm going to put my name down!

(Chorus)

We can't solicit funds, I thought you knowed,
That would be a hideous crime, 'way down the road,
I got a brother in a southern jail,
And he needs money for his bail, so
I'm going to put my name down!

(Chorus)

We're going to have Clark Kerr's job, I thought you knowed,
We're going to see him unemployed, 'way down the road,
We're going to give him that good old deadline,
Make that headline or make that breadline,
I'm going to put my name down!

(Chorus)

Take the students back, they said, I thought you knowed,
At least until you've proven them guilty, 'way down the road,
Clark Kerr simply uttered "No",
The Constitution's red, you know,
I'm going to put my name down!

(Chorus)

We're going to break the rules, I thought you knowed,
Yes we're going to talk and think, 'way down the road,
What do we want, why the mess?
The Constitution, nothing less!
I'm going to put my name down!

(Chorus)

BATTLE OF BERKELEY TALKING BLUES
(words by Dave Mandel)

Let me tell you a tale of campus sin,
Of tables and regents and a big sit-in,
The day the students built a mountain
Atop a police car near Ludwigs fountain...
Defying law and order... thinking, God forbid!

It all started out near Sather Gate,
September 30th was the fateful date,
The rebels sat, tin cans in hand,
A threat to traffic on the Regents' land...
Sabotage by the I.S.C.; the Intracampus Slate **Conspiracy.**

The rebels were ousted, the tables banned,
The deans thought they had won their hand...
Then came a sight they never thought they'd see,
A genuine sit-in in the halls of Big C...
Civil Disobedience...an essay come alive...education in action.

Then Sproul Hall spoke in tones of woe:
"From our marble steps you'll have to go;
We wouldn't threaten, but we'll tell you true,
We might be forced to suspend you too!"
"Policy, y'know...regulations...we can back 'em up, too. Call out
Knowland's police."

The students left the steps that night
But returned to the tables in a show of might.
The cops tried to split them, but to no avail;
Four hundred gladly went to jail...
or built their own...a jail surrounded on all sides by
prisoners!

Then came a show of patriotic might
Rotten eggs bursting by the dawn's early light;
Red-blooded lads from Fraternity Lane
Proudly upholding Cal's great name, shouting
"We want our car...we want our...we want...we......."

Friday eve brought a glorious sight
800 cops just itchin' for a fight;
Clark was bluffing, Mario knew,
But they signed a pact and the cops withdrew...
They'll write a book about it...they'll call it A Motorcycle For
Your Thoughts.

The FSM is now in action;
At the Multi-U there's a multi-faction.
Free speech is coming 'cause some spoke out...
To get our rights we'll have to shout,
But don't worry...it's o.k. ⨯ if you wake the people up, 'cause
morning's come.

HEY MR. NEWSMAN

WORDS: Richard Kampf; music: a
traditional blues
Copyright 1964 Fantasy/Galaxy Records

Hey Mister Newsman, how come you're taking pictures of me? (2x)
Is it 'cause of my long hair
Or 'cause of my boots up to my knees?

Hey Mr. Newsman, Abe Lincoln, he had long hair too (2x)
Or did you want Abe Lincoln
Would have a crewcut just like you?

You call me a Commie, say that all my friends are red, (2x)
But we've been freezing here for freedom
While you've been sleeping in your nice warm bed.

Don't know if I'm subversive, just want to say what I please. (2x)
Strange how us subversives
Keep fighting for democracy.

Yes, my hair is long, and I haven't shaved in days, (2x)
But fighting for my freedom
While clean-cut kids just look the other way.

My boots are old, and my collars don't button down (2x)
But you don't need no tuxedo
When you're fighting for the rights of man.

THERE'S A MAN TAKING NAMES

TUNE: There's a Man Takin' Names
(Leadbelly); words: Dan Paik
Copyright 1964 Fantasy/Galaxy Records

(Chorus)   There's a man goin' round takin' names (2x)
           You may take my buddy's name,
           But you gotta take me just the same.
           There's a man goin' round takin' names.

I read my Constitution long ago (2x)
      I read the Bill of Rights, read it nice and slow
      I don't know much but this I know
They ain't got no right to take my name.

There's freedom in the air, baby mine (2x)
      If it's a crime to speak your mind
      I may be guilty, but I'm feeling fine
There's freedom in the air, baby mine.

Tell me which side are you on, baby mine (2x)
      You gonna stop, turn, hide your face
      Just when it looks like we'll win this race?
Which side are you on, baby mine.

WE DON'T WANT YOUR KIND PROTECTION

words:Peter Krug   copyright 1964
music:"I don't want your millions mister" by Peter Krug

We don't want your kind protection
Of our young and tender brains,
All we want is a chance to think freely
Give us back our rights again.

We don't need you to defend us
In an ivory tower so high,
All we want is education,
Our search for truth you can't deny.

If the leaders of the future
Cannot tell what's wrong or right
If just to hear is enough to corrupt us
The future will be a sorry sight.

We did not get to where we are now
By being lazy, wild or dumb
We want all sides to every story
So we'll be ready when our day comes.

In times gone by a University
Was a place where men of thought
Could come and weigh all concepts freely
And for that freedom we have fought.

Now students and teachers must think only
What administrators say
And if they are in disagreement
They're called ingrates and driven away.

We don't want mass education
From IBM machines so blind
But just to be treated as human beings
Our cause is freedom of the mind.

$$\tfrac{1}{2}$$

   Suggestion: When singing the second verse of the English
translation of "Die Gedanken Sind Frei" (see "Songs of Work
and Freedom" by Joe Glazer and Edith Fowke) make this
substitution: old line- "My thoughts will not cater to
duke or dictator"
                 new line- "My thoughts will not cater to
administrator"

PRESIDENT KERR   by Genevieve Hailey
                                    tune: William Worthy
                                    (spoken Wildwood
                                          Flower)
                              chorus: Dr. Freud

    It's of a band of students,
    A brave and noble lot,
    They demonstrated for the free speech most of us have got.
    When they tried to fight the red tape
    This is what the red tape said,
    "You say we're denying freedom
    Well then, you must be a red"

      Chorus: O President Kerr,
              O President Kerr,
              We regret our cause is causing such a stir.
              You uphold the law so well;
              We're suspended if we tell,
              Free speech is not a commie line we sell.

    Now, two thousand students sat outside
    The hall where Kerr was hid.
    They knew there wasn't any stronger
    Way to make their bid.
    They demonstrated for their rights.
    Their freedom must be won.
    And by and by the press said, "Hi!"
    And joined in all the fun.
                        (chorus)

    Well, the rumors started flying;
    The papers told the truth.
    They said those students were setting up
    A "We Like Russia" booth.
    Those commie agitators and the party plot they preach,
    Why, they've got the students yelling
    "Marx and Lenin and Free Speech"
                        (chorus)

    Well, elections they were coming
    And the Chancellor thought it best,
    That to get a nice bond issued
    He should cover up the mess.
    He proposed a moratorium,
    Discussions would begin.
    It's the only way this dispute can quietly be done in. (chorus)

    Fifteen hundred marched outside and set up tables too,
    Their rights denied, expelled they tried
    To do what they must do
    The Constitution guarantees free speech to everyone;
    They're fighting still, as free men will,
    Until their rights are won.

TIMES ARE GETTING HARD

words: Kitty Piper
tune: Times are getting
hard, Boys.

Times are getting hard, boys, rights are getting scarce.
Times don't get no better, boys, going to leave this place.
Going to San Francisco State, where even speech is free,
They care more for learning there than for bureaucracy.

Had a cause a year ago, took a little stand.
Dean of Students office took everything I had.
Got kicked out of school and lost my job at the U.C.
To protect the image of this university.

HOLD THE HALL

tune: Hold the Fort

copyright 1964 by
Sylvia Kalitinsky and
Lee Felsenstein

We met today in freedom's cause and walked into the hall,
For since they would not talk with us we had to stop it all,

(chorus):   Hold the hall, for they are coming,
             Movement men be strong,
             Side by side we sit together,
             Victory will come!

In the hall now, see the troopers, nightsticks waving high,
Failing to provoke a riot, harder still they try,
      (chorus)

See their numbers still increasing, hear the sirens wail,
Still, they cannot stop our singing, all the way to jail,
      (chorus)

Through the day they slowly labor, drag us off to jail,
But they can't arrest ideas, in their might they fail!
      (chorus)

****

    As the police got around to us a Negro demonstrator stood on a
table and told this story: "When I was on trial for my part in the
Auto Row sit-ins last year a cop took the stand and said, '...and then
they sang the Star-Spangled Banner sitting on the floor! '
"The prosecutor asked, ' you mean they sang the national anthem
sitting down?' with righteous anger in his voice.
" ' That's right,' said the cop, 'sitting down! '
" ' No further questions! ' said the prosecutor.
" Then the defense attorney cross-examined the cop.
" 'You mean to say they sang the national anthem sitting down! '
" ' That's right,' swore the cop,' sitting down! '
"'And when they sang the national anthem,' continued the defense
attorney, ' Did you take off your hat?'
" ' No.'
" 'No further questions! ' "

They have tried to stop discussion that
    might hinder their great plans;
"You must learn to make your millions and
    forget your fellow man!"
But we rose up as a movement and defied their stern commands,
The movement makes us strong!

(chorus) Solidarity forever!
          solidarity forever!
          solidarity forever!
          For the movement makes us strong!

In their hands they had the power to arrest us one and all,
To imprison us and drag us from their sacred marble hall,
But they're dealing with a concept that is bigger than them all,
For the movement makes us strong!
(repeat chorus)

They had thought the institutions they had built would always last,
And they blindly tried to force us into molds that they had cast,
Ah, but we are of the future and they are of the past,
And the movement makes us strong!
(repeat chorus)

Some people think a college is made out of
    stone
But a college is more than just buildings alone,
It's professors who lead, students who learn,
Who aren't forbidden to talk out of turn,
(chorus):
Well, you talk out of turn, and what do you find,
Administration tryin' to clean your mind,
Throw you off campus, you can't use their halls,
And the Constitution says they can't do it at all!

Well, the civil rights movement, as we all know,
Started in the colleges not too long ago,
Many gave up their youth for freedom now,
But we can't advocate it 'cause the rules don't allow,
(chorus)

For how many years were we running scared?
We knew what was right but we never dared,
But now we're standing up and we're mighty tall,
If they want to take one they've got to take us all!
(chorus)

FREE SPEECH CAROLS

Oski Dolls
(Jingle Bells)

Oski Dolls, Pompon Girls, U.C.
    all the way!
Oh, what fun it is to have
    your mind reduced to clay!
Civil Rights, politics just get
    in the way.
Questioning authority when you
    should obey.

Sleeping on the lawn in a
    double sleeping bag
Doesn't get things done,
    Freedom is a drag.

Junk your principles, don't
    stand up and fight,
You won't get democracy if you
    yell all night.

We Three Deans, by Barry Jablon
(We Three Kings)

We three deans of Berkeley are,
Fearlessly demanding our car.
We'll stop the riot, and have
    peace and quiet.
Bring out the feathers and tar.

UC Administration, by Sanderson
(O Little Star of Bethlehem)

UC Administration,
Your clumsy punch card mind
Has put your back against the
    wall
And tied you in a bind.

Yet in the darkness shineth
An Oakland cop's flashlight
To strengthen all your argu-
    ments
And prove your cause is right.

Hail to IBM, by Ken Sanderson
(Beethoven's Ninth)

From the tip of San Diego
To the top of Berkeley's hills
We have built a mighty factory
    to impart our social skills

Managers of every kind.
Let us all with drills and home-
    work
Manufacture human minds.
    (more- see below)

Silent Night, B. Jablon

Silent night, silent night
Nobody talks on the left or the
    right.
Five hundred policemen armed to
    the teeth
Circle the car like a black
    Christmas wreath.
Sleep in heavenly peace,
Sleep in heavenly peace.

Call Out the Deans. Barry Jablon
(Bell Song)

1. (men): Call out the Deans,
    And the Marines,
    Call in a cop,
    Throw them a sop.

2. (women): We shall not leave,
    We don't believe,
    Your empty words,
    They're for the birds.

3 (men): We want justice, liberty
    and freedom!
  (women) (repeat 2nd verse)

4. (men 1) (repeat no. 1)
  (men 2) We want justice, liberty
    and freedom.
    We want justice, liberty
    and freedom.
  (women) (repeat 2nd verse)

5. (all) We want freedom!
****

(Hail to IBM - cont'd)

Make the students safe for
    knowledge,
Keep them loyal,
Keep them clean,
This is why we have a college,
Hail to IBM machine!

Masters of Sproul Hall, by
   Dustin Miller
(Masters of this Hall)
Masters of Sproul Hall announced
   the news today
Students have no rights except
   to idle play.
If you want your rights, you have
   to cross the street,
Or the Regents will declare your
   education incomplete.
To the Oakland Tribune the stu-
   dents went one day,
But the Chancellor declared
   that's not healthful play.
Why not use the sandbox, try some
   basketball
If you want some clean fun,
   Buy an Oski Doll.

God Rest Ye Free Speech,
   by K. Sanderson

God rest ye Free Speech Move-
   ment-niks,
You must remember when
Good Mario, our Savio, did speak
   to speak again,
To keep us all from Chancellor
   Strong
And his committee men
To save our university (making
   us free)
And the first amendment
   guarantee.

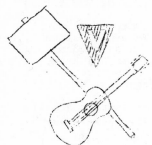

O, Come all ye Mindless,
   by Barry Jablon
(O Come All Ye Faithful)

O, come all ye mindless,
Conceptless and spineless,
Sell out your integrity
   to IBM.
Don't make a commotion,
Strong wants a Promotion.
Do not fold or spindle
O, do not fold or spindle
O, do not fold or spindle
Or mutilate.

Joy to UC, by D. Miller
(Joy to the World)

Joy to UC
The word has come
Clark Kerr has called us Reds
If you are 49%
You can't work for the govern-
   ment
The knowledge factory
Turns out more GNP
Without your subversion
On its property.

FIAT (NOT TOO MUCH) LUX!

FROM THE FSM CHRISTMAS CARD

INDEX

Page references to pictures are in *italics* and those to footnotes are followed by the letter *n*.

People's first names are listed as they usually appear in the text. Acronyms, rather than full names, are used for the most prominent organizations: FSM, CCPA, etc. In the text, the University of California at Berkeley is referred to by its full name, or as Cal, the University, Berkeley, or by other shortened forms—in the index, all are listed under the full name and cross-referenced as *UC*. The city of Berkeley is referred to as *Berkeley, CA* in this index, although not always so in the text. References to the Regents of the University of California are shortened to *Regents*. The term *administration* here includes references to President Kerr, the Chancellor, and several deans of the Berkeley campus who managed the University side of the free speech controversy. Bancroft Way (the southern boundary of UC campus) also appears in the text as Bancroft and as Bancroft and Telegraph—all are indexed as *Bancroft Way*.

When cross-referenced in the index, several major events that occurred in the fall of 1964 are referred to by the words or acronyms in italics. On September 16, all student organizations banned from political activity on UC property at Bancroft Way (*ban*). On September 30, eight students requested to appear in Dean Williams' office for illegal activities (*The Eight*); first Sproul Hall sit-in begins (*SH1*). On October 1, second Sproul Hall sit-in occurs (*SH2*), while outside the *police car sit-in* is taking place. On October 2, students agree to negotiate *pact*, ending the police car sit-in. On November 23, third Sproul Hall sit-in occurs (*SH3*). On December 2, fourth Sproul Hall sit-in begins (*SH4*). On December 3, graduate students call a *strike* of classes. On December 7, Clark Kerr addresses the student body at the *Greek Theatre meeting*.

This book is set in Linotype Bembo by
Wilsted & Taylor,
Oakland, California